THROUGH SOPHIE'S EYES

THROUGH SOPHIE'S EYES

A MEMOIR

SOPHIE KUSSMAUL
1875-1968

Cahaba Press
Eureka Springs, Arkansas
Birmingham, Alabama
2014

Published by Cahaba Press
483 County Road 231
Eureka Springs, AR 72631
www.cahabapress.com

Cover Design by Happenstance Designs and *Penguin Graphics II,* Eureka Springs, Arkansas

Cover Photograph: M'lle Anna Held's eyes—Library of Congress: LC-USZC4-12048
Copyright © Sinclair Seevers 2008
Edited by: Sharon Laborde Horton

Printed in the United States of America

First Edition   2008 by Happenstance Books
Second Edition   2014 Cahaba Press

ISBN 615961177
ISBN 9780615961170

Library of Congress Control Number-2008920022

Preface

Just why I am writing my life history, I really do not know. It would not interest any outsider, but I thought perhaps <u>some</u> time, <u>some</u> day, my only child (Little Sophie) might find it. She would be the only one who would enjoy to hear the true story of her mother's life. She, alone, understood me. Perhaps my youngest grandchild, Noreen, might like to read it too.

Looking back now over the sixty-five years and more, I can see that though nothing very unusual happened to me my life was really a little different from the average person. Two days of rain for every one of sunshine. Still, I am glad I lived—not just existed.

Now, before I start my story, I want to make a few remarks for the benefit of my parents, or any boy or girl that ever expects to be a father or mother. I think if fathers and mothers would observe these five rules, it would spare them, as well as the child, untold misery and after regrets.

First: <u>Never</u> lie to a child – for just as sure as you lie to a child, that child will in turn lie to you. Sometimes a child will ask a question and it may be easier or pleasanter for the parent to evade the truth, and out pops the lie. Sometimes, out of love and consideration for the child, the parent will tell another lie to save the child's feelings. But believe me, sooner or later the child will find out the deception – and ever after be a little suspicious.

Second: Never make a promise to a child unless you are <u>positively</u> sure that you can keep it. Often a parent will say to a child that if they do this or that, I will take you to a picnic, or I will give you – and mention something the child would love. And when the time for fulfillment comes, just say, "Oh, I cannot bother with that now." Little do they know of the bitter heartache, the keen disappointment caused by their lack of keeping a promise.

Third: Never insist on unconditional obedience. So many times I have heard parents brag that their children obey them blindly. They say a well brought up child never questions why they should obey every command, unquestioningly do as they are told to do. I say a child has a perfect right to know why he or she should do, or not do, certain things. A child is just as much a human being as the father or mother. If such people want unquestioning obedience, let them try to train dumb animals, not their own kind that also can reason and think for themselves.

Fourth: Use a child as an equal, not as a pet or an inferior being. Some people use their children as if they were little angels and must be guarded from everything worldly, while others, every time they want to discuss business or any little family affair, send the children away, saying, "You kids run out. You would not understand what we are talking about." The children will troop out, sullenly, defiantly, and why not? How proud and happy they would be if the father or mother would say, "Perhaps you would like to make a suggestion?" But no, they are made to feel that they are left out – do not really "belong."

Fifth: Remember that a child any time after three or four years of age knows and understands its father and mother much better than the father or mother ever understands the child.

Now as I am only going to write down my own life story, I will not give the history of my parents. But I will have to give a brief description of them so it will be easier to understand my life and give me, so to speak, a background and, in a way, explain why I did so many things.

My father was, without any exceptions whatsoever, the most highly educated man I ever knew. Later in life, I became acquainted with lawyers, doctors, a senator, bishop, author, and numerous business men with college educations, also a few professors, in a social way. None of these men had the deep, thorough education my father had. Still, he settled down on the small farm on which I still live and expect to die. He loved nature and preferred the plain, humble things of life. He was a thoroughly good man, clean minded, honest, hard working, and a good provider. A true husband, very affectionate towards his wife. I can truthfully say that in their forty odd years of married life, he never even gave my mother a cross word. I do not think there ever was a father who loved his daughter more than my father loved me. I knew this perfectly well, but I am sorry to say we did not get along well together. I have heard too many older people say, "Now I see where my father was right or wrong. If only I had listened to him, my life would have been much happier." Well, I cannot say that. Now, looking back, I plainly see that I always was in the right in our countless quarrels, and my father was in the wrong. In build, he was quite tall, broad shouldered, but rather thin. Coal black, straight hair, shiny black, piercing eyes, and a very dark skin.

My mother, too, was the best educated woman I ever knew. She also had been an extensive traveler. She had visited forty-two countries in her younger days. Then after she married my father, she settled down on our little farm and took up all the countless duties of a poor man's wife. I loved my mother more than the average daughter loves her mother. It was more like a worship, like one feels toward a saint. To this day I often wonder how anyone could live so long in this world and remain so pure. My mother never scolded me, never punished me. When I was naughty, she just looked sad. She loved my father and me very tenderly. My mother was rather short, not fat, but just a little inclined to be plump. Her hair was light brown and wavy, her eyes deep violet (beautiful eyes), her features were delicate – a beautiful face. Complexion light, a pure clean skin.

Now here is something hard to explain. In a way they were not proud; still they were very proud. They considered themselves far, far above all our neighbors. It was always "we" and "those people." A few times when I grew older, I said to my mother, "Why are we so much better than other people?" My mother looked at me and said, "God loves these people just as much as he does us, but we must not forget that we are different." My father would often say, "Mr. So and So or Mrs. So and So are quite nice people for such as these." Maybe my mother would say, "After all, what can you expect of such people?" Even as a very young child, I often wondered why we were so much better. Somehow it did not seem right.

My father made one great exception – Indians. Any Indian was considered an equal. Young as I was, I felt the great change come over his entire attitude when Indians were mentioned, or the few times when real Indians came to us. He would thaw out to them as he never did to our white neighbors. Well, is it any wonder I grew up a strange, lonely child? Grew into a shy, lonely, heartsick young woman?

Editor's Note:
Sophie's memoir has been very lightly edited. Only a few changes have been made for clarity and redundancy. She was educated at home by her parents in German, but writes that she was always able to understand English from her earliest years. During her sixties, she began writing her memoir in English in composition books. Sophie's vivid, strong voice speaks for itself and gives a true picture of the hardships and triumphs of life in America during her remarkable ninety-three years. Her granddaughter, Sinclair Seevers, promised to have the work published. That promise has now been fulfilled.

Most of Sophie's family photographs were lost in tragic fires. A few of the survivors are on the following pages.

Elsie Monsee Kussmaul

Mother of Sophie Kussmaul
Granddaughter of Emperor Frederick of Germany

Elsie Monsee Kussmaul

Taken at Yoost Photographers
Oneida, New York
1919
78 years of age

Joe Henry
Sophie's great love

Charles Estey

Albert Miner

Levi Miner
Albert's younger brother

Little Sophie Estey

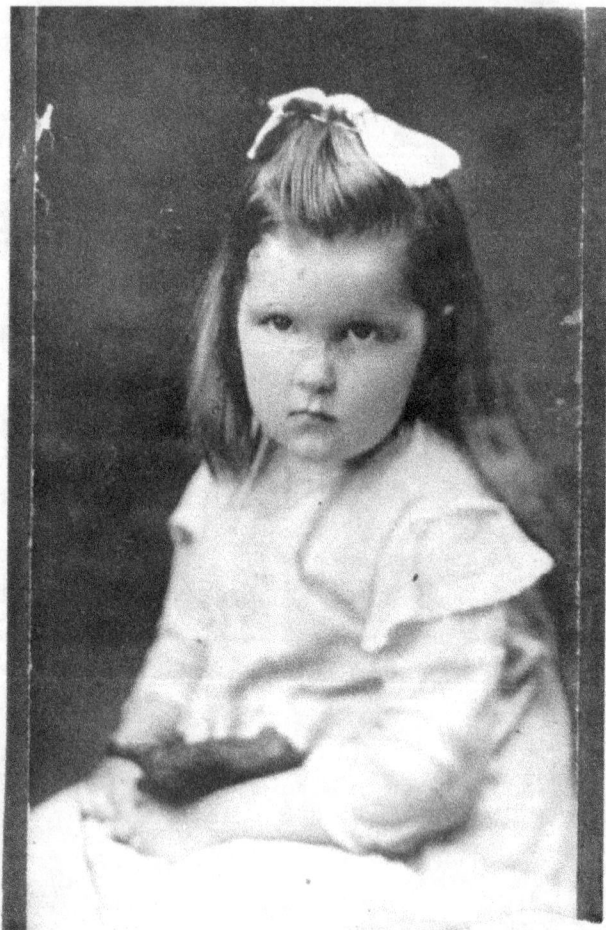

Little Sophie

Little Sophie

Sixteen years old

Sinclair Seevers, Sophie's Granddaughter

CHAPTER 1

When I was born, I had coal black, shiny hair nearly six inches long and piercing black eyes. I began walking when only eight months old, and by the time I was ten months old could run as fast as an average child of five years. Yes, my mother often spoke about it. I would leave my bed and run out of the house down into the swamp woodland. By that time, the latter part of October, the days were getting cold.

My poor, dear mother was almost frantic. She would go in search of me, calling, while I hid under some bushes or tree roots. Then she would lock the door, so if I got out of my bed while she was getting breakfast, I could not run away in my little nightgown. But although I was only a baby, I raised the window and skipped out. In the long winters, I would play, and during the day spent hours silently looking down to my beloved swamp woodland. But late in the afternoons, I would always go to the west window and often said to Mother, "I want to go there," pointing to the west. My mother would say to me, "Do you want to go to the Powers' house?" (Our neighbors) I would shake my head and say, "No, way up that way." Again, my mother would say to me, "You mean way up the road?" I would give a little choked sob; I never cried, and say, "Way up that way where the sun is going."

In spring, summer, and autumn, I lived an entirely outdoor life, mostly in the swamp woodland below us, but just as soon as it was nearing sunset, I would come up and stand on the west side of our house and gaze westward. I do not think I was an unusually smart child, but for some reason (how I was never

1

told), I could tell the time by the clock, even to minutes, before I was three years old.

I have heard some people say that they can remember back to the time they were two-and-a-half years old; others claim to have distinct memories of their life from the age of three years, while some say that they cannot remember back further than to their sixth year. Be that as it may, I have no doubt but what people differ in such things, the same as in other things. After carefully searching my brain and memories, I can truthfully say that my memory goes back to four years and about two months.

The reason I happen to know I am right about this is for the following facts: years later I heard old people tell that though they had always lived here (New York State), there was only one winter, from the middle of February to the middle of March, that the snow, which had been unusually deep, froze up so hard that the heaviest teams, with loads of giant logs weighing tons, could travel anywhere cross lots, over low marshy swamps, over rail fences (wire fences were at the time unknown), over brush-grown pastures. All was one white, smooth, snow field. Well, I had been four years old on the twenty-first of December, and my first memory dates back to being in our little sleigh. I think that kind of sleigh was called a jumper. There was hay in the bottom and bed quilts. Nellie, the little sorrel mare, was hitched to it. My father and mother and I were in the sleigh. We were going cross lots to Mrs. Mary Jane Dixon's. Once my father looked over the smooth white surface and said, "I think we are crossing the rail fence here."

A little later on, we passed so near to a big hemlock that the branches brushed our faces. That hemlock still stands. This ride is as clear in my memory as if it had happened yesterday. Another time we rode to North Bay, also cross lots, passing under the big pine tree below Flanagan's and coming out back of Anchard's, now Symour's place.

A third time we drove straight across from our place to Mulholland's on the next road. Once we drove back to what we called the "Hacabaum." In fact, that day it was christened. My mother and I stayed in the sleigh. My father went and cut down a tree. I said to my mother, "Bad Papa, hurt tree." My mother said, "No, good Papa, he cut tree to make warm fire so your footies

2

will keep warm." Then I said, "More hacabaum, Papa." Hacabaum means cut tree. Ever since, that part of our wood was called "Hacabaum."

I cannot recall ever being in the house that spring or summer. The time was divided between the farmyard and my beloved woodland. At home, I was with the hen, baby chicks, ducks and ducklings, the two cows, a spotted calf, and Nellie, our horse. I can still see my mother take out a handful of extra choice grass, or an apple, or slice of dry bread, or a small ear of corn to the horse and gently stroke her face and say, "My poor, dear little horsey, my dear Nellie horse." I did not mention our cats. They were never regarded just as animals; they were part of the family, and when it was decided to keep another young baby kitten out of a litter of four or five, always two were kept.

Our spring, summer, and early fall evenings were always spent on the veranda looking towards my woodland. Those evenings were divinely beautiful, a memory almost sacred. My father and mother sitting together talking quietly. I sat near my mother in a small rocking chair. I always was silent. I listened to the night sounds, frogs singing, the sweeter notes of the toads, the subdued hum of many insects, the cheerful chirping of crickets. Sometimes the booming sounds of a nighthawk, and once in a while the sweet thrilling haunting song of a whip-poor-will.

There were the sweet smells of early spring, damp ground, lowland scents. Later, the heavy fragrance of lilacs, then apple blossoms, roses, new mown hay, clover, the aroma of apples, grapes, and buckwheat blossoms, corn in tassel, and a hundred other alluring smells.

There was the beauty of seeing the stars, one by one coming out. Sometimes there was moonlight playing hide and seek through the moving clouds. Oh, how beautiful it was to watch the moonbeams through the heavy foliage of the trees, see the enchanting silver light shining on the bend in the road.

Sometimes my father would sing. He had a grand voice and had belonged to a glee club. Some of the time he would sing German songs, other times the dear old songs of Stephen Foster: "Old Folks at Home," "Nellie Gray," "Old Kentucky Home," and many others. There was one Latin song I loved. At that time I loved my father as much as my mother.

Once in a while, not too often, the Freeman girls would come and stay a few hours with us. Sometimes, the Dixons. But generally we were alone. At times my mother would put her arms around me and say, "What is my little sweetheart thinking about?" I would, young as I was, answer, "You would not understand." I was never made to go to bed. As I can remember, I stayed up till I wanted to go to bed.

These summer evenings continued with very little change for the next twenty-five years. Of course, in later years my thoughts changed. Yes, even now after sixty-four years, in summer the moonlight, the night sounds and smells are the same. The road, though, lacks something. Perhaps it is because the moonlight that used to shine on the faces and forms of my father and mother now shines on their graves, just a few feet below where they used to sit on the old verandah.

> Mine were childhood play days
> Happy days they were
> Full of flitting fairies
> Through the summer air

It seems that summer was extra dry. By what I heard later, in those days many of the neighbors were still clearing land. The farm which was later known as the Reamore Farm was then owned by Fred Powers. That entire pasture land, from our line to the McLaughlin line and from what is now the little Cleveland place way back to the Yager line, was at that time a dense forest. Giant pines, hemlock and hardwood trees.

Mr. Powers had started to clear a few acres quite near to our line, just below where the Cleveland place is now. He had cut the best trees and piled the brush on the stumps, and was waiting for a heavy rain to set fire to the brush piles and the stumps. The men would always wait till the first drops of rain would fall, then fire the brush piles. Unless there was an unusual downpour, the brush and stumps would burn for hours, but the rain would wet the ground so the fire could not spread.

With us, an east wind always was a sure sign of rain. Well, as I said, that summer was unusually dry. Then the latter part of August, for three days and nights the east wind blew hard. On the

4

third day, the sky was completely hidden in black clouds. It seemed like twilight all day. Then a few drips of rain fell and everyone expected a cloudburst. Mr. Powers rushed out and set fire to his brush piles. Within a few minutes, the wind turned west, the rain stopped and the sky cleared. Out came the blazing red sun, every sign of rain vanished as by magic. The fires roared and spread. Fred Powers called for help. His hired man, the two McLaughlins, Littlefield, and my father fought fire all night long.

The women, my mother included, made coffee and sandwiches and pails of lemonade and carried it to the men, as they dared not leave the fire. Still, the fire gained headway and by morning, it was raging on our land and the mighty forest I just mentioned was a roaring furnace, flames shooting up the tall trees. It got to our wood, the entire Yager lot, and on Dixon's. Not one drop of water in any of the creeks. Most people's wells were dry. People for miles around came and fought in six hour shifts. McLaughlins, Powers, Littlefield all kept their teams harnessed day and night, a double wagon loaded with their best furniture so as a last resort they could hitch the horses to the wagons and leave.

Our Nellie was kept in harness day and night; our one horse wagon loaded, all but the bedding that was to be thrown on the last minute. I loaded my dolls and best playthings on my little express wagon, but of course did not realize that we were in danger of losing everything. The men went and took eight of the strongest horses and hitched four of them to a heavy iron plow. One man sat on the plow to hold it down, one held the handles, and two of them drove the teams. They started at the McLaughlin line over Powers' land, ours, Dixon's, on to the Dixon road. The heat from the sun and fires, the choking smoke, the virgin land that had never felt a plow, made it hard for the teams and men.

After the first four horses had strained and pulled a few hundred rods, they were unhitched and the four fresh ones hitched to the plow, then again the first ones and so one. They made what is called a back furrow, a fire brake. It took nearly all day, as they made a double back furrow.

Well, even then, the fire kept jumping the fire brake. I cannot say just how many days this lasted. I only know I have heard my father fought day and night for over ten days. After a few days, he would drop on the ground for a few moments sleep, then up again.

After all our buildings, I mean by "our" all the neighbors' too, were out of danger, the forest kept on burning for weeks; the very ground was on fire. After a while the rains came, but it took more than one heavy rain to kill that fire. Yes, even to this day, sixty-five years later, I can still find places in the wilderness on Dixon's where the old fire brake still is visible.

In those days, the school year in our country school was divided into two terms. The winter term began the beginning of October and ended about the last of February. Then a short vacation, a week or ten days, and the summer term began. It closed about the first week of July. The winter term was almost always taught by a man teacher. That fall, while the fire still smoldered, my father applied for the position to teach the Red School, better known as the Yager District.

The three of us were in Camden and for some reason my father wanted to see one of the professors in the Camden High School. There, a little incident happened that made an indelible impression on my wind. Just why, I have since often wondered, but I can see the thing still before me as clear as if it had happened yesterday.

My father and mother and I sat close to the desk of the professor. He was quietly talking to my parents when a bell rang, and it seemed to me an endless amount of big boys and girls formed in lines and each one picked up a tiny inkwell from his or her desk. The long line filed by the professor's desk and there each one handed him his or her little empty inkwell. The professor filled them out of a large bottle, and then the students marched back and put their little inkwells on their desks and went back to their studies. The professor smiled and said, "Today is inkwell day."

Soon after, it was necessary for my father to go to Rome to take his teacher's examinations and obtain his teacher's license. I had never seen a train close by, much less, of course, ever rode on one. I do not remember how we got down to the depot that morning, probably with Nellie, and left her somewhere till night.

My father and mother warned me not to be afraid when the train should come. I always had been perfectly fearless, never

6

was afraid of the dark or animals, nothing. But when we stood on the little platform of the North Bay Station and that horrible ugly screeching black monster roared up, made the very platform shake under our feet, and the black smoke poured up, I was terrible scared, but I never flinched. I never cried or made a sound, but once in the train I was enchanted.

I do not remember how we got from the O.D.W. Depot to the Central in Oneida, but at the Central, the noise was even more terrifying. Rome was horrible, people everywhere. We went up a high building in an elevator and left my father there. Then something nice happened. My mother took me in a very large store and there were dolls and dolls and more dolls, little tiny ones, medium sized ones, and one giant one. Some had real hair, some china heads, some were beautiful wax dolls. My mother told me to pick out one. I said I wanted that biggest one. She tried to tell me some of the others were so much nicer, but I only want that big one.

Well. She bought it, but I could not carry it, as it dragged on the ground. Then we went into a photographer's studio, and I sat in a little chair with my doll in my arms, and we had our picture taken. I had this photo till the last fire. I do not remember how we came home.

Soon, my father was teaching. He left home each morning before I was awake. He had to walk about a mile and a half, build his own fire, and get the school house warmed up before nine o'clock.

I was very happy with my mother. In warm days, I still played outdoors most of the time. At noon, my mother did the chores, unless the weather was very windy or cold, I went with her, played in the hay mow, stroked the calf, climbed on Nellie's back, patted the cows, looked for eggs, knew and loved each hen and duck.

But when my mother thought it was too cold or rough for me to go out, I would stand by our bedroom window, which faced toward the north. The stable door of the barn faced south, so I could see my mother go to the door, open it, and after a little while she would let out first one cow, then the other, then the calf and lastly Nellie. But for some reason (or was it a gift?) after the first cow came out I would clearly see maybe a deer, or bear, or camel, or perhaps an elephant or lion or tiger. Then the other cow would appear, again one or two wild animals, then the calf, more things like a zebra or donkey. Then Nellie, and the whole procession would march to the spring and then back into the stable.

Of course, as there was no window at the end of the stable, after they all entered they were swallowed up by the darkness inside. I did see those other animals just as plainly as I did our own cattle. I never saw them when I was with my mother in the barn. I had no more fear of them than I did of our own beloved animals. I often told my mother, and she said I just imagined I saw them. I was very much hurt, as I really did see them as distinctly then as I did our cows.

In later years, I often wondered how my small, delicate mother, who had never done the least work except teaching, could ever do the real had work she did do, cooking, baking, sewing, mending, knitting, and when my father was not a home, the barn chores. True, I do not think she ever did a washing. For years, every two weeks a boy from North Bay drove up and took a big basket of dirty clothes home. In a day or two, he brought them back washed and ironed. Later, Mrs. Dixon came to our house every two weeks and did our laundry. Also, once a month, as far back as I can remember, Mrs. Dickson came and swept, mopped and cleaned out each room.

One day, sometime in November after the noon chores were done, my mother hitched up Nellie, and we went to visit my father's school. He was very well liked, as he introduced many new ways of teaching. He never threatened to lick a boy, but somehow he kept perfect order. Well, that was a wonderful new experience for me. There were over forty pupils there, the children ranging from five years of age to twenty-two. There were not only the ones that belonged in the Yager District, but half the boys and girls that belonged in the Haskin District, and even a few from North Bay. I sat in silence and watched every face, every movement. Just before dismissing the school, my father leading, the entire school sang, "Oh, Where Is My Wandering Boy Tonight?" That song had just come out. I can almost hear it yet, my father's really beautiful voice and all the happy young people singing with all their might, yet also with deep feeling. Well, we rode home together.

Chapter 2

My parents were very poor at that time, but we always had a wonderful Christmas, the one and only holiday they ever kept.

As I look back over the years, I can see the beauty, the glory, yes, the holiness of those Christmases. I would be five years old the twenty-first of December. I cannot remember my birthday, but I am sure my mother gave me something.

For weeks before Christmas, my dear mother told me about the Christ-child. She told me in her sweet, simple way, and because she herself had such an implicit faith, it entered my heart as nothing ever would again. She told me that the Christ-child, born so long ago and now living in heaven with his Father, God, came down to earth each Christmas and brought a Christmas tree and lovely things to the little ones of this earth.

While my mother baked Christmas cakes and cookies and trimmed up our little home, she and I would talk about the dear Christ-child. Somehow, the time before Christmas and during Christmas week always seemed different, as if the presence of the coming Christ-child was glorifying the very atmosphere. Only the last few years, it is losing some of the old enchantment. But of all the beautiful, yes, Holy Christmases of my childhood that first one I remember will always stand out as apart from all the others.

That morning I had my first vision. I slept in the big bedroom next to our living room, and that opened into the winter kitchen. All at once my father and mother rushed in, woke me up, and acted excited, saying the Christ-child had just brought the tree. Perhaps I could still see him. I jumped into my father's arms and we rushed through the living room. I caught one fleeting glimpse of a dazzlingly lovely tree all sparkling in silver, gold, and many other colors. It was lit up by dozens of little wax candles. But my mother tore open the front door and there I saw the Christ-child flying heavenward. He was perhaps ten or twelve feet from

10

the ground and swiftly winged his way up. His body gleamed like bright silver, so did his beautiful wings. He had very light curls and wore a shimmering golden crown on his dear head. On the crown was a silver star.

It was still night, probably about 5 o'clock and the sky was blue black with a few stars here and there. I did see this, and though I have wondered through sixty-four years since then, in my mind this vision is as fresh as ever, one of the holiest things that had ever come into my mind. Well, I was still in my father's arms when the door closed, and I gazed on the most beautiful tree I ever saw, even though each year after our Christmas trees must have been the same as my mother saved everything. Of course, in my early years I thought the Christ-child literally flew from heaven with the tree and gifts.

Under the tree was an unbelievably lovely wax doll, golden curly hair, eyes that would open and shut, even little teeth, and little tiny golden earring in her ears with blue stones. She was dressed exquisitely beautiful. She also had a whole wardrobe in a nearby box. There also were two plainer dolls, smaller, one with a china head and the other, plaster. There was a red velvet box containing what I then thought was a set of silver dishes (they were polished pewter). Another box of delicate china dishes trimmed in blue and white. Picture books and some toys. Bags of good colored candies and the first oranges I had ever seen. If heaven had opened up, I could not have been any happier.

Now I must explain some things. In those days of so long and long ago, the people where we lived did not keep Christmas. Over half of them did not even know that it was Christmas. Some had a good dinner, but otherwise went about their work as usual. The few that kept it, did like this: got a tree, hung a few presents like mittens, stockings, shoes, perhaps a homemade rag doll for a girl and maybe a homemade little cart for a boy. No one even knew about tree ornaments or candles. They would hastily strip off the present and throw the tree out. Even in Oneida, no store carried Christmas tree trimmings or candles, not even nice wax dolls.

My mother's sister, my aunt Sophie, lived at that time in Constantinople, Turkey, in the European quarter of that city. I was named after her. She had no children and was well off. So she sent my mother those exquisitely beautiful tree ornaments. There were dozens of glass balls, gold, silver, blue, green, pink, red, purple, all sizes. There were gold and silver baskets that folded up, gold and silver crosses, chains made of all colors of paper, tiny Santa Clauses and a lot of other things. There was a little wax Christ-child to be suspended from the ceiling above the tree.

The tree stood on a small stand in a little box. The box was covered with black cloth and in large golden letters was written: "I am a good Shepard." There on some green moss stood a little china doll dressed like the old time shepherds. In his hand he held a crook. All around him were tiny sheep in the deep green moss. My mother made the box and sheep and dressed the shepherds.

My mother wrote to her rich friends in New York to send us the candles and holders. They sent the set of china dishes and some toys. My aunt sent the wax doll, her clothes, and the pewter set. My father got the two heads for the plainer dolls and my mother made their bodies and clothes. There was no such thing as oranges in North Bay at that time. Candy, yes, but only stick candies.

Of course, I did not know about these things till years later. But young as I was, I remember people coming to our house from miles around, people we had never even seen before, asking to see the tree. I also noted how awed they were. Rough looking men took off their hat and bowed their heads when they walked in and saw the tree lit. We kept it till after New Years, then one morning it was gone. My mother said the Christ-child came and got it, but would bring it back next year. After that first morning, it was carried into the living room.

Well, life went on as before, my father teaching five days a week in the little red schoolhouse. On Saturdays he went to Oneida, leaving our house even earlier and coming home at night about seven o'clock. He had an algebra and a Latin class in the forenoon and a French and German language class in the afternoon. I often heard him say that he made a lot more money from those classes in a few hours than he did from his five-day school work. Sundays, he would go into our woods in the forenoon and cut wood in a pole length. In the afternoon, draw it home with Nellie. Each weekday night, he would go after supper, light the lantern, and saw the pole wood up with a bucksaw. We kept two fires going day and night, and still he managed to get many a cord cut ahead for winter. In those days, no one had ever heard of an oil cook stove.

Right here I want to say something about our lantern. The kind everyone uses now, has been using for over sixty-years, was not even known in those days. They were built square, a kind of light, thin frame of iron, the four sides each a seven by nine window pane. On of these sides was the door. It opened and was fastened with a little hook. Inside this little glass case, exactly in the middle of the tin bottom, was a hole to hold a large tallow candle. All the farmers made their own candles by drying out the tallow from their beef, adding a little beeswax and a little lard. This was melted and either poured onto forms, with a piece of twine for a wick fastened so it would stand up straight in the middle, or they made dip candles, taking the strings and dipping them in the melted tallow. When they cooled off, they were dipped again and again until they were thick enough. The tallow was kept warm, not hot; so each time the candle was dipped, it increased in size, the warm tallow sticking to the cold candle. The top of these lanterns was also tin, sloping upwards and ending in a little cone-shaped pipe with a hole to let the candle smoke out.

Although my father had such a wonderful education, it seems he had forgotten some of the names of our state capitols and metropolises. Of course in those bygone days there were not yet forty-eight states. Some were still territories, but these too had their capitols. For a few nights after supper, my mother would take the big geography book and read out loud: "New York State." My father would answer, "Albany is the capitol. New York City, the metropolis." And so they would go from state to state. One night, my father made a mistake. He called one of the capitols a metropolis. I piped up quick and gave the right answer. There was a silence. They both just stared at me, then my mother said, "And how did my little sweetheart know?" I said, "I know them all." So my mother began to name each state, and I made no mistake through the entire list. They were awestruck. I was only a few weeks over five years and up to that time had had no lesson of any kind.

A short time after this, my father, who loved higher mathematics, was explaining to my mother how they measured the distance between certain stars and planets in miles and asked her to write down on our little blackboard two billion miles in figures. My poor, dear mother, who was overworked, wrote instead two trillion miles in figures. Of course my father saw at a glance her mistake. I went and grabbed a piece of chalk and wrote two billion in figures. They almost acted frightened. Then I wrote hundred, thousands, tens and hundred thousands, millions, billion, trillions, and quadrillions. My father said I was a genius, and I would go far in mathematics. My mother kissed me and had tears in her eyes. How little they dreamed of the great, bitter disappointment I would prove to be to them in later years.

And alas and alack, little did I dream what sorrow, terror, hatred, and desperation was in store for me about the thing called an arithmetic book. To this very day, when I see an arithmetic book, a weak, sick feeling comes over me. Well, each day my mother and I lived the same dear, quiet life. At noon hour I either played in my beloved barn or watched the animals, real and unreal.

Then about the middle of February, my father said that the children were all planning on a big last day. It seemed it had always been the custom for the teacher to have the pupils speak pieces and sing songs on the last day of the school term and that this year, there were more than twice as many pupils than any other time, and my father being liked so much, the entire school was determined to have a great time on that last day. So for about two weeks, each night my father and mother would look through their books of poems and their song books picking out the right kinds of poems and songs for the very tiny ones, the little boys and girls a little older, and so on to the grown ups. My father kept the full school hours as always, but after four o'clock till five, he rehearsed them. He told my mother they all were doing wonderfully well. My father, who was a poet, composed a beautiful song which went with the tune of "Home, Sweet Home." This was to be the last song, the end of the entertainment, and was to be sung by the entire school.

Sophie Kussmaul

Only last winter, Ike Eckel, one of the few remaining pupils of my father's school, mentioned that last day and the song my father composed. Ike is seventy-six years old now.

About a week before school was to be let out, my father said one night at supper that the older boys and girls were going to decorate the school room. Then he said he intended to keep school as usual the last day of February, which ended the school term, then take the entire next day, which fell on Saturday, for the entertainment. All at once, he said, "I want you and little Sophie to come. I will speak to Mr. Anchord (he has a splendid fast team of young horses) to come after you at ten in the forenoon and come after us all at four in the afternoon. I will leave here the same as every morning and get the schoolhouse warmed up, and the older ones can get it all cleaned up and start to decorate it. I may have to rehearse a few of the little ones once more and them we will have lunch for us three. The real entertainment is to start at one o'clock and last till four. I except quite a lot of people, as most of the pupils have invited some of their family or friends."

I always was a very quiet child and the great news almost stunned me. I had never for a moment dreamed of going to the last day. I looked at my mother and saw a look of joy spread over her dear face. She who had traveled so much, seen so much, been to so many great theatres, concerts, everything, had now been living, I might almost say, in isolation for eight years. I, who scarcely every left our little home, would be all at once going to see and hear such a marvelous thing. Oh, what joy filled my little mind, and to think that my mother and I would eat out of lunch pail or a basket. That, too, would be just wonderful. Oh, joy, to ride there and back with the lovely, fast dancing young horses. I was too happy to sleep for hours. The next days were filled with a happy anticipation. It was not like the holy joy of Christmas, but I think in another way it was as big an excitement.

Somehow the days went by and the great day had come. I, who was always fast asleep when my father left in the morning, was up and at the breakfast table, but too happy, too excited to eat. It seems we had had an unusually mild winter. That morning, the sun was shining brightly, but I do remember my father saying that he thought it would turn cold. After my father left, I kept running to the east window to see if Mr. Anchord was

15

coming. My mother kept telling me that it would still be over two hours until ten.

Well, I knew that, but I thought there just might be a chance he would come earlier. My dear mother went upstairs and got a very beautiful basket out of one of the trunks. I had seen it before, but today it had a new meaning--it was to contain our lunch.

My mother had almost an endless collection of all kinds of souvenirs, things she had collected from the many foreign countries she had visited. My father only had a very few such things. But this basket was a gift from the Seneca Indians to his father, who had once come from the old country and stayed with the Senecas. He took the basket back to Europe and when his youngest son, my father, left home for America, he gave him this basket and told him why he should so highly prize it. Well. The basket was woven square, with a tight fitting cover, but the beauty of it lay in its exquisite workmanship. Through the entire filling of a basket are the strands that go around the longer, thicker sticks that go up and down, called the standards, and woven all through this basket was a beautiful design of beadwork representing trees, ferns, flowers, grass, and moss. On one side was a deer.

My mother made some sandwiches, cut thick slices of a rich fruitcake, and put in a few large red apples. She wrapped the sandwiches in a snowy napkin and the cake in some thick white papers. Then she fixed my hair, put on my best dress, dressed herself, and got our coats near the fire. It was getting much colder, and the wind had begun to blow stronger.

It was ten o'clock and no Mr. Anchord yet. My mother got my little thin coat to wear under my heavy one. It was eleven o'clock, and I just kept running from the east window to the clock and back again. It was twelve o'clock. My mother tried to have me eat something, but I was too excited. By this time, the windows were frozen over, and I had to blow on one little spot to look down the road. My mother got out two heavy shawls, one to wear over her coat and the other to wrap all around me after I got in the wagon. At that time, most women wore shawls. There was no snow on the hard frozen ground, but the sun had disappeared by now and the wind got stronger. It was one o'clock. I did not cry; I never did; but I could see the great disappointment in my mother's sweet, gentle face. Two o'clock, half-past two, three o'clock, and I gave a little cry, "He's coming." But the next second I could see through the frozen window pane that it was a one horse buggy driving in.

My mother opened the door and an icy blast blew in. A man jumped out and said, "My wife is almost froze to death." He half carried, half led her into the house. He said he would put the horse in the barn. My mother unwrapped the woman, made some hot tea, and fed it to her with a spoon. The woman shook so she could not guide the spoon. Neither could she speak. The man came in, and he was almost as bad off. It turned out that the man was a soldier friend of my father's and had come to see him on some business.

About half-past three, Mr. Anchord drove in with his prancing young team. He came to the door and said, "Well, Mrs. Kussmaul, are you ready?" I had never seen my mother out of patience before, but she spoke up and said, "We have been ready ever since ten o'clock this morning, the time you were supposed to come after us. Now, I have some half frozen people here, and besides, it's too late anyway. The entertainment is about over now. This has been a bitter disappointment to my child and myself."

My father came home abut five o'clock and told my mother he tried to put off the entertainment as long as possible. He said, "I shall never forgive Mr. Anchord." In later years, I learned just how he never forgot or forgave.

At bedtime it started snowing. When I woke next morning, my mother told me that about nine o'clock the night before, the Gasers left. They had a buggy and were afraid they would not be able to leave later as the roads would be impassable. They had a lot of cattle at home and could not leave them too long. The wind would be on their backs. They lived on the other side of Rome.

Chapter 3

I did not get up, no, not for the next six weeks. I became very ill. I never knew just what ailed me, only that I had a terrible fever. My mother told me later on that for six weeks I never ate a single thing. She tried to coax me to ear, to have me drink milk. I had always been fond of milk. But when she put a spoonful in my mouth, I would shiver and spit it out. After about a week, I said I wanted some of the Christ-child's golden apples from heaven, oranges. My father walked to Camden and back, sixteen miles, and got a dozen oranges and a dozen lemons.

After that, I drank lemonade, a few spoonfuls at a time, and the juice from the oranges. My good father made that long trip three times. They moved me into the kitchen on a little bed. Neither my father or mother undressed for six weeks. I do not think I had any pain, but each night I was out of my head, and I got so weak I could not even turn over in bed. I cannot recall that we had any callers. The cats were a great comfort to me. I so loved to hear them purr. I would lay there and gaze at them.

My mother often told me I hardly ever spoke. She would ask me if I wanted this or that, and I only shook my head. Then, after about five weeks, I said I wanted to see a flower. Though it was the beginning of April, it was still winter; the winter had come so late. My father started at once for Mrs. Dixon's. She always had potted plants. He had hardly gone when old Mr. Powers came. He was known to be a very mean, disagreeable man. He asked my mother, "Where is Otto?" She told him I wanted to see a flower, and he went to Mrs. Dixon's to see if he could get one. Mr. Powers gave a grunt, got up, and went out. In about fifteen minutes, he came back with a little paper sack and handed it to my mother. He said, "If that is what the young one wants, here it is. I went over to Margaret's. That was Mrs. Littlefield. If I live to be a hundred years old, I shall never forget the great joy those blossoms gave me. I can still see them, three big spikes of full bloom geraniums, one a dark scarlet, one a salmon color, and one snow white. Perhaps that is the reason that even now the geranium is so dear to me. A short time later, my father came back with a potted plant in full bloom that was also a geranium, a double pink one.

The fever left me; I slept, woke up, looked at my flowers, and went back to sleep. Still did not eat. After six weeks, I woke up and said to my mother, "I'm hungry." My mother half laughed, half cried, and said, "Some nice toast, or an egg, or canned berries?" I said, "Meat." My father went out and killed a hen; my mother dressed it. I watched her. While it was cooking, I said, "Smells good." Then every little while I asked if it was done. At last it got done. I ate and ate, but my mother was afraid to let me eat too much at once. About this time, my father brought me each day great big branches of pussy willows. I would pick them off and put them in little dishes. Well, I got well.

The snow was gone, and spring seemed to come overnight. I lived outdoors from early in the morning till bedtime—the same dear, dear evening spent on the verandah. Everything was just the same again except one thing; my illness left me with a cough. Now, I think if I had playmates, I would have gotten over my cough. As it was, it was forever brought to my mind. My good, dear, sweet mother would come out to me where I was happily playing and ask me anxiously, "Was my little honey girl coughing again?" Then, I know not why, I would cough. I really did not do this on purpose. Then my mother would look dreadfully sad. She would tap her chest and say, "Does it hurt you here when you cough?" She came out every few minutes to ask me if I was warm enough. If the west wind blew, she would move my playthings on the east side of the house and vise versa. Forever watching me, asking me if I had coughed while she was in the house.

I was not a bad child, but I did do a few very naughty things. Just why I did them, I do not know. Here is one of them: I generally only played on the east side. My mother had a row of chicken coops there. In each coop was a mother hen with her brood of chicks. At the end of the row were two coops, each with a hen and her family of ducklings. Well, my mother had two tiny dishes in each coop, one with feed, the other for drinking water.

In front of the two coops, with the ducklings, a pan of water so they could bathe and swim in it.

I spent hours each day watching the little downy chicks and ducklings. Often my mother was with me. She, too, loved to see them. All the coops were built tight on three sides. In front, there was open-work laths nailed a few inches apart to let light and air in, and at the bottom, a space where the little chickens and ducklings could run in and out.

Well, I made up my mind; I would teach the baby chicks to swim as well as the little ducks. So I would grab up a few and put them in the water. Of course, the mother hens were frantic, but I knew they could not get at me. But they made such a racket, my mother came rushing out. Well, I was very fleet, and when I heard her quick steps in the house, I flew about ten or fifteen feet off and was innocently playing when she came out. She picked the soaked, shivering little chicks out of the water, and said she could not understand how they ever got in.

This happened again and again, but I learned to be very cunning. I would go into the house, perhaps to see what time it was or after a drink of water, but really only to find out what my mother was doing. If she was in the bedroom, which overlooked the yard where the coops were, I would go back out and play innocently for a while. But if by any chance she was working in the kitchen, I would run out and catch all the poor little chicks I could and dump them in the water. When some of them tried to struggle out, I would push them back in. I got bolder all the time, as I had never been caught.

The old hens made a deafening racket, as I had chicks from four or five coops. I was having a glorious time. All at once, there stood my mother. I shall never forget just how she looked at me. There was some anger in her face, but a lot more sorrow, disappointment, and yes, even a little surprise. She scolded me a little, but what was worse, she told me she could never trust me again. She pitied the poor, half drowned chicks and then did a very wise thing. Instead of punishing me, she went and opened up all the coops except the two that had the duckling's foster mothers. I was afraid she would tell my father that night, but she never did, and neither did she ever mention it again. Of course, with the old mother hens at large, I could not catch and torment their chicks anymore.

As the spring, summer and early fall passed by, I was only in the house at mealtimes and at night. On rainy days I played in the barn or on the verandah. Soon it was the first week of October and a cold wind was blowing. I had been in the house more lately. We sat at dinner. In came Johnny Shwartze and told my parents that his father had been taken very sick in the night and wanted to see my father and mother. He went on to North Bay. The Shwartze family lived about four miles in the opposite direction from North Bay. After he went, my mother said, "Do you think it will hurt little Sophie to take that long ride in this cold wind?" My father said, "No, if you bundle her up well." Oh, I was excited. We drove there with Nellie. My father and mother went with Mrs. Shwartze into the sickroom. I stayed in the kitchen with Willie and Lizzie, who were a few years older than I, and Emma, who was just my age.

After a while, they took me out into the apple orchard. They had quite a few trees and they were full of all kinds of lovely apples. The ground, too, was covered with apples. It seemed that Mr. Shwartze had not been well for some time, so no apples had yet been gathered. The next thing I remember, I was sitting on the ground in the high grass, my little back against a tree trunk, eating away on such a big apple I had to use both hands to hold it. Never before or after can I remember an apple tasting so delicious. The three Shwartze children also sat in the grass munching apples. I was happy. All at once, I saw my mother running towards me. She looked frightened and both arms were outstretched. She grabbed me up and said, "No coat on, nothing on your poor, dear little head, and sitting on the cold ground, and that apple." I still hung onto the apple and ate faster and faster.

At home, I had an apple or two every day, too, but my mother would first wash her own hands, though they looked clean, then carefully select an apple, peel it very thin, cut it up in small pieces, put them on a clean little plate, and then, much against my will, wash and wipe my hands and say, "There, little lamb, is an apple." Well, that day I ate one, skin and all, that was not wiped, and my little hands were not carefully washed. I was very happy. On the nice ride I saw so many things: other people's cows, horses, and hens, other houses, trees along the road. And best of all, I heard my father promise Mr. Shwartze that we would come again next day, and every day till he got better.

I mentioned in my preface that my father had spent a year in a medical college. Well, we went there every day for about a month. If it rained, the children and I would play in their barn. Not till a year or so later did I hear my mother tell Mrs. Anchord how she had worried herself almost to death about my cough and that for some strange reason it had stopped the very day we went to Shwartze's and I was exposed to that bitter cold wind. Mrs. Anchord laughed and told my mother that if she had not reminded me all the time about my cough, it would have stopped long before.

It was about the middle of November, a dark gloomy day. I had been in the house all day. My father had worked in the woods in the forenoon and for a wonder, was home the rest of the day. I do not mean to say that he never went visiting around the neighborhood, but in spring, summer and early fall he always worked on the farm. The rest of the year in the woods, unless he was teaching.

Well, I cannot find just the right words to express the "something" that seemed to be in the air that afternoon. My father, who was by nature a very silent person, seemed more quiet, more reserved even than usual. My dear, sweet mother, who always went about her work with a smile, seemed listless, sad. I was never a child to ask questions, but I felt the tension. I knew not what it was. There was no quarrel between them, only silence. After a while, my mother tied up her head in a white kerchief. She often did that when she had one of her severe headaches, but on other occasions she would talk to and smile at my father, but today there was silence.

After supper, perhaps it was about half past six, the night was black; all at once we heard some stamping on the doorstep and then a knock. I shall never forget the look of agony that came over my mother's face as she glanced at my father. She got up and opened the door. Two men walked in. They had a lantern with them. One of the men was Higa Humistan, a man who quite often came to our house. The other one I had never seen before. The three men visited quietly for a little while. I do not think my mother spoke a word. After perhaps half and hour, the stranger got up and said, "Well, we might as well get her." My father, Higa, and the stranger went out together. Then my mother broke out into hysterical weeping. I had never seen her weep before.

After some time, I went up to her and asked her what was the matter? She was still shaking with sobs, but trying hard to control herself. She took me in her arms, and said it was her headache. She also had such a cold. Well, I asked no questions, but somehow I felt there was something wrong besides her headache. Then she took me into the bedroom and began to unpack one of her great big trunks, bringing out things she brought from the old country. I had seen them before, but loved to see them again. She told me about the different countries where they had come from. Well, after a while my father came back in the house. They looked at one another, but did not speak.

Next morning, I awoke. The sun was shining. My dear mother came to me, knelt down in front of my bed and said, "I have to tell you something. Nellie died last night." She looked at me with so much love and tenderness, yes, and sadness that I could not answer her. Then she went on and said, "Nellie was not well for some time, and that was why those men came last night. They tried to help her, but it was too late, and that was why I cried so much." Well, I never spoke a word, asked no questions, but young as I was, I reasoned out that my father never could have got Nellie out of the stable alone and so of course she must still be in her stall.

I had never at that time seen a dead animal, but somehow it sent a terrible feeling of horror over me. After a while I got up, ate my breakfast, and started playing in the house. I, who always, unless the weather really was bad, made a dive for the door. My mother looked at me and asked in a surprised tone, "Is my little honey girl not going out to play in the sunshine?" I just said no.

After some time had passed, I would go out of doors to play again, but not until sometime in April did I ever enter the stable. How I longed to play in the hay, hunt eggs, look at all the hens, ducks, and above all the cattle. The barn had always been my winter playground. But nothing could induce me that long, yes terrible winter to enter it. Some instinct told me it would be terrible. So as I had never heard my father mention her removal,

I took it for granted that Nellie must still be in her stall. If only I had asked my mother, what horror, what fear, what nightly nightmares I would have been spared.

Winter set in very early that year. Even before Thanksgiving we were snowed in. In those days, there was a rail fence from McLaughlin's corner down to McCormack's corner. So, of course, that caused great drifts of snow to pile up on our road. Wire fences were not even heard of then. Of course our modern big snow plows did not come for nearly sixty years later. The R.F.D. was unknown as well. Our road being what was termed a back road, it was generally not opened at all. So when the first big snowstorm came, we were snowed in. Then, once a week, my father took a large basket of eggs (we had about one hundred hens that winter) and an empty bag, walked or struggled over and through the mountains of snow to North Bay. I would eagerly await his return. The large bag was full of groceries, thrown over his back, and the basket was also full. Sometimes the storms were so terrific that it was two weeks between his trips.

Baked stuff was not heard of. Except in Oneida, every one did their own baking. Neither could any one obtain canned goods. Once in a great while, the road was opened. It was done this way: eight or ten men went ahead with shovels, then a team of horses hitched to one bob floundered through, then two teams, four horses, hitched to a scraper were driven through a few times. All this took all day. The next day, the farmers used the road from before daybreak till night. Wood was drawed to North Bay. Logs to North Bay Saw Mill. Hay was drawed by, loads of grain, potatoes, groceries brought home. The road scarcely ever lasted a day or two. Some winters it was not even opened up once.

That winter broke all records for coming so early, no mid-winter thaw, and lasting into April. My dear mother wrote to my Aunt Sophie to send her a first reader and an ABC book in German. My father and mother, who never spoke an English word amongst themselves or to me, had very wisely decided to teach me to read and write German before I learned to read and write English. Strange, though I never heard an English word spoken at home and saw such few people, I understood every single word spoken when anyone did come to our house.

24

Sophie Kussmaul

One day, it was the end of November, my father, coming home from one of those North Bay trips, handed my mother a small square package with many stamps. She undid the heavy cord and many wrappings. It contained three books. One, the smallest one, a German first reader or ABC book. Then there was another book, larger, and I think the most beautiful book I have ever seen. It was bound in light yellow leather, trimmed in blue and gold. Its pages were rich, smooth paper, clear print, and for every little story an exquisite colored picture.

I was still looking at the pictures when my mother read out loud a sentence from her sister's letter. "According to your description of my little niece, she will probably learn to read in a few weeks and then be able to read the little stories in the little book herself." My mother smiled proudly at me. I imagine my mother had written to my aunt the winter before about my really uncanny way of reading and writing the figures into the millions and so on, also about how I knew all the state capitols and metropolis. Just then I opened up the big book. It was *Grim's Fairy Tales.* I gave one smothered cry and fled into the next room. My mother followed me in and asked me if I got hurt. I fairly shivered with fear and whispered to her that it was that picture. My mother went back. The book was still open where I had left it. There were some dwarfs and a witch. My mother tried to calm me, telling me that millions of little boys and girls loved that book. Two or three times after that, she coaxed me to look at some of the pictures, but each time such a great terror came over me, she had to give it up. I saw her put it into a bureau drawer. I would make a circle around the bureau. Finally she put it upstairs. I never got over that fear. I was forty-eight years old when the house burned up and still when I was upstairs alone, a creepy feeling came over me when I thought of that book. Of course not nearly as bad then as when I was little, but still a feeling of horror.

The next day my mother took me on her lap and said, "Now my little honey pet is going to learn to read." She pointed at the letter of the alphabet, said "A - B - C. Now, you say it." I looked at the letters, at my mother, then gazed out of the window. Again and again my patient mother repeated those three letters. I did not answer. At last she tried just the A. It made no difference.

Each day for weeks she tried with infinite patience to teach me those three letters. By spring, I could read three little words. I never learned the whole alphabet. I did not try to be stubborn. I do not know why I could not learn. I used to look at my mother's tired, sad face, then I would bend over the same page we had for four or five months, but everything look meaningless to me. About the same time my reading lessons started, my father produced a little arithmetic book, a beginner's arithmetic book. I heard him tell my mother, "I suppose I could start her on the third or forth book. A child who could read and write the figures into the quadrillions when she was just five years old, without any teaching, should be able to do all the examples in book three or four now that she is nearly six years old."

Well, he got the little book and a slate and wrote down one and one, two and two, and asked me to add it up. I sat there, stared at the figures, and dimly wondered why they stood on top of one another. My father saw I had not added them up, as he called it. I did not even know what he meant. He explained. I did not understand, he got angry, said I was just stubborn. The more he scolded, the less I knew what he wanted me to do. How little I realized what was before me. From then on, all my winters, until I was twenty years old, were just on long stretch of misery. I hated, hated arithmetic. I could not learn it.

My father had no patience. I hated him too. He kept me at that despicable arithmetic for hours every day, Saturdays included. I never got any further than the average child of eight or nine years. At twenty, I quit. Death itself would have been much preferable to any more such so called arithmetic lessons. To this day the very sight of an arithmetic book makes me feel sick.

In this nightmare of a winter, there were two diversions. First, the holy blessed Christmas. I had been six years just before Christmas, and until after Christmas, there were no lessons. My mother's reading lessons bored me, but I did not fear or hate them.

Then some time in the winter, about the first of February, our road was opened. For a great wonder. The next day, though bitter cold, it was clear and no winds, a lot of people went by, using the road. About five o'clock, to my great surprise, a beautiful bay horse with a string of bells, the first I had ever seen, and hitched to a shiny cutter, drove into our driveway which my father had shoveled out, to be in keeping with the open road. A great big man got out, dressed in a long fur coat and fur cap. A large woman followed him to the door. She also was dressed in heavy expensive clothes. My father was in the barn, so he introduced himself to my mother. He said his name was Ceigler, and he was a soldier comrade of my father's. The woman was his wife. The lived between Rome and Utica.

My father came in, and they went and put their horse in the barn. My poor mother tried her best to prepare a good supper. We were very poor at that time and it so happened that my father had not been to the village in ten days. He intended to go down the first thing the next morning.

So in spite of all my mother could do, we had a very plain supper. Mr. Ceigler said they always had cake for supper. While we were still at the table, the wind came up. At bedtime it was snowing, drifting. In the morning, one of the worst blizzards I can remember was raging. Mr. Ceigler went to the barn to feed his horse. He came back and said he could not find any oats or ground feed. My father told him he had none. "Well," he said, "you have hens." I can make corn do for once." My father told him we had scarcely enough corn to carry us through the storm. He got mad and said, "You got nothing, not even a decent meal to eat." My mother baked pancakes for breakfast. They both declared they always had sausage or fresh meat with their pancakes. My mother said we were out of meat. Mr. Ceigler sniffed, and said, "Well, why don't you kill some hens?"

After awhile my father really got mad, the two men had a row, and the woman said, "Willie, dear, let us go home." But no living creature could have lived and traveled a mile that day, not the next, or the next. For three days and nights the blizzard raged, the worst and the longest storm I can remember. The woman told my mother about their lovely home, a big farm. They kept a hired woman and two hired men the year around. One the third day, the two men go into a fight in the kitchen. The woman screamed and ran into the living room saying, "Oh, my Willie, my Willie." At last it was over. The woman wept and washed her husband's bloody face. Mother said to my father, "You must remember they are our guest." My father replied, "I do remember it, but that so and so does not." The woman said, "Willie, let us go. We might better perish on the road than stay here." The man glared at her through his battered face and answered her, "There is no road."

That night the wind stopped and through the intense cold, the high snowdrifts had become hard. We heard then get up about one o'clock and leave. They hitched up their horse in the dark. When morning came, my father went to North Bay. It was forty-five below zero. But before he left, he took a picture we had in the house of two large fat hogs, one a boar and the other a sow, put them in an envelope and addressed then to Mr. and Mrs. Ceigler. On the back of the picture he wrote, "In your haste, on leaving our quiet home, you forgot your likenesses." Well, we never heard from them again.

Chapter 4

At last the long winter was over. There still were some old drifts left, but the sun shone warm and bright, the damp ground smelled good. The robins and blue birds were flitting about and filled the spring air with their sweet, cheerful songs. Again I was out of doors most all day, but down in my woodland retreat there was still too much snow and water to play. Of course, I did not enter the barn. On one forenoon, when I was playing near the house, a man, woman, and a little girl came to our house. They were carrying a great many baskets. For some strange reason, I, who always ran and hid when anyone came, except the Dixons, went into the house at once. Those people were full blooded Indians, the first I had ever seen. For once my father was in the house, shelling corn for the hens. He told my mother to get something for them to eat. My mother put bread and butter on the table. He told her if there was any cooked meat to put it on too. I gazed long and earnestly at them. Yes, I even went up to the little girl and held her hand, then slowly, shyly went up to the woman.

My mother looked astonished, as I had always shunned everyone. Even the very few children that did come, I would not make friends with. After they had eaten, my father bought a big clothes basket, a bushel basket, and a market basket, also some lovely bead work. The woman gave me a small basket and a bead necklace. Just before they left, my father looked at the man and said, "Oneida?" The Indian nodded, hesitated and said, "Seneca." My father nodded. After they went away, I went outdoors again, but something came over me, a great longing. I wanted that child for a playmate, and for years to come she seemed near me. I had, in a way, that same homesickness, that call of some unheard voice from far, far away as I did when I looked westward.

Each spring one or two little calves were born. For me, that was a great occasion. One morning, it was about the middle of

April, my father came in from the barn and said, "Diana had a red and white heifer calf." On what a joy! A heifer calf meant we would keep it. The little bull calves were always kept till they were fat and then sold. But instead of rushing out to see the calf, I did not stir. My mother looked at me in surprise and said, "Why does my lambie not go out to see the little bossie?" I did not answer. I was longing to run out, but out there was the horror. After breakfast, I went out to play in the warm sunshine. The grass was getting green. My mother came out, smiling, and said, "Are you not coming out to see Diana's baby?" Well, that was a little too much, so I followed her. The stable door stood open so the sun could shine in.

But the nearer I got to that door, the slower I walked. Now the way the stable was in those days, the cow stations came first, the horse stall was at the farthest end. Diana stood nearest the door. So, slowly I went near. I thought maybe I could see the calf by not going in, so cautiously I crept to the door and gave a quick terrified glance towards the horse stall. It seemed empty. So I went in and put my arms around the dear little calf, but still felt the horror must be near. I thought it probably was in the barn part. All that day, I ran back and forth to the calf, but dared not look into the other part. The next day, I crept close to the door that opened into the other part and peaked through a crack. Still no horror. I opened the door a wee bit and looked. No horror...then I walked in. Everything was the way it always had been. Oh what a good feeling. Then, all at once, I thought it must be back of the barn. I dared not look. So I ran down into the pasture. I thought from there I could see back of the barn and still not be too near. I looked. Nothing. I cautiously went closer. No, everything was all right. Then I began to be happy again. That haunting terror no longer existed.

I knew those unreasonable, cruel, outrageous arithmetic lessons were over till late next fall or early winter, and at that time, that seemed as far off to me as ten years would seem now. My reading lessons, too, would be over with for a long, long time. They were not so bad, just a little tiresome. The other terror was stowed away in a trunk in the garret. I hardly ever went upstairs, and if I wanted to go up into the really nice, big room beyond the garret, all I had to do was run through the garret, give on quick glance to where the trunk stood that held it. Well, I was happy, life was beautiful. Spring was in the air. Lillie, our gray and white mother cat, had two lovely black and white kittens in a big basket in the woodshed. Daisy, the little heifer calf, was just learning to eat grass. Diana, Blacky, and Spotty, the cows, were out to pasture. Soon there would be dozens of little baby chickens, little ducklings. Wildflowers were everywhere.

My father had taken a German class to teach in Cleveland, a night class. So he worked on the farm from dawn till four in the afternoon, washed up, changed his clothes, and walked to Cleveland. The class lasted from seven thirty to ten; then my father walked home, about eight miles each way. He got home between twelve and one, but was out at work again at daybreak. That meant about four in the morning. He did that three times a week till the first of September.

Way back in March, my mother received a letter from her sister that she intended to come out and spend the summer with us. My dear mother, who lover her so much and often spoke of her, was very happy. You see, these two sisters had always been together and now for nearly nine years had not seen one another. My mother was very poor, my Aunt Sophie very well off. Also, Constantinople, Turkey is a long way from North Bay, New York. In each letter the two sisters wrote to each other every week, she was speaking of her intended long trip.

My Aunt Sophie and her husband were to travel to Germany together. There he would put her on one of the big steamships going to New York, and then she would come on to us. He was to visit his people. Well, my parents got Mrs. Dixon to clean the house from top to bottom. Poor as they were, they got a new carpet for the living room and bedrooms. The kitchen floor, recess and pantry floors were repainted, also the floor of the big room upstairs. At that time, linoleum was unknown. All the wood work in all the rooms was also repainted. All the rooms were papered, the summer kitchen and back room scrubbed, new curtains bought. I think Mrs. Dixon worked for us every day for about a month. She always went home at night. All this was very pleasant for me. It was a joy to see my little, frail mother look so happy.

Through Sophie's Eyes

Well, time flew by, and it was the beginning of June. One morning at breakfast, a boy brought my mother a telegram. It was the first time there was such a thing as a telegram. He said it arrived the night before at North Bay, but there was no one to deliver the message. It was from my Aunt Sophie. She has arrived in New York City, would stay overnight and then would take the first rain to Oneida the next morning, arrive at North Bay on the Ontario and Western at six fifteen, and then hire a rig to bring her to us.

Of course, this meant today, as the telegram was delayed in delivery. Oh, I was wild with excitement. For once I did not go to my woodland. I played near the house, running in often to see what time it was. Well, it was about eleven o'clock, my mother was very busy in the summer kitchen, cooking and baking things for supper; my father had just come in from the garden. All at once, a black team hitched to a wagon containing two women drove into our yard. One woman was slim, the other tall and large.

My mother gave a little cry and just flew out. The big woman had jumped nimbly from the wagon and the two hugged, kissed, laughed, and cried together. I stood there in wonder, silence. My father said, "That is your Aunt Sophie." The driver of the team beckoned my father; they unloaded the largest trunk I had ever seen, also, a smaller trunk and two traveling bags. My father asked the driver how much she wanted for bringing my aunt and trunks, but she said she had already had her pay. My mother said the telegram said she would not arrive at North Bay until after six-fifteen at night. My Aunt laughed and said, "After I sent the telegram, I thought I might as well take a night train to Oneida. I got to Oneida at seven this morning, but had to wait there for the nine-thirty for North Bay. Well, anyway, I got here."

My mother rushed around and got dinner on the table. That was a happy meal. After dinner, my father went out to work as usual. My aunt got a key and started to unpack the big trunk. I would never have believed that so many things could go even in a large trunk. Every chair in the room, the sofa, and even the table were piled up and still the bottom of the trunk was not reached. There were new sheets and pillow cases, bedspreads, two new linen table cloths with napkins. Yards and yards of pink and blue gingham for my mother's house dresses, and a few yards of light brown cloth to make a Sunday dress for my mother. There was not many ready made dresses in those days, but my aunt brought out of the depths of her trunk a pasteboard box of delicate lace, a white muslin petticoat also trimmed with lace, and two pair of sheer, white stockings. "There my little namesake is something for you to wear to church." I glanced at my mother, touched the things with a brown finger, and wondered if people wore white things if they went to church. As yet I had never been to any church.

Then came a light blue thin coat and bonnet for spring and fall and a heavy dark brown chinchilla coat, lined with red silk for winter. My dear mother kept saying, "How lovely." There were half a dozen new white shirts for my father and a black suit that my aunt said was last year's style, just as if it mattered. Then there was a square box, inside a music box that played four pieces. Then a box full of ribbons of all shades and colors and dainty laces. Another larger box with dozens of pieces of silk and velvet and lots of buttons. Then a dozen new white linen towels with red borders. Story books, pictures, and a lot of other things.

I think my poor aunt was much hurt and disappointed in me. She probably thought I would show my delight, but I just stood there in silence. Then she unlocked the smaller trunk. On top was a great big, heavy shawl for my mother. At that time, women all wore shawls. Then, oh joy, out came a ten pound box of figs, then another ten pound box of dates. Never had I even heard of those things, much less ever tasted them. These two boxes were of tin and my aunt said, picked and cured just a few miles from Constantinople. Out came two five pound pasteboard boxes, one full of delicious chocolate candy, the other of mixed white candies. I really was not a greedy child, but I stuffed myself for once. Then all at once, I left and ran to my woodland play house. There I stayed until I smelled supper. When the west wind blew, I could always catch the odors of cooking.

I came home tired but happy. My dress was torn, my face, hands, dress very dirty. My aunt looked at me in horror, asked my mother what was the matter. My mother smiled at me and said, "She was playing." My aunt said, "But why don't she play in the house?" I wondered how anyone could play in a house in summer.

We had supper, then my father started his chores, and I did mine. I fed Daisy her milk, fed all the baby chicks and little ducklings, and when the new milk came in, took a small bowl of it to the mother car and her little kittens. Then I went and sat down shyly near my aunt on the verandah. My mother was still busy in the kitchen. My aunt asked me many questions. Then she said, "Did you enjoy the nice little stories in that book I sent you last fall?" I said, "Yes." Then she said, "Run in the house and bring it out." I did. Then she handed it back to me and said, "Now read me a story. I want to hear it with your sweet little voice." I was silent. Then she patted me and said, "Oh, I do not care which one, any of them." I looked at her and said, "I can not read." At first my aunt just stared at me then said, "Did your mother not teach you to read?" I said, "She tried to." Then my aunt called my mother out and said, "Elise, did you not teach little Sophie to read?" My mother looked sad and said, "She was so young. We will really start this coming fall."

Well, my aunt soon found out that I could not even write my name. My aunt sniffed, and said to my mother, "You wrote and told me the little girl could read and write the figures into the billions, trillions, and knew as much about geography as a average girl would know at ten years when she was just a little past five years. Now she is six-and-a-half years old and cannot even write her name." Then she laughed. I felt she was disgusted with me.

Well, in after years I often thought it must have been like this. I probably heard my father say that it took seven figures to write a million and so on to quadrillions. I could count up to a hundred ever since I was three years old, so I imagine I counted the 0's and the one. I could only read and write them with a 1 and a string of 0's. Probably the capitols and metropolises sounded to me like poetry. I was a born poet. Therefore, I could remember to say them.

After a while, my father and mother had their work done and also came to sit on the verandah. They talked together, and I sat in silence and listened to the night sounds. Oh, how I loved them. About half past eight (it really was not dark yet being the longest days), all at once my aunt said to my mother, "Is this not the time you put your child to bed?" My mother said, "She never goes to bed until we do unless she asks to go before." My aunt sniffed again. I wondered why she thought I should go to bed and the rest stay up.

So the days went by. Each day I felt that my aunt looked at me as something not quite up to what I should know and be. One day after dinner, I hastily grabbed a piece of bread and a chunk of meat and stuffed it into one of my pockets. I pressed down on it, as there were other things in the pocket. My aunt looked on in horror and said, "What are you going to do with that food?' I said, "Eat it." My aunt said, "What else have you got in that pocket?" I pulled the bread and meat out and turned my pocket wrong side out. There was a snail's house and about a dozen dead pollywogs. I think Aunt Sophie nearly collapsed. She said in a weak voice, "What are those little dead creatures?" I told her they were dead pollywogs. I had caught them for the little ducklings, but they would not eat them now. I said, "They like to feel them wiggle in their little bills and throats." She said, "How can you touch those dead things?" I calmly put bread, meat, snail's house, and pollywogs back in my pocket.

So the summer days went by. One day it rained, and I played all the forenoon in the barn. After dinner, my aunt called me back as I was going out again. She produced a lovely workbasket. The basket was round and finely woven. It was lined with scarlet satin. There was an oblong leather box lined with purple plush. In it were three sizes of scissors, all shiny like silver, the smallest one being only about two inches long. There was a needle book made of thin yellow leather, the leaves inside were white flannel. There were dozens of needles in it, from big darning needles to the smallest, and white pins. There were three sizes of sewing awls. Tape, black , white, blue, and red sewing silk. Black and white thread from the finest to the coarsest. A tape or yard measure, and many other things to complete a sewing outfit. I looked long and earnestly at the things, but did not touch any of them. After a while my aunt said, "And would not my little niece like to learn to sew?" I replied, "Someday I will learn to make baskets like this one." Later on I did. My aunt looked at me and said, "You make baskets?" I said, "Yes," and ran off to the barn.

A few weeks later, I heard my aunt say to my mother that she was sorry I knew so little. Of course, she meant my not being able to read and write. I said to her, "Auntie, it is you who knows so little. I know a lot." I think she would have been very angry with me, but somehow she must have seen pity in my face for her, so she said, "Well, little one, you certainly cannot learn anything down there in the woods." I said, "Come with me, Auntie." Well, she did follow me. When we got to the spring, she halted and said, "What are all those tiny moving black things in that slimy stuff?" I told her they were newly hatched pollywogs and they would eat that stuff that had been around their eggs. When it was all eaten, they were big enough to eat tiny flies. Then when they had grown to about five times their present size, they would get tiny little front legs, but still keep their tails, as they needed them yet. Then, little hind legs would grow out from under their tails. Then the tails would drop off and the little black pollywog would become a brown or rather a gray little frog. Slowly he would get lighter colored until he was a bright green with a white throat and belly.

Then we went on through the cedars and hemlocks to the fence. My aunt said, "These trees (the poor woman did not know they were hemlocks and cedars) look so dull. Are they dying?" I said, "Why, no, you see, it is this way. God always waits till every leaf tree and shrub have their new leaves and look their best, then he makes the new needles on the needle trees push out the old ones." Just across the fence were a few raspberry bushes, the berries not yet ripe. My aunt asked me what kind of berries they were. I showed her that some of them were black raspberry bushes, some red ones. I told her the black ones had so much longer stems and then bowed their heads way down to the ground during the fall. The dead leaves and grasses would collect around them so the ends, or bowed heads, would be covered up. During the winter, the part that was covered would start roots and so in spring each bowed head, now rooted off at the bottom, would spring up again, and from the roots would spring another new plant. But the red raspberry bushes were not like that. They grew up straight, not so tall, and never bowed their heads to the ground.

Their roots ran from the main bush under the ground and then a foot or two from the main bush in all directions would spring new plants.

By that time we had reached my house. In those days, now sixty-two years ago, back of where the few lone hemlocks now stand, was a dense forest, mostly hemlocks, a few leaf trees, and a large pine tree. Against the trunks of two giant hemlocks that grew so close together that their trunks formed a thick wall was the back of my house. On two sides, where the young hemlocks grew so close together that they formed the side wall, I bent their tops over my house and tied them together with vines. That made a thick roof. Besides, being under those giant old hemlocks, under their heavy branches, no rain, unless it was almost a cloudburst, could leak through the roof. I had carefully cut off or pulled out any brush that had been on the ground, my floor. I had collected all kinds of mosses and had so arranged them to form patterns, light colored ones in the center, then a ring of darker ones, then another ring of deep dark moss for the floor.

On one side was a small bench covered with shining birch bar. On it were little snail houses, an oriole's nest, a few bird eggs. On the other side were chickens. On another little bench, also covered with birch bark, were little boxes made out of bark. In one I had a lot of cocoons, big and little ones. My aunt had to bend her head a little when she entered my house. She asked me what those things were in that box. I told her they were baby butterflies. They as yet only had a body, no wings. I opened one and told her what kind of butterfly it would become. Then I showed her some big, fat, white grubs I had dug. These are going to become June bugs. Do you see their little brown heads? Then to her horror I put then in my pocket for Speckles, my pet hen.

She saw the silvery bird nest. I told her how the orioles hang their nest way out on tree branches, how the robins built mud nests and then line them with down. She shrieked; she saw a wasp. I told her how the wasps caught the horrid spiders. Then I told her how the mud wasps built their homes. There are always two together. When they work, one carries a small pellet of dirt in his feelers, the other one a tiny drop of water. The first one puts his pellet on the started mud house, the second one his drop of water on top of the speck of dirt, then they step on it to press it down and go for another load. We heard a shrill note on a tree close by and my aunt said, "A birdie." For once I laughed. I told her it was a tree toad, but if he saw us he would change his color to the tree he was on.

We were just starting back home when my aunt gave a little gasp. There was a giant toad in front of my house. I told her I was glad he was there; he caught thousands of flies and mosquitoes. She thought he was too clumsy to catch those things. I told her he had a long sticky tongue. He would dart that out and the flies would stick to it.

Well, we came back home and my aunt told my mother she had learned more from me in an hour than if she had read half a dozen books on nature. A stange child.

So the summer went by. On the last day of August, my aunt left us for her faraway home in the Orient. Mr. Anchord came with his young team and took my aunt and her two traveling bags to the North Bay station. The two trunks with all their contents she left with us. For my dear good mother, this parting was heartrending; for her it was again the same workaday existence and the probability of never seeing her beloved sister again. While for my aunt, though of course she too hated leaving my mother, before her lay the long voyage, first the days travel to New York City, a short visit there with her friends, then the ocean voyage across the Atlantic, then the happy reunion with her husband, who would be awaiting her at the seaport. Then together back to their love home in the tropical country.

Chapter 5

Well here was the second of September, a glorious night, with a full moon shining. The three of us sitting together on the dear old verandah. For a long time we were all silent. I was thinking of my aunt, of the little Indian girl I had met in the spring, of the woodland, the little wild animals I loved so much, the kittens, the glory of life. I also knew just what my mother and father were thinking, but also knew that they did not know my thoughts. I knew that my mother was following in her mind her sister. She, too, had made that trip. She pictured to herself the large white house, the wonderful tropical garden with its almost countless flowers, palm trees, fountains. The golden moonbeams falling through the green foliage, the white, winding pathways and the inviting trellised arbors.

Yes, she was thinking back to the time when she walked those very paths with her sister and, yes, the man who loved her so dearly. But those days were gone. They had been the happiest of her life. She was also thinking of my father, a man so highly born and educated, tilling his life away on our little farm. She was thinking of me, of my future. Yes, and with dread in her heart of the coming winter.

My father. Oh, yes, I knew what was in his mind. He worried about supporting us. I felt this in a vague way. He was not dreaming of the lovely night, but of the long ago, his boyhood, his dreams of the life ahead, and now, all had come so different. Oh, I knew.

Then my father broke the silence. He said, "Yesterday was my last day in Cleveland, and the money I earned there all summer went as fast as I earned it. I am certainly not complaining, but it cost us more than twice as much to live this summer." Then a pause. Then my father spoke again. "I sold Blacky today. She really was a poor cow, and there is not enough hay to winter three cows and the calf. The man will be after her in the morning." My mother replied, "Oh, my poor, poor Blacky."

Of course, I hated to see any of our animals go, but I really cared the least for Blacky. She used to try to hook me. Well, perhaps she did that because I always tormented her. When the cows were stantioned up and I was sure my father and mother were not near, I would take a long stick and tickle her heels or poke her in the belly. Not enough to hurt her, but just to make her mad. She would turn her head and glare at me and blow through her nose. When she caught me out in the barnyard, she tried to catch me with her horns.

Then my father said, "My school will not begin till the eighth of October. I will not draw any pay till six weeks after. The cow money will have to go to put a new roof on the house so we will have to be very saving." Another long pause, then we saw coming up the road in the bright moonlight a man walking rapidly. He turned into our lower driveway between the dear old maple trees, the same old maples that are still standing. It was one of the Eckels. For a little while he talked about things I do not remember. Then he said he had been chasing around all day after hop pickers. He was to get up a load of twenty pickers, ten men and ten women.

In the next county, there were large hop farms. They sent out all over to get enough pickers. All at once he said to my father, "I thought maybe I could get you." Then he went on to say that a good picker could make a dollar a day. In those days a man had to work ten hours at heavy farm work for fifty cents. He told of the good, hearty, three meals a day. How each person's fare out there and back was paid; it made it look very tempting. He said it would last between two and three weeks. My father said he would go in a minute, but he could not leave my mother and me alone. My mother, though so frail and little, was a very brave woman. She said we could get along fine for that time, beautiful weather and only a few chores to do. You see, they had been married about ten years, and my father had never spent a night away from home in all that time.

The man said all the pickers were to be at the North Bay Station the next afternoon at five o'clock. After he went, my father said, "Well, I have an acre of corn to cut, and it's a bright moonlight night. I will go at it at once." I was up for breakfast, the corn was all cut. The man came after Blacky. My father tied the corn stalks in bundles, about ten to fifteen stalks to a bundle, about eight to ten bundles to a stock. This was an exciting day for me. I followed my father around outdoors. My poor mother tried to be cheerful, but I could see the tears in her eyes. She packed my father's work clothes in a large satchel. In those days suitcases were unknown. My father worked till after four o'clock then hastily changed his clothes and was off. Then my poor dear mother wept.

For a week, things went lovely. One day my mother and I walked to North Bay, got the mail and a few groceries. Even that was an unusual thing for me. I was happy, played outdoors or followed my mother. I helped with the chores. We slept in the big bedroom downstairs. Then one morning we woke up with an awful fright. There was such a terrible roar that we could feel it. It came again and again. We knew what it was. We had often heard it at a distance, but never so close by. It was the Cleveland's monster red bull. He was the largest and ugliest bull that even the oldest neighbors had ever seen.

We heard afterwards that he weighed a ton, twenty hundred pounds, after he was dressed. So imagine how much more he weighed when alive. My mother and I jumped out of bed, and peeked out of the window. Looking in, his eyes were red with rage. He pawed the ground, roared and gave low grumbles of rage. We knew very well if he gave one mighty push against the old wooden door, the old door would fall in like pasteboard. We left the kitchen so he would not see us.

Out in the barnyard were our two cows waiting patiently to be put in the stable and be milked. My mother dared not go out because of the bull, though in front of the house, kept walking about and would see my mother cross from our back woodshed door across the barnyard to the stable. Strange to say, the bull showed on interest at all in our cows. After a while, he lay down and began chewing his cud. Then my little mother rushed out the back way, put the cows in the stable, milked, and turned them out again. I watched through a crack in the back door. Yes, she got back all right, but in closing the back door that led into the barnyard somehow it made a loud banging noise. Instantly, there was a mighty roar and the bull came with a rush, leaped lightly over the barnyard fence, and glared around, sniffing in the air, then pawed the ground, and gave bellow after bellow. Our cows looked at him then went quietly off to graze. The bull paid no attention to them whatsoever.

For at least the past twenty years, it is against the law to keep a bull over a year old in a pasture, but in those long gone by days a farmer could do as he liked. Also, in those days of over sixty years ago, sometimes for days no one passed by on our roads. We listened for a rig so we could signal for help, but no one passed.

We ate cold stuff, as the cook stove was in the kitchen and the least noise seemed to arouse his fury. He would wander around, go in the garden, eat our cabbages, but he always kept an eye on the house. Late in the afternoon our cows, the calf was with them now, came home from the back pasture. Every little while the bull would jump over the fence and look towards the back door, then again jump back and run around in front of the house bellowing and foaming at the mouth.

My mother and I went upstairs to sleep that night, as we did not know what moment he might break into the house. My mother said if he should try to come upstairs, his great heft would break the stairs, but if he should manage to mount them, we would have to climb out of the window onto the roof of the verandah, down the butternut tree, and make a run to the neighbors for help. Well, sometime in the night, we woke up with a terrible crashing noise, as if the whole house was falling down. Our very bed shook. There was a splintering of boards, a mad roaring of the giant bull. Tumbling and smashing noises and then silence. We peeked out cautiously from the windows and there he was going under an apple tree, eating apples. Well neither one of us slept again that night. In the morning we saw he had broken down the door on the west side of the house that led into the back room, smashed an old table and a few chairs, and walked out again. My mother saw him lay down under the tree and made a quick dive for the barn. He could not see the barnyard from where he was.

42

Sophie Kussmaul

She got the cows out again, barely got in the house with the milk when he woke up. Another day of terror, only cold stuff to eat. We could not even get a drop of water as the pump was in front of the house. No milking that night. No one passed by. We had a quiet night; my mother whispered to me that he probably went home. But in the morning we heard him roaring in the back room. My mother could not close the place where he had smashed in the door, as the least noise brought him straight back.

We got through the day somehow, again no milking. It seems he had slept a lot that night, and was now on the alert more than ever. At about four in the afternoon, we heard a rig come down the road. It was Jim Brown. For once the bull was at that moment in the barnyard. My mother ran to the road, waving her hands, in a few seconds she told him. He promised to send help.

In about an hour, Mr. Cleveland and one of his hired men came on horseback, two more men on foot with pitchforks, with Nero, the big Shepard dog. Well, they got the bull home and put him, by coaxing, in this old stanchion in the barn. Mr. Cleveland went to North Bay, sold him to the butcher. The butcher came out, but when he saw the bull, he dared not take him out. He put a rifle bullet through his brain, killed him in the stanchion. Then eight men got him loaded up.

After a while my father came home and said he would never leave us again. He never did. Then he hired two men to shingle the house and woodshed roofs. They had to tear off all the old shingles. I sorted them over, drawed them into the woodshed in my express wagon, neatly piled them up for kindling wood. I loved this work, thinking I was grown up. Soon after this, my father's school started.

Our school was only a small one, six to eight pupils, mostly grown up boys and girls. The pay, too, was less than half what he had received in the Yeager District. From the very first day he told my mother that the pupils did not seen to like him. He also said that he did not feel the same way toward then that he had felt towards the ones in his first school.

My German reading and writing lessons were again undertaken. I began to see into them a little better. I also had geography now, which I loved and learned fast. At night after supper, oh horrors, the arithmetic lessons from two to four hours.

I still ask myself what for? My father would work himself into a rage, yell, then tell my mother I was stubborn, sulky, self-willed, but he would break me of that; he would make me learn. Of course, all this made my sweet, gentle mother feel very sad. She would beg him to have patience with me. She would come and kiss me and whisper, "Try and understand."

It made me sullen and defiant.   I hated arithmetic...my unreasonable, tyrannical father also. I did try to understand, but if I stared at my example, trying to make sense out of it, he would say to my mother, "See, she just sits there and sulks. She don't try to study."

So it went till my eighth birthday, the twenty-first of December. Then till After New Years, I tasted freedom. Then my so called lessons began again and lasted into April.

We had a lovely Christmas.   Amongst the many things I received, there were three that gave me pleasure for years to come.   There was a present from my father and mother, a beautiful hand sleigh painted a dark green background, with a big bunch of red, pink and white roses in the center. My mother's rich friends from New York City sent a large box of watercolors and direction how to mix them; also two large books with outlined pictures to color. In those days, crayons were not yet heard of. My Aunt Sophie sent me four drawing books. One was a beginner book, the second was of animals; the third, people's faces, from babies up to old men and women. There were pages with only eyes, others with only lips, and others with only ears and so on. The forth book was drawings of houses, castles, bridges, little cabins, rooms, hallways and so on. I cannot say just how much pleasure I got out of those things. They brightened my lonely winters. Of course, just as soon as spring came, I did not touch them again till next late fall and winter.

I cannot recall that my mother or I went to a single house to visit, or even to North Bay to the store. We were snowed in as usual. Our road was not opened even once. Very few people came to see us, other than the Dixons, quite often, and the Eckels came a few times. Saturday mornings my father would wallow through the high drifts. Sometimes, as the snow was frozen so hard, he would walk on top without sinking in. We only had about twenty-five hens that winter, so there were not so many eggs to sell. My mother always waited eagerly for his return, the only time for a week that she could receive any mail.

One clear, cold day, sometime about the middle of January, after we had our noon chores done and eaten our lunch, my mother said to me, "Little sweetheart, let's go and visit your father's school." Of course, I was overjoyed. I still remembered going a few years ago to the Yeager District School. Yes, that time I was not quite five years old, but I did remember the happy faces of all there, from the tiny ones up to all the many young men and women, and oh, the singing.

We walked over the hard frozen drifts, and got there just after school was called for the afternoon session. There were only eight pupils there. My father wrote something on the blackboard and called to Harvey Wilsy to come up and write the answer to it. Harvey was a young giant of nineteen years of age, broad shouldered, red of hair, and red of face. Instead of going up to the blackboard, he grasped the back of the seat in front of him with his two large red hands and said, "I won't come." My father turned around quickly and asked, "What did you say?" Young Wilsy repeated, "I won't come." My father just made a spring over to his seat, grabbed him around the throat with an iron clutch, and at the same time gave a kick against his hands so they dropped their hold on the other bench. Then there was a brief tussle and my father dragged him to the blackboard, and there gave him a hard kick on the place where people sit down, and said, "You did come!" Sullenly, Wilsy did his work on the blackboard. When he got done, instead of resuming his seat, he marched through the room, took his coat and cap, and said, "I won't be back."

Harvey Wilsy was born and raised in Rochester, but was on a long visit to his grandmother, Mrs. McLaughlin, and his uncle, Charles McLaughlin. My father called up two big girls to the blackboard. While they were busy at their lessons, across the sill there was Ira Candee, a young man of twenty-two…tall, but not so powerfully built like young Wilsy. He kept whistling, stamping his feet, then began singing, "Harvey is a good boy, teacher is a bad man." My father turned toward him and said, "Shut up." He answered back, "Shut up yourself, you darn fool." My father yanked him out of his seat; there was a fight; then my father grabbed him, called to my mother to open the door and threw him bodily into the snow. My father went back to the blackboard, breathing very hard, his long black hair mussed up, one coat sleeve half torn out. The two big girls, Nellie and Jenny Freeman, had gone back to their seats.

My father glanced around the school room, called Uber Cannon, a boy of nine years, and Edith Freeman, a girl a half year younger than myself, to the blackboard. The lessons went on as if nothing had ever happened. On one of the benches sat Jimmy Corcorn, a young man of twenty years. My father told my mother that he always behaved, but was so terribly dull it was almost impossible to teach him anything.

Well, my mother and I stayed until school was dismissed at four o'clock; then the three of us walked home together. About the first of March, the school term closed. There was no speaking, singing, or decorating of the school house.

A few weeks after that exciting day at school, on a Sunday afternoon, we heard a knock at our door. In marched Harvey Wilsy in his flashy Sunday clothes, a very, very bashful, respectful, and awkward young giant. He told us he was going back home to his mother in Rochester next morning and came to say goodbye. He stayed perhaps an hour, then got up, shook my father's hand a long time, and said, "You were the best darned teacher I ever had." We never saw him again.

It was about the middle of April; one day my father came home leading on old, old horse. She was the thinnest horse I ever saw. My mother looked at it with horror. My father told her the man who owned her was going to kill it, so he gave it to my father. He said she no longer could eat hay, but would fatten on the grass. Well, we boiled corn and bought ground feed. We had no hay culler, but my father took wisps of our best hay, cut it up fine with a sharp knife, and mixed it with her feed. She also picked the young tender grass, but did not fatten up. But there was a strange thing. Although she looked like a skeleton and just crawled along, she was terribly strong. He name was Nellie, too, but she was not gentle and affectionate like the Nellie my mother had loved so much. She always laid her ears back when she saw any of us. She also bit and kicked. Luckily, she had no iron shoes on, so her heels were not so dangerous.

Sophie Kussmaul

Many a bite and kick I got from her that summer. Though she had no back teeth left (they are called grinders), her front teeth were long and sharp. She was only of medium height, but I could not reach up to harness her, so I got a box to stand on and then I could throw the harness over her back.

That was a happy spring and summer...Mrs. Dixon cleaning house, no more lessons till fall, and a horse. I was very proud of that horse. Mr. Anchord came and did the plowing, but I did all the dragging. Yes, acres of it. The old horse went so slow you could hardly see her move, but I kept at it all day and every day for weeks. I would drag the same ground many times till the soil was all mellow. Later on, after the corn and potatoes were up, I started to cultivate the garden, again day after day. I really got great pleasure out of that work.

It was the first of July; we were sitting on our verandah in the twilight, and a horse and buggy drove into our yard. It was Mr. and Mrs. Brayton from Utica, who kept a three-story summer hotel on the North Bay shore of Oneida Lake. My father and mother had known them well for years. The horse was a hired one. After a little while they said that they had heard about my father's swimming feats, how years ago he had swam across Oneida Lake and so on. They said they had four half grown children whom they wanted to learn to swim. Also, amongst their hotel guests were five or six that also wanted, while staying close to the lake, to take swimming lessons.

My father told them that he did not even have a swimming suit. Mrs. Brayton laughed, said she had thought of that and had brought from Utica three suits, one for my father, one for my mother, and a little one for me. So it was arranged that the lessons should begin next afternoon, three times a week until the last day of August.

I had seen the lake a few times, but so far had never taken a bath in anything but our washtub. My father told me that if I walked out into the lake up to my mouth without screaming or in fact making any kind of noise, he would give me a silver dollar. In those days, a silver dollar meant more than a ten dollar gold piece would today.

He took me by the hand, and we walked out slowly. Each step the water got a little deeper. It felt cold and seemed to take my

47

breath away. Before me lay, to my way of looking at it, an endless waste of horrible cold water. On we went. It reached my mouth; I threw back my head. Another step, a wave washed over my head. I never made a sound. My father glanced down at me, turned around, and we walked back to shallow water where my dear mother waited for us. Then I said, "Do I get my dollar?" My father said, "Yes, you are a brave girl." That repaid me better than the money. I was no coward.

We went as far as Anchord's with the old horse. There I unhitched her and we walked the rest of the way to the lake as my father and mother were too much ashamed to go through the village with such a thin, slow, head drooping horse as we had then. After each lesson, my father gave me a short swimming lesson too.

Well, the last day of August came, the last time we all were together. The next day, the hotel guests were to go back to their city homes. About ten days later, on a warm, twilight Saturday night, we were on the old verandah as usual. Again, we saw a rig drive up through the dusk. It was the Braytons. They said they were going back to Utica the following morning on the ten o'clock train. If we could manage to come real early in the morning, they would enjoy to go in the lake once more…just their own family and us.

Next morning, after a very light breakfast, we went down. I think we left home about six o'clock. They wanted us to eat breakfast with them after our swim, but my father said he wanted to get home. The Braytons kept their caretaker and his wife in the hotel the year round. After we had the old horse hitched up again and were on our way home, we had gotten as far as what we always called the Nichol's corner; my mother and I saw my father was fast asleep. We crawled slowly on, when to our surprise, yes, horror, we saw way up at the McCormic's corner a runaway team come flying down toward us. They were still about an eighth of a mile away but coming at such a terrific speed it seemed only a few seconds when they came down the steep little Flanagan hill. That was the end of everything.

The team had been hitched to an old heavy wagon, just the front wheels, by what is called the reach. Two planks had been laid across lengthwise. On these were seated Mr. Goodman, owner and driver of the runaways, and next to him, his wife, and next to her, their son, a man grown up but simple minded. It seems that coming down that short, steep hill something hit the horses' heels. They already were badly frightened, but now were crazy. It took only a few seconds for this to happen. Just below the hill on the little bridge, I saw how the three Goodmans were tossed up high in the air. Also, the two planks they had been sitting on, instead of landing on the road, were flung below into the little creek. At that place, too, the rear wheels were left near the road, after turning a complete summersault. On rushed the maddened horses. From the time I had first seen them, I got on my feet, started whipping and pulling on our old horse to get her out of the road. However, the team was so desperately fast, our old horse, so terribly slow, that all I did manage to do was to get her and the buggy partly out of the road, but the one front and hind wheel were still on the road.

The wild team rushed on and their heavy front wheel caught between our wheel and axel, cut it off like a streak of lightning, the same with the hind wheel. This did not even slow up their terrible speed. Now if our buggy had been six inches nearer to them, they would have crashed right into us. Well, then and not till then, my father woke up. We told him what had happened. My father and mother hastened down to see what had happened to the Goodman family. I unhitched our horse, hung the few things we had in the buggy on the hames, got on her back and started for home.

Mrs. Goodman broke a leg and arm, the son broke his shoulder and nose, but Mr. Goodman escaped with a severe shaking up and a few scratches. Mrs. Flanagan sent one of her boys to North Bay after the doctor. We heard afterwards that one of the colts, the four-year-old, had only been hitched up three or four times before and the other one, a three-year-old colt, that morning for the first time. Also, that Goodman had an old half rotten harness. When she pulled on the lines, they broke. The colts were very large. A few weeks later, I heard a neighbor tell my father that we got punished for going swimming on a Sunday. My father replied that the Goodman family got punished much worse than we did and they were on their way to church.

Through Sophie's Eyes

It was about the middle of October; my father was cutting our year's wood across the creek. He cut the trees down and then sawed them up in stove length with the crosscut saw. The limbs were trimmed and cut into pole wood. My father would walk out after breakfast, and start cutting. I would harness and hitch up the old horse and slowly crawl out there. My father would fill up the old wagon with either the block wood or the pole wood, as I was not strong enough to lift it on the wagon. But at home I would drive into the barnyard back of the woodshed and roll off my load. While my father was loading up, I would wander around in the deep woods. It was almost half a mile from our house to the creek. I made two trips in the forenoon and two in the afternoon.

The early autumn woods were very beautiful. All the leaf trees were masses of gorgeous colors. All the needle trees fairly shone with the bright slanting autumn sunshine shining on their dark green branches. The many different kinds of mosses that during the hot weather had faded now regained their beauty. Though the summer ferns had bower their heads and died with the first frost, all the different winter ferns were now in their glory. Then, too, there were lots of wintergreen berries. Oh, how good they tasted. Along the creek, which was dry now, the bushes of spice berries were loaded with their long red fruit. These were not good to ear, but I loved the smell, and to this day, when I go back there at this time in the fall and get the odor of those leaves and berries, all those sixty odd years seen to have melted away. I look about me and almost see my father, the old, old horse, and the one horse, heavy wagon with the spliced thill.

Once in a while there was the "shirr" of a partridge, the shrill note of the blue jay, the soft twitter of the little wood birds, the chirping of crickets, and the chatter of squirrels. Sometimes a rabbit would run across my woodland road, sometimes a black crow would fly across. Yes, looking back over the years of my childhood, these few weeks when I drawed out our years' supply of wood were, I am sure, the happiest weeks I ever knew.

But after a while, the wood was all drawed up, the weather that had been so mild and dry changed, the sun was hid under heavy clouds. It rained then snowed. All the green grass was either frost bitten or covered with snow. The poor old horse had no more grass to eat. Each morning she had to have help to get up. The neighbors told my father that just as soon as she did not try herself to get up that no six men could lift her up. Well, we knew the end was near. I had heard about this all summer so, in a way, was prepared for it.

My father gave her an extra good feeding of ground feed. My mother and I gave her a big pan of sweet apples and then my father led her gently into the back lot, accompanied by Julius Janes with his rifle. Of course, my mother and I did not go with them. Afterwards, my father said that one shot from the rifle through her brain killed her. She never suffered even a moment. Then they dug a deep grave. After it was covered with dirt, they wheeled about a ton of big stones on top.

Later on my mother and I visited the grave. Although I had driven the horse constantly for half a year, I cannot say I grieved too much. Of course, I felt bad, but knew from the first that we could not make her live through another winter. Then, too, I had gotten so many bites and kicks, I was not so sorry than if she had been gentle. Right here, I will say this. Although those three terrible days and nights when we were in real danger of that ferocious bull, they were nothing compared to the horror I suffered for over six long months when I thought Nellie lay dead in her stall. I say again, tell children the truth.

Winter set in extra early that year, so of course, my hateful so called arithmetic lessons also began earlier than usual, and I could not learn them. After four long, terrible winters, I could add up fairly well, but I never really learned to subtract. I could see that you could take five from eight or three from six or four from nine and so on, but I never could understand how a person could take a bigger sum from a smaller one. They claim you can borrow from another figure huddled close by…but why? Why not let it all drop. Then there was long division and short division. I never could see into that muddled up affair. Then there was the thing called fractions. I never got into them. I only saw that there were a lot of smaller figures, perhaps children of the larger ones. Well, after fifteen years from fall into late spring, at from two to six hours daily, I finally got the multiplication table into my tired, weary brain. Then I quit. But I'm getting ahead of my story.

By this time, thanks to my poor, dear, patient mother I could read the lovely little German stories by myself. Amongst them,

Heidi. I made rapid progress in geography and did fairly well in history.

That fall my mother started me reading and writing English. I learned this surprisingly fast. For amusement, I drew and painted with my water colors. Outdoors, I played in the snow and spent much time in the barn. Our three to four cats were just part of our family. I cannot recall any time when my father was in the house that he did not have at least one cat on his lap. I was not allowed to play rough with them, but I dearly loved them all.

About a week after our old horse was disposed of, one cold, snowy day, my father came home from North Bay and said, "I got it." My mother knew at once what he meant. For a year and a half, he had been trying to get his soldier's pension, but as it turned out, he got more than twice as much as he thought he would get. He also got what is called back pay, meaning his pension started from the very day he applied for it.

We were happy and for one day he skipped my arithmetic lesson. There is an old proverb that misfortune never comes alone, but in this case, things were reversed. Less than a week after we heard about my father's good luck concerning his pension, he received a large white envelope from the Old Country covered with large red sealing wax stamps. This letter contained the information that a distant relative whom he had only seen a few times when a boy had left him an annuity, meaning that as long as he lived, he would receive a certain sum each month.

The first week in December, we all went to Oneida. That day I shall never forget. I always was a late sleeper, never got up till long after my parents had breakfasted. But as the train left the North Bay depot at eight o'clock in the morning, I was up without being woke up, washed, combed, and dressed and eating breakfast by lamp light with my father and mother. Soon after, we heard the merry jungle of sleigh bells. There was Mr. Anchord, whom my father had engaged, with his lively team. It was not quite daylight yet when we got into his big sleigh. I think he brought at least six or eight blankets to wrap us up in. Oh, such a happy ride. The horses felt fine; they trotted along, jingling the bells and throwing the fine snow. How the runners cut through the cold snow. When we got to the little North Bay station, it was daylight but no sun, a dark cloudy sky. We did not have to wait very long for the train to come roaring in. Then the ride to Oneida. This was only my third train ride.

My father and mother went from store to store. They bought and bought. They bought clothes for themselves and for me. Coats, shawls, dresses, underwear, yards of cloth to be made up, bedding, curtains, shoes, boots, slippers, dishes and groceries. Each place we bought at, my father had them box it and gave orders to have it at the Oneida depot in time so it would be sent to North Bay that day.

We had gone to a restaurant once before in Rome. This was my second visit to a restaurant. We ate a full dinner. In the afternoon, we again went shopping, but more slowly, as what we were to buy now we would carry with us. We spent a long time in the 5&10 cents store. I was fascinated. My father's big satchel was crammed full, my mother's smaller grip, also. Then I had my first ice cream soda. Oh, that was delicious. My parents and I walked, I think, for miles. Every once in a while they saw something they wanted. When five o'clock came, we all were loaded down with bundles. We went to the same restaurant, had a light supper, and when we got out on the street again, lo, it was all lit up. No electricity...gas...but how wonderful it looked to me. Then we walked to the station. Every step seemed marvelous. We had to wait for our train, but that did not bother me. There were too many exciting things to watch. At last it came, and we got on. The train was all lit up.

When we got to North Bay, Mr. Anchord was at the station. He and my father loaded up the big sleigh. It was so full of boxes and bundles we had hardly room to sit. Mr. Anchord looked at the load and said, "Did you people buy out the whole town?"

It was a bitter cold night, but to our joy the house was still warm. My father had banked the fires in both the stoves that morning. A happy Christmas. I was now nine years old. A long dreary winter and again the marvel of springtime.

Chapter 6

Three things stand out clearly that happened in my life that summer, and two more that happened in the early fall. Here is the first one. As much as I loved my mother, I found out she had deceived me. I still loved her just as much only I never forgot, thought perhaps she might do the same thing again. My father always repaired the entire pasture fence before he turned the cows out, but of course, every little while he went over them again. It was May, a lovely day, the green grass with patches of blue and white violets, lilac bushes in full bloom, the air sweet and heavy with perfume of apple blossoms. Millions of bees flitting about, robins singing. At dinner, my father said he would have to go back in the woods and look after the fences. Our cattle had already been in the back pasture nearly a month. My mother had taken her mending out on the verandah. I played on the ground just below. She and I were happy visiting together when Eligh Humiston came along. He asked after my father. My mother told him where he was. He sat down and they talked about things that did not interest me; then I heard Eligh say, "I know where you can get a real good young horse cheap." He mentioned the man's name. "He is selling out and moving to the city. The horse is a good worker and a fair road horse, very gentle." Of course, I listened eagerly; then my mother said, "What color is he?" Eligh said these words, "Why, he is a dark sorrel, just about the color of the little mare you loved so much, and do you know, she is still alive and looking well. Don't you see her going by here once in a while?" I glance up quick at my mother. She, too, looked at me. I went on playing. After a little while, Eligh said, "Well, I will go and see if I can find Otto." After he had gone, my mother came down to me, gently put her arms around me, and said, "Dear little honey girl, I must tell you something. Do you remember that dark dismal night in November, about four or five years ago when Eligh and that strange man came with a lantern and after they and your father went out, how I wept and when you asked me what was the matter, I told you I had such a headache?" I said, "Yes." But I felt myself stiffening up. Then she went on. "Next morning I came to your bed, said Nellie died last night." I said again, "I do remember." Then she told me, "Nellie did not die. Your father sold her to that man, but I did not want to tell you so you would not grieve. I wanted to save you that sorrow." I did not answer. I think the subject was never brought up again. But I kept thinking to myself, Oh, why did she not tell me the truth. If I had known she had been sold, I would have felt bad for a day or so. But I never could put into words the terror, the horror I went through for the next six months. Each night I went to sleep with fear in my heart. I would awaken in the night shivering with horror. The fear, the dread of what I thought must be in that stall never left me in the daytime. Still, I never spoke of it. Now, I found out the truth.

Now I must tell another story. I must give the entire picture of it so anyone can fully understand it. It was only a short sentence spoken by my father, just a few words, but it changed my entire attitude towards him. These few words spoken sixty years ago, I never forgot or forgave. My father is in his grave for over thirty-one years now, but I still feel the bitter injustice of those few words. Again, I say treat children as equals.

From the time our cattle first started to go into the back pasture, meaning way back across the creek, about the latter part of April to the end of September, they always came home to be milked at six o'clock. I can still see them trooping down the old lane. We never had to go after them. Most farmers had to spend from half an hour to an hour each night rounding up their cows. The secret why ours always came home was very simple. Each night they found something good to eat in their mangers. For the first few weeks in early spring, my father put a small forkful of old, dry hay in their mangers. He claimed that when they first filled up on so much juicy young grass it did not have the full nourishment. They devoured it with great relish. Later on, when the grass about our home got big enough, he would mow some each day. Each cow got exactly the same amount and the yearling that went with the cows, a half portion. Still later on, each cow found a few stalks of sowed corn or a quart of ground feed on coming home.

It was now the latter part of June. My father had mowed the yard just below the verandah and the little grove. At dinner, he told me to rake it up and bring it into the stable for the cattle. I had helped to do this countless of time, as I did alone for quite a few summers. So after dinner my father went back to his work. He was hoeing corn next to what is now Reamore's. My mother took her mending basket, as usual, on the old verandah, and I, to make a game of getting the grass in for the cows, first took the rake, raked it up in long windrows like the farmers in big hayfields. Then with the pitchfork I made it up in little heaps called haycocks. Then I got my express wagon, on which I had built a miniature hayrack, a complete imitation of a real hayrack. Oh, it was lovely. Warm bright sunshine, no wind, the giant rosebush on the little grove loaded with sweet scented double roses. My dear mother smiling and talking to me all the time. I took the little wagon and pretending I had a horse hitched to it, would say, "Get up," then "Whoa," and started to load up. When my wagon was full, I took it up the broad path and then to the little gate, opened the gate, pulled my wagon through, closed the gate, and pulled my load across the green barnyard, opened the small red door into the barn, pulled my wagon in, and put my first load in for one cow.

I made four trips exactly like the first one…three full loads for each cow and half a load for the yearling. Each single time I opened the gate, I closed it carefully behind myself, though I was to pass right through again. From my very earliest memory, this was one thing my father was very, very strict about. He always made me close every door, gate, or bars, no matter if I was to return in half a minute, so of course, I was so used to closing everything behind me, I know I would have done so had I walked in my sleep. Soon after I had my grass all taken in, my mother said she would have to start getting supper, as she always used the summer kitchen that was on the west side of the house during the summer months. As I liked to be near her, I followed her to the west side and played near the open door of the summer kitchen.

Sophie Kussmaul

We always ate in what was the backroom of the house in summer. There was the west door from which it was only a step to the summer kitchen and the east door that led out to near the gate where I had drawed the grass. After supper was ready, my father came in from his work through the west door. We were about half through eating when all at once we heard cattle walking and grazing close by. One glance through the opened door showed our three cows and yearling in our yard, the gate wide open. All three of us rushed out. My father opened the stable door and called them in. In five minutes everything was over; we were back at the supper table. My father looked furious. Then he turned to me and said, "I have always forbidden you to leave that gate open." I told him that I had closed it. He thundered at me and called me a darn little liar, saying if I had closed it the cattle would not have gotten out. I, too, was boiling mad. In the first place, I knew I had closed it, and in the second, what right had he to call me a darn little liar when I had spoken the truth. My poor, sweet, patient, peace loving little mother, who loved us both so much, looked at us. She knew there was a terrible crisis coming into our lives; then she spoke. "Otto, the child is right. I was there all the afternoon and saw her close the gate each time." I gave her a quick grateful glance and went on eating. But my father could not swallow another mouthful. His dark face turned as pale with rage as it could, red spots gleamed on his high cheek bone, his black eyes sparkled with fire, and his whole body shook with his terrible temper.

When I finished my supper, I went back to the west side to play where I had left off at supper time. The west door was wide open. I did not intend to listen, but where I was playing, just back of the open door, I heard my father say, "Elise, I am surprised at you that you should take the child's part against me." My dear mother answered, "Otto, I could not do different. She was entirely in the right. I saw her close the gate each time she went through it." Then my father said the words that I never forgot or forgave. He said, "If it had been the other way around, I would have taken your part, even if I had known she was in the right." Something shot through me like fire, a hate, yes. I despised my father!

Through Sophie's Eyes

It was the beginning of July. Haying time...this summer only the second time that our grass was to be mowed with a mowing machine. Each year, an acre or so had been mowed by hand early, early in the morning. By about nine o'clock, when the dew had dried off, the heavy swaths of wet grass were shook out with a pitchfork. In the afternoon, the hay was raked up by hand, meaning with a wooden hand rake. Then made into haycocks and let stand overnight so the hay could sweat and cure. The next day it was drawed into the barn. I can just remember what was called revolving rakes. We never had one, but the farmers thought it a great invention, a wonderful improvement to the hand rakes. A horse was hitched to it, a man had to walk behind the rake and lift up a certain part that would drop the raked up hay.

Well. Mr. Littlefield bought a mowing machine and a buggy rake. A buggy rake is what every farmer later on had; it was soon just called a hay rake. My father hired Mr. Littlefield to mow our meadows. He brought down the mowing machine and the new buggy rake. Mr. Littlefield owned three horses. He explained just how the rake worked. Of course, I was much fascinated with it. Then he turned to my father and said, "I think your little girl could run the rake. I know that she done a man's work with your old horse two years ago. Now I am sure she could take one of my horses and do the raking."

I could never find the words to express my unbounded joy. Oh, I to drive a neighbor's horse! I to be trusted with a new machine! I to do a man's work! I could hardly keep from shouting with joy. I glanced at my father in fear that he might forbid it, but to my unutterable relief, he only said, "Well, she might try it." Next day he brought down Jack, his black horse, and I helped to hitch him to the rake.

I shall never forget how hard it was for me to dump the rake. It took all the strength I had. Our hay was very heavy; it had to be about every eight or ten feet. The horse walked quite fast, so it kept me dumping or lifting all the time, and the horse was hard bitted, meaning that I had to pull hard on the lines to turn him. I did the work so well that Mr. Littlefield said no man could have done better. In fact, so well that when our haying was all done, he asked my father if he would let me rake for him. Again, I looked at my father fearing he might refuse, but all he said was,

"Yes, if she wants to." If I wanted to? Oh, what joy! Mr. Littlefield at that time also owned the farm afterward known as the Reamore farm, so I got the job of raking on both the big farms.

When night came, I was so tired I could hardly move. My little hands were swollen and blistered and callused, every nerve tingled, and every muscle ached. I was only afraid my mother would notice, so I pretended not to be tired at all. Luckily for me, the heavy raking only came in the afternoons. In the late forenoons, if I raked at all there were only the scatterings, or after rakings, so I could drive maybe fifty or sixty feet without dumping. Added to my great joy in raking, Mr. Littlefield gave me different horses to rake with. I had one, one day, another one the next, and so on till I had raked with all three of them.

At last all the hay was raked. I was sorry. That was a happy summer. Came September and I made a discovery. From my earliest recollection, my mother had told me over and over again about her family, the places they had lived and so on. In winter, when I was housed up, she and I were all alone, and I would ask her to tell me again about this or that. She told me about her first home in Venice, and how when she was only five-and-a-half years old, they moved onto a great and beautiful estate owned by some relation of her mother. This must have been an earthly paradise. Her father was the caretaker. She told me about the old palace in which they lived, about the dairy, over one hundred Swiss cows, about the twenty work horses, the four beautiful coach horses, the saddle ponies, and the wonderful poultry: peacocks, pheasants, doves, and of course, hens, ducks, and geese. There was a small army of workmen and maids and their own personal cooks and servants.

Her older sisters were well and strong, attended boarding school for most of the year, but my mother had been very frail and delicate from birth so they kept a governess in the home for her. My mother told me so many, many times about their lovely park, how she and her governess would take their books into one of the rose arbors to study, how the fountains would play near by, about the stately swans therein. I felt as if I knew all about her home, her family. Yes, in a way I lived with her bygone

59

childhood. In later years, she told me about their home in Cordsruh (Karlsrule?), her many travels.

As I said, it was September. I would be ten years old in December. I was working in my flower garden when all at once it came to me that I knew nothing of my father's people. In a vague way, I knew that he had some brothers and sisters. Yes, I even knew that one or two of his sisters had lived here in our home before my mother and father got married. So all at once, I wanted to know something about my uncles and aunts on my father's side. I say today that I had a perfect right to know. So, I left off my work in the flower garden and ran into the kitchen where my dear mother was at work.

I asked her a lot of questions, such as, how many brothers my father had, their names, and where they now lived. My mother told me how many there were and their names but was not sure just where they all lived. Then I asked her the number and names of his sisters. Again, she told me the number and their names, but was not sure where they all lived now. I kept asking her some questions, and after a while, ran outdoors again.

At dinner, all at once I said, "Wouldn't it be nice if my Aunt Albertine would walk in now?" The moment I said this, a heavy black cloud came over my father's face. He looked at my mother and said, "Have you been telling the child about my family?" My poor, dear mother answered, "She wanted to know how many brothers and sisters you had, and their names." Then there was a silence. My sweet mother tried to make light conversation, asked my father how the corn and potatoes were coming, told him about the beautiful beans in the garden, told him how lovely Mrs. Dixon had laundered the curtains. But there was no use. My father never spoke a word. In the afternoon, I was breaking in a bull calf to harness. I had been at that some days now, when my mother came to me and very, very gently told me never again to mention my father's people before him. I asked her no questions, but I felt hurt. Why should I not know? They were my people too.

Chapter 7

Now I will run ahead of my story, for some years, then come back to where I left off. I noticed, once in a great while during the years to come, say when I was fourteen, sixteen, eighteen, twenty, that when I came into the house unexpectedly that my father had spoken to my mother about his people, but the moment I entered the house, he stopped talking. I was an outsider. I knew he never got or sent any letters to them, for from the time I was eleven years old I was, with very few exceptions, the only one who went after our mail to North Bay. When I was about twenty years old, the R.F.D. started, and I managed generally to rush out to the mail box first. When I was about twenty-two years old, I brought into the house a letter addressed to my father in a strange handwriting. It came from Heidelberg, Germany. He opened it, and my mother asked, "From whom is it?" I being in the house, he merely said, "You can read it to yourself when I get done." After that, for the next fifteen years, when he received a letter from his people, it was always the same. He started reading it aloud to my mother. If I happened to come in, he would stop, fold it up, and put it into his pocket. I was an outsider.

Well, it was November again. Lessons, snow, cold, dark dreary days. But oh, wonderful happy news. My Aunt Sophie was sending my mother a lot of money, a lot for those times, to buy me an organ, a good organ. I had been longing for an organ for years. Oh, how I loved music. I always knew sometime I would get one, but it always was in the distant future and now, yes, now, I would really, truly get it soon. I tormented my poor mother so much that the next morning, we three walked to the North Bay station before daylight. On the way down, we stopped to Mr. Anchord's, and engaged him to meet us that night at the station.

Through Sophie's Eyes

We went to Oneida and bought on organ. My mother had been an accomplished pianist. Now, after not having touched an instrument for so many years and in spite of the fact that an organ was somewhat different from a piano, after just a few days practice it all came back to her. In one of her big trunks she had many music books, beginner books, easy to play little tunes, the great and beautiful works of Beethoven, Bach, Mozart, Straus, Schubert, and many song books.

With my good mother's infinite patience and my great love of music and natural talent, I learned to play very rapidly. At night after supper, during the long late fall and winter evenings, my mother would play the difficult music. Then she would play songs, some in German, some in English, French or Italian. My father, with his really grand voice, would sing them. Sometimes she would join him in singing. Just why I do not know, but I never went into the room when they played or sang. I stayed in the next room and read or wrote poetry or drew pictures. Right here I want to mention few things that I always thought strange. I still cannot understand them.

I loved my mother more than the average of daughters loved their mothers. This I can easily understand. In the first place, she was such a wonderfully good mother. Then I had no brothers and sisters, no playmates, no schoolmates. My dear mother was my teacher, playmate, and companion. She told me about Jesus, the beauty of true, simple religion. In fact, she was my all. I never loved my father the way I loved my mother. Of course, in a way I loved him too.

Here is the strange thing. I looked like my father. I inherited most of his traits of character, my wild nature, my great love of the out-of-doors, the love of Indians. In no way did I take after my mother. My father was a poet, yes; he wrote some very beautiful poems. My dear sweet mother never wrote a verse in her life. If she read some really lovely poetry, she would appreciate it, but here was their difference. If my father read out loud a poem or recited one, he put feeling, expression, in every line, but no matter how touching a poem might be, my mother would read or recite it in a sing-song way. "Jack and Jill went up the hill." Always that light lift to it.

Sophie Kussmaul

Now while I am on this subject, I must mention one more thing that my father repeatedly did that hurt me very, very much. It was that if he found an extra beautiful poem in a paper, magazine or book, he would read it to my mother. My mother would say, "Oh cut that out so our little girl can read it." Then he would always say, "She would not understand or appreciate it." I would understand and appreciate a good poem much more than my mother. Another thing, when he said, "we," he always meant my mother and himself, never me. Still, I knew he loved me. I knew he would have given his life for me.

When my sweet mother wanted me to do some little chore, she asked me to do it. I gladly, joyfully did it. When my father wanted me to do the same little chore, he ordered me to do it. Why should I take orders from any one? I was free.

That winter I started to translate German stories into English, and English stories into German. As always a happy Christmas. For indoor amusement, I had my music. I read book after book, both German and English. Also drawing and composing poetry. For out of doors, I spent most of my time with the bull calf, now a big, strong yearling. I had spent days, yes, weeks breaking him into the harness. Not a yoke like an ox, but I made him a collar with hames and tugs, also a back pat, bridle and lines. I had quite a time getting him used to the bit, but after a while, I could ride and drive him. I made a small bob, with wooden runners.

We did not have so much snow that winter till after the beginning of February. So all through the latter part of November, all of December, except the holy Christmas, and through the long month of January, my father worked in the woods. I drawed out our year's supply of fire wood with my horse. I would hitch him to the bob, get on his back, and ride out to where my father was working. There I would either fasten one big log to my bob, with a chain or half a dozen poles, the heavy ends resting on the snow. I always walked home, as the load was heavy enough for my horse. Those were happy times indeed.

Now I will tell how I was dressed. That was more than half a century before the modern snowsuits for girls had even been heard of. Since I was five years old, I wore rubber boots, always boy's boots. My mother cut down an old pair of my father's pants. I wore them over my dress, tucked into my boots and tied the top of my boots so no snow could get in.

After the beginning of February, winter set in with full fury. That ended the work in the woods...lessons, music and reading indoors, the daily chores at the barn outdoors. We had no company. At rare intervals the Dixons came, but now we were snowed in. Now I must relate a little incident that happed the latter part of February. But in order to tell this story, I must give an entire picture of things before I played a part in it. This was long before people in the country had any daily newspapers. My father kept a weekly paper, but we were always well supplied with reading matter. My mother's rich friends in New York City sent out bundles of newspapers, story papers, and magazines each week. So, when my father made his weekly trip to North Bay, he always found them at the Post Office. In winter he had a lot of time to read and often read items of news to my mother

One day he read about a terrible murder that had been committed. A woman had been found foully murdered in her home. Her husband came home at night and found her. They lived way out in the country and by the time her husband got a coroner it was morning. The coroner said the woman had been dead twenty-four hours. Not till then did the search for the murderer start.

In those long gone by days, there were no radios, automobiles, or State Police. In the country, or even in small villages, no telephones. The only clue they could find was that a neighbor living about a mile from where the crime had been committed, had seen a tall, well dressed man, who carried a small black satchel, going in that direction at about the same time, or just before, the husband left for his work. Then my father said, "Now, that is not very far from here." Then he went on reading something else and the matter was forgotten. Now to my own story.

The snow was deep, the road drifted high; no one went by for days, yes, weeks. I was in the cow stable; my father wallowed through the deep snow down to the spring to shovel it out. He told me to wait till the spring was shoveled out and then turn out one cow at a time. He would stay down there and dip water. When one cow had drank and come back to the stable, to put her in and send the next one down, and so on, so they would not hook one another on the narrow path.

I have related what I wore in the winters. But I also wore a short old coat. I had found a very wide leather belt, which I also wore, and to my dear, gentle mother's dismay, had made for myself, out of an old leather boot, a sheath to hold a butcher knife. This sheaf I had fastened with a leather strap to my belt, on my right side. With great patience and lots of hard work, I had whittled myself a hard wood club, about two-and-a-half inches thick at the big end, tapering to about one inch at the other end. This I had dangling on a short strap on the left side of the belt. I was very proud of my weapons. Well, my dear, good mother had knit me a nice, warm hood or cap, blue and red, but I thought that altogether too tame, so I went and covered it with hen feathers, standing up straight. To my great joy, I had found a dozen brass rings, about an inch across. They just made a complete circle about my head, and concealed the quills of my feathers. Then I cut off three bunches of long hair from the ends of the cows tails, one black, one white, and one red. With a strong cord I tied the end of each bunch so the hair would not come out, and fastened the three bunches to the back of my bonnet.

As I waited in the stable for my father to wave his shovel as a sign that he was ready for the first cow, I took the dung fork, and started to clean the stable. All at once, I saw a man walking over the mountain high snowdrifts. At one glance I knew he was a stranger, well dressed, carrying a small satchel. To my great surprise, I saw him turn into our yard. I could not see him enter the house, but as he did not appear on the road above our house, I knew he must have gone in.

By nature I was very shy of people. The few that did come to our home, with the exception of the Eckels and Dixons, generally did not see me. I stayed out of doors till they had gone. So, of course, when I saw this strange man enter our house, I did not intend to go in, but all at once I heard the most horrible noise, a squawk, a screech. Quick as lightning, it all flashed through my mind. The thing my father had read about… the murderer, a tall, well dressed man carrying a small black satchel. Of course, I thought that horrible screech came from my dying mother. I gave a yell and fairly flew across the barnyard. First there was the little henhouse. I hopped through that, gave another yell, rushed through the woodshed, another yell, through the backroom, another loud yell, through the pantry, another yell, one more leap and yell, and I was in the warm winter kitchen. In my desperate haste, I had not dropped my dung fork. What did I see when I arrived when I came to my poor dying mother? Well, she sat near the table with some papers in her hand, and the villain; I just got one glimpse of him. He sat in the comfortable rocking chair near the fire. Near my mother on the table, was our old dinner horn. It had been out of commission for a year or two, so I had quite forgotten it. We had not used it any more because instead of giving a loud clear toot, it made such an awful noise. My mother looked at me, reproachfully. I bounded back into the pantry. She followed me, saying, "How could you come in like that?" The she told me to get my father. It all came to me. She took the horn into our big bedroom, opened the window, and blew it, never dreaming of the results, yes the same bedroom window at which I used to stand and see all those strange animals.

Well I thought I might have a little fun too, so I ran, or tried to run, down to the spring. The snow was so deep I fell, tumbled, and rushed on again. When I got down there, I panted out, "There is a strange man in the house. Elise wants you to come up there just as quick as you can." Well, he did go quick. Spry as I was, it was all I could do to keep up to him. I followed him into the pantry, but did not go into the room again where I had so disgraced myself. I found out what it was all about. The man was a fire insurance inspector. The company sent him out to inspect chimneys, stove pipes, garrets.

As this was a bitter cold day, our open garret ice cold, and my dear little mother so delicate, she wanted my father to take the man upstairs. The large room beyond the garret was always warm and comfortable in winter, as the pipe from the heating stove below kept it warm. Well, after a little while my father came out and told me to finish the chores. I did, and then peeled through the pantry door. The three of them were drinking coffee and eating cake. I stayed out till after the stranger had gone. I found out he had been a college man. My father said it seemed so good to have a gentleman in the house for once.

Chapter 8

In April, my father bought a horse, chestnut in color, another Nellie. I worked, drove, and rode her all spring, summer and fall. I also had my own vegetable and flower garden. When not occupied with those things, I either went fishing or berry picking. As soon as early, early spring came, my lessons stopped. Much as I loved my music, I very seldom played now. The outdoors lured and claimed me. When we had rainy days, I would take a book or magazine and go either into the barn or one of the little outbuildings and read.

Mrs. Eckel had been engaged to stay with us, from the first of April to the first of November, to do the housework. My mother, who never had been strong, was not even as well as usual, though she never complained, always was patient and cheerful. Mrs. Eckel was not a young woman, but she was well and strong, and she thought our little housework was for her almost a vacation. At that time I did not realize just how lucky we were to have gotten her. She never got out of patience and tried her best to please us all. She was a woman who never seemed to get in our way. For example, the evenings we three had always spent together during the spring, summer and early fall months had really been the only pleasant times we were together. In winter there was always that horrible arithmetic in the atmosphere. When spring did come, my father worked on the little farm. I either worked outdoors or ran wild. I never was in the house. Mrs. Eckel, just as soon as the supper dishes were washed, would retire to her room upstairs. During the longest days, that often was two hours before sunset. My father and I did the chores. Sometimes he would hoe till almost dark.

When we stayed on the dear old verandah, I had my hammock on the furthest end and my father and mother each had a comfortable chair close together. I never talked much. When they talked of things concerning the farm, the crops, the animals, the needed repairs on some of our buildings, then I listened. But when they talked about a new star or planet that some astronomer had just discovered or any such stuff, I drifted off to my own thoughts. About the West, forever and always, especially early in spring and autumn, the longing to go towards the setting sun was upon me.

Why, I never knew. Neither my father or my mother had ever been west; neither had I ever heard them talk about the West. From my earliest childhood, my dear mother had told me about her travels in the many old countries. Often she would say to me, "When you go to Switzerland..." or "When you go to Scotland, be sure to go and see..." and then she would tell me of some extra beautiful thing to see, meaning that she took it entirely for granted that sometime I would be going to all those countries. Still, I never thought of them.

I would listen to the night voices from out the woodland floating up softly, sweetly on the night air. Every once in a while the haunting song of the whip-poor-will. This summer passed by like so many others. There was only one little incident that left an impression on my mind.

For some years past, Sylvan Beach had developed from one small hotel called the Forrest Home, with perhaps a dozen small houses under the trees near the lake, to a summer resort. Hundreds of wealthy city people built little summer homes there. The bathing beach became famous. Long sandbars stretching out into shallow water, no stones. Small stores, dance halls, stands with all kinds of novelties, a large merry-go-round. Tables and benches under the trees, free for the use of picnic parties. Ice cream for sale at a dozen places.

Every day, band music, and on special days, brass bands from near by towns came and played by the hour. I had heard of all this many times and though I knew that most of our neighbors went there a few times each summer, and though, when the southeast wind blew, I could hear the music float over the miles, I really had never wondered why we could not go there too. To me, it was the same then as when now I hear about some special feature of interest in Newport, Saratoga, or Atlantic City.

One quiet summer afternoon, a Mrs. Will Hemingway came to see my mother. She was a farmer's wife, living about one and a half miles from us. Mrs. Hemingway and my mother sat on the verandah. I generally hid when anyone came, but for once I came and got into my hammock. After a while, Mrs. Hemingway said, "The real reason I came over today is this. We went over to Sylvan Beach a few times this summer, took a basket of lunch along, and ate it on one of those free tables, and at the end, bought a dish of ice cream. If you bring your own dish and spoon, they give you all a person can eat. Our children had a ride on the merry-go-round and waded in the lake, and all it cost us was five cents a dish for the ice cream and ten cents for the two little one's ride on the merry-go-round." Then she went on to tell my mother that there were two brass bands coming to play, one from Norwich, the other from Oneida. She said they were going over again, and as they had a two seated wagon, and a good team, they thought they could drive around by our place and take us along. She told my mother just to pack up a lunch and that we all would eat together at one table. She told us about what she would take. "Your little girl and my two little ones... (She had a boy and girl about my age) can play in the sand, or go looking for shells while we older ones visit. The bands will play most of the time." I was so happy I could hardly contain myself from shouting for joy.

My sweet mother said she would tell Otto. If he thought best, we would be delighted to go. Mrs. Hemingway went home. Soon after my father came to the verandah from his work. My mother told him at once what Mrs. Hemingway had said. This is what he answered. "That is about the most foolish thing I ever heard of, traveling five miles and eating stuff you could eat at home. They must be crazy." My mother gently said, "They have such good ice cream for sale cheap." My father said, "We seem to get along all right without that stuff."

For once I ventured to speak. I said, "They will have band music." My father said, "I heard all the brass band music I ever wanted to hear when I was in the army." Then he turned to my mother and said, "Write a note and tell them we are not going.

Little Sophie can take it on the horse." That was a bitter, bitter, disappointment and one that I did not forget. After that, when I heard the band music from the long distance, a strange feeling came over me.

In the autumn, Mrs. Eckel went home and lessons began, and I started to help in the house. My mother was far, far from well. Perhaps I went about my housework a little awkwardly as I had never done it before, but my gentle, patient mother never seemed to notice what I was doing. In December, I was twelve years old. I really did not mind the work I was doing. In a way it was a novelty for me. The laundry still went out, once in a while, Mrs. Eckel came for a day to give a general cleaning up, but my dear mother, I felt, was sorry that I was doing such work and here I must say that she did something that in later life always was a mystery to me. It was this. My mother was by far the best educated woman I ever knew. Add to his her extensive traveling, which is so broadening to the mind, and on top of all this, her great insight into human nature. She had a great gift to read peoples thoughts. In this, too, she made one terrible mistake.

Well, here is the mystery: I never went anywhere. There were absolutely no rich people in our neighborhood. Still, when she saw me scrubbing a floor or cleaning woodwork, she would say to me, "My poor, dear child, I am so sorry to see you do that kind of work, but after you grow up and get married, you will have it easy. Then you can have a beautiful home and servants." I was then in my thirteenth year and in my mind saw a grand mansion, such servants at my beck and call. Not till years afterwards did it ever come to me how impossible it would have been for me to find such a fairytale husband.

December found me thirteen years old. That January, my father, who tormented me all those years trying to teach me subtraction and the things called long and short division, gave up in despair. Just why the two kinds of division had fences around them, I never knew. The fences did not encircle them all the way around. So much yelling, threatening, declaring I would have to learn on my father's side, and hate, fear, despair, and revenge for my wrongs on my side. We started on the multiplication table. I was kept at it until I was eighteen years old. Well, I did learn it at last. Yes, I could answer it backward or criss-cross. My tired little mother had been strictly forbidden to help me with my arithmetic, but after I had been at the multiplication table five winters and could not make any headway, one day she confided to me that any figure could be turned around, such as four times five or five times four, or six times seven or seven times six. That gave me a clue to the whole darned mystery and in just one more year I mastered the entire multiplication table. Then, oh horrors, my father started me again on subtraction and the partly fenced in things called division. Well, I was in despair.

Each fall, yes, each day after I was eighteen, I had made up my mind not to submit to another lesson, but each day when my stern father got the slate and arithmetic book, my resolution failed me. I sat down, not meekly, but sullenly. I can only compare myself to the trained lions and tigers of the circus. From little tiny things, they learned to fear their master's cruel whip. My father never whipped me. If he had, I fear I would have killed him. So day by day, month by month, year by year, the lions and tigers, though grown strong and probably intending each day to pounce on their master, still when they came face to face with him and his whip would shrink from him. So I felt too. We went back to subtraction and division till I was nearly twenty-two years old. Then I revolted. But now I must go back to my thirteenth year.

This winter passed very much like all the others. Besides my studies, I really helped a lot in the house. I started washing and ironing the smaller pieces, learned to bake good bread and make yeast. For in those faraway days, or were they not just a little while ago, all the farmers' wives made their own yeast. I still know just how it was done. That was the reason why every farmyard had one or two hop poles laden with hops in their backyard.

Came the fourth day of April. The snow gone excepting the remnants of some of the bigger drifts. The ground was bare, cold, damp and muddy. It was not raining, but the sky was dark and gloomy. I had had no more lessons since the first of April. Of course, I was outdoors looking for pussy willows. I heard a heavy wagon approaching from below. My first impulse was to run home and to the back of our house to look at it. But for some reason I swiftly went near to the road and crouched down amongst a bunch of thick willows. When the horses came near, to my surprise I saw at a glance that they did not belong to our neighborhood. Neither did the driver. But what else did I see that made my heart beat so fast and wild? What was it that sent my blood racing through my veins with joy? Oh, you who read this would never understand. On the seat with the driver sat a little old woman and a large man, both of them very dark. The wagon was piled high with old furniture. Even I, in my excitement, saw how cheap and old and worn it was. But perched upon the load was a young Indian woman. Close to her on one side sat a little girl of four, and on the other side a little boy of six. In her arms she held a baby. Clinging on the load somehow were a girl of twelve and one of ten. I afterward found out their ages.

Slowly the team dragged the heavy wagon on up through the mud and passed our house. Then I sprang up and ran as fast as I could back of our house, up into the orchard, swung myself into an apple tree to get one more look at those dear, dark faces. Slowly, they went on, and then turned into the yard of the old Powers' house, now called the Cleveland Place. The house had stood empty for two years. Well, I sat on that apple tree limb like one in a dream; sat there until the last piece of furniture was unloaded, the team turned around, the driver past our house. Now, I think, most children of my age would have rushed into the house, told their parents the great news of the new neighbors. But instead, I hid behind an outbuilding and thought and dreamed of the wonderful thing—Indians living next to us, children of my own age.

Mrs. Eckel had already come to stay with us a week or so before, but that day she had gone home and was not coming back till the next day. After a while, I smelled supper cooking, so I went into the house. My dear mother smiled at me and said, "Did you see the load of furniture go by?" I just said yes. My father said, "They must be very poor. Such terrible looking stuff, and I think four or five children." After some time I told them that the new family had moved into the Powers' house, but did not tell them that they were Indians.

Next morning at breakfast my father said, "You are wondering what we could do with all the skim milk." We were milking four cows, all very heavy milkers raising only one calf. My father never kept any pigs. "As soon as the cows get on grass, they will give a lot more milk that they do now, so why not go up and tell those poor new neighbors to come down and get a pail full each day."

After breakfast we went up. Yes, they were real Indians, basket makers, and from that day the two girls, Libby and Susie, did not only come every day for their milk, but stayed with me most of the time. We three were always together. When I worked with the horse, or in one of my gardens, they followed me; then we went on fishing trips. Later on, we went on berry picking trips. In between I would sly up to their mothers' and learn to make baskets. My dear mother did not quite approve of my going to their home, but something like a magnet drew me there. Mrs. Webb taught me how to weave all kinds of baskets. I made large market baskets, egg baskets, comb baskets, round and square work baskets. She taught me how to bend the standards, split one, how to shave and polish the splints for the fillings so they would be smooth like silk, how to twist the points and curl one row, how to make the double brim, and how to dye some of the splints red and blue.

Many times we would go together down into my beloved woodland. My little house was no longer there, but just a little beyond was a giant pine tree with large, thick branches almost to the ground. We would often go and sit on the larger limbs, or swing on the smaller branches. The branches and needles were so thick that even if it rained, we stayed quite dry.

Our evenings on the verandah were as they used to be. My little friends never came down at that time. Mrs. Eckel still went upstairs by herself soon after the supper was cleared away. Still, they were not the same. A dark and terrible shadow was looming over us. My sweet mother had, for some time past, had a lump in her left breast and at last consented to have old Doctor Nicholas examine her. He said it was a tumor and might turn into cancer, but he gave her medicine and said it might be driven away. My father never sang anymore at night on the veranda. Came the tenth of July and two cousins of Libby and Susie from Canastota came to spend their school vacation. They, too, were Indians, but seemed much better off. They were dressed very nicely and altogether made a better appearance. The oldest was a boy of fifteen, rather small for his age but of perfect build. His name was Earnest Foster. His sister was thirteen, both of them very handsome. So the five of us were together. My mother often said to my father that she did not think it proper for me to be around with that boy. But my father, who always seemed suspicious of other people, only said that there were four girls and only one boy.

At first, we five were just children. But after a few weeks the boy and I became sweethearts. My first love affair. I was just thirteen-and-a-half years old. It seemed new and strange, but mighty pleasant. Somehow I grew up. We five would sit together on the limbs of the big pine tree, Earnest and I close together. He said as soon as he was eighteen he would come and marry me; we would live in a little home in the woods. Somehow it seemed so much dearer to me than the beautiful mansion with an unknown husband. Child that I was, I never thought of how we would make a living, never thought of myself doing the hard housework. Of course, I never breathed a world of all this to my mother.

On the twenty-fifth of August, he said good-by to me. They were going home that very day. The five of us were on the pine tree. Softly he took me in his arms and kissed me, the first and last kiss he ever gave me.

Our school opened on the second of September, and Libby and Susie attended. After that I did not see they very much. On the fifteenth of September, after school, they came running and came into the house and said their cousin Earnest was dead. That fall a diphtheria epidemic broke out in Canastota, and a great many children died. A queer feeling came over me, as I must not show my sorrow, a feeling of loneliness.

My mother got no better. That October we went to Oneida to see Doctor Carpenter, the uncle of the Doctor Carpenter of today. He plainly told my mother that it was cancer, but he did not want to operate just yet.

My fourteenth birthday. I always received a great many presents on my birthday, more than most children ever got for their Christmas. I always woke up early, so I could see the candles lit on my cake. The table was spread with a snowy white cloth. In the center of the table was my big birthday cake, on each side a smaller cake. Then on the best small dishes we had, glass, silver, and a few hand-painted china plates, there were from six to eight kinds of candy, each kind on a different plate or dish. Also, different kinds of nuts, each kind on a separate dish. Raisins, oranges, dates, figs. At one side of the table my father's presents to me, and on the other side, my dear mother's.

On my plate, always my aunt's gifts. She was living so very far away from us. Always sent some lovely jewelry. This year my father's gift to me was "The Youth's Companion." Of all my beautiful presents, I liked that the best. For the next fifty-two weeks, each week I received my copy. The stories were exactly to my liking. Then for the next four years, it was renewed for me each birthday.

Just a few days after came Christmas. The same lovely, yes holy, Christmas, the tree with the same ornaments as of the other years, but the dark cloud of sorrow hovered over our otherwise joyous time. Still, perhaps just on that account, the day seemed even more holy, more sacred.

Then followed a hard, sad winter for me. Most of my lessons were dropped, except arithmetic. My mother, who had loved the French language, tried to teach me French. I hated it. But she looked so sad and kept saying it might be her last chance to teach me, so I took it up. I did most of the housework. Hardly ever saw my Indian friends, and ever before me was the dread of the operation, which was to come in the spring. By this time, the lump in my mother's breast was more than twice as large.

But being so young, I was only in my fifteenth year, I still looked ahead to spring. At least, I thought, I would again be with my Indian friends. Came the second of April and the whole Indian family, except the old grandmother who went to live with her daughter in Canastota at the time her grandson had died with the diphtheria, came to call on us to tell us all goodbye. They had rented the place for a year and were to mover out on the fourth. They told us Mr. Littlefield would take their furniture to the North Bay Station early on the morning of the fourth. They asked my father if I could take down the woman and the five children and a few bundles to go on the next train.

Next day it rained all day. The day after, it was dark, the roads a mass of mud. I swallowed my breakfast, got the horse, ready, and went after them. I had always trained myself not to cry, but to keep perfect control. So this morning, though my heart was torn with sorrow, I kept quiet. The Indian woman with the two smallest ones sat on the front seat with me, Libby, Susie and Willie on the back seat. We slowly went along through the deep mud. I talked to them in a quiet way till I got them to the little North Bay Depot.

But when we said goodbye to one another, in spite of all I could do, I broke down and wept. Yes, I shed bitter, bitter tears. After they went into the little depot, I started up the long hill; a great loneliness came over me, but I had by now regained my composure.

I saw children, young girls like myself, on the sidewalk laughing and talking happily together. It hurt me somehow. The only people besides my parents that I had ever liked, yes, loved were gone from me forever, one in an early grave and the others to unknown parts. Now after I had regained at least an outward calm, everything would probably have gone all right. By the time I had reached home, I could pretend indifference. But my mother had asked me that morning to stop on the way home at Londen's to get a few groceries so as to save another trip to the North Bay grocery store. I hitched the horse and went into the store. Though I had stopped crying, my voice still was a little tremulous, and I suppose my eyes were red and my face swollen. Mrs. Londen said, "My poor child, is your mother any worse?" I shook my head and said no. But she kept at me. "Did you get hurt?" I said no. Then she said, "Well, what is the matter with you anyway?" Then in spite of my best efforts, I blurted out with a wild sob, "The Webb family all moved out this morning and are going far away." Mrs. Londen stared at me a moment, then said, "Why that is nothing to feel sad about. They were only Indians." Well, I stopped crying. Something like fire swept through me, and ever after I felt bitter towards her.

As I have said so often, I could not get on good with my father, but at the same time we were much more alike than my dear mother and I had ever been. When I came home, my mother smiled at me and said quite lightly, "Did you get them to the train in time?" I nodded. Somehow, I felt she was glad they had gone. My father, always silent, did not speak, but I sensed sadness about him. That evening he wrote a very beautiful poem about the Indian family who had lived near us for just one year.

Now after fifty-five years, though all my people have passed on to the better land, and generations have sprung up, again gone to oblivion, when I think back to that one year, a mixed gladness and sadness comes over me, and in my mind I see the dear old scenes vividly before me.

Looking Back

I gaze on the moon and wonder
As I gaze on its golden beams
If it's the same moon of my childhood
And my happy dreams

I dream of my Indian companions
That were so dear to me
As we played in the lowly swampland
And under the old pine tree

When life was all before me
A glorious book unread
With joyous years a plenty
And never a thing to regret

Softly now, from out of the distance
Ever at the close of day
Comes a thought of memory floating
Then as fleetly fades away.

Chapter 9

So life went on. Mrs. Eckel came back to stay with us again til autumn. The birds sang, the grass became green again, and the trees were in bloom, but though the world seemed fresh and happy, the dark cloud that hung over our lives did not lift. Came the tenth of May, the three of us went to Oneida, but these trips no longer filled me with joy. The hours spent in the doctor's waiting room I shall never forget. Today, they were going to set the day for the operation. But when they came back to me, my mother told me it was not yet decided when it would be. Foolish child that I was, I was so glad, just as if that would help matters. Then every two weeks, my parents went to Oneida; I took them to the little North Bay Depot in the morning and went after them again when the six-thirty train from Oneida came in. Mrs. Eckel was at home, so I was not alone, though I really only went into the house long enough to eat my meals. Then at last the day was set for the operation, the seventeenth of June.

The sun was brightly shining, birds twittering in the nearby trees. The three of us were on the verandah listening for the whistle of the ten o'clock train at North Bay which was to bring the two doctors. The table for the operation was ready in our living room. My mother had showed Mrs. Eckel what clothes to put on her after the operation if she lived through it, if not, what to put on her if she died. I did not eavesdrop, but I knew she did not know I heard her. Then we heard the shrill whistle. We looked at one another in silence. Of course there were no automobiles in those by gone days, and we knew it would take just about half an hour for them to be driven up with the hired rig my father had engaged to meet them.

How fast that half hour seemed to fly by, yet how slow. Then a strange thing happened. One by one, our three cats came on the verandah, jumped on my mother's lap, looked at her, kissed her face, and slowly went away. They sensed something was wrong.

I will not dwell on the operation. I stayed back of the house till the doctors left, but I saw plenty. My mother was just coming out of the ether, seemed to know us, then sank back to oblivion. Blood everywhere. My father never took his clothes off for the next six weeks. He stayed with my mother all the time. Mrs. Eckel did the housework. I did the chores, went to North Bay every day for the mail, our groceries, and such things.

Here I must mention one thing. It was left for me to wash my mother's big sore. The first day and half, it was not washed. Then I had a job I dreaded. There were sixteen stitches to be taken out, the strings from four arteries. In those days things were done different in that line than now. The doctors had given me full directions how to do it. After seven days, when the cut was supposed to have healed enough to hold together, to take a very sharp pen knife and cut every other string and very gently pull it out. A few days later, the others. The stings that tied the four arteries inside the wound hung outside for about an inch. After five days, I was to pull on them just a little so they would not heal into the flesh, but not to pull too hard because then, if the end of the artery was not healed, my mother would bleed to death. That was my job, and I was barely fourteen-and-a-half.

My mother really picked up fast, but kept telling us that at the end of the cut there always was a dull pain. That fall we went back to Oneida to see Doctor Carpenter. He did not like to speak about the pain at the end of the cut, said it would pass away after a while.

So another December and came my fifteenth birthday. I did most of the housework and had my daily arithmetic, which I could not learn. Also, some other lessons. For recreation I had my organ, my books, and the "Youth's Companion." We had very little company, and I had no young friends.

By the time spring came again, there was a lump as big as a hen's egg at the end of that cut, or rather by now red scar. The Oneida trips were again made to Dr. Carpenter. He kept telling my mother to wait. First, he said to wait till fall, when the weather would be cool. When fall did come and my dear sweet mother had a lump as big as a large sized goose egg, he said he would operate the coming spring.

Mrs. Eckel was with us part of that summer. This December brought me to my sixteenth birthday. A terrible, sad winter. Each day my patient mother's dear face showed more and more suffering. Hard, steady work for me and that horrible arithmetic.

When spring came at last, the lump on my mother's side was fully as big as a baby's head, and by now had turned a dark blue or purple. On the seventeenth of May, lacking just one month to a day for being just two years from the first operation, we had the second operation. I will not give the details, only I had again the job of washing the wound and taking out the stitches and the strings from the arteries.

After this operation my mother did not rally so quickly. In her sweet patient face there was a look of discouragement. Though the great wound healed up rapidly, she kept telling us that above the cut, yes, way up under her arm, the same sharp burning pains she had suffered never let up. Yes, they got worse all the time. My father went to Oneida, told Doctor Carpenter about it. He kept saying the pains would let up after a while. In July, my poor mother went to Doctor Carpenter herself. He examined her, gave her some medicine, and told her to come again the first of August. By that time you could plainly see a dozen or more little lumps. Doctor Carpenter said it was too late to operate; there was no way left now to save her life.

We came home. Out on the verandah, my mother said, "Get all the rest you possibly can tonight and tomorrow, we will go back to Oneida and go and see every surgeon in the city." Well, they went…came home in despair. They had gone from one doctor to another, always the same answer—too late. A few days later they went to Utica, saw six more doctors, again were told too late. On the twelfth of August they made one more trip, this time to Syracuse. Then again, they went to nine doctors and again were told it was too late to operate.

They had to stay in Syracuse one night. Well, after that, though my mother never complained, life for us all certainly was a horrible, sad thing. Mrs. Eckels tried her best to make us comfortable, the dark shadow getting ever blacker. All the doctors had agreed on one thing. They said it would be about three to four months before the end would come.

In the beginning of my book, I said I was writing my life story, not those of my parents. But these operations were so entirely a part of my life that I must include them as such. So each day went on, till about the sixth of September; we could begin to see that the entire side of my mother's lump, the cut was beginning to turn blue, and almost daily after that it showed plainer.

It was the nineteenth of September. Mrs. Eckel had gone to bed. We three were on the verandah, a warm moonlit night. We were very silent; my father had to go to Oneida the next day on business. I took him down in the morning; he walked home from North Bay at night. Mrs. Eckel had supper heady, and we waited for him. When he did come he acted strangely excited. Then he told us his story. After he had attended to his business, there were some five or six hours to wait for the train. So he went to spend some of that time with Mr. Suitzer, an old friend of his who kept a shoe store. My father sat there not speaking, and I suppose looked very sad. Right here I must say I had never seen my father smile.

Well, Mr. Suitzer spoke to him and said, "My dear friend, you seem so troubled. Is there some way in which I can help you?" My poor father, who never shed a tear, gave a great sob and told him the whole terrible story, ending, "Now it is too late... too late." Mr. Suitzer was silent for a few minutes; then he said, "There is one doctor you have not gone to yet. It is Doctor George Menzie of Oneida." At first my father said there was no use to go, so many good doctors had all agreed there was no help and now another month had gone by. But more to please Mr. Suitzer than any hope of help, he went to see Doctor Menzie. My father told him the whole story, from the time now over three years ago when my mother first felt the little lump in her breast up to now.

Doctor Menzie listened very attentively, then said, "Bring your wife out tomorrow, and I will make an examination. So next morning, the twenty-first of September, the three of us went to Oneida, and I went into the office with my parents. At Doctor Carpenter's, I always stayed in the waiting room. Doctor Menzie made the examination, never saying a word. Then he started pacing rapidly up and down the little room. While he was still pacing, my father said to him, "Doctor, do you think you can save her life?" The doctor turned around quick and glared at my father and yelled, "No!" My poor father said, "Then you will not make the operation?" Doctor Menzie took his fist and started pounding a small table. I thought he was raving crazy.

Then he said in a loud voice, "Yes, I will operate." My father said, "But why, if there is no chance to save her?" Doctor Menzie said, "If I do not operate, this woman will suffer the tortures of hell, will probably live about two more months, and each week, each day, yes, each hour, the pains will get worse, until death releases her, and if I make the operation she only also has about two more months to live, but her suffering will be practically over. She will get weaker all the time, and finally just pass out." Then he added, "But this will finish me as a surgeon. All the doctors will call me a darn fool. As you said, about two dozen good surgeons refused to make the operation, so they would not have the name of operating on a patient who was doomed to die, but his woman shall not suffer such agonies."

Then my mother asked him when he could make the operation. He said it ought to be done the next day, but he had some other cases he had to attend to, so they set the day of September the twenty-fourth, which came on Saturday. After we left the doctor, my good dear mother went and bought a lot of things for my birthday and Christmas. The next two days, she wrote a great many letters, as she thought she would never arise from the operation table. Imagine, through all those years of her suffering, she never mentioned it in her letters to her sister, so they would not feel badly. She also wrote a long letter to me, which she put in one of her big trunks, upstairs, with the newly bought Christmas boxes. On the twenty-third, she went out and patted each cow, and the little calf, the horse, thinking she would never see them again. The cats...Oh, how did they know something was wrong; they would not eat, just looked at my mother and mournfully meowed. She went into our gardens, picked a few flowers. Next morning after a light breakfast, we got the operating table ready again, this was the third time. At half past ten they came, Doctor Menzie and Doctor Otto Pfaff, who is still alive today and known as a great surgeon.

Sophie Kussmaul

When everything was ready, Doctor Menzie said, "Listen, this woman always was frail and delicate, and now, after her long and terrible suffering is in a weakened stage, may not be able to survive this operation, so I do not want to feel responsible if things go wrong." Then I said good bye to mother and ran out into our summer kitchen, where there was a fire to keep lots of water hot. I crouched down in my great despair and there was my mother. She followed me out to see me once more, to tell me not to feel so bad. Then and now, I know just how the near and dear ones feel when they say their last goodbye to a man or woman about to be executed. Only with this difference, the condemned ones had committed a terrible crime, but my pure good mother had never even had a bad thought.

Mrs. Eckel kept coming and going, telling me how things were going. I had my watch with me...one long hour, two long hours, three long hours, would it never end? Then Mrs. Eckel came in again, saying, "Well, they have killed your mother, gave her too much chloroform."

I never stopped running, through room after room, till I reached the operating room. This is what I saw. The ceiling, walls, window, curtains splattered with blood, the floor slippery and reeking with it. The two doctors, who had on white shirts with their sleeves rolled up above their elbows, were so completely soaked in blood that it literally dripped from them. In the center of the room, the operating table. Oh horrors! That, too, was drenched in blood. On it lay my mother, her head, which also was covered with blood, hanging way down. The two Oneida doctors blowing into her mouth, fanning her, holding ammonia to her nose. What little I could see of her face that was not covered with blood was waxy yellow, like a corpse. Her side and her whole back like raw beef.

The doctors had laid back all her skin so as to work better. The nurse spoke and said, "There is no use to work on her any longer; she is dead as she ever will be." My father said, "She is not dead, she will come back." Then there was a faint, very faint, flicker of her eyelids and a few moments later, a little sigh, hardly perceptible. They put a few drops of brandy between her lips. Doctor Menzie said, "Now we will have to work fast and get her sewed up as we cannot give her any more chloroform."

My father asked him if it would not be terribly painful for her to be sewed up without the anesthetic. The doctor said no, as in the first place, the chloroform was still so strong in her system that it would numb all pain, and in the second place, she was so very, very weak, through loss of blood, that that too would help her to be in a kind of faint. I went outdoors, did not cry but trembled all over. After a little, I went back into the operating room. They had just finished sewing her up.

The nurse did not do a thing. The doctors started washing her off. I washed her face and the bloody hair. I also helped to put on a clean, dry, loose nightgown; then my father and two of the doctors carried her carefully, gently into the bedroom. The doctors and nurse went and washed their hand and faces, the two Oneida doctors put on their coats over their still wet and blood soaked shirts. Then the four of them calmly went into the room next to where they had operated and sat down to eat a hearty lunch Mrs. Eckel had gotten ready for them. Good Mrs. Eckel was half sick with it all, but went to work at once to clean up the room of horror. Soon after the doctors had eaten, the man with the carriage came to take them to North Bay to catch the four forty-five train back to Oneida. My mother was still entirely unconscious when they left. Doctor Menzie gave my father full directions what to do.

Then followed a month which I shall never forget. Good Mrs. Eckel did all the housework, got the three meals for my father and myself, churned the cream into butter, canned and preserved fruit, made jellies and pickles, washed and ironed and kept the house clean. My father spent his entire time with my mother. Now, looking back I wonder how he ever got along with so little sleep. After I had eaten my breakfast, done my outdoor chores, I would sit by my mother one hour. My father threw himself on the couch in the living room and dropped to sleep the moment he lay down. Just one hour afterward, he would jump up and say he was rested, fit till the next morning.

During that long month, there was very little change in my mother's condition. Most of the time she slept, and when not actually sleeping, was in a semi-conscious state. She always had been a very small eater; now when she needed nourishing food so much, and still did not have the strength to really eat, my father would feed her a half of a soft boiled egg, or a tablespoonful of Port wine, or a couple of teaspoonfuls of beef tea, or a few spoons of milk, a spoonful of orange juice, and so on about every hour day and night, never waking her up, but when she seemed to come out of her sleep for a few moments. Still, the terrible cut healed rapidly. Once a day we would slip a rubber blanket, which was first warmed, under her blanket and I washed her big sore and re-bandaged it. There were one hundred and six stitches this time.

We had a great many callers; people we had hardly known would call to see my mother. My father only admitted a few, but thanked them all for calling. I remember in particular two rough looking men in work clothes, just men we slightly knew. They asked permission to see my mother. They softly tiptoed to the door of the bedroom, stood there a few moments with bared, bowed heads, turned to go away with tears in their eyes. A rough appearing Irish woman came, stood a few moments gazing at my sleeping mother, then crossed herself and went silently out of the room. Mrs. Eckel told me that night that Mrs. Baird, that was the woman's name, told her she felt as she was in the presence of an angel. Those were what my parents called the common people.

About four weeks after the operation a beautiful bay team drove into our yard. To our utter surprise, Doctor Menzie walked in. He hired a fast livery team and driver to come out to see if it was possible that my mother was still alive. Of course, he came at his own expense. He carefully examined the sore, kept saying wonderful, remarkable, wonderful! My father asked him about the further care of my mother. He smiled and said that my father did not need any of his advice.

So the weeks went on. In the first week of November, my mother was propped up for the first time in bed and tried to feed herself, but she fainted. After another two weeks, the twentieth of November, we wrapped her up in a warm robe, and my father carried her into the living room, into a big rocking chair with many soft pillows. She looked so thin, so white, but smiled at us sweetly. From that day on, she gained rapidly. By the first of December, she could walk a few steps and eat at the table.

Through Sophie's Eyes

Mrs. Eckel stayed with us till the middle of December; then I had all the housework to do, but my father did the outdoor chores again and kept two fires going day and night.

Now I must go back to the first of October of that year. All day I heard the sound of many axes, and again the next day. Then I heard form some of our callers that they were going to cut down every bit of the dear woodland below us. At first I could not believe it, but there were from ten to twelve men on the job, and in a short time I could begin to see open spaces. In the house was my dear precious mother hovering between life and death for weeks, and outside they were cutting and slashing down my beloved woodland, every blow from the ringing axe cutting into my heart. Yes, they cut down the big, noble old pine tree, everything.

For once, we had a mild autumn, no snow till way into December, so the wood cutters were at work all the time. When the people came calling, they all spoke of the great improvement and how pleasant it would be for us to have the woods cut down. I felt bitter and though my parents said nothing about it, I knew they too felt bad.

Of course, my mother did not know about this until nearly December. The twenty-first of December and my sixteenth birthday. My darling mother had me bring from upstairs the box marked for my birthday. The night before I had baked my own birthday cake. My father came upstairs to wake me up and when I got down, my dear mother, weak as she still was, had the table ready, as in other years. The same display of candies and nuts in or on the same dishes, my father's, mother's and aunt's presents, everything the same. Only this year, my mother was so much better than the year before.

Came Christmas, a happy time. Still, in spite of the fact that my mother was daily regaining her strength and telling us that she did not have those terrible, cutting, burning pains anymore, there was still the dread specter hovering near us, the constant fear that the cancer might break put again, somewhere, anytime. Once a month my father went to Oneida to report to Doctor Menzie. After New Year's, my arithmetic lessons began again. As I had all the housework to do now, my terrible arithmetic came after supper.

Sophie Kussmaul

In the last four or five winters, I had only mastered the two's and three's of the multiplication table. One morning after my father and I had had an extra stormy session the night before about figures, my gentle mother told me that any figures could be turned around, such as six times five or five times six. That gave me a new hold, a key to the multiplication table. Yes, I had learned it, knew it backwards, cross ways, any old way. I still know it, by cracky.

Every winter, the young people had parties, dances, sleigh rides. By now our road was generally open; at night we could hear the merry jingle of sleigh bells, and sometimes the happy laughter floating on the night air. As I had been raised so alone, I really did not miss it so much. Still, after I had worked all day at the cooking, baking, cleaning, washing, ironing and so on, and after supper sat down grimly with the despicable arithmetic, and heard sleigh bells and the joyous voices of the young people going by, a strange feeling came over me.

Shy as I was, not used to young company, still I felt a sort of longing to go with them. Then one day in February Mrs. Eckel was with us. A short time before she expected her husband to come after her, she began to talk about those parties. Said that besides the usual dances and parties for games and such, this year there were so many surprise parties; the girls would bake a big cake or a few dozen cookies or doughnuts or make a batch of sandwiches. One of the boys would furnish the team and sleigh, another one a pound of coffee or sugar, or something else in that line, and they would fill a big basket and go to some house and surprise a boy or girl. Would play games, sing, sometimes dance, eat and plan whom they would surprise the next time. She also told us about long sleigh rides they made together. In those days, movies were not even heard of. Then she turned to me and smiled, saying, "Well, Sophie, they are all coming to surprise you tomorrow night."

I was so astonished I could not speak. Then she went on, "It is about time you had a little fun in your life, something besides sorrow and hard work, and after they are here, they will invite you to go with them all over." It was the first time in my life that any one was really coming to visit me, and a whole load of young people at once. I knew them all by name and sight. I was in a dream of happiness for a few minutes. I was very romantic by nature and had read dozens of novels, so I pictured myself a sweetheart, a young, pleasant boy or young man who would sit near me on the sleigh rides, who would notice me, be my partner at games, and so on, a boyfriend as all the other girls had.

Then Mrs. Eckel's husband came after her, and my mother and I had been alone only a few moments when my father came into the house. My mother started to tell him about what Mrs. Eckel had just said. At a glance, I saw his displeasure. He said, "And did Mrs. Eckel really think I would let my daughter run around nights with a bunch of young ignorant forward young fools? Well, she is not going. If they come here tomorrow night, I will receive them civilly, but tell them plainly that she can not leave the house." So next night they came, seven girls and five boys. Charles Dixon furnished the team, asked my father's permission to put the horses in the barn as it was a cold night. I played the organ, they sang, we, or rather they, talked. When the basket of food was unpacked, handed around, my father refused to eat any of it. I can not say that he really was impolite. But I felt a strain, something seemed wrong. When they got ready to leave, they planned their next party. It was to be at Fred McCormack's. They told me to be ready at seven thirty, two days from then and bring a dozen cheese sandwiches. I had no chance to answer. My father told them in a very polite way that I was only a child, too young to be out nights. Some of the girls laughed, told him I was in my eighteenth year; they had gone out now since they were sixteen.

One of the boys went over to my father, said to him, "Will you not trust her with us? I will look after her myself." My father stiffened up and said, "I have spoken. She cannot go." Imagine the feeling of shame, of humiliation that stole over me. I had been old enough for the last three years to do a nurse's work about my mother's wounds and stitches. I had been old enough to do the entire farm chores for three years in summer. I had been old enough to do the housework alone for two winters. I had been old enough to do most of our marketing, selling eggs and butter, buying the groceries, but was a child, too young to have a little pleasure.

Sophie Kussmaul

Next day, my darling mother, ever trying to make peace between me and my father, said to me, "My dear little Sophie, your father was right last night when he thought it was not proper for you to go out at night. He loves you as few fathers love their daughters, and it certainly would not look well for you to go out like that without a chaperone." I ventured to say that the other girls did not have a chaperone either. My mother said, "Well, these girls and boys grew up together, and besides, you must never forget that they are the common people. You belong to a different class." Oh, how I hated, yes hated, that. Were we not all God's children? Did not Christ love us all alike? I loved my people, the common people.

Chapter 10

So my life went on. Work in daytime, arithmetic at night. I had some time in daytime to play on the organ and read. My mother had gained more and more strength, spent hours every day mending, darning and making over clothes of all kinds. The work had been sadly neglected for over a year. That was one thing Mrs. Eckel did not do. Neither did I, and my mother's left arm was so much affected by the cancer that she could hardly move it.

Mother had begun to help me with the lighter part of the housework, and in her goodness to help my education, kept speaking to me in French. I did not like French, told her so, but she kept saying that later on when I traveled in the foreign countries, I would find it useful. Well, I was right about this. Here I am, sixty-nine years old, and never had an occasion to use French.

Came the sixteenth of March, I was very busy, had tapped our maple trees, kept running after my sap, was boiling it outdoors, making delicious syrup and soft maple sugar. I loved this kind of work. My father went to North Bay after groceries. My mother, who by this time was much improved, was getting dinner. I saw Fred McCormack, with one of his lovely young horses drive into our driveway. I went into the house, not dreaming what his errand might be.

After making a few remarks about the weather, he said his sister, Marion, was giving a St. Patrick's Day party the next night, just a little music, a few games, and supper. He said she was sending me an invitation and handed me a neatly written envelope. I was much confused and felt the hot blood mount to my face, yes, into my very hair and down into my throat. Of course, he noticed it, and I being very shy and bashful anyway, that made me feel all the more uncomfortable. He turned to my mother, saying that if I could come, he would be glad to come after me and also bring me back home. I shall never forget the look on my mother's face. Yes, I felt sorry for her. I knew she hated to deny me this pleasure, still, she felt in duty bound to do so. So she very politely told Fred that I was still so young and had never been out anywhere without my father and mother. He bowed, mumbled something about their having counted on me, and left. Fred McCormack was at that time, and for many years to come, the most popular young man of our neighborhood. He was about six years older than I.

After he went away, my mother said to me that it would have been most highly improper for me to have gone out alone with a young man, and especially so at night. The next night as I sat sullenly at my hated arithmetic, I heard the merry jingle of the sleigh bells as they passed our house. Well, all this did not keep me from dreaming, dreaming of a sometime lover who would come into my life. And I pictured to myself the glory of such a love.

Came spring and I started working out of doors. Happier days, my darling mother felt better than she had for years. She again took up the lighter housework. I did the heavier part of the housework and work on the farm and in my gardens.

Came the twelfth of June. The three of us went to Oneida. The reason we made this trip was that Doctor Menzie wanted to make a through examination of my mother, also take a blood test. He said that if she passed the examination, the blood test, there would not be any more danger or chance of the cancer returning than if she had never had it. But we all, the doctor included, feared that it was still lurking in her system. So we were back in the same little office where he had made that other examination. Carefully, inch by inch he went over the parts where the cancer had been. Then he asked my mother dozens of questions, such as if she ever had any pains inside. Finally, he took her blood test. The sample had to be sent to Buffalo. Well, when he got all done, he smiled and said that as far as he knew, she was perfectly free of cancer. He would write and let us know how she passed the blood test in a few days, but he assured us he was quite confident that she was cured.

No one knows how I felt during that examination. No one knew the thrill of great joy that passed through me when he announced her cured. My father and mother both thanked him for saving her life. Doctor Menzie turned and looked at them both, then he solemnly declared, "Do not thank me, thank God; he saved her. She was far, far beyond help." The rest of the day was a happy one for us all, and funny as this may sound, in our great joy we bought a nice present for Mrs, Eckel. Of course, we were happy again, but still awaited a little fearfully the answer from the blood test. That came in a few days, no trace, of course.

Life seemed good, and each day my mother seemed to be more like she was years ago. We spent the days as of old, working at our different occupations, the dear, long summer nights again on the verandah. Once in a while, a neighbor or two came to visit us. Once in a while, I took my mother out in our buggy, sometimes just for a short ride, other times to call on some of our friends. When there was a sick person that my parents knew, they always went to see them.

Now, looking back over all my years, I know that this was the happiest summer of my life. In the first place, the grim shadow of sorrow that had hung over out lives for so many years had gone. The summer before, the dreaded specter, cruel death, had ever camped on our threshold. Even the woodland below us had regained a little of its former self. The wood cutters had not bothered themselves to cut down the smaller trees, and when spring had come and clothed them all in their new fresh green leaves, and each twig and branch of the thousands upon thousands of young trees and shrubs sent out six to ten inches of new growth, as I called it the healing touch of Mother Nature, another forest was springing up.

Oh, those wonderful nights on the verandah. My father and mother sitting close together, talking in a happy, contented way to one another. I lay in my hammock dreaming dreams of the life before me. Ever in my dreams appeared a lover, a good and handsome young man all dress up like a prince. He would come to me and love me, take me to my West. For I still and always had that intense longing to go west. Thus our summer nights on the verandah were spent.

> Then came years of maidenhood
> Fanciful and sweet
> Visioning a lover
> To make my life complete
> Or was it yesterday?

Sophie Kussmaul

Now I must go back a little in my story. There was a family by the name of Bagnell living about three miles from us on what is called the California Road. They were not any particular friends of ours, but still we always had been on neighborly terms with them. Mrs. Bagnell was a very large, powerfully built woman, muscular. Her husband, on the other hand, was a very small man. They seemed very affectionate toward one another and Mr. Bagnell was known to be a very peaceable man. But once in a great while he would go on a drunk, and then he became ugly and abusive. On an average, this only happened about once a year or so. The neighbors would laugh and say that when he came home and started tearing around, his wife would spank him. How true this was, we did not know, but she certainly could licked two like him.

In April, we heard that Mrs. Bagnell had been stricken by a strange ailment. The North Bay doctor and a Camden doctor had been called, but neither one really knew just what was the matter. She seemed unable to arise out of bed, yet, after the most careful examination, they could not find the least thing wrong with her. At times she would go four and five days without eating, or drinking, not even a mouthful. Then again, she would eat very hearty. She also at times did not even know her own family, would try to speak, but could not do so. Again she would know everyone and could talk, but could not, or would not get up. The doctors declared that she did not have a shock. Quite often my parents would talk about going to see her, but as this was a very busy time on the farm, it was put off. Fence, haying, crops to rush in, hoeing, cultivating, oat harvest.

Came the eighteenth of July. On this day something happened in my life that seemed to change everything. We had had a very good summer for crops. Lately it was beginning to be rather dry, but once in a while a refreshing shower would come in the night, just enough rain to freshen up the crops. But miles away the north woods had caught fire. All day there was a smoky haze in the air and early in the morning much stronger, one could smell the woody fire smoke, also the faint odor of ground burning. Not too strong, but fragrant.

The morning was calm, beautiful. My mother was getting breakfast. My father and I were doing the outdoor chores. We were eating breakfast in the back room as we always did in summer. All at once, my father said to my mother, "We have so often spoken about going to see Mrs. Bagnell, now the farm work is caught up for a while, and I do not think it is so oppressively hot today; the ride will do you good." No matter where my father went, he always wanted to go in the morning. After the meal was cleared away, I went out and harnessed and hitched up the horse to our top buggy, drove from back of the barn to the front of the house, hitched her to the hitching post under the big maples and went upstairs to put on a fresh, thin summer dress.

By that time my parents were ready and took their seats on the seat of the buggy. I always sat in front of them on a low stool and drove the horse. When I was out alone, I always drove just as fast as I could make the poor old horse go. But when they were with me, I seldom drove out of a walk. So we slowly went along. There seemed to be a great peace in the very air. We saw how some of the farmers were still making hay, others cutting their oats.

Although fifty-three years have past by since that day, looking back I can see everything before me as if it were today. It must have been about half past nine o'clock when we arrived at Bagnell's. We all went into the bedroom. Mrs. Bagnell looked at us a long time, then called each one of us by name, shook hands, and again seemed to drowse off.

We went into the living room. Mr. Bagnell was there, and their eldest daughter, Mary Jane, who had come home to keep house since her mother's illness. Then, one by one, the three boys, ranging in age from twenty to twenty-five, came in. Johnny, Christie, and Willie. Here was a strange thing. I was always so terribly bashful, especially before a young man. But although I plainly saw that all three of them kept looking at me every moment, for once I did not blush or look nervous. Well, it was about eleven o'clock and my father said it was time to go home.

After we got back in the buggy, my mother asked my father what he thought of Mrs. Bagnell's ailment. He said that probably Mr. Bagnell was drunk and struck her on the head, probably a bone was pressing just a tiny bit on her brain. I think he was right about that.

Sophie Kussmaul

Then my mother spoke again, saying, "Did you notice how rude, how very rude those Bagnell boys stared at our little daughter?" My father answered, "I cannot keep men from looking at her, but if any of then ever should come to call on her I would make a quick stop to that." So we slowly drove home.

We were now on this side of Mr. Cleveland's house, now known as Charles Congdon's place, had reached the stone pile which I always called the halfway mark between Cleveland's house and ours. To my great surprise, just a little ways ahead, under the maple tree which is still standing, were two men sitting on the ground and eating their dinners out of dinner pails. This maple tree is just on the line between what was then Cleveland's farm and Littlefield's, now known as Congdon's farm and Arthur Nash's farm. On Littlefield's side there was a pasture, on Cleveland's a big hayfield which had been cut and the hay taken off some time ago, so what could those men have been working at? All this passed through my mind in a few seconds. By now, we had reached the spot where they were sitting on the ground. The older one, who sat eight or ten feet further from the road, spoke to my father. His name was George Young, a man who lived in North Bay and was known to do any kind of work, from digging a grave, to working at planting, hoeing, haying, cutting wood, for a living. His wife took in washing and went out cleaning, scrubbing. But the younger man? He sat much nearer to the road. He looked at me with the kindest look, the pleasantest smile I had ever seen in a man. His head was bare, his heavy dark brown hair wavy, his beautiful eyes brown. He wore a dark brown drooping mustache. At that time, almost every man wore a beard or mustache. He had the pleasantest, truest face I had ever seen. Yes, to this day I have never seen a man's face like his.

When he looked at me, something like electricity shot through me. A thrill like something divine. A bliss not of this earth, but heavenly. I seemed to be in a sort of trance the rest of the short way home. I drove to the front door to let my parents out and then drove back of the barn and unhitched the horse, took care of her. I walked to the house in a sort of dream. My mother had the table set, said she just put on a cold lunch as it was already past twelve o'clock. She would have a cooked supper for us. As if those things mattered. I have not the least idea what we ate, nor the least idea of what they talked about. Each day after the mid-day meal, my father would lay down on the couch for a short nap. My mother would take a book, lie back in our big easy chair, read a few minutes, and then, too, have her nap. I always kept very quiet during that time.

I went out on the verandah and into my hammock, took up the book I had been reading the day before. But I could not read. I only saw his face, his dear smiling brown eyes. Then, through the young leafy trees of the one time forest, I saw the two men going towards the big hemlocks. When the woods were cut down the autumn before, the men, by order of Mr. Cleveland, left nine large hemlocks on and very close by to our line fence. At the present time, there are only three of them left. Well, to my wonderment, I saw that when they had reached the one nearest toward the road, a distance of perhaps two hundred and fifty feet from the little tiny bridge on the road, they stopped and started digging at the very roots of the hemlock and close to our line fence. This indeed was a mystery to me. Though they were quite a distance from where I was in my hammock, and though there were the young leaf trees and our own little cedar trees between, I could distinctly make out the two men. He was taller, he moved a little quicker. Ever and again, I heard his voice floating up on the still hazy air.

I was in such a dream of happiness that I hardly heard my mother when she came on the verandah with her mending basket. She smiled at me and said, "Isn't my girlie reading?" As if I could read. Then she talked to me about different things. But not about him. She had not even seen the men, now at work, did not seem to have even heard his voice. Then my father came on the verandah, said he should go and work in the garden. Then he heard and saw the men working at something. For a few minutes, he seemed mildly interested, then began to talk about something he had read in the newspaper. All at once, I, who had never stopped looking down, saw him going towards the road and then coming up towards our house. I was almost afraid my mother would hear my heart beat; it was beating so loud and wildly. He came right up to our verandah and asked my father for some drinking water. He was talking to my father, but looking at me. Yes, with that good true look in his dear brown eyes.

My father asked him where he came from, his name. He laughed softly, said he was born in North Bay but for the last ten years had worked most of the time in Oneida. But he still made his real home in North Bay, with his mother. His name was Joe Henry. Then all at once, it all came to me. I had so often seen a kind, pleasant looking middle aged woman in the North Bay Post Office and little grocery store. I knew her name to be Mrs. Henry. So this was her son. Well, he told my father, still looking at me, that Mr. Cleveland had hired Mr. Young and himself to dig a ditch to drain the swamp. He laughingly said that they thought it would only take ten days or two weeks, but they found that the ground was just a network of tough roots that had to be chopped and grubbed out of the ground. Still smiling at me, he said it would probably take a month. Then he walked lightly back to his work, with the little tin pail of water for his partner.

After he had gone, my father spoke of the work they were doing, what it would mean, what a great improvement, that it would also help to drain our side of the lower pasture, that as long as it had been dry so long, now was the time to do that work, if heavy rains should start coming, it could not be finished, and so on. But not one word about him.

My father went into the garden to work. I took my berry pail and wandered off for a little while. That summer there were hardly any wild berries, but I managed to find a few. That first night on the verandah after I had seen him, everything seemed enchanted. More of heaven than earth. The night sounds, sweet and low, through the hazy, smoky air. I slept little that night, was too happy to sleep. But when I came downstairs in the morning, my mother looked at me and said I must have had a good refreshing sleep, I looked so fresh and bright.

In those days, men worked ten hours a day instead of eight. So at seven, I heard their picks, axes, and voices, his voice, coming up through the smoky haze. So it went on for a month, no rain to speak of and I seemed not to be living in this world. I seemed to have entered paradise.

Came the nineteenth of August, a hot, dry forenoon. The haze in the air had become denser, thicker, but oh how I loved this weather. Ever since, through all the many, many summers since, when this time of summer comes with its heat, hazy atmosphere, and quiet days, I go down to where the big ditch was started at the foot of the old hemlock, of which there is only part of the trunk left. Years ago it was struck by lightning and then slowly died. But there is still some of the ditch left. But that, too, is caving in and filling up. I go there, kneel down and pray, as if it were a shrine.

Through Sophie's Eyes

I listen, yes, the same sounds as of those olden, golden days. Crickets chirping, bees buzzing, a few birds twittering, grasshoppers hopping about. I listen, but one sound is lacking, the dearest one of all, Joe Henry's voice. So I come back home, my lonely silent home. I gaze down the drive—way down the road. I can almost see him coming, and who knows, perhaps his spirit is as near to me as my thoughts are ever and always with him. For over twenty-six years now, he has been sleeping about a mile from here in a little cemetery, but I am still roving around on the ground he used to trot.

Well, as I said, it was the nineteenth of August. I had picked two bushel baskets of string beans that forenoon, and now my mother and I, each with a bushel in front of us, were busily snipping them to be packed in big jars for winter use. My father was somewhere on the farm. I saw him coming up the road with his little tin pail after water. He came to us as we were working at the beans on the shady verandah.

As always, I felt the hot blood mount to my face. Luckily there was a large potted plant between my mother and myself so she could not see my face. Joe came up, said the ditch was done. He came nearer to me, looked me in the face, and said he would miss our cool water, hesitated, stood there a few moments; then he said his mother would like to have me call on her. Oh, how glad and happy I would have been to go to her, but knew my parents would be horrified. My mother answered for me, said I just went to North Bay to get the mail and groceries. Soon after that he went slowly down the road.

After he left, my mother said, "How perfectly ridiculous. How absolutely improper that would be, you calling on a young man's mother just because we let him have water. Just a common laborer." That night on the verandah I was both very sad and very happy. That sounds as if I was contradicting myself, but it was like this. I felt desperately lonely; he might never again come up the road to us. I also was very unhappy, for I knew if he ever came without a good excuse, both my parents would guess why he came and that would end it all. Then again, such waves of joy, such bliss would come over me when I thought of how he had looked at me, how he had shyly asked me to call on his mother.

Then I remembered, when I was thirteen-and-a-half years old, how I had thought I was in love with my little Indian sweetheart. How, when my dear mother used to say to me that after I grew up and got

98

married, I would have a lovely home and servants. Then I used to picture myself, a beautifully furnished mansion. But strange to say, never a husband. Then a few years later, I would vision a handsome, stylish garbed young man coming to me, speaking of love the way I had read in novels, bringing handfuls of expensive jewels, taking me, his bride, to the golden West.

Now, oh what did mansions with servants, lovers with pearls and diamonds mean to me. Was not one glance of love from Joe Henry's eyes worth more to me than millions in gold and silver. So the evening passed by.

Chapter 11

Now I must go back a little in my story. There was one mystery about my mother I never understood, yes, even less today after my experiences of life. Though she was by far the best educated woman I ever knew, and in after years I became acquainted with many college educated women and such, I know she still had absorbed more real, deep learning. Added to this were her many travels in dozens of foreign countries, and above all, a great gift to read human nature. Years later, I met people who had known my mother in her younger days. They all remarked that it was almost uncanny the way she could glance at a person and as they said, read their very thoughts.

Still, she made one terrible mistake in that line, something that caused me many distressful hours, something that at the time almost made me frantic. About a mile-and-a-half from us by the road and only a half mile cross lots, on the next road, lived a family by the name of Corcoran, a farmer's family. They were just in comfortable circumstances, just ordinary people. They had quite a number of boys. All of them had homes of their own, except the second youngest one. His name was James, but everyone called him Jim. I always had been extremely bashful, especially with men, but in this case there was a vast difference. I feared him; even as a little child, when he came to our house, a feeling of fear crept over me. I think I mentioned him in the beginning of this book when I described my mother's and my visit to my father's school the day of the fights. Those fights did not in the least make me nervous. But every once in a while I would glance over to where this James Corcoran sat and an uneasy feeling would creep over me.

He was between twelve and thirteen years older than myself. In later years, I found out, he was not liked in our neighborhood. Once, even I heard his own mother say, "God pity the girl that ever becomes Jim's wife." Yes, those were her very words. He was cruel by nature,

100

abusive when drunk...seemed utterly without feeling. There was just one good trait about him—he was a great worker.

Here was the great mystery. My mother liked him, claimed he was a good man. She of all people with her great discernment of human nature. I really think that that was the only time in her entire lifetime that she ever was mistaken about a person. Here connected with this was another mystery in a way even greater. From my earliest childhood, she would talk to me in such a way that she took it for granted that if I got married, I would have a very rich husband, a highly educated husband, perhaps a nobleman.

At the same time, once in a while she would say what a horrible thing it would be if I married one of these common men, picturing a life of indescribable hardships, and worst of all, degradation. Still, at the same time, this was when I got a little older, fifteen, she would hint to me what a good husband Jim Corcoran would make, saying in a sweet tone that if I married him, I would always be near my old home. How he would keep at least one hired girl for me, how I could change and rebuild the farm house, while everyone knew that he had no money, besides was mean, and miserly with the little he did have, excepting with himself. He drank quite heavily and gambled. When I plainly told her that I hated him, she would smile and say that all girls say that about the men they begin to love.

There was this difference between Jim Corcoran and all the other young men I knew. When I met any of them on the road, store, post office, or when by chance I happened to be at a neighbor's house and one of them stopped there, they would greet me with a pleasant smile and nod of the head, perhaps make a remark about the weather or inquire about the health of my parents. I was not embarrassed. But when I met this Jim Corcoran, I very, very seldom was on foot, either on horseback or in the buggy, and he would stand still, leer greedily, hungrily at me, his eyes devouring me. But if I met him in the store, post office, a neighbors, or if there happened to be anyone with him on the road, he never spoke to me, no, did not even seem to see me.

One of my few pleasures in spring, summer, and early fall had been to take horseback rides on the lonely byroads. But I had to give them up for a number of times, though miles away from his home, I would run across him. I would turn my horse around and ride away at full gallop. Of course I never told my dear mother about those things. When he did come to our house, sometimes to either borrow or return a farm tool, he always was politeness and respectfulness itself, before and towards my mother and myself.

My mother, who always used any of the other young men with cold politeness, would talk to this one in a friendly way, and would either manage to tell him what a good cook I was, or that I never went out with anyone. Of course this was years later than where I dropped my story about Joe's last day on the ditch.

In July, a girl by the name of Florence Mickels, born and raised a little beyond the Schwartz family whom I mentioned in the very beginning of the book, got married to a man by the name of Conner. This girl, who was about a year-and-a-half older than myself, had worked for us once in a while for a few days at a time. A good, pleasant young girl. The man she married we only knew by sight and name. We had heard that they had rented a very old house, just outside of North Bay, but not on the road where the Henry's lived.

One day at dinner my mother said she would like to call on her. So the next afternoon, when I made my trip to the grocery and post office, my mother went with me. After I had gotten our provisions and mail, we went to the little old house. I had gone by it countless of times, but had never been inside of it.

While I was hitching the horse to the hitching post, Florence ran out to welcome us. She seemed so happy. She conducted us into their kitchen. The floor was bare, but scrubbed and scoured spotlessly clean. A plain table with a cheap, but snow white cloth, was set for two. There was another old table, her work table, a homemade bench on which stood a water pail and wash dish, a cupboard with a few dishes. Three or four second hand kitchen chairs. An old cook stove. There was a kettle on the stove and a fire in the stove. The stove was badly smoking. Florence told us the stove had been given to them from her parents. Some time they would get a new one. She cheerfully added, "But it is a good baker and cooks our meals."

Then she took us into the living room. On the floor was a faded rug carpet, a present from her people. A second hand couch and a few old rocking chairs, gifts from her husband's folks. The walls were newly papered with a cheap wallpaper. She and her husband had done that after working hours. A small table with a lamp and a few pictures on the wall. She showed us their bedroom, a clean, bare floor, with a homemade rug in front of the bed. Her husband had bought a new bedstead with springs. She had bought a mattress and pieced some quilts. Her mother had given them two pillows. On a row of nails hung their clothes. When we left, she proudly showed us their six hens and a rooster. I can still see them. They were Plymouth Rocks, she said, "And they lay and keep us in eggs. Next spring I will set some of them and we will have chickens."

There was such genuine joy in her voice, such a happy, happy light in her eyes. Well, my mother and I had no chance to talk our call over. I had brought her two letters from the post office, and the very moment we got back into the buggy she started to read them. They were from her beloved sisters, both so far and far away.

When we got home, I took care of the horse but did not go into the house. Instead I ran down into our pasture and crawled into a thick clump of cedars. My heart was full to bursting. For the first time in my life, I felt jealous, or perhaps the right word was envious. Why, yes, why, should this girl, only a year and a half older than I, have everything worth living for and I have nothing? I thought of her neat humble kitchen, the table set for two. I pictured to myself how she would look and listen for the voice and step of the man she loved coming home. Then they would sit down together and eat the meal she had cooked.

I also pictured their long winter evenings together in that homey living room. There they would plan for the years to come. Years of youth, and the later years of their fuller life. Or perhaps they would go out together with the other happy, joyous young people for the evening. I would spend my winter days doing housework, but not for the man I loved better than life.

Each day there would be hours of that horrible arithmetic, and evenings I would hear the merry jingle of sleigh bells coming ever nearer and nearer, then echo themselves away in the distance. After a while I would go upstairs to my lonely room. Why, I thought, I could not even speak about him to anyone. I had no girl friends. The few girl friends that I might have had, I never had a chance to visit with. When a young girl did come to the house, my mother never left us alone.

I remember once a very nice girl came to see me, about my age. Her name was Sadie Yager. We just had my room upstairs repapered. I took her up to show her the room. My mother followed us up, sat down, then said, "We had better go down now." Yes, I thought bitterly, I dare not even think about my great love before my mother for fear she might read my thoughts. Then I heard the call for supper. After we had started eating, my father asked my mother if she had made her call on Florence. She said, "Yes and I felt so very sorry for her. The poor girl got nothing. Just a little old shabby furniture. Everything looked so poor and bare, and she tries so hard to be brave about it. I could not help thinking how much better off our little daughter is. She got everything to make her happy, and nothing to trouble her--a good, comfortable home, a father who provides for her, and not a care in the world. While that other poor girl has nothing, married to just a laborer." My father spoke and said, "That is the trouble with these people. When a girl gets to be eighteen or nineteen years old, they imagine they are in love, get married to some poor laboring man, and from then on enter a life of drudgery. There should be a law forbidding any girl to get married under twenty-four or twenty-five years. A girl of eighteen or nineteen does not know any more about love than a baby of a year old."

Well after that, we had more rain, and the smoke had cleared, the weather was cooler, but still no frost. Came the twenty-eighth of September, a beautiful mild Sunday, and again that morning the smoky haze was in the air. The reason for this was, where the fires had been raging so long, they had had less rain than we had. But the rains in our vicinity, together with a brisk southwest wind, had thoroughly cleared the air for a time. But now after a few days without any rain, and a breeze from the north, the smoke had come floating back and mingled together with the sun's hot rays. There was absolutely no air stirring. Everything looked exactly the way it had during those blessed days of summer, when he so often came up the road and into our lower driveway.

It was Sunday afternoon, about three o'clock. My father and mother were sitting together in their accustomed places on the verandah. I was in my hammock, but not laying down. I was sitting in it, busily at work on an egg basket. For a number of days I had been cutting and shaping splints, both for the standards and filling. Then I had shaved them smooth as silk with a piece of sharp glass. Now I was weaving the bottom of the basket with the standards, which, after the bottom is completed, are turned up and the filling wove into them. This was a difficult job. It is easy to make a square or long basket, but to fix the standards to make a round basket is a lot more difficult. To weave the splints around, after the standards are shaped, is easy

104

enough. Still, interested as much as I was in my pleasant work, every once in a while I would gaze down the road, thinking of him and in my mind visioning him coming up the road and turning into our driveway as he had done dozens of times.

It really had been only about five weeks since the last time he had wandered up. Still in a way, it seemed now like a thing of the long and long ago, while at the same time it also seemed only yesterday. My parents were visiting together, and at times, as was their want, fell into long and thoughtful silence.

Now, though I was only about ten feet away from them, sitting up in the hammock, my face close to the meshes of the hammock, I could see their faces as plainly as if the hammock had not been between us, while they could not see my face at all. Again I was dreamily gazing down the sunny road when, oh, what did I see? Or was it just a hallucination of the mind. No, I did see it. My blood rushed into my face. I felt weak and dizzy. I heard my father say, "That man looks familiar. I know that walk." Then my mother said, "It seems to be that ditch digger." By this time he was turning into our driveway. She added, not too well pleased, "I wonder what he wants here now."

Yes, it was him. But not in his work clothes, stained with earth and dirt from honest toil. This Joe was all dressed up like a rich man. But with the same dear true look in his handsome face. He walked up to our verandah, bowed and politely greeted my parents, hesitated a moment, then walked a few steps to where I was. Looked me straight in the face, then smilingly said to me, "So you can make baskets?" I did not answer. He picked up a splint and said, "Will you teach me to weave a basket?" Then I did a very, very foolish thing. I said no. He looked at me for a second, hurt, surprised, and went and sat down near my parents. Now I will try and explain why I snubbed him. I had gotten a glimpse of my mother's face as she glanced at Joe when he spoke to me. I felt, yes I knew, that she had read the love in his face, his very voice, as he looked at me. At that second something flashed through my mind I had overheard last winter. It was the next day after the young people had invited me to go with them to the next party. I overheard my father say to my mother, "Of course, now she is only a child, and we can keep her from mixing with these people, but what will we do if in later years she should fall in love with one of these men?" My mother answered so quickly that even then it came to me that she had planned this long ago. She answered, "We will send her at once to my sister in Constantinople for a year. By that time she will have forgotten all about that nonsense." I knew that they both loved me so very, very much that this parting would almost kill them, but that at the same time, they would make any sacrifice to their own feelings to save me, as they thought, from such a marriage.

Well, all this had come back to me like a flash. So now, my only hope left me, as I then thought, would be to let her think I cared nothing for this man. From where I sat, I could see all their faces. My father talked to Joe. About half a dozen different things Joe told him about his work in Oneida. Up to this time, they had had a horse drawn street car. Now they were putting in a trolley line, and Joe had passed his examination as motor man. There was a pause, then he told my father that he did not like Oneida, and if he could find more work around North Bay, he would much rather stay at home, saying it took nearly half his earnings to pay his board and at the same time keep up the little home for his mother. He said even if he could only earn half as much around here and could live at home, he would still be better off. My father fully agreed with him.

Then Joe said that he had heard my father hired some work done on the farm, and that he would be glad to get that job. I could see displeasure in my mother's face. My father said that all the farm work was done for this season except for digging the potatoes, and he could do that himself, that I always picked them up. Then he said that he had a little job, but as it was rather hard work, he might not want it. It was a few days cutting wood in the woods. Joe gave that glad little laugh I loved so well and said he liked to cut wood.

My father always cut a year's wood ahead, so we always had dry, seasoned wood for the long, cold months. He told Joe that he had about a dozen big hard maples across the creek, trees that really were too large for one man alone to cut and work up. In those days no one ever used a buzz saw. All the farmers cut up the log wood with a cross cut saw. Two men, one at each end of the long saw. The limbs were cut up with a buck saw. Joe listened with that happy look in his face that I loved so much. My father said that he thought each tree, besides the smaller limbs and branches, would yield at least three cords of wood. He went on to say that while they were cutting, I could be drawing it home.

Sophie Kussmaul

While this conversation was taking place, I was so exquisitely happy that mere words could not begin to describe it. I pictured in my mind how he would be coming to us every morning, not just to get some water but to stay with us all day. Of all my outdoor work, I had always loved this, the drawing of our year's wood the most. I who loved nature so much. October in the dear woods. With all glory of autumn. Now added to this joy would be the great delirious happiness of him with us. I also knew that would mean he would eat dinner and supper with us. My thoughts went winging their way on. Yes, after that, he would come to us often, as a guest, a friend, my sweetheart. I was even carried on in fancy to a little home of our own.

I suppose that all of us in some way at some time, picture in our minds the life in the betterland, the joys of the Eden to come, and in a vague way see as in a dream the glories of the Promised Land. But no anticipation of that divine glory could have been greater, sweeter, than the joy, the ecstasy that surged through my very being. Added to this was that I felt, yes I knew, that my father liked Joe. Except when my father's terrible temper broke out, he always had such perfect control of his features that it was hard, indeed, to read his thought. But I, who knew him so well, sensed that he did approve of Joe.

Now I must relate something about my parents. There never was a kinder, more considerate, affectionate husband in the world than my father. He idolized my mother, and I knew would have gladly given his life to save hers. Still, he was supreme boss, without being bossy. Everything indoors, as well as outdoors, went exactly as he decided. So I felt very happy, even though I knew my mother was not pleased about the woodcutting arrangement.

But all at once she bent over him, brushing some imaginary dust off his shoulder, said to him in a low voice in German, "Npma Ipe Nicht." This meant in English: do not take him. My father kept on talking to Joe as if he had not heard her. Branched off so easily, so naturally from his talk of the big maples. Began to discuss the merits of other woods and so on to poplars, saying they were no good green, but when seasoned, made a quick, hot fire. Then on to the time when men burned up the best hard wood in piles to clear land. So on and on, ever further away from hiring Joe. At last Joe spoke, said to my father that any time he was ready to start cutting to let him know, that he would leave off any work he might be doing. I saw it pained my father, but he said he really had not yet made up his mind about those

107

big trees, perhaps he could not cut them after all. Joe looked up at him quickly, then at my mother, and then said he must be going. He came to me, made some remark about my basket. I did not answer. Then he held out his hand, said goodbye, looking me straight in the face. I did not take his hand. I knew my mother was watching. How gladly I would have thrown my arms about his dear neck and sobbed and laughed out my love for him.

Slowly he walked down the road. My father turned towards my mother and asked, "Why did you not want me to hire him? I like the man. He looks like a good, honest man." My mother said, "He is very much interested in our daughter. I suspected that a long time ago when he kept running here all the time after water, was glad when that old ditch was done. I thought that would end it, but a blind person could see the love in his eyes every time he looked at her today." My father was silent. Then he said, "Impossible. Why she is only a child." A pause, then, "I am very sorry. I like the man, but of course if that is the case we will have to stop his coming here."

I felt rebellious, bitter, but dared not show it, for I knew if either one of them had guessed my feelings, what little bit of freedom I had, such as riding, or driving to North Bay, or on rare occasions to ride somewhere else, would have been taken from me.

Came the sixth day of November, a dark, gloomy day. The ground was still bare, but frozen as hard as a rock. The wind was blowing from the northwest and threatening snow. It was Sunday, and we had just finished eating our dinner in the cozy winter kitchen. There was a bright fire in the kitchen stove, blooming plants at the windows, an enormous black and white cat dozing and purring on a cushioned chair. Two fat, sleek kittens, one gray and white, the other one all yellow, playing together on the floor. Through the open door into the living room, one could see the cheery looking light from the coal stove, all Isinglass doors. The room looked very warm and inviting. As I said, we had just finished our dinner when there was a knock at the door. My father opened it and in walked Joe Henry. He greeted my father and mother, then, with a quick step, came to me. I felt as if I wanted to fall into his arms, but instead did the silliest thing I could have done. I ran upstairs.

I despised and hated myself for doing this, but again, it was fear of being discovered, for I knew as yet my mother had not guessed my secret. As I said in the beginning of this book, children know their parents, but parents do not know their children. I heard my mother say something to Joe that, though I loved my mother far more than I think the average daughter loves her mother, sent a bitter feeling surging through my being. This is what she said: "I think my daughter was a little surprised, disappointed. She had been expecting Jim Corcoran." This was the last straw. I felt like rushing down, getting into the middle of the room, and shouting out loudly that I did not expect Jim Corcoran, that I hated him, and then turn to Joe and invite him into our pleasant living room. These were my thoughts, but I knew if I would dare do such a thing, that the very least my parents would do would be to order Joe out of the house and me upstairs, then follow me up, with an unending lecture, shaming me. And that each day for months to come I would again and again be reminded what an unforgivable thing I had done. I crouched down, trembling, quivering, in a little heap in the corner like a wounded animal.

I do not know just how long I was there, I imagine only a short time, when I heard the door below open and shut. I got up, went to the east window, and saw him walking down our driveway and slowly down the road. That was the first and last time he had ever been inside our home.

Now most girls would have wept, made a great commotion about their feelings. But due to the strain of blood I had inherited from my father, and the strong effort of self control I had always practiced from my earliest childhood, I came downstairs calmly. At a glance I saw a look of triumph on my mother's face. She said, "Well, I do not think he will ever bother us again." My father again said, "I am sorry. He is a good true man, but does not belong to our class." Then he lay down on the couch and took his usual nap. My mother picked up a book and half lay down in her big easy chair. I went into the living room. Though I could not see my mother, I know she was not sleeping.

In winter, I could not spend my evenings out of doors; I always went upstairs to bed early, hours before my parents did. But this Sunday night, I went up even a lot earlier than usual. I wanted to be alone, throw off that mask of pretending and perhaps shed a few tears of sorrow that seemed to be drowning my heart. I had scarcely got into bed, and put out my candle, when I heard my mother come softly up the stairs through the garret and into my room. She came up to my bed, put her candle on the little stand close to the head of my bed, bent over me and kissed me. Then she asked me if I was sick, she had noticed that I had looked pale all the afternoon, noticed that I had eaten hardly anything for supper, gone to bed even much earlier than usual. I told her I felt all right. I thought if only she would leave me alone.

But she kept at me, wanted to know if I had a headache, sore throat, if I felt sick at my stomach, to be sure and tell her just what was the matter. She wanted to know if I would not rather come downstairs for the night. If I wanted lemonade, and so on and on, when all I wanted was to be alone. After a long time she went down again. I lay there hour after hour, thinking, thinking. About midnight I heard someone softly stirring downstairs then coming up, and again into my room. My mother had put on a heavy, warm dressing gown over her night gown, fleece lined slippers and a fresh long candle.

The night was cold, but my room was quite comfortable. On she came on tiptoe, asked how I felt, thought maybe I had eaten too much of the roast duck for dinner, or perhaps caught cold because I had stayed outdoors all the afternoon, and a dozen other things, all but the true cause of my misery.

When I came downstairs next morning, there was a foot of snow on the ground, and still snowing. After breakfast, and the outside chores done, my father got out the old, tattered arithmetic book, slate and pencil and announced firmly, "Today we will start your arithmetic lessons." He drew some of those half fences on the slate, put some figures inside the fence, and some outside. Why, God only knew, I am sure. I did not. Then he talked to me how to do my example; yes, that is what he called it. So I bent over my slate, looking at the figures, and vaguely wondered why, if he wanted some more put there, he did not do it himself.

Now to this day, I do not know just what possessed me to do what I did. This I do know. I did not do it to be naughty. After a while, I took up my slate pencil and got busy. My father was pacing up and down the room. After a while he bent over my shoulder, pointed a forefinger at my work and said, "What is this?" I had drawn a thick stem of a running vine at one of the fence posts, then the curving twisting vine up the post and along the top rail. There were small, delicate side branches or tiny vines, lots of leaves. The bigger leaves were veined and shaded off a bit. I answered, "That is poison ivy."

My father took the wet sponge that dangled on a string from the frame of the slate and wiped it all off. Made another sort of fence and put in some figures which suited him. I looked at the thing a long time then put some very neat figures in a little open fence corner. They were not the ones he wanted there. Well, it did not matter. My figures never seemed to suit him. My poor darling mother often would say to me, "Oh, my child, it is so easy. Do try to learn it."

I never answered her out loud, but I would mutter under my breath, "Easy like heck." Came the twenty-first of December and my eighteenth birthday and Christmas. Everything good and beautiful as in all the bygone times at this time of the year, but my heart was very lonely. I forgot to say that just a few days after Joe's last call at our house, I saw in our local newspaper, in the North Bay News Items, that Joseph Henry has obtained and accepted a job as motorman in Oneida.

Chapter 12

This winter was long and very lonely. My arithmetic started again the second of January and lasted till about the first of April. There was just one thing that dreary winter that sent joy and peace into my life. I had another vision. A very beautiful, yes holy, thing. It was about the middle of January, a cold clear night, not a breeze stirring.

I was asleep upstairs when I suddenly awoke with a little start, not in the least of fear, on the contrary, rather of joy. I saw a light streaming in from the open door which led into the big garret on the west side. In winter, when the west wind blew, I always kept this door closed, but on a windless night like tonight, I often kept it open as my father kept a hot fire going in the kitchen stove below. This light did not have the horrible red glare of fire, which in later years I learned to dread so much. It was a clear light, just tinged a trifle by gold. I jumped up quickly, ran into the garret to see where it came from. It was streaming in from the west windows. I ran to one of them and to my surprise and wonder saw outlined against the dark blue midnight sky towards the northwest, not too far from the horizon, and yet not too low down either, the three words, in large golden letters "In His Name." The beautiful thing about this was that each letter of those three words had been formed by small golden stars. I stood there for a few moments transfixed then ran downstairs to awaken my parents to share the glory with me.

My father was sitting by the kitchen stove. He used to be up most all night to keep the house warm for my mother. He hardly ever had a light, unless he was reading. I rushed into the adjoining alcove, where my mother slept, gently woke her up and told both of them what I had seen. But by the time I had gotten them to the west window, the vision was fast fading, just a faint glow left on the sky.

Sophie Kussmaul

The next day I wrote a poem about my vision. If I still had it, I would put it down here in these pages. That winter I wrote a few more poems. My mother would read them in her light, sing song way and say, very pretty, very pretty, but they all sound so sad. A young, happy girl like you, without a care in the world, should write something merry, something light and cheery. Well, even that winter came to an end, and spring came once more.

In April, my father subscribed for a daily newspaper. I think he was the very first one of all our neighborhood farmers to take a daily paper. Of course it became my job to go after it each day. So each night after supper I would saddle up the horse and ride to North Bay after the mail. Though I knew every foot of the road, I still enjoyed these trips very much. But there was, even here, one drawback. It was that for a good many years, every night after Jim Corcoran had his chores done, he went to North Bay, summer and winter, week day and Sunday, to sit in the hotel barroom till late at night.

So each day, just before I reached the Nichol's corner, I would give a quick look to see if I could see him come. If so and I had time to reach the corner first, I would whip my horse into a trot and get ahead of him. But if he already was past the corner, I would ride on a very slow walk so as not to overtake him. Then I knew he would be in the hotel. I had no fear of meeting him on the way home, but sometimes, when I did not see him on the way down, I was always in fear of meeting him on the way home. A number of times, if I saw him in time, I would ride into Mrs. John Dixon's yard, stay on my horse, talk to her a few moments till Jim got past, and then hurry home. Still, in spite of my vigilance, sometimes I met him. If no one was in sight, he would stand still, look me over greedily, and try to talk to me, but if anyone was near, he never seemed to see me.

Well, came the ninth of May. It had been a hot day for the season, and I had worked out of doors most all day with the horse. I left home about half past six. Though the day had been rather hot, now, with the westering sun, it was just agreeable warm and mild. Though by now, I have lived through nearly seventy months of May, never have I seen a more perfect May evening. I cannot describe its beauty. Such things must be felt more than seen. The golden rays of the sun shimmered on the tender, green grass, on the apple trees that were clothed in pink and white bloom. It shone on the young leaves of tree and bush. Millions of honey bees were still flitting and buzzing amongst the sweetness of the flowers. Birds were singing and warbling their love songs.

I generally made the horse trot at least part of the way, but tonight first because she had been working quite hard that day, and lastly because I was drinking in the sweet loveliness all about me, I let her go on a slow walk. I think that only those of us gifted with the eternal spirit of youth could fully comprehend the glories of nature spread out before them on that May evening.

When I was nearing the Nichol's corner, I gave a quick, searching glance in the direction from which Jim Corcoran might come, and as he was not in sight anywhere, I kept on slowly towards North Bay. The Post Office was in the same building where it is today, only the people have changed. I was just going to dismount when I glanced up. Was I dreaming? No, there coming up the little hill, just below the Post Office, on the sidewalk was Joe Henry. He had his good clothes on, carried a small grip. This was Saturday night and he was coming home to his mother's for Sunday. I had heard that he only had every three Sunday's off. I did not jump off the horse. A feeling of numbness seemed to creep over me.

Joe saw me, came straight up to where I was, looked me directly in the eye, searchingly, then smiled at me and said he would hold my horse for me while I went into the Post Office. I went in, but as I had some letters from my parents to mail, had to wait my turn at the stamp window. At least I came out again. Joe was stroking my horse's head. I mounted; he still held the bridle reins. Began talking to me, how I had been, about the lovely weather, other little matters.

He was not afraid to have people see him talking to me. Jim Corcoran never saw me before other people, and here tonight were at least a dozen people near us. Now I have often heard that a person is actually struck dumb for a moment by great fright. But I was momentarily struck dumb by great joy. My heart beat so fast it nearly choked me. I lost my power of speech. Still I did not want to leave him.

In later years it came to me that he thought I was too proud to speak to him. Just how long we were together, I do not know, but all at once Mr. Miller, the Post Master, called to Joe he wanted to see him. As if in a dream, I turned my horse towards home. Again, slowly, I was riding back, head bent low, but my heart and thoughts soaring high. I was in such a daze of happiness as to have quite forgotten the possibility of meeting Jim Corcoran.

So when I had nearly reached the Nichol's corner, suddenly I was brought to earth by a loud, "Hello, Sophie." I looked up quick. There he stood, both legs spread out, leering boldly at me. I gave the horse a little cut with my whip; he broke into a coarse laugh. Then, when I was past him, I pulled my horse back into a slow walk again. I wanted to keep on dreaming.

My dear mother always knew just about how long I would be gone if I only had to go to the Post Office as I never stopped to visit anywhere. Now tonight, I was much later. Both my parents, having got their work done, were waiting for me on the verandah. I rode up, gave my father his paper, took the horse to the barn, unsaddled her and turned her out to pasture, and went upstairs the back way to change from my riding habit into a loose dress.

The sun was not yet down. But I had scarcely got to my room when my mother followed me in. She looked at me and smilingly said, "Did you see him tonight?" In my confusion, I said a low yes, blushing scarlet. My mother kept watching me, then said, "I knew it the moment you rode up to the verandah. I saw your happy face. Did he tell you that you are handsome? Did he say when he was coming here again? Did you invite him to come? Did he ask after your father and me? Or was he so busy telling you pretty little things. You cannot fool your old mama. She knows her little girl." She went on till I was almost frantic, for after the first question, I knew she was referring to Jim Corcoran. I had intended to go and lay in my hammock as on other nights, but she followed me to the hammock and began talking about what a nice farm Jim had. So I went into my flower garden and started to weed out a few beds. But she came out there too, saying I must have had a long visit with Jim, I was gone so much longer. I tried to tell her that he only said, "Hello, Sophie," but she only laughed. She knew how happy I looked and that I was gone so much longer.

That summer I started peddling berries and a few vegetables. Only the last few years, about twenty-five or thirty small summer cottages had been built along the lakeshore below the village of North Bay. The Braytons, whom I mentioned in the beginning of this book, had a great many of their friends interested in the location for summer homes. So almost all of the new little summer houses were occupied by friends and acquaintances of the Braytons.

They, the Braytons, told us of the great new opening for berries and fresh vegetables, and in turn, told all those cottagers about my splendid and highly educated parents. So they paved the way for me, assuring me of good sales, and then that I was not just a farmer's peddling daughter. I must say that those six weeks of house to house peddling did me a great deal of good. In the first place, it took me away from myself, from the everlasting thinking. Then it opened up a new view of life for me. I learned more of human nature, people, than I could have learned in most any other way. If I had met these same people in society as their social equals, they, perhaps even unknowingly, would have been on their constant guard, trying as it were to appear a little different to hide their politeness, their true selves. On the other hand, if I had gone amongst them as a servant, they would have felt their superiority and in a dozen little ways have let me feel it. But as a free vendor of the things they so much wanted, I really saw them in the raw. Just human beings to barter with.

Well, this was the first money I had ever earned from outsiders. My Aunt Sophie always had sent me an allowance. Since my fourteenth year, my father paid me for work I did on the farm, excepting my daily chores. Both my parents would have felt disgraced if I had gone out to work for anyone. But to sell good stuff, that was all right. Also, no matter how lowly or hard one worked for themselves, that was all right. Well, I made good money. As I had always done with my allowance, what I earned on the farm, I put every cent of it in the Oneida Savings Bank. I admit I worked very hard that summer raising vegetables and picking hundreds of quarts of wild berries. We also had a lot of cultivated berries. I still did the harder part of the housework for my mother. She, in turn, spent hours each day looking over my wild berries and putting them in baskets for me.

At night I would pack my vegetables and berries and right after breakfast start out to sell them. Of course, during those six weeks I did not go after the mail at night, but generally got back by nine or half past nine each day.

I could write a long chapter about my experiences as a peddler, but will not do so. Came the twenty-second of August, I had made my last trip that day. We were on the dear old verandah a pleasant summer evening. My mother broke a long silence saying she would like to go and visit Mrs. Myers once more.

Chapter 13

Now I will have to go back a good many years in my story, give a quick description of this Mrs. Myers. I cannot say just where, when, and how my mother and Mrs. Myers became acquainted. The first time that I can recall ever seeing her, I was between eight and nine years old. Of course, the moment I saw her alight from the carriage, I vanished. First I hid under a bush to admire the beautiful horse. Mrs. Myers had given the driver instructions to call for her in an hour's time. Then I ran into the woods, returning only after I knew she had gone. The next year she again made a short call. I knew that each Christmas she and my mother exchanged greetings. She sent me little presents, such as were suitable for an average little girl, but what did I want with such stuff? When I was between eleven and twelve years old, Mr. Anchord came to tell us that he had a little business in Cleveland and if my mother wished, she and I could ride out with him and call to that rich old Myers woman while he attended to his business. There were all sorts of rumors concerning the Myers. Years ago, before I was born, a rich man came out from New York City, bought an acre of ground, and built and furnished a grand house. He had the wilderness of the grounds made into a little park, a smooth lawn and a large flower garden. It was said that he spent money lavishly, throwing it away as if it were dirt. People said he was queerly.

But during that entire summer of building and furnishing, converting of the grounds, his wife never came out. But every summer afterwards, she came out from about the middle of June to the end of August, while Mr. Myers would not come till about the middle of September, stay a month, and go back to the city.

Sophie Kussmaul

From the time he had finished building, he hired a young couple, Mr. and Mrs. Nathan Brown, as caretakers. They lived in one wing of the great house. Mrs. Myers always brought out with her a personal maid. Well, that had been the first time in my life that I had been to Cleveland. Oh, how I enjoyed the long drive near the lake. How I was surprised, astonished at the richness of that house, I, who had only been in farm houses.

We were only there a short time when Mr. Anchord called for us. Then, the next time that Mrs. Myers called to see my mother was when I was fourteen. Then I understood about the attraction they had for each other. I overheard their conversation. It seemed Mrs. Myers was about twenty-five years older than my mother. It seemed that in her younger days, Mrs. Myers had traveled in the old countries.

I listened as they talked about things they had seen in Edinburgh and Glasgow in Scotland. The Westminster Abbey in London, England. I saw the tender light in my mother's face, the faraway look in her eyes, when Mrs. Myers spoke of Heidelberg, Germany. Here in this far, far distant country, away out on our little farm, was a woman who, like my mother, had seen that dear, romantic city on the river Rhine.

So they talked of the picture galleries they had both seen and enjoyed in Italy, of the imposing St. Peters of Rome, the magnificent Notre Dame of Paris. The great beauties of the Alps of Switzerland. Yes, these two, at different times, had seen the same things.

Of course my mother had traveled through far more counties than Mrs. Myers, but my mother had another attraction through her. She was the only woman whom she knew in our neighborhood who had had a real education, natural refinement.

She came out once more, just a little over a year ago, a few weeks before I had first seen Joe Henry. I was working in the hay field and did not want to be seen by her. But just before her hired rig came for her, I went to get a drink of water. My mother was excusing our humble home when, to my intense surprise, Mrs. Myers said, "My dear Mrs. Kaussmaul, you are far, far richer than I am. You have a daughter. I have no child."

That night at supper, my mother said, "Mrs. Myers looked ill." At Christmas, as always, she sent greetings, little presents. That night at supper we planned on going to Cleveland the next day. In the morning, I washed and polished our top buggy, gave the horse a good cleaning and an extra feeding. Cleveland was about eight and a half miles from our place, meaning a seventeen mile round trip. Instead of our twelve o'clock dinner, we had a lunch at half past eleven.

At twelve, my mother and I started for Cleveland. Our horse was getting old and the day hot, so we drove on a slow walk. At two o'clock, we arrived at the beautiful house and grounds. I hitched the horse to a hitching post, under a vast elm tree. I admit I felt a little nervous when we walked up the broad path through the large park like yard. Nathan Brown, the caretaker, was trimming a hedge. My mother rang the bell. Of course, we expected that either Mrs. Brown, the caretaker's wife, or Mrs. Myer's maid, or perhaps Mrs. Myers herself would open the door for us.

So, imagine our consternation when we beheld the apparition before us. I almost lost my self-control; even my mother gave a tiny little start. This is what we saw. A man over six feet tall with I think the broadest shoulders I have ever seen. He was not what could be called fat, but just well filled out. Everything about him was enormous, but the most startling thing about him was his head. That, too, was very large. He had very heavy snow white hair, so white it shone like silver. He wore it so long that it completely covered up his ears, hung over his coat collar. He also wore a thick long heavy beard that rested on his chest and covered most of his face. That, too, was glistening white.

Besides this, he had a heavy long moustache and eyebrows, a whole handful of white hair over each eye. What little was visible of his face, his forehead, his nose, and the upper part of his cheeks, was of a yellowish whiteness. I said everything about him was enormous, excepting his eyes. They were small, a pale blue.

After a moment, this creature made a very deep bow then said, "Mrs. And Miss Kussmaul." My mother assented. Then he said, "I am Mr. Myers, the husband of your friend, Mrs. Myers." My mother said hello and asked if Mrs. Myers were at home. At that, he threw both his gigantic arms and hands up and said in a low tone that Mrs. Myers expired last February. He told us she had been in poor health for a long time, but that the end had come very easy. My mother and I turned to go, but he fairly insisted on our resting a little while. After we were comfortably seated, he rang the bell, telling Mrs. Brown to bring us some refreshments. Then he went to the door, called to

Sophie Kussmaul

Nathan Brown, telling him to take out two loaves of bread, break them in small pieces, take the bit out of our horse's mouth, and feed her the bread, piece by piece.

He turned to us, saying he kept no horses out here so had no suitable horse feed, but he said most horses are fond of bread. Then he went on to say that in New York he had several horses, very fine horses. By that time, Mrs. Brown wheeled in a dainty little table, covered with a snow white cloth, embroidered with silver and gold threads. On this table were two deep silver dishes, with a fruit salad, consisting of sliced bananas, sliced pineapple, pieces of oranges, and a few drops of lemon juice, all thickly covered with powdered sugar. There were two cut glass dishes heaped high with vanilla ice cream and in the center of the little table, a silver platter of white layer cake cut in thick slices, with a pink frosting. Never before had I enjoyed such a feast.

While we were eating, Mr. Myers talked. He addressed my mother, telling her how often his wife had spoken of the refined Mrs. Kussmaul, and here he made me a very deep bow, about her lovely young daughter. Never before had I been used to such manners. Still, I wanted to get away from him. I felt something was wrong. When at last we got up to go, Mr. Myers again bowing very low, said to my mother that he had a favor to ask. It was permission to call and meet her husband and the father of the most charming young lady. So it was arranged that he come next day as he intended returning to New York City the day after.

He came, hired a rig and driver from Cleveland. He handed my father a box of expensive cigars, then after a low bow, he presented my mother and me with an enormous box of delicious confections, bound with a ribbon, saying, "For the ladies." Still I did not like him. I soon left the house, climbed up a tree and sat down. After a while my mother called to me. Mr. Myers came to me, and though I ignored his outstretched hand, he grasped my small warm, brown hand in his enormous white cold hand. A shiver ran through me. I quickly pulled my hand away. Well, I had to listen to some of his compliments, but thinking tomorrow he is going away. So what was my horror when he turned to my father, saying he would not now go to the city for at least another month. Again bowing low, he said, "And with your permission, I would enjoy calling often during my stay out here."

Two days after, he came again, told the driver to unload something, which at that time I knew not what. It was an ice cream freezer full of ice cream. As soon as I had eaten my share, I skipped out, went into the woods so I could not be called back. Just two days later, he came again. Gave my father a bottle of old wine, my mother a basket full of beautiful flowers, and handed me a small box, which he requested me to open at once. It contained a lovely bracelet. The bracelet was of exquisite workmanship, heavy gold, stuffed with large emeralds. My mother said afterwards it must have cost at least three to four hundred dollars. I handed it back to him, refusing to accept it. In this, both my parents took my part, saying that in the first place I was too young to wear such expensive jewels, and in the second place, it would be entirely out of keeping with the rest of my things, and my surroundings. In the third place, it would not be proper from an almost stranger.

He seemed much annoyed, said he had sent a telegram to New York to his bank to have them express out the bracelet and a few other things. After we were alone, my father said he had told him he loved me and wanted to marry me. A great horror broke out over me. Of course I told my parents how I dreaded him, asked them to order him out of the house if he came again.

To my disgust, they both said they could not do such a thing as he belonged to a better class of people than the people around here. My mother wrote to her friends in New York, Judge Tappen and his wife, requesting them to find out about the social standing of the Myers, giving them the address he had given us.

To all our surprise, the answer came back that he had been a very rich man, but had lost about half a million on the stock market, but still was wealthy. He was a nephew of the Goelet family of New York City's wealthiest people. But he was considered extremely eccentric. Imagine my good dear, sweet mother hinting to me that if I could put up with him for a few years, I would be independent for the rest of my life. But I must give both my father and mother credit for this. Neither one of them urged me to accept him as long as I had such an aversion towards him.

The next time he came, he brought me a magnificent diamond ring. It must have cost a thousand dollars. It was one his wife had. He begged me to wear it as an engagement ring. I absolutely refused. After that, I was on a constant lookout and whenever I saw the team approaching, I vanished. He did not leave for the city until the beginning of November.

Well, my arithmetic lessons came then. Came the twenty-first of December, my nineteenth birthday. I was down to the North Bay Post Office on the twenty-fourth, got a post card that a big box was down at the express office, addressed to Mr. and Mrs. and Miss Kussmaul. That was before Parcel Post came into effect. I brought home the box. It was from Mr. Myers.

It contained two dozen large, very sweet oranges, two dozen big pears, two dozen giant red apples, and one dozen grapefruit, the first I had ever seen. One dozen large lemons. Also a ten pound box of delicious California grapes. I had never seen, heard of, or tasted them before, but my mother said when she was in Constantinople, they had them every day. The big box also contained a whole stem of bananas.

Well, we all did enjoy that Christmas box. As always, Christmas was happy, though I felt lonely. What would I not have given to see Joe Henry, even for five minutes. After New Year's the same old winter set in, housework, arithmetic, quarrels with my father, loneliness. My books and organ.

I was kept at the thing called subtraction. Well I could see into the first part. I could understand that two could be taken from five, or four from six, but how in heck's name can a larger figure be taken from a smaller one. They have some way to borrow. I say to heck with that. It is mean and dishonest. Why should a neighbor figure pay their debts? Why in the devil's name run in debt anyway? Well, I could not master subtraction.

Right here I want to say something. Although I cannot do the so called easy examples that the average boy or girl can do at nine years of age, while I who had been at it about twelve long winters from two to six hours a day cannot do it, I can add and know the multiplication, by jingo. I can take three kinds of berries, each kind selling for a different price, go from house to house, at each house people taking some from one to three kinds, each family a different amount, also some vegetables, and in a few moments I know how much money is coming to me, and can make the right change, even while talking to people. So why study arithmetic.

Chapter 14

In winter, I always went to bed early. My father and mother would visit together. I felt like an outsider. When my mother and I were alone together, we enjoyed one another's company. Often while I was doing the housework, my dear mother would read to me. Many were the books she read to me during those hours. At other times, she would be mending or darning and tell me of her travels, life in far distant countries. But in the long evenings, my father was always at home. I cannot remember even one evening he was not at home summer or winter, except those few weeks when he went hop picking. So in a way, I felt less lonely upstairs in my bed than down with them. There at least I could think in peace. I would dream of the West. Oh, how I longed to go to that unknown West. I would again think with joy of every time I had seen Joe. One night as I lay in the quiet darkness I remembered how, when I was fifteen and sixteen, I used to fancy that a rich man would come to me, bringing jewels and offering me wealth, beautiful horses, a grand home. Oh, I now thought, how silly, how utterly impossible in my humble existence. Then all at once it came to me, why there did come such a one into my life. But, horrors, the man, all the wealth in the whole world, could not compensate for a life with that apparition.

Then I had a dream that very night, such a lovely dream. I dreamed of a garden, a very vast garden, beautiful beyond all description, soft tender young grass literally studded with little flowers of all colors. Bushes, shrubs and trees loaded with blossoms. The very air was laden with their rich perfume. A warm, bright, yet mild sunlight over it all. Ever and ever changing soft lights, from gold to silver, from rose to green, from blue to purple. From somewhere, from everywhere floated the most exquisite music, heavenly strains of harmony. In this Eden, hand in hand, I and my beloved Joe were roaming, not walking or flying, just floating along together in a nameless bliss.

God in his wonderful mercy
God in his love supreme
Hath sent me consolation
Through a beautiful golden dream

The rest of that winter, as always, was sad and lonely, but the thought, the remembrance of that dream, was an ever present comfort, consolation. It helped me through many a weary day, through many a stormy session with my father.

In the fore part of winter, many letters came from Mr. Myers. In each one he told us that just as soon as spring came, he would be a daily caller. That filled me with horror. For the first time in my life, I did not look for spring to come as a deliverance from the hated winter, the more hated arithmetic lessons. But when March came, the letters stopped suddenly. I was filled with a new dread. Perhaps he, the apparition, had already arrived in Cleveland.

So towards the end of March, we read in our local newspaper, in the Cleveland Items, that Mr. George Myers of New York City and owner of the Lake View residence near Cleveland, had suddenly died of a heart ailment, that the Lake View residence was now owned by a man, also from New York, called Mr. Williams. Perhaps it was wrong for me to be glad to hear of the death of a man who loved me, but I felt so much relieved, so happy to think I would never see him again, I, who hardly ever laughed.

In less than two months after this, there was again a new item from Cleveland. It stated that the beautiful mansion, Lake View, had burned down, with everything in it. The handsome grounds that had been cared for at such an expense had in a couple of years' time gone back to wilderness. About thirty years ago, one day when I was in Cleveland in a car, I tried to find the place. Even the giant old elm tree had vanished. A few cheap summer cottages had sprung up, the rest was just a wilderness.

Through Sophie's Eyes

When spring and summer came, I was very busy doing some of the housework, raising vegetables to sell, and picking over one thousand quarts of berries. I peddled about eight weeks. I made a few trips to Sylvan Beach, but our horse was getting very old and slow and as I could sell all my stuff at North Bay, I gave up going to Sylvan Beach.

Nothing new happened that summer. Our evenings on the verandah were quiet and serene. I would lie in my hammock and gaze at the stars and dream of my coming life. How bright, how long, how very long stretched the road before me. What a happy, happy way to travel. All would be pleasant, glorious just beyond and it seemed to me endless. Why even one year ahead seemed so long, so far away. I would probably have sixty or seventy of those long years ahead of me. Now looking back, what a short time it took to travel that shining road ahead.

Yes, and where was all the glamour? Where was the glory and joy envisioned by me in those long ago nights on the dear old verandah.? But after all, were they so long ago? Why it seems looking back to those peaceful evenings like a day and night. Yet none that I then loved is here now.

As I lay there in silence and heard in the distance the train on the night air, a great longing would sweep over me, and I would think with a pain in my heart, if it only would bear me away and away. Still, here is something very strange. I longed to go far and far away, to places wild and free and beautiful, but at the same time I loved this little plot called the home place so much that I knew even before I had ever left it that I would die out of home sickness if I had to leave it forever.

Well spring and summer passed by and in the lovely October weather I was again drawing home our winter's wood. Yes, I was happy. How I loved this autumn job. Come November, it set in with rain, sleet and snow, dismal days and dreary nights. On the tenth of November the rain raved and fairly shook the house. At times sleet and snow came so thick a person could not see ten feet ahead of them. We burned a lamp all day because of the dim daylight. Late that afternoon, Matthew Dixon came to our house on a little business. About the first thing he said was that it had been a bad day for the funeral. Of course my father asked him, "Whose funeral?" He replied, "Mrs. Henry. Joe Henry's mother." I shall never forget the feeling of anguish that came over me. Yet I must not show it. Matt made a few remarks about the funeral. None of his family had gone to it. He thought probably no one went excepting the family. He did say, "Joe is a good fellow, I think," for which, in my heart, I always thanked him. He talked about a few other things and then went home.

The next morning was cold and dreary. No sun. I had not slept much for the sorrow in my heart about the Henry's. When I came downstairs, as always, my parents had had their breakfast. About an hour later, my mother was sitting in the living room sewing and my father came in from the barn looking stern and forbidding.

Now I mentioned in the forepart of this book that each fall I had firmly made up my mind that I would not submit to any more arithmetic lessons, but always just at the very last moment, all my courage failed me. I just felt weak and bitter and sullen. I suppose this fall under the same ordinary circumstances I again would have given in at the last moment. But there is a saying that even a worm will turn.

Well, as I have said, my father looked angry when he entered the back door. He threw off his coat and cap, marched to the desk where he always had kept the arithmetic book and slate, pulled them out, planted them firmly on the table. A faint, sick feeling came over me. Then he yelled out, stamping his foot on the floor, "This winter you will learn. I will keep you at your lessons all day and make you study." I cannot put into words the look of determination, yes of blind obstinacy, nor the loud harsh tone of his voice. For a second a terror seized me. Then, born of despair or hate, or both, something like living fire shot through me. I made one spring to the table, grabbed the hated book, made another spring to the cook stove, in which burned a hot fire, threw the book in, made a quick grab for the slate, threw it on the hard bare floor, where it broke into a hundred pieces, took the little slender slate pencil, broke it in two, threw it down after the broken slate. Now all this took only a few seconds. Then I whirled around, facing my father. I fully expected he would kill me, but I faced him, told him I would never again take an arithmetic lesson from him, never.

I remember seeing my dear, sweet, gentle mother standing in the doorway white, scared, and oh, so sad. My father was silent. There he stood, tall, straight, and dark of face. His coal black hair and shiny black eyes, the boiling anger in his every feature. We stood there facing each other. All my fear of fifteen years had left me. I gave a

127

wild laugh. My mother said afterward that in a second we had been transformed from two white civilized people into two Indian savages.

From that day on, I had lost all my fear of my father. We often, often after that had bitter quarrels, but we were on equal footing. After that awful scene, my father and I did not speak a word together for many a week. Not till Christmas did he eat at the table with me. I never came downstairs till after their breakfast, at dinner and supper he came to the table, filled his plate and cup, carried them into the living room.

Came the twenty-first of December and my twentieth birthday. Christmas and then beginning of January, a letter from my Aunt Sophie that they were leaving Constantinople for Wiesbaden, Germany, and after they were settled there, she would once more come to spend the summer with us. My dear mother was very happy and that helped her through the winter.

On the second of February, I went to my first party. I went with Mrs. McLaughlin and her family. I enjoyed it, and saw how much I had been missing. After that, I went to two or three more before spring.

To my dear mother's great disappointment, my aunt did not come out. They did not get settled in their new home till late in spring so she put it off for another year. I will go over this spring and summer quickly, much work, berry-picking, peddling, summer evenings on the verandah.

Came the sixteenth of September, and now I must go back to something, even to the time before I was born. As I said, my mother had been a governess in the family of Judge Tappen and his wife, very, very good people. This Mrs. Tappen had told my mother that she surely would some day come out to see her. So from my earliest recollections, from early summer till some time in September, my mother was always in a state of anxiety. She of course had written to Mrs. Tappen about our plain little home. Still, she kept telling me that Mrs. Tappen would be shocked at this and that. I, in my total ignorance of the kind of life really rich people lived, could not at that time understand just what she meant. So when early summer came, she would get letters like this. Mrs. Tappen would write, saying they were going to Carlsbad, Germany, for six weeks. They went almost every summer. On their return, they would go to the Adirondacks for a few weeks, and try to stop off at Utica, either on their way to the mountains or on their return trip home.

Then my mother would give a sigh of great relief, saying, "Now, for six or seven weeks, we know she cannot come." At the end of that time, an everlasting cleaning up would begin again. Now my mother really loved Mrs. Tappen, but no one who does not know the circumstances could fully realize the difference of such people's surroundings.

So it went on from year to year. My mother had not heard from Mrs. Tappen for some time. Of course we imagined she might appear any time. Still, we thought, being the middle of September by now, we would be safe till next summer. So on this sixteenth of September I got a letter for my mother in Mrs. Tappen's handwriting, postmarked from Fordham, New York, the suburb from New York City where Mrs. Tappen lived. As I drove into the yard, I waved the letter joyfully, told my mother all our worries were over, Mrs. Tappen was back home and now would not come out. I stayed in the buggy till my mother had read the letter to us.

Mrs. Tappen wrote that she was leaving her home on the twentieth of September for Richfield Springs, and would remain there until October first. She said she had carefully consulted the railroad time tables, saw that she could make perfect connections from Utica to Oneida, then to the I.D.W. to North Bay, and so would either come to us direct from New York or from Richfield Springs, or on leaving there for New York City. She asked my mother to write back at once to let her know if she could hire a livery rig at North Bay.

At that time, automobiles were not yet heard of. But a Mr. George Butler, who lived just opposite the little North Bay station, kept a fast horse and twice a day, when a passenger train pulled in, he always was at the station hopefully waiting for a would be fare. Very seldom did he get one. So my mother answered the letter at once, telling Mrs. Tappen about the conveyance she could obtain, and my father took the letter down the same day, walking to save our old horse another trip.

Now Mrs. Tappen mentioned that she would have to bring her maid along. This made a lot of extra planning. We only had one spare bed. In summer, the three of us slept upstairs, each in a single bed. Now we knew it would be impossible to put the maid and Mrs. Tappen in the same bed. I offered to sleep on the couch or even the floor for one night or so, as to put my single bed in the room with Mrs. Tappen for the maid. But my mother said she knew Mrs. Tappen would go upstairs and see that I had to give up my bed. So after my mother and father had talked it over, they decided that he and I should drive to Camden the next day and buy a cot bed with a new mattress.

We drove very slow. It took nearly all day to go and come, as our horse was failing rapidly. Well, I just cannot describe the cleaning, rearranging everything. Then twice every day, the excitement at the time the Oneida train was due at North Bay. We would look at the clock, wait and wait for Mr. Butler's long legged bay horse to drive in with Mrs. Tappen. Then when that time was over, I would hasten to North Bay to see if there was a letter telling my mother when she would come. No letter came and the excitement grew worse each day.

My father had his farm work to do, so of course could not look spic and span. So we had a wash dish, water, soap, and towel out at the barn, also a clean shirt, so if Mrs. Tappen came, he would clean himself up a little before coming to the house. I really think that if we had expected the President's wife, we would not have been more excited. If possible, the last day of September and the first day of October were the worst.

Of course, as we were so sure of her coming, we thought now she surely will come to us. Well, on the first day of October, after the last train from Oneida had come, I went to the Post Office and found a letter from Mrs. Tappen to my mother, postmarked Fordham, New York.

As usual, I stayed in the buggy as my mother opened the letter. Out fell a crisp new twenty dollar bill, and a five. Mrs. Tappen excused herself for not writing and telling my mother why she could not come to see her. She was called back to New York on very important business and so she decided it would be better for my mother and me to come to New York for two weeks to visit her instead, from the eighth of October to the twenty-second.

I was so intensely surprised, so overjoyed, I could hardly believe it. Here I was nearly twenty-one, had never spent a night away from home, and for years had longed to go at least six or eight miles over a new territory. Now, oh, a long day's journey and have my sweet mother with me.

Well a few days later, my mother and I went to Camden once more with the poor old horse. That was the last time I ever drove her out there. We bought a cheap suitcase and a few things we had to have to make that trip. To me, it seemed as if we were making a trip half way across the country. Came the seventh day of October, a dark, dreary day. It rained steady all day.

My mother and I packed and unpacked that suitcase many times. We cooked and baked for my father. I knew my mother's heart ached at the thought of leaving him. Since her marriage, she had never spent a night away from home. I also knew that she would not have accepted the invitation had it not been for me. Well, came the eighth of October; we were all up at five o'clock. I ran out with the lantern, harnessed the horse, and said good-by to each cow. The weather had turned colder. Now it was snowing and a cold west wind blowing. We ate our breakfast in silence by the dim light of the kerosene lamp. Although I could always read my parents thoughts much better than they ever could read my own, I know, after almost fifty years, really know better what ran in their minds that morning than I did then. Although I had never got along good with my father, I knew that he loved me as few fathers did their daughters.

Probably these were the thoughts that ran in his mind. He was looking back to the time when I was a baby, then a little toddler who followed him around the farm, then a little older when a batch of kittens, a new calf, a little garden was my life. Then, how much interest I had taken to get our hay and crops in. Later when I started peddling and was proud of my little profits. Now I was to enter the big world, the rich side of life, and when I came back home, I would never again take up the homey, quiet, simple life that he so loved. And I suppose all my years, that at that time seemed so long, so very long to me, to him, looking back, now only seemed like a dream, now the awakening to reality.

My mother, yes, I am sure I now know and understand what she then thought. She was torn between two things. First, she felt guilty about leaving my father. Through her mind ran the memory of the last time she had made that trip from New York City. It was to marry my father. A light hearted, trusting girl, the years of hardships here, yet sweetened by the love they had together, the heart rending years of those operations, the unending care, love and devotion he had bestowed on her, the many little sacrifices they had made for each other.

On the other hand, she, who had spent so many years in travel, and then been shut up here for nearly twenty-five years, to once more get a glimpse of the life she had been used to, and above all to introduce me to what she thought was my future world. I was quiet as always, looking ahead for the wonders that I was to see. Perhaps this would fulfill the call, the very longing of my heart and mind to go far and far away.

We left at seven o'clock. The roads were muddy, snowy, a cold west wind blowing, a dark sky. Slowly, very slowly, we went down to the little North Bay station. Then, for the first time in my life, I really felt sorry for my father. To this day I can see that picture before me. The old horse slowly creeping up the long hill, my father huddled on the seat. We, at least had had the wind on our backs in coming down. Now we were in the warm little station while he had to face the storm all the way home, take care of the horse, which I had always done, and then go into the little quiet home, the first time in almost a quarter of a century and not find my mother there.

Well after we got on the train, I thought less and less of that, and when my dear mother would wistfully say, "I hope Otto got home all right," I would lightly say, "Oh, yes, of course he did." Still, a little stab would enter my heart. When we got to Oneida, the snow had changed to a pouring rain. My mother took a cab to take us to the Central Depot, also a new experience for me. Once in the elegant coach of the Grand Central train, every mile was new for me.

We arrived at Albany about two-thirty. There we had to change trains. That, I thought, was terrible. Trains roaring in from everywhere, people running about, noise, confusion, and to my utter surprise, my mother perfectly calm. Well I must tell about a little incident that I witnessed, in itself really of no consequence at all to us, but something that stayed in my mind forever.

Amid all the confusion were some baggage men tossing out trunks and boxes from a baggage car when all at once, they flung out an extra large, old, very old, trunk. It struck the hard concrete pavement of the great platform, and as it struck the hard platform, it burst in two, spilled out all sorts of garments. They, like the trunk, were old and worn. There also were other things: pictures, photos, little baskets and boxes, an old family album, and a dozen little such things. In falling, they scattered out on the platform, people rushing by, some stepping on some of the things, others, hastily, sidestepping them. But there came a little old woman, and even in those long ago years she looked old fashioned. She rushed up to the broken trunk, threw up her hands, gave a little cry, and frantically started picking up her little treasures, throwing them back into the wrecked trunk. I do not know how it all ended. Perhaps some kind person gave her a long strap or rope to fasten her trunk together, perhaps this little old woman had always lived a quiet life somewhere out on a little farm, perhaps now that she was so old, she had lost the ones dearest to her, and with an almost breaking heart had gathered together the few household goods of her little home before she left it forever to go where? Perhaps to a son or daughter. Who knows?

Our train came, and we started on that beautiful trip along the Hudson River. Now I am not going to describe my trip. I could devote a whole chapter to the beauties of nature along the way, but as I am just writing the story of my life, I will skip about this trip. If God lets me tarry long enough, I may sometime write a book about all my travels.

Before we reached Yonkers, it was too dark to enjoy the scenery, but how beautiful the towns looked in the glare of electric lights. It seemed to me we were a long time in the great city of New York before our train finally pulled into the Grand Central Station. Noise, confusion, thousands of people rushing in every direction, the immense buildings, the sparkling lights. I was bewildered. Still, I saw some things that touched my heart: the frantic sobbing farewells as some went away and others stayed, the burst of joy as some traveler came and was embraced in loving arms, the shy ones, perhaps their first trip alone. All this only took a few moments and then my mother and a short, very staunch little woman were clasped in each other's arms. Then I was introduced to Mrs. Tappen.

Somehow we got into another train. A half hour's ride to Fordham, a much smaller station. There waiting for us was Mrs. Tappen's carriage, drawn by two shiny bay horses and coachman. I had never before, except in pictures, seen a closed carriage. The driver was seated outside on what was called a box.

We drove a little less than half a mile along a grand residence street. Large houses, beautiful grounds. I say all the houses were large, but there was one little story and a half house, just distanced by one more large one, before we reached Mrs. Tappen's place. This little, white painted frame house had a carved wooden raven over the front door. It had been the home of Edgar Allen Poe, the author of the Poem. "The raven, never flitting, still is sitting, still is sitting, just above my chamber door." Well, much as my mother had prepared me, I still could hardly believe the lavishness about me. I felt scared. I knew Mrs. Tappen meant to be very kind to us, but everything was so entirely different from my home life.

I forgot to mention that Judge Tappen had died less than a year before, but his mother, a lady of ninety-six years, was still alive. She had three rooms and a bathroom for herself and her attending companion.

After a late supper, we were shown our room, a very large room with two single beds and a fully equipped bathroom. I found out next day there were four such large guests rooms, each one with its bathroom. Next morning, as soon as we stirred in our room, there came a knock at the door; a maid entered, saying Mrs. Tappen had sent her requesting that she do my hair. Up to now, I had always worn it just pinned up tight. Well, I did not like this, but sat down quietly. Then Mrs. Tappen came herself, looked at our clothes, and said, "We will have to do something about this at once." We had a delicious breakfast, but I felt awkward. The serving maid noticed it too.

Mrs. Tappen spoke through a speaking tube to the coachman, ordered the horses be brought up at once. Well, we went back to the city, into Wanamaker's Department Store, and Mrs. Tappen bought so many real beautiful and expensive things for us; I was quite overwhelmed. But she also bought me a corset, a thing I hated, something I had never worn at home and something I made up my mind I would not wear after we got home. But as long as she paid our fare out there and, of course, was going to pay it back, fed us on delicious food for two weeks, took us out every day, spending more money on us in those two weeks than we did at home in a year, I submitted to the horrid thing while out there.

Now as it would take at least fifty pages to describe all I saw in those two weeks, I will not undertake to do so, but just mention a few things. Mrs. Tappen took us to Wanamaker's, Stearn, Macy's, Siegel and Cooper, and a few more of the largest stores in the city. Five times we went to the best theaters on Broadway, each time a different one. I must say I thought I had entered fairyland. Some concerts. Eaden Musee, the world in wax. The largest churches on Fifth Avenue, crossed the Brooklyn Bridge. A circus at the Madison Square Gardens. The Battery, an aquarium, the Museum of Natural History, the Museum of Art.

Sophie Kussmaul

We took a trip to Staten Island, one to Ellis Island, one to Long Island. We climbed up the Statue of Liberty, took long drives through Central Park and the Bronx, and Riverside, to Woodlawn Cemetery and a dozen more beautiful things. Each day while roaming we had lunch in some expensive restaurant. When the two weeks were up, she bought tickets for our return trip on the Empire State Express as far as Utica. We brought home with us a large and small trunk, both filled to the limit.

As the fast train did not stop in Oneida, we had about half an hour wait in Utica. We did not leave the station. I was sitting quietly, deep in thought, when my mother smilingly asked me what I was thinking about. I could not tell her, for these were my thoughts. I had seen thousands of young men walking on the sidewalks; we met them riding on the trolleys, the elevated trains, the subways, on the trains, and even a dozen or so I had been introduced to. Yet not one of the many had in the least appealed to me. One glance of the good, true look of Joe's smiling face, his dear brown eyes, meant a thousand times more to me than any other man ever had, or ever would.

Of course it was dark when we got to North Bay. My mother hired Mr. Butler to take us home as my father had written to her that Nellie, our old horse, had failed so much that he did not dare to drive her so far again. Oh, how small the little station looked. How small and dark the road, the way home appeared to me. When we had turned that little bend in the road just below our home, we could see the faint gleam of the kerosene lamp, still, cold, dark, dreary, after all the brightness, the glittering lights, the bustle and hustle, the display of great wealth. Yes, in spite of all the bitter heartache I had known here, a great joy, a feeling of gladness entered my heart, for now I was coming home to my Home Sweet Home.

I shall never forget the look in my poor father's face, such love. My father never was demonstrative, but he looked at us so happily, so glad to have us back. He had grown thin and older looking in those two weeks. He told us about the horse. He dared not hitch her up again. She could hardly get home that morning. So three times a week, he walked down to North Bay to get the mail and send letters to my mother. He said we would have to get her killed. No one had called to see him, but the cats had proved good and true companions. Everything looked plain and shabby, and now I understood why my mother had so dreaded Mrs. Tappen's visit. But though I had had such a wonderful time, I was glad to be home again.

Well soon after this, we had a man come and shoot and bury our old horse. Strange, though I had used her for almost nine years, I did not feel too bad about it. I think the reason was that for years I had wanted a horse of my own, but we could only afford to keep one. My father agreed to let me buy one. I had plenty of money in the bank as I had never spent a cent of it. Well I bought a young bay horse, Billy. He was quite fast and road easy, but he kicked and bit. Still, I made him do a lot of farm work.

Sophie Kussmaul

Chapter 15

Came the twenty-first of December, my twenty-first birthday. A happy Christmas, a fairly good winter. I rode and drove my wild horse. In March, my mother got a letter from my aunt that she was coming out for sure.

Came the twelfth of June, my aunt arrived. My dear mother was overjoyed. I did not peddle this summer as there was so much more housework and besides, my aunt, mother, and I took a drive almost every afternoon. So the summer went by.

On the second of September, my aunt left us for her long journey home. My mother and I accompanied her as far as Oneida. Although my sweet mother tried her very best not to lose her self-control, at the last moment, when her sister had torn herself away to enter the train, my mother broke into hysterical weeping.

From her earliest childhood, she had never been separated more than a few months at a time from her sister. Even while on her long travels, they had always managed to meet somehow. Then came the first long separation of nearly eight years. Still, they were both much younger then. After that there was the longer one of about fourteen years. Now, in all probability this would be the last meeting, the last parting. Still, my mother had my father and me left with her; her home life would go on as before. It was left for me, in my later years, to come to know what it is to part with the ones nearer and dearer to you than life itself. When, after the parting, there was no one left to come home to. Nothing but memories, and loneliness of body, heart and mind.

Well, nothing unusual happened that fall. December brought my twenty-second birthday, and Christmas. Another spring and I again

137

got ready to peddle. In May, a man by the name of Joe Estey bought a small place just half a mile from us, on a cross road. I passed by a few times and saw that he was making some improvements on the house, and planting a large garden.

When in July I was peddling, I always had a large order of berries and vegetables to deliver at a summer hotel, so of course I had to carry my stuff into the large kitchen. This year I found a new cook had been hired for the summer season. From the very first, I took a great liking to her. The attraction seemed mutual and we introduced ourselves to each other. She told me that her name was Mrs. Everson. She was a widow of forty-five, and as soon as Labor Day came and her work at the hotel was over, she would go and keep house for her brother, Joe Estey. I was delighted and told her that I lived close by. That fall I called on her a few times. She and her brother, who was twelve years younger, often came to our house. I liked them both very much.

They were a strange family. On their father's side, they came from a very high class of people. Were related to President William Henry Harrison, the Kirkpatrick family, a famous judge of the Supreme Court. But on their mother's side of the family, just poor working people. They, too, were very poor, and my father was glad to get a man to work for him by the day who lived so near by. I was not in love with this man, though I liked him very much as a friend.

On the twenty-fifth of October, to our utter surprise, my mother received a letter from Mrs. Tappen. Again, twenty-five dollars in crisp new notes and an invitation to come out on the first of November for a two weeks visit. She, herself, intending to leave New York on the eighteenth of that month to spend the winter in Pasadena, California. My mother answered at once, thanking her heartily for the kind invitation, but assuring her that though she would enjoy the visit very much, she could never bring herself to leave my father again, but she would love to have me go.

So it was arranged that I make the trip alone, but take a train at Oneida that would take me straight through to the Grand Central Station in New York, and not have to change trains in Albany like before with my mother. Dear Mrs. Tappen was there, and took me home. Now as I said before, I will not spend the time here for my descriptions, but I must say this. The first time I was in New York, both Mrs. Tappen's married daughters and their families were in

Europe. But now they both were back in their homes. Well, I had been frightened at the richness of Mrs. Tappen's home, but still I was not prepared for the extravagant luxury I was to see at Mrs. Fairchild's. I had been to Mrs. Tappen's two days when she announced that while we were sightseeing in the city we would drop in to her daughter's for lunch instead of going to a restaurant.

Well, I thought that sounded homey. She hailed a cab. There were quite a few automobiles in the city by this time, but still a great many more horse drawn conveyances. To my surprise and a little tremor of terror, the cab drew up at a mansion on Madison Avenue. We walked up some broad stone steps. Mrs. Tappen rang a bell. Instead of a maid opening the door, a butler stood there. He looked so much like a statue, I stared at him a moment to see if he were real. He was quite tall, fairly broad and straight. He had a shiny silk shirt on, a scarlet velvet coat heavily embroidered with gold braid, also scarlet velvet breeches that buttoned below his knees, white silk stockings, and low shoes with great gold buckles.

Of course he knew Mrs. Tappen, but not me. In an instant of time, from somewhere he produced a silver tray, and holding it out to me, said, "Card, please." For me that was a stunner. But Mrs. Tappen said, "It is all right, William, the lady is with me." He made a bow and we entered the hall. The butler who had led us in had first asked for my card in the vestibule. Well, this house was four stories high besides the basement, where were the kitchen, store rooms, laundry, and the servants' dining room. This vast hall had a skylight. In the middle was a very, very broad stairway, a spiral stairway, a circling one.

There were great long mirrors on all sides, paintings ten to fifteen feet high, and the whole place aglitter with electric lights. The butler preceded us into the reception room. From there, through heavily brocaded draperies, was visible a vast elegant drawing room. On the other side, I glimpsed the dining room. This, to me, looked like a vast jewelry store, the display of polished silver, sparkling glass, delicately painted china. The very furniture polished to such a degree that it reflected other objects. Everywhere the glitter of electric lights. A number of maids in uniforms were noiselessly flitting about. Mrs. Tappen said to me, "Come." I followed her up one flight of the great stairway. We entered a room which she called her daughter's private sitting room. There we found Mrs. Fairchild. She was dressed in a very heavy silk robe. Of course I was much frightened. I saw a good kind woman before me in spite of all the rich lavishment surrounding her.

Soon after, two young girls rushed in. They were Mrs. Fairchild's two daughters. The oldest one, Edith, was a little past seventeen, the younger, Grace, just sixteen years of age. Both of them were attending a finishing school near by and coming home for their lunch. Mrs. Fairchild introduced me to them. Well, Mrs. Fairchild had looked me over with kind, understanding eyes, but these girls looked me over as a sort of curiosity, coldly superior. I felt as if I would sink through the very floor. My clothes were all right, as Mrs. Tappen had fitted me out the day before from my hat to my shoes. Mrs. Tappen's maid had that morning done my hair, in a very uncomfortable style, but which they approved of. But as I have said, there were large mirrors everywhere and when I shyly glanced up, I saw the reflection of the five of us in a great mirror on the opposite wall. Mrs. Tappen in her late seventies, Mrs. Fairchild in her middle forties, the two young girls and myself. Then for the first time, I saw the great difference. They all looked very white, too white I thought. Faces and hands white with just a little color in the cheeks of the girls. All their fingernails were manicured. There I sat amongst them at least three shades darker, partly owing to the left over summer tan and partly to the blood I had inherited from my father. My hands and nails, though clean, did not look like their dainty ones that had never done any work or ever been exposed to the sun and weather like my own.

Then came the chimes of the luncheon bell. We went down into that glittering, sparkling dining room. There was a manservant. Mrs. Fairchild glanced at him and made the slightest motion with her hand. He bowed and pulled out a chair for me, and bowed towards me. I sat down. This man served the food, but there also was a maid servant who filled the water glasses and brushed off imaginary crumbs from the table, removed the dirty dishes, and passed the finger bowls.

There were three forks and knives at each place. I was so frightened, I ate very little and was immensely relieved when at last we left that place. A few days later, Mrs. Tappen said at breakfast that we were going to spend the day with her other daughter, Mrs. Mills. A new terror came over me. Mrs. Mills lived at 145 West Forty-Second Street. But to my great joy, things were not quite so stylish there. Three servants, besides the cook. There was a lovely young daughter of fourteen and a dear little boy of twelve. Those children took to me at once. I told them of my out of door life, the wild and tame animals. They kept clapping their hands and asking me all the time to tell them more about my home life.

So when the two weeks were up, I came home. Yes, despite the late dreary fall weather, despite everything, I was glad to come back. A few days after I came home, our new friends, Joe Estey and his sister, Mary Everson, came to spend the evening. They brought with them another man, a brother named Charles Estey, who had just arrived from New Jersey. This brother was older, about fifty years of age, but as he was very lively, he seemed much younger. He was a little man, brown hair and eyes, and wore glasses. He had been a professional dancer and a comic actor in the New York theatres. He also was a good musician and was the best on the violin. So we really had an enjoyable evening.

After this, Charles came almost daily, or I should say, almost every evening. He would play and sing for us. Sometimes, I would play on the organ, and he would accompany me. From the very first, he fell madly in love with me. My parents knew about this, but for once tolerated him to come. The reason they made this exception from all other men who had shown even a slight interest in me was, I think this. In the first place, he was old enough to be my father. In the second place, he was penniless. All he owned was his violin and the clothes he had on his back, so of course they thought it would be an impossibility for me to have any more regards for him than those of friendship.

In the third place, though so poor and only with a common school education, still they felt a certain link between this family as they had brought proof of their paternal ancestry, none better in this country. In the fourth place, both my parents being so fond of music, his coming passed many an otherwise dreary evening. They took it for granted that I, too, only looked at his coming, his love making as a passing entertainment. December brought my twenty-third birthday.

This winter was not so bad. I had my horse, my music, and the Estey friends. I must say this--although my folks did not object to Charles coming, they both strictly forbade my ever going to visit his sister, saying it would look as if I ran after him. I had the memory of the beautiful New York trip, the lovely clothes they had given me, the good books and magazines they were sending. But ever and always my thoughts went back to my one love, Joe Henry. Yes, tender was the memory of him.

But no one knew about this, nor did anyone know about the intense longing I always felt for the West. I can only compare this longing to homesickness. Then there was one more thing that was very annoying to me, that my own dear mother was forever bringing up Jim Corcoran. I despised, hated and in a way feared him. I will mention one little incident. It was Sunday afternoon. Charles was at our house. He had really out done himself in making me compliments. Of course my mother as always was present. Then my mother very artfully, cunningly, made a remark to the effect that I loved Jim Corcoran and that he loved me. I was quite furious and as always, blushed. To my utter surprise, Charlie looked at me and said, "Sophie, is this so?" I fairly shouted out, "No!"

I saw my mother, gentle as she always was, looked angry. After Charlie left, she told me that it was very improper for me to say what I did. Well, the winter melted into spring. I was busy outdoors. One day, some time the latter part of May, my father, mother, and I had been to North Bay. They wanted me to drive around the square on our way home so they could stop and visit Mr. and Mrs. Corcoran, Jim's parents.

I really liked the old people. They were so entirely different from their son Jim. When we got there, there were two young men in the house. One of them was James Kinney. He was one of their son-in-laws, and a man whom we had met there quite a few times before. Mr. Kinney was married to Jim's younger sister, and owned and operated a cigar factory in Oneida. They introduced the other man as Frank Fisher, the partner of their son-in-law. This man was of medium height and a trifle overweight, with rather heavy features, but really with a good natured expression. Sandy hair and gray eyes. He kept looking at me in his rather dull way, but I was so used to having people look at me, I scarcely noticed him.

Well, after an hour or so, we went home. To our great surprise, next morning while we were still at the breakfast table, Mrs. Corcoran drove into our yard with her gray horse. She was well up in the seventies and very plump. She came in, laughing, and said she had an important message to deliver

We could not understand at first what she meant; then she told us. She said that their friend Mr. Frank Fisher had fallen in love with me and had begged her to come to us and break the news. I could see plainly that she expected we all would be delighted. I listened in silence, was neither glad nor displeased, really quite indifferent. My father and mother at once told her just to tell him not to bother about coming.

She said that he and her son-in-law had grown up together and now for the last five years had been partners. How saving he was, how he had been boarding with her daughter's family and always stayed at home after working hours. How he had never had a girl before, and so on. Well, she took it for granted that we all would think that she was conferring a great favor on us to help get such a husband for me.

Well the following Sunday he came. He rode his bicycle out. Awkwardly, slowly he walked to the verandah where we all were. My father and mother received him with cold politeness. I merely bowed my head. He presented my father with a box of cigars. He stayed and stayed, just sat there dumbly. At last my mother brought out some sandwiches and milk, saying we would not have any supper. Still he stayed on. At long last he left, saying he would come again next Sunday. None of us invited him. Next Sunday I went away. He was there for hours, my mother told me. Then he started coming out at night after working hours. My father kept throwing out plain hints. I would leave the house when he came.

So this went on for some weeks. One weekday--he had only come Sundays and weekdays after working hours--for a wonder I happened to be in the house one forenoon with my mother when we saw him coming on his bicycle. My mother said she would end his coming once and for all. I had just time to run and hide in the recess. Soon after he came, my mother told him that he was only wasting his time to keep coming as I was very much in love with a young man in our neighborhood. Of course I knew my mother meant Jim Corcoran. But I thought, anything to get rid of this man. He kept on sitting there for perhaps half an hour, never spoke a word, then slowly went away.

Well as I am not going to refer to this thing again; I will go ahead some years in my story. Years after, we heard from the Kinney family that he never went to see a girl. When asked why, he always said he had loved once and would never want to have another one. Yes, even ten years later, he would come home from his work, eat supper and go to his room.

Well, I really only had the two hotels down on the lake shore left to sell my stuff to this summer. Almost all the cottagers I had first known had sold or rented their summer homes. Besides, now there were a dozen peddlers where I had been the only one. So twice a week, I took berries and some vegetables to Sylvan Beach. I found a small restaurant, with very pleasant people. They always bought from me. Their name was Lewis. Their home was in Oneida on James Street, but they ran this summer place for about two months each summer. At that time, I little dreamed that these people, or rather Mrs. Lewis, would help to change my entire after life. But more about this later on.

Charles Estey obtained a job in Utica and could only come home every two Sundays. But he wrote to me two and three times a week. Such love letters. My parents always read those letters before I did. I only wrote to him every two weeks, a short letter which my father always read before I sent it out. So the summer went by. We still spent our evenings together on the verandah, my father and mother sitting close together, either talking to one another or just in silent meditation. I lay in my hammock, living in a world of my own, living mostly in the future, a future that was forever calling and beckoning me away. Beckoning me on to the great, the beautiful, the wonderful life ahead.

I made my last peddling trip on the last day of August. Came the third of September, Sunday. This day started like thousands of other days. A warm, pleasant, sunshiny day, quiet, serene. Well soon after breakfast, my father and I got into a terrible row. This was not just an every day disagreement, but a bitter, bitter, quarrel. I cannot now recall what it was about, only this much; that I had made up my mind not to submit to his orders. Well, this was early in the forenoon. By late afternoon, everything was, to outside appearances, all over. A strained quietness. But I know I was still seething, boiling mad within. I also knew that after such a row, my father would stay angry for weeks to come. I had noticed from early childhood that when he had come

Sophie Kussmaul

out ahead in one of our bitter sessions, he would, after a day or so, forgive me. But if I held my ground and would not give up to him, he would stay angry for weeks and months to come.

About four o'clock in the afternoon, Mrs. Meaney, Paul Meaney's mother, came to make us a call. She acted a little absent minded. After a while she half laughingly told us that she had gotten herself into a mess. She had agreed to get up a load of fifteen hop pickers for a Mr. Clinton Oliver, a small hop grower near Augusta Centre. She said she thought that would be an easy matter, but when she had about half her number together, some backed out. So she had to find new ones to take their place. This very morning, a woman whom she had counted on for sure came to tell her that she could not go.

I heard all this in an entirely disinterested way. Then, all at once, she turned to me and said, "Sophie, I do not suppose I could get you to go?" In a second's time, I had my mind made up. I looked defiantly at my father and spoke up, "Yes, I will go. I am twenty-one." My poor mother looked as if I was going to destruction, my father was silent. Then I asked Mrs. Meaney when her load was to leave. She said, "Tomorrow morning on the eight o'clock train."

When we got to Oneida, there were two teams with large wagons waiting for us. For Mrs. Meaney had only gotten up one load of pickers, there was another load of sixteen at Oneida. Well, we had a pleasant ride of about twelve miles. Right after dinner, we changed into our working clothes and went into the hop yard. I loved the work, and the smell of the hops. There were only twenty pickers; the rest of the loads were box tenders.

I will not go into any description here about the hop yard. I will leave that to another time when I can describe a large yard and its management. Everything here was rather quiet. The men, or as they were called, the boys, were not at all interesting. Came Saturday night and the Olivers had planned to hold a dance in the hop-kiln. Men and girls from the neighboring hop yards came by the dozens.

I never was a dancer. Once in a while I had been dragged into what is called a square dance, but I always got confused, mixed up. I was introduced to a young man from a neighboring yard. His name was Augustus Penfield. As I did not care about dancing, we sat together and watched the others. After that we had supper, and he said he would come over the next afternoon, Sunday. Well he came and we took a long walk. Wednesday night there was a dance at the place where he was picking, so he came after me and brought me back.

We got done hop picking at Oliver's Friday night, so I came home Saturday. I thought it best not to mention about Augustus when I came but, to my dismay, in about a week's time, I received a letter from him. His home was in Utica. Of course my father opened it first and found out it was from a young man. There was absolutely nothing wrong about the letter, but my father wrote to him not to write again to his daughter. Well that was the end.

Sophie Kussmaul

Chapter 16

December brought me to my twenty-fourth birthday. This winter was about like the last with plenty of work. Charlie's lovemaking, music, reading, and when the roads were open, my horse and cutter rides. Very early in spring, in March, Mr. Corcoran died. His wife, who was about seventy-eight, never got over his loss, and in June she too passed into the great unknown. For nearly a year they had kept a hired woman, as it took most of Mrs. Corcoran's time to care for her husband, and after his death, Mrs. Corcoran failed so rapidly she could do no housework. Well I will not say my mother was glad that Mrs. Corcoran died, for she really did like her, but soon after the funeral she surely thought now Jim would propose to me. I knew that he never even dreamed of doing so. The summer passed by. I had only been peddling twice a week. Too many others now on the road peddling. September, there were rumors that Jim Corcoran went to see a girl in Maple Flats. As I had said before, no girl that knew him seemed to have any use for him. He still kept the old lady as housekeeper. When my mother heard about his going to see a girl, she just did not believe it. It was early in October, a perfect day, all the glory of summer without its great heat, and all the abundance of early autumn. As yet no frost. My flower garden more beautiful, really, than in mid summer. My father walked to North Bay in the forenoon. My mother and I had been making mixed pickles. We had cooked a good dinner, as we knew my father would be home promptly at, or just before, twelve o'clock. Right here I will say this. In all the many years my parents had been married, my father had never even once kept a meal waiting. We ate slowly, leisurely. My father was telling how Mrs. Anchord, who had been sick, was getting better, and a few more such news items. Luckily, I was just done eating and was getting up from the table when my father looked up and said, "Oh, I almost forgot to tell you that Jim Corcoran got married this morning." I could have shouted for very joy. What a relief. Never again would I have to hear from my mother that she knew he loved me. In getting up from the table I glanced at my mother. Such compassion, such pity in her glance at me. I felt as if I wanted to laugh, to sing. Well, I have said before that each day, the year around, they took a short nap right after dinner. We just either covered the left over food on the table or hastily put it away. We never washed the dishes till after their naps. I took a book and went out on the verandah into my hammock, as the weather was like summer.

Oh, I felt happy, happy. I had scarcely got settled when my mother, who never missed her noon rest, came to me. She bent over me and kissed me tenderly, looked at me so sorrowfully, then began to tell me not to take it too much to heart, that I had been to blame for not encouraging him, how hard he had tried to win me. I kept telling her that I did not want him, that he had never wanted me. I begged her to go and get her rest. But no, she said she would not leave me alone and that after a while it would be easier to bear. I got really out of patience with her.

Later in the day, she followed me into the garden, everywhere. Once I heard her tell my father that I took it very much to heart but tried not to show it. Well my father was much wiser. He told her that I was not so foolish as to care for a man like Jim. He told her she imagined all that stuff. Well, for once he was right. At last I went upstairs to bed, but my mother followed me up, trying to comfort me, and so it went for days and weeks.

All the time, I would have given almost anything for one look of Joe Henry's kind face and true brown eyes. Well, December brought my twenty-fifth birthday. Another winter, another spring. I really did not peddle this summer. Once in a while I took some berries to the one hotel. The other one burned down. Once in a while I took some stuff to the Lewis restaurant.

This was the year of the Pan American Exposition at Buffalo, New York State. I went with a party from North Bay--Mr. and Mrs. Dexter Nichols and their little daughter Sara, Mr. and Mrs. Joseph Cook and their daughter Lena, and another married daughter of theirs. We left home on the nineteenth of August. Well, I will not try to describe the beauties of that grand fair. We boarded in the city, went to the fairgrounds as early as they opened up each day. We spent ten days at the fair and two more, one at Niagara Falls and one day on a little trip into Canada. I must say those fourteen days, and one to go and return, were happy days for me. I brought home quite a few souvenirs from the fair.

I had intended to go as a hop picker in Mrs. Rose's load on the fourth of September. I arrived home on the second. I had not been home over an hour when Mr. and Mrs. Belcher drove into our yard. She made me a proposal to go with her to Morrisville to pick hops.

Now I must say a few things in explanation. The Belchers were considered nice people. They owned a very nice home on the lake road between North Bay and Jewel. Mrs. Belcher's brother had owned the electric light plant at Morrisville, and also three small houses in that village, one near the electric light plant, which was situated about a mile outside of Morrisville on the road to Caden. I had been there a few times with Mrs. Belcher. After Mrs. Belcher's brother's death, she inherited his Morrisville property. For this reason, she had to make frequent trips out there. But as all this property was heavily mortgaged, she had some difficulty in selling it.

Now this was the offer she made. The little house near the light plant was completely furnished, even to knives, forks and spoons. She did not like to stay there alone, and she thought it would be necessary for her to remain in or near Morrisville about two to three weeks to settle up her business affairs there. Her husband could not accompany her, as some one had to stay at home. There were three small hop farms in that neighborhood, and so she thought if I could go there with her, we could keep house and pick hops. Saying this would be so much pleasanter for me than to stay nights in a place with so many strangers. Of course my mother fully agreed with her, as she had not at all liked my going in Mrs. Rosa's load.

Mrs. Belcher wanted to start on the following day, on the late afternoon train. That gave me scarcely a day at home. We arrived at the little Morrisville Station before dark, took the stage to the Village, a distance of four miles, went into a grocery store and bought some provisions for our housekeeping. We walked the last mile. This was truly a novelty for me, and I felt independent. Next morning we started to pick hops for Mr. Ward Foster. We carried our noon lunch. The distance was less than a quarter of a mile. Every evening Mrs.

Belcher either went to see people about selling, or some one came to our place about those houses and above all the light plant. I did almost all the cooking and so on, but I felt as if I was in my own home.

The people in the Foster's yard were all pleasant, but nothing very wonderful. On Saturday we got done at Fosters, were to start to a Mr. Fuller Monday morning. His yard was about two miles from us on the road to Eden. He was to pick us up each morning and bring us back at night with his hop wagon. Well Saturday night, Mrs. Belcher and I went to Morrisville to stock up on food for the next week. While we were in the little grocery store, Mrs. Belcher introduced me to a man by the name of Wilbur Henderson.

He was a man of about forty, very well built, an intelligent, handsome face, just a suspicion of gray on his temples, gray eyes, and rather light hair. I liked him at once. He was the first man I really liked since I met Joe Henry seven years before. Of course it was not like that time; still I did like him. When he asked Mrs. Belcher's permission to call the next day, I felt happy. Yes, he came. I felt like receiving him in my own home, only more so, because at home, no matter who came, even a girl of my own age, they were always made to feel that they were my parents' company. I never was left alone in a room with any one.

But here, Mrs. Belcher went into the next room and took a long nap, leaving us alone. After a while, we took a walk, came back, and had Mr. Henderson stay for supper. To my delight, he told us he had hired out as Yard Boss, both to Fullers and Harts. Hart was the third place we were to pick hops. Well, that was a happy, happy week. I got up early, cooked our breakfast, packed my lunch, and soon after eating, the big hop wagon would stop for us, Wilbur Henderson running to the door to see if we were ready. All day, if he could spare a few minutes, he would come to our box. Then the ride home at night. He said he would hire a rig and take me out Sunday. Well, the days flew by on wings. Sunday came, so did Wilbur Henderson, with a beautiful dapple gray horse and a shiny buggy. He took me to Hamilton, about ten miles from Morrisville. A lovely drive. We had a good dinner at a hotel there.

Mrs. Belcher, who had known him a long time, gave him a grand recommendation. I was very happy. I pictured to myself the time when I would introduce him to my father and mother. I felt sure they would like him. Another happy week in the hop yard, and the promise of one more nice ride on Sunday. We expected to get done about Monday night of the next week. Wilbur had asked me at least a dozen times if I had a sweetheart at home. He kept saying, "Now tell me the truth. Do not deceive me. Is there no one where you live that means anything to you?" I told him the truth, that there was no one at home that I loved.

Came the last Sunday, I was up early. I expected him about eleven o'clock. At ten o'clock I was all dressed up in my very best. Heard a knock at the door, rushed to open it, and there stood Charles Estey. I had completely forgotten him. He came by train, but got on the wrong road and instead of having walked the five miles, must have covered at least ten. I did not know what to do with him. After all, he was my guest; still I did not want my last day spoiled with the man I loved. We were talking, the door was open; I did not hear the wheels of Wilbur's buggy. Charles as always was just again telling me how much he loved me, how he had missed me. There fell a shadow across the floor. We looked up. There stood Wilbur, anger, disappointment in his face. I jumped up, went to him, explained that this was an old friend of mine. He sneered. Charlie said, "She is my sweetheart." Mr. Henderson left. Outside stood the same lovely horse and buggy. I went into my bedroom and shut the door. My heart was filled with bitterness and sorrow. Later in the day, I came out; we had a late dinner, and then Charles went on his way.

I knew he would never tell my parents. For this reason--it would have hurt his pride to have them or any one at home think that he was not the whole thing with me. So next day, the last to Hart's hop yard, Wilbur was coolly polite. All the joy had gone out of my heart. The day after, I left for home. To my great joy, I found that my father and mother had made up their minds to go to the fair. I think I was even more happy about this than I had been when I was getting ready to go there myself. My darling mother, who had traveled so much in her younger days, had now with the exception of those two weeks in New York, not been away from home in over twenty-eight years. My father, who had bought our home place seven years before he had married my mother, had now been here about thirty-five years. The only time in all those years that he had been away was the two weeks when he went hop picking, and that was just to work. Really, by what I gathered, he had never in his younger days gone anywhere for pleasure.

Lately, after so many, many years, I have often wondered if that was not the cause of his great disapproval, his not understanding that a young person like myself could crave pleasure. Neither, I suppose, could he understand that I could fall in love. He himself had never in his life gone to see a girl, never felt what love was, till he met my mother. Then he was just past forty years of age. She got his first love, his only love. I am perfectly sure that if she had died the first year of their marriage, he would never again have remarried.

So on the twenty-eighth of September, I took my parents to the little North Bay Station to start their first pleasure trip together. True, they had gone to Utica and Syracuse together about eight years before to be told that there was no help for my mother, that she was doomed to die in agony, but now they could taste a little happiness. We had made arrangements with Charlie's sister to come and stay at our house nights, as my folks did not think it proper for me to stay alone at night.

They left on a Monday and returned on the following Saturday night, hiring a rig at the North Bay Station to bring them home. They both looked and acted like two happy, tired children when they got home.

The coming December, I was twenty-five years old. Nothing special this winter, spring, or summer. Came September, I went in a load of hop pickers to a Mr. Christopher Kilts, up on the hills about six miles from Oneida. Now this time I got into a large hop yard. There were eighty of us, besides the family and the help in the house.

There are always four pickers to a box. A box is divided into four parts, each part holding nine bushels. There is a canvas roof over the box to shade the pickers from the sun and light rains. When it rains hard, the picking stops. A box tender had eight pickers, two boxes. He has to cut the hop vines and pull the poles for the pickers. Each box has a certain amount of poles, which is called a set. When those are picked, comes the call, "Clean up around your box." Then the two boxes are moved into the next set. There is always a yard boss. He walks from box to box, sees that the hops are picked clean. This means that no little ones are left on the vines. He also sees to it that the boxes are really full before they are emptied.

With him is a helper, who does the hard work. When a picker's box is full, he or she yells, "hopsack." The helper empties the box full of hops into a large sack. The boss gives the picker a ticket and also marks the number of your full boxes into a little book. At the kiln is a hop drier. At night the bags are collected and taken to the hop kiln.

I had some fun there, but things were not like they were at Morrisville. Sundays some of us, perhaps twenty-five, would go on long walks. About every other evening there was a dance in the hop kiln. I met a man by the name of John Engles from Rochester. We spent our evenings together, walked together on those Sunday trips, were good friends, but neither one of us was serious. He invited me to come visit him in Rochester, said his mother would be kind to me. Of course I never went.

Hop picking over, a long dreary autumn. Came December and my twenty-sixth birthday. Charles Estey came, but I could not be so friendly. This was the second winter I did not play music with him.

I did not peddle any more, so the summer went by. Late in August, Mr. Kilts came to our house. He wanted me to get up a load of twenty hop pickers. Well, I did. I spent days riding my horse all over, but at last I got them together. Again, John Engles came to Kilts's. We chummed around together.

December came and my twenty-seventh birthday. Another spring and summer. I got up another load of hop pickers. John Engles and I picked at the same box this year. I came home, everything quiet, no excitement, when to my great joy, on the first of December, my mother received a letter from Mrs. Tappen. She said she would like to see me again, but as she was not feeling well at all--she was about eighty-three now--she could not take me out sightseeing. So she had talked it over with her daughter, Mrs. Mills, and this was what they had decided to do. She, Mrs. Tappen, would pay my fare both ways, but I was to stay most of the time to Mrs. Mills, who could take me out daily. Once in a while she would send her carriage to Mrs. Mills and have me stay at her home for a day or two. So of course, I got ready to go at once. I left home on the fifth of December. This time I decided to take another route. I had found out that I could take a train at North Bay on the Ontario and Western road that would take me direct to Weehawken, New Jersey, opposite New York City. So I wrote to Mrs. Mills to meet me there, instead of at the Grand Central Station in New York City.

I had two reasons for wanting to go that way. In the first place, lovely as had been the scenery along the Central, I had made two trips, really saw it all four times, going and coming, but this way every mile after leaving Morrisville would be new to me. My other reason was I would not have to change trains. Although I knew that the train on the Ontario and Western did not travel as swiftly as the one on the Central, I knew I would arrive at my destination at about the same time. If I took the Central, I had to wait in Oneida about two hours.

It had, of course, been dark some hours before I arrived at Weehawken. When the train pulled into the station, I had no trouble finding Mrs. Mills. Although Weehawken is the terminal of the Ontario and Western railroad, it is quite a small station. Where there were thousands of people milling around at the Grand Central, there were scarcely fifty people here.

Now since then, I have seen very many beautiful things on my travels. I think I can truthfully say that I have seen all the really worthwhile scenery in all our States, but never before or since have I been so impressed with anything the way I was when we left the station and boarded the ferryboat to take us to city. Before us, gleaming with millions of electric lights was New York City. Just to one side, Brooklyn also aglow with lights. Like a golden bow connecting these two was Brooklyn Bridge. This great structure also was a sparkling mass of lights, the reflection of which was mirrored in the river below. All around us were crafts of all kinds, row boats, motor boats, large and small sailboats, tugs, barges, steamers, each and all aglitter with lights and again, reflected in the river below. From somewhere came floating the Star Spangled Banner. I was awed with it all. I could not utter a word.

Everything I beheld was so new and strange to me; it seemed as if I had entered fairyland. Did I say everything? Well, there was one thing that was not new. There was a full moon, and a few stars in the cloudless heavens above. These, too, were reflected in the dark waters of the river below. Strange, amid all this wonderful glory, the sight of that moon sent swift memories rushing over me of the countless summer nights spent on our lovely quiet verandah, nights of bitter heartaches, nights of a great love to come, nights of golden dreams.

Then swiftly, my mind was racing ahead. I felt I knew that wherever I might be roaming, be it thousands and thousands of miles from home, no matter where, the heavens above me would always be the same. So, too, the love of God would never change.

Sophie Kussmaul

Well, we arrived at New York City. People rushing about, noise, confusion. Mrs. Mills was kind to me, kept me going from place to place. The few days I spent with Mrs. Tappen were also enjoyable. Although by this time automobiles were very plentiful, Mrs. Tappen still kept her carriage and coachman. So each day I spent with her, we took long rides together.

I left Mrs. Mills on the twentieth of December for home. I will have to say something about the difference in the climate in the comparatively short distance from New York City to our home. When I had left home on the fifth of December, we had about a foot of snow on the ground. In and near New York City, the ground was still bare and the weather mild.

When I left Weehawken on the twentieth of December, it was just getting daylight. Everywhere it looked like Indian summer. I traveled for hours before I first beheld a little snow here and there, but each hour after that, I noticed more and more snow. When my train stopped in Oneida, there was only one passenger to get on board. This man was Gerald Corcoran. He lived about two miles from us. He was an older brother of Jim Corcoran, but a very different sort of a man. He had a wife and eight children, the older ones married and with families of their own.

Well he seemed pleased to see me and sat down in the seat beside me. Of course he asked me where I had been and if any one was to meet me at North Bay. I told him I would try and hire some one to take me home. Mr. Corcoran said he expected his daughter Gertie to meet him at North Bay with a horse and cutter, and he would have her drive around the square and take me home. But when we got to North Bay, the snow was over three feet deep, and Gertie said that both the crossroads were blocked. So I had to go home with them. They wanted me to stay with them over night. Well, after a late supper, Gerald said if I was determined to get home, he would see what he could do. He went out and hitched up two big mules to a bob sleigh and said if anything could get through, they could. Well they did. At times they wallered through snow up to their necks, but slowly, steadily went on. We got to my home about eleven o'clock. For a wonder my parents were still up. Oh, how glad they were to have me home again.

I, of course, at a glance noticed how plain everything here looked compared to the rich splendor of our New York friends, but, how homey, how good things looked to me. In the big roomy winter kitchen was a cheerful wood fire in the large cook stove. On the floor was an old, but clean, thick carpet. On the table, a kerosene lamp with a green shade. On the couch, nestled between the cushions, our two oldest cats. On the window sills, plants in bloom. In the living-room, a bright, glowing coal fire, and near by on a big cushioned chair, a gray and white half grown kitten, the family pet. On the center table, another green shaded lamp.

This was home, my home, sweet home. Of course my father and mother thanked Mr. Corcoran many times for his kindness. Next day was my birthday. I was twenty-eight years old. My darling mother, though not sure when I would return, had baked my birthday cake the day before.

I had only seen Charles Estey a few times since spring, as he had been working in Utica. A few days after I came home, he called, saying he had bought out his brother Joe. He seemed very proud of that, and I think was trying to impress me with it, just as if I cared the least little bit what he bought or had.

Another dear old Christmas and then a long, lonely winter. On the nineteenth of March, Mrs. Everson, Charlie's sister, came to tell us goodbye. One of her sons who lived in Camden had two tiny children. His wife was never really well, so his mother was going to live with them, care for her son's wife and help to bring up his children.

I felt terrible bad about this. I loved this woman far better than any girl of my own age that I knew. But, again, I kept all this to myself, showing indifference. On the first of May, Joe Estey came to bid us farewell. He had bought a small farm on the road between Camden and Taberg. I knew I would miss him, the dear old friend.

I worked on the farm, in the house, picked berries for our own use. We spent our summer evenings as before on the verandah. At times, the call of the West was so strong within me that it almost was a physical pain. A pleasant fall, no snow until after December. On the twenty-first of this month I became twenty-nine years of age.

Charlie came quite often. One day my mother and I were together when he came. First, as always, he told me of his great love for me and so on. I hardly heard him. Then all at once, he asked me to marry him. I was neither glad nor angry. I just looked at him and laughed out loud. He seemed hurt. My mother told him that if I ever did marry, it would be to a man who could offer me a much better home than the one I now had, give me some comforts of life, and a few of its pleasures. He left, stayed away for a while; then he came calling again.

Chapter 17

Came the sixth of April, and the turning point of my life. But before I begin this story, I will have to go back some years. I think I mentioned in the beginning of this book that when I was between eight and nine years old, my father had an annuity left to him from the old country, from which he received, four times a year, a check, which he always took to the Oneida Savings Bank. There he had the check cashed, deposited half the amount in the bank, and kept the other half. This done, he would go and buy the things we either could not obtain at North Bay or, if so, had to pay almost double for them at our little stores at home. Of course in later years, when most people owned an automobile and were able to go further for their things, the prices at home dropped too. When these things were all done, my father had still six to seven hours to wait for his train home. He hated those long hours of waiting. Sometimes he went to spend a little time at King's. Mr. King was a soldier friend of his. But most of the time, he just sat patiently in the waiting room. He would always buy a good book, read it there, then bring it home to us. So after I had made my first trip to New York City, he said I would be perfectly able to make those quarterly trips to Oneida, tend to his business at the bank, and buy the things as he had done. He said, and I think he was very wise, that it would be good training for me, in a way prepare me for my later life.

At the same time, it relieved him from a duty he so much hated. I was delighted, felt important. So, the next time the European check came, he took me with him to Oneida, introduced me at the bank, and explained to them that after this, I would come in his place. He also showed me the stores, where he got the best bargains and so on.

158

Sophie Kussmaul

Now for about eight years, I made those quarterly trips to Oneida. It so happened that once in a while I had to make a trip in between, but not very often. Now, in all those years, I did exactly the way my father had done. First took care of the bank business, then bought the things they had put down on the list, went to the same little restaurant my father had always gone to, and then to the depot for my long wait. In bad weather, I would sit there by the hour and read. In fair weather, I would bring my parcels down, give them to the ticket seller, whom I knew, and sometimes go to King's for a few hours or take long walks. I, like my father, hated those long waiting periods. In later years, I sometimes called on the Lewis family, the friends I had made at Sylvan Beach. They lived on James St., but entirely out of the real city. They always kept a few boarders.

Now whatever I did, or where ever I went, or whom I saw while in Oneida, I always told my mother all about it. Up to this time, I never had a secret from her. Well, on this lovely spring day, after I had finished all my errands, I parked my purchases at the depot and walked back to Madison Street, wondering just where to go. Then I remembered reading in our local paper that Mr. Lewis had died in January. I had not called at the Lewis's for over a year, so decided to go there.

When I rang the bell, instead of Mrs. Lewis opening the door, there stood a young man, a very handsome young man. I had always much preferred dark people to light, but this man was light. He was of medium height, rather slight of build, yet of perfect proportions. Light hair, blue eyes, and good features. He bowed very politely, and I asked him if Mrs. Lewis was at home. He told me she was. I stepped into the living-room and she soon came. She introduced us. This man's name was Charles Spear, but he generally went by the name of Charlie Sheppard. The reason for this was that his father's name had been Charles Raymond Spear. He died before the boy was a year old. His mother remarried when he was about two years of age. His step father's name was Charles Sheppard, so after a while the boy was known as Charlie Sheppard.

Well, he stayed in the room with Mrs. Lewis and myself, sometimes joining in the conversation. I admit I was fascinated. Never before, except at my New York friends, had I seen such perfect manners. Every move was graceful, every word, sentence correct. I could not help but notice that he looked at me with admiration. I also noticed that his hands looked as well cared for as the hands of the rich people I had met in New York City. All the boarders I had ever seen at Lewis's were working men. They came in to their dinners, and off again to their work, but this man, it seemed to me, had enough money to live on without soiling his hands.

About half past four, I got ready to leave, as I knew Mrs. Lewis, who did all her own work, would soon be busy in her kitchen, as she had two more boarders who were working in the Lee Chair Factory that would expect their supper at six o'clock. Mr. Spear jumped up and asked me if he might accompany me to the depot. After we left, he pulled out a heavy gold watch and said, "Why it is nearly two hours to train time. Let us sit awhile in the park."

I can still see the little park, young, tender green grass, the giant elms and maples just leafing out. Birds singing and nesting. A warm sun glinting through the new leaves. We sat down on a bench. He asked me a lot of questions, said he wanted to know where I lived so he could come to see me. Then a great fear came over me. I knew my parents would find out I had met a strange young man. Still, I thought if they met him, they would surely approve of him. Why he was a real gentleman. He was not a laborer. I told him it would not do to come to my home, explained how my people were, said we would have to think up a way for him to meet them without their knowing that I had already met him.

Then he asked for my address. He would write to me. Again I said that would not do. We had the R.F.D. I told him I hardly ever got a letter, and if I did, my father always read it first. Then when I answered it, he would read that letter too. All at once I said to him to write to North Bay. I would buy a Post Office Box there that very night. I did not feel that I was doing anything wrong. Here I was, well past my twenty-ninth birthday, and up to now, had had no freedom at all.

After a while, we walked to the depot. He stayed with me till the train came. I was very happy. Yes, I bought a box at the North Bay Post Office before I went home, but I began to feel guilty, more so when I saw the good honest look in my parents' faces.

A few days after, I had to go to North Bay. When I entered the Post Office, at a glance I saw there was a letter in Box 50. My heart beat so loud, I was afraid Mrs. Miller, the Post Mistress, would hear it. On my way home I read it a dozen times. It was truly a splendid letter. Expensive stationery, beautiful penmanship. No spelling or grammar mistakes. Very affectionate, though not so ridiculous as Charlie Estey's expressions. I longed to show this to my mother, tell her how and where I had met him. I felt she would understand, but as I had got this at North Bay, she would ask me why I had not given him my right address. So I thought I would wait till after he came to our house. I thought then they would say he was one man in a million.

Now I ran into another difficulty. Up to now, I had never written one word except at the table downstairs. But I knew the moment I would even get the pen and ink stand, either my father or mother would ask me what I was going to write, then lean over my shoulder and look. So after a long time, my father was not in the house, and I managed to smuggle a sheet of paper and an envelope, ink stand and pen and carry them to my room. I felt like a criminal. Carefully, I put them on my little stand. Then I heard my mother come up the stairs. I barely had time to thrust the things into my bed. There she stood, smiling and saying, "What is my lambie doing up here all alone?"

Now I knew she did not come to spy on me, as she never dreamed I was going to deceive her, it was just her affectionate way, wanted me with her all the time. So I went down with her, then a fear came over me if she would miss the inkstand. After a while, I ran up, hid it in my dress, and when she left the room, replaced it.

Next morning I took one of my drawing pencils, hid the sheet of paper and envelope in my dress still in my bed and ran into the woods. There I felt safe. I wrote my letter, it was all crumbled up, hid it under a log, and waited till they wanted something from North Bay.

So our correspondence went on for a month; as I said, once in a great while I had to make an extra trip to Oneida. This did not happen very often, sometimes once a year, and at other times, not in two or three years' time. So I really was much surprised when on the fifteenth of May, my father wanted me to go to Oneida to draw some money for him. I wrote to Mr. Spear that I was coming to Oneida on the seventeenth.

Through Sophie's Eyes

When I arrived at the Oneida Depot, he was there to meet me. If possible, looking even more stylishly handsome than before. I felt proud of him. I kept thinking that if my parents could only see him, they would at once like him, tell me how lucky I was to find a cultured gentleman here where most of the young men were all so crude. Well, we walked together, I went to the bank, did a few more little errands. It was still morning. We took a walk, and then sat in the park. He told me of a plan Mrs. Lewis and he had; how he could come to my home, get acquainted with my people, and of course after that the rest would be easy.

He took me to the best restaurant in Oneida, not the little one I had always gone to. Ordered an excellent lunch, and pulled a big wad of bills out of a monogrammed billfold to pay for it. I no longer felt guilty about my big secret. In fact, I felt as if I was going to give my dear parents the best surprise--a rich, handsome, young, healthy, affectionate, highly educated son-in-law to be.

About two o'clock, we went to Mrs. Lewis's. There they told me their plan. Mrs. Lewis would need butter and eggs at her Sylvan Beach restaurant. She knew I lived on a farm. Mr. Spear could go after them. She told me this summer she was going to open her restaurant much earlier, as her two boarders were now leaving for a job in Syracuse. She intended to open up at Sylvan Beach about the fifteenth of June and she laughed, said Mr. Spear could make his first trip after butter and eggs on the twelfth.

Now it was left for me to tell them that my friend Mrs. Lewis wanted to buy eggs and butter from my people, and as she could not come herself, would send one of her boarders after them. Well, I thought I would not have to lie to them, I would tell the truth. I went to Mrs. Lewis's to spend some of my long waiting hours there. She spoke about the eggs and butter, offered to send a boarder after them. That would be the truth. So when I came home, I tried to tell my parents about it. My father said it would be a good thing, as it would save the trouble to take them to North Bay. I was happy, of course. I thought just as soon as my parents once saw this wonderful man, they would be delighted, and my mother would kiss me and say, "My dear child, I do not blame you one bit. He is just lovely."

I kept getting such grand letters from him. I hid them all in a tin box under a log in the woods, intending to show them all to my mother when they understood. At long last the twelfth of June came.

I was terribly excited, but tried to appear calm. My father was at work on the farm. I did not dare to dress up much, so as not to appear to my mother as if I cared.

The door was wide open. A knock. There he stood. My mother admitted him. I introduced them. Mr. Spear was politeness itself. My mother, too, but to my dismay I saw that she was not charmed with him. He tried to talk to me. I was not the same, easy, pleasant girl he had met twice in Oneida. Here, before my mother, I was shy, awkward. He stayed perhaps an hour then asked if he could come again on Friday--this was Tuesday and get the same amount of butter and eggs. My mother said he could. After he left, I asked my mother in a casual way what she thought of him. She hesitated then said he was well mannered, made a good appearance. But I felt she did not like him.

The next day, I went to North Bay, and got a long letter from him. He said he had noticed that my mother did not seem to like him, but I should not worry, he would soon win her over. I felt much easier. At last, Friday afternoon came. My father did not go back to his work after his noon rest. He sat, as was his want, on the end of his couch, next to the window. In my mind I can see him yet. He was reading his newspaper and as always, held it up in front of him.

When Mr. Spear came to the door, my mother received him then introduced him to my father. I can not say that my father looked at him. He acknowledged the introduction by a slight nod of the head, gave him a swift glance, and again held up his newspaper, went on reading. Mr. Spear showed surprise in his face. My mother, in spite of her politeness, was a little cold towards this man, but my father reminded me of a bronze statue. Well, I felt that instead of being delighted with this man, neither one of my parents approved of him. He tried to talk, first with my mother, then with me. I did not know what to do. After a while he again pulled out his fat wallet, counted out the money for the butter and eggs, and absolutely refused to pick up the change my mother had handed him. He got up, asked my mother if he could have the same amount of produce on the following Tuesday. My father broke his silence for the first time since Spear had stepped into our house. He decidedly said no, that it was all we could do to supply our old customers.

Mr. Spear glanced at me, then bowed and left us. My mother said to my father, "You did not like him? But how could you tell as long as you never even really looked at him?" My father said, "I did look at him. I saw enough. He is no good. I should call him a swindler." My mother then said that she, too, saw something in his face, the first time he came, that she did not like.

Imagine my disappointment. Well, after this he kept on writing to me, asking me to meet him here and there. He would hire a saddle horse at Sylvan Beach, I would ride my horse. I must say this--we did nothing wrong. I felt that we had tried to meet in my home, but could not.

This year I started for Mr. Kilts's hop yard on the second of September. I gave Mr. Spear my address. He wrote to me almost daily. One day, on a Thursday, just when the whole big bunch of us were going back into the yard after dinner, Mrs. Kilts called me back, said there was a gentleman at the front door who asked after me. I wondered who that could be. It was Charlie Spear. He had hired a rig and drove out to see me. We sat down on a bench in the big front yard, under a giant pine tree, and he told me how he had missed me, said he would come Sunday morning and take me out for all day, said he just had to have a long talk with me. He soon left. I went back into the hop yard. I seemed to be floating through the air. He had again assured me that nothing would ever change his love for me.

Came Sunday, after breakfast I went upstairs and dressed carefully, then came down and went on the broad verandah facing the road. Oh, joy, there drove into the driveway a shiny, rubber tired carriage drawn by two prancing, young, bay horses. I ran out to him, got into the seat beside him, waved a happy farewell to my crowd and we were off. This was one of the happiest days of my life. It was still summer, though here and there was a faint touch of autumn color on some of the maples. But, oh, how very beautiful everything looked. We rode for many miles over the Madison hills, at last coming to Peterboro. There we put the team into a hotel barn. Mr. Spear ordered them well fed.

He ordered a sumptuous dinner for us. After eating, he said we would let the horses rest a few hours. We took a walk near the shady little creek near the village. We sat down and there he asked me to marry him at Christmas. I said I would. We sat there a long time. He told me he would never let me do any more hard work; he would keep a maid for me. We planned a home, a little home in this earthly paradise.

Since then I have crossed that little creek countless of times, seen the grassy knoll on which we sat, under the shady trees, seen and heard the water run and murmur its way along, but under such different circumstances. Well after a while we went back, got the now rested team and started on our way back.

Yes, this day will always stand out as one of the happiest in my life. We made arrangements that when I left Kilts, he would meet me in Oneida. We would spend the day together, and I would take the six-thirty train home. When I reached Kilts, it was just getting dusky, the girls seemed awed. I thought they were a little jealous. They only had boy friends; I had a prince.

Next morning, I noticed at breakfast their heads together talking in low tones. Women whispered and everyone seemed to glance at me. After breakfast Mrs. Kilts said she wanted to see me, so instead of going out with the happy bunch, I went with her into her bedroom. She locked the door behind us and asked me how long I knew this Mr. Spear, where I first met him, if my parents knew him and how much did I know of his past life. I felt she did not like him. She confessed that she had never seen him; it was only what she had heard. But she said since I was nearly thirty years old, and had a father and mother to protect me, she did not want to say too much. Besides, maybe the things she had heard were not so. Of course I wanted to know what she meant. Well, after a while she told me that he had served a year in States Prison in Binghamton, New York, had a wife and child in Cortland, and was a professional gambler. I seemed to grow cold. I told her I did not believe any such things. Well, she said to be careful.

The joy had gone out of my life. Still, maybe this was all a mistake. But perhaps the gambling was true. He never worked, still had plenty of money and all the other stuff. I just did not believe it. People were jealous. Yes, that was it! Well, hop picking was nearly over.

The last day came. We got to Oneida. Mr. Spear met me. My folks never suspected anything. I think they thought that everything was over with us from the time my father had told him we had no more butter and eggs to sell to him.

Came the twenty-second of October, a dark, dismal morning. I was baking bread, raised biscuits, and an apple pie. My mother was sorting over some beans. My father had just come in from doing chores. There was a knock at the door. My father opened it. In walked Charles Spear. He politely handed my father a box of cigars, my mother a box of lovely house roses and ferns, me a big box of chocolates. This was an utter surprise. He acted so very nice that both my parents did thaw out to him. Of course he stayed for dinner, said it was the best dinner he had tasted in a long time. My father tried to draw him out as to how he made his living, but with little success.

He stayed with us till four o'clock, since the last train left for Oneida at four forty-five. After he left my father said, "There is something I do not like. Still, there seems to be a lot of good in him too. The cats liked him and that is always a good sign. Beware of a person whom the animals are afraid of." I was very thankful for this.

The first of November my father said that he was going to find out all about this man. Of course both my father and mother knew why he came. My father said the truth would not hurt anyone, if he was as bad as he still thought he was, it was better to know all about it before it was too late, and if he was all right, so much the better.

Well, my father went to Oneida three different times. Each time he came home with worse and worse news. So at last on the third of December, old as he was, he started for Binghamton, to stay there over night and get the real truth about his life there.

No one knows just how I suffered. Mr. Spear and I had planned such a beautiful life together. I was to have all the comforts of the rich, without living their restricted ways, no city life for me. He had offered of his own free will to help my father and mother. There was another thing, though. I did not love him the way I had my Joe Henry. I was very proud of him. All the older girls I had known were now married long ago and had families of their own. Also those of my own age, and now come to think of it, most of the girls eight or ten years younger, were either married or happily engaged. While I, who had always longed and dreamed of a great love, was almost thirty

166

years old, and, I thought, now that I could get a wonderful husband, he was being hunted down like a wild beast.

I remembered my first childhood love affair, how I had to keep it secret because I felt how my mother would be shocked. Yes, I even had to hide my grief when I heard he had died so soon after. Then came the one great love of my life, Joe Henry, and how he was used, fairly driven from the house. Then, when the young people wanted to take me with them to parties, that too was forbidden for fear that I might meet some young man I could care for.

When Charles Dixon stopped at our house and wanted to take me for a drive, with his fine young horse, my father strictly forbade it, although Charlie promised to bring me home long before dark. Then came the Fisher episode. He, too, was driven from the house. I remembered half a dozen other times a young man would call, would be froze out. I will admit all of these, with the exception of Joe Henry, I did not care for. Then there was Wilbur Henderson, as good and true a man as ever lived. He had a good recommendation and a man whom I could have loved and respected. Charles Estey had to come and spoil that.

Now why could I not be left alone? Well, my father came home the next day. In spite of everything, I felt sorry for him. He looked old and tired, said he hated to play spy but felt it was his duty to do so. Well, he brought no news; I was so thankful. He said he met an old soldier friend of his the moment he stepped off the train at Binghamton. He told him his errand in town. This friend took him home. My father felt very ill. The man told him he had a son in Binghamton who knew almost everyone and another son in Cortland who was a detective. My father should stay with him till morning, then go home and he would get in touch with his two sons, tell them to leave no stone unturned. As soon as he got the information, he would write to my father.

No one, unless they had been through a similar experience, could even begin to understand just what I went through the next few weeks. To begin with, the weather itself was depressing. There was no snow on the ground, the fields, meadows and pasture all were a brownish gray, all the leaf trees bare. The sun hardly ever shone, a dull, heavy gray sky. No happy birds singing or flitting about, the only thing alive seemed to be a few crows and once in a while an owl.

Through Sophie's Eyes

The air was cold and chilly all the time. Each day I would watch the clock, at one o'clock our mail man would come. Oh, what news he would bring. I knew my entire future would depend on that letter. If the report of his former life was good, why then we could be married. I would have a lovely home we had planned together, and life would be a happy, joyous thing. I reasoned, after all, so far people had only hinted at things. Even my father admitted that all the things he had heard against him in Oneida were only hearsay. Still, even I at times saw something in his face I did not like.

But if this letter confirmed the things that had been hinted at, then of course all would be over, and what a life would then lie before me. So each day at mail time, my heart would beat wildly; I would fly to the mail box. There always was some mail, but no letter from Binghamton. Now added to all this suspense, a dozen times a day my dear mother, who I knew tried to comfort me, would gently remind me that if I had only encouraged Jim Corcoran, I would now be happy married. Oh, I told and told her that I hated, despised him, and also knew he never cared for me.

Well, it did not help matters. She would look sad and call me her poor, dear, little lamb, and so on. My father, who generally never spoke much, would go over the thing all day, would say that in the first place he did not see why I wanted to get married anyway. Then go over the same thing countless of times, that he saw at one glance that that man was no good. At the same time, I received two letters a week from him; then came a letter saying my mother had written to him. I saw that letter later on. She had written in such a way that he could not very well come again.

Came the nineteenth of December. As every day, I rushed out to bring in the mail. Being so near Christmas, there was quite a lot, mostly for my mother, and a few parcels and a letter for my father. At one glance, I saw the Binghamton stamp on his letter. I could hardly get to the house, my legs shook and trembled.

My father read the letter over a number of times, then a silence. Oh, what was in that letter? Then he got up, stood there straight and dark, with a look in his face I shall never forget. He said that, calling the man a name I cannot write down here, was worse than he had thought he was. He read us the letter out loud. I can not remember it word for word, but the meaning of it was this: Charles Raymond

Sophie Kussmaul

Spears, Sr., the father of the man I knew, was a good, true, manly man, but he married into a very low family. The mother of his boy was a very handsome girl, but what is called a fast girl. Mr. Spear put a certain sum of money out in trust in some way that his wife could not touch it. This was for the boy's education. Well, young Charles was a bright boy, finished high school with honors at sixteen, and entered Colgate College at seventeen. Did very well there, had two years there. Then, at nineteen, he got a girl in trouble, had to marry her. They had a baby boy soon after. He left her. Broke into a bank at Cortland, he and two others. They were sentenced to a year and a half at hard labor in States Prison. After he got out, he became a professional gambler. Lived a year with one woman in Cortland, a year and a half with another one at Binghamton, and with a third one some time near Syracuse.

There were some other little things, too, such as being arrested a few times for minor thefts, and so on. Well, my father said if I did not give him up after all this evidence, he would go out, find him, kill him and then give himself up. I felt bewildered, heartsick, helpless, and it seemed as if I had come to the end of everything. I got up, put on a coat and something on my head, went out. The sun for once was shining, rather dim as if through a mist. I sat down on the little front porch, not the long verandah on the east side of the house. I had not been there long when I heard my mother say to my father, "She takes it very hard. I am so sorry for her." I did not want to be pitied. I got up, went down into the little pasture, then on to the old hemlocks, just across our line, to the one where they had started the ditch from. I sat down at this tree's roots, leaning my back against its trunk.

I crouched there so near by where my little woodland playhouse had been. Not so far, either, from where the mighty old pine had stood, where I and my beloved Indians had spent a happy summer, and right here at my very feet was the ditch that he had dug. I felt the warmth of the sunbeams on me, dim though they were. I seemed like a severely wounded animal wanting to crawl off by itself. I thought of the first time I had met Charlie Spear. Then it was April, spring. Of each time afterwards. Of the day we went to Peterboro, the plans we made that day. Of what Mrs. Kilts had told me, the dislike my parents had shown towards him, and now this letter. Yes, I said to myself, it is all over. I just knew what the neighbors would say. Well,

Sophie did not get that handsome young man. I bet she will be an old maid.

So I huddled there for a long, long time. I was too tired in body and mind to clearly think anymore. I began to shiver. The sun was nearly down, going towards the west. Then all at once, like an inspiration, quick as lightning a new thought was born in me. I would go west. The great apathy that had come over me left me, a thrill of new life surged through me. Yes, I would go west at once. I had plenty of money, had been putting almost every cent I got into the bank in Oneida. I would be thirty years old day after tomorrow, and since I could remember, that had been my dream--to go west. Then it came to me that the holy, sacred time of Christmas was almost here, the one time in all the year when my father and I had never had a quarrel. Peace and love had always reigned supreme in our house, from my birthday till New Years day. I remembered my first Christmas when I had seen the Christ-child as he flew towards heaven. No, I could not leave here till after New Years as maybe this would be our last Christmas together. So I got up and walked home.

Chapter 18

I stood there, head high, announced in a firm voice that I was leaving for California. In those days, very few people ever went to California. My father rose up, said it was unthinkable, improper, impossible. I was too young; he still looked at me as if I were a child, said a young girl would need a chaperone. I just stood there and repeated, "I am going west." My sweet mother, who had traveled through dozens of foreign countries alone, and as a guide, even before she was thirty, smiled sadly at me and turned to my father, saying it would be the best thing for me.

The next day, I went to North Bay, and at the Post Office, as I expected, I found a letter from Charlie Spear. Of course my first impulse was to read it. For over half a year, I had received two such beautiful letters each week. But I had made up my mind that I now must make a clean break, forever. So I took the letter, marked out the address to me, and re-addressed it to him. The next day was my thirtieth birthday. Both my parents were kindness and consideration itself to me.

Came Christmas, they gave me more things than ever before. Christmas week was sad, yet very beautiful. I think my father and I were closer together that week than we had ever been before. Somehow, holy as that time had ever been before, this year it seemed to have a new meaning. It seemed to link all the years of my childhood and girlhood to the new life before me. I must here say that on the very next day after I had made up my mind to go to California, I started to answer some of the information for travelers' advertisements concerning routes, prices for tickets, stopovers and such.

In a few days, they came--folders, booklets, timetables of all kinds. Of course in those days, people only traveled by rail. Greyhound buses were unheard of. Automobiles were already plentiful, but to drive one from Coast to Coast was not yet thought of. I also want to say here that as Christmas came on a Monday, I had intended to leave on the second of January. The day after New Year's. I found that if I bought a nine months ticket at Chicago, I could get it almost as cheap as a one way ticket would be.

I mean that such a ticket would take me to California and back to Chicago on half a dozen different routes I might choose from. Also, it enabled me to stop over anywhere. I had made my plans but had not figured that the weather might interfere. We had had some snow in November, then a thaw and not any more snow to amount to anything till the twenty-first of December, my birthday. After that, it kept on snowing till by the time New Years came, our road was impassible. Of course, things were not as bad as they had been years ago concerning our road. The rail and board fences had been tore down, and since we had the R.F.D., the roads were kept open better than before, but still as all the work had to be done with horses and men shoveling instead of the modern motor drawn big snowplows, we still often were snowed in for days.

So on the fourth day of January, our road was opened. This was Thursday. Next day, I had to make one more trip to Oneida to draw most of my money out of the bank and buy a good, strong suitcase. I had plenty of good clothes. I had intended to make this trip between Christmas and New Years, but on account of the snowstorms, could not do so. So on the next day I went to Oneida. When I got to the Oneida Depot, a strange feeling of loneliness came over me. Now for over seven months, every time I had got there, there was Charlie Spear waiting for me. Now he would never be waiting for me again. I started walking up Madison Street. The air was bitter cold, a dark, unpleasant day. I was deep in thought when all at once I heard a pleasant, familiar voice calling to me. It said, "Hello, honey, where are you going?" I turned around quick. There was Charlie Spear, looking at me with his handsome young face. He was just a year older than myself, but people took him to be twenty-four or twenty-five at the most.

For a moment I was so surprised I did not answer. Again he spoke. I coolly told him I was going to buy a suitcase, draw some money and start for California. Then I walked on. He fell in step with me, said he must talk with me, said he had a perfect right to know what had changed me so. Well I had to admit that he did have a right to know. So we agreed that after I had my business done, I would meet him at the Madison House.

The large sitting room in the Madison Hotel was warm and cheery. For once there was no one else there. We found a sofa at the farthest corner. I told Charlie about the evidence we had received concerning his past life. Well, he did seem a little uncomfortable. Then he said, "So you have so little faith in me that you believed that stuff. strangers told you. Now I would not believe a thing against you. If I heard such things about you, I would have gone to you and whatever you told me, I would have believed." He admitted about his forced marriage, but declared that he was absolutely innocent as to the baby, said it was a frame up. He had taken the girl out a few times, had not loved her. Said she got into trouble with another man. But as he, Spear, had some money, she and both her parents swore that he was the father of the child to be. He claimed, and that part was really true, that after the forced marriage, he never lived with her. As to serving over a year in States Prison for breaking into a bank, that he said was true. But he told me he had got in with some bad fellows. They all had been drinking and before he really realized what he was doing, he went with them, as he had then thought, on a lark, and he said that should not make any difference to us now, as he intended to spend the rest of his life atoning for that one mistake.

As to living with three different women, he just laughed, said that story probably started as he had been boarding at those places. Then he showed me the letter my mother had written to him. I was stunned. I knew it was her handwriting. In a way she only wrote the truth. Still it was a masterpiece of mischief and trouble making. Really he could hardly have come to our house after that. Well, he said he would go with me to California; we would start a new life together in the new country. I could come home after a while and tell my parents I was happy and they would forgive us. I could either go back to him in California or if I would rather live near my parents, he would come out here. I could choose where I wanted to live. I told him I could not live with him without being married to him. He said he would not expect me to.

173

Through Sophie's Eyes

We would get married in Chicago. So we arranged everything. Monday I was to take the train to Oneida Castle instead of Oneida. There I would take the West Shore to Syracuse. He would leave Oneida on the Central for Syracuse. There we would meet, take a train for Buffalo, from there to Chicago. The next day, Saturday, I went about my usual Saturday cleaning up, the same as I had done for so many years. Once in a while I felt a little tug at my heart. Would I ever handle those little household goods again? My father went up to see Mr. Reamore. He hired him to come Monday morning to take me to the North Bay Depot to take the eight o'clock train. My father never liked to drive a horse. Besides, the snow was quite deep. Mr. Reamore would bring a young, strong team.

Both my parents were going to accompany me as far as North Bay. Sunday my dear sweet mother and I packed my new leather suitcase very carefully. Also an alligator skin satchel I had been given in New York some years before. In those days, women only carried very small purses, or handbags, not the giant ones of later years.

In the afternoon, I went out to say farewell to each cow, also my horse, Billy. I had ridden, drove and worked him for nine years. I glanced at my saddle, harness, and buggy. I went into the hen house. How the hens and ducks came to meet me. In the house our four cats followed me around, kept looking at me and meowed. It reminded me of the way our other cats had acted the morning of each operation. That evening my mother followed me upstairs, sat on the edge of my bed a long time. She tried to be cheerful, but I knew her heart was heavy and very sad.

At last she went down, but I could not sleep. I lay there in the silent darkness for many hours. All at once I woke up after a short nap and heard my father and mother talking downstairs. I got up and went down. It was five o'clock. My dear mother was preparing a regular feast for my last breakfast, I who always ate a very late breakfast and then only a light one.

Well, somehow the time went by. At seven-thirty, Mr. Reamore came with his lively team. I can still see my father and mother as they stood close together on that cold snowy platform of the little Depot that dark morning of January the eighth, waving to me till they looked like two black specks and my train had gone around the bend.

At Oneida Castle, I did not have long to wait, but when I got to Syracuse, I found I would have to wait three long hours before I could take a train to Buffalo. I felt much alone, though so many people were rushing about. An hour dragged itself by, then another hour. Did he lie to me?

Another half hour, then as a train pulled in again there he was. He rushed me into the nearby restaurant, said he had not yet had his breakfast. For me, it was an early dinner. At last we were on the train, his arm about my shoulders, and what guilt I had felt vanished. I felt quite happy. Was it not my life I was to choose and lead?

It was long after dark before we reached Buffalo. Again a long stretch of time lay before us before our train, on the Wabash, was to take us to Chicago. First we went to a restaurant for a full meal, and back to the large waiting room where we chose a seat as far back as possible from the main rush of traffic, also more away from the glare of the many bright lights. We sat close together watching the ever changing crowds come and go.

There was a middle-aged man who we noticed passed by us a number of times. He kept looking at both of us, but more at me. I paid no attention to him; I had other things to think about. Charlie said to me in a low voice, "Do you know that man? He seems to know you." I told him that I had never seen him before.

It was after eight o'clock when we left for Chicago. We were told that the train would arrive there the next day about one in the afternoon. After we were comfortably seated, all at once that same man passed through the aisle, again looking at me. About every hour or two he would do the same. We hardly slept at all, just a short nap now and then. Came morning, daylight, no snow on the ground. We stopped for half an hour at a railroad restaurant for breakfast, and just as we sat down at a little table, that same man came direct to us and asked me if my father's name was Otto Kussmaul, if I was his daughter, and if my name was Sophie Kussmaul. Of course I said yes. Then he said, "Who is this man here with you?" Before I could answer, Charlie Spear spoke up. "My name is Spear, Charles Spear, and this lady is my wife. We are on our wedding trip to California." Well, the man told us that he had been born and brought up at North Bay. His name was Seff Dickonson, a brother to Jay Dickonson. That he had known my father very well, but for the last twenty years had lived in Chicago. He had been out to his brother's for the holidays then stopped off at Buffalo for a few days to visit with some friends, now was going back to his home in Chicago. He said that on some of his visits to North Bay he had seen me with my father and that I was the very picture of him. He wished us good luck and went his way.

Well, we both thought that this man would probably not return to North Bay for years and if he did, would have forgotten to say anything about seeing us together. At one o'clock we pulled into Chicago, registered as man and wife at a near by hotel and left our luggage there. Then we went and had dinner, and from there to a drugstore to look at the City directory. We found the names of a number of ministers, chose a Methodist minister by the name of John Thompson on Locust Avenue. We went there, found him at home, told him we wanted to get married. He said we would have to have a marriage license. They were just starting that then. I stayed at the parsonage with his wife and daughter. He and Charlie went after the license. They seemed gone a long time, came back, and we were married.

The minister's wife and daughter were our witnesses. I felt better then. I thought, Charlie really kept his word. By this time it was quite late. We went to a theatre. Back to our room at eleven o'clock. We made up our minds to stay in Chicago a day or two to rest.

I will not describe the things we saw in Chicago, but I think I liked the large zoo at the Lincoln Park the best of anything I saw. On the morning of the twelfth of January, I bought my nine months ticket. Charlie bought one to Sacramento, California. We took our seats on the Union Pacific at eight o'clock in the morning.

I want to show the difference of those days and now regarding travel. This road was considered First Class, but it took us five days and five nights to reach Salt Lake City. There were always and forever little things to delay us. Once our giant locomotive broke down. It took over half a day to send for another one. Once the track was tore up, they had to send a hundred miles for a gang of workmen, and so it was about nine o'clock at night when we reached Salt Lake City. I was half dead for want of sleep, as I could not sleep on the train. Charlie, too, was good and tired. We went to a restaurant, had a good supper, then to a nearby hotel, and took a room for three days and nights, of course paying in advance.

We did not get up until noon the next day. Eating, sleeping and sightseeing. We explored the Mormon Temple, the Mormon Tabernacle, the Beehive, and some other things in the city. One day we spent on the shores of the Great Salt Lake. Everything went on very smoothly. Charlie was always polite to me. I could find no fault about him. Still I felt no real love for him. I was very proud of him, he was so handsome, so attractive, but I also felt that he had no real love for me. We went to the same restaurant we had gone to for the last supper there. We were going on to Sacramento in the morning.

While we were finishing our supper, we saw two men enter the restaurant, one a policeman in uniform. Of course that meant nothing to me, but I noticed Charlie turned deathly pale, acted nervous. The men gave a quick glance around the restaurant. There were about fifteen to twenty people scattered about at the various tables. Their glance rested on us. Then they went to the desk where the meal checks were paid, talked to the man there. He, too, looked towards us. Then they came direct to our table, asked Charlie if his name was Charles Raymond Spear. Poor Charlie. I did feel sorry for him. His face turned to an ashen pallor. Of course, he admitted his name. One of the officers put his hand on Charlie's shoulder and said, "You are under arrest." They wanted to know who I was, and so on. Then Charlie did one nice thing--he said I was absolutely innocent, to let me go free. He begged them to let him get his suitcase. They consented. They walked one on each side of Charlie to our hotel room. I followed meekly behind. One of the officers drew a pistol, stood guard. The other one opened and examined his things in the suitcase. They said he could keep it. Then they went through my two bags. They, too, were okay.

Before they left, they examined our bed to see, I suppose, if there were any weapons hid in it. They assured me that I was perfectly free, as my husband would have to serve from ten to fifteen years for a few other things after they got him back to New York State. We said goodbye to one another; he was marched off with the officers. I never saw him again.

Then a very strange thing happened. I, who never could sleep after the least excitement, went to bed and slept soundly till morning. I was afraid on leaving the hotel that all the employees would stare at me. But to my great relief no one did. I think the reason was that all the night help had been changed to the day shift help. I took my baggage straight to the Depot and ate breakfast in the adjoining room. I did not dare go back to the restaurant where my Charlie had got nabbed.

Now before I had left my home, I obtained an address of a man we had well known, a Mr. Higgins. He was now married and lived on M Street in Sacramento, California. I had intended to hunt him up, and if I could arrange it, board with his wife for a while, or they might find me a good decent place to board for a few weeks. Of course this was before I met Charlie that fateful day in Oneida.

I had sent Post Cards and a couple of letters home, just signing myself Sophie. Before leaving home, we had made arrangements that my parents would write me at Sacramento, California, General Delivery. After two days and one night I arrived at Sacramento just before dark. The scenery was gorgeous. I will describe it in my book of travels which I intend to write.

I had no trouble finding these people. Mr. Higgins was overjoyed to see some one from his old home. I think he asked me about every one for miles around. Mrs. Higgins was a friendly little woman. They had three little boys. I boarded with them for two weeks. When Mrs. Higgins had the time, she showed me around the city, but most of the time I strolled around by myself. I spent hours each day in the park. The thing that impressed me most was an old Fort. That Fort was built a few years before the great gold rush of 49. At that time, Sacramento was just a little settlement. The old Fort was built of very large logs. Everything was still intact, exactly as it was when used so many years before. The Fort, all the block houses, and the high stockade. Inside were almost countless Indian relics. Also the first prairie schooner that had ever crossed the vast plains. I spent a couple of days looking over this Fort.

After two weeks I started for San Francisco. Of course I did not tell the Higgins family about my little marriage adventure. I left on an early train and arrived at the Bay of San Francisco. There I had to take a ferry boat to cross the ten mile bay. That was over thirty years before the great bridge was built. When I arrived there, there were about a dozen cabs, sent there by the different hotels. Mr. Higgins had given me the name of a good, comparatively cheap hotel. I forget the name. So I took the cab there and paid for a room for three days. After dinner there, I took a trolley to go to the Golden Gate Park, of which I had heard so much.

I had not been in the park over ten minutes when I saw by far the largest greenhouse I had ever seen. It truly was immense. It must have been at least thirty feet high, as big tropical trees grew in that house. So long and wide that I almost thought I was dreaming. Of course I went into it. There was a rich perfume everywhere and such masses of flowers as I had never imagined could grow. I saw begonias whose leaves were over two feet long and eighteen inches across. To my surprise the place was almost deserted.

There was a large fountain raised a few feet on a sort of mound. All around it, steeply sloping down, was cement, and forming a ring just below this was a little tiny gutter to catch the overflow of the spray on this cement. Most of the spray of the fountain fell back into the vast basin below it. This outside cement was terribly slippery. No one was ever supposed to venture on it. Well, I stood there staring at the fountain. The thing that fascinated me the most was this--the fountain shone and shimmered with all the colors of a rainbow.

From gold to silver, from blue to pink, from green to purple, forever changing. So I tried to solve the mystery. I had always been, and still am, sure on my feet, so I took a few quick steps up that steeply slanting wet cement so I could peer into the fountain. Now just how this all happened I never knew, but I fell down on both knees with such force that for a few moments I felt sure that both my legs were broken.

Never had I felt such pain before. Then this thought entered my mind. Here I am nearly four thousand miles from home with two broken legs. Then the pain, though still terrible, let up just a little bit. I tried to move one of my feet. Yes, I could move it a little. Then I tried to move the other one. Yes, with great pains shooting down to my very toes, up to my hips, I could move my legs. Oh, I was so glad. I looked ahead of me. There was no one in sight. Oh, yes, about a hundred feet ahead of me, I saw two men at work amongst the tall plants. They were so far away I could not call to them. I put both my hands on the wet cement and tried to raise myself up. The pain made me weak, and faint. All at once, I heard a very pleasant voice say to me, from behind, "Can I assist you to your feet?" I nodded my head and a pair of strong arms took hold of me under my arms and raised me up on my feet. I could stand up.

Of course I could not see this man as he was still behind me, but he pointed to a small bench about twelve feet away and almost hidden by masses of pink roses. He still had a firm, but gentle hold of me. He said, "Do you think you could walk to that bench with my help?" I nodded my head again, and gently he helped me to it, sat down beside me. The pain, though letting up a little, was still so severe I had not yet looked up at the man or spoken a word to him.

Then he said, in his gentle voice, "If you will give me your address, I will go and get a cab to send you home." Then for the first time, I looked up at him and spoke. I saw a medium-sized man, mild, black eyes, hair that was so dark brown it could have been called black, and a rather handsome, but very good looking face one could trust. I told him he could not send me home as I lived nearly four thousand miles away. He was surprised. Then he offered to get a conveyance to take me to a hospital. I decidedly objected to that. In those days women all wore long skirts. But weak and faint as I felt, I was determined to see for myself. So I lifted my heavy skirt, folded it across my lap, and behold, both my knees were just a bloody mass. There did not seem to be a bit of skin left on them. Neither was there any of the stocking left. I mean covering the entire place of the knee. It surely looked sickening.

I had always trained myself not to cry or make a fuss. I dropped my skirt again. The man beside me jumped up and said, "Wait here for me. I am going to get a cab and take you to a first aid. There is one on Market Street connected with a drug store." He was off. Well, there was not much chance of my running off. I was much better, but still in great pain. About twenty minutes later, I heard the rattle of wheels. A cab drawn by a gray horse drove up to a door quite close to where I was sitting.

My new but unknown benefactor ran in to where I was, gently helped me on my feet, and half carried me out into the cab. It was really only a short drive to the drug store on Market Street, one door of which had a First Aid sign. It must be that the nurses had been told of my coming. They at once put me in a comfortable easy chair, and without asking any questions went to work on my knees. First they sponged them off carefully, then put some kind of powder, then oil on them. Just when they were bandaging them up, the man reappeared. He had vanished after I entered that First Aid room. He handed one of the nurses a tiny package, saying, "The lady needs these stockings." I did not seem surprised. It seemed quite natural.

Sophie Kussmaul

One of the nurses took off what was left of my stockings and put on the new ones, a much better pair than I had before. But she insisted on fastening them below my knees, said it would irritate them even over the bandages. All my life I had always pulled them over my knees, and there wore a tight round elastic. I do not know if the man paid for this treatment or not. He gently helped me up and took me to the other part of the drugstore. There he ordered two ice cream sodas. After that he asked me if I felt able to go back to the park. I said I did. He again called a cab, and we entered the park at a different street. We walked a little ways, then sat on a bench under a large palm tree.

He said to me, "We can not do much walking today. We will have to sit down most of the time." Then we started to get acquainted. He asked me a lot of questions--how I happened to have come so far from my home, if I intended to stay here, if I had brothers and sisters, what kind of a town I had lived in, and so on. I told him the exact truth about everything. That since my earliest recollection, I had had such an intense longing to go west and particularly to California. I did not lie to him in anyway whatsoever. But I did not mention my little marriage adventure from Chicago.

Right here I want to explain a little matter. Just before we hunted up the Minister to marry us in Chicago, we went into a jewelry shop and bought a wedding ring. Oh, how proud I was when Charlie slipped it on my finger after the minister had pronounced us man and wife. How proud of it I had been until that fateful night at Salt Lake City. Still, I would have worn it until I came home, but as I intended to go to the Higgins I knew it might seem strange to them, as of course I would go there as Sophie Kussmaul. So the next morning, before leaving Salt Lake City, I sewed up my ring in the little bag in which I carried my money, all but a little change. This bag I wore next to my body, fastened to my underclothes.

I told him my name and exact age; then he told me about himself. I knew I felt that he was telling me the truth. This was his story. He had been born, educated, and raised in England. They were neither rich nor poor, but managed to keep two servants. When he was twelve years old, his father died. After that, they only kept one, the cook. He was an only child. At sixteen, his mother also passed away. Then he went to live with his mother's sister and her husband. He continued on with his school. When he had finished his education, he accompanied his uncle and aunt to Canada. He arrived there the day he was twenty-one. Soon after he joined the Mounted Police. At twenty-five, his aunt died and as he had never liked the bitter cold winters in Canada, he had come to San Francisco on his own. He said he had been very fortunate, found employment in a paper mill after being in the city less than a week. He said he was still in the same mill. His name was Ernest Galway and his age was twenty-nine. He said although he had worked there about three and a half years, he had never taken a vacation. But he had made up his mind that he would now take a months vacation.

He said that he had always wanted to explore the park, but so far never had seen much of it. The Golden Gate Park covers over one thousand acres. I asked him how long he had now spent in the park. He laughed and said he had not been in it over ten minutes when he found me. Well, we would walk a little, then sit down again. As proof to what he had told me, he showed me pictures of his English home, school reports from his professors, pictures of himself as a Mounted Policeman. Many, many check slips from the paper-mill. At half past five, I said I wanted to get back to my hotel. He jumped up and said we must first eat our supper. We walked slowly to Market Street. Went into a good restaurant and he told me to order anything I liked. Well I was going to be modest; still I got a good meal.

He accompanied me on my trolley trip to my hotel. Then he asked me when I got up in the morning. I said about seven o'clock. He said not to order breakfast, he would be waiting for me in the lobby, then we could go to a quiet little place, eat together, and then to the Park.

I slept real well, but when I woke up and tried to move, my legs were so lame and sore I thought I could not walk on them. But after I got up and washed and dressed myself, I got along all right. I came downstairs. Yes, there he was. Seemed glad to see me. We took a trolley, went to a little eating place, again took the trolley to the park.

I will not describe the wondrous beauty of that famous park here. That, too, will have to wait. But I feel that I want to put one thing into this story. Every once in a while we would come to a beautiful white statue. Some of them presented figures out of mythology, others just perhaps an angel, a horse, a lion, and so on. I saw them with the eyes of youth. To me they all seemed chiseled out of pure white marble. The sun shone on them so brightly, they were glistening and gleaming. Twenty-five years later, I was again walking in that park

with my first grandchild, little Joe, on my arms. I saw that instead of
marble, they were carved out of wood and badly in need of paint.

Chapter 19

After lunch we strolled up the Strawberry Hill, a little eminence in the park. There Ernest asked me to marry him. He told me he was not a rich man. He had been putting by a little money each month and had a good job. He told me he could provide me with a good comfortable home, but I would have to do my own housework.

I would have to be alone most all day, but we could spend our Sundays together. I knew he was sincere. I told him I liked him enough to marry him, but I had started out to make this trip and I wanted to finish it, but if he cared enough for me to come after me when I got home, I would be willing to marry him. He was well pleased and satisfied, even said he respected me for wanting to be married at my parents' home. Well, about three o'clock we left the park. Ernest insisted on my going back to the First Aid place to have my knees redressed.

Then we looked for an engagement ring. We went to a number of jewelers on Market Street before I found just what I liked. Of course there were dozens of exquisite diamond rings, but they were all very expensive. At last I found a gold ring set with three pearls and quite a large green emerald in the center. The ring was a perfect fit.

Ernest put the ring on my finger, then kissed my rather brown finger and said, right there in the jewelry store, "My little Indian princess." I had never been called that before. It made me very happy. That night we went to a theatre. Next morning again he was waiting for me. Another happy day at the park.

Now I will relate something in this story which will condemn me in the eyes of the world. But I said in the beginning of this book that I would give the full and true story of my life here. So far, I have. Every detail, every date, every name of any person or place I have mentioned was always their real names. So I will continue to tell the truth, no matter what the world may think of me. Furthermore, I will shock whoever reads these pages more yet, for I will say that I am glad for what I did. I never regretted it. Yes, even now, after thirty-nine years, I still say that I am glad. I will also say this--that I was as much to blame, if there was anything wrong done, as Ernest Galway. I will also say that up to now no one ever knew about this chapter of my life--not even my only daughter, in whom I confide a lot more of my life than I ever did to my mother or any of my husbands. Well, here is the story.

I knew Ernest loved me in a clean, honest way. He told me that he had never been with a girl or woman in a sexual way. This I found out to be true after our first night together. I, too, loved him and was nearly four thousand miles from home. I had been married or I would not have gone into this. I will here again say that he did not persuade or talk me into this. I had left home with the intention of enjoying a honeymoon, so why not have one. So we agreed that I could stay in Frisco as long as I choose. He had a month that was his own. So we decided to take a room somewhere for our nights together. Our days we would spend mostly in the park and some of them on the Pacific beach.

He told me he could not take me to his room as his landlady was a very strict woman. He would tell her that he would be absent for a month on a vacation, but to hold his room for him. I found out later on that all this was true. Well, I got my baggage; we rented a room with a private bathroom. Then I spent the happiest month of my entire life, before or after. Of course, there had been very happy days, but never a whole month of absolute love and contented happiness. I felt safe, I mean about this. In the first place, Ernest had faithfully promised that if I should find myself in the family way, to send him a telegram at once from wherever I might be, and he would take a train the same day, come to me, and marry me. I knew he was sincere about this. Besides, I thought if he should fail me, all I would have to do was to show my marriage certificate and put on my wedding ring again.

I knew then and I know now that the angels in heaven looking down on us sanctioned what we did. This man was my perfect mate in every way. He was willing to come to my home, either get work in a near by town or, if I would rather, buy a small farm near my old home.

Of course I did not love him the way I had loved Joe Henry. That love was not just of this earth, it was sublime. And I knew even then that never again would I taste such blissful glory. The feeling I had had for Wilbur Henderson was different too. I knew he was a good man; I respected him and could easily have learned to love him. As to Charles Spear, I was fascinated with him, proud of him. He was so handsome, so well polished, so polite. I admit in a way I loved him. But even from the first, once in a while I felt that there was something wrong.

But this man and I seemed just to belong to each other. I really felt much more married to him than I had to Charles Spear, though a Minister of the Gospel had really married us.

The Golden Gate Park seemed like Eden to us. Almost every night after our supper, we went to a theatre, once in a while after the theatre to a night club. There again we ate and drank good wine and listened to the music. I had seen and been on the Atlantic Ocean a number of times, but it had always looked cold and dark and somber, unfriendly. So when Ernest proposed one morning that we spend the day on the beach, I was a little disappointed, but said nothing. But when I beheld the ocean, I truly was surprised. We walked and sat in the warm, clean sand for hours. I would gaze at the immensity of the waters before me. All ashimmer in green and silver, flecked with the sun's golden rays. When the tide went out, we would walk on the still wet, but hard sands, looking for shells. Then again, sit down and gaze over the vastness of the waters. Far, far off toward the skyline would appear a faint puff of smoke, or was it just a delusion of the eye. Yes, there it was again, then nothing more, again it came, and so after perhaps twenty minutes of uncertainty, there it was, blacker, bigger, and soon afterwards there appeared a dark dot of something under the smoke. Slowly, steadily, it grew in size and shape till it formed itself into a mighty ship.

Somehow a great joy would come over me when the enormous ship with its cargo of human freight, which had come from so far and far away, over the deep depths of the almost endless wastes of the waters, had arrived safe in the harbor. Again over the shimmering waters, away off, would appear, disappear, appear again a white speck on the skyline. That, too, seemed to play hide and seek in the distance till after a while it came nearer and nearer. It was the sail of a sailing vessel. Like the wings of a great bird, it brought its ship safe into the harbor.

Sometimes we would watch a great steamer getting ready to leave. Hundreds of people would go aboard; others would come to see them off. At last with flags and music of the ship's band playing, the ship would start on its trackless way to somewhere. There was always a tiny tug at my heart to see them go, get smaller and smaller and finally vanish from sight as the distance swallowed them up.

Well, we spent five days of our golden month on the beach. One day we had dinner at the famous Cliff House. Soon, too soon, this month passed by. Our last day spent in the Golden Gate Park had come. Our last night together. First we went to the theatre and after, not to a noisy night club, too many people, too much noise. We went to a quiet little drinking place, ate a lunch, and sipped wine. Neither one of us spoke much. Then came the last drink. We clicked our glasses together; Earnest said, to meet again in Frisco. Why I answered the way I did, I never knew, but I said, "To meet again in heaven." Then slowly, arm in arm, we walked to our little room.

Now before I go on with this story, I want to relate a queer circumstance. San Francisco is noted for its foggy and rainy winter season all through the months of January, February, and March, but during the five weeks I spent there, there was not one hour of fog, nor a drop of rain. From sunrise to sunset, golden sunshine. At night the heavens gleamed and sparkled with thousands of bright stars. Wherever we went, we heard people remark about this. Even the oldest residents had never before experienced such a perfect winter.

Well, I will skip the sadness of our parting. Next morning my train left for Los Angeles. Shortly after six o'clock, Ernest went with me to see me off, then to his job at the paper mill. When I left Sacramento, I gave orders at the Post Office to hold my mail until I sent them a new address. So I had not received any letters from home in a little over five weeks. About ten days before I left San Francisco, I wrote to the Sacramento Post Office and had them send on my mail to Los Angeles. Of course I also wrote to Los Angeles Post Office to hold all my mail there until I called for it. I wrote two letters a week to my mother while in Frisco, besides sending home Post Cards. My train was due to arrive in Los Angeles that night soon after ten o'clock, but on account of a washout on the track we were delayed and never pulled into Los Angeles until eight o'clock next morning.

This was March the ninth. I got a room and then found my way to the Post Office. There were seven letters from my dear mother and to my surprise a letter from Charles Estey. My mother wrote and said he wanted my address. Well I did not bother to write a letter back to him, but sent him a picture Post Card. I read all my dear mother's letters according to the dates. How lovingly she wrote to me. All the simple little happenings at home touched my heart. I was beginning to feel homesick. She said the cats all missed me so much, especially Blacky. She would look for me everywhere. Well, I wrote her a long letter, told her I had just that day arrived in Los Angeles.

I also wrote to Ernest. Mailed them, ate supper and went to bed at eight o'clock. The last night in Frisco, I had only slept a few hours and last night on the train, had never closed my eyes. The next day I never got up until noon, ate, went to a little park, then by trolley to the Post Office. There I found a long letter from Ernest, he missed me so. He told me that he had confided to his landlady about meeting me on his vacation, but of course not that we had been living together, and that we were now engaged to be married. That he was coming to New York State after me some time in the spring. He told me he had to tell someone, and that this woman seemed almost like a mother to him.

The next few days I spent resting up. I would go to bed at seven or eight at night, get up at about ten next the morning. Eat, rest in the park, eat, take a trolley down to the big Post Office, rest in the park, eat supper and again go to bed. After a while I spent three days doing my duty. I mean by this that different people at home had given me addresses of their relatives living in Los Angeles. They wanted me to hunt them up and carry them some messages. So I spent nearly a whole day looking up and finding George Vericn's daughter.

She was married and seemed much pleased to see someone from her old home at North Bay. I stayed there for quite a few hours. Next day I went on the hunt for a cousin of Annie Wright. This time, quite a ways out of the city. Next day I sought and found George White's sister right in the very heart and noise of the city. Then I spent a few days sightseeing. I will only mention here a few of the things I saw and did.

I took a trip a few miles out of the city and visited a bamboo farm. They raised many acres of bamboo, and in nearby shops manufactured it into light furniture. I would have loved to buy some to bring home, but how could I get it over thousands of miles. I also visited a broom corn ranch. They shipped thousands of bales of broom corn all over the States to be made up into brooms. One day I went to see a pineapple plantation. I spent some time on Spring Street and bought quite a few souvenirs to bring home. One day I took a trip to the lovely Pasadena. Of course Los Angeles was less than half as large a city then as now.

On the nineteenth of March, I really began to feel homesick. I wanted to see and feel our own home springtime. A great longing came over me to go back home. Then, too, I was thinking, Ernest would come to me. Yes, I would start and by easy stages travel homeward. So I made my last trip to the post office, gave orders to send all my mail on to Denver, Colorado, and wrote to Denver to hold my mail there. It was quite late when I got back to my room. I carefully packed all my belongings so all I would have to do in the morning was to wash and dress, pay my bill, leave the key, and go my way. Just before I went to bed, I looked at my timetable. I found out that a train would leave Los Angeles at eight fifteen.

So I made up my mind to get up early as to have plenty of time. I forgot to mention that when I arrived in Los Angeles at the great big railroad station in the heart of the city, I took a trolley that would take me to a suburb to a small, quiet hotel well out of the city. So of course I took it for granted that I would have to go back to that station to resume my travels.

Next morning I was up at five. Before six o'clock I was in the little restaurant in which I had eaten most of my meals since I had come to Los Angeles. The same pleasant waitress was there who had always waited on me in the forenoon. I was so early that I happened to be the first and only customer, so after she had served me, she sat down at my table. Seeing my baggage, she asked me if I was leaving. I told her I was leaving for the east and going by way of Salt Lake City, that I was going downtown to take a train at San Pedro Station. She looked at me surprised and told me the San Pedro Station was not downtown. In fact, she laughed and said it really was out in the desert.

Then she carefully explained to me that they had just opened up a new road, and that it led directly out of the city into the vastness of the desert, that it really was more of a trail than a road. But as Los Angeles was growing so rapidly, expanding all the time, it would probably not be long before that new section would be developed. But as yet, she said, it was only a lonely trail leading to a tiny station. I listened and was very thankful in the first place, that she had saved me from taking the long trolley trip back into the noisy city, which I always hated, and in the second place for telling me about getting to the little quiet station. She fully gave me the right directions. I was to go up one block, turn to my right, there would only be a few more houses, then no more pavement, just an open road. When within half a mile of the station, there would be a gentle rise of the ground, on the top of which was a rather high wooden bridge over a river. I think this was the San Pedro River. Then just a few hundred yards further on was the tiny depot.

I thanked her and was on the point of picking up my bags when she said I would have to take a cab, as it was three miles out there, and not one house on the entire road where I could stop and rest. I glanced at my watch. It was not quite half past six yet. Why I would have nearly two hours to make it in.

My baggage was not too heavy; I would walk. It was a perfect morning, beautiful bright early sunshine, a clear blue sky. I would enjoy that walk. I easily found the direct road. Yes, it really was just a wagon trail. After I had walked about half a mile, I saw ahead of me what looked to be dozens and dozens of tiny houses and tents. I was puzzled, the waitress had positively told me that there was not a single house on that three mile stretch from the city to the little station. Another half mile and now I could clearly see what those little houses were. They were covered wagons, dozens of them. Also many, many small tents. Now here and there the smoke from a campfire. As I came to the edge of the encampment, I found that they were Gypsies. But the vast camp seemed so quiet. Only a few old women were about, busy over the little fires cooking breakfast. Here and there, there were a few half naked children. Where were all their horses?

I walked a mile further on and I spied way off in another direction a large herd of horses grazing on a green looking stretch of ground. Near the road and camp, the desert ground was all bare and brown. Now I came to the rise of land, no hill, just an elevation of the ground. When I reached the summit, there before me was the rather high wooden bridge. When I got to the highest part of the bridge, I stopped. Just as the waitress had told me, there only a few hundred yards ahead was a very small railroad station.

It really was much smaller than our station at North Bay. I gazed down at the little river, perhaps fifteen feet below. Although it was such a small stream, in the middle it looked quite deep and swift. Well, I picked up my baggage again and went to the little railroad station. There was not a soul there. I glanced at the clock. It was just twenty minutes to eight. I got my long ticket out, gave it to the station master to stamp, told him I wanted to go to Denver, Colorado, by way of Salt Lake City.

Although I had bought a nine month ticket in Chicago, I would have to get it stamped every time I stopped off, or rather every time I resumed my journey, with the date I restarted. And if for any reason I did not use it the day it was stamped, the entire ticket would be void.

He handed it back to me, stamped. I said to him, "So the train will leave for Salt Lake City at eight fifteen?"

He answered, "Yes, eight fifteen tonight." I said, "Tonight?" He again said, pointing at the timetable, "Eight fifteen p.m." Then I glanced at my own timetable. Yes, he was right. In my haste the night before, I had not stopped to see if it was eight fifteen a.m. or p.m. Well, this was a nice situation. My ticket must be used today or I would lose the entire value of it. Not a house in sight. Why, I could not even buy myself a lunch. Here I would be stranded for twelve and a half hours. Then a bright idea flashed through my mind. I would check my baggage and go back to the city for the day. So I started walking back. Oh, how lovely the desert looked.

Every little while I would stop to inhale the pure desert air. When I got back to the Gypsy camp, there were a great many more people stirring about. Some of the women asked me if I wanted my fortune told. I just shook my head and passed on. After a while I was again out in the open.

I entered the city and wondered just how to spend the day. I could not go back to my hotel room as I had paid and left that morning. It would be folly to rent a room for a few hours. I could sit in the little park, go twice to a restaurant, and walk about. Anything would be better than to stay at the station not even able to buy food. I had hardly got to the city when I saw a boy coming toward me with his arms piled high with circulars which he was handing to every one he met. He pushed one into my hand. I was just going to drop it without even looking at it. I thought it was advertising some sale, such as furniture, or clothing. But I did happen to glance at the heading. It was advertising an eighty mile sightseeing trip along the coast in observation cars.

These cars are just open trolley cars. The trip would include stopping at Venice, Santa Monica, a famous rose garden even in this land of roses, a visit to a private museum open to the public for this one day, an art gallery, and a stop on a beach famous for finding moonstones and fine shells. There also were some other interesting stops to be made. The entire trip, including all these stops, only cost one dollar. Of course the luncheon stops, at twelve and five o'clock, were not included. But oh, how I wanted to take in this trip. To my joy, I saw the time they were to be back at the starting point was six o'clock. That would give me plenty of time to get to the little station before dark. They were to start at nine fifteen. It was already nine ten. I asked someone from where we were to start. I was told it was only about a block, but I should hurry.

Well, I did. There were five open cars. They were just ready to leave, but I got on the last one in time. Nothing could have been more beautiful. We were on our way back when, to my horror, I saw the sun setting, and I knew we were still many miles from Los Angeles. All at once the car seemed just to crawl along. Yes, it was now six thirty and getting dusk; seven o'clock, seven fifteen, and still not in the city. I thought about my ticket. Seven thirty, we arrived at our starting point. Three miles to make in three quarters of an hour. Well, I would take a cab. I inquired where I could get one and no one seemed to know. Someone said I might get one by walking a few blocks toward the city. Of course that would take me further and further away from my depot. Now it was twenty minutes to eight. I would walk. I half ran. The streets were lit up as bright as day. Then I came into the open country. No lights, and how dark it seemed after the brilliantly lit up city. Not even a moon. I could hardly find the trail. I really felt it more with my feet, then saw it.

I could not run, or I would fall down on the rough road. I walked fast, fast. Then I saw the red glow in the sky from the Gypsy campfires, then the campfires themselves. I felt glad. They seemed like a beacon to me. I remembered the friendly looks they had given me in the morning. On I hurried, breathing hard. I knew the camp was about halfway from the city to the depot. Could I hold out? My heart was pounding. I almost ran. Then I came to the camp. But, oh what a difference from morning. There were hundreds of Gypsies now. How they all stared at me. A group of five or six young, husky men would stare at me, then give a shrill whistle, and I would see another bunch step out of the darkness from somewhere ahead. The road itself through the camp was all lit up, bright campfires and swinging lanterns. The further I got, the more Gypsies I saw.

Sometimes fifteen or twenty, mostly men, would follow me. Then they would call to some others ahead. I knew there was no use for me to turn back; it was just as far back to the city as to the depot. I admit I was frightened. I heard later on that there were over one thousand Gypsies in that camp. Lucky, I did not have much to carry, just my little purse and a small box of seashells I had picked up that day.

A new terror came over me. For the first time it came to me that I wore two good rings, a gold chain around my neck with a gold watch. Although I only had a few dollars in my purse, they might think I had a lot of money. On I went, faster and faster. At last I got out of their camp. Then the road looked darker than ever. I knew I still had over a mile to make. The noise from the camp died down, but a new and awful terror came over me. I heard a man walking behind me, but I dared not look around. I tried to walk still faster. I could hear my heart pounding. I could also hear the man's footsteps. When I walked extra fast, so did he; when I slacked up a little, so did the footsteps behind me. I expected every moment that he would either grab me or stick a knife in me.

I recalled every horrible murder I had ever heard or read about. Again I tried to increase my speed. What would he do? How would he kill me? On, on I hurried. I came to the rise in the road that made me breath still harder. I felt I would drop, but on I went. I reached the wooden bridge. Just a little ways behind me, I heard that steady tap, tap of his steps on the wooden bridge.

All at once a new horror came over me. I thought I now knew why he had put off killing me. He would wait till I got to the highest part of the bridge, rob me, kill me, and throw me in the swiftly running stream. In desperation I made one more effort to speed up my steps. Oh, now that I reached the height of the bridge, I saw the light of the little station. I was going downgrade, still I heard the steady tap, tap behind me. Now I was off the bridge, only about two hundred yards more, then safety. I tried to run, the footsteps ceased. Somehow I got to the depot. There were about ten or twelve people in the tiny waiting room. How they all stared at me. I glanced at the clock. It was eight fourteen. I rushed to the ticket window and asked the man if the train to Salt Lake City had gone. He said not yet, it would be there in about one minute.

With trembling fingers, I got out my baggage checks. While he handed me my baggage, the train roared in. I grabbed my suitcase, satchel, box of shells, purse and staggered out. The conductor gave me one quick glance; then he said to the bystanders that he would have to help this lady in first. He took my suitcase, satchel, and little box in one arm, with the other he half lifted me aboard. Then he put me in the first seat near the door, put my stuff in the rack above my head, looked once more at me and kindly asked if I would be all right. I thanked him and said I would be all right. Everyone stared at me.

All at once I saw myself in a large mirror. My hat was way down on one side of my head. My hair, which I always wore pinned up to my head in coils, was all loose, hanging down over my face, neck and sides in tiny black strands. My entire face and even my throat were fiery red. My black eyes looked shiny black. After a little while I combed my hair and pinned it up again. That made me feel some better. Then I went into the little wash room, washed my face, throat, arms and hands. I began to feel much more like myself again. I took off my shoes. About midnight, we stopped at a small desert restaurant. I was very hungry and ordered a full meal. Here is a queer thing about myself. No matter how tired I am, I cannot go to sleep on a train, bus, or car, not even after going without sleep for two or three nights.

After we were all back on the train, most of the passengers went to sleep. Then all at once a new thought entered my head. Perhaps that man who followed me out of the Gypsy camp meant no harm at all. Maybe he was a white man, perhaps even a policeman, from Los Angeles who thought it was his duty to see that no harm came to me. Anyway I was not molested. Well, I never knew. Then I began to figure. It was twenty minutes to eight when I left the city, fourteen minutes after eight when I arrived at the little station. I covered those three miles in thirty-four minutes, a trifle less than twelve minutes to the mile. I was young, strong, and naturally always quick on my feet, but I do know that I never could have made it if not that fear and desperation had driven me on.

At last dawn broke over the desolation of the desert, then a golden sunrise. I would love to describe the beauties of the desert. My train was supposed to arrive that coming night at nine o'clock at Salt Lake City, but as usual, there were some delays, so we never pulled into Salt Lake City until four o'clock the next morning. That made two days and two nights without a wink of sleep. Added to that, that terrible experience at the Gypsy camp. I felt I must get some rest somewhere. I did not want to go back to the hotel where Charlie Spear and I had stopped. Although I had been perfectly innocent, still if any of the help there would recognize me, they might or probably would link me to that dreadful episode.

I found a small hotel just a little ways from the depot. There I ate a hearty breakfast and went to bed at five o'clock in the morning. I slept until one in the afternoon, ate, took a walk, and also found out that I could either take a train to Denver that night at seven o'clock or one the next morning also at seven o'clock. I decided to wait until morning. I had two reasons for that. The main reason was I knew I was going to travel through some very beautiful mountain scenery. The other reason was I wanted to get thoroughly rested before making another long trip.

All this happened nearly forty years ago and the western railroads were not what they now are. So I took a hot bath and went to my room and bed early, giving orders to be called at six o'clock the next morning. I got a good rest and left Salt Lake City on the twenty-third of March. The scenery was grand and the air so clear a person could easily look off over a hundred miles in any direction.

This was a lovely day's travel, and I was sorry that I had to travel that night and miss seeing so much of that wild rugged country. But I never could describe the glory of the sunrise. How the first golden rays kissed thousands of mountain peaks while the valleys were still in darkness. Some peaks seemed to turn to silver. I rode again all day. We arrived in Denver late that night. I found a hotel and went to bed at twelve o'clock.

Next morning I walked about a few hours. I had intended to hunt up the post office, but somehow did not. Thought I would do so the first thing next morning. In the morning I inquired at my hotel what sights were the most worth seeing. They told me about eight or ten buildings such as churches, a museum, library, and so on. Then they explained to me that in summer, Pikes Peak was the greatest attraction for tourists. But now, there was just one excursion train a week running to the base of the great mountain. There was a good hotel there, where anyone could stay as long as they wanted, or run out of Denver in the morning, eat dinner there, and come back to the city late in the afternoon. They said it happened that this day was the day they ran the excursion train out there and that if I wanted to take in that trip I would have to go in about twenty minutes. Of course I wanted to go, so put off going to the post office one more day.

I shall never forget that day. The weather was perfect. Though the thermometer read only ten above zero, the air was so clear and dry it did not seem any colder than it does in New York State at twenty-five above zero. There were about twenty-five of us on that coach. Never before or since have I come across a bunch of more agreeable people. They were all so jolly, so happy, so homey, that they all seemed much more like friends than strangers. The scenery became more and more lovely at every mile. I was young and strong and in perfect health. Added to all this, my heart was full of joy and happiness. Was I not soon to be back home where a loving father and mother were longingly looking for me? Where soon, very soon, as good and true a man as ever lived was coming over the almost endless miles to claim me for life. Yes, I was very happy that day, the last really happy day I had for many years to come.

The view from the hotel was grand. We had been gently climbing since leaving Denver, and now in the clear dry air, we could see the city of Denver lying below us like a vast picture, and rising seemingly into the sky was the snow covered mountain. Close by the hotel was a small store filled with all kinds of souvenirs from Colorado-- postcards, mining things, gold and silver nuggets, and a thousand other things.

I bought a silver hammer, a small piece of gold, and one of silver ore, an Indian head carved out of bronze, a few real Indian arrowheads carved out of flint, and of course a bunch of postcards. We had a most excellent dinner at the hotel, then about three in the afternoon we went back to Denver. I had been collecting so much stuff I had to go out next morning and buy another satchel. My little pasteboard box with seashells and moonstones was ready to fall to pieces.

Chapter 20

This was the twenty-seventh of March; a day I shall never forget. I joyfully repacked my things. Oh, how I would enjoy to unpack them again when I got home. In the afternoon, I inquired my way to the big post office. At the General Delivery window, I received two letters forwarded from Los Angeles. One was from my mother, but where was Ernest's letter. I saw at a glance that the other letter was not in his handwriting. So far, he had written to me almost daily. I went back to the window and asked the clerk to look once more. No, there was no other letter. I felt hurt, a little bit offended. Well, it was after dark when I got back to my hotel room. Now if I had been like most girls or women, I would have been curious to find out who had written to me from San Francisco besides Ernest. But I think I was born without curiosity.

So I slowly, carefully read my mother's letter first. How loving she wrote to me. I could plainly see between the lines that both my father and mother were very lonely; they were longing to have me home with them again. As I was reading about all the little happenings at home, I, too, was becoming more and more homesick.

Then I picked up the other letter. I cannot give it here word for word, not after nearly forty years, but the meaning of it is still as clear in my mind as it was that night. It was written by Ernest's landlady. She began by telling me that what she had to write to me was very hard for her to do, as she knew it would hurt me terribly, but still it would be better to receive the blow than be kept in ignorance; the suspense would be harder to bear. I had not the slightest idea what she meant. Then she went on to tell me that Ernest Galway had been boarding at her house for

198

three and a half years, that she had kept boarders now for over forty years, but she had never had such a model boarder as Ernest. In fact, she said he seemed just like a son to her. I remembered how Ernest had told me that his landlady seemed almost like a mother to him.

Then she went on to say that in all the long time he boarded there, he had never gone anywhere, never taken a vacation until this winter he took a few days over a month vacation. When he came back, he confided in her that he had met the first and only girl he had ever loved. That he and she had become engaged to be married in the spring. That he was leaving San Francisco just as soon as he got word from his sweetheart that she had arrived at her home in New York State. Why, I thought, this is all good, joyful news. It showed me that Ernest had really told me the truth about everything. Why did she say she knew it would hurt me so much? Then I went on reading. She said there had been a terrible explosion at the paper mill. Well, she was enclosing the piece about it from the San Francisco News. I looked dumbly around, saw no clipping. Then I fumbled in the envelope. Yes, there it was. I pulled it out, scanned hastily through it, and then came the list of the dead. There were six names of those that were instantly killed and there was his name. I can still see it before me. Ernest E. Galway. Then it went on to state that, giving the names of the five others, they all had families to whom the entire city was extending their sympathy. Ernest E. Galway had no known relative. Then came the list of the men injured.

Just how long I sat there, I do not know. At last I went to bed, but not to sleep. I thought I would take the first train to Chicago, and then keep on going straight toward home. Oh, I was longing for my mother. She would understand my grief and comfort me. These were my feverish thoughts during the long, long night. But when morning came, reason also came back to me. I knew my mother would not understand. I could never tell her the whole truth, not ever the fact that we had lived together for a month. I knew her so well that I knew she would condemn me, that in her eyes I had committed an unforgivable sin. If I just told her I had become engaged to a stranger, she would have censored me to have been so unwise and that it was probably much better for me that everything was now all over. It probably saved me from a lot of unhappiness.

No, I could not confide in her. I would have to go on as always and lock my sorrow into my heart. I gave up going home at once. I would stay here a few days longer till the worse was over. I wrote to Mrs. Robert Mason, Ernest's landlady, thanking her for sending me the information. I wrote to my mother telling her not to write again as I would soon be coming home.

For a few days I stayed most of the time in my room. Here at least I could be alone. As much as I loved my mother, I knew unless I went into the woods, I could never be alone to think. If I went upstairs, no matter what she might be working at, she would drop her work and follow me up and say, "My little girlie must not stay up here alone. Come down so we can be together." Now I knew she only did that on account of her great love for me, but I wanted to be alone so I could think.

I stayed on in Denver a few more days. I did not care to go sightseeing. I took long walks in the wonderful clear, bracing, cold air so I would get tired out and be able to obtain some sleep. After a few days, I was getting over the worst of it. I reasoned things out with myself. I would make myself think that after I got home and took up my old life again this one month of perfect happiness would be like a blissful dream to look back to. At least there would not be anyone or anything at home to bring it all back to me daily. I also felt quite confident that my hasty marriage to Charles Spear would never be found out. I would hide both my wedding ring and the really lovely engagement ring from my Ernest and then no one would ever be the wiser.

On the second of April, I made my last trip to the post office and gave orders to forward any mail that might come to me to my home address. Next morning at six o'clock I left for Chicago, arriving there on the fifth of April. How dark, dreary, smokey, and windy the city looked to me. I was all tired out, as I could not get any sleep on my long train journey. I took a room and stayed there until the early morning of April 7. Here my long round trip ticket expired.

I bought a ticket for Buffalo on the Nickel Plate Road. I arrived in Buffalo at eight o'clock at night on the eighth day of April, took a room and left next day at eleven in the forenoon. I had intended not to stop over any more now until I got home, but again we were delayed and our train never pulled into Syracuse till ten o'clock that night. So I had to take a room once more, and on the morning of the ninth of April I left for Oneida. Dear old Oneida. How good it looked to me. Still I felt a strange tug at my heart--memories. The days of my early childhood, when hand in hand with my mother I walked about the streets in wonder. Later on, those heartbreaking trips about my dear mother's operations. Still later on, my many little trips there to do my father's errands. Then the day I met Charlie the first time. Why, I thought, that was just about a year ago. It lagged just a few days of being a year. Still, I had lived a whole lifetime since.

It was only two o'clock and my train on the Ontario and Western would not leave for North Bay until after six o'clock. I carried all my luggage to the depot where I had left my things so many times before. Then I thought I would go to Mrs. Lewis. I would not in any way at all mention Charlie Spear. Still, she might begin talking about him. I felt sure she did not even suspect that we had gotten married. Well, I went there, but the house was all closed up, a sign For Sale on the front door. I was stunned. Her next door neighbor called to me saying Mrs. Lewis had suffered a bad shock in January and went to live with a sister in Rochester. Well, I thought, that ends another chapter of my life.

So I went back slowly to the depot. It seemed as if my train would never come. At last I got to North Bay. I could have easily walked home, but I wanted to get all my baggage home with me so I hired Billy Janes to take me home. Both my parents were so glad to have me back. My father, who never showed his emotions, for once did show me how much he loved me. I really felt like the Prodigal Son. The cats, especially my Blackie, were happy to have me back.

I will go over the next few months. I took up all my old work again. Each day, my parents seemed to outdo themselves to be kind to me. I knew what my father was thinking. He thought now that he had saved me from that bad man, I would never get married to anyone, would always be at home, his little girl.

My mother thought something like now that I had made this trip alone, I was prepared in the years to come to travel about in Europe and there find a good and rich husband.

I must also say this. For the next few weeks after I got home, we had a great many callers. They all wanted to hear about my wonderful trip. In those days, very few people from around here had ever been to California. Charles Estey, too, kept coming quite often. I showed him some of my souvenirs. Well, he was the same as ever, telling me how much he loved me. I used to go to the woods when I saw him come.

So the rest of April, May, June and July passed by, the three of us living together in perfect peace and harmony. Our dear old summer nights spent together on the old verandah. Everything was exactly as it had been in other years, only if possible with more love and consideration shown me. Yes, it was all the same until the second of August.

Now before I go on with this story, I want to mention and explain a few things. I never wrote many letters to my aunt, and I had never told her about my meeting Charles Spear. But after my return home from the west, I wrote and told her about my wonderful trip, nothing more. But I think my mother wrote to her that I had had an unhappy love affair and to forget as much about it as possible I took that trip. None of us ever told our New York friends about my going west. Strange as this may seem, neither my parents, or I think any one else, had ever heard of Charlie Spear's arrest. I suppose the reason was that in the first place he was taken direct to Cortland, not Oneida. In the second place, in and around Oneida, Sylvan Beach, and so on, he was only known as Charlie Sheppard. So if by any chance anyone had read about him, they would not have suspected that Spear and Sheppard were the same man. Never once since I came home did either my father or mother ever allude in any way to Charlie Spear, for which I was truly thankful.

So up to August second, everything went on very smoothly. A typical mid-summer day. The sun rose blood red in a rather hazy blue sky, the air, though sweet and fresh after the cooling night, already had that faint odor of distant smoke, that same haze and smoky atmosphere of that other summer now thirteen years in the past. There was no dew to speak of; still the ground was not parched. I had helped my father do the outdoor chores the same as on that other day. My dear sweet little mother had our breakfast ready. We ate in the old back room.

All was peace and love amongst us. My father said he was going to North Bay as there were a few things he wanted to do there himself. I almost always did our marketing in the village, and if my father went there or any other place, I always took him with the horse as he did not like to hitch up or drive a horse. So I said I would go out and harness Billy. But he said not to, as he would rather walk. Explaining that he wanted one of his shoes fixed and might have to wait there an hour or two. He also had a small iron hook to take to the blacksmiths. There, too, he might have to wait, and on the way home, he wanted to stop in to Londen's and Anchord's. My father very seldom went anywhere to visit, but Mr. Londen and he had been together in the army, and Mr. Anchord had always been ready to help us.

My father told me as he left not to try and do any outdoor work, as it would be a very hot day. I cleaned out our downstairs rooms, and then helped my mother prepare our dinner, as we knew my father would be home at twelve o'clock. We saw him coming. How straight and fast he walked. I felt weak. I too well remembered that when he was very angry, he always straightened up and walked very fast. We put the dinner on the table as he was coming into the house. I shall never forget how he looked. His face was livid with rage; his piercing black eyes fairly glistened. He glared at me like a wild animal, then sat down on the couch near the window. My mother gently told him that dinner was ready on the table. He did not even answer her. She asked him if he was sick. No answer. She said, "Otto, dear, try and drink some tea. That might make you feel a little better." He gave a grunt.

I tried to swallow some dinner, but the food seemed to choke me. All at once, he leaped to his feet, pointing a trembling finger at me, and began to call me all sorts of horrible names. My poor mother looked at us, her face deathly pale. After he had yelled at me till he had to stop for breath, my mother asked him what it was all about. Then he told her that I had lied to them, had deceived them right along, and that I was no longer his daughter. He told her that a man who used to live near North Bay had seen me and a name I cannot write down here on the train together, and that we had brazenly told him that we were on our wedding trip to California. Now that only was partly true. I remembered that Charlie did tell him that, but I had said nothing. My poor mother looked heart broken.

My father raved on, said that when I had promised, after reading that letter from Binghamton, not ever to see this--again that name--man, I had not intended to keep that promise. God knows I did not intend to ever see him again at that time. My father went on to say that I degraded the holy time of the

Christmas week. Then all at once, he said that he knew all about everything. Here he was entirely mistaken. He claimed that he had spent my money and then dropped me. Now the real truth was that I paid for all my fare tickets and Charlie paid for his. The few days we were together in Chicago and Salt Lake City, Charlie paid for our rooms and meals. But I could not say a word. I just had to stand there and take it.

But I was very thankful for one thing. Now I was sure my father did not know about Charlie's arrest. But there was one thing that always puzzled me, and to this day I never found out the true solution. Did my father see this man Dickonson that morning at North Bay or did he hear the news from his brother, Jay Dickonson. I distinctly remember how he had told us on the train that he only came back to his old home town about every two or three years for a short visit. As he had been here for the Christmas holidays, why would he be out here again now in August? Well, perhaps Jay Dickonson had been out to see him in Chicago and brought home the news. I never found this out.

So the days and weeks dragged by. Every time my father came to the house, he would go over the same thing, accuse me of having lied to him, of having run off with--again that name--and having lowered myself and lived with him, adding a dozen or more other things. My mother did not scold and rave the way my father did, but I think the way she went on even hurt me more. She went about with a long, sad face, kept saying to me she was sorry that she had not died during her last operation as that would have saved her all this anguish. Our beautiful evenings on the verandah, as in the old times, my father and mother sat close together, I a little further off in my hammock. I always silent. My parent's conversation ran on something like this. My father would say, "I can bear it, but my heart aches for you. You should not have to suffer so much. You who were always so good and pure, why should you be cursed with such a daughter?" Then my mother would answer him, "Oh, my poor dear Otto, it is harder for you to bear than for me. You were such a wonderful father." That is the way it would go on.

Sometimes after I went upstairs at night, my mother would follow me, sit down on the edge of the bed, and ask me if I did not have any conscience, if I did not feel any remorse, if I had no feeling. But never, never thinking that I had any trouble on my mind. Still, it was

August, and I could spend a lot of time outdoors, wander about in the woods.

On the second of September, I went hop picking. That was a great relief. Of course as every year, there were a lot of new faces. Still there were a good many there that I had met and liked in other years. Again I saw no one seemed to have heard about Charlie's arrest. A few of the girls asked me if I still went with that handsome young fellow that took me out last year. One or two of the girls wanted to know who my fellow was this year. After I had been there about two weeks, one afternoon a heavy thundershower set in. We had to stop picking and go to the house. Mrs. Kilts called me into her bedroom and locked the door exactly as she had done the year before. She asked me if I knew where Charlie Sheppard was. She said no one had seen him in Oneida for nearly a year. Again it seemed no one knew about his arrest. Well, the picking came to an end. I was sorry, though I had worked very hard. I was happy there. Such a jolly, friendly crowd. I felt carefree, in a way quite happy.

Now although I knew my father so well, had always known how unforgiving he was, still I hoped that after I had been away from home now for nearly three weeks, he would not be throwing those things in my face all the time. But I was sadly mistaken. I had hardly reached home before he started in again. For a few more weeks, I spent a good part of my time out of doors. Then late in October the weather changed to cold, rainy days. Early in November winter set in. There was no break in the weather till spring. This was the hardest winter I ever lived through.

Never a friendly word or look, nothing but sarcastic remarks and a great pity for each other. My one great pleasure in winter had always been my organ. I loved my music. I had hardly ever played in summer, so when the first really rough day set in, in late October, I went in to play. Oh, if I could only play my beloved melodies again. I was longing for them. I had hardly touched the keys when my mother came in to the room saying my father could not stand to hear me play, I did not deserve to play. I could still read, but how could I enjoy a book in the same room where he was forever telling my mother how wicked, how sinful I was.

One night I took a book up to my room. My mother followed me up, said my father said the place to read was downstairs. Came my thirty-first birthday and for the first time, no celebration. Then our holy Christmas, but no tree. Both my father and mother said it would be a sacrilege to have a Christmas with such as me in the house. What a winter.

I know that whoever reads this book will wonder why I did not leave home. Well, there was a good reason, or rather many reasons. In the first place, I was not trained for any profession or even a trade. In those days, girls could not go and get a job as they do now. All I could have done was common housework. The way I had been brought up, that was unthinkable. I still loved my mother very much. Oh, how I loved my home, the little farm, the animals. No, I could not leave all that to toil at hated housework for others.

At night when I lay in my still dark room for hours at a time, how I wished that Ernest had lived. Then we could have gotten a little home close by, but now he and my one happy month spent in Eden was only a bygone dream, a chapter of my life spent in another world.

Chapter 21

Very few people came to our house that winter. In the first place, on account of the severeness of the weather. In the second place, my people were so wrapped up in their bitterness that they were not pleasant company. But the few that did come were told that they, my father and mother, had so very much grief, sorrow to bear. Although they did not in so many words tell them that I was to blame, still by looks and in other ways, they made it plain to them that I had brought sorrow and shame and disgrace to them. They would glance at me.

Charlie Estey was the only one who, when he did come, had not changed towards me. I no longer made the trips to Oneida for my father. He went himself. Well, even this winter came to an end. Once more spring came, and I could be out of doors more. But my father hired a man to do the work on the farm that I had done for so many years and had so loved doing.

Came the sixth day of June, a lovely, warm, bright sunshine without really being hot. Our peonies were still in full bloom, thousands of early roses filled the air with their sweet perfume. Robins singing joyfully. All out of doors was lovely peace and beauty, but in our little home was hatred and bitterness.

For some reason, all that forenoon my father raved on about my wickedness even more than usual. My mother, who never used bad language, would look at me in such a way that it really hurt me more than my father's loud accusations. As we were sitting at the dinner table, the door wide open, I had been trying to choke down a little food. During all my father's loud ravings, I had always maintained a sullen silence. But there is an old saying that even a worm will turn.

Through Sophie's Eyes

Now, after ten months of continual nagging, throwing into my face a dozen times a day how thankful I should be to be tolerated to live with two good people, and so on, all at once something snapped in me. I lost my self-control and said, "I will marry the first man who wants me." At that very instance, there was a step over the threshold of our open door, a shadow, and at the same time, there stood Charles Estey. He fairly leaped towards me, saying eagerly, "Sophie, did you mean what you just said?" To tell the honest truth, I already regretted what I had said, but I looked defiantly at my father and said, "Yes, I did mean it." Charlie fairly danced about the room. He again declared how much he loved me, how very happy he was.

I was silent, so were my parents. In a way I was glad to think I would be released from this earthly hell and still be so near to my old home. I knew Charlie loved me. But I also knew that the beautiful life I still hoped to enter sometime, somehow, would have to be given up. I would have a much smaller, plainer home than I now had and no more long trips. But I would not now back out. I left the room and went out on the verandah. Charlie followed me out. My father, as always, laid down for his afternoon nap. But for once my mother did not take her nap, she followed us out. Charlie said he had come to tell us that he had just received a letter from West Monroe from some people he knew there. They wanted him to come out there at once to paint their house.

He said he was glad to get that job and if I was willing, we could get married at once, and he would take me with him, pay my board. Neither my mother or I really liked this hurry up business. After all, she was my mother and wanted to give me at least a little wedding. So the three of us talked it all over. Charlie thought it would take from four to five weeks to paint that house. My mother and I thought that would give us plenty of time to get ready. She wanted to see to it that I had a decent setting out to start my housekeeping.

Charlie admitted that he did not even have a good suit of clothes to get married. Well to this day I do not really know just how I felt about the whole thing. In a way I was glad to get away from this unbearable life. I suppose there is no girl but gets a thrill at the thought of a home of her own. But the great joy, the blissful happiness of looking forward to become a bride was utterly lacking.

That night my father said it was a foolish piece of business, to say the least, but as he no longer considered me as his daughter, he did not care what I did. My mother and I wrote to our friends in New York City and to my Aunt Sophie in Europe. We just told them that I was going to marry a poor man, but one who had loved me for years. We could not bring ourselves to tell any of them just how poor he really was.

Dear old Mrs. Tappen, who was now well up in her eighties and not in good health, sent me a check for fifty dollars, saying I should buy myself whatever I needed or wanted the most with that money as she was not able to go shopping. In those days fifty dollars went further than a hundred does these days.

Mrs. Fairchild sent by express three large boxes. Everything was exquisite, but sadly out of place for my future surroundings. One large box contained bedding, two large new down pillows, sheets and pillow cases of the finest linen, lovely soft woolen blankets, a couple of silk quilts filled with down. Another box contained table linen. Six large beautiful damask table clothes. Dozens of napkins to match. There were a pair of large draperies, heavy green velvet richly embroidered with gold braid.

The third box was smaller. That contained silverware, a dozen table knives, a dozen bread and butter knives, three dozen forks, a dozen table spoons, a dozen teaspoons, a dozen desert spoons, a dozen soup spoons, all the other extras. Also a silver coffee urn. Mrs. Mills sent simpler things, but even those were better than my new home surroundings were to be. She sent me an entire kitchen outfit. Ten aluminum kettles of all sizes, three sizes of frying pans, strainers, plain tea and coffee pots, bread, pie and cake tins, egg beaters, long handled roasting forks, bread and butter knives, paring knives, mixing bowls, and countless other really useful things. Also kitchen hand towels, tea towels.

But in a way, my aunt's gift surprised me the most. She, like Mrs. Tappen, sent me fifty dollars. But she made a special request. It was that she wanted me to spend it on a little wedding trip. She said just because I was going to marry a poor man, I should have that little luxury before settling down for life. She said if I used it up to buy things, it would not go far, but beginning my married life with a happy little trip would stay in my memory forever, and I could always remember her by it.

Charlie wrote me two love letters each week. He came home over Sundays every two weeks. He was permitted to come to the house, but not invited to stay for supper. While he was there, both my parents would lead up to the subject that it was a disgrace for a man to take a girl out of a good comfortable home if he could not at least provide one as good or better for her. Then there would be a pause, then one or the other would go on to say that a man would not do so, only a selfish brute.

I had no chance ever to see him alone. So one day I managed to slip him a little note telling him where to meet me in an hour's time. Our marriage was only about two weeks off, and I must see him alone. He came to the place I told him to come. I told him about my affair with Spear, the whole truth. He said it would not make any difference with him. I felt as if he had a right to know about it. But I never ever told him about my month with Ernest Galway. In the long winters, I used to piece quilts. Not the last winter. I had been too harassed to do such work. I had six of those quilt covers. The last few weeks, my mother had bought cloth for the other sides of them and cotton batting for the filling and together we quilted them.

One day I went to Oneida, and with part of the money Mrs. Tappen had sent me I bought a really beautiful set of dishes. There were one hundred and fifty two pieces in the set. White china trimmed with gold and little blue flowers. When I bought that set, I thought they would last me a lifetime. At this writing, yes even twenty years ago, there was not one piece left. I did not get any new clothes to get married in. I had so many, many beautiful dresses that our New York friends had kept sending me. Well, we set the day for the eleventh of July.

My parents had Mrs. William Hemingway from North Bay bake and deliver the cakes. There was a lovely wedding cake and two or three other cakes. Thin sandwiches, cold sliced meat, and a salad. Also a gallon of delicious ice cream that saved us a lot of work. I only invited two people, Mr. and Mrs. Carol. The minister also stayed for refreshments. My father hired Mr. Reamore to take us to the depot at Jewell, as we had heard there would be a crowd waiting for us at the North Bay station.

We went to Oswego and stayed there overnight. The next day we started for the Thousand Islands. We were gone just a week. I stayed at home the first night we got back as nothing was ready at Charlie's little home. Next morning, he came after me. We walked to his house, as he said, to look it over. Now years ago, when his brother

Joe had owned the little place and his sister Mary had lived there, kept house, I had been there quite often. Though the house was very small, his sister had kept it clean. She had that rare knack of neatness and order combined with the feeling of cozy comfort.

I have been in nice clean houses where there always existed a feeling of coldness, a constant fear that some chair or even a book might be misplaced. But here in this little house, there had always been that rare feeling of home. Of course I heard that when Charlie's sister moved out, she had taken with her the things she had brought to the house. Later, when Joe Estey moved out, he in turn took most of his furniture with him. But Charlie had told us that he had bought a lot of Joe's things, as he put it. Enough to keep house. Well, when Charlie opened the door of what was to be my new home, I was not prepared for the sight that met my eyes. The room we entered was so cluttered up and filthy that mere words would fail to describe it. The floor looked as if it had not been swept for months, not really scrubbed for years. There were little heaps of old rags and parts of old shoes and other rubbish scattered on the floor. The really good cook stove was a messy looking thing, covered with rust, dirt, and a few unwashed old kettles.

The walls were a sight. Most of the wallpaper was torn off completely or hanging down in tatters. What was left on the walls was covered with dirt and mold. There were three windows in the room, so dirty the glass looked dim. No curtains. The big table also was sticky bare and dirty. A few old chipped, dirty dishes piled on it. A few old kitchen chairs standing around the room.

There was a large built-in cupboard where Charlie's sister used to keep her dishes, on the lower part of which was a small drawer for the silver and below that a larger one for table linen. I opened the doors of that cupboard. If possible, it was much dirtier than the room. I opened the door that went upstairs. There really was only an attic. No one could stand up in it. But I did not go up. The stairs were so cluttered with all kinds of rubbish, they were impassable.

I went to the cellar, door. I remembered the cellarway was quite large, with shelves like a small pantry. But that, like the rest, was horribly dirty. We went into the bedroom. Again, an unswept, filthy floor with rags, dirty old clothing, worn out shoes, old papers and so on. The wallpaper moldy, dirty, and half of it torn off like in the kitchen. More bare dirty windows. The old bedstead and springs were in fairly good condition. The mattress was a disgrace. I had not spoken a word. I was fairly overcome with disgust. Charlie kept saying, "We will have to clean up the rooms." I still did not say anything, but I was wondering why he had not cleaned them up before taking me there. He had been home a full week after he got back from West Monroe. Well, I thought, I brought this on myself. He asked me where I wanted to begin to clean up. I said the cupboard. He built a fire in the dirty looking stove, and I carried water and put it on to heat. To my surprise, Charlie sat down. Started telling me how much he loved me, how beautiful I was, how happy he was, that he had never loved any one half as much as me, and so on and on. But he did not try to help me. There was no washing powder, but I found a piece of soap.

In all my thirty-one years I had never undertaken such a dirty job. It fairly made me sick at my stomach. The day was quite hot. I kept at it and by eleven o'clock the cupboard was clean. It had taken me a little over two hours. I had no papers to lay on the shelves. I would bring some from home when I got my dishes. All this time, Charlie had not stirred out of his chair. I was getting hungry, but I saw no food.

I said, "What about dinner?" Charlie said, "There is a bag of potatoes in the cellarway and a kettle on the stove." I tried to clean out the big iron kettle, then went and got some potatoes. Charlie handed me his jack knife, saying that was what he always used to peel potatoes with. Well, I got them on cooking and asked Charlie what else there was. He said he was sorry, there was nothing else, but he would go to North Bay in the afternoon and bring home some food. I tried to clean off the table a little, washed up the few old dishes, and set the table. There were only steel forks and knives. We had boiled potatoes and salt, and cold water to drink.

All during dinner, Charlie kept telling me how happy he was, how good and sweet I was, how good the dinner tasted, so much better than that restaurant stuff we had had on our trip, how good I had cooked the potatoes. I asked him where he kept his broom and mop. He told me he did not have any, but he would borrow them from Jake Eckel, a neighbor living close by. I went to my purse and gave him money to buy a broom, a mop stick, and a package of soap powder to clean the floors. At home I always went out on the verandah into my hammock to rest a while after dinner. But now I got ready to go home to get my dishes.

Of course I did not tell my mother how terribly dirty the house was or about my poor dinner. I went into this of my own free will and now I would stick it out, come what might. I looked at my entire set of dishes, but out of the whole box of exquisite table silverware from Mrs. Fairchild, I only took six knives, six forks, six teaspoons, and a couple of tablespoons. I plainly saw that all the rest of those things were absolutely out of place. I took one of my six damask table cloths and no napkins. But I took two of my dainty tea towels to put under our plates to save getting the lovely table cloth dirty. Also a big armful of clean newspapers. I did not yet take any of my kitchen pots, pans and so on. I wanted to first clean up a place for them. I did take the sheets and quilts from my own bed. The lovely bedding Mrs. Fairchild had sent would have to wait till I had a place for them. I hitched up my horse and took the things to the house.

Charlie had gotten home. He proudly pointed to the table. There was a can of salmon, a loaf of bread, and half a pound of green tea. He helped me unload my things. I would have asked him to take my horse back, but felt that my parents did not want him to come there. When I got back, it was half past two. Charlie was sitting comfortable on a chair in the midst of all the dirt. I wanted to get my dishes in the cupboard. I asked Charlie to pick up all the dirty rags and rubbish from the floors and carry it out. Well, I have never seen a more surprised look on a man's face. Well, he got up and said, "Why, yes, I will do anything for you, my sweet little wife." He carried out armful after armful, then sat down again.

I thought he would start sweeping, but he did not even seem to think of it. I cut and laid the clean papers on the cupboard shelves and arranged my lovely dishes on them. What a transformation. Then I gave the table another good scrubbing, put ten or twelve thickness of newspapers on it, and then the damask table cloth, but it was much too big. So I looped it up all around. Then I set it with my dainty dishes. Now the cupboard and the table really looked very nice. But, oh how the rest did look. All the time I was working, Charlie sat on his chair, telling me over and over again how happy he was, how glad he was that he had a good home for me. Well, I got supper.

In the morning, I asked him what to do about breakfast. He said there were a lot of boiled potatoes left from yesterday and that I should warm them up. I said there was no lard of grease. Again that mild surprised look. "What do you want lard or grease for? I never use it. Just mash them up, throw them in the frying pan with a little salt and water, and heat them up." Well, I did and made some green tea. I tasted the potatoes but could not eat them. Charlie ate two heaping platefuls, assuring me they were real good. I ate a few slices of dry bread and drank water. I could not drink that tea. At home, we had coffee with rich cream, eggs, toast with plenty of good butter, sometimes breakfast food with milk and fruit, or pancakes with bacon or ham.

Here was starvation food, but I was told how good and sweet and beautiful I was, how happy I made him. While at home for the last ten or eleven months, I was reminded a dozen times during each meal how bad, how wicked, how sinful I was, and how very thankful I should be to be tolerated to live with such good people. This day I spent in scrubbing the floors and windows. I told Charlie I was going to Oneida the next day to buy some things I needed. He declared we needed nothing, but I was firm about this. If I was to spend the rest of my life here, I would make it look as good as I could.

What use would my lovely bedding Mrs. Fairchild had sent me be without a bed, and what should I do if any one wanted to come to us over night. Well, I went and of course Charlie went with me. I still had over half the money Mrs. Tappen had sent me and a few dollars of my aunt's money left. I also had some left in the Oneida Savings Bank, though my western trip had lowered it sadly. Well, I bought a good bedstead, spring and mattress for my spare bed to go with the lovely bedding Mrs. Fairchild had sent me. I also bought a good mattress for our bed, a cheap carpet for the bedroom. I picked out a green carpet with yellow flowers to match those lovely green velvet draperies trimmed in gold. I also bought three sets of white and green curtains for the bedroom and three sets of white curtains for the kitchen. White and gold wallpaper for the kitchen, which also was our living and dining room. Green and white wallpaper for the bedroom. The next day I got my horse and fetched the things home.

After I had the carpet down, the beautiful bed made up, the heavy draperies dividing the bedroom into two tiny rooms, the curtains up at the clean windows, the cellarway shelves cleaned and filled with my kitchen things, the little house in a way was lovely, all but the walls. I would paper them little by little.

I had another disappointment. As I had remembered the house, there would be plenty of room for my organ in the corner next to the bedroom. But after seeing the place again, I saw plainly it would not work out. We only had three windows in this room and if I put the organ in that corner it would have covered up the entire window. If I turned it the other way, it would block up the entrance to the bedroom. That was a real disappointment. I loved my music. Charlie, too, was disappointed. I had a real nice sofa at home that I had bought some years before. I had made half a dozen lovely sofa pillows for it. They were really too good to be used, but I got the sofa and pillows and put them in that corner. The sofa went under the window. Charlie was delighted. He nestled himself amongst the silken cushions.

Now I must relate something that really made me bitter. It was that my parents always had kept three or four cats which they thought a great deal of, and I always had had one of my own. My beloved Blackie had died, but I had raised a kitten pussy gray. Of course I had intended to bring her to my new home. So one day after I had the house cleaned and furnished, I carried her to her new home. My mother told me she would let me have a cupful of sweet milk every day for my kitten. The moment I entered the door, Charlie sprang up, saying I could not bring a cat into his house, that if I did not take it back at once, he would kill it. A hot feeling of resentment welled up in me, and my first impulse was to defy him, tell him I would keep my kitten. But I knew that if he did not actually kill it, every time he got it he would kick or stone it.

So I picked it up again and carried it home. My mother was greatly surprised. I told her the kitten seemed so frightened that I would wait a while longer before I took it again. When I got back I felt sullen. I did not say anything, but I made up my mind that the next time I would not give in. Charlie tried to act sweeter than ever. Next morning at breakfast I said I was going to pick some huckleberries. Now ever since I was a very little girl, I had picked berries. This was one of my greatest pleasures during the summer.

This year had been the first time in my life when I had not started picking just as soon as they began to ripen. The reason was that just about a week before my marriage, they had started to ripen, but I was very busy; amongst other things, I helped my mother to quilt my six bed quilts.

Through Sophie's Eyes

Today was the first of August. All through my hard labor of cleaning, I had longed to get out into the berry lot. Besides, my mother had told me that if I could bring them a few to eat, she would can all I could use. Of course I knew she would furnish the cans and sugar. I also knew that as long as I picked so close to my home, I would eat dinner there. Now I really had thought that Charlie would be quite delighted about my saying I was going to start picking huckleberries.

To my utter amazement, his face changed in a second's time from his mild, smiling self to one of furious anger, and in a stern tone of voice he said, "You are not going berrying." This outburst of rage came so sudden, I was silent. He went on. "You are not going to kill yourself with that beastly work of picking berries. You have a good home and I want you to stay in it." I tried to reason with him, told him, "The work here has been very hard for me and I love to pick berries." It did not do any good. If possible, he got still more angry at me. I remembered how I gave in the night before about the kitten. I had done so for the sake of the kitten. Now I would not give in. I did not yell or argue, I simply said I was going and walked out. I got home about seven o'clock. My parents were still at breakfast. They made me sit down and have a cup of coffee and some cookies. Oh how good that felt on my poor empty stomach. But of course I never admitted at home about my starvation diet. Then I started for the berry lot.

At that time we did not have any berries on our land, but just across our line fence, on LeGrand Cleveland side, there were acres and acres and more acres of huckleberry bushes. It was a perfect midsummer morning. Everywhere I looked I saw the thick, dark green leaved bushes, laden with berries. I felt almost happy again. I would put a few handfuls in my pail, then a big handful in my mouth. I had only been there a little while when I heard a step. I looked around and there was Charlie Estey. I said, "Why didn't you bring a pail?" He glared at me and said, "I did not come out here to pick berries, I came to see what you were up to." I looked at him in utter surprise and said, "What else would I be up to besides picking berries." Then livid with rage, he yelled out, "The reason you are so darned crazy to get out here in this berry lot is to meet some man!" Now I knew why he did not want me to come. I saw he was crazy jealous. But even then I did not dream how much misery he would cause me by that evil demon of jealousy.

Now I got good and angry and we had our first quarrel, a bitter one. He went home and I stayed till my pail was heaping full. Went to my mother's house and took out about a quart to take home to eat for supper and breakfast. I was still very angry at Charlie, but kept quiet. I never mentioned about our quarrel to my mother. When I got home, Charlie was repentant, said he loved me so much he was always afraid of losing me. I said if he carried on so again the way he had, he would lose me. I went after huckleberries almost every day; then a few times I went looking for blackberries. For some reason or other this year there were not many.

Now I will have to go back a little in my story. Before I had become engaged to Charlie, I had promised Mr. Kilts to pick hops for him. So he booked me as one of the pickers. He knew he could depend on me. I told Charlie about this before we got married. I saw at once that he felt terrible about it. But here was one peculiar thing about Charles Estey, or shall I say a noble thing about him. He considered a promise as something sacred. So slowly, sadly, he said that as long as I had promised Mr. Kilts, he supposed I would have to go. But he added, "Let this be the last time." So when the second of September came, I started once more for the hop fields.

To my great joy, Mr. George Griggs, our mail man, engaged Charlie to paint his house and barn. So we locked up our little house, and I left for the hop country, and Charlie went to stay at Mr. Griggs' until I should return. The Griggs place was about four and a half miles from our home. Charlie declared after I got back, he would walk there and back each day.

It seemed good to get back to the Kilts's. Such a friendly, lighthearted bunch of people. Not till this year did I appreciate the good food. Of course now that I had left my parents' old home, and went there for a meal, I was used decent, but all the time I was there I had to listen to all kinds of pointed remarks about Charlie not working, not trying to make a cent. I just had to listen to this, as I knew it was the truth. But just the same, it hurt me terribly. All the time I was in my new home, though Charlie never ceased to make love to me, telling me over and over again of his great love for me, at the same time there was that bitter jealousy. I knew he never trusted me, and I knew he was secretly watching me.

Hop picking came to an end. I had been gone nearly three weeks and had earned twenty-five dollars. When I got to Oneida I saw a lot

217

of things I would have liked to buy, but something seemed to tell me not to spend my money. While I had been to Kilts's, my mother wrote to me once a week, giving me the dear home news. Every other day I received a love letter from Charlie. He generally used up a whole page calling me sweet names such as: lovey dovey, little honey sweetheart, precious darling, honey bunch, dear little girl wifie, little blackeyed angel, little lambie pet, and so on. The next page was filled with him telling me how much he missed me, how sorry he was that he had ever said anything to hurt my feelings. Still, now that I knew him so well, I could read between the lines that he was jealous.

When I got to North Bay, Charlie was waiting for me at the depot. I had scarcely got off the train when he grabbed me, hugged and kissed me before everybody. He carried my suitcase in one hand and with the other arm tight about my waist, we walked through the village. Luckily it was dark. When we got home, to my surprise there was a five pound jar of butter, two dozen eggs, a basket of nice ripe tomatoes, some sweet corn, and a loaf of bread on the table. He told me that Mr. Griggs had asked him if he would take farm produce for pay instead of money. I really was glad. Well, to go a little ahead of my story, I will say that later on, when the painting was all done, Mr. Griggs brought us one hundred pounds of buckwheat flour. I loved buckwheat pancakes. Also twenty pounds of dry beans, ten bushels of potatoes, thirty pounds of salt pork and another five pound jar of butter.

Charlie bought a couple of sacks of flour and I baked our bread. My mother gave me twenty-five quart cans of sweet canned huckleberries, and the McLaughlin family, who owned a farm close by, but lived in Camden, told me I could pick all the apples I wanted. I gathered many bushels of pound sweets, northern spy's, russets and greenings. Our little cellar was full. Charlie and I got up early these days. I cooked his breakfast and packed his lunch and he would leave home before daylight as it took him about an hour and a half to walk the nearly five miles to his paint job. I was busy too. Here again, I must go back a little in my story.

Before I married Charlie, I made an agreement with my mother. I was to do their washing and of course she would pay me for it. My mother had never done a washing in her life. From the time she was married up to when I first began to do the washing, they had always hired it done. During the few weeks while I was hop picking, there was no washing done. When I got back, I would catch up with it. The time I went west, they tried and tried to find a woman to do the washing. At last they found one. She charged an enormous price and did poor work. Now strange as this may seem, I rather liked to wash, preferring it to any other housework.

I told Charlie about my intended washings. He was bitter against it, that is, he was bitter against my going home to do it. He said I should run down in the morning, carry back the dirty clothes, wash and iron them, and then carry them back at night. Now at home I had a cool place on the back porch to both wash and iron. In my new home, I would have had to do all this in a hot kitchen, to say nothing of carrying a heavy basket of clothes back and forth half a mile each way. Besides, at home I would get a good, hearty dinner. At first I did not see why Charlie was so bitter about my going home, but I found out it was all on account of his insane jealousy. Whenever I got out of his sight, he was brooding about my meeting some man.

At home we always had had a great many houseplants. In summer they were kept on the long verandah, during the late fall and winter months, in our heated rooms. In our winter kitchen were three large windows with broad, deep window sills which could be removed again in spring. In this room was a large cook stove and from the time the weather began to get cold in the fall, until early spring, my father kept a good wood fire in this stove, which also heated the pantry and alcove. These three windows were filled with blooming plants such as geraniums of different colors, double petunias, calla lilies and always a monthly rose or two and a lemon and orange tree, with their sweet blossoms. In the big living room adjoining the kitchen was a large coal stove, which like the wood stove, my father kept going night and day. This also heated the big bedroom next to it. In the living room, like in the kitchen, also were three large windows, with the same broad window sills that could be removed in the spring. These windows were filled with half a dozen kinds of coleus, fuchsias, and primroses.

At the one window in the bedroom, the only window facing north, were several kinds of ferns. My bedroom, which was above the living-room, had two big windows, which I always kept full of odds and ends of all kinds of plants, as it never froze in here. My father took a great interest in the plants. I have seen him going from window to window, carefully examining each plant. On extra cold nights, he would carry the dozens of pots away from the windows on tables and chairs, and next morning back to the windows. Now when Charlie Estey used to come calling, he always admired our really beautiful plants and flowers. If we went anywhere, he always would notice people's flowers. I remembered how his sister had always kept a few plants during the winter. So right after I had become engaged to Charlie, I started some slips for my new home. Of course I realized there would not be room for many plants. Still there would be the three windows in the kitchen and though they were smaller than those at home, I still thought I could put three or four small pots at each window.

While I was away on my little trip to the Thousand Islands and during the three weeks I spent picking hops, my mother watered them for me. The first few days after I got back, I was very busy catching up with the washing and other work. But on the thirtieth of September I took the plants to my new home. As I said before, Charlie was still painting for Mr. Griggs and did not come home until after dark. I must say that I have never seen a healthier, nicer looking bunch of young plants. The geraniums were bushy, stocky, and already had tiny clusters of buds, promising blossoms all through the winter. I also had a few beautiful leaved begonias, and brightly colorful coleus. When I looked at the now shiny clean windows, with their thin, snowy white curtains and rich, fresh looking plants in them, I really was proud of them. The moment Charlie came in, he saw them and was delighted, saying those plants made it look so much like a real home.

Tired as he was, he bent over each one, and then exclaimed joyfully, "Why they are budded." Then he wanted me to tell him what color they would be. I told him there was a deep dark red one, a pink one, a salmon colored one, and a snow white one. These were the geraniums. So each day before leaving he would look at each plant, and again at night, and claimed he could hardly wait for them to open up.

October was a lovely fall month, hardly any rain, no wind, and warm pleasant weather. I really was quite happy now. Since Charlie had started that paint job, my parents had stopped throwing out so many pointed remarks about his laziness. My mother was almost as kind towards me as in the old times, and my father just ignored me. I was in perfect health and had enough to eat. Of course I still missed the good rich food I always had been used to, but still, I had enough and besides, now that Charlie was away all day and peace at home, I generally helped my mother a little about the house in the forenoon and ate my dinner with them.

Charlie assured me a dozen times each night and morning of his great love for me. Now silly as this seemed to me, it was still far more pleasant to listen to this than it had been to be constantly reminded about my great wickedness, my sinfulness, my general lowness of nature.

Well, I noticed from the very first hour of my return from the hop fields that Charlie had something on his mind. He looked grief stricken, absentminded. But I had never been inquisitive and never asked him what was troubling him. So the month of October slipped by. Now I must explain something. Mr. Griggs did not have a very large house or barn. Still, Charlie had been at this paint job now ever since the second of September and now it was the fifth of November. The house and barn were now done, but he had a few rooms inside yet to paint. An average painter could have done all this work in about three weeks time, but the reason why people hired Charlie was because he was an expert painter, neat, and when a job was done, it was done to perfection. That was the reason he only painted a building by the job, not by the day or hour, meaning that he and his prospective employer would agree on a certain sum of money to be paid after the building was done.

The weather suddenly turned much colder. One night about the middle of November, the ground started to freeze as Charlie came home. After our supper, I moved my plants from the window sills on to the table. The geraniums were now in full bloom. Charlie looked at them, then at me, and said I might as well leave them at the windows as they would soon all freeze anyway. I hardly knew just what he meant. I asked why would they all freeze. He looked at me with such a look of surprise that I really did not know what to think when he said, "When the winter really sets in, the water pail freezes up solid every night." Well that was a new one for me. Then I said, "But your sister's plants never froze winters. They were lovely." Charlie said, "When my sister was here, Joe kept fire day and night." In wonderment, I said, "But we would have to keep fire, too. Why even then there would not be a fire in the bedroom." Charlie looked at me, mildly, much hurt, and said, "It will be all I can do to get enough wood to keep fire in daytime."

Well, the weather warmed up again. I still had hopes of keeping my plants. Now I must relate something else. Of course during the ten weeks that Charlie had been at his paint job, he had had no time to either get or cut any wood and the very little supply we had on hand was used up long ago. True, the weather had been unusually mild so we really only needed fire early in the morning to cook breakfast and again at night to cook supper. I usually ate dinner at my parents, and if not, ate a cold lunch at home. There was not a stick of wood on Charlie's little plot of ground. But for the last month or so, I had been making daily trips over in John Brown's woods, gathering up all the dry wood I could. Carried it home, broke it up for firewood, and made one or more trips after more wood. But as the weather began slowly to turn colder, we needed more and more wood. Charlie assured me that as soon as he was done at Griggs, he would start cutting wood. I knew that he had made an agreement with Paul Meaney to cut wood on shares with him. The agreement was that he, Charles, and Paul would work in the woods together, Paul to keep two cords out of every three, Charlie one cord. I thought that this was a fair offer, as Paul was to furnish the wood and deliver Charlie's part at our door with his team of horses.

Lately every two or three evenings, Paul would come to see if Charlie was done with his paint job, telling him to hurry up so they could go and start cutting while the weather was dry. Later on there would be heavy cold rains, and then deep snow. Now I am going to go ahead of my story and then come back again to the fifteenth of November.

Little by little I found out that if we had wood enough to last for a day or two, no matter how good the weather might be, Charlie would not go to the woods to cut more. I cannot tell how many times that winter, and later on other winters, when we only had enough wood for one or two days, and for winter the weather was fine, that Paul Meaney would come to our house at breakfast and try his best to get Charlie to go in the woods with him. He would try to reason with him, explaining that now there was only a little snow, but in a few days the snow would be so deep it would be hard to even get into the woods and almost impossible to drive the horses in to draw out any wood. But Charlie would not go.

After Paul went, he would settle himself in a chair with a book and say, "We are not out of wood yet." The thing I never could understand was that he felt the cold much more than I did. Lots of times we were caught in a big snowstorm without a stick of wood. Then he would waller through the deep snow and carry a few sticks from John Brown's woods. When the storm was over, he spent hours to dig a road into Paul's woods so he could bring us some more wood. But this did not teach him a lesson. Then he would again sit down till this load was all burned up. We went to bed early to save wood and during the coldest weather we often were without fire, even in the daytime. At night we never had a fire.

Here was the strangest thing of all. In the hottest days of summer, when I only needed a little fire to warm up a few potatoes and make some tea, I would pick up a few chips so as not to heat up the house, but every single time, Charlie would go and fill up the big stove with hard wood. The heat was sickening. I know he burned up enough good wood that way to carry us through many a cold day and night. It did not do any good for me to tell him that he was not only wasting wood, but making me actually suffer with the intense heat.

Now I will return to my story where I left off. It was the sixteenth of November, a cold, raw morning. Charlie left before daylight as usual and as soon as I could see, I made a number of trips after dry wood. It was quite a long ways from our house and the wood was heavy. A little before noon, I went to my old home. Oh, how good it looked and felt. The two large stoves throwing out heat, the many plants, some of them in full bloom, the cats purring happily, the rich odors of dinner cooking. My mother had a big dripping pan in the oven with a giant pork roast. I had hardly gotten into the house when my father, who hardly ever spoke to me, said in a very decided tone of voice that I would have to get rid of Billy, my horse, at once. He could not bother to take care of him. As long as the weather had been warm, he was out to pasture day and night and made no work, but now that the weather was getting cold, he would have to be in the barn and make a lot of extra work.

Well, that was a hard blow for me. I bought him about eleven years before, had never thought of parting with him. But I did understand my father's side of the question. My father had always been very good to all his animals. For some reason, he had never cared so much for a horse as he did for the cows. Ever since I was very little, I took most of the care of the horse. My father always got me to hitch up and drive him wherever he wanted to go. The times I was hop picking, it always was warm weather, the horse out to pasture. While I was roaming about in the west, the horse, of course, was in his stable. But my father never hitched him up once. He would either walk to North Bay or hire Mr. Reamore to take him.

I sat right down and wrote to Edward Watkins, a horse dealer in Camden who I slightly knew. Now I must relate a strange thing. Mr. Griggs, our mailman, came at about one o'clock. I gave him the letter and asked him when it would reach the Camden Post Office. He told me it would be afternoon of the next day. I said I was sorry, as I wanted Mr. Watkins to receive it sooner, if possible. About half an hour later, I was just leaving, going to my own home, when Mr. Watkins drove in the yard saying he received my letter about the horse. I could hardly believe it. It was like this. Only about half a mile up the road, Mr. Griggs met Mr. Watkins, handing him my letter. Well, I do not even like to write about this. Mr. Watkins said he was getting old and it being late in the fall, he could not give me more than twenty-five dollars. In my mind I can still see him tied behind Watkins' buggy and trotting down the road for the last time. Well, one more link to my old home life was broken.

I went home. I wanted to be alone. I was cooking supper when Charlie came home about an hour earlier than other nights. He told me at once that he had finished his paint job. Then I told him about my selling my horse and a strange look came into his eyes. Then he asked me how much I got for him. I told him. Then there was a long pause.

Charlie got up from his chair, walked about the room, looked at me, went to the door, back again, and then came straight to me, saying, "You got twenty-five dollars hop picking and today you also took in twenty-five dollars, fifty dollars in all." Then he kept repeating fifty dollars, fifty dollars.

We sat down to supper in silence, but I noticed that Charlie acted very queer. After supper he spoke. "Sophie, I would like to make a bargain with you." I said, "It takes two to make a bargain, but let's hear it." Then he told me this story. About six or seven years ago, he had bought this little home, feeling sure at that time of winning me. Each summer, or rather each fall, he made a payment to his brother Joe. The better I knew Charlie, the more I found out that he never worked in winter. Well, about three years ago, when people told him I had a handsome fellow in Oneida whom I was going to marry, he gave up making his payments. Said he no longer cared if he even had a home or not. His brother had not crowded him, but while I was away hop picking he had received a letter from Joe telling him he was sick, had been sick all summer, and not able to earn any money and not raise much food, and if Charlie could possibly make a payment, it would mean a lot to him, as he was in actual need of food. That explained why Charlie had looked so grief stricken.

He went on to tell me that he lacked just fifty dollars in finishing to pay for his place, and here he stopped. Another long pause, then he went on and said that if I made that last payment, he would deed the place over to me. I said I would do so. Then he said that he would go right up to see Gene Holmes, who at that time lived on the Charles Brown farm, now known as the Clark farm. He wanted to hire a horse and buggy for the next day so we could go to Joe's.

Right after breakfast next morning, we started for Camden. From there it was still four more miles to where Joe lived. When we got there, it was about ten o'clock. Joe had bought a small farm of eight acres, part of which was only brush land. He had a small, very old house, but it was immaculately clean. No woman could have kept it cleaner. But oh, when I saw Joe, I had not seen him for about seven years, my heart ached for him. When he, his sister, and Charlie used to come to our place to spend the evenings, he was a red cheeked, healthy looking young man. He was eleven years younger than Charlie, and at that time had a happy, jolly way about him. Now I saw a pale, thin, old, sad looking man before me. But he looked at me so kindly, called me sister. A strange feeling came over me. What would my parents think if they ever knew that such a poor man called their daughter sister?

Charlie made the last payment on the place and Joe gave him the deed and the receipt in full. Poor Joe, he was so glad to get that money he had tears in his eyes and shook and trembled from excitement and weakness. Then he heard a car coming--there were a lot of automobiles on the road by this time. He ran to the door and waved to the man to stop. As the house was close to the road and the door open, I heard him tell the man to bring some good groceries and fresh meat, handing him a bill of the money he had just received from us. He came back saying the man, his next door neighbor, would be back soon. He had a small barn, but no cow or horse, but there was some good hay in it for our horse's dinner.

When the neighbor came back with the food, I helped Joe cook dinner. Every kettle and dish was perfectly clean. But I discovered that there was not a thing to eat in the house but potatoes. Now I must say something here about those two brothers. Joe had always worked very hard, from a boy up, took care of a number of brothers and sisters. Even now, he owned his little place free of debt.

While Charlie never liked to do hard work, I think I know the reason for that. When he was quite young, he danced and played the violin in New York Theatres and for a few years made money, which he spent as fast as he made it. So probably that spoiled him for real work afterwards.

Well, we ate dinner happily together. Soon afterwards, we started on our rather long drive home. That night, Mr. Griggs brought a load of farm produce, which I already mentioned. Next morning Charlie and I walked to North Bay to see Sandy Rae. He was the Notary Public. We wanted him to transfer the deed over from Charlie to me, but Mr. Rae told us that that could not be done; we would have to get a third person for that.

So Mr. Ray, Charlie and I went to Gleason's. Mr. and Mrs. Gleason at that time had a small grocery store at North Bay. Charlie made his place over to them, and they in turned deeded it back to me.

Came the eighteenth of December, with a bitter cold wave from the northwest. The thermometer steadily sinking till it dropped to thirty-five degrees below zero. Our wood supply was very low, as Charlie did not go into the woods for the last two weeks. I brought all my plants as near to the stove as possible. Pinned six or eight thicknesses of newspaper around each one, and then built a sort of tent over them, throwing a bed quilt over the hole. Charlie thought if we let the fire go out at seven o'clock, there might be enough wood to last the next day. In the morning I heard him breaking the ice in the water pail with a hammer. I got up and carefully lifted the coverings of my plants. The sight of those poor frozen plants fairly made me sick. Every one frozen black, even the dirt in the pots frozen as hard as a rock. My geraniums, which had been laden with bloom only the night before, now were just a blackened little heap on their pots. I said nothing, but I could see Charlie, too, felt bad. Well, first I had to give up my organ. Then my kitten. Then my horse. And now my plants.

Sophie Kussmaul

Charlie put on his overcoat and cap and crouched near the stove saying he would have to go into the woods the next day.

Chapter 22

Came the twenty first of December, my thirty-second birthday. No celebration, just another day. The next day I went home to do a washing and both my father and mother invited us to come and eat Christmas dinner with them. I was glad; still I was afraid they would in some way throw out some sarcastic remarks. But the day passed by peaceable, as all Christmas days had ever done. Still, I felt and so did Charlie that both my parents did not like him. The Christmas tree in the living room looked very good to me.

Now I will go over the time from January first to the twenty-fifth of April in a few sentences. I only went home about once a week to do the laundry work, when the weather was too severe, often only every two weeks. There were a number of reasons for my not going there oftener. Every time I did go, Charlie sulked for a couple of days, declaring I probably met some man at home. Since New Years, my parents had also started something new to torment me with. From the time I entered their house to the time I left, they would make all kinds of remarks to each other of how low, how disgraceful, how despicable it was for people to get married and have no children.

Then one of them would say that even animals, if they mate, have little ones. Then the other one would answer that some people are much lower than animals. Then my mother would sigh and say, "I always had hoped to have a grandchild, but even that is being denied me." They would keep that kind of conversation up indefinitely, then change to the subject to how he, my father, had always had wood ahead for a year, then allude to some lazy rascal who never had any ahead, and that his wife had left him on account of being so shiftless. Then the other would say that a woman who would not leave a man like that is a darn fool. They would keep up this kind of conversation till I went home.

Sophie Kussmaul

Still, the winter was not too bad. Charlie, excepting for his unreasonable jealousy, was still as lover-like as the first day. Of course I never mentioned one word of what my parents said. I brought home big armfuls of newspapers, story papers, books and magazines that our New York friends were still sending to my mother each time I went to my old home. As Charlie was fond of reading, it helped to pass the otherwise dark, dreary winter. We also had another very pleasurable diversion. We were planning to have a very large garden the following summer. So I sent for three or four seed catalogs. I think we spent hours each day looking them over. I would compare prices and so on. I told Charlie that if he paid for the plowing and dragging and bought the fertilizer and seed potatoes, I would buy all the other seeds. I had been getting a dollar a month from home for my laundry work, and I never spent a cent of it. Of course I knew it would not take all of my wash money to pay for the seeds. I still remember what I got: both early and late sweet corn, both summer and winter squash, both water and musk melon, citron cucumbers, both early and late cabbage, cauliflower, early and late tomatoes, summer and winter turnips, beets, carrots, parsnips, lettuce, radishes, pole beans, string beans, and a lot of dry winter beans, sweet and hot peppers, and half a dozen kinds of flower seeds. Just as soon as the snow went off, I filled all kinds of old pots and pans with dirt and started my tomatoes, peppers, and celery in the house. I had also bought three kinds of onion seeds, onion sets, and a lot of pea seed. No one could realize how much real pleasure I derived from this work.

A little later on, I built myself a hot bed. I took a shovel and spaded up the ground close to the east side of the house where the bed would get both the morning sun and most of the afternoon sun. I went home and wheeled back a heaping wheelbarrow full of horse manure. Put that in the place where I had spaded and again covered it up with fine dirt. Into this I sowed two kinds of cabbage seed, one kind of cauliflower. Also a few seeds of my radish and lettuce for early use. Then I went home and borrowed six big window frames with their glass and covered up my hot bed. By the time the ground in the garden was ready, I had hundreds of strong, healthy cabbage and cauliflower plants to set out.

Well, to go back a little in my story, during the fore part of the winter, we had fairly decent food. Now in March, we had to go back to buckwheat cakes for breakfast and clear potatoes for supper. Of course there was no butter, grease, meat, eggs, or syrup to eat with our pancakes. Charlie did not earn one cent during the entire winter.

Came the twenty-fifth of April. I was hungry all the time, but never let my parents know about that. Charlie said he was going to see Gerald Corcoran. When he returned, he looked very happy. He told me he and Mr. Corcoran had made a bargain. He was to plow, drag, and mark out our land. He also was to furnish the seed potatoes and eight hundred pounds of fertilizer, and Charlie was to paint his house for pay.

The house was not very large, and Charlie thought he could finish it in about three weeks. He was to start work that very afternoon. He had to go to North Bay before dinner. Well, I was very, very glad, as I was a little afraid he might not get the ground fitted as he had no money. I almost forgot my empty stomach. I was boiling our daily potatoes when Charlie bounded into the room. He was so excited and out of breath he could hardly talk. He put an armful of groceries on the table; then told me Dexter Nichols wanted him to paint his house and store, all in one building, and take his pay in groceries. Charlie told me he thought he would be able to begin on Mr. Nichols's house about the twentieth of May. Well, we had the first real dinner for many, many weeks. I felt so thankful and happy.

Right after dinner, Charlie left to start his painting. Next day, Mr. Corcoran plowed our ground and the day after, dragged and marked it. He did a wonderful job. The ground was all mellow and easy to work. Charlie, who never liked to do any kind of work besides painting, now got up each morning long before the sun came up and planted potatoes. He painted till six o'clock, walked home a mile, ate supper, and then worked on our land till dark. I put in the smaller seeds.

There was an acre and a quarter of land. The house, yard, and little outbuildings did not take up much space, and every foot of that plowed ground was planted to something. Never have I seen crops grow the way ours did that summer. The farmers in the neighborhood would stop by and gaze at our wonder crops, and all declared that we raised more from our acre and a quarter than any farmer from six to eight acres.

Charlie never missed a day, rain or shine, at his paint jobs, as he so arranged his work that he painted blinds, inside jobs, under porch roofs, and Mr. Nichols's rooms on rainy days. Every hour left him of daylight at home, he planted, hoed, and dug on the land. I never did any of the hoeing, but I planted all the smaller seeds, weeded, and set out many hundreds of plants.

When the huckle and black berries were ripe, I would pick all the forenoon, eat dinner at home, rest a few hours in my hammock on the cool, shady verandah, then about five in the afternoon go to my own little home and cook a good supper for Charlie, who always came home at six-thirty. After supper we both worked in the garden just as long as we could see.

I really ought to have been happy this spring and summer. Everything we had planted was turning out far beyond our fondest expectations. I was in perfect health, had plenty of good food to eat. Charlie, excepting for his disgusting jealousy, was kindness and love. Since Charlie started to work in spring, my parents had stopped throwing out so many sarcastic remarks. I could spend many hours there. I could also go roaming about again in my search for berries without knowing that Charlie was forever stalking me, slinking behind bushes and thinking I did not know he was there. Oh, the innocence of people. I knew he thought that as long as I did not see or hear him, I could not possibly know he was near by. But my sense of smell had always been very highly developed and no matter how clean a person kept themselves, I could always catch their scent a long ways off.

As I said, I ought to have felt lighthearted and happy, but I felt far, far from happy. There had been, and still was, a dark, threatening cloud hovering over me. It started early in spring, the latter part of April, and instead of lifting, grew in size of darkness. The thing I had at first only suspected was now a certainty. I was going to have a baby. I said in the beginning of this book that I would write the full truth about my life, and I will continue to do so, but I suppose that whoever reads these pages will be shocked. I did not want a baby. I did not like babies. Always in my daydreams of a happy married life, I had pictured to myself a loving husband, a lovely house, beautiful surroundings, trees, flowers, and animals--horses, cows, sheep, lots of poultry, and at least three to four cats. But I had never even thought of a baby.

The only time I had ever given thought of a baby or little ones was when in my great love for Joe Henry, I had seen in my mind a plain little home, simply furnished, a happy, rosy cheeked little Joe, and little Sophie running joyously about at play. But even then I had only visioned them as children of five or six years of age. Never as babies. When there was a new baby in our neighborhood and I took my mother to see it, she would bend over it, look at it with tender adoration in her face, exclaim to the young mother how happy she must be, what a sweet little thing it was. Draw my attention to its little hands and so on. While all I could see was a homely, red, wrinkled, squirming something. Years later when my own little daughter was twelve, thirteen, fourteen, fifteen and we went to Camden or Oneida and she saw a baby carriage on the sidewalk, she would run ahead a few steps and eagerly peer at the small occupant.

Her face, like my mother's, would fairly glow with love and admiration, and she would pull me back so she could look at it once more. Then, instead of noticing the many pretty things we saw, she would talk about the lovely baby. I have often read in stories and poems of the great joy that comes to a married woman when she first finds out that she is to be a mother. I can truthfully say that I did not experience such feelings. On the contrary, I felt terrible about it. But I was not wicked enough to, as the saying goes, get rid of it. That I considered a great sin.

Charlie, why he acted half insane with joy. After I told him I thought I would have a baby, he would talk about nothing else. He would fairly laugh for the very joy of thinking of it. He would assure me that he would much rather have a baby than a million dollars. I would look at him to see if he had gone mad. He would give a happy little laugh and say he hoped it would be a little girl. He would call it after me and then he would have two Sophie's. I kept putting off telling my mother. Sometimes I thought that now that they felt better towards Charlie and had made thousands of remarks about what they thought of childless couples, they might be very glad to hear the news. Still, somehow I could not quite bring myself to tell my mother. The first few weeks, yes, the first two months, I was still hoping it might not be so. After I was sure, I would think at night that the next morning I would talk to my mother. But when I got there each time, there was something to make me wait.

Came the fifteenth of August. I got Charlie's lunch done up, he left for work, and right after that I felt life. In plain English, for the first time I felt the baby move within me. From that very second a great change came over me. I felt a great thrill of glory shoot through my

232

very being, a joy so great, so sublime, yes, even holy, as I had never before experienced. All the dread, all the feeling of fear for my own safety vanished, and I dumbly wondered why I had not rejoiced in the knowledge of the thought of being given one of God's little ones to rear and raise to His glory. Now I was going home to tell my mother the happy news. But when I got home, my poor mother, who never was really well and strong, had one of her sick spells--a nervous attack. So for the next few days I kept my news from her. On the twentieth of August, she was much better. I made my berry trip, ate dinner with them, and then went on the verandah knowing that as soon as my mother had had her nap, she would join me. Then I would tell her my happy secret. Well, she came out, so did my father, something he hardly ever did in daytime. I waited patiently for him to leave us, but he said he thought he would take it easy as he had a headache.

Now my mother hardly ever had any callers, but it so happened that the next two afternoons, some one came. The day after, the rain poured down all day and I did not go home. Then came Sunday. I never went home on that day. I always spent Sundays with Charlie. Monday afternoon, I had hardly got into my hammock when my mother came out to me. She did not take her nap. She looked me straight in the face and asked me, "Do you expect a baby?" I was utterly taken by surprise, so much so that I stammered out, "I believe so." My mother looked hurt, offended, said a real daughter would have told her mother, and I was no real daughter to her.

I tried and tried to explain to her that I had for a long time intended to tell her, but I knew she did not believe me. She even insisted that Charlie had forbidden me to tell her. Well, the real truth was that Charlie was so delighted about it that he wanted me to tell my mother even before I was quite sure myself.

After a while, I took courage and asked my mother how she knew. She said to me, "Your body does not show it, but your face does." Well, that was a new one for me. Now I thought things would run on smoothly. My father could never throw my childless marriage in my face again, and for the last four months, Charlie had really worked very hard. But I was sadly mistaken. The very next morning when I entered their house, my father did not answer my good morning. Then he started in saying that it was a sin, a crime, for a man who had nothing to bring a poor innocent child into the world to starve to death, and that he himself was not going to support it. Again, as in winter when he preached about the sins of childless marriages, all of his remarks were directed to my mother, not to me, so I really could not answer him.

After that, there was not a day when I went home that he did not allude to the subject in some cutting way or other. When my mother and I were alone, we often spoke of the coming baby. On the twentieth of September, Charlie finished his work for Mr. Nichols. Paul Meaney came and wanted Charlie to start cutting wood, as the woods were not dry. He told Charlie that if he went out to his woods and cut and picked up old, dry wood, he would draw it to our house for nothing. As we were all out of wood, he did go to pick up a load, but instead of doing this in one day, he would go to Paul's woods for perhaps an hour, maybe the next day not at all, and so the time dragged by till the last of September when Paul brought us such a big load that his strong team could hardly draw it.

Again Paul urged Charlie to start working in the woods now while the weather was so pleasant instead of waiting till the snow came the way he did last year. After Paul went, I told Charlie in a nice way how good it would be to get all of our winter's wood cut and brought home before winter set in. Then he could stay in a warm house through the winter. He looked at me with adoration in his eyes, telling me I was right, how well I could manage things, how he loved me more all the time, and so on. Then he added, "But first I will have to pull and stack the beans and dig the potatoes."

Of course that sounded reasonable and after all, I thought, it would only take a few days. But things went very different. As long as he worked fully ten hours each day at painting, he would work frantically at home. No one could have done more work with the hoe than he did. But now he would sit and read by the hour, or else just sit there and tell me how happy he was, how good I was, how thankful he was to think I was going to have a baby, and so on, by the hour. He would go out, work at the beans a few minutes, and then come in again and say, "Oh, it won't rain for a few days. There is no hurry."

I did not go home much now. In the first place, I was canning. I canned up a few bushels of tomatoes, made all kinds of pickles. Then if I did go home, my father would rave about the sin of bringing a baby into the world to starve to death.

Sophie Kussmaul

Charlie would scowl and get his jealous tantrums if I mentioned cutting wood and would look at me surprised, saying we were not out of wood. As to the potatoes, he said he would have to build some bins in our little cellar, which was true. So he spent a number of days, part of the days hunting up some old boards. At last he got them from Mr. Holmes. Now he could have built those bins in half a day, but again he would only work at them a few minutes at a time.

To make a long story short, it was now the fifth of November. Charlie had taken until now to build the bins, dig, and put the potatoes in them--we had fifty bushel of lovely potatoes--dig and pull our carrots and turnips, put them in the cellar, and our enormous cabbages. By now, that big load of wood was nearly all gone. It started to snow. I have often since wondered at the great patience of Paul Meaney. Time and time again he would come and try to get Charlie to go into the woods.

Well, on the sixth he did go. The snow came very early that fall. After sitting around the house most of the time for the last six weeks while the weather was so perfect, now in the first snowstorm, he had to go, as we only had a few sticks left.

Now I must go back a little in my story. When I made out my seed orders, I had thought there would be just enough, yes plenty, for the two of us. But everything bore in such abundance as I had never even dreamed of. Besides all the tomatoes we could possibly eat and can, I sold ten bushels--five dollars worth. I sold both sweet and hot peppers, dozens of large cauliflower heads, some cabbages, and a bushel of onions. Altogether, I took in over twelve dollars from such things as we could not possibly use ourselves. I put every cent of this carefully away for the time when my baby should be born. Also, every cent of my wash money since April. Now everyone who reads this should know that one dollar in those days went farther than three today. Yes, I think it would be safe to say as far as four does today.

I also want to say that for the four months painting job at Mr. Nichols, Charlie did not receive one cent in money. Each week Charlie brought home a few, very few, groceries. He had to buy himself shoes, socks, shirts. He really needed those things. So when the job was done, there was very little left. I insisted on getting a sack of flour, a pound of coffee, a pound of tea, and five pounds of sugar to put away when I would be sick, and a woman would be with us for a couple of weeks.

That finished the whole of the paint pay. Now we had lovely vegetables of all kinds, pickles and sweet canned black berries and huckleberries, my mother having furnished the sugar for them. But no meat, butter, milk, or eggs, and of course no grease to cook with. Sometimes bread and oftener none. This year, as last, I got a lot of apples.

On the twenty-sixth of October, my mother invited Sara Dixon to her house, also told me to be sure to come that afternoon. The reason was Sarah Dixon was a dressmaker and had made a specialty in making and selecting baby wardrobes. So my mother told her to make out a complete list of everything a baby needed from birth and up to one year of age. Sarah told my mother that was a little unusual, as people generally only bought for the first three months. Then my mother said she knew that, but she might not live long and then the poor child would not have anything. I felt the hot blood mount to my cheeks.

After the long list was made out, my mother and Sarah arranged to go to Oneida to pick out the things. I, of course, was to go with them. My father hired Mr. Reamore to take us to the depot and come after us at night. We went on the twenty-ninth of October. My mother did not only buy the amount on the list, but always two or three times the amount. Such as, instead of three little shirts, she would buy six; instead of three long dresses, eight; instead of two nightgowns, six. So on through the list of things. Sarah looked on in surprise and even the girl clerk smilingly said, "You must be expecting twins or triplets." Then besides the long list of things, she bought yards and yards of the finest Indian linen, yards and yards of dainty lace, a lovely long baby coat of the finest white mohair lined with heavy white satin, and of course a bonnet to match. Lastly, a bassinette, something that was just coming into style in place of the old time cradle. Everything she bought was pure white, to tell the truth, out of keeping with my home.

I went to my bank and drew twenty-five dollars, thinking maybe my savings were not sufficient for the birth expenses. That left me next to nothing in the bank. Of course the things were left at my mother's house for the present. I went home every afternoon for a few hours and hemmed the six dozen diapers. My mother hemstitched the six lovely white fine woolen blankets in heavy white silk, also embroidered them. Then Sarah Dixon was hired for a couple of days to come and make up the dainty Indian linen into long and short dresses and little under slips. No millionaire's baby had a finer wardrobe.

Chapter 23

Came the twenty-first of December, my thirty-third birthday. Again an invitation for Charlie and myself for Christmas dinner. Although I knew that my parents felt so bitter against Charlie, I also knew they would keep the peace on that day. Well, we went and there was the dear, dear Christmas tree in the living room with the same ornaments and trimmings on it as in the olden days. Yes, the same as on that early Christmas morning when I saw the Christ-child flying from earth to heaven. Even while I stood there looking at the tree, I felt the new life to be within me. Yes, everything passed off very quietly, very peaceable. Still, I who knew my parents so well, knew also that they felt a bitter hate in their hearts against Charlie. When we went to our little home that night, we carried the bassinette between us. It was filled and piled high with the exquisite baby clothes. Charlie had not yet seen them, but when we got home, he unpacked them and was so childishly pleased he would kiss each little dainty garment. Finally I put them in my dresser drawers or he would have spent half the night with them. I am glad to say I ran down home every afternoon for a few hours during the Christmas week.

On New Years Day, Charlie went to Paul Meaney's woods to, as he said, "Get a load of wood home for the baby." It was a clear, cold day with about a foot of snow on the ground and as Charlie carried his dinner with him, I went home for dinner.

Although my parents were known to live so well, they never celebrated New Years by a special dinner. I did not know then how long it would be before I came to my old home again. I left for my own little home about two in the afternoon, filled up the big cook stove with wood, and walked to Paul Meaney's woods. It really was only a little over a mile cross lots, but the snow was much deeper than on the road, as the wind blew it off the road more. I wore rubber boots, but in some places it came far over my boot tops.

Paul and Charlie were sawing with a crosscut saw and did not hear or see me come. They both were much surprised to see me, but oh, how good it seemed to be in the woods again. Then the sun that had shone so brightly disappeared behind heavy snow clouds. Paul said he would try and draw us a load of wood that very night as he feared we would have a heavy snowstorm. I waded home through the deep snow, got supper, and soon after Charlie came home. It had already started to snow and drift.

After supper, though it was dark, Paul came with a cord of good, hard wood. By morning there was a roaring, blinding snowstorm and bitter cold. All day it raged, but by night the wind went down and it stopped. For a wonder, on the morning of the third, they opened up the roads. In those days, it was a much bigger job than now. The men shoveled for hours, then drove horses through, and lastly plowed out the roads.

They called Charlie out to help shovel. That day I baked bread, swept and cleaned out the cellarway, laid clean papers on the shelves, and did a dozen other little chores. At seven o'clock that evening of the third of January, I had my first birth pains. Charlie ran up to Mr. Reamore's. He hitched up his fast horse, drove at top speed after Mrs. Rosa, the midwife I had engaged. She lived between North Bay and Vienna. Before eight o'clock, Mr. Reamore had brought her to our place. Certainly quick work. She worked over me all night, all next day, and the next night.

In the morning on the fifth, Mrs. Rosa said I needed a doctor. Poor Charlie, he was all tired out. He and Mrs. Rosa had only snatched a few mouthfuls of food and kept drinking strong coffee and tea. Charlie came back from North Bay frantic. Said he had telephoned to Cleveland, Camden, Vienna, Rome, and Oneida to half a dozen doctors each place. Always the same answer. I struggled on, Mrs. Rosa did her best, but she still could not bring the baby. Both Charlie and Mrs. Rosa asked me if I did not want to send for my mother. I said no. She was so delicate I thought the excitement would be too much for her. Another long, long day. Between pains, I would doze off. Mrs. Rosa fell asleep leaning against the wall. Charlie fell asleep kneeling at my bedside. A night of horror! Morning. Charlie again went to North Bay, telephoned all over. The answer as the day before was that a flu epidemic was raging and every doctor was overworked. Charlie was in the hotel and said I was dying for lack of a doctor. Someone told him there was a doctor in New London, his name was Middleditch, and he was at home. He would come regardless of who would call for him for any other sickness. Charlie telephoned. Yes, he would come as soon as the horses were hitched up.

Charlie almost staggered back home. Told the good news. The weather was bitter cold. Mrs. Rosa had been getting me out of bed and walking me to the stove. There I would squat down and after a while walk back to my bed, only a few steps. Charlie had not been home more than half an hour. I was squatting on the floor in front of the stove, where I could look down the road, the window being quite low, when I saw what I can still see in my mind. Two small horses, hitched to a cutter, coming on a full fast gallop. It was over twelve miles to New London. One man jumped out, ran to the door. The other, the driver, seeing we had no barn, asked Jake Eckel permission to put up his steaming, panting team. The doctor gave me one glance, said to Mrs. Rosa, "Put that woman to bed." I tried to get up, but all at once I felt as if I had no legs. I could not stir. The doctor asked me if I had any pains. I told him I had no more pain anywhere.

I saw the quick glance between him and Mrs. Rosa. I also saw him throw his instruments on the stove shelf, also the sharp, small, glistening knife. Mrs. Rosa and Charlie carried me back to bed. It was now quite dark and our dim kerosene lamp was lit. Sleigh bells. My father and mother came in. I heard afterwards that Mr. Reamore had been in the hotel and heard the one-sided conversation over the telephone. So he drove home by way of my parents, told them I had started to be sick on the third, how he had gone after Mrs. Rosa for me, and now it was night of the sixth and still no baby. They told him to wait five minutes. They filled a basket with good food, put on their coats, and had him drive them to my home. Then everything went very fast, but to me rather dimly.

The doctor had made a quick examination, and then put his instruments in boiling water. Mrs. Rosa was running about, Charlie kneeling at my bed, my mother stooping over me with love and compassion in her face. My father was in the kitchen. Then the chloroform, the cry of a baby. Semi conscious, I could hear, see, but not move. My mother came close to me and said,

"Everything is all right, all over with, afterbirth and all. You have a lovely baby girl."

I whispered, "I want to see it." Mrs. Rosa brought it to me, wrapped in a blanket. It certainly was a beautiful child, not red, not wrinkled, not bald, not skinny. Mrs. Rosa was seventy-four years old and had been a midwife for fifty years. She said it was the most perfect newborn baby she had ever seen. My mother told her that I, too, had been born with thick, long black hair. My baby's hair was light. Mrs. Rosa said all Indian babies were born with heavy long hair. The doctor was washing himself up. I called to him in a weak voice and asked him how much his bill was. He stared at me, said it was twenty-five dollars, but if you have to pay for it, it will be fifteen. I motioned to Charlie and whispered to him, "Get my purse out of the dresser." I took out the fifteen and handed it to the doctor.

Dim as the light was, I noticed there was blood everywhere. I heard afterwards that in his great haste, my life and the baby's depending on seconds, in the very dim light, the doctor had cut an artery, and I had come so near bleeding to death before they could stop it that the doctor himself said it was a miracle that I lived. Therefore, I was too weak to feel any more pains, and also too weak to move. I could move my hands, but not my arms or head.

Charlie fluttered about from me to Mrs. Rosa, who was dressing the baby. My father kept silent, came to me once, looked at me, and I felt that he had suffered for me in his heart. It was twelve midnight when the doctor left. He said he did not dare leave me, gave Mrs. Rosa directions what to do for me. The baby cried. Mrs. Rosa said it was hungry. She put it to my breasts, but there was no milk. She said if I did not have any milk in my breasts before the child was born, I would not have any now after my great loss of blood. She said this before my parents. My parents had cows, offered milk, but Mrs. Rosa said it would not do because they were not fresh, so the baby would have to have other milk till my parents' cows freshened.

Charlie wanted to rush down to North Bay at once, wake up Dexter Nichols, and buy a nursing bottle, nipple, and a can of condensed milk. Mrs. Rosa forbade him to do that, said it might cause his death, four days and four nights with hardly any food or sleep, on the constant go, and now at one o'clock on a bitter cold night to undertake the three mile trip, going and coming, nothing short of suicide. Then some of them made coffee. Oh, that smelled good. Mrs. Rosa brought me a cup of strong coffee with rich milk in it. Bread with thick butter on it and meat. I dimly wondered where the things came from. I could not move. She had to put the food in my mouth, hold the cup to my lips.

Then I saw them at the table. This was the first time my father and mother had ever eaten in my house, and really it was their own food they had brought with them tonight. This was the seventh of January, two o'clock in the morning, the first meal Mrs. Rosa and Charlie had eaten since the third of January, and for that matter, I either.

At three o'clock my parents left. Sick as I was, I worried about my mother. She always had been so delicate. Now the big excitement and then walking home in utter darkness, the thermometer ten below zero. Mrs. Rosa did not undress, but went to bed in my lovely spare bed, the first person to occupy it. Charlie sat up in the rocking chair near the stove so as to keep fire for the baby. I dozed off. I would wake up, hear Mrs. Rosa breathing. Charlie would sleep, then jump up and kneel before the baby's couch and go to sleep on his knees.

It was getting daylight. I heard Charlie fill up the stove and go out. Mrs. Rosa got up, got breakfast, and fed me. Then Charlie came back. He had been to North Bay, pounded on Mr. Nichols's door till he woke him up, got the nursing bottle, nipple, and a can of Red Cross milk. The baby had been crying for a long time. Well, Mrs. Rosa fed her and now it was really daylight, I saw her for the first time plainly. Mrs. Rosa said the baby should have Horlick's Malted milk. It was a dollar a quart bottle and she would need a bottle a week till April, when my father's cows would freshen. Here was a problem. I knew I would have to pay Mrs. Rosa, and also Mrs. Belcher, who was to come as Mrs. Rosa had another case coming any day now. I was too weak to talk much. I whispered to Charlie to raise me up, get my writing paper, pen and ink. After he had lifted my right arm in position, I wrote to Mrs. Mills of New York City, telling her in as few words as possible all the circumstances and begging her to send me twelve bottles of the Horlick's Malted milk as soon as she possibly could.

In order so she would get it the next morning, Charlie again walked to North Bay through the bitter cold. About noon, my father came bringing fresh pork, fresh beef, milk, eggs, cookies, cheese, and a lot of other things. He said my mother wanted to come, but he would not let her come till it warmed up a little. It was now twenty degrees below zero. Dear, good Mrs. Rosa stayed until the tenth, then she was called to another birth. While she was there, she took good care of me day and night. Also the baby. Did the cooking and washing. I paid her ten dollars. Mr. Reamore went and got Mrs. Belcher. All she did was to eat, sleep, and tell Charlie what to do. I could feed myself, but could not turn over in bed without help.

Mrs. Belcher did change the baby and wash her diapers. She would sit by the hour and read. Charlie did the cooking. She and Charlie got in a row. She went down to my parents' house and stayed while my father got Mr. Reamore to take her home. So when the baby was ten days old, I was alone with Charlie.

Charlie did his best. Cooked, washed the dishes, waited on me, changed the baby, cleaned and mixed up her bottles--the malted milk had come--and went practically without sleep, keeping fire all night, feeding and changing the baby every few hours. But it seemed that he had never in his life washed out anything, so he just threw the dirty diapers in a heap. It was lucky my mother had bought so many. One thing worried me. I knew we must be out of wood again.

After the baby was twelve days old, Charlie said he would have to leave me for an hour to go out and get a cord of wood from Paul. As soon as I was better, he would pay him back for it by cutting for him. He got our big rocking chair in front of the stove and spread a thick quilt over it. He raised me up out of bed on my feet, but my legs could not hold me and I slumped down. Everything turned black before me. Charlie lifted me back into my bed. But he had to leave me, said he would hurry back as soon as possible. He did. But this was the first time in my life I was afraid to be alone. I thought if the house would burn up, I could not have gotten up. And in the kitchen on the couch lay my baby. I could not have saved her either.

Two days later, we tried the getting up business again. This time, with Charlie's help, I walked to the chair. After resting, I told Charlie to put a kitchen chair beside me, fill a dishpan half full of warm water, and bring me a bar of soap and the pile of soiled diapers. Slowly, very slowly, I washed them out. Told Charlie to empty the water, again half fill the pan with warm water, and I rinsed them out. Told Charlie to hang them out on the line. There was a beautiful sunshine outdoors. I lost consciousness. When I came to again, I found myself in bed. Still, I was gaining, very, very slowly, but each day there was a little improvement.

My mother came to see me twice. They had to hire Mr. Reamore to bring and take her back. But she did not bring me anything to eat. Since Mrs. Rosa and Mrs. Belcher had left, they never brought or sent me a mouthful. I heard afterwards they were not going to feed Charlie. So weak, sick, desperately in need of real nourishment, I had to go back to potatoes and vegetables, not even a spoonful of grease to heat them up. Our flour was gone. Once in while Charlie brought home a loaf of bread. I still had some canned berries. After paying Mrs. Belcher, I had just five dollars left. Often I was tempted to break into that for meat, but I had a reason for not doing that. The reason was I had made up my mind to buy a little pig in spring so next winter to have meat. Also garden seeds, as I knew I would not get them if I did not buy them myself. Now, here was a good thing about Charlie. He never asked me for a cent or touched a penny of it. My baby was getting all the good malted milk she could drink, had her daily bath, and never was left wet. No child ever had better care. Her clothes would have been suitable for a little princess. How she grew. How very beautiful she was.

Well, in one way I was happy. I loved my child. I knew Charlie fairly worshiped her and if possible, showed me more affection than ever. When the baby was four weeks old, Charlie went back into the wood business with Paul Meaney. This winter was not quite as cold as the winter before, but since the baby came, we had fire night and day. I was longing to go home. It seemed as if I had not been there in many months. But I was still so weak I could hardly do the most necessary housework and knew I could never walk half a mile through the snow, let alone come back.

Came the twentieth of February, a beautiful, sunshiny day. I was getting much better, though still far from well. I had thought of walking home and leaving the baby with Charlie. Still I hesitated, being afraid I might not be able to walk back. Then about eleven o'clock, Mr. Reamore drove up to our door, saying my father had hired him to come and get me, bring me home, and at three o'clock take me back. I was overjoyed. I bundled up the baby and took her food along. Charlie did not like it. In the first place, he did not like the idea of his not going, too, and then he really hated being parted from the baby even for a few hours.

We got home, my mother took the baby, and I could not remember ever having seen her so happy while she looked at it. My father, too, in his silent way, seemed very pleased to have us there. They had a wonderful good dinner. Oh, how good it seemed to eat just that one meal. We went into the living room and all the cats were there and had come to welcome me. My pussy gray, in particular, was glad. She purred and clung to me. Plants and flowers everywhere. Then my father and mother did a very wrong, yes wicked, thing. Whoever may read this book may say it was not right for me to say such a thing about my parents, but I am going to write the true story. Now that I am looking over the years, both my parents are in their graves now for many, many years, and I still say that what they did that day was very wicked.

The only excuse I can make for them was that they did it for their great love for me, but in a way it was a selfish love. I say again that parents should not try to lead their children's lives. Let each person lead their own life. After dinner, when we were all happily sitting together, my father began by saying the only sensible thing I could do was to stay. When Mr. Reamore came, I should just leave the baby, go back with him, load up the things I needed right away, bring them back and stay. He, my father, would hire Mr. Reamore the next day with his team and heavy sleigh and fetch all my things home. I was so surprised, stunned, I could hardly answer. Then my mother very persuasively added that I owed it to my child. The poor little innocent thing should have a real home. That man should not have her.

By now I was getting angry. I heard afterwards that they had this all planned to do before my baby was born. Up to now, my father had talked quietly. Now when he saw I resented his plan, he flew into a rage. Both of them said the reason I did not nurse my baby was because Charlie had forbidden it. I told and told them I had no milk. They both just sniffed and said it made no difference. They just stuck to it that it was Charlie's idea, and I was a darn fool to listen to him. My mother said it would have been so much better for the baby if I had nursed it. My father yelled out that a low person like Charlie would not give a darn about a baby.

They raved on until Mr. Reamore came after me. Amongst other things, they said they would never allow Charlie to enter their house again. I said then I would not come either. Then my mother said I was cruel and heartless to take the one joy from her, the baby. Finally, I said I would bring her down once in a while. If I wrote a hundred pages, I could not tell all they said that day.

When I got back that afternoon, Charlie was so glad to have us back, said how he missed us, how he kept watching the road, the clock. He knelt down beside the baby and said he hoped I had a good time. Well, I did not tell him one word of what they had said.

Came the sixth of March, a warm day, I carried the baby home. My father never spoke a word to me. My mother used me politely, loved the baby. They had been sending their washing to North Bay by Mr. Reamore. I said I could do it again now. Well, for me it meant twenty-five cents a week and one full meal. For my mother it meant to have the baby with her for a few hours. When Charlie was in the woods, I also went there once or twice a week for a little while.

On the second of April, one of the cows at home freshened and a few days later I started my trips there daily after a quart of new milk. I made those daily trips spring, summer, autumn, winter for four years. The only time I ever missed a day was once in a great while during an extra hard blizzard. But on the other hand, in the hottest days in summer, I had to make two trips a day so the baby would have sweet milk, as it would sour so quick.

Chapter 24

Now I am going over the next four years in a hurry. They were such terrible years for me that even now, in memory, I do not like to dwell on them. In the four years, my father never spoke to me. Once in a while he would make some sarcastic, cutting remark to my mother concerning Charlie or myself. My mother always helped him out. For example, "The Jaynes have a baby, but that father supports it, and of course also his wife." The answer, "Any man would support his child and wife. Even a beast would do that." Or maybe he would say, "I read in the newspaper about a woman who left her husband because he did not support her." The answer, "Any woman with the brains of a goose would leave a man like that."

At home, Charlie would still tell me of his great love for me and so on, but he made my life miserable with his unreasonable jealousy. If I happened to look up or down the road, he claimed I was expecting some man. When he was not painting, I knew he always was hiding somewhere around my old home, and when by any chance a man called to see my father, no matter if he was married or eighty years old, there would be a bitter row that night. Some of the time I had enough to eat; other times, I did not.

Here is something I could not understand and still do not. It was that at home, ever since I was a young girl, I did a lot of housework, helped to do the barn chores morning and nights, worked in the fields, the gardens, and for about two months in summer, picked a great many berries. Still, I always had a chance to rest after dinner. As long as the weather was warm, I would lie in the hammock on the verandah for an hour or so and read, in colder weather in the house. Now, although I had apparently so little to do, I never could sit down

247

to rest no matter how tired I was. It just seemed impossible. I am not superstitious, but sometimes I actually thought there must be a curse on the house.

Well, I did buy a little pig in the spring and Charlie did manage to buy the feed for it. I also bought garden seeds and helped in the garden, but we never again had such a bumper crop as the first year. I picked and sold a few berries each summer, took in a dollar a month for washing, sold a few vegetables. I used every penny of my own money for extra food for my baby and to buy the spring pig and garden seeds. Luckily, I had had so many, many clothes given to me from New York that I did not buy a single garment.

After two years, my shoes all worn out, I wrote to Mrs. Fairchild and Mrs. Mills, begging them to send me some of their used shoes. They did, but both of them said that now I was married, my husband should buy my shoes. My parents kept on buying expensive clothes for the baby. When she was four months old, they bought her a lovely baby carriage. Now maybe people will say that if my parents always threw out so many bitter things at me, why did I still keep going there? There were reasons enough. After my baby could eat a few things, each day I was there, my mother fed her good, easy to digest food, soft boiled eggs, light custards, bananas, and later on, meat, fresh fruit and all kinds of nutritious food she needed and I could not buy for her.

I only ate there on wash days, or when I picked berries in the forenoon, leaving my baby with my mother. How happy she was when down to my old home. So the time went by. Hatred on my parents' side, jealousy, hunger, and toil on the other side. Never any diversion. No, I even had to give up my reading. I never had an idle moment and at night I was too tired to read. Sometimes I did not even undress, except my shoes, and when December the twenty-first came, I was thirty-seven years old.

Of course there was the Christmas tree at home. I took my little girl, who was now nearly four years old, down in the early morning as my mother wished. It was still half dark outside and they had hung heavy blankets at the windows inside so the lights on the tree would look better. Oh, it all was so lovely, so holy, and peace in the house. If only Charlie could have come down with me. They had given my little girl an enormous amount of beautiful presents. My mother and I had returned into the kitchen, little Sophie between us. She just fluttered from one thing to the other in her childish happiness. The tree in the living room was still lit. I looked in and what I saw, I shall never forget. My mother had always been very religious and had taught me to pray, had so many times told me the beautiful story of the Christ-child, the life, the love, the death of Jesus. Some of the beautiful verses of the Bible. I knew my father was no infidel, still I had never heard him talk about religion. What I saw under the lighted Christmas tree on that early Christmas day, or rather morning, was my father kneeling under the tree. His head, that had always been held high, was bowed low in silent prayer. His hair which had been as straight and black as a raven's wing was now snow white. This sight touched me strangely.

Was he now thinking back to the time when he was a little boy in a faraway country, in the long and long ago, when he frolicked around another Christmas morning with his father and mother, who now had been turned to dust so many years ago? Perhaps, too, of his six brothers and sisters who had been with him under just such a tree as now. He did not even know if they were alive or not, and if alive, in what part of the world. Perhaps his entire life passed before his mind, the long, long road that had stretched before him in his youthful days, and now he saw he had suddenly come to the end of it all.

Perhaps he was thinking of the little farm where he had toiled now for nearly fifty years, trying so hard to make it into a home for the ones he so dearly loved. Perhaps he also remembered that on that very spot where the tree now stood had stood the operating table, with my mother's blood-covered head hanging down, and the doctors saying it was too late. Perhaps, too, he saw me, a little child, a young girl, and now here was another little Sophie. Though he hated and despised her father, after all, she was still his grandchild. God in heaven only knew what passed through his mind. For me, it was a holy picture.

After a while, he came into the kitchen. My little girl was wildly excited with her treasures and eager to show them to her Papa Charlie, as she always called her father. We packed all her many things in her covered sleigh, which her grandparents had given her three years ago.

Came the sixth of January and my little girl's fourth birthday. The winter went on as usual. The forepart of the winter, we had good fresh meat, but by the middle of February, that was used up. I still made my daily trips home after the quart of milk. Little Sophie still loved her milk. On fair days, I took her with me. I only ate there on washdays. I saved every cent I got hold of to buy extra food for my little girl. She had never yet gone hungry, and I did not intend that she ever should.

About the first of February, I started coughing. I did not get any better, but each day, no matter how cold or rough the weather was, I made my trip home after the milk. I got so I could cough all night and when I tried to eat, it strangled me. Came the tenth of February, I was getting much worse. A cold northwest wind was blowing. Charlie was bitter against my going after the milk, said the child could get along without it for a few days. Little Sophie kept running to me, her little painted cup in her hands, saying, Mama, please milk. Well, I bundled up and coughed my way home, stayed a few minutes, and started back. Now I had to face the northwest icy blast. I coughed and strangled till I fell in the deep snow, rested, and had another spell. Sometimes I thought I could not get up again. Somehow I reached home. I got so bad after that that each time I had one of those coughing spasms, I nearly strangled to death, could not swallow a mouthful. I longed for a cup of hot milk, but I would not touch my baby's milk. I was so weak and tired, but when night came, I would not lay down.

The moment I laid down, I had another coughing spasm. Came morning, the wind had turned into the north east, if possible colder, rougher than the day before. Of course I could not eat. Charlie absolutely forbade my going after milk. That was not necessary. I knew very well that I never could have made even one third of the way one way. Things looked bad. I worried about my baby's food. I realized it might be many days before I could get out again. As well I knew; I did not have just a cold. About eleven o'clock Mrs. Meaney, Paul Meaney's mother, drove into the yard with her horse and cutter. She parked the horse on the south side of the house where the bitter cold wind would not strike him, put a heavy blanket on him, and came into our house.

I tried to welcome her, but the moment I started to talk, I strangled so bad I almost choked to death. The poor woman was frightened. She said I ought to be in bed and have a doctor. I tried to tell her that I would be all right, but was worried about my little girl's milk. Then Charlie told her that I had been down yesterday and of course got much worse. She stared at me then said, "Why don't Charlie go about the milk?" I hesitated then gasped out, "They do not want him to come there." That had been the most I had ever said to any one against my parents, while they told everyone that came there what a terrible man Charlie was, and how good they themselves were. Mrs. Meaney said nothing, but as sick as I was, I saw a strange look in her face. She said she was on her way to Vienna to see her mother, Mrs. Mahonny. I asked her if she would be kind enough to stop at my mother's and leave the empty bottle and on her way back call and bring me the milk. She gave me a strange laugh and said she would not at all mind to stop there.

Well, the day dragged by, my little Sophie running to the east window to see if Mrs. Meaney was coming back. Childlike, she started looking for her hours before I knew she could come back.

The afternoon wore on, the weather getting rougher, wilder. Still no Mrs. Meaney. I began to fear that the back roads over which she was to return had gotten impassable and that she went home by North Bay. Just at the beginning of dark, she drove in, brought the milk and a letter from my mother. I felt frightened. Probably some bitter mean accusations. Mrs. Meaney gave a loud laugh and said, "Tomorrow Charlie can go and get the milk." Charlie spoke up and said, "They won't let me come in the house." Mrs. Meaney gave another laugh and said, "Oh, yes, they will let you come in. In fact, they want you to come." She laughed again and left for her home. I opened the letter with trembling fingers. Out fell a five dollar bill. In those days, that meant about the same as fifteen or eighteen dollars would today. I started weeping as I had never wept before. The tears rushed down my cheeks in streams. I had to read that letter over a number of times before I could really believe the news of it. I could not hand it over to Charlie, as it was written in German. When I could control my cough and emotion enough to speak, I told him that my mother said they both felt very sorry to hear how sick I was, that my father was sending me some money to get a doctor and whatever I might need. She said I should not try to come after milk till I was well again, that Charlie should come down after it each day. She would come to see me just as quick as they could hire Mr. Reamore to bring her to me.

I must say this. Although my little girl was now four years old, my father had not been in my house since the night she was born. My mother came twice soon after, but now it was more than four years that she had been there.

Early next morning, Charlie went to North Bay and got Dr. Wilsey to come. He stopped at the store and bought a few things he thought I could eat. He rode home with the doctor. Dr. Wilsey said I had whooping cough. Said there were about twenty-five cases around North Bay, but that I was by far the worst of any of them. After he left, Charlie went to my parents' home. I answered my mother's letter. After he left, I knelt down and prayed, asking God to let real peace come to us. Well, after a short time, Charlie came back with a basket full of good food, besides the milk. He said that both my parents had received him kindly, told him to be sure and come each day. My mother came twice to see me. My father kept sending money. They also sent more food.

On the fifteenth of March, they sent Mr. Reamore after me. When I got home, I was sad to see my father looked very ill. My mother had always been delicate, often, often very sick. But my father always was well. Now what a change had come over him. He was more kindly towards me than he had been since I had come home from the West. When I saw my mother alone, I asked her just what Mrs. Meaney had said that day. My mother got a little nervous and replied, "Mrs. Meaney is a very outspoken woman." Then she changed the subject, and as I noticed that she did not like to talk about it, I said no more. But a few weeks later, when I was quite well again, I went to see Mrs. Meaney. I told her that she accomplished a miracle making peace between Charlie and my parents. I thanked her then asked her how she did it. She gave that same laugh and said, "I told them just what I thought of them. I had wanted to do that for a long time." Then she told me that she told them that I was sick unto death, needed a doctor and food. That I was their only child and while they were living in comfort and plenty, that they ought to be ashamed of themselves. They were always helping others, but let their own child live in actual want. I stared at her and asked, "How did you dare to talk like that to them?" She laughed again, said, "I dared to do it all right. I knew they could do no more than to order me out of their house, but for once I was going to have those proud people know just what I thought of them."

I asked her what they said. She said they both started in on Charlie, that the reason they did not help me was because he was no good. Then Mrs. Meaney said she told them that Charlie was as good as they were. Again, I said, "How did you dare to talk like that to them?" She laughed out good and loud and continued, "I told them a lot more. I told them that the whole neighborhood was talking about them, saying that they were hard hearted people, that they thought a lot more of Charlie than they did of them." Again she laughed, said they were always running Charlie down, talking about him, hiring men to do the farm work, paying them high wages, and then saying how lazy Charlie was, why they did not hire him. She also told them that Charlie never spoke a mean word about them. I thanked her again. She laughed and said, "Oh, I enjoyed telling them. They looked so surprised they forgot to get angry."

Well, when the snow went off in the beginning of April, my father hired Charlie every day. I went down about half past ten and helped my mother with the dinner. My little Sophie was very happy. She loved us all, and my father was a changed man. I had never seen him so kind and gentle before. But dear God, he was failing fast. Still, somehow I could not believe it. He never had been sick, always so strong and rugged, why of course he would be all right again.

April, May, June, we were a happy, peaceful family together. Charlie really worked hard, did all the work on the farm excepting the team work. I was at my old home most all day. Little Sophie would bring my father presents each day--a pretty pebble she found on the road, a wild flower, a bird feather, and so on.

Came the Fourth of July, a hot day; my father was sitting under the big maple trees in front of the house. He did not complain. My poor dear mother looking sadder, more worried, telling me she feared it would not be long now. I just could not believe it. I told her he had never complained. In the distance we heard the canons fired. My father looked up and said in a far away voice, "Look, that was the way the battle between Petersburg and Richmond began." Then his head sank down again. It was early evening, a quiet solemn night, a strange light all around us, a beautiful light. We all felt it more than we saw it. Little Sophie went up to her grandfather and said good night. We went away. He looked after us strangely.

Now I just cannot bring myself to speak much about the next day, the fifth of July, only this much. At two o'clock in the afternoon, my father went to sleep on the same couch in the same room where he had always taken his naps. He was sitting outdoors under the old maple trees all the forenoon, then walked slowly into the house, sat down on the couch near the window, looked at us, gave a deep sigh, and closing his eyes, went to sleep, sitting up, never again to wake up. This was the first death in our family, the first link broken forever.

Through Sophie's Eyes

I will go over the next few days swiftly. Even now, after the long span of years, it pains me too much to dwell on my mother's great anguish, her agony of heartache, the great sorrow of losing my father. She did not rave and tear her hair, but even through it all, she was thoughtful for our little Sophie. Now just why this one little thing impressed itself so deeply in my heart, I never knew. But I do know that if my mother had screamed and made a big scene, I probably would have forgotten it long ago. But this thing I can never forget.

The undertakers left our house about at midnight. I had put my sleeping child on the bed in the big bedroom next to the living room. This was the first night she had ever spent here. Charlie went to our little home. My mother and I stayed up until two. She was utterly exhausted, had not closed her eyes the night before. She lay down on her bed in the recess. I lay down on the bed with my little girl. None of us undressed. There came the light that comes between night and day. I heard my mother moaning. I got up. She, too, was up. We walked out of the house. It was at least half an hour still before sunrise, but dawning comes early in July. This was the sixth.

The summer had been unusually hot and dry. This morning promised another hot day, but as yet there was a pleasant, cool air. No wind, a few notes from a half awakened robin, a wonderful sense of peace all about us. At that time, there was a large apple tree a little north east of the verandah. Now there are good sized maple trees where the apple tree stood. Under this apple tree was an old cook stove. I made a fire in it to heat some water to make coffee. My mother could not eat. There the two of us stood. My mother looked all around, then said, "The world is so empty." That was all, but it impressed me far, far more than if she had said a thousand wild words.

My father had so loved his little home farm, its seclusion from the outside world and filled with bitter sweet memories of nearly fifty years of life spent there, that he had often expressed the wish to be buried there, even after death, that, all that was mortal should remain under the ground over which he had walked countless of times. So we made arrangements to have him buried just below the little grave of my baby brother, his first child. I will not go over these first days. We had the funeral on the eighth of July. There were sixty-eight people present, neighbors, and today, looking back, I can only remember six still being alive. I and my little girl stayed with my mother. Charlie was with us most of the time, but as we had planted a fairly large garden, and had a pig at our little home, we thought it best he should stay there nights till after the pig was butchered and the garden stuff gathered.

I also had another reason. I thought it would be easier for my poor mother to get used to the new life slowly. I fitted into the picture, had been born and raised there, and I was flesh and blood of my father, had lived there for about thirty-one years, for the next six years had been there almost daily. She, my mother, loved my child doubly so because my father had also loved her. Although peace had come between us, I felt that my mother still resented Charlie. Good Christian woman that she was, she would always look at Charlie as an outsider, an intruder. Now before I go on with this story, I must relate something I could never understand.

As I just said, I had lived at home for over thirty-one years. In all that time, my mother and I had never quarreled. Then I lived with Charlie six years, and with the exception of his jealousy, he and I had also never quarreled. I know both my mother and Charlie had fervently made up their minds to be agreeable to each other. That I know. Yet, after he once came to live with us just before Thanksgiving, they had one row after the other. Neither one seemed to blame, or if turned around, both were to blame. If I tried to make peace between them, my mother would say to me, "Sophie, I am surprised at you, that you stick up for that man against your poor old mother." Charlie would say, "We got along all right, lived happy together, and now, no matter what I do, you turn against me, join in with your mother." Then both of them would be on the constant lookout for offenses, each one thinking the other one had done this or that just to be mean. I could write many chapters on this subject, but I will now go back to the time after the funeral.

In a way, everything went on the same, yet nothing seemed quite the same anymore. It was pitiful to see how much the cats missed my father. They would look for him, listen for his voice and footstep, especially his cat named Tippy. It seemed as if a hush had fallen over everything. The grief of mother was pitiful to see. Now I have heard so many, many times that death wipes away all hatred, that after a parent dies, the son or daughter admits that they had always been in the wrong, never the parent. Now as this is a true story, I will say I could never have said that in our endless quarrels my father was right and I in the wrong. Not then or even today, now after he has been resting in his grave for nearly thirty-two years.

I still say he was too strict, too unforgiving, too bossy. But after his death, I also began to see his great love for me. He wanted to plan and run my life after the pattern he had laid out for me. I also saw him again, in memory, I a little child following him about the barn, the great joy in his silent face at Christmas times. Saw him in the little red school house, saw him wallowing through the deep snow with our week's supply of groceries, and saw him kneeling under the Christmas tree his last Christmas on this earth.

I shall never forget the evenings after the funeral on the verandah, Charlie going home after supper. My mother would sit in her chair, my father's chair empty at her side. I would lay in my hammock, my sleeping child beside me. Everything was the same. The white winding road in the moonlight, the big maples shading the lower driveway, the sweet night, the dear night sounds, crickets chirping, once in a while the deep cry of a night hawk, and even late as it was in summer, a distant call of the whip-poor-will.

I say everything was the same. Oh, no, just below the little grave, with its white picket fence, was another grave, a much larger one and a new one, too new. My mother and I would talk together then lapse into long silence. I would go back to the olden days, the evenings when we sat out here together and my father would sing the olden songs in his really beautiful voice. Later, when I was dreaming of the future, my mind so often, so tenderly and yearningly went back to the days when Joe Henry would walk up the road and to our verandah. Yes, he was the only man I had ever loved, loved with a pure love, as I think few girls ever love a man. Then, fleetingly, I would think of my beautiful five week's honeymoon in dear old Frisco. Those five weeks ever did and ever will stand out as the happiest of my life, like a chapter out of another world, another existence. True, I did not feel the glory of love I did for my Joe, but the setting, the background, was incomparably lovely, and ever the thought of the West brings that picture before me.

Chapter 25

So the summer folded into autumn and late in November, Charlie came home. Mr. Reamore brought all my things back and I furnished my large bedroom upstairs. Little Sophie was delighted. She had always hated to see her Papa Charlie leave towards night. I could see my mother did not like the new arrangement, but tried to take it sensible.

Here is where our new troubles started. I could mention a dozen things that caused trouble between my mother and Charlie, but I will here only mention a few. When my father died, of course his big pension stopped and so did his annuity from the old country. Of course he had laid by a small sum for my mother. But after the funeral expenses were paid there was not so very much left in the bank. My mother received her widow's pension, but naturally it cost more for four of us to live than it had for those two. Added to this, the prices at that time were just mounting up on account of the war-- World War One. So they tried to settle things like this. My mother said she would buy all the groceries, pay the taxes, and furnish the milk, cream, butter, and eggs. Charlie was to cut the wood for the winter kitchen cook stove and get it drawed to the house.

Now that sounded real good to me because with Paul Meaney Charlie had to help cut three cords to get one while here in our own woods, he only had to cut for us. But Charlie declared that he could not cut alone, and as he had no money, my mother had to hire a man to help cut, then hire Mr. Nash to draw it home. As to the food question, my mother always had been an extra small eater and there were four of us to eat. There never was a meal eaten but my mother would mention how big the weekly grocery bill was. Charlie let no meal pass but what he figured out how much cabbage, carrots, potatoes cost. While the pork lasted, that also was brought up. But in February that was eaten up, so my mother was expected to buy meat and fish each week, as they belonged to the groceries.

They never quarreled about these things, just looked hurt. Well, came the twenty-first of December, my thirty-eighth birthday. Then Christmas, the first one without my father and the first one with my little girl living in my old home. My dear mother had bought enough Christmas presents for little Sophie as a dozen little ones generally received.

Still, for me it was rather a sad Christmas. The great grief of my mother went to my heart, and I felt sure it would be her last Christmas. She was so frail. But of course, in a way, I was happy in the knowledge of my little daughter's happiness.

On the sixth of January, my little Sophie was five years old. I will not write much about this winter. My poor mother was bravely trying to bear up. She was never really well, but did not complain. Still, a dozen times a day, sighing, she would remark how happy she had been till my father died, and now everything was so different. Then she would add, knowingly, that she was glad that he did not know how things were going on now.

Charlie would look at me wistfully and say, "I wish we were back in our own home. We were so happy there." My little girl, at least, was perfectly happy. Came April, the snow went early and by the middle of April the ground was dry enough to plow. I put in a garden. As there was not enough pasture, my mother had to sell one of our four cows. I hated to see her go, but I could plainly see that not only the lack of pasture, but also a great shortage of feed was coming. No cornstalks or sowed corn. Though everything was so high, cows brought very little.

On the twenty-first of April, I hired a horse and buggy and Charlie and I and little Sophie drove out to Cleveland to see Barney Delehunt. Mr. Delehunt was a real estate agent, and I wanted him to sell my little place. He knew about the place and gave me very little encouragement. Said it might be many years before he would be able to sell it. He said it was too small for a farm, on a side road, not even on a mail route, not suitable for people with children, being too far from a school or church. Unsuitable for a carpenter or any other

Sophie Kussmaul

mechanic as it was not near enough to a village. But, he said, he would do his best to try and sell it.

On the nineteenth of May, at dusk, a car drove into our yard. Mr. Delehunt came to the door. I was feeding a calf. He called to me, saying he had a prospective buyer out in the car. I got the key for the house. Then Charlie, little Sophie, and I got into the car. This was the first time any of us had ever been in an automobile. The man's name who was with Mr. Delehunt was Townsend. He was almost a giant, tall, broad shouldered, and very powerfully built. He was eighty-four years old, but could easily walk thirty to forty miles in a day.

By the time we got to the house it was about dark. Mr. Townsend glanced about and said it was just what he wanted. We made arrangements to meet him next day at Cleveland at Mr. Delehunt's office. We hired a horse and buggy and at two in the afternoon, the place had been sold and bought, Mr. Townsend paying me the cash.

The next day little Sophie and I walked to the North Bay depot in the morning and took a train to Oneida. I put most of the money in the bank and kept only a few dollars. I bought a lot of things for little Sophie and we came home that night tired, but happy. Well, this spring and summer I really worked very hard. I did all the chores, took entire care of the vegetable garden, and helped my mother in the house. In fact, I did most of the housework.

We had no more ducks, and only about half as many hens and chickens as in the old days. My mother hired the grass mowed. I raked it, with a neighbor's horse, helped to draw it in. Picked a lot of berries. We had fresh berries on the table every day for ten weeks starting with wild strawberries, raspberries, huckleberries, and lastly my beloved wild blackberries. My mother and I canned dozens and dozens of cans for winter use.

The spring and summer before, Charlie had really worked hard on the farm; then he got paid for all he did. Now, though he, little Sophie, and myself got our living, a good living, he kept saying he was just working for nothing. Of course my mother's pension would have been enough for her, but not for four people, so every little while she had to draw on the reserve she had in the bank.

I had intended to buy a horse right away after I sold my little place, but as fate would have it, horses were very high and our feed supply low. I did not want to use up too much of my money, as I had my heart set on improving the house and building a new hen house. Of course, in a way, I still missed my father, but I think it is in God's plan that children should not grieve too hard, or long, for the loss of a parent.

Still, I was quite happy this spring and summer. Both my little girl and I were in perfect health. I was home. Though I did ten times the work, then experienced that utter exhaustion I had always felt in the other home, of course now I had my three full meals a day and a short nap after dinner. As of old, I took a great interest in the farm. Life seemed very good to me and the future still beckoned me on with a silver wand.

One thing I sadly missed was our dear evenings on the verandah. My mother would not come and sit with us, not this summer, because Charlie was here. I know how her heart ached, alone in her dark room. Charlie would come out a few minutes, then complain about the night air, go upstairs, close the window up tight, light a lamp and read. Then every few minutes, open a window and yell down to me to bring up the child, I was exposing her to the night air.

So the spring and summer passed by. Came the sixteenth of September, Mr. George Verian came to our house. He was living with his sister and her family, but he owned a house in North Bay, on the back street. He wanted to get Charlie to paint his house, pay him by the job. Charlie had .not done any painting for two years. The house was not very large and Charlie thought he could do it in about a month. I said I would dig and bring in the potatoes. The other work I did anyway.

My mother said nothing, but I could see that she was very glad. I knew the reason. She thought that now for one month Charlie would be away all day. Well, as Mr. Verian had the paint down at his North Bay house, Charlie started work the next morning. Charlie always liked getting up early. I got up, cooked his breakfast, packed his lunch pail, and he left soon after six o'clock. He was barely out of the house when my mother made her appearance, and then little Sophie ran downstairs. We ate breakfast together and for the first time since my father's death, my mother looked and acted almost happy again. I went out to do my chores, and as always, little Sophie was with me. We had our dinner together. Of course, Charlie came home for supper.

The next morning, the eighteenth, everything went the way it did the day before. After I had done my out door chores, I built a fire in the summer kitchen stove and started to make and bake a batch of pumpkin pies. The day was quite hot. Little Sophie was playing near by under a shade tree. All at once I heard the sound of wheels coming up the lower driveway. Of course where I was I could not see the front of the house, and as I heard the rig stop, I ran around the corner of the house to see who was there. There was a large white horse hitched to what was called a democrat wagon. The driver was just jumping out of the back of the wagon box. For a moment I stared; then I knew. There was another man squatting on the floor of the wagon box with his arms around Charlie, holding and steadying him, but what a Charlie, covered with tar and blood.

He knew me, but could not speak. His mouth, too, was dripping blood. The man, whom I did not know, told me that Charlie had slipped on the roof as he was tarring it, and fell on a paved walk below. It seemed that in falling he had stretched out his arms instinctively to break his fall. They also told me that the doctors were on their way up. Yes, they were even then driving into our yard: Dr. Wilsey and Dr. Button, the latter a good surgeon from New York City who was spending the summer at North Bay.

In falling, he had gotten tangled up with the tar bucket. Well, I will give a list of his injuries. One arm, below the elbow, was broken in two places, the other arm in three places, two of the bones sticking through the skin an inch. At first they wanted to amputate this arm, but I begged them not to. They found that his collar bone was broken and also two ribs. His nose and jaw and his tongue were badly cut. Added to all this, there were small pieces of glass sticking out all over his face as he had smashed the glasses he always wore.

Well, poor brave Charlie, he never lost consciousness through all the bone setting. After that was all done, and the glass picked out of his face, they went and washed the blood off from him, but could not do anything with the tar. They pulled off his paint and tar spattered clothes and asked me for a dressing gown or bath robe. Neither Charlie nor I ever had one, but I knew there were two in the trunk upstairs where my mother had packed away my father's clothes. I ran up, got one of them, thinking that in such a case and my father now being dead over a year, my mother would not object. However, well, I will not say any more. Both doctors told me that Charlie must not go to bed, but be kept in a sitting position. So we fixed him up in a large easy chair, with pillows all around him so he could lie back comfortably. But they asked me for a long scarf as they said he would probably be out of his head at nightfall and try to get up. If so, he would fall on his face, hurt his arms, ribs, and collar bone anew. They gave me orders to put a few teaspoons of fresh water in his mouth whenever I had a chance.

His food, of course, would exist of thin soups, broths, and milk for weeks until his tongue and jaw were healed. But as I could only feed him a few spoons at a time, he had to be fed every hour or two. Of course I also had to do the same for him as for a baby as he could not wait on himself. Now it was impossible for him to go up to our room, so he stayed in the winter kitchen, which really was, in warm weather, a living room. I slept on the couch in my clothes as I was up every hour or two. My mother and little Sophie slept upstairs in our room for two weeks, which I am sorry to say my mother bitterly resented.

After two weeks, I carefully helped him up to our room. I could not lead him, as I must not touch his arms. He now went to bed at night and up in the morning. The first few days, both doctors came twice a day; after that, Dr. Luddon alone, but still twice a day for two weeks.

I must say this. Mr. Arthur Nash came every day, offering to do what he could. Also, always stopped on his way to North Bay to see if we wanted to send for anything. The doctors told me, as Charlie got better, that they never thought he could get well. He already was sixty-eight years old. Of course I had all the outdoor chores to do just the same, also our washing and cleaning and cooking. My mother looked after and amused little Sophie most of the time.

After a few weeks, when I could leave Charlie a little longer, I gathered our winter vegetables, picked the apples and grapes, dug the potatoes, wheeled them into the cellar. I bought two pigs this past spring instead of one, as we always were out of meat by about the middle of February. So I had one of them killed the first of November and the other one not till the middle of January, the latter one a great big hog, and so we had pork all winter, and salt pork.

The next day after it was killed, I cut it up. Came Thanksgiving. Charlie for the first time since his accident eating at the table. Up to now, I always helped to feed him, but today he started eating without my help, excepting that I had to cut up his meat, butter his bread.

Sophie Kussmaul

For a good many years, my parents had started their coal fire in the living room from the first to the tenth of November according to the weather. Charlie, who always seemed to feel the cold more, was extra sensitive to it this fall owing to his terrible smash up, so on his account we started the coal fire by the middle of October. Coal had jumped up to twice the old price. My poor mother had to draw more of her savings from the bank. We also knew that Charlie could not cut a stick of wood, so my mother and I tried to figure out about how many cords we would need. I drew some of my savings and together we bought the wood.

The twenty-first of December, I was thirty-nine years old. A very happy Christmas for little Sophie. January sixth, and her seventh birthday. She ought to have been in school, but in the first place, we lived a mile and a quarter from the school house. In the second place, she was very shy and not used to children, with me all the time. So I thought I would not begin to send her till school would open again the following September.

The winter went by slowly, my poor mother more or less sick all winter. Charlie blue, but in fairly good health. I and my little child kept well. But to our dismay, we had to buy more coal and more wood. Spring came at last and I bought Kitty, a big black horse with a white face. I paid one hundred dollars for her and as she was still quite a young horse, thought she would last us for many years to come.

I started the farm work, drawed out the manure, went into the woods and picked up a few loads of dry, scattered wood. We got some land plowed; I dragged and marked it, planted it, put in a piece of oats. We hired the grass mowed. I raked it up and with the help of my little girl drawed it into the barn, then got the oats in. Now, I thought, Kitty can go out to pasture. I hurried to get some berries picked for winter use. Kitty was lying in the pasture, could not get up. I did not know what ailed her. She did not seem to be sick. We carried hay, grass and oats to her, and of course, water. She ate and drank, but did not get up.

After two days, I sent for Dr. Boshart at Camden. He examined her very carefully, admitted she was a young horse, but had a weak heart. Would never again get up. Two days after that she died. This was on the first of August. On the twenty-fourth of August, I bought

Queenie, a bay mare, for forty dollars. I knew she was old, but what I did not know when I bought her was that she had been doped with arsenic.

Well, the day after Labor Day, the fourth of September, our school opened up. I took my little girl to school. The teacher's name was Miss Elenore Shanly. It made me heartsick to leave her at the school. She looked so frightened, desolate and forlorn. She did not cry, but when I started to leave her, she gave me such an imploring look, begging me with her eyes to take her back home, but I knew I must not. Before leaving home that morning, she put all her cows and horses out to pasture. Her grandmother had made her about twenty little cloth cows and half a dozen horses. There were stantons for the cows and little box stalls for the horses. She told me if it rained to be sure and put all her cattle up, showing me again the proper place for each one. Then she went and said goodbye to each of her many dolls. I knew her grandmother took it much to heart, too, but she bravely kept telling my little girl how nice it would be in school, children to play with.

Well, the first day seemed endless. I went after her. Both the teacher and all the children were good to her. She learned very fast, but never liked school. The next day after she started her school, I started building my new kitchen. The old backroom was torn down and I had a real kitchen built. After this, the winter kitchen would be our living room and if we had company, our dining room.

Our old living room I turned into a parlor, of which I was immensely proud. Mr. Atwell Annis of North Bay did the carpenter work. At the same time, I had a brand new hen house built. Jim Dixon did the work on that. I was very busy, but happy.

By the beginning of November, the kitchen was complete, also the hen house. We had our big wood cook stove moved into the new kitchen, and the coal stove moved from the old living room. But here a new problem popped up. Now there would not be any heat under our big room upstairs. So we had a chunk stove that had been in one of the outbuildings moved up into our room and set up. This would mean an extra stove to buy wood for. The new kitchen was not connected with the old one. There had been a pantry but I took out the shelves and made a lovely little freshly papered and painted hallway between what would be the new living room and the kitchen, but that would not help either the kitchen fire or the living room fire to help each other. That, too, meant more coal or wood. I had intended to use the new living room for a dining room when we had company. I set the big table, put on the silencer under the rich white damask table cloth, set the table with my gold and blue trimmed china and the heavy silver. Then I threw an embroidered cloth over the whole table. The beautiful dishes and silver showed through. I was very happy.

But there were a few things that worried me. Queenie was getting thinner and weaker. I fed her more ground feed in a week than I ever fed Billy or Kitty even during their hardest work. I only used her now to take little Sophie to school and sometimes, if the weather was bad, to go after her. I doubled her feed. Still I saw she was failing fast. Yes, I gave her more now in one day than I had ever given a horse in four days. She was so gentle, so affectionate.

Came the twenty-first of December, my fortieth birthday. Of course for a long time I knew it was coming. Still, in a way, it seemed so strange to me. Why I had only been thirty a little while ago. Yes, really, and only twenty not so very long ago either. But I shook this off. Life was still all before me. Yes, it called to me with a sweet voice. It beckoned me onward.

A lovely Christmas, but a very sick Queenie in the barn. She died on the twenty-ninth of December. I had taken my last cent out of the bank to pay for the building. I could not ask my mother for money to buy another horse. For the last two Christmases, since Charlie had got smashed up so badly, Mrs. Fairchild had sent me twenty-five dollars, but both times I had used it to help my mother buy wood, and in spring to buy two little pigs to raise and fatten for the coming winter.

I had written to good Mrs. Fairchild once in a while during all these years, and after Charlie's accident told her all about it. In fact, I had sent her a newspaper clipping about the accident. Before this, she had sent me clothes and shoes, never any money. I think that my mother had written to her telling her that my husband was lazy, so she probably thought it would only encourage his laziness to send me money. But after this terrible accident, she sent me those twenty-five dollars at Christmas time. Now I swallowed my pride and told her all about my buying Kitty. I told her the full truth, that I paid one hundred dollars for her, and that I had taken the money from the little place I sold. That, now, I did not have a cent left. That I needed a horse to get my child to and from school in winter. That was long before school buses were even heard of. That I did need a horse on the farm, and begged her to help me buy one. This was the truth. But I did not tell her about Queenie. I let her just think that I only had bought the one horse, thinking that if she knew I had lost two horses in nine months, she would think I was to blame and not try to help me buy another. Also, I did not mention the fact about my new kitchen and hen house.

To my great joy, by return mail I received one hundred dollars from Mrs. Fairchild to buy a horse. Now who ever reads this must know that even though the prices had come up greatly, that still a hundred dollars meant a lot more in those days than they do now. I took little Sophie to school a few mornings on her hand sled. Luckily there was not very much snow and she walked home.

Came the sixth of January, my little girl's eighth birthday. She did not go to school. Late in the afternoon, a man by the name of Edgerton drove into the yard with an iron gray horse. He had heard I wanted to buy a horse and of course highly recommended Frisky. She was only four years old, weighed about twelve hundred, was perfectly sound, and would work double or single. She was gentle and a fairly good road horse.

He wanted one hundred and twenty-five dollars for her. He insisted on leaving her with us a few days. The next morning I hitched her up and took my child to school. I drove to Camden, went out every day with her. She seemed all right, but still I did not like her. Friday afternoon after I had brought home my little girl, Mr. Edgerton came. I told him I did not want his Frisky. He was much surprised. That evening Mr. Le Grand Cleveland called to see us. Of course we talked about horses. He said he had heard that Charles Perrigold had five or six horses and wanted to sell part of them. Mr. Perrigold lived where Jerry Sands lived later.

Then like a flash, I remembered when I had picked black berries on the old McLaughlin farm, a beautiful snow white horse that had been in the pasture there with her colt. She was not only beautiful, but had such a gentle, intelligent face, beautiful dark eyes. Oh, I thought, if only I could get her. I knew she must be at least twelve or fourteen years old.

Next morning, Saturday, I asked Charlie to go up to Mr. Nash and tell him I wanted to hire him to take us to Perrigold's after dinner. It was bitter cold, way below zero, but we bundled up well and Mr. Nash took us to Perrigold's, a distance of a little over five miles. We went to the barn. There were six horses there, that is, four horses and a two year old colt and a yearling colt. I walked straight to Mollie's stall, the snow white mare I had in mind. Yes, she was beautiful. But, oh, in the next stall I saw a horse that was far, far handsomer. He was one of her sons. He was, I think, about the handsomest horse I had ever seen. He weighed between ten and eleven hundred. Like his mother, he was white, but where his mother was snow white, he was silver white. His coat fairly glistened and felt like the softest silk. His head was held high on a perfectly arched neck. I think he had the heaviest mane and tail I ever saw on a horse. They, too, were silver white and soft like silk. He was not really fat, but so well rounded that you could hardly see the line between his body and hips. Though he had a small body, you could not feel a single rib. His legs, though built strong, were slim. His face and eyes looked almost human. His father had been a registered Arabian stallion, his mother, Mollie, half Arabian, half mustang. He was not yet six years old, would be the next May.

I asked Perrigold how much he wanted for him. He said that Prince was not for sale. He would sell Mollie for seventy-five dollars, a bay horse for ninety dollars, and an iron gray for one hundred dollars. He said to Prince, "Shake hands." He lifted his front foot and placed his hoof gently into Perrigold's hand. Then he said, "Bow to the lady." Prince began to nuzzle each one of his master's pockets. Perrigold said he generally put a slice of bread, an apple, a potato, or a lump of sugar or some tobacco in his pockets when he came to the stable. When he said, "Prince, kiss me," Prince took his soft white lips and gently touched them to his master's cheek. Perrigold said, "I cannot sell him. He seems like my own son." But I kept at him and finally he said, "Will you be good to my horse?" I readily promised. Yes, I really did mean to keep that promise. But, oh how little I realized that day what was to come. Well, this is now all in the past, in the long an long ago. So in the end I talked Perrigold into selling me the horse. He had been offered two hundred dollars only a few days before. This was true, as we heard afterwards. I agreed to buy him for one hundred and fifty dollars and to pay one hundred today and give a note for the other fifty for six months. This was the first time in my life I had ever run into debt. As happy as I was about my horse, it bothered me. Of course my little Sophie was wildly delighted with the lovely horse and too young to understand the grave responsibility of raising those fifty dollars. Neither did it in the least worry Charlie. He just said, "Just write out to that Fairchild woman and tell her to send you fifty dollars."

Now I knew good as Mrs. Fairchild was and though she was so very wealthy, that if I asked her again for money, in less than two weeks from the time she had sent me a hundred dollars, she might never again give me a penny. Though I was so happy on the way home, I dreaded to tell my poor mother. I knew that neither my father nor mother had ever owed a cent in their lives. I had often heard my father say that no one should ever buy anything unless they could pay for it. Now I ran into debt for fifty dollars knowing I had no way to pay for it.

When I got home and had my Prince in the barn, I fairly dragged my poor mother out in the bitter cold to see him. She admitted that he was very beautiful. She had always been very fond of horses, but she told me I did wrong to buy him and that I should have bought one of the others, for which I could have paid. I knew she was right about this. I said I would pick a lot of huckleberries to sell. At that time, they only did bring six to eight cents a quart. My mother said, "Child, you are head over heels in your farm work." Well, again I knew she was right. She added, "You have a child to support."

The next day was Sunday, clear and cold. I got an early dinner, then hitched up my Prince. I still had my light harness, good cutter, string of sleigh bells, and my two lovely, heavy, warm robes. I took little Sophie for a long ride. I asked Charlie to go with us, but he said it was too cold; he would stay by the fire.

This is one day I shall never forget. The roads were fine for sleighing, and I really think my horse enjoyed it as much then as we did. We seemed to be flying along, mile after mile. What thrills of joy surged through me as we passed by cutter after cutter. How people stared at my horse and outfit. I was so happy. Yes, exultantly happy. I did not have to work my horse with a whip. If I just shook the lines, he seemed to break out into new speed. Little Sophie gave little low laughs. She was too happy to talk.

After supper that night, when I was going upstairs with Charlie and my little girl, my mother called me back, said she wanted to talk to me. I went up, got little Sophie settled, and came back downstairs. My mother said that the only way I could get out of that horse deal was to go to Rome the very next day, draw fifty dollars out of her bank and pay Perrigold. That touched me very much, as I knew she did not have much money.

We got up very early the next morning. I drove to North Bay, left Prince to some of my friends, took the eight-ten to Oneida, then a train on the Central to Rome. Back to Oneida, then North Bay and home in a snowstorm. That night little Sophie started with the measles, which had been in the neighborhood for some time. She had them very light. Our roads were impassable for a few days. Then Charlie and I drove to Perrigold's and finished paying for my Prince.

The winter passed by, a busy spring house cleaning, gardening, farming, the daily chores. I was happy, my mother and Charlie never really quarreled. I know they both tried to keep the peace. Still, they were so different, their childhoods, bringing-up, environment. In fact, their entire outlook of life was different, and so even while they really tried to be agreeable to each other, without knowing it, they offended each other. Charlie tried to help with the farm work.

When little Sophie was not in school, she was with me always. How glad she was when the long summer vacation came. Those were happy summers. Happier, much happier than I then knew. Now in my seventieth year, I can judge better about some things, see the things out of the past clearer. I know, yes I am certain, that my child was the only person on this earth who really understood me. My father and mother both loved me very much, but neither one of them in the least understood me. Playmates, schoolmates, and young girl companions, I had none. I had four husbands, besides my little honeymoon affair in San Francisco, but not one of these men ever read my heart. My Aunt Sophie also loved me, but we were strangers. My rich friends were more than good to me, but the life they planned for me, though luxurious, would have been terrible for me.

When my little Sophie was still very young, I always confided in her, used her like an equal, not the way I had been brought up. My good mother always made me feel that I was something very precious, something very tender, very sweet, something that must always and forever in a thousand ways be given to understand that I must never have an opinion of my own. I was just a child. They must decide for me. In short, I was entirely cut out of their life.

Through Sophie's Eyes

While my little girl and I were true companions, I felt she understood me then and also in her after years to come. Well, our busy, happy summer went swiftly by, too swiftly. On Labor Day, I took my little girl to Sylvan Beach. Then came her second school year.

During the month of October, Charlie and I and Prince went daily into the woods and got out some of our winter wood. Not all, by any means, as Charlie really was not able to do much hard work. In November, I took my little girl to Oneida and spent every cent I had earned from my huckleberries. I bought her a good winter coat, new shoes, stockings, underclothes, and two new dresses. I never had to buy anything for myself, as good Mrs. Fairchild still kept sending me clothes and shoes.

Chapter 26

Came the twenty-first of December, my forty-first birthday. A wonderful Christmas. The sixth of January and my child's ninth birthday. A long, dreary, busy winter. Charlie was not so well, never went out of doors. My poor mother, who always felt worse in winter, was weaker, sicker than usual. My little girl and I kept well. Thanks to Prince, I managed to get her to school most of the time. Many, many times he would waller through the deep snow up to his head, lay down, struggle up, and flounder on again. Of course there were some days when it was impossible for me to get her to school.

Spring came at last. Both my mother and Charlie felt much better when they could get out into the sunshine again. Came the twenty-ninth of May, the day before Decoration Day. A perfect May day. I had been working in the garden most of the forenoons. Little Sophie was in school. My mother cooked the dinner. Charlie had walked to North Bay. He always hurried right back, or at the most, stopped in at a friend's house. But Charlie loved to visit. He would stop and talk to anyone he knew. Yet in one way he was like my father. He never kept us waiting for him at meal time.

So promptly at a few minutes to twelve, he came home. We had a good dinner. My mother ate in silence, once in a while smiling at me. Charlie kept chatting. He was full of the news he had gathered on his North Bay trips. He said that Legrand Cleveland was putting in fifteen acres of sweet corn, that Albert Flanagan said the crows had pulled half his field corn, that Symore Flanagan had bought a new horse, that James Nichols and his wife had set out one thousand strawberry plants. Also quite a few more things like that.

I saw my mother look absentminded, probably did not really hear what Charlie was saying. I had felt mildly interested as I knew all the people so well and always liked to hear about farming. By now my mother and I were done eating, but as Charlie had talked so much, he was still busy with his pie. All at once he looked up, straight at me, and said, "Oh, I almost forgot to tell you that they buried Joe Henry today." All my life I had practiced self-control, but for a few moments I could not speak, even move. Charlie added lightly, "He was a good sort of fellow. I used to know him alittle, years ago." Then I heard my mother say, "Was that not that ditch digger who used to come here for water?" That roused me. There was something in her very tone of voice that indicated that he was only a ditch digger. For the first time in my life I felt a strong resentment welling up in me against my mother. When my father died, terrible as it was for her, she could at least indulge in her great grief. Yes, even for years after, she had the pity, the sympathy of her own and her friends. Her sorrow, her loss, was respected. I had loved Joe Henry as much as she had my father. This I knew. No mortal woman had ever loved a man more than I did my Joe.

Still, even in death I must hide my grief from her, and the world. As I had said so often, we never washed the dinner dishes right away. I grabbed what food there was left on the table, went to my hammock. My mother went to get her half hour nap and Charlie went to get a book and read, probably for hours. My heart was pounding so hard I could scarcely breathe. I looked towards the road. There was the lower driveway between the two big maples, and the white winding road, gleaming in the sunshine. Yes, everything was just the same as then, as when he came up the road, turned into that driveway, and walked lightly up to our verandah. Then a great ache came into my heart. Would I never again see him? Never again see his straight, graceful form lightly walk toward me in the summer sunshine. Never again see his smiling face, his dear brown eyes, look at me.

All at once, the words that my mother had uttered in the early morning after my father's death came back to me, "The world is so empty." Yes, the world was so empty. Then a new thought came to me. Although I had not seen Joe for years, so many years since then and now, years filled with joy and sorrow, mostly sorrow, years filled with some honeymoons, hunger, labor, strife, years in which I had not seemed to think of him, still, there must have always lingered the thought of a sometime reunion between us. I turned my head, looked down towards the swampland just as if I might again catch a glimpse of him through the young undergrowth, the way I had then. But now there was a dense young forest where at that other time there were only young saplings. Why yes, since that golden, heavenly summer, twenty-four years had rolled away. I got up, hurried down our little pasture, through the cedars to the big hemlocks on the line, to the last one, where the big ditch had begun.

All about was silence. On either side, the wild vines were growing over the old ditch, earth crumbling into it. I knelt down, listening. It seemed as if I must hear his low, merry laugh, his soft whistle once more. I got up, walked back home to my hammock. Just then my mother came out with some mending. She always was mending for us. She smiled at me and began talking about the lovely day. I did not answer. She looked at me again and said in an anxious tone, "Why my poor child, you are so pale. You look ill. What is the matter with you?" I told her I felt all right. She said I must have over worked in the garden and that I should not do any more work that day.

Well, I certainly did not feel like working. Later, she told Charlie I was not well. He wanted to give me half a dozen kinds of patent medicines which I absolutely refused to take. Soon, little Sophie came home, happily, from school. Next day, Friday, would be Decoration Day, then Saturday, Sunday. Three days without going to her hated school.

Sophie and I went to the spring to catch a few pollywogs. She, only about nine and a half years old, said to me, "Mama, Grandma and Papa Charlie think you are sick. The old people don't know any better. I know you feel bad, terrible bad down in your heart." Silently, there on the mossy bank, I took her in my arms. She asked me no questions, but as ever, we understood one another. At suppertime, I forced myself to eat a little. My dear mother worried about me, said I should not work so hard. Charlie said I should take a big dose of salts and a tablespoonful of Slone's Liniment, which I refused to do. That night was a nightmare. I never closed my eyes in sleep.

Next morning after the chores were done, I took my little Sophie back into our woods. Oh, the woods, the weather were so lovely, so restful to my weary, aching heart. We went across the creek. We looked for wild flowers. How cool, how tranquil the brook looked, hurrying and ebbing its way swiftly over the mossy pebbles. How the warm, bright sunlight shimmered through the green young leaves into the clear water. Birds warbling joyously, my child carefree and happy. Only I seemed sad, hopelessly sad.

We came home, decorated the two graves, and filled half a dozen vases with out beautiful wild flowers. But I was thinking of a new grave, one I could not decorate, one that held the one and only man I ever really loved.

Came Monday and school. Daily life duties went on. Came the mailman, bringing my poor mother a much belated letter, a letter from her sister's husband saying that her best beloved sister had died in April, my Aunt Sophie. My mother took it very much to heart. I felt sorry for her, but personally I could not grieve so much. She said to me, "You never lost any one you loved. You cannot know what real grief is." Oh, that hurt. I watched my chance and when she was not looking, snatched a sheet of paper and a pencil and made a quick rush for the old hammock. Though I was in my forty-third year, I knew that if she saw me take the paper, she would ask a dozen questions, would insist on seeing what I wrote.

In my heart I carry a burden
Of a story all untold
Of one I loved so dearly
Now sleeping neath the mold

Through him I knew the glory
That God gives once to man
The bliss, the joy of loving
And know you are loved again.

But I could not tell this story
At home, to the ones I loved
For they were proud and haughty
And at my lowly Joe would scoff

And so I kept this story
In my bosom all untold
Until my youth was fading
And my heart was growing old

And then one day at dinner

Sophie Kussmaul

My father spoke and said
Oh, I almost forgot to tell you
They buried Joe today.

Other men have claimed me
And thrice I've been a bride
But the love I had for Joseph
Has never dimmed or died

Came the twelfth of June, a perfect June day. Little Sophie had gone to school, and I went to North Bay after a few groceries and pig feed. All at once while I was in the village, a great longing, a great desire came over me to drive around by way of Charles Dixon's so as to pass the old Henry place. It was about a half mile further and the roads were much rougher, and I only seldom went that way.

After Joe Henry's mother had died, the house had been shut up and only once in a while Mary Henry, Joe's older sister, came home to look after the place. I had heard that about two years ago, she had come home to stay. She had worked in Oneida ever since she was eighteen. After the many years, the people she worked for had died and as she had always saved her money, she had retired, to spend the remaining years of her life at her old home. I had not seen her in years. So I turned my horse's head to take the road leading by her house. I pulled Prince into a slow walk. I saw the dear old house. A neat little front yard, a large dark leaved peony, laden with dozens of rich red flowers in full bloom. I saw a gray haired woman working in the vegetable garden back of the house. I had not seen Mary Henry in years, and though I remembered her as a rather young woman with brown hair like her brother Joe's, I still at a glance knew who she was.

A stab of pain shot through my heart. To my amazement, when she saw me, she beckoned to me to stop, to drive in. We had never really been friends. The very few times in years gone by I had met her in a store, or on the road, we just bowed to one another. I had always longed to know her better, to love her as I might have loved a sister. But strange as this may seem, just because I so loved her, I put on that mask of indifference. I drove into the yard, hitched Prince to the hitching post. There was something peculiar about her. Though she had signaled for me to drive in, she stood in silence while I hitched my horse. Then I followed her into the house through a very neat little woodshed leading into a spotless kitchen. Then into a cozy, homey little living room. She motioned for me to sit down on a sofa.

The emotions swelling up in my heart almost choked me. This was the first time I had ever been in his house. I sat near an open door leading into a small bedroom, a snowy white bed and a dresser, and on this dresser was a small framed photograph of Joe as he looked when I had first seen him. A faintness began to steal over me. I was brought back suddenly by her voice, the first words she spoke to me.

"I suppose you know my brother Joe is dead?" I could not answer. I dumbly nodded. She went on. "If you had not been so proud, so stuck up, thought yourself so much better, he might be alive today, but of course that means nothing to you." I was so completely stunned, so utterly taken by surprise, I could not speak. I half whispered, "I do not know what you mean." She went on and told me of the great love Joe had had for me, how I had avoided him, openly snubbed him time and again. "Proud like your parents." I felt like weeping, like throwing my arms about her neck and telling her the truth, that I had loved him better than life itself. But I seemed frozen. After a while, she got up, went to a writing desk, pulled out a small drawer, and took out what looked like a leather envelope. She came back and sat down in front of me again and said, "This is what he carried in the breast pocket of his coat for over twenty years." She pulled out my likeness. I stared at it, mumbled that I had never given it to him. She gave a shrill, hard laugh, said, "Oh, no, you would not even give him a kind look." A pause, then she said, "He went to Yoost (the photographer who had taken my pictures every year since I was a year old) and bribed him to give or rather sell him a copy." I was sixteen when that photo was taken. I do not know just how long I was there. After a while I left drove as slowly as possible. I wanted to be alone. My heart was filled, both with unspeakable joy and unspeakable sorrow and remorse.

When I was driving into our lower driveway, I saw my mother standing on the little front porch waiting for me. She looked anxious, worried, asked if I had an accident, if something had happened to me. She said I was nearly two hours later than usual. I told her I was all right, drove on the west side of the house, unloaded the groceries at the kitchen, and took the horse and buggy to the barn.

I seemed to be in a sort of dream. Things seemed strange to me. The dear old days of that golden summer of long ago seemed to have come back to me. It seemed as if Joe's spirit was near me. I came into the house from the back yard. My dear mother was telling me how she had worried, how she had been keeping the dinner hot for me. Charlie was sitting near the kitchen stove, although it was such a perfect summer day. All at once he leaped up. I saw his face was livid with rage. Then he started in yelling, calling me all the vile names he could think of, saying he knew why I was so late, said he saw it in my face before I left home that I intended to meet some man.

He accused me of committing unspeakable things, roared out that that was the reason I went around by Charles Dixon's. I had arranged to meet some no good on that lonesome road. He raved on and on, yelling, stamping his feet, and acting like an insane man.

I stood there speechless. Then all at once I became very, very angry. Ever since the twenty-ninth of May, I had been battling with my great sorrow in silence, carefully hiding my intense grief. Then today, the old wound of my heart was torn open afresh. The new revelation of Joe's life showed me what might have been. My nerves were at a tension of breaking. Now they gave way. I, in turn, told Charlie what I thought of him, all the bad names I could think of. In short, all my bitterness of heart and mind broke loose, all my pent up emotions gave way. I remember, as in a dream, how my poor gentle mother looked at me. This was the first real quarrel Charlie and I ever had. But not the last one.

When Charlie had raved himself into exhaustion, he went upstairs and I knew, though he had had no dinner he would not come down again that day. My poor mother, who had carefully prepared and then kept heated, a good dinner, begged me to cool down and eat. Strange as this may seem, that horrible row did me good. I had been so deep in my grief, so alone in it. Now, after this storm, I felt a little better. My mother, pale and sad looking, and I sat down to dinner.

I was relieved about one thing. Now she could not read in my face my great heartache. Whatever emotion I would show, she would connect with my row with Charlie. When little Sophie came home from school, she asked me where Papa Charlie was. I said upstairs. She ran up, came back, and said, "Papa Charlie is mad." He did not come down for supper. I never slept a minute that night, but when

Charlie thought I was asleep (we slept in separate beds), I heard him go downstairs barefooted. He went into the kitchen and ate.

Next morning, he came down to breakfast. We ate in silence. So the summer and fall went by. Came the twenty-first of December, I was forty-three years old. A happy Christmas. The sixth of January and my little girl's tenth birthday. Now I will go over the next two years as nothing very important happened during that time. I worked out of doors in spring, summer, and fall. Of course, in the house too. The price of huckleberries had come up from six to eight cents a quart to from fifteen to eighteen cents a quart. I used to get up long before sunrise, pick eight to ten quarts, come home about seven o'clock, soaking wet, eat breakfast, which my mother had ready for me, do the morning chores, and then, if the weather was fair, work in the hay or oat field all day, do my evening chores, and rush back to pick berries till it was really dark.

On rainy days I would catch up with the washing, cleaning and baking. The winters were terrible. Those two winters, Charlie spent most of his time in bed. So I had to carry all his meals upstairs. Also, many cords of wood, as we had to keep the fire in our upstairs room going day and night. My poor mother was very weak and sick but tried to help. Besides the barn chores, I had to get my child to school if I possibly could get through the snow filled winter roads.

Well, again it was December the twenty-first and I was forty-five years old. Christmas and the sixth of January, my child twelve years old. Now excepting for Charlie's frequent outbreaks of jealousy, he really was his old affectionate self, telling over and over again how much he loved me, how he had never loved anyone like me, how good I was, how beautiful. I do know that he almost worshiped his little girl.

This winter was one of the worst I ever lived through. Our school was closed for a few weeks as all the country roads were impassable. Charlie had an attack of pneumonia right after Thanksgiving and did not come downstairs again until April. So, of course, I had to take his three meals a day up to him and keep the stove in our upstairs going day and night. My poor mother, who never was really well and always a lot worse in winter, was much worse this winter than usual. She suffered with a very painful spinal disease. Still, she tried to help me. Now she never complained about her suffering, but it was very depressing to be with her. She would tell me a dozen times a day how unhappy she was, that she missed my father more each day, that she hoped soon to be with him, that she prayed to our heavenly Father to let her die soon.

Charlie would moan and groan so loud at times that we could hear him downstairs. When I was with him, he would keep saying that he feared he would never get well again, that he was afraid he would not live till spring. How sad he felt, what a life he had, and so on. We kept getting out of pig feed, chicken feed, groceries. No roads. A few times I took a bag and walked a mile and more through the icy blast wallering in the deep snow and carried home fifty pounds of feed. A few other times I got to North Bay somehow and brought home groceries.

On one of those horrible trips, I froze both my feet, both my hands, and both my ears. For weeks after, I could not get a shoe, boot, or even a slipper on my feet. They bled and maturated on each foot. I lost some toe nails. I bound bags on my feet, as I had to keep going just the same. Half the time that winter I never undressed when night came, just laid down for an hour or two and tended the three stoves. My little girl and I kept well. She was a great comfort to me and helped me with the barn chores.

Beginning of December, our pump gave out, and the rest of the winter I had to carry every drop of the water from the spring. The snow being so deep and drifting all the time, I had to keep shoveling it out, sometimes twice a day. Then on the sixteenth of February, such a blizzard set in as we seldom had. It raged day and night till the nineteenth. We had no roads before, but now we were snowed in mountain high. Not one bit of pig feed, chicken feed, and nearly out of all kinds of food except potatoes, apples, and cabbages. Only enough coal for one more night. We had been burning coal in two stoves.

The morning of the nineteenth was bitter cold, but clear and no wind. All at once, I heard men's voices yelling, and to my great joy, I saw a dozen men shoveling and two teams hitched to bob sleighs. They were breaking out our road. I was so thankful. Our mailman, Mr. Elmer Matthews (Mr. Griggs had resigned) had not been able to get through for three days. For two weeks before that, he made his long trip afoot, carrying the mail bag over his back.

Well, when I found out we were going to have a road, I started to shovel out our driveway. My cutter lay buried in the snow, as I had not been able to get it to the barn for some time. I had turned it bottom-side up. I shoveled it out and got it on the driveway. Then I shoveled and dug a narrow path to the barn. I had been going over the drifts, but today I must lead Prince out. It was about two o'clock when I had him harnessed and started to lead him out. He raised his beautiful head, high up, snorted and looked around. The snow on each side of the narrow path was much higher than his head. I looked him straight in the face and said to him, "Prince, if you ever were a horse, try and be one today." I knew that he could not understand my words, but I was sure he knew what I meant.

He looked at me with so much understanding in his face, his eyes, that he really seemed more human than just a horse. All the way to North Bay, the men had been able only to cut through the deep frozen snow enough to make a road wide enough for one sleigh to travel. On each side, the snow banks or walls were from eight to ten feet high. As there was only room for one sleigh, what to do if you met one? Of course I, like everyone else, carried a shovel in my cutter. But even then, it would be an awful task in the bitter cold to dig through the frozen bank to let a team pass. Well, I did not take my little Sophie on this trip. In the first place, she could not stand the cold as well as I could, and it was fifteen below zero. In the second place, I did not like to leave either my mother or Charlie alone too long in the condition both were in, especially on such a cold day. In the third place, I knew she would have all the barn chores done by the time I got home.

I must say this: I could trust her perfectly with all the barn chores. She loved that kind of work and did it right. In the fifth place, I knew I would have my cutter packed full. Well, I got to North Bay without meeting anyone. Went down to the depot first. There I ordered two tons of coal to be brought up in the morning. Bought three hundred pounds of pig and chicken feed. Then went back through the village to Dexter Nichol's store. I filled up the cutter so full with groceries that there was no room for me to sit. So I walked behind the cutter, and when I saw it was about to tip over, steadied it.

Luckily, I met no one, but Prince fell down a number of times. But good horse that he was, he got up again and struggled on. At last I reached home. It was now twenty below zero and as my fingers were so stiff with the intense cold, I could not unbuckle the straps. It was not yet quite dark, so we fed the poor hungry hens and loudly squealing pigs. Little Sophie carried all the groceries in the house. Of course I had to unload the heavy feed bags. My poor dear mother, as weak as she was, got supper ready.

My mother said she worried every minute while I was gone, knowing about the dangerous roads and the intense cold. I took a good hot supper up to Charlie and told him I had made the trip without an accident. I named over the many, many good groceries I had gotten. Told him joyfully that we had enough pig and chicken feed for the next two weeks. When I got all done, he just said, "To heck with that stuff. We will all freeze to death." Then I told him that I had ordered two tons of coal to be brought up in the morning. As tired as I was that night, by starlight I shoveled a road from the driveway to the cellar window on the west side where the coal was to be dumped into the coal bin in the cellar.

Chapter 27

The winter came to an end at last. Early in April, spring came to stay. Never have I seen snow go faster. Day and night alike, it was warm. I did not try to put in so many crops. We could no longer get any of the back pasture fenced, so I had the two cows at home all the time. That made more work, as I had to stake them out. Yes, both my mother and Charlie were a lot better when the weather got warm, but my poor frail mother never again was as well as in other springs.

About the middle of April, Charlie went to Rome on a short visit to some of his relations. When he came home, he kept telling us what a wonderful man he had met while in Rome. A man who had come from a good family, who used to be well off but now was poor. An interesting talker, a good looking man in his early fifties. Charlie kept saying he took such a liking to him that he had invited him to our home on a visit. I was mildly interested, and when Charlie wrote to him, enclosed an invitation in my name.

We corresponded for a few weeks. I was delighted with his letters. Interesting, faultless in spelling, and perfect in grammar. It was the tenth of June. A lovely early summer day. Flowers in bloom everywhere, hundreds of roses near the house, the long verandah filled with blooming plants. It was Sunday; we were at dinner in the kitchen. I heard a step on the back porch. The door was wide open, but through the closed screen door, I saw a man. Before he could rap, Charlie sprang up and welcomed him in, and introduced him to us as his friend, Mr. Edwin Fisher of Rome. He was in no way connected with the Frank Fisher from Oneida of my childhood days.

Sophie Kussmaul

The moment I met him face to face, I fell for him. He was so sure of himself. He was a very handsome man and did not look over forty or at the most forty-five. He stayed with us a week, then went back to Rome and came out on weekends.

In August he stayed with us over half the time. He greatly reminded me of Wilbur Henderson. Looking back, I can plainly see that I was infatuated with him. At the time, I thought it was love. We would make plans for the future. He intended to come and live with us as a boarder. I would have been very happy had it not been for my mother. Slowly, very slowly, she got weaker and though she never complained, I know her suffering was increasing.

All through August she daily got up, tried to help me, went out on her beloved verandah, and at least once a day to my father's grave. In the beginning of September, she still got up each morning, but acted very strange. She would take me to be her sister. At other times, she would say, "Oh, Father, I am so glad you came." Then she would talk to him. Each day she got worse. By the twelfth of December, she could no longer get up. I sent for Dr. Wilsey as our good Dr. Ludden was dead.

I do not want to dwell on the next eight or ten days. They were terrible days and nights. On the twentieth of September on a Monday, at five o'clock in the afternoon, she passed away, a smile on her dear face and whispering, "Oh, Mother, you came to me." The funeral was on the twenty-fourth, the same date on which her last operation had been. A mild, sunny day, but be it superstition, be it imagination, call it what you will, the very air, the very atmosphere, seemed charged with sorrow, a desolation, a sadness. Her grave was just below my father's, as close to it as they could dig it without disturbing his resting place. Now before I go any further with my story, I want to relate something that will probably seem very strange to whoever reads this. In a way it seemed strange to me, though I think I found the right solution.

From my very earliest childhood, I had loved my mother more I think than most children love their mothers. It bordered almost on worship. I linked her with something almost divine. She always had been so tender, so loving, towards me. Then too, she had always been a semi-invalid and then those heartbreaking years of her operations. Added to all this, I had never gone to school, never knew what it was to have childhood friends, schoolmates, playmates, or girl companions. So my mother was all in all to me. Though I knew way down in my heart that my father loved me, still, we were always strangers. There never was that intimacy between us as there so often is between fathers and daughters. I was an outsider. But here is the thing I now want to mention. I felt ten times as bad when my father died than I did when my mother died. In the first place, though my father was not in the least afraid to die, he hated so to leave my mother. This I knew. On the other hand, my mother had been longing, yes praying, to go. In the second place, my mother for years had been a great sufferer, especially the last year, and I knew that she never again would be free from pain. So all things considered, I felt it would only be selfish to wish her to stay, to stay and suffer, to stay and mourn.

The hardest part of my grief at my father's death had been the knowledge of my poor mother's inconsolable grief. Now of course, this does not mean that I did not feel very bad about her going. She had been eighty-two and a half years old. Now I must say another thing. Ever since Charlie got so badly hurt, Mrs. Fairchild had kept sending me small sums of money, some months more, some less. Still, though it had been a great help, it was no regular allowance. Some time before my dear mother died, she begged Mrs. Fairchild to help me until my little girl was educated and could take care of herself.

My good mother assured her that she herself would need no help, as she had her widow's pension, but of course that would stop at her death. So to my great relief, Mrs. Fairchild sent me each month a sum much bigger than my mother's pension had been. She also for many years sent me a large box of groceries each month and all my clothes and shoes. At Christmas time, some lovely presents for my little girl and to me, an extra check.

A short time after the funeral, Mr. Fisher came back and stayed most of the time with us. We often talked about our future. Fisher advised me to get a divorce from Charlie. I did not want such a scandal. Thanksgiving, my forty-sixth birthday, Christmas, New Years. Fisher left us for a while. Up to now, I had not once overstepped the line of decency with him. The sixth of January and my child's thirteenth birthday. The next day Charlie left for Rome, to stay with his relations until April. I gave him enough money to pay his board and get what he called treatments from a chiropractor, in whom he had great faith, and who had promised to make a new man out of him.

A few days after Charlie left, Fisher came out and spent the winter with me. Now as I am writing my true life story, I will also here tell the whole truth. From the time he came, the ninth day of January, to the last day of March, when he left, we lived together as man and wife. I never thought I was doing anything wrong. Now I will have to go back a little in my story.

My little Sophie started that fall at our district school, but she did not like her teacher, Miss Katherine Kinny, so after one week I made arrangements for her to go to the North Bay School for that year's school term. Here is something else I must mention here. Years before my Aunt Sophie had died, they had made their wills. Her husband, who was my uncle by marriage, was to have two thirds of their property, and as they had no children of their own, his part was to go to his sister and after her death, to her two sons. My mother's sister's one third was to go to my mother, and after her death, to me. But although my aunt had been dead now some years, the property could not be divided until after her husband's death.

My dear mother and her sister had never missed a week in writing to one another in over forty years, but after her death, her husband and my mother only exchanged letters about every two to three months. I wrote to him after my mother's death. He answered it in October. I was a little hurt that he had not written to me at Christmas. I sent him Christmas wishes. Then on the twenty-sixth of February, to my surprise I received a letter from Europe in a strange handwriting. It was from a firm of lawyers telling me Mr. Bulling had died the last of October. He was eighty-six years old. They were informing me that they now wanted to settle up the estate, that my mother's share came to sixty thousand dollars. As she had passed away, I was to inherit it. I was fairly stunned as I had never expected to receive more than eight or ten thousand dollars. But the letter went on to say that right now, owing to the War, the Marks were still way down and they were advising me to wait until they came up to, or nearly to, their old value. But in the meantime, there had also been a life insurance left to my mother which was now made over to her one and only child, myself. This was for two thousand dollars. But that, too, had dropped in value, but not so much as it was in French Franks. They told me what to do, get in connection with the French Council in New York City, and so on.

Well to make a long story short, by the twentieth of April, I received fifteen hundred and thirty-five dollars from this insurance through the Oneida Savings Bank. Fisher left me on March thirtieth and went to Norwick to a hospital, intending to come back to me as soon as he got better. Now I will skip ahead a little in my story then come back to this date.

Fisher wrote to me very often while at the hospital. At first, very hopeful letters, then not so hopeful, then for a week no letter came, then an announcement from the hospital informing me of his death. A few days after this, a letter from a tailor friend of his telling me that Fisher had requested him to send me his few belongings. They came to Camden by express. I drove out and got them. Now before I close this chapter on Fisher forever, I will say that I never had felt in the least guilty about my three months intimacy with him. I do know this. If I had been married to Joe Henry or Ernest Galway, it would never have happened. As it was, I was lonely and for the last fifteen years I had been working far beyond my strength, most of the time strife, quarrels and misunderstandings, mixed with sorrow. I do not know if it would have happened if I had been married to Charles Spear or not. Here is one more thing I want to say. It is something that I never understood, something that always has been a complete mystery to me.

Charlie had been so terribly unreasonably jealous about every man that I have known him to fly into an uncontrollable rage if I merely bowed or smiled at a neighbor in passing. He had bitterly, cruelly accused me of having done low things if I went home in broad daylight. He had sulked for days if he saw me looking either up or down the road, declaring I had been looking for some man. But now that he knew I really had been living with Fisher for three months, he said very little about it. Naturally I felt bad when I heard he had died, but I cannot say I really grieved.

Now once more I will have to briefly go back in my story. For years, ever since my little Sophie was about nine years old, she wanted a Shetland pony. For the first year or two, she would only say how much she would like one, then by the time she was twelve years old, she would keep telling me to buy her one. Now I would have been glad to save and save to get enough money together to buy her the pony.

But in the first place, there just was no such animal in our neighborhood, and besides, I knew they were expensive and I had Charlie as well as my child to support. So the first thing when she came home from school that night on the twenty-sixth of February, I told her about my coming inheritance. She jumped up and down for joy, saying over and over again, "Now you can buy me a pony. Now we just got to find one." To tell the truth, I was as eager to find one as she was. I answered advertisements in newspapers, one place in Montana where a Shetland pony ranch was advertising.

The answer came back--any color, any age, either male or female. One hundred dollars. The freight would be around sixty dollars more. Then I would still have to get a saddle, bridle, harness, and cart. I answered other ads. One place they no longer had Shetlands, and so on. We were both disappointed.

My money got to Oneida on the twentieth of April. Charlie, little Sophie, and myself went to Oneida the very next day. I bought a lot of things for my little girl, a few things for Charlie, and nothing for myself. All the time we were wondering where we could find a pony. This was Friday, so of course the next two days there was no school. All I heard those two days was pony, pony. Monday, the twenty-fourth, little Sophie went to North Bay to school as usual. At half past four, she came bounding into the house, and I had never before seen her so excited. She was half laughing, half gasping for breath, hopping around. She was trying to tell me something, but was so out of breath, all I could make out at first was pony.

When she could control herself, she told me that she had met a cute little brown Shetland pony hitched to a two wheeled cart, harnessed in a light yellow harness, and a woman and a girl in the cart. Little Sophie's cheeks were fiery red and her eyes seemed to bulge out of her head. I looked at her and was really afraid she had imagined all this. In all the years of my life, I had never seen or heard of a Shetland pony in or near North Bay. So I was afraid the excitement about getting a pony had been too much for her and now she had probably met a small horse and her great imagination had done the rest. We ate supper, I did my barn chores, and then I hitched up Prince. I wanted to go and see Jimmy Dixon about getting him to do some plowing. Of course I took little Sophie with me. She was still babbling away about the pony, saying, "And he shook his head like this." Well, when we got to Mrs. Dixon's, the first thing Mrs. Dixon said was, "Oh, just think, the cutest little pony hitched to a little cart just went by here." Little Sophie looked at me triumphantly and said, "Now do you believe me?" Mrs. Dixon went on to say that a family had just bought the Faulkner place, up on the hill, and they were the ones who owned the pony.

So as soon as I had made the bargain with Jimmy, we started for the Faulkner hill. Little Sophie was so terribly excited she whipped Prince into a gallop. Yes, the pony was there all right. So I made a bargain to buy him for one hundred and twenty-five dollars--pony, cart, harness, saddle, and halter. The pony's name was King. He was under seven years old, weighed two hundred and twenty pounds. I paid five dollars down that night. Next morning I went to Oneida and drew some money and that night after supper, but before I did the chores, we went to Storms, the name of the people on the Faulkner place, and I paid for the pony.

I drove Prince home, and just behind me, my little girl, seated in the pony cart, was driving her own Shetland pony home. Beside her in the cart was the pony's saddle. I really think that was the happiest day in her life. When we got home, she unhitched him, put on the saddle, and rode up and down the road while I did the chores. Charlie, too, was perfectly delighted.

That summer I had more building done. I built a large, beautiful bedroom next to my kitchen on the north east side, and a new kitchen on the northwest side of the kitchen. I made the kitchen I had built a few years ago into a dining and living room. So in winter, I would put my heating stove into this room, the kitchen on one side, the bedroom and the dining, living room on the other side would be warm and comfortable.

I also had a large clothes closet added, and a new woodshed. I bought lovely, heavy exminister rugs for the two front rooms, and other things. I hired Mrs. Storms for a week to paper the two large front rooms, the big bedroom, and the alcove with Oatmeal paper. When I had everything done, the house truly looked lovely. I was very happy. Of course, I thought I was to enjoy it for as long as I lived. I also made some other improvements, such as rebuilding fences and buying three purebred jersey yearlings. Of course, I did not have a cent of that money left by the first of September. But that did not worry me as my monthly allowance from New York City would go on, and besides, I reasoned, when my real inheritance would come, I would put that out at interest and live on the interest. Besides, I had my farm.

Well, this coming fall was mild. Little Sophie again went to our District school. The twenty-first of December, I was forty-seven years old. A happy Christmas, the sixth of January, little Sophie's fourteenth birthday. Nothing unusual happened that winter. Another spring, a hot summer. My little girl and I would get up long before sunrise, go out and pick berries. Oh, looking back to those days sends a queer sensation over me--half joy, half sorrow. We both were in perfect health, brimming over with life. There picking berries in the early morning, watching the eastern sky grow rosy, then the first, bright sun rays sweeping over the higher waste of wildness about us, and in the lower places, the fog vanishing like ghosts in the night.

We both were happy. My little girl had always loved poultry and now I had gotten her two or three kinds of ducks, half a dozen kinds of hens, some with large topknots, turkeys, bantam chickens, and above all, her pony. We made plans together from then on to eternity, never thinking, never dreaming that a Divine Providence might change all.

Poor Charlie. He was patient, happy for our happiness, but slowly getting weaker. He was suffering with asthma, but I was so busy, so happy with my child and our future plans that in a way I was just being swept through that beautiful summer. Charlie got so he had to have help in walking about. The weather was so hot, so dry, and his breathing had become so difficult; he had stayed out of doors altogether the last few weeks. I had fixed him a bed on the back porch.

Came the first of September, an extra hot day. I had been picking berries all the forenoon. Little Sophie had stayed at home on account of the great heat. We had a quick dinner. I was anxious to get back to picking so as to fill my crate. Poor Charlie, he could not eat a mouthful, was gasping for breath. There was no air stirring. I wanted to hustle off to the berry lot. He looked at me, asked me not to go, not to leave him. I told him I would be back as soon as I had gotten my ten quart pail full. The berries were not as plentiful as they had been. Again he said, "I wish you would not leave me." I told him I would leave little Sophie with him. Before I left, I helped him to walk around the house from the back to the front yard, in the shade of the big maples, and got him settled in the big rocking chair. Then hurried off to the berry lot. He looked after me sadly.

First I picked over on Mr. Cleveland's, then on Jim Dixon's, and when my pail was level full, crossed over on ours again. I came a little north of the big stone pile near our wood road. I was just beginning to heap up my pail when I heard the pony's hoof-beats coming along the wood road. I was a little peeved at little Sophie for leaving her father. She was going after our cows, which were in the Yager lot. When she came close, I said to her, "What made you leave your father? I told you to stay with him till I got back."

She smiled happily at me then said, "Oh, he is much better. Why he got up and walked all the way around the house and up the steps on the back porch without any help." I really was surprised. Then she added, "He kept asking after you." I do not know just why, but all at once a great fear clutched my heart and I hurried home as fast as I could.

Over the olden wood road, down the long lane, up the little old pasture, through the clean, green, back yard. Yes, there I could see Charlie sitting on the couch on the back porch, one hand resting on his knee, the other one firmly holding on to his cane, his head slightly bowed. He had his cap on his head, a habit of his even in the greatest heat of summer.

But why did he not look up when I opened the gate? It always gave a little creaking sound, and so many, many times when I opened it, he would look up quickly, knowing I was coming home. But not this time. I closed the gate, hurried up the little path to the back porch. I called, "Charlie." He did not look up. I touched his hands. They were still warm. I pushed his cap back, bent down to look at his face, spoke to him. Dear Charlie, no answer, and I knew I was too late. Then I felt more guilt, more remorse, for not having stayed with him these last few hours then I ever had in being untrue to him. Quickly I rushed to the barn. For a wonder, I had left Prince in his stall instead of out in the pasture. I put a bridle on him, leaped on him bare back, and galloped down the little pasture, up the old lane, over to the wood road, and on, on at full speed.

On the other side of the creek, I overtook my child, and her pony. She looked at me surprised, said, "What is the matter? Charlie is better, isn't he?" I could not utter the words, he is dead. So I said,

"Yes, he is better, much better." I said, "Let the cows go to heck. I want you to go to Arthur Nash and have him go to North Bay and telephone." I could not say any more. But as ever, the bond of understanding between her and myself was so strong that I felt she knew.

Again, I want to go over these next few days as quickly as possible. When the undertaker from Camden came, he said he could not take care of the body until we had a Coroner's inquest, as we had had no doctor for the last three days. So they telephoned to Rome. At about ten o'clock that night, the Rome Coroner came, pronounced it heart failure. It was about two in the morning when the undertakers left. Good Mr. Nash stayed with us till they went away in case he could in some way be of assistance to us. The night was unbearable hot. Mr. Nash stayed on the front steps. Next morning right after breakfast, little Sophie hunted the cows, and after she got back, I went to North Bay and telephoned to half a dozen of Charlie's relatives.

He died on Friday, late in the afternoon. The funeral was to be on Monday afternoon. I sent word to Mrs. Storms to come and help me clean up the house, as the front part of the house had not been used in so long; it still was dusty, needed airing and freshening up.

Well, Sunday a lot of people came calling. Monday they started coming soon after twelve o'clock noon, though the funeral itself was not to begin until two o'clock. We had a prayer service at the house at two, the funeral services at the North Bay Methodist Church at three, and the burial at Camden Cemetery. There had been a reserved lot there next to his sister Mary's grave. Now before I drop this part of my life story forever, I must tell of a little incident that happened at the grave, in itself a few words spoken, a short sentence, but it made a lasting impression on my mind. For me, those few words meant so much. They revealed in a way a lifetime. I must describe the scene.

It was right after the grave had been filled up. All the friends and neighbors had left, most of Charlie's relatives also. The grave was filled up and a mound of dirt rounded up over it. Someone, I suppose the gravediggers, were putting some of the many flowers at the head of the mound, picking up their shovels and picks, leaving. There was now no one left except Joe, Jim Estey, my little girl, and myself. We, too, were just leaving. I saw Joe on one side of the grave, Jim on the other side. Both stood there with their heads bowed in silence. Then at the same instance, each one reached out his hand. They clasped them tightly, a moment's more silence, then Joe, in a tremulous voice, said, "Us two are the only ones now left, out of ten." They still stood there with bowed heads and clasped hands across their brother's grave and Joe again repeated those words, "Us two are the only ones now left out of ten." Then they moved away, each one to his own home.

Like a flash I was carried back to over twenty years ago when Joe, Charlie, and their sister Mary used to come to us and spend the long winter evenings with us. They always were so jolly, so pleasant. Charlie would play the violin and sing. Sometimes they all would sing. Sometimes they all would sing while I played the organ. Sometimes they would sit by the hour and tell us little stories of their childhood when the ten of them were at home. We could easily see how poor they had been, but we could also see how happy they had been together--six boys and four girls. Now only two old men left.

Someone brought us home in an automobile. At home, everything was the same. The cats came to welcome us, the hens and ducks and pigs and calves wanted their suppers. Prince and King stood in the barnyard. I had kept the cows at home that day. They had to be milked. Yes, everything was the same. Still, nothing seemed the same. Charlie was gone forever.

Well, life had to go on. My little girl went to school. I picked a few more berries then did my fall work. December the twenty-first and my forty-eighth birthday. A beautiful Christmas. The friends from New York City sent more things, lovely things, than ever. There were the same dear old ornaments on the tree as in my childhood days. Little Sophie was happy, but for me there seemed to be something that was different, something that was lacking.

Came the sixth of January, and my little daughter's fifteenth birthday. The winter passed by. My little girl went to school. I did my chores, went to North Bay once a week after supplies, and did my housework. If possible, we two grew closer together than ever. Often one or another of her schoolmates would invite her to a birthday party, but she never went, always said, I do not want to go to those silly people. I want to be with you.

When I had bought the Shetland pony, my little girl only weighed seventy-five pounds. Now she weighed one hundred and twenty pounds. And the pony weighed less than he did when I bought him. So during the winter I kept saying we must find a small horse, one weighing about six hundred pounds. I inquired about for such a horse, but with no results.

On the twenty-third of December, there was a play at our school each year. I went to it as my child was in it, and besides it always was at night, and I had to be there to bring her home. But this particular night I shall never forget. I had been to at least a dozen of the best theatres on Broadway, New York City, one in Chicago, about a dozen of the best ones in San Francisco, and since to so many, many I cannot recall. But for some reason, this school play touched my heart. It stayed with me in my memory.

It was the olden story of the Divinity, the baby in the manger. It really was beautiful. I sat there as if in a dream. I felt the glory, the holiness, about me. Today as I write about it, a sadness steals over me. My child, who was all the world to me, who never wanted to be away from me, is now in some far away country. I do not even know where. For looking back, it seems like a vision out of the better land.

April came. I was working outdoors. My little girl, who hated her school, would hurry home and help me on the farm, the outdoor life she so loved. But I needed a man to help me. I hired Jake Meinhart a few days, but he was very slow. I had one or two others, but I really got nothing done.

One day I said to little Sophie, "I wish I could get George Smith. He would do more in one day than the others did in a week." Of course she wanted to know who he was. I told her that he had worked for my father ever since I was three years old, a few days at a time, and I heard my father often say that he did more work in one day than any other man in two, and the best of it was, he did all his work right and could be depended on. But the year before my father died, he moved to Florence with his family. I had met him a few times during all those years when I happened to go to Camden.

Chapter 28

It was really a happy spring. We both were in perfect health. School would be out early this year. Then we would be together all the time until after Labor Day. This was something we did not like to talk about. This coming June, my little girl would leave our district school forever. Instead of staying home with me, she was to start high school in Oneida. So I had already made arrangements with some of our good friends to get her boarded from Monday till Friday. The people's name was Mr. and Mrs. Frank Patton and they lived about halfway between Durhamville and Oneida. They had a small farm, and I knew that next to our own home, my little Sophie would be much happier there than anywhere else.

Still, I knew she hated, yes hated, to go. In the first place, she did not like school life, and in the second place, she was not the kind of girl to mix with others. Mrs. Fairchild had promised to take care of us until my child was educated to teach. After that her money and the monthly box of groceries were to stop. I could make my living on the farm and besides, we had figured that when my little daughter would be teaching, she still would live with me. Oh, those dear, dear plans. Yes, of course she would always stay with me on the farm we both loved so well.

April faded into May. I think this was the most beautiful May I had ever seen. The weather was warm, not hot; we had just enough rain to keep things growing. I worked very hard, but never seemed to get tired. We both got up early. We did our morning chores together. I had gotten a lamb and some rabbits for my little girl. We ate breakfast together. Then she went to school and I worked on the farm. I always had an early supper ready. We ate and she would either follow me around on the farm or we both would work in the garden together. We did our chores.

We most always spent our evenings on the verandah, as I had in the olden days. But sometimes on moonlit nights we would take Prince, unless he had been working that day, and go for a moonlight drive. I always let him go on a slow walk. We went on the lonely roads, sometimes along the California road. I can see it all before me yet. The winding, lonely road through the semi wilderness. The moonlight flecked with shadows from the trees. The haunting song of the whip-poor-will, the sweet odors from the forest. The great peace all around us. We would sing "Nita Juanita." Slowly, slowly drive home.

Came the twenty-first of May, I was in the barn milking. All at once little Sophie rushed out to me, telling me there was a strange man at the house wanting to see me, said he knew me. I finished my cow, and as we got back to the house, I saw George Smith. Now I do not mean to say that I was in love with him, absolutely not. But I was delighted to see him. In the first place, since my earliest recollections he had been to our house. For four years he had worked for Mr. Cleveland and somehow he had stopped to our house almost daily. Well, we visited, he told me about himself, his children all grown up. His wife had left him to live with one of her married daughters in Sherrill. He was now staying at his brother's house, Robert Smith, on the California road, in fact, the old homestead, the house he had been born in. But he said he would soon be a near neighbor to me as he had already made arrangements to buy the place I used to own.

I had sold it to a Mr. Townsend, and then it passed through a number of other owners. Well, he agreed to start working for me the very next day. In a surprisingly short time, my farm work was in fine shape. Mr. Smith, now established so near by, would run in almost every day. Came the twelfth of June, George Smith had worked for me this day; we were at supper. When we were nearly done, he looked at my little girl and laughingly said to her, "If you grow much more, you will be more able to carry the pony than the pony is to carry you." Then he turned to me and said, "Really, when I saw her coming up the road tonight, I thought she is getting too big for that pony." I told him I had been trying to find a small horse for her, one that would weigh around six to seven hundred pounds. As an afterthought, I asked him if he happened to know of such a one. He looked thoughtful then said if he had only known about my wanting such a horse, he could have gotten me a grand pony.

The man next door to where he had lived in Florence had a five year old pony, perfectly sound and gentle, iron gray, with a snow white mane and tail, weighing less than seven hundred pounds. But he added he had sold it to a rich man near Syracuse for his young son. Then just as we were getting up from the table, he said that a man by the name of Miner had a small black horse he wanted to sell, as he was going west.

Of course my little daughter asked a lot of questions about that horse--how much the man wanted for it, how old it was, its name, if it was a good saddle horse, how much it weighed, and so on. George Smith laughed and said he really did not know a thing about the horse, only that it was black, a good road horse, and the man wanted to sell it. He told us that when he had been to his brother Wesley's, he saw it go by a few times. He thought it probably weighed around eight hundred. His brother Wesley had said the man wanted to sell it as he was going west. Otherwise, he did not know a thing about the horse. Of course, my little Sophie was excited, wanted me to start right out to look at it. I asked Mr. Smith where that man by the name of Miner lived. He told me they had bought the Will Yeoman's farm, the second place from his brother Wesley's.

Yes, I had been to Yeoman's, so I knew just where it was, a trifle over three miles from our home. My little girl kept saying I should hurry up. I told her just as soon as the dishes were washed and our chores done, I would hitch up Prince. She begged me to let the dishes go. Mr. Smith said he would do the chores. So about twenty minutes after we had heard about the black horse, we were on the road.

When we were turning into the driveway, we saw a rather stout woman sweeping off a rug on the front lawn. At one glance I saw she was Indian. I glanced at my little girl. The understanding between us was so strong that I knew she, too, had seen it. We both loved the Indians better than white people. I spoke to her, said I had heard that her husband had a small horse to sell, and we would like to see it. She said, "The horse belongs to my son and he is not at home. May not be back till late and got the horse with him." So I asked her if he would be home tomorrow night, as we would not be able to come till after school let out, as tomorrow was the last day of school. She said he would be home as he was painting Nick Dixon's barn.

When we got home, we found all the chores done and all the dishes neatly washed and piled on the table. I really was not much surprised as Uncle George, as my little girl called him, had done that many times before. He had gone home and would not be back for a few days as he had some other jobs to do. The two of us were on the verandah, first talking about the dear Indian woman we had just met. We both had taken a great liking towards her. After a while we were silent. I was thinking back to the night before the first day of school for my little girl. In a way it seemed like a tragedy. My poor, dear, tender hearted mother felt so bad about it, though she tried to appear cheerful before my child. Charlie, too, was much worried, imagining all kinds of things that might befall her at school. Still, he would say to me, in her hearing of course, "Now we will no longer have a baby girl, just a little school girl."

Tonight I was filled with strange thoughts. I was carried back to that eve of the first day at school, to this eve, the last day of school. That evening I still had my mother and Charlie with me and neither yet had known the bitter grief of Joe Henry's death. In between then and now, Fisher had come into my life and again passed out of it. And at that time, I had a little helpless girl, almost still a baby, and now a girl going on sixteen years. Then the eight years ahead of us at District School seemed to stretch away into distant years to a time far, far ahead, and now why it only seemed like a dream and the awakening there from.

So in the morning after my little girl had left for school, I worked in the garden till noon. Came in the house and ate my lunch. I had intended to go back into the garden until three o'clock and then take Prince and drive to the school house. My little Sophie had told me a dozen times that morning to be sure and meet her there at half past three, as being the last day, school would be out earlier. She kept saying, "Then we will see that nice, good Indian woman again and the little black horse." To tell the truth, I was as anxious to see the Indian woman as she was. This woman, besides being Indian, had a strange fascination for me. I also was curious about the horse.

Just as I got up from my lunch, I heard the sound of wheels on my upper driveway. I glanced out and saw an old looking buggy, a black horse, and a young man. He jumped out lightly and came to the door.

Through Sophie's Eyes

I saw he was very handsome, fairly tall, slim, young, graceful of movement. His hair and eyes were coal black, his features regular and beautiful, rather of dark complexion. He asked me if I was Sophie Estey. I said yes. He said his name was Albert Miner, and he had heard that I wanted to buy his horse. Then I glanced at the horse, and at one swift glance I knew that I did not like it. In the first place, it was too big for a pony, and in the second place, had very large clumsy feet, and in the third place, an ungainly body, and besides all this, I did not like the head, an unfriendly face. I told this man at once that the horse was not what I wanted.

Of course he told me how good she was, a good road horse, a good saddle horse, that she was only eight years old. Her name was Babe. He wanted me to ride her. We unhitched and unharnessed her, put my saddle on her. I rode her up and down the road a few times, trotted and galloped. She was quite fast, but did not ride too easy. I thought if I could get her cheap enough, and my little girl should like her, I might buy her and keep her until I could find what we really wanted.

Well, I did not get back into my garden. This man and I went to look at Prince and King, the calves, pigs, chickens, ducks, rabbits, sheep, and cats. My cows were way off to pasture and my heifers and yearlings out for all summer. He took a great liking to all my animals. But the thing that touched me the most was when I showed him two tiny kittens, their eyes not yet open, both of them were gray and white, and told him I would have to kill them, as I had three cats. He kissed them and said, "Oh, no, no, do not kill the dear little things." Well, in the end, I did not.

He kept staying. We talked about the West. He had been out to the Mid-West, not the far West. At last, I told him I had to go and meet my little girl. He said we could drive up with his horse and buggy. When we got quite near the school yard, we stopped, as none of the children had yet come out. We visited like old friends. He told me he would be twenty-nine years old on the third of September.

Then the children came out, a few at a time. They carried their books. Said farewell to one another, some of them never to come back to this school. Then my little girl stepped out, books and lunch box in hand. I saw her give a quick, disappointed look. She was looking for me with Prince. I waved towards her, beckoned to her to come. She reluctantly came, asked me why I had failed her. I explained. After we got home, she, too, rode the horse. After a while, she took the pony and as usual went after the cows. Albert still was with me. After I had my chores all done, we all ate supper together. I told him that next day, on the fourteenth of June, Flag Day, our school and about six or eight other districts would have a picnic at North Bay in Phelps's Grove. I invited him to go with us. Well, he stayed till after midnight, promising to come bright and early next morning to take us to the picnic.

Next morning at eight o'clock, Albert came, with his black horse and dressed in his best clothes. We left my house a little before ten. I had him hitch his horse to my carriage, as his old buggy did not look good. We watched the games, and then ate a big picnic dinner. It started raining. People went away. We, too, left early and got home about two o'clock. My little girl sat down to read. Albert and I went on the verandah. There he told me that he loved me, wanted me to marry him. I told him I would. He thought we ought to get married at once, but I said I wanted to wait until the first of January. I said Charlie had not been dead yet a year. But my real reason for waiting was I was getting a pension for my child until her sixteenth birthday. If I married before, that would stop.

We walked into the house and told my little girl. That evening after supper and my chores were done, Albert took us to his father's house, and told his mother the happy news. She was a little surprised then came to me with tears in her beautiful black eyes. She looked at me, seemed to look into my very heart, and said, "Will you be good to my boy?" I looked back at her, straight into her eyes, and said, "I will." His father came to me and kissed me and called me daughter. I also met his younger brother Levi.

Never in my life before was my heart so touched. It felt tender towards these, my people. While we were visiting, Albert ran upstairs to his room, came back with a suitcase and an armful of clothes. His mother asked him what he was going to do. He said, "I am going to stay with Honey." She did not quite like this idea, said he should stay home until we got married, but he said he could not wait so long. We went home and Albert stayed with me. Little Sophie liked him, and we both loved his mother.

Of course I loved Albert more than I had Charles Estey or Edwin Fisher or Charles Spear. But not as much as I had loved Ernest Galway, nor not the tenth part as much as my Joe Henry. I knew then and I knew later on that such a love would never again enter my heart. Still, I was happy. Yes, this was one of the happiest summers of my life.

Levi, Albert, little Sophie, and myself were together most of the time. Sundays we would go home. Both his father and mother called me daughter. That summer I heard the song "It Ain't Going to Rain No More" for the first time. Levi was always singing it. Now when I hear it, a pain shoots through my heart. It is like an echo from that happy, carefree summer. I know, too, it was one of the happiest ones for my little girl. Although I now had such a beautiful home, all kinds of animals, the farm in good condition, money in the bank, and still my more than generous allowance from New York City, I was still expecting my big inheritance from my aunt. But I must say this--I had never yet told Albert about this. So no one can say he wanted me to get that fortune.

So the happy summer went by. Came the fifth of September and my child went to board at Patten's. I tried not to let her see my heartache. It was terrible to pack her things. Came the seventh of September, we were still up, though it was dark outside, and I heard her voice calling. I ran towards the road. There coming up the road was my little Sophie, half laughing, half crying. She clung to me, said she had been dying with homesickness; she had been away so long. She begged me not to send her back.

Now here was a problem. I could not send her back to board, as she was so unhappy. I could not keep her at home for several reasons. In the first place, she lacked four months of being sixteen. At that time, the law was that she would either have to go back to our district school, although she had passed her eighth grade with high marks, till she was sixteen, or I would have to get her a working permit and she would have to be employed. Well, both of these alternatives were unthinkable. If Mrs. Fairchild found out that I did not have her finish her education, her money would stop. So the only way out seemed to be to have her go back and forth to Oneida each day. This was terrible.

As the days got shorter and shorter, she had to be up long before daylight, eat, dress, and ride the pony to North Bay, put him into Florence Dixon's barn, and walk quite a little ways to the depot. There take the eight-ten to Oneida, walk a mile and a half to high school, walking very fast so as not to miss her first class. The same distance on the way home. The worst of all was she would have to wait three hours at the Oneida Depot if the train was on time, much longer if it was late. So of course it was always long after dark when she got to North Bay, and then the two miles of lonely road home. I would walk to meet her, was always afraid something would happen to her.

She would come home tired out, only to go through the same thing again the next day. Sometimes she left in a pouring rainstorm, or came home late at night in a rain or snow storm. Besides all this, she hated school life. About the middle of December, the school nurse said she should stop school for a time as her eyes were being strained too much. I always had my doubts about this, as she would read fine print by the hour by the light of a poor kerosene lamp the rest of the winter, with no ill effects. But I was glad to have her home. She was to stay home and rest her eyes until the following September. I forgot to mention that in August the black horse died. I bought a sorrel from Mr. Skinner by the name of Captain.

Chapter 29

Came the twenty-first of December, my forty-ninth birthday. A lovely Christmas, the same dear old ornaments on the tree as in the olden times. Yes, it was a lovely Christmas, and I knew not then that it would be the last one in my beloved home, or rather, my beloved house.

Came the first of January, a bitter cold but clear day, and my wedding day. The wedding was at Albert's parents' house. I had sent out quite a few invitations, but no one came except Mr. and Mrs. Thomas Andrews. They stood up with us. We had a grand dinner.

On the sixth of January, my little Sophie became sixteen years old. Nothing unusual happened that winter. Came spring, a busy time. We were planning a belated honeymoon trip, wondering if we all three should go by train or take a horseback ride into the Adirondack Mountains, go to Malone, Albert's home where all his mother's relatives still lived. I do not know which one of us thought first about getting an automobile. They were still a little scarce, only the richer people had one. Anyway, one evening at chore time I was out in the barn and heard an automobile stop at the house. Albert came running out to me, telling me in an excited way that Lyle Richie was at the house and had a good Ford car he wanted to sell.

Lyle Riche lived near Jewell and had a car repair shop, and also bought and sold cars. I went and looked at it. It looked nice and shiny, but I really did not know a thing about automobiles. I knew this much--the tires looked quite good. Richie wanted one hundred dollars for the car. Of course Albert and my little Sophie said to me, "Buy it." Albert said he knew how to drive a car. Well, I paid fifty dollars down, was to pay the other fifty in twenty-five dollar a month payments.

Richie went home. I finished my chores, hitched up Prince and we three drove to Jewell. Joe Corcoran was there. Joe drove the car home for us. Albert and little Sophie rode in it, and I drove the buggy home. This was the second of June. The next day and the day after, we kept the car going, our new plaything, Albert driving. I had never driven a car. On the third day, Albert was sick., and I needed something from North Bay. Albert said I should take one of the horses, but I took the car. My little girl went with me. I kept stalling it, but somehow I got to North Bay and back without any mishap.

We went to Miners, Cleveland, Camden, North Bay and a few miles on the back roads every day, no great distance from home. We were planning to go on our delayed wedding trip to Malone. Finally, we set the date for starting on the fourteenth day of June, Flag Day, and just a year from when we had become engaged.

My dear little girl was simply overjoyed. Although we had been running around in our new car, new for us, we had as yet not gone any further from home with it than we often had been with the horses. I had taken my little Sophie to Utica once by train to go to a very large circus, Barnum and Bailey and Ringling Brothers combined. Once also we had gone by train to Eaton and spent the day there in the beautiful hills picnicking. A few times I had taken her to Rome, always, of course, by train, but this was to be quite different.

Oh, we were all so happy in getting ready. I packed and repacked our things half a dozen times just as if we were going to start out on a trip of six months. I made arrangements with George Smith to stay at our place during the time we were absent. I knew everything would be seen to the same as if we were there. So on the morning of the fourteenth, I was up at a little after four o'clock in the morning and started to cook breakfast instead of going out to start the outdoor chores. That seemed very strange to me. Soon after I was up, my little girl, who never liked to get up early, was up and all dressed for the trip.

I can see her still. Her eyes were shining with happiness. She was so excited. Albert, too, was up hours before he usually got up. Right here I will say this; as long as I was married to Albert he never helped me with my chores, either morning or night. We were all done eating breakfast at five o'clock. Mr. Smith came to see us off, but I did wash up the dishes.

Through Sophie's Eyes

We pulled out at fifteen minutes after five o'clock. It was Sunday morning. It had rained a little in the night and the grass and all the leaves on the trees were dripping. The sun was just nicely up and every raindrop sparkled like diamonds in the golden rays of the sun. There was no wind and the air was laden with the sweet odors of the fresh young day. We all were very happy and after we left Rome, every step of the way was new for us all.

It all seemed heavenly beautiful. I was in perfect health, so was my little girl, and the three of us were on our first automobile trip, Albert's and my wedding trip. As we were rolling along through the beautiful country, it seemed to me we were going into, entering the greatness of life. Our first stop was a little refreshment stand this side of Boonsville. It was now about nine o'clock and having had such an early breakfast, we stopped and had sandwiches and coffee.

In those days, autos did not travel as fast as they do now, and we in our Ford Motel T went about twenty miles an hour. But to us, who were only used to horses, this seemed very fast. Well, as I said so many times before, I will not try to describe the scenery in this book. We stopped a number of times for lunches and also so that Albert could rest from driving. But when we got to Bankor, the car suddenly balked. Albert, who did not know much about a car, could not start it. We pushed it along to a nearby garage. Whatever it was, it cost me six dollars and we were much delayed besides. At last we went on, got to Malone, the queen city of the North. It was long, long after dark, even for those longest June days. Albert had a little trouble in finding his aunt's home, his father's sister Lizzie.

At last he found it. It was after eleven o'clock. He kept ringing the bell, and then tooted our auto horn. An upstairs window opened, a head came out, a voice wanted to know who was there and what was wanted. Albert cheerfully called back that it was himself and his wife and stepdaughter, that we all were hungry, wanted supper, were tired and wanted to go to bed. Well they let us in, fed us, and made up some beds for us.

His Uncle Frank had to go to work the next morning, so at six o'clock they called us for breakfast. Albert ran to the head of the stairs and called down that we were not getting up yet, not till eight o'clock. Finally, we came downstairs. The woman was washing, but stopped and got us some breakfast. We stayed there two days and two nights. That is, we ate there and slept there. During the day, we went about sightseeing, dropping in for meals. One night we went to the Malone Theatre.

When we left there, Albert backed into a car in the heart of the little city and was fined. Now I had a little money with me, but I knew we were almost three hundred miles from home and I would have to buy gas and oil and food on our trip home. Also, I wanted a few dollars in case something happened again on the road with the car. Albert said, "I will telephone to Aunt Lizzie. She can run down and pay it." Well, he telephoned and the poor woman left her housework, took a trolley, and came and paid the fine.

We went by two or three of his mother's relatives. I loved them all. One of his mother's sisters lived on a small farm, another one on the outskirts of Malone. We stayed at each place a day or two. Then we went on to Chasm Falls, then to Owl's Head. There I think we went to five more of his mother's relatives. One day my little Sophie and I went up on the very top of Owl's Head. There we could look around for many, many miles to Indian Lake and Wolfe's Pond on the south, and to Canada on the north.

Everything and everyone reminded me of the Indians. After a few more days, we started for home by a round about way. At West Chase we saw a wild life reserve, Lake Champlain, Lake Placid, Bloomingdale, Swan Lake, Laranac Lake, Paul Smith's, and a dozen other lovely places. We were very happy; then we had more and more trouble with the car. At last about ten miles north of Sandy Creek, it gave out entirely. We left it there, never to get it back.

We got a ride into Syracuse and the next day, by train, came to Oneida and then home. We had been gone nearly two weeks and although I lost my car, for which I still had to finish paying, it was one of the happiest trips I ever made. Mr. Smith had taken care of everything at home.

Chapter 30

Well, another few months of lovely summer. Then my little Sophie started to go to school in Cleveland, riding either Prince or the pony back and forth. It was eight miles each way, but far better than the Oneida trips. As in Oneida, her classes were out at three o'clock and about five she was home. But there was one difficulty. She found a good place, for whichever horse she rode, about half a mile from her school. But these people had no barn. As long as the weather was pleasant, the horse had a large yard with good green grass to eat, but when the snow came, what then?

Came the fourth of October and Captain broke his leg and had to be killed. This was on Sunday. On October eleventh, on Sunday just one week later, our beautiful home burned up. No insurance. We saved quite a lot of things and piled them in the barn, but I think that was the hardest blow I had had up to that time. For nearly fifty years, I had saved, first little things, then more and more expensive ones, built, furnished, and loved my house. Even while I stood there, seeing all go up in flames, I kept repeating to myself, "Thou shalt have no other gods before me." I felt I had loved my house too much. Yes, I fear I did worship it.

For a week, we stayed at Miner's. It had one little advantage. It made the daily school trip more than three miles shorter for my little girl, as the Miners were living about four miles from Cleveland. But as I had all my animals, excepting the pony and Prince, at home, cows to milk, pigs, calves hens, ducks, and cats to feed, I either had to make two trips a day from Miners to my place or, as I generally did, take a lunch with me and stay down all day. We knew that we could not keep this up all winter.

Sophie Kussmaul

I went to see George Smith, got him to let us move into his house, which once had been my house. He let us have it, rent free. He went to live with his brother Robert. We had saved a lot of my best furniture but there was no place to put it in this small house, so I brought just the most necessary things to keep house with. Mr. Smith left his cook stove, table and chairs, and one bed for us to use.

Sad and terrible as that blow had been, I was looking ahead. My inheritance would soon come, and I would build another house. I still had all my beloved animals and most of my best furniture. Of course, never again be able to replace the many, many things I had lost. But life was ever calling, calling me onward.

After the snow came, I went to Cleveland and looked for a boarding place for my little Sophie. I found a good place, quite near the school house, with a Mr. and Mrs. Stanford. I knew the woman very well. She, too, was part Indian. Albert was sick most of the time. I had to get up early Monday mornings. I went home before daylight and fed my animals in the dark barn. I never took a lantern with me for fear of fire. I hitched up Prince and brought him to our new home. There fed him, blanketed, and hitched to the cutter. Then I went into the house, cooked breakfast, and got my little Sophie up and ready for school. We used to leave just before the day really broke. I took her to her boarding place and drove home.

Every Wednesday afternoon, she would take a train leaving Cleveland about four o'clock and arrive at North Bay about half past four, walk home, a little over two miles, and again on Thursday morning I had to go through the same performance as on Monday. But that gave her one night in between the week at home. Friday night, she came home the same way as Wednesday night. Luckily, the weather was not as severe as it generally was so late in the year.

Came the twenty-first of December and my fiftieth birthday. How proud I had felt on my tenth birthday. I thought, now I am no longer a child. On my twentieth birthday, how I longed to try my wings. Though I so loved my dear home, I felt a longing to see the world, to go to the land of my dreams, the Golden West. What heartache surged through my breast on the very eve of my thirtieth birthday, and also what a sense of exultation at the thought of entering into a new life. Then all of a sudden came my fortieth birthday. Somehow that thought seemed a little unpleasant for, after all, where had the years gone to? Well, I shook that thought off. Yes, I still had most of my life before me yet.

Now I was really fifty. Why, that could not be possible. Yet I knew it was so. But life was rushing me on. My little Sophie had quite a long vacation this time, from the twentieth of December to the fourth of January. She busied herself making little Christmas tree ornaments for, of course, we would have a tree. But though I said nothing, even the tree with its attempts at trimmings hurt me very much. Never again would I see the same precious ornaments on our Christmas tree I had seen since my fifth birthday, the morning on which I had seen that Holy vision, the Christ-child flying towards heaven.

Still, in that lowly home of ours and after my great loss, there in the early dawning of Christmas morning, I felt the quiet, serene holiness of that day. On New Year's Day, we went to Miner's. Our first wedding anniversary. The sixth of January, my little daughter stayed at home, her seventeenth birthday. Then school again. We did not have very much snow, just enough for sleighing. Mr. Wallace La Celle had given us some wood, all cut in sled length.

The wood was on the old Jim Brown farm, now known as the Clark farm. The woods were a long ways from the road, over in fact, to the California road. I had drawed out a few loads, but as I knew my little girl loved to ride into the woods, I waited till the coming Saturday and Sunday so she could be with me. Saturday came on the thirteenth of February. We did our barn chores together and the rest of the day we drawed wood. We got most of it out.

Next day was Sunday, the fourteenth of February, Valentine's Day. I did the morning chores alone, brought Prince home, fed him in the yard. It was a mild, dark day. We had an early dinner. Then my little girl and I took Prince and got the last two loads. Prince acted tired. I promised him a good rest as there was not to be any school in Cleveland till Tuesday. Well, he got his rest. It was about three o'clock when we got the last load of wood unloaded. Then we went down to the barn, did the chores extra good and careful. The weather was so warm, yet looked like snow or rain.

My four cows and yearling and pony all went down to the spring. We cleaned out the stable. I threw down hay from the mow and little Sophie filled up the mangers. We had grain in the barn. I fed the ducks, hens, and guinea hens. The barn part was so full of furniture it was hard to get around in it. I remember my little Sophie went and got a book out of the lovely bookcase. Then I went and milked the four cows, Florence, Jersey, Flossie, and Dora. They were all going to freshen in the spring, but I still milked them once a day. Then I fed my two cats, Twilight and Merely. Then I carefully closed up the door, took my pail of milk, and we started home.

Always when I got to Cleveland's house, I stopped long enough to change my heavy pail to the other hand. While I was doing this, I half turned around and, oh what I saw I can never, never forget! It could not have taken us over two, or at the most three, minutes to walk up from the barn to where we now stood, and what I saw was an enormous black volume of smoke rolling up from the north side of the barn and a red flame of fire. I, who always was so fleet of foot, felt as if I was frozen. I said, "For God's sake, save the animals." My dear good little girl started to run back as fast as she could. I tried to run fast, but my legs felt numb and my heart seemed like lead within me.

When I got to the driveway, the entire yard was filled with dense clouds of black smoke through which I saw the entire barn in great flames of fire. But I did not see my child. I think for the next few moments I suffered the greatest anguish of my life, not only to know that all my beloved animals, also all that was left and saved from my dear home, was in that inferno, but above all else, my child. I had said to her, For God's sake, save my animals. I stood there. I could not move. I seemed paralyzed with horror. Then I saw her coming towards me out of that dense blackness of horror and with a face so indescribably sad that no words could picture it.

If I lived to be a hundred years old, I could never forget how she looked and the words she spoke to me. She said, "I was too late." But in spite of that scene of horror, a great joy welled up in me, a great thankfulness. I had my child. Even now, after almost twenty years, I do not like to think about that day, so I will pass over it as quickly as possible.

There we stood, and in that inferno of flames were my beloved animals, all my beautiful furniture saved from before. Once, for a fleeting second when the smoke lifted, I caught a glimpse of my beloved organ. All my tools and buggies and hay were in that barn. In November, I had bought an old Ford car. That was out of doors, but I also had bought four brand new tires. They were in the barn. I suppose they were the cause of that dense black smoke, they and the hay.

Well, after a little while, a few people came. Albert saw the smoke and came. When he reached the driveway, he fell down flat on his face. I think he fainted. Well, this was a hard, hard blow for me. I was now cleaned out of everything and had my child and Albert to support.

The next morning Twilight came to our house. His hair had been badly scorched, but otherwise he was unhurt. He was the only living thing that escaped out of that place of horror. I had never brought him down to our house. I had bags of feed in the barn, also mice. So I left two of my cats at the barn. Each day I had taken down to them a few scraps from the table, and after milking, left a dish of nice warm milk for them. Later, I had often wondered if Twilight had sometimes come to my new home at night. How did he know where I lived? I had another cat, Hans. He had been in our new home since I moved there in October.

On the twenty-fourth of March, I walked to Mr. Justin Skinner's. After the fire, we had deep snow. I bought a blue cow. Her name was Fanny. I had a hard time to bring her home. The roads were terrible. She would lie down, rest, struggle up again, and by night I got her home. There was that tiny shed that Charlie had called the paint shop just big enough to put her into.

Good Mr. La Selle had been bailing hay on the same farm where he had given us the wood. There was quite a lot of hay left at the stacks after he got done bailing. He gave me that hay. So each day I took a long rope and went up there, about half a mile, rolled up some hay, and snaked it down home.

After the fire, my little Sophie went back to Cleveland to school. She took a train from North Bay at ten a.m. and, of course, missed her first class twice a week. Neither my little girl nor Albert would go down to my dear old home. The place where the barn had been was a place of indescribably horror. So on the sixth of May, I heard that the Breitenbeckers at Vienna had an old horse for sale. I walked there, bought the old horse. His name was Spike. Rode him home on horseback and next day fixed up pieces of an old harness that we had laying around our new home. The one-horse lumber wagon also was there. Then I hitched Spike to the old wagon, put in an ax and a chain, a whiffletree, put on a pair of old overalls and an old sweater and old gloves, and set out to do the most horrible job I had ever done in my life.

I drove to where the barn had burned, unhitched the horse from the wagon, fastened the heavy chain to one of the carcasses, put on the whiffletree, and hitched Spike to it to drag off the carcass, but this did not work. The horse pulled and they went to pieces. They had been partly burned, partly rotted, and party eaten by dogs. So I unhitched him and hitched him back to the wagon, took the ax and chopped each carcass in small sections so I could load it up. Prince, the pony, four cows, and a yearling. I drawed them back in the lot on a pile. When the last bone had been taken back, I stripped off my overalls, sweater, and gloves, threw them on the pile, too, and went back home.

The next day I took the horse and wagon and went to where Mr. La Selle had given me the hay. I drawed two loads of the poorest hay down to where I had piled the carcasses and completely covered them up. Next spring when only the bones remained, I got Mr. Smith to dig a deep hole and bury them.

Now, I had been determined not to give up my home, to move back there to build. But of course it would have been impossible to go back there with the horror of those decaying animals. My husband had absolutely refused even to step on the farm as long as they were there, and I had no money to hire it done, as this was not just common work.

So the spring melted into summer. I bought another good horse from Mr. Justin Skinner. We plowed the acre of ground where we lived. But each day I took the cow down home in the morning and went after her at night. I hired Jake Minehart to mow my grass. Then I raked and drawed every bit of it, alone, to where my old barn was and tried to stack it. I had never made a haystack, and so it did not shed water as it should and when winter came, the late heavy fall rains had soaked it through and then froze the hay like ice.

Well, I must go back a little in my story. We thought if little Sophie had an automobile, she could enter the Camden High School and drive back and forth until the roads got impassable, and then board at Camden. She was ready to take up third year high school at Cleveland at that time. They only went to the second year of high school studies. I did not now have the money I had a few years ago and so I told my little girl if she paid part of the money for the car, I would pay the rest. We picked out another Ford car, Model T, from Keller in Oneida on Cedar Street. The car was one hundred dollars, the same price I had paid Richie. My little girl drawed forty dollars out of her bank, and they drove the car home for us. I signed a paper that I would pay ten dollars a month till it was paid for, which I did do.

The next day, we tried to start the car, but try as we could, we just could not start it. Different ones of our neighbors worked at it, with no better results. So there it stood in our yard. At last I wrote to Mr. Keller about it. He sent out a man and it worked at times. So the car was likely to stall any time, and none of us had a driver's license. Here I must say that when we made that trip to Malone, Albert had no driver's license. Never had had one.

I found a boarding place for my little daughter in Camden with a Mrs. Flaggs. I took her out Monday morning, got her Wednesday afternoon after her class was out, and took her back again Thursday morning, got her home Friday afternoon. Now I want to go back to one day of my haying in July.

Of course all the days down there were about the same during my haying. I had always loved the work in the hayfield, but this was different. Yes, very different. It was a hot day even for a July, a Sunday, but I went down there just the same. I would rake hay for a little while. That was easy for me, but harder on the horse, then load up a small load, draw it to where I had started my stack. This was hard work for me, but easy for my horse. This was the picture of that day which I will always carry in my mind. Blackened trees where my house had stood, around a yawning cellar.

An attempt at a haystack where the haymow had been, a dark spot where the animals had been housed for so many years and where, though I had removed every vestige of them and the sun and rain had been using their cleansing powers now for about two months, there still was a deathly sickening odor from that gruesome spot. In other years, there were happy calves frolicking about, hens cackling, chickens running all over chirping, ducks quacking, a few lazy cats purring, flowers growing, but now only silence and desolation. The only thing alive there that day, besides myself and Barny, my mustang, were flocks of black crows. They hovered over the one time happy home and over the three graves of my people.

Well, to go back, came the twenty-first of December and my fifty-first birthday and Christmas, which somehow lacked something. The sixth of January, and my little daughter's eighteenth birthday. The weather had been very cold, but up to now, the snow had not been as deep as usual. I forgot to mention that about the middle of October, Harry Andas had come to visit us. He had been coming for a few years, and as we had no barn or place to store the car, we let him take it to his father's farm, about five miles north of Camden, for the winter.

The Matthews family had moved to Rome and as their barn was empty, told us we could put our animals in there for the winter. This was good for the two horses and my cow, but the thing was this. My hay was at home in a frozen stack. We lived about halfway between the hay and the Matthew's barn. I had no sleigh, only a sort of stone boat. So each morning I had first to walk down to Matthew's barn, feed and milk the cow, come home, cook and eat my breakfast. When my child was home, she had breakfast ready for me. Then go back to Matthew's barn and hitch up a horse to the stone boat and go home where I had stacked the hay, chop some of the frozen hay in blocks, and take them back to Matthews barn. As I only could take a small amount at a time, I had to make at least two trips a day. If it looked like a storm coming, I worked at this hay business all day so as to have enough on hand to last a few days. At night I had to walk back and feed the animals. Not once did Albert help me with this work.

We got through the winter somehow. Spring came quite early. In April we got our car back, then we would take little Sophie back and forth each day to Camden, but only for a little while, then the car refused to start again. On the nineteenth of June, my little daughter passed her third year high school examinations with high marks. I was proud of her.

We picked a lot of berries that year, drove the horses while the car stood in the yard. Again Albert had some of the neighbors try to fix it. I took it down to Clayton Montross, left it there a week, paid him eighteen dollars. It ran for a few days, then the old trouble again.

Came the twelfth of August, my little girl and I had been picking huckleberries in the afternoon. The three of us were at dinner and all at once Albert spoke. He said, "I know a man who could fix that car so it would run." I asked him who he meant and he said Ray Wilson.

I laughed and said, "That will not help us any. The last I heard, Ray was in Texas. He may not be back here for years to come." There was no more said about this.

After dinner, my little girl and I went back to pick more berries. Albert said he would walk down to North Bay. At supper, he looked up suddenly and said, "Whom do you think I saw in North Bay today? I saw Ray Wilson." I certainly was surprised. Then he added, "I told him about the car, and he said he would come up tomorrow and look at it."

The next day was Sunday and sure enough, Ray appeared. He went and lifted up the hood and in only a few minutes came to the door and said the car was in running order. He took us for a ride in it. We made arrangements that he came the next Sunday early and we would all go on a fishing trip to Chazee's Pond, about eight miles from Constantia.

During the week, I drove the car down home twice each day and a few times to North Bay. I did not have a license. So on the nineteenth of August, we made our fishing trip and after we got home and I was getting supper, Albert told Ray about his many ailments. Now I want to say this. In the first place, Albert was always talking about how sick he was, how sick he had always been, and so on. In the second place, I want also to say that from the very first day I met Albert, he told me how he longed to go to California, how he had always wanted to go there. That, of course, attracted me to him, for I was forever longing to go there again. Always thinking that when my child was through school, we two would make that trip together. After I had Albert, we often spoke about it. But now, after all my losses, I even had to draw every cent out of my bank, and my inheritance had not yet come, and this longed for dream seemed an impossibility.

While he was telling Ray all about himself, he added, "I will never get well, never get any better unless I can go to California. That is the only place on earth where I might recover again." Ray said to him, "Go out there with me this fall. I am going in about three weeks." Albert groaned and said, "I will not leave my honey," meaning myself. Ray said, "Let us all go together." I laughed and said, "Yes, we can all go together." Of course I took this as a big joke. Ray left after supper and the subject was not again brought up.

Chapter 31

Next Sunday, the twenty-sixth of August, to our surprise, Ray came. As he entered the door, the first thing he said was, "Well, are you people all ready to go to California?" I spoke up cheerfully and answered, "Oh, yes, all but to pack our suitcases." Ray saw I was taking it all as a joke, so he said he really meant it. I glanced at him. He did seem in earnest about it, yet I could not really believe it. He stayed for dinner and he and Albert made plans about going. I think Ray was working in Utica at that time and this day left soon after dinner. After he left, Albert was much excited now we were all soon going to start for the Promised Land.

I still thought all this talk was only the building of air castles. The next Sunday, the second of September, Ray came again. This time I saw he really was in full earnest. So we began to make plans. Ray at that time only had a half ton truck. He made us this offer. I was to furnish the car and the food, he was to buy the gas and oil and take along two tents. He also said he would get a trailer to carry most of our things so as not to crowd us too much in the car. I let Albert's cousin, who at that time lived five miles north of Boonville, have one of my horses, Barny, until we should come back in spring. The other horse, Albert's horse Robin, we let Mr. Sheppard have for the winter. I boarded my calf, a blue and white yearling, out to Minehart's till spring. My poor, faithful blue cow, I sold back to Mr. Skinner. I also had another cow and calf and a hog, which I sold. I took my hens to Mrs. Gleason to pay her fifty cents a hen in spring, and she was to keep what eggs they would lay. I had four cats. Three of them, I was to take with me, but Jerry, who was always so afraid of people, and everything else, I left with Mayolia Eckel, who lived near us. She promised to be good to him and I think she was, but this was a terrible hard thing for me, to leave him behind. He died in November and Mayolia wrote to me that each day he would look and listen for me up to the last hour of his life.

Now I will go back in my story to almost a year. Something happened to me that I forgot to mention, but I feel my life story would not be complete without this. I had my fourth vision. A very, very beautiful thing. That and my first vision, when I saw the Christ-child on Christmas morning, were the two most sacred things that had come into my life. My husband was away from home, my little girl off to school. It was a dark, gloomy day in October, the fifteenth. I was digging potatoes on the piece of ground next to our wild land. Of course I was alone, as not even my buildings were standing yet. I was in great trouble, sorrow was creeping up on me; there just did not seem any more hope for me. I can not here give the details of my anguish. I had often prayed for deliverance, but somehow my heart did not seem in my prayers.

But there all alone in the gloom of that dark October afternoon, I knelt down on the potato ground, closed my eyes, and bowed my head and really prayed. I said, "You can help me. I have as much faith in you as the woman of old who touched your garment and you made her whole. Now I will also touch your garment, and I know you will answer my prayer." Well, I swear I am telling the truth. When I reached out to go through the motion of touching His garment, my head was still bowed and my eyes closed. I felt something, a tingle like electricity shoot through me. I looked up and I saw Jesus. Only for a moment, his kind face. He seemed transparent, vanished. But I still felt that tingling. I jumped up, I was happy, joyous. That night my prayer was answered in a very miraculous way.

Came the twenty-sixth of September, and at four in the morning we pulled out. I was happy. Now we would start on our great adventure. But I did feel very guilty about Jerry. We went to Miner's, said farewell, and had breakfast with them. The sun was just coming up; we were getting into our car; she was weeping. The last words Mrs. Miner said were, "Oh, my boy, I will never see you again." This was terrible, and for some miles I felt saddened.

Life was calling and beckoning to me. After leaving Syracuse, every mile was new to me. Ray drove, but our old Model T only averaged twenty miles per hour. We got to Buffalo after dark. That

316

is, we camped a few miles this side of Buffalo. Now as I have so often said, I will not describe this trip. We made camp every night. I cooked a good supper and got food and everything ready so I could get a quick, hot breakfast. I made sandwiches. At about twelve o'clock we would either get a few bottles of soft drinks or coffee, according to the weather, and eat our sandwiches.

On the tenth of October, we made our first real stop with a Mr. Ice, who owned a very large ranch and had seventy acres in corn. Albert was sick and needed to rest. This ranch was in Oklahoma about ten miles from a town about the size of Camden, or perhaps a little smaller, by the name of Geary. We camped there for five days. Ray and I picked corn. They call it shucking corn. We took a team and heavy wagon, drove through the cornfield, two rows on each side, broke off ears and threw them in the wagon. Little Sophie cooked our meals. We stayed there five days. On Sunday, we went to a real western rodeo.

Our next stopping place was Amarillo, Texas. We stayed there four days. Then on to Albuquerque, New Mexico. There we made camp in a beautiful cottonwood grove. I think we stayed there a week. After this, we did not stop again. We arrived in Los Angeles on the twenty-second of November. The first two nights we camped in a park the city was developing, meaning that they were turning the natural beauty of nature into an artificial park.

Then we were fortunate enough to obtain a bungalow rent free. We were not in the heart of the city, more in the open and only a little ways from Pasadena Avenue. We had some lovely neighbors. Our next neighbor was a wonderfully good woman. Her name was Mrs. Moore. My little girl and I were trying to make this semi-tropical temporary home of ours seem a little like Christmas. So on the nineteenth of December, she and I went up a large hill in this to-be park. There we collected masses of mountain holly, dark green leaves with big clusters of red berries. We broke off great big branches, all we could possibly carry, and decorated our rooms.

Mrs. Moore came, was horrified, said it was strictly against the law to even break off one little twig. Well, nothing happened to us. We just got away with it. But about an hour later, she came in again, looked a little queer. Said she and her son were going down town and wanted to take my little girl with them. I knew these people were all right, or I would not have let my child go with them.

After they left, I picked up a book I had been reading, settled myself on the little vine covered porch, but after a few minutes I lost all interest in my story. I could not concentrate on it. I picked up a garment that needed mending, but after a few stitches, I put it away. A vague feeling of uneasiness was creeping over me. I picked up a broom, started sweeping, but the confinement of the house stifled me. Albert was sleeping. I walked about the yard, then up one of the streets, back home again. I was so nervous, felt as if something was going to happen. I did not know what, but a sense of fear or dread came over me. I looked at the clock every few minutes. Why did not Mrs. Moore come back? Albert woke up and went to the grocery store on Pasadena Avenue. I heard a car stop, but it was not the Moore's coupe.

A policeman stepped out and a woman in uniform and my child. She looked pale as death. The man did not come to the house, but that strange woman in uniform followed my child in. It seemed as if I had turned to stone or ice. All that I could think about was that my child had stolen something and been caught at it. The woman in uniform, who I later found out was a police woman, spoke. She said to me, "I want to speak to you." I felt like a sort of machine. I could move, but not think. I led the way into our bedroom. There were two chairs there. The woman sat on one, my child on the other. I sat down on the bed. Of course, I still had only one thought in my mind that my child had been stealing. Then the woman began. She said to me, "Are you this girl's mother?" I nodded. She went on. "I suppose you know the condition she is in?" I stared at her, dimly wondering what she had stolen. I managed to say, "What do you mean?" She bluntly replied, "She is going to have a baby." For a moment I was stricken dumb. Then a great rage welled up in me. How dare this woman say such a thing? Before my little innocent child, I jumped up and yelled out, "That's a lie." I turned to my child and said to her, "You tell her she's lying." To my utter amazement, my child looked at me and said, in a low tone of voice, "But it is so." Everything about me turned black. I could not speak. The darkness cleared. I looked at my child and for the first time saw her. Yes, it was so. How could I have been so blind? I managed to say to her, "Who was it?" She looked me straight in the eye and answered, "Henry Smith." I will try and skip over most of this.

Mrs. Moore had seen that I did not have the least idea about my daughter's condition. She was an intimate friend of Aimee Semple McPherson, the great evangelist. Got her to help us out. After this woman left, I went out into the yard and sat down under a giant sycamore tree. I have not the slightest idea of how long I sat there. At first a numbness of grief seemed to possess me. Then slowly my brain began working. I had always known that my child was not perfect, as none of us ever is, but I had been so proud of her innocence, her purity, and always had said to myself that no matter what else she may do, she is morally clean, as pure as the angels above us. I thought of the years we had planned together to get her educated so she could make her living. I thought of how I could now provide for her and Albert. Of the terrible disgrace we would have to face on coming home in the spring. My mind was racing ahead. All I could see was sadness, trouble, and disgrace for all of us. Yes, I was thinking of that good, pure, true mother of ours, Albert's mother, and why, oh why, should she have to suffer.

Then at once my mind now active, raced backward to the time I felt life within me for the first time, the glory born in my heart at that time. Then to the night my child was born, the thrill of rapture that surged through my very being at the sight of her. To the first time she smiled at me, the first time she reached out her tiny fat arms toward me, to her first awkward kiss on my cheek, to her first word, Mama. To the time she took her first toddling steps and a little later followed me around the room on unsteady little legs, always clinging to my skirts. To our dear hand in hand days, her first day in school, and later we always were together, always would be together, why it could not be otherwise. And now she had done the one, for me, unforgivable thing. But I could not hate her. She was still my child.

After a while it came to me that on another nineteenth of December I had been crushed with grief--the time my father had gotten that letter from Binghamton with the evidence against Spear. That time I had gone to the old hemlock tree at the very roots of which Joe had started to dig that ditch. At that time I made up my mind to go to California. Now here I was in California with another crushing blow.

Then Albert came to me, sat down close by me, put his arm about me. I laid my head on his shoulder. We did not speak. All at once an inspiration flashed through my brain. I began to see light ahead. I said to Albert, "You and I wanted a baby, a baby of our very own, and now why can we not adopt my child's baby, that really would be our child." To my joy, Albert kissed me and replied, "Sure, honey, God may have answered our prayers for a baby this way."

Supper that night was only a pretense. Then in the perfumed, flower filled early night air, I took my child for a walk. We went as nearly as possible away from the traffic. I still remember we slowly walked along a street where there only were a few new bungalows, flower bordered walks, and to this day when I see verbenas, I remember the masses of them that night, with their own peculiar sweet odor. We walked up a little terrace and there found a rude bench and sat down. I told her of my plan. So we all could stay together, the baby would be adopted. She would be its sister, and when we went back home, no one need ever know the truth.

I would write to Albert's mother, tell her the real truth and our plan to adopt it. She would keep our secret. I would write to Mrs. Fairchild and tell her Albert and I had a baby. That would not really be a lie, as the baby would be ours. So we talked the matter over together in the starlit night air of Southern California. The next day, we had another interview with the policewoman, as a girl of my daughter's age, at that time, would be sent to a reform school unless her parents or guardians would pledge themselves responsible for her and her illegitimate baby to be.

The day after this, the twenty-first of December, my fifty-second birthday, we had obtained permission from Mrs. Aimee McPherson to apply for entrance to the General Hospital of Los Angeles, to register for birth delivery and stay at that place for ten days, the bill to be paid by that wonderful woman Aimee Semple McPherson. Came Christmas Eve, we went to a concert, or rather song service, at the Angeles Temple. We had a fir Christmas tree at home. My little girl had made a few little gaudy ornaments. For the first time, we had colored electric light bulbs on the tree instead of wax candles. The next few days, I was quite busy hemming two dozen of diapers. I forgot to mention when we came home Christmas Eve, there stood a lovely blue and white bassinette on a swinging frame on our verandah which was filled and piled high with really beautiful baby clothes of all kinds and a few exquisite, lovely blankets. In a way, the next four days passed swiftly by. Then about four o'clock in the morning of the twenty-ninth of December, my child woke me up. She thought her time had come. I woke up Albert and asked him to go to our next door neighbor and wake them up and have them telephone to the General Hospital to send out an ambulance at once.

I had spoken to those kind people before, explaining our necessity to have a telephone message reach the hospital, and they had assured me they would send it at any hour, day or night. I hurried and made some coffee to keep us all up. My child was nervous, could not eat, but drank her coffee. At five-thirty, the ambulance arrived. I went with my child. The electric lights were still on, but daylight was also creeping in from the east. When we arrived at the hospital, I made final arrangements to have them send me a telephone message at once if she needed me or if anything went wrong and, of course, just as soon as the baby would be born.

Then a nurse came and ushered us into an elevator up to the delivery room. All the way up, my child had clung to my hand. We stood in front of the delivery room. She still clung to me. A nurse said to her, "You will here have to part with your mother." She looked at the nurse so pitiful. The nurse gently pushed me away and said to her, "Your mother can not have the baby for you." I entered an adjoining room and sat down to wait, my heart pounding away like mad. A few minutes later, the same nurse came to me, handing me a small bundle of clothes, saying, "Here are your daughter's clothes. You had better go home, as the doctor, who just made his examination, said it might be four or five hours before the baby's born. Everything is normal."

Three times before in my life, I had been handed a bundle of clothing. The first time, when the undertaker handed me my father's clothes, saying, "Here are your father's clothes." The second time the undertaker's wife had handed me a bundle saying, "Here are your mother's clothes." And again, when they handed me Charlie Estey's clothes. Now here they handed me my child's clothes with the same remark. Such a little bundle. They were still warm.

I went home. I could not concentrate on anything. The hours dragged by slowly. Albert, too, was very nervous. I was out of doors. I saw the woman who had the telephone come towards me. She said, "I just got a message from the hospital." My heart stood still. Would she tell me the worst? She went on to say, "Your daughter gave birth to a baby boy at fifteen minutes to eleven. She is as well as can be expected. The baby weighs five pounds and three quarters." Oh, how glad I was. She lived through it. It was a boy. Of course we would have adopted a girl just the same, but I knew that both Albert and myself wanted a boy, and I also knew that my little daughter would much rather have a little brother than a little sister.

Now back in our little bungalow, while I was telling Albert about the message, I started weeping, the first tears I had shed since that policewoman brought my child home. I felt like rushing off to the hospital, but I knew I could not get admission to the maternity ward till two o'clock in the afternoon, and then only for five minutes. Again at eight o'clock at night. Also for just five minutes.

We lived seven miles from the hospital, but it was rather a round about way to get there. First walk to Pasadena Avenue, there take a trolley, I forget to where. There get a transfer, walk a block, then take another trolley to, I also forget the name of that street, and walk over to the street where the hospital was. Albert and I had to stand in line by the big gate, as the clock in a little tower close by the gate lacked a few minutes of being two o'clock. I felt weak. At last we went inside, up the elevator. There I asked the desk nurse to let us see the baby. She motioned to another nurse. She took us along the long hall to a glass enclosed room. That is, the side of the room next to the hall was all glass. This nurse took a key and told us to stand out in the hall. I gave her the baby's name. I looked into this room. There seemed to be dozens of tiny babies there. I found to my dismay, when the nurse showed me my child's baby, a little red, wrinkled creature, bald, with I thought a deformed head and oh, such a thin little neck and arms. The nurse held him up for us to see and said, glancing at the card attached to him, "This is Baby Estey." But she never knew what memories those words brought back to me. For over a year after my child had been born, our friends in New York City and Buffalo had sent her countless post cards and little trinkets, always addressed to Baby Estey. Now to hear that name again. Albert had his arm about me. I

322

stood there, weak and trembling, but in spite of my first disappointment, I was happy my child was okay.

Then we were allowed five minutes in the maternity ward. There were sixty-four beds in it, thirty-two on each side, and each one contained a young mother. Hastily as we walked through, I glanced from side to side and then I saw my little Sophie. She did not look, at least to me, to be more than just a child. She had not yet seen her baby. She would not be allowed to nurse it until eight that night. In a way I was glad, thinking it would spare her for a few hours to come the shock of seeing the homely little creature.

Again promptly at eight o'clock that evening, we were at the maternity ward. The nurses were wheeling in the little babies, each one to his or her mother, each baby wearing a tag with its name and number, the corresponding name and number being on another tag attached to the bed post of its mother. When the nurse stopped at my daughter's bed, I held my breath. Oh, how my poor child would be disappointed. As the nurse handed her the tiny red, squirming mite, she reached out her arms for it, nestled it to her breast, and smiled at it. I thought she had not really seen it yet, so I said to her, "In a few days, he will look better. Yes, in a few weeks time, he will look all right." To my intense amazement, she looked at me with a happy smile on her face and said, "Why, he is beautiful now. How could he be any handsomer?"" Well that was a stunner for me. I said no more. Then as I looked at her lying there with her new born baby boy in her arms, a strange thought swept over me. She was so childlike herself, and it was still so near to Christmas, all at once I thought, and so lay the Mother of Jesus with her baby clasped to her breast.

So for ten days, twice each day, I made that trip to see my little girl for five short minutes each time. Some of the times Albert went with me. On the eleventh day, a neighbor of ours took me out to the hospital in the morning. I took my daughter's clothes along, and a few things for the baby. What the baby had on, stayed in the hospital. What a difference this trip from the hospital was, compared to the one to the hospital.

I will just give a swift description of that winter. I took entire charge of the baby, all but feeding him. He really rapidly improved in looks, but he never was as handsome as my little Sophie was at the same age.

Chapter 32

Albert was homesick. He wanted to get home to see his mother. He had so hoped to get well again by going to California. Instead, he was not nearly as well as before we got there. I sold our Ford, as it could not make the trip home again. I bought a Ford one-ton truck. I hired a carpenter to build us a house car on it, and then we were told that the truck would not have the power to carry such a load over the Rockies. So I sold that, too. Ray bought a Chevrolet and was going to drive us home in that. We shipped half a ton of our things to Camden by freight.

So on the seventh of May, we left Los Angeles for San Francisco. When we reached San Francisco, Ray said he would have to spend a day there to do some work on his car. I was delighted. I took my little daughter to the Golden Gate Park, carrying my little Joe in my arms. Albert stayed in bed most of that day. We went to some of the identical spots in the park where I had spent such a very happy honeymoon with Ernest Galway. Yes, I remembered those dear places. But there was such a difference now. That time, though in winter, for five glorious weeks the sun shone bright and warm all day. I heard old timers remark about it at the time. Never before had they seen such a long spell, at that time of year, without fog.

But today in May, it was very foggy at times. A mist like rain descended and the day was dark. Where all those lovely marble statues had gleamed in the bright sunshine, why now I saw they were only carved out of wood and badly in need of paint. We went up to that eminence where there are two great palm trees, at the edge of the park overlooking the Golden Gate and the Cliff House. Oh, how often I, or rather we, had stood there towards the end of the day and saw the sun slowly sinking into the Pacific Ocean, the waters gleaming, shimmering, blue green and silver, tinted with gold. But today through the foggy mist, all looked dim and gray.

Then there was another change, a great change. That time, like now, I was planning to go home, home to where my father and mother were waiting to welcome me. I would tell them about the good man I had met, the happy news about his coming to marry me. Yes, I was going to my home, sweet home. Life was all before me and I was happy. I was young in body, heart and mind. Today, here I was standing again on the same spot planning to go home, with my grandson in my arms, my daughter at my side, and to my home where there was no longer any one waiting for me, not even my house, of which I had been so proud. Nor the barn, with my beloved animals. I wondered where did all those years go to? Still, my child thought it a lovely place even with the gloom of the fog.

We stayed there till it got dusk, then I took her back to our camping place and got supper. The next morning we resumed our journey, only stopping at cabins at nights, as Albert was so anxious to get home and see his mother. So the days went by. We went by Sacramento and through the rugged country of Nevada. When we reached Salt Lake City, Albert wanted to rest, so we stopped over one day on the outskirts of that city. Then we steadily pushed onward until we reached Lincoln, Nebraska, on the seventeenth of May. Albert had been complaining all day about a severe toothache and that night he slept very little on account of that. He said he must have the tooth out. I left my little daughter and Baby Joe in camp. We were outside the city. I went with Albert to have his tooth out. We stopped at the first dentist's office we came to, but the dentist, after going over Albert, refused to pull his tooth. So we went to the next one and the same thing happened. When the third dentist refused, Albert questioned him and insisted to know why. The dentist hesitated a moment, then said, "The condition you are in, the shock might be too much for you." Albert got angry and said to me, "Find me a doctor's office. Any doctor will pull my tooth if I pay him." So we went into the first doctor's office we came to. The doctor looked at Albert, listened to him. Albert told him all about himself, our trip to California seeking health, now about our going home to his mother's. The doctor listened, then said, "If you want to see your mother, take the first fast train out. If, as you said, you are traveling by auto and stopping nights, it will take too long. You will not live to get there." Then Albert said something that I shall never forget. "I will not leave my honey." The doctor put something on his tooth that stopped the pain and we went back to the camp.

I kept telling Albert that the doctor did not know what he was talking about. Really, Albert acted much better than he had since we left Los Angeles. We always ate our homemade sandwiches at noon, stopping at some place, and according to the weather had either hot coffee with them or soft drinks. But to my surprise, at noon Albert said to me, "Let us have a full dinner today." We stayed in the car and had the waiter bring it out to us.

All that afternoon, Albert seemed very cheerful, made all kinds of plans what we should do when we got back. He felt sure I would soon receive my inheritance, as I had had a letter concerning it a short time before we left Los Angeles. So the afternoon went by. A little past six o'clock, we came to a small town, the name of which was Gothenburg, on the North Platte River, a small stream. We saw they were advertising a large auto cabin camp. So we went to the camp. While Ray was unpacking, I went to the tiny grocery connected with the camp to buy some food. We had supper. Our last supper together.

Right after supper, Albert went to bed and a few minutes afterwards was asleep. My little daughter washed up the supper dishes and then too went to bed. I, as every night, washed up all the baby's clothes and diapers so as to have them ready to pack again in the morning. Just when I was all done and ready to go to bed with Albert, he gave a horrible yell, more like a strangled scream, and started waving his arms as if he were fighting off something. I asked him what he wanted, told him he was all right, that I was there with him. Of course, I thought he had a bad dream, a nightmare. My little girl had jumped up out of her first sleep. This only lasted a few moments; then Albert sank back and went to sleep again.

I was just getting ready for bed the second time when he again started in yelling. This time, when he did, I knew it was not just a bad dream. I thought he must be having a fit, so I ran out to where our automobile was and woke up Ray, who slept in the car. I told him to get a doctor as quickly as possible. I really think it was not over five minutes before a doctor arrived. Afterwards, I found out why he came so quickly. Ray was in the car and just had to start it, drive to the office of the camp only a few rods away, and they told him there about a doctor who lived close by. They telephoned to him and he was at home. Ray gave him the number of our cabin, he jumped into his car and got to us while Albert was screaming and throwing himself about. The doctor managed to force a few drops of something between his lips. "If he has another convulsion, he is gone," the doctor said. Even while he spoke, Albert began to draw himself up, made horrible faces, clenched and unclenched his fists, and started screaming like a maniac. In between, he would call out, "Oh, Mother, Mother, where are you. Your boy is dying." This convulsion lasted about ten minutes. Albert became quiet, went to sleep, and a few minutes later the doctor felt of his pulse, listened at his heart, and pronounced him dead. It lacked a few minutes of nine o'clock.

The doctor said he would send an undertaker. Shortly afterwards, an undertaker and his helper came, carried out the body. Then I did a strange thing. I undressed and went to bed. It was still warm from Albert's body. I went to sleep and slept till morning. All this happened on Friday, the eighteenth of May. When I awoke, it was six o'clock, and I saw I was alone in the bed. Then the whole terrible thing from the night before came back to me. My little girl was awake. She had taken it much to heart. I got breakfast; Ray came in to eat. I had to make some arrangements at once.

I only had a few dollars, just enough to buy food and rent cabins till we reached home, and I knew there would be a good many expenses. I also knew I could not borrow any money from Ray, as he only had figured on having enough to buy gas and oil to take us home, and he was in deathly fear all the time that the car might break down and no money to buy parts with. So I had to think and plan for this emergency. Albert's mother had told me that he, Albert, would get a little money at her death as he had refused to have a share in the farm as Levi had done. So I reasoned, Why not let this go for his burial. He certainly would never now need it in his life.

I knew, though a telegram message would travel the many, many miles in a short time, I could not send one to North Bay before eight o'clock, as there would not be an operator there till eight or perhaps a little after. Well, I also knew that the undertakers were waiting for instructions what to do with the body. After the message got to North Bay, it would again take some time to deliver it and receive an answer. I knew the North Bay operator had no automobile, and it was a trifle over five miles from North Bay to Miners. So wrote out the message, condensing it as much as possible, asking his mother should I have Albert buried out here or have his body sent home. Also, how much should I spend for a casket?

This was the hardest thing I had ever done. This good, true, loving mother; why it would break her heart. If only I could have prepared her a little, but this telegram would be so cruel. Still, I must send it. So I gave it to Ray, telling him to take it to the telegraph office and at eight o'clock send it out. I went to the undertaking parlor and told the man that I had sent a telegram home and would know in a few hours what to do. They told me that as this man had died so sudden, the coroner requested an autopsy.

At ten o'clock, the answer to my message came back. It said she would pay all expenses. I should have the body sent home, use my own judgment as to the choice of the casket, send her the bill and she would pay the expenses. I took this out to the undertakers, picked out a casket. This was a responsibility, using another person's money. I dared not take anything too cheap, especially to be sent two thousand miles. On the other hand, I knew I must not be extravagant, as our dear mother did not have very much money. I also had to get a cheap new suit of clothes to put on Albert.

This was a long, long day, Saturday. I think the Miners could not get to the Oneida bank in time that day, as the bank closed at noon. So they could not get to the bank till Monday morning. They had the bank send a telegram to Gothenberg, as the undertakers held the body and casket till they got their pay. So of course we stayed at the camp till the body was shipped.

Came Sunday morning, the camp was quiet. We had an early dinner, were just through eating when we heard a low murmur of voices, a step, and a man stood at our open door. Back of him were quite a number of men and women. The man bowed, introduced himself, and said he had heard about our bereavement. The man who owned the camp had told the minister about us and he, after the sermon, had spoken to his congregation to give us a little assistance. Then he handed me a five dollar bill and stepped back. Then each one of the men walked up to me and gave me a dollar bill. Then the women formed a line and each one in turn handed me something in the food line. I do not remember just all we received, but I do recall baked loaves of bread, still warm from the ovens. Another gave a big cake; a number gave home baked cookies. Some brought home canned fruit, others tinned milk, beans, meat, and so on. In fact, there was so much of this stuff that we still had a supply of it on hand after we reached home.

Monday morning about ten thirty, the undertakers got the telegram and the notice of the bank at Gothenberg that the money was ready for them. They told me there would be a train going east on the Union Pacific at just twelve o'clock noon. They would have the casket at the depot on time to go east. Now they told me it would cost double fare to send a body, but I or any one of us could also go on that fare. But as things were, I decided it would be impossible for any of us to avail ourselves to take that way home.

I, as the wife of Albert, would naturally have been the one to go that way so as to be on hand to attend his funeral at home. But I certainly could not let my little daughter travel two thousand miles unattended with Ray Wilson. I knew if I sent my little daughter home by train, she would be terribly lonely and frightened, so I decided the three of us and the baby would stay together. I hurried back to our cabin, cooked dinner. Ray got everything packed and in the car excepting our dishes. We ate, got the last things packed, and went to the Union Pacific depot. A few minutes later, the train came. We saw them load up Albert's casket. The train pulled out and for a few miles we kept up with it, as the highway ran only a few rods from the railroad tracks. But after a few miles, the train slowly but steadily was gaining on us, and in a short time we only saw the distant puffs of smoke, and then not even that. Albert was on his way home to his mother, and she would be waiting for the arrival of her boy's body.

This was the twenty-first of May. We no longer took any cabins at night. We traveled practically night and day. I wondered then, and I still wonder, how Ray stood this continual driving with next to no sleep. Before sundown, we would stop along the roadside, cook and eat our supper, then back into the car for an all night ride. Early in the morning we would again stop. Ray would throw himself down on the ground and instantly drop asleep. My little daughter cooked breakfast. I heated water, gave the baby his bath and washed his clothes, which I hung up inside the car to dry. She and I would eat, make sandwiches for our midday lunch then wake up Ray. He would hastily eat and while he was eating, we washed up the dishes and packed them away again, and so started another day.

While Albert was alive, each night when I put Joe to bed, from a tiny little mite up to the night when Albert died, he would come and bend over him and tenderly kiss him goodnight. Saturday and Sunday night, while we were still in camp, he looked all around questioningly for his good night kiss, looked a little disappointed, and then closed his eyes in sleep. But Monday night, our first night on the road, at the time I changed his clothes for the night, a very strange, yes, a very beautiful thing happened. Baby Joe first gave a quick, searching glance about, and then his face wreathed in smiles reached up his little arms, still smiling happily, and went to sleep. Now I am telling the full truth in this story, and both my little daughter and I felt the presence of Albert near us. I will go further. We both saw something very faintly, stoop over Joe, then vanish. Never after this did Joe look for him again.

One morning before daylight while we were traveling in Iowa, our car, which had been making a queer noise for some time, balked completely at the foot of a steep hill. Ray said the rear end was gone. So that day, till after dark, my daughter and I camped there while Ray took out that part of the car and carried it two miles on his back to get it fixed. That delayed us another day.

Chapter 33

On the twenty-seventh of May, a little past midnight, we arrived home, to the house we had left on the twenty-sixth of September. The next day we went to see Albert's mother. Of course, we had been too late for the funeral. The dear, good woman assured me that I had managed well; that no one could have done any better than I had under the circumstances. She loved Baby Joe, but I knew her heart was breaking for her own boy, Albert.

The next morning Ray left for a month. I went to see Jake Meinhart, got him to take us to Justin Skinners where I picked out a black cow. I bought her for eighty-five dollars. I paid down ten and was to make monthly payments. We went on to where Robin was, about five miles further on. I had brought my saddle and bridle along. My daughter rode Robin home, as I had the baby in my arms. Next morning I walked to Skinners, about ten miles, and led the cow home. I had a very hard time getting her home, but at last I got her home okay. Next day I walked to Meinhart's and fetched my blue yearling home, Queen Victoria.

Mr. Miner had come and plowed about four acres of ground for me. I put in half an acre of potatoes, a large garden, and was going to put the rest of the ground into buckwheat. I had received my monthly allowance from New York as soon as I got home. I also went and bought two six week old pigs. Went to Mrs. Gleason's and got my hens. Well, I was very, very busy, but in a way quite happy. I was perfectly well; I had my daughter and my darling baby Joe, whom I loved more each day. But I was longing to get home. Strange as this may seem, the place where we were now staying did not seem like home although I had once owned it and spent six years there. In fact, it never had seemed like home to me. I had fixed the little pasture fence and kept Robin and the yearling there, and each morning after I milked the cow, I led her home and at night went after her; again. I also had to go back and forth a number of times a day to work in my garden. This was terrible--on the road back and forth all day.

I made up my mind I would get home to live somehow. About the first of July, Ray came back. The next day I had him take us to Albert's cousin, who lived near Boonville, so I could bring Barney home. I rode him fifty-five miles without getting out of the saddle. Ray procured a very large tent from somewhere and set it up near the road, just below the little green grove my child and I had planted. Mr. Miner brought me a tiny pig pen built like a house. I built a small yard around it and fetched down my two pigs. I took the one horse wagon and brought down our few belongings into the tent. I also fetched down a few old boards, nailed them to the little maple trees below where the barn used to be, and laid some of the boards on top for a kind of roof and fetched my hens down. To my great surprise, although they had been away from this, their old home, they still remembered the place. I was happy. I had made a break and was back home. I would stay.

Ray was not with us, but he helped me with the haying. I got my buckwheat in and had a fine garden and potato patch. Though the baby took up much time, my daughter and I still managed to pick and sell a few hundred quarts of huckleberries. Besides my monthly allowance, I raised one hundred dollars and went to Camden to Danas and bought doors and windows and some boards to start building a cabin. Came the last of September, as we only had an oil cook stove, the tent began to get cold at night. The stove we had been using where we had lived did not belong to us, and so we could not move it.

I went to Camden and bought a large secondhand cook stove, which they delivered for me, for fifteen dollars. About this time, Mr. Miner started building my cabin. I had to run in debt to Danas Lumber Company for a lot more building material, but I did get him paid up after some time. Well, Mr. Miner got the cabin done after a while. We had an early fall of snow about the middle of October which delayed the building. I sold Barney to Mr. Miner, as I really had no place for him. Ray brought us an old building, which he put up and which was large enough to hold Robin and the black cow and the yearling. I had a few old boards left and Mr. Miner built me a small hen house, so attached to the little barn.

The snow all went off and on the twelfth of November we moved from the tent into the cabin. There was a kitchen and a bedroom with a clothes closet, and a woodshed. Mr. Miner got me a share in the Grange House at Jewell which was being torn down. I drawed thirty-five one horse loads of old boards and rafters home.

The weather was mild and no snow. Came the twenty-first of December and my fifty-third birthday. We had a Christmas tree. The twenty-ninth of December, Joe was a year old. He did not only walk, but could run, as he had started to walk when he was only nine months old. The sixth of January, my daughter became twenty years old. The weather continued good for winter. Of course there were some cold and windy days, but the snow held off wonderfully. I still drawed old boards. For some time I had planned going to Oneida. They no longer ran the trains, and I was puzzled just how to go and come. All at once I made up my mind I would drive Robin to Oneida and back. This was the twenty-fourth of January.

I was coming home from Jewell with a load of wood when I made up my mind to go with the horse. This was a beautiful day. The winter sun was shining, the ground bare and partly thawed up. No wind. I made up my mind to go very early the next morning, as we surely could not expect this wonderful weather to last much longer. It was about one o'clock when I came home and then told my daughter that I had made up my mind to drive to Oneida and go the very next day. She thought that would be a very good idea.

That afternoon, we made out a long list of the things we needed. I had no grain for Robin, but I gave him a lot of good hay for his supper. Now I had intended to leave home about five in the morning, as I knew it would take about five hours to drive out there. That would give the horse a long rest in Oneida while I did my business, and then the five hour drive home.

It was a full moon. I woke up at two o'clock and woke up my little daughter. Something urged me to start just as quickly as possible. She got up, cooked me a quick breakfast, and I went out and gave Robin some more hay to eat and harnessed him, filled a bag with hay and put it in the buggy, got a couple of horse blankets in the buggy also. Went in the house and filled a quart can with milk and got a couple of pounds of butter packed to take to Mrs. Bowman, where I was going to leave my horse. I got Robin hitched to the buggy and left home at exactly three o'clock.

This trip I shall never forget. The moon was full and there was not a cloud in the sky. The ground was frozen; still it did not seem very cold. There was no breeze, no sound of any kind. I let Robin walk, knowing he would have to cover over thirty miles before we got home. A great silence seemed everywhere. I drove through North Bay. Never met a person. No one or nothing was stirring. As I was half way down, I heard a cat meowing. I stopped the horse and there on my right, running back and forth a couple of feet only, I saw a large gray and white cat with one of his hind feet in a steel trap. The poor cat was looking at me and calling for help. The trap was only a few feet from the road in a ditch, and in the bright moonlight I could see almost as well as in daytime.

It took me a few minutes to find a stick to spring the trap. The cat was watching my every movement. At last he was free, and instead of running off, he first came to me, looked at me as if to thank me, then rubbed his head against me and rapidly limped off up the hill a little way, then crossed over to the left and disappeared in the bush. Not till ten years after, I heard whose cat it was. It belonged to the Drake family.

I drove on, silence all around me. Through Sylvan Beach, up over the high bridge, and turned to go by the Jug Point Road. As I was going over Maple Hill, I noticed that the moon was not quite so bright anymore, as if a veil was over it. When I reached State Bridge, I could hardly see where the moon was. I had brought no lantern as I thought I would have the full moon all the way out and, of course, daylight all the way home. A very fine snow, more like a frozen mist, started falling. Before I got to Durhamville, the moon had entirely disappeared, a dark, heavy sky, and by now real snow falling. As I was driving through the village of Durhamville, I saw the first signs of life since I left home. Lights in most of the houses, dogs barking, a few people on the sidewalks. There were not so many automobiles in those days as now and of course still less so early on a winter morning.

The snow was coming faster, thicker. I turned into Lake Street. About a mile from Durhamville, I came to Bowman's. To my great joy, I saw a dim light, a kerosene lamp, burning. It was getting daylight. That is, it was still much more night yet than day, but there was the early, early dawn. Mrs. Bowman was getting breakfast for her two sons, Bill and Dan, who were working on the night shift at the Oneida Asbestos Shingle Mill. To my great disappointment, they had no shelter for my poor horse. All they had was a little hen house, built so low that no horse could have gotten into it. So I unhitched him, tied him to the buggy, put both the horse blankets on him, gave him the bag of hay I had brought along, and left him.

Mrs. Bowman wanted me to eat breakfast with them, but the food was so horrible I could not eat it. I swallowed a cup of boiled green tea without any sugar, but I was glad to sit near their fire, as the long ride had chilled me. Although I was anxious to get on my way on account of the ever thickening snow, I knew that I could not get into the bank before nine o'clock, and that would be the first place for me to go in order to get money to buy the things we needed so bad at home.

I left Bowman's at half past eight, leaving my horse to rest. It was about a mile to the bank. I had brought a suitcase from home. Into this, I put the many little things we needed. I went to a grocery and bought two large boxes full of good groceries, leaving them, together with my suitcase, at the store till I came after them with the horse. I went into a vegetable and fruit market thinking I would get a few bananas. The man there was very friendly, so I told him how the winter before I had so much damaged fruit and vegetables given to me in Los Angeles. He fairly jumped up, asking me in what part of Los Angeles I had stayed. It turned out that he, too, had lived on Fifty-six Street near Pasadena Avenue. He said he also had some things I could use. He filled an orange crate, a bushel, heaping full with apples, late pears, oranges and lemons, and about four dozen bananas. Then he got another crate and filled and heaped it with all kinds of vegetables. I thanked him.

I went into a restaurant and drank two cups of good hot coffee, ate a few fried cakes. Then I hurried back to Bowman's. By now, there were between two and three inches of wet snow on the ground and it was snowing very fast. I only had on shoes, no rubbers, and by the time I got back to Bowman's my feet were soaking wet and ice cold, but I dared not stop there. I knew what was before me.

When I got Robin hitched to the buggy, I had quite a hard time to turn him towards Oneida. He wanted to start for home. Well, I got back to the city, loaded up my groceries, suitcase, and vegetables and fruits. Just when I was crossing the Central track, the twelve o'clock whistles were blowing. The snow came thicker and faster all the time. I went along the State road. Robin was walking fast. I knew he was thinking of reaching home, and so was I. But when we got to Durhamville, I stopped at the feed mill and bought a hundred pounds of chicken feed and a hundred pounds of pig feed, thinking this might be the last time I could get out for a long time to come.

I no longer had the pigs I had bought in the spring. One of them I had killed just before Thanksgiving, and the other one soon after Christmas. But I had bought a fall pig to winter over. Well, my buggy was so full now I had hardly room to sit. The old miller asked me how far I had to go. I told him twelve miles north of North Bay. He looked at the sky. It was snowing faster than ever. He looked at my horse, he looked at the over loaded buggy, then he said, "You will never make it." By this time, the snow on the ground was at least four inches deep, which made the buggy pull harder. Now the wind was coming up, just a gust at a time, but it came from the northwest. Robin walked fast, his head lowered. It was steadily getting colder. My feet felt like clumps of ice. I took off my wet shoes and sat on my cold, wet feet. By the time we reached State Bridge, the wind began to blow a little stronger and tiny drifts began to lay across the road. I also noticed that Robin did not walk quite so fast any more.

When we got to Maple Hill, he stopped for the first time. Was breathing hard. Then made a new effort, walked fast for a few yards, came to a drift and almost stopped again, but went slowly on. The snow kept getting deeper. At last we crossed the Sylvan Beach Bridge and to my great joy met the big snow plow. Then up to the top of the hill of the Y, the road was all scraped out and Robin seemed to take new courage. We also had been sheltered a little from the wind. But when we got to the top of the Y hill, to my dismay I saw the plow had come from Vienna and the road leading to North Bay was badly drifted. Robin would go a few yards, stop, breathing heavy, plunge ahead again. The snow in places was ten to twelve inches deep and it was hard to pull the wheels through.

When we got to North Bay, the road was not so bad through the village, but the moment we struck the road leading to Nichols Corner, the snow was deeper again. Robin walked slower and slower. I knew the worst was still to come. While we were still on this road, I tried to put on my shoes, not knowing when I might have to jump out. But they were frozen so hard I could not get them on. We turned the corner to go on the Flanagan Road. An icy cold wind was now blowing, which we had to face. This road was drifted much worse than the others, the drifts coming to the hubs of the wheels. Robin did his best, but to my horror, I saw he began to stagger. I was much afraid I would have to unhitch him, ride him home, and lose my entire load. I did not whip him, as I knew he was doing his very utmost. He put his head down lower and his ears began to droop. Somehow we got to the foot of Flanagan Hill. It was drifted full and a steep little hill to climb. Robin stopped at the foot of the hill, trembled, panting, looked at it, and plunged ahead, the wheels in the drifted snow sinking to the hubs. I shall never forget this. Robin staggered, trembled, swayed, still half plunging, half swimming on. I knew if he stopped on that hill, he could not start the load again, and I also knew that if he fell, he could not get up again without help. Would he make it to the top? Slowly, foot by foot, he crawled on. Yes, he reached the top.

He breathed so hard that it shook the very buggy, his head way down, his ears drooping. The icy northwest wind was getting stronger. The snow was dry, whirling about us. Robin made another effort. It was still uphill to the McCormack corner, but not very steep, but all the time the road was filling up more and more. He would stagger ahead, stop, sway, and try again. Oh, I thought, if we can reach the next corner, our road would not be quite so bad. I had handled horses all my life and knew he was absolutely exhausted, but I also knew that he sensed a real blizzard was about to break and his only chance to save his life would be to reach home, his stall. I, too, was over half froze. I could not get out and walk, as I only had my wet stockings on.

Well, we did turn the corner. He stopped and fell on his knees, but after a few moments struggled up and went on. We reached Congdon's. He stopped, staggered on. The snow was not quite so deep here, but I noticed he kept staggering from side to side, stopped, and then struggled on. At last we came to the foot of the little hill just below my home. That was drifted deep. Robin raised his weary head, looked at it, and then turned his head to where he could see his little stable. He desperately plunged into this drifted hill, half falling down, swaying, almost stopping. On again, we got past the mail box. At that time my cabin stood quite a few rods from the road and I saw the driveway was drifted full. He made the last supreme effort. I drove directly to the kitchen door. I knew then, and I know now, that if it had been ten rods further, he would have gone under. My little daughter opened the door. I told her to put her boots and coat on and unhitch the horse and put him in his stable. I half jumped, half fell out and went into the warm kitchen. It was just five o'clock. I saw the windows were all frozen.

I took off my cold, wet, and frozen clothes, got into dry ones. Little Sophie came in. I got her to unload all my things into the kitchen. I unloaded the two hundred pounds of feed. It was getting dusky fast. I went to the little stable, unharnessed Robin, rubbed him all over with dry bundles of hay, and then put about a dozen bran bags on him, as his blankets were just a frozen mass. My daughter had filled his manger with good hay. Now the blizzard had really broke. It was now quite dark, and this awful storm raged for three days and nights. But I knew we had food enough in the house for two months, and so did our animals. I came into the kitchen through the woodshed and the first thing I saw was dear little Joe, a big orange in one hand and a large red apple in the other. My little Sophie was putting a good, hot supper on the table. I still remember one of the things was an enormous pork roast.

It was now five below zero and the wind was fairly roaring outside. At bedtime, nine o'clock, it was ten below. Oh, how thankful I was to be at home and have my poor horse in a warm, dry stable.

Well, the winter passed by. It was April. Nothing unusual had happened. Came the twelfth day of April, a clear, bright day, just a bit cool. My little daughter went to North Bay after dinner on horseback, riding Robin. I was sitting on the kitchen floor playing with Joe. I sat there in such a way that I really was facing the west window, but at the same time I had the glass door, which was on the south side of the house, on my left side. Joe was standing near me. He had his back to the glass door and was facing north. As I said, the sun was shining brightly. While we were in this position I just described, all at once a shadow fell across the floor, in fact across the glass door. Joe whirled around to look. I looked and we both saw a man close to the glass door, looking at us. The man was Albert Miner. He had an eager but very sad look in his face. Joe looked surprised. The vision had vanished, but it was so real. I jumped up, ran to the door, and flung it open, but there was no one there. I glanced at the clock. It was just two o'clock. My child came home about a half hour later.

Sophie Kussmaul

Joe had been very quiet since he saw that vision. Now he rushed to my daughter and told her in a very excited tone about the nice man who had looked in at us. My daughter turned to me and said, "Who was it?" I said Albert. So April melted into May. I was really very, very happy. I was perfectly well, I had my daughter and my dear little Joe; they both were well and happy. Spring was in the air and in my heart. Life seemed like a beautiful poem.

If anyone had told me there could be, there would be, a change, I would not have believed it. But what did happen was so absolutely terrible that even now, after sixteen years, I can not bring myself to write about it. That wound never really healed. So I will go over it as swiftly as possible. On the twenty-second of May, I felt depressed. I knew not why. My child and I made such beautiful plans that same day, of course including Joe, for our future.

Note: The pages which originally followed were either lost or destroyed by Sophie Kussmaul, perhaps because they were too painful for her to read. However, her granddaughter, Sinclair Seevers, remembers reading them and the following is her effort to reconstruct the events they related. "Little Sophie" has also written her story of the events.

My grandmother made up her mind to go to Rome to buy another horse. That would take her most all day. Her daughter got up a few minutes after she did. It was still dark outside. Grandmother fed the animals and came back to the house. Little Sophie had breakfast ready for her. She ate a good breakfast. Little Sophie then said a strange thing. She said, "The quicker you go to Rome, the earlier you can get home." Still, at that time, my grandmother did not think anything was wrong.

My grandmother went to Rome, bought a spirited gelding. He was very dark brown and his name was Shadow. He was a nice young horse, strong and reliable yet gentle. Before reaching home, she had a terrible feeling of loss. The closer to home, the stronger the fear became. The house was not yet dark, but she did not see her child or little Joe. Where was her little Sophie? Her baby Joe? She went out to the stable and called, but no answer. The next few days she was numb. Her darling child and little Joe were gone. Her heartache was so painful, the loss so unbearable. Surely her children would come home.

Well, they never came back. Her little girl and baby Joe just vanished. She could not eat, could not imagine going on alone with her darling children lost.

Finally, Ray's mother told her that Ray and Sophie had gotten married in Rome on October the twentieth, seven months previous. That Ray took his wife and Joe. My grandmother could not believe this. Ray was already married to Mrs. Bowman. She could not understand. She was sure her daughter had been very happy with her, and baby Joe had a good home and good care. They both loved him so. She had no idea her beloved child was even thinking of such a terrible thing. My grandmother wondered why her child did not confide in her.

Little Sophie's Story:

Having a baby out of wedlock was a terrible disgrace. My mother even went as far as saying that of course a girl would rather commit suicide than face the disgrace. Also, the baby was in disgrace all his life.

So my mother and Albert got the idea to say that Joe was their child. It seemed a way out. I was only nineteen and had no way of taking care of him by working. So when we went back to New York my mother told everyone she saw that Joe was their baby. A few people believed it. She was fifty-one, so most people probably only pretended to believe it.

Albert died on May the eighteenth on the way home from California. Ray kept after me to marry him. The chief reason I did was a chance to get away from New York and start my own life. I really had no life of my own. Everything went completely as my mother wanted. It would not have occurred to me to fight over this. She had always ruled everything, and she had the farm and the money to feed us.

On October twentieth, I married Ray. We both knew there would be big trouble if she knew it. Quite complete of doing anything to get her way. So we kept it unknown to her. The next spring, Ray had an offer to work on a job in Laramie, Wyoming. Jobs were already getting scarce. The Depression was starting. He wanted to go.

Sophie Kussmaul

I knew my mother would do anything to stop my going and of course taking Joe. By that time she loved him, and besides it would expose what she had told people. I didn't know any way out of it. Ray just said to leave without telling anyone we were going. It seemed the easiest way. My mother went to Rome to buy a horse. While she was gone, we left. It was early, about nine in the morning. We traveled all day and got into Pennsylvania that night.

When my mother got home, she was furious, as I had known she would be. She went right away and called the State Police. She told them I had taken her baby and that Ray had taken us away. There was the Mann Act in New York. If a man took a young woman into another state, he committed a crime. The police, of course, investigated and found out we were married. They also asked her if she had any papers proving Joe was her child. Of course she didn't, so they could do nothing. Ray had the idea she would get over it in time. I knew she would not.

Well, we went to Wyoming on the job he was offered. He worked about three months. Then that job was finished. She still told everyone that Joe was really her baby and I stole him. If people believed her, I don't know.

Ray couldn't find work around Wyoming, so we went back to New York, not to North Bay, but to Syracuse. There Ray found a construction job at Pompey. They were putting in a new road, the New York Freeway. At Pompey, it was called the Cherry Valley Turnpike. For a couple of weeks we lived in a tent. Then Ray became acquainted with Frank Kelly and his brother Tom. They had an empty house and let us move in. It was dirty and old, but we cleaned it up. We stayed there about three years. I became very attached to Pompey. We got to know our neighbors and soon had friends. I became pregnant with Vick that fall. Money was short, but we got along. In the spring we planted a garden. I forgot to say that Ray went back to North Bay and brought his mother to stay with us.

Of course, we got all the news from back home from her. Ray still thought my mother would get over being angry and everything would be fine. I knew her better and was sure everything was not fine. She had thought a lot of Joe, and most of all she felt I had defied her by leaving with him. She still thought if only she could find us, she could break up our marriage. Then, having no job or money, I would go back and live with her again.

341

Through Sophie's Eyes

The Depression got worse. There were no jobs. Ray's mother wanted him to come back to the farm. He was willing, but I was dead set against it. I felt there would be trouble. I wanted to stay in Pompey.

Sophie's story resumes with Chapter 34.

Chapter 34

Came the first day of June, Sunday. It was sometime in the afternoon. I was working in my garden. I heard a car drive in. My heart was pounding. Surely someone was bringing my children home. It was the Bowman family: Mrs. Bowman, Dan, Ralf, and little Gladys. After only a little while, Mrs. Bowman began to talk about my daughter's disappearance. Somehow, it did not hurt me to have her talk about this. All at once I started weeping. These were the first tears I had shed since I had found my children gone.

Mrs. Bowman was very kind and tender. After I stopped crying, she asked me if there was anything she could do for me. To my surprise, I said, "Yes, leave Ralf with me." I had not ever thought of it before till the very moment she spoke. She looked at Ralf and said to him, "Do you want to stay with Sophie?" He nodded his head. Well, they went away, and Ralf stayed. I looked at him, wondering if I had not better stayed alone. Well, I showed him my large garden. Some of the things were coming up. I showed him my three acre oat field. The oats were up, but the grass and clover seed were not yet up. I showed him the acre of ground I had got ready for potatoes. We went back and I showed him my two pigs, the black cow, the blue and white heifer, the calf, the two horses, my hens, I had about sixty-five, my ducks and baby chicks, my guinea pigs, and lastly, my two nice big cats. One of them had two kittens. Ralf loved all the animals.

All at once it came to me he would want some supper. As I said before, the last ten days I had practically not eaten at all. I had an oil stove and an oven to go with it. I made some nice light biscuits, fried some eggs, made some cocoa with rich milk, and put on a big dish of fresh butter. I only put on one place and one cup and told him to sit down. He asked me where I was going to eat. I was just going to tell him I did not eat anymore when before I knew it, I got another plate and cup and sat down at the table. I drank my coffee in the morning standing near the stove. At noon, I grabbed a slice of bread and went under the apple tree with it and a tin dish of milk, and at night, just milked into my mouth.

Well, I really ate supper that night. It seemed good to have Ralf praising every bite he ate. Then I did my chores. Ralf followed me step by step. I did not go back to work in the garden. We sat on the front doorstep, Ralf talking. When it got real dark, I felt as if I must now wander off into the far woods, but I could not leave Ralf. Why, he was even afraid of the shadows of the trees near the cabin. I fixed him a bed on the sofa in the kitchen near the door. To my disgust, he closed and bolted the door. I had no screen doors so in warm weather, I just had kept both doors wide open. He ran to each window and put a nail in so it could not be raised. He begged me to close my outside door and asked me to be sure to leave the door open from the kitchen into my bedroom.

After he was asleep, I opened my outside door again. It seemed strange to me to stay in bed. I did sleep most of that night. I got up early, went and started my chores. Soon after, Ralf came out, tried to help me, but was afraid of all the bigger animals. After I had the chores done, I would just have made some strong coffee but I knew Ralf needed breakfast. So I stirred up some sour milk pancakes. Remembered I had some bacon left, fried some eggs. Got some maple syrup. Ralf was eagerly watching every move I made, and in between made up his bed very neatly and swept the kitchen and set the table.

To my surprise, I ate a good breakfast. Ralf kept telling me that that was the very best breakfast he had ever eaten. After breakfast he helped me with the dishes. Then we went into the garden and I planted a few more things. Ralf tried to help me, but I soon found out that he was much better at housework than farm work. About nine o'clock, John Covell came. He brought Elmer and Homer and twelve bushel seed potatoes. I harnessed up Robin and hitched him to the one horse lumber wagon and got them started to draw manure for the potato ground. Then went back into my garden with Ralf.

About eleven o'clock I went into the cabin and started dinner. The Covells brought their own dinner. Ralf was with me step by step. From then on, I ate three meals a day and slept most of the night. Of course that desperate heartache for my children was always with me, but that boy was so good, tried so hard to help me, to please me, in a hundred little ways, that I slowly began to be myself again.

Came haying, Mr. Miner mowed my grass. I raked it up. Ralf and I drawed and stacked it. I paid him ten cents an hour for what he did in the hayfield. I had an enormous crop of huckleberries. Ralf and I picked hundreds of quarts. A man named Friday picked them up three times a week. Mrs. Wilson came over almost daily to pick on my land. Miners often came to visit me.

The second day Mr. Covell and the boys were at the potato planting business, I received another letter concerning my inheritance. I saw it would be necessary to go and see James Gallagher. If I drove a horse to Cleveland, it would take me half a day. So I asked John Covell how much he would charge to take me to Cleveland if I bought the gas. He smiled at me and waved his hand over the potato patch. The day was very hot, and he said I would be doing him a favor to give him the excuse to get away from that hard work for an hour or two. Of course he left his boys at work and I left Ralf.

I was in hopes that now at last things could be settled, but we found that as long as my parents' marriage certificate had been destroyed by fire, I would have to bring absolute proof of their marriage. I told him what year, month, and date they had been married in Utica by a Protestant German Minister. Mr. Gallagher said he would be going to Utica in a few days and have the records searched. About a week later, he wrote to me that when he was in Utica, he found the old minister and his wife. They were still alive and both of them, although fifty-seven years had come and gone, still remembered my father and mother. The marriage ceremony had been performed in their private home. So again, John Covell took me to Gallagher's. Now I had to get in touch with the German Consulate in New York City, and so this business dragged on and on for months.

To come back to John Covell, he was a very different type of a man than he appeared to be. Of course I had told him about my great sorrow, how I missed my children, especially my baby Joe. He had tears in his eyes. Told me although he had six living children, he still mourned for a little baby boy that had died when fifteen months old.

How he still could see him in his mind, how he toddled about, smiled, and so on, though ten years had now passed by. He tried to comfort me, said he would have to go to Rome the next day, asked me if I would like to go with him for the ride. So next morning he brought the boys to work, and I went with him to Rome.

Everything on the way out there delayed us. We had two flat tires, the gas pump would not work, and so on. We did not get to Rome until twelve o'clock noon. John Covell said he could not go too long without eating, so we went into a restaurant and had dinner. I offered to pay half the bill, but he would not accept my offer. While we were eating, Wesley Smith came into the restaurant. He saw us, came to our table, shook hands with us, talked a little, and walked away looking very knowing. Later, I heard that he told people that he had seen John Covell and me at a hotel, letting people think we had taken rooms there.

In July, John Covell and his family moved from Camden to North Bay, out the back road into the old Bill Wright house. Then he, John, would run up to my place every day. I went to Rome and Oneida with him countless times and once to Syracuse. A few other places. On days when we did not go out in his car, he would run up after supper and visit, sing for me, and he certainly could sing.

The summer went by. I canned a lot of berries of all kinds. Made a lot of jelly and half a dozen kinds of pickles. Bought and canned a bushel of pears and a bushel of peaches, always with just one thought, for my children. I had never stopped looking for them. They would surely be coming home, yes, perhaps that very day. It was now October. Ralf was still with me. He wanted to stay all winter. I told him he could stay with me till my children came home.

At haying time, I let Mr. Miner have Maggie to pay him for cutting my grass and to furnish me in wood for the winter, as my inheritance had not yet comes. Besides, I had not enough feed for two horses, or stable room in winter, and I really only needed one. Of course I would keep Robin. He was not over ten years old, as Bashart had definitely told us he was eight years old about two years ago.

Now that haying was over, I often made three to four trips into what we had always called the wild land after my huckleberries. So I used to ride Robin out there, tie him to a tree where he would be in the shade, fill my pail, then climb on his back, tell Ralf to hand me the full pail, and ride slowly home so as not to spill my berries.

346

Sophie Kussmaul

Came the third day of August, I rode Robin out in the morning as usual. Ralf always walked at my side. I noticed that Robin was trying to break out into a fast trot all the way out. I kept pulling him back so Ralf could keep up with us. After I tied him to the tree, he started to whinny loudly and often, and kept stamping his feet. I also noticed that about a dozen crows kept circling over him. The berries were so plentiful it did not take me very long to fill my ten quart pail. I got Robin untied, got on his back, and he acted so wild I could not take my pail. In spite of my trying to pull him into the little pasture, he rolled over half a dozen times. I thought it must be that the flies were tormenting him. Ralf and I went and had a quick lunch, so as to get back to pick more berries. To my surprise, I saw Robin laying down flat. I did not like this position. Ralf thought he was sleeping.

About four o'clock, we came home with our pails filled full and found Robin dead. In a way I was not too much surprised, after I had seen the crows circling about him, as he had had a few sick spells before, and that was the reason Albert had him given to him. Of course I felt bad, but this was such a small thing compared to my real sorrow, and such a little loss to what I had sustained that I did not grieve over it. But poor little Ralf, he wept bitterly, would not eat any supper, ran out to the dead horse and laid his own head on the horse's head, threw his arms around his neck, and wept hysterically. I knew how terribly quick a dead horse would start to smell in hot weather. If I waited until morning to send a letter out to the Rome Rendering Works, they probably would not receive it until the day after. So I wrote a note to Marjory Montross, who at that time had a grocery store and telephone, to telephone to the Rome Rendering Works for me, giving the reason. I sent Ralf down with it, and he brought back the message that they could not come after the horse till the day after tomorrow. But at least I knew by that time it would be disposed of. Ralf cried half the night. In the morning, it already began to smell very strongly and was all bloated up. I knew by another night and day it would be much, much worse.

Ralf no longer went near it and kept on crying. Mrs. Wilson, who had been coming over cross lots every day, came home with us at noon to eat dinner with us. Of course, during the hot forenoon, the smell had increased. To my disgust, she went up to the horse, felt of it, and came back to me. Asked me how much the man would pay me for the carcass. I told her nothing. Then she wanted me to help her

347

skin it. She said we would get five dollars for the hide, two and a half apiece, and I should cut up some of the horse and put it into the hog yard. The hens, too, would eat a lot of it. Of course I refused. She said that was very wasteful.

By next forenoon, the smell was unbearable, but about ten o'clock the man from Rome came. He assured me the horse was still in fine condition to work up. On the fifth of October, Mrs. Bowman came and said she was very sorry, but she would have to take Ralf away from me. She could get him into the Shingle Mill, and she needed his earnings very badly. Bill and Dan were past twenty-one and spent all their money buying old automobiles, gas, oil, and paying fines. But they still ate and slept at home.

Ralf was now just eighteen, small for his age, but he had gained twenty-two pounds while staying with me. Poor Ralf. He cried like a boy of five years; he did not want to leave me. I felt sorry, too. I had gotten so used to him. He was half child, half man.

The next day was dark and dreary, no sunshine. A car drove in and to my great surprise, Jake Miller, his wife Stella, and their five year old little daughter came into my cabin. I had not seen Jake Miller for over twenty-two years. At that time he was a boy of fourteen years. He had picked hops at the same box with me, to Kilts's. His father was an Oneida Indian. His mother was a white woman. I knew him at one glance. Stella, his wife, was a full-blooded Oneida Indian. I took to her at once. Ernie, their child, was a beautiful little girl. Jake told me they had gotten burned out and had heard of an empty house in or near North Bay, but found the house had been sold. He knew I lived somewhere near North Bay, so inquired after Sophie Kussmaul.

I had them for supper, and all at once an idea hopped into my mind. Could they not come and live with me? At first they hardly knew what to say, but in the end they said they would bring out some things the next day and stay for a while. Anyway, the next day they came with a trailer containing bedding, clothes, and a lot of groceries. We got along very well together. Jake had a job at Sylvan Beach, was gone all day. Stella and I picked a lot of Princess Pine. The little Indian girl was with us, but was no bother at all.

Mr. Covell had gotten a job in Camden and so could not come but on Sundays. These Sundays he and the boys dug and picked up the potatoes. We had a great crop; each one got a hundred bushels. I sold mine as I had plenty I had raised myself. The weather was beautiful, quite warm for the time of year, and the little rain we did have fell at night. So the month of October went by. Jake finished his job at the beach on the third of November. On the fourth, we all went to Syracuse. Jake went looking for a job. He hired out to work at the Franklin Auto Works, to begin the next day. The weather was still so warm that he slept in his car outside the city, eating in restaurants. Of course, he came home Saturday nights and left us again Sunday night. Stella and I kept on picking Princess Pines.

Came the sixteenth of November, a Saturday. A cold north east wind and rain. Jake came home, half frozen. Said he took some rooms in Syracuse and would take his family there as he could no longer trust the weather to come out each week. By morning, the ground was white and a cold north wind blowing. They packed up and after we had a good dinner, they left, and again I was alone. Now the weather was bad. More and more snow fell, cold bitter winds blowing, dark and dreary days, and long nights.

During the weeks Stella had stayed with me, three of her married sisters and their families had often come to my place, and I liked them all, but I was only thinking of my children. They would surely be coming home now. Winter was here. Came the twenty-seventh of November, Thanksgiving Day. The day was clear and cold. I did not intend to do any cooking. No, that would only bring other Thanksgiving days back more clearly, happier days than today.

At eleven o'clock, John Covell drove in. He came to take me home to have Thanksgiving dinner with them. I was glad. Now I could partly forget myself and eat a good dinner. I visioned a large roasted turkey on a platter, or perhaps a good fat goose, or maybe a couple of tender, brownly roasted ducks. Or perhaps a big roast pork. Perhaps a baked or even boiled ham. Of course, all the rest that goes to make up a Thanksgiving dinner. The moment I entered the house, I gave a quick sniff to find out what we were to have. I smelled no meaty smells. After a while we sat down to dinner of mashed potatoes, boiled onions, hot biscuits, and canned huckleberries. The whole family ate hearty, happily. Mr. Covell smiled at us all and remarked, "Many, many a time I would have been thankful for a dinner like this." He brought me back to my lonely little home.

The winter weather continued cold, snowy, dark days. Came the fifteenth of December, a thaw set in with the snow going very fast. By the eighteenth, the ground was bare again, muddy like early spring.

Through Sophie's Eyes

On the nineteenth, Sunday, John Covell drove up to see how I was getting along. The day was so warm I had my cabin door open. I told him that I wanted to go either to Oneida or Rome before Christmas. He said he would be laid off from his job at Camden on the twenty-second and had to go to Rome on business on the twenty-third, would come after me.

Came the twenty-first of December and my fifty-fourth birthday. The day was like summer. I spent most of it in the woods. I cut and carried home a Christmas tree. I would put it in the woodshed, and when my children came home, my little daughter could trim it. I felt so sure they would be home for Christmas. Why, it could not be otherwise. As I said, the day was very warm for the time of year. I kept thinking, if we only could go to Rome tomorrow and not have to wait till the day after.

The next day was much colder, but still a good day for winter. Late that afternoon, the wind shifted into the northeast, a bitter cold wind came up, and at nine o'clock the ground was frozen as hard as a rock. The wind came up stronger. The sky had been overcast all day and now not a. star showed in the heavens. I moved my bedding from the bedroom into the kitchen, made up my bed on the sofa near the stove. I got up a few times in the night and put wood in the stove. I thought it would be impossible to go to Rome in the morning. I was very much disappointed as I wanted to be ready for Christmas for my children. I felt so sure that my little daughter would not leave me alone on that day.

I went to the little stable and fed my animals and chickens and ducks. The air was icy cold and a strong wind from the north east. I ran into my cabin, got a good, hot breakfast, and ate. All at once John Covell drove in, asked me if I was ready to go to Rome. I was surprised, told him we would freeze to death and a big snowstorm might break any time. He assured me that he had a good heater in the car and some heavy blankets, that if I bundled myself up, I would be quite comfortable. He thought being so bitterly cold, we would have ample time to go and return before the snowstorm broke. Why we ought to be back home by two o'clock. I hustled around and got ready in a few minutes. It was half past nine when we left my home. Yes, it was not bad at all in the car, but the roads were so icy the car kept skidding. We had to go to his house, as his wife also wanted to go to Rome.

Sophie Kussmaul

Well, she had not even begun to get ready, and by the time we left their house, it was nearly eleven o'clock and a fine snow was falling, coming ever thicker and faster. It was twelve o'clock when we got to Rome and there were already two or three inches of snow on the ground, and the air was thick and full of more coming down. Of course, every store and shop was full of shoppers. I hurried around from place to place so as not to keep them waiting, as I knew every hour the storm and roads were getting worse. I bought a lot of groceries, thinking this might be my last chance to get out for a long time to come. I remember I bought *Desert Gold*, a book by Zane Gray, for my daughter's Christmas, and a small black horse on wheels for baby Joe. Also six or eight pounds of different kinds of candies, a few pounds of mixed nuts, figs, dates, California grapes, oranges. I was going to give them a happy holiday week.

A little past one, I had all my things in the car, but where were the Covells? The storm was ever getting worse and worse. If we only could get started. At two o'clock Mrs. Covell appeared and as John was not there, she ran back to the stores. Soon after he came, waited, and then went looking for his wife. So it was half past three when the big snow plows went. The going was bad. It was nearly five o'clock when we got back to Covells. Already night had set in and there was a blinding snowstorm. They both wanted me to stay with them overnight, but I told them I must get home. I had only fed my animals that morning. If I stayed with them, the back roads would be impassable maybe for days to come. At that time our road was not yet opened by the big snow plow.

Mr. Covell took Elmer along and two shovels, thinking he might still make it. We got through the village all right. As we were on the road to Nichols corner, right in front of Symore Flannagan's, the big Nash skidded off the road into a ditch. They pushed, shoveled, pried, but could not budge it. At last I went to Symore's. He got a lantern, hitched up his team, and pulled the car out. He took no pay, but advised us to give up going to my place, said the cross road would be drifted full. I should go back with Covell. Well, we got to the corner, turned to go on the Flanagan road, went a few rods, and slid into another ditch. This time we all knew we really were stuck and I could not go back and get Symore to hitch up again. All around us was snow darkness. Whirling, drifting snow. None of us had a flashlight. Covell again urged me to come back home with him. I told him I was a mile from his house and only a little over a mile to my home. I would get home all right. There were some empty bran bags in the car. We turned on the dome light, and I sorted over my things. I put about twenty-five pounds of the things I wanted the most in one bag. They put my groceries in the two other bags. We left the car. They went to North Bay. I started home.

I had on overshoes, but of course every step I took, I sank in the deep snow far above my knees. I could not see where I was walking. The snow was coming down faster than ever, snow above me, deep snow under me, snow all around me, and darkness. The bag over my shoulder seemed to get heavier, my legs weaker. I would struggle on a few feet, stop to get my breath, then on again. By some born instinct I found my way. I was now battling, step by step, up the Flanagan hill. Falling down, getting up, floundering on. I remembered how just eleven months before I had that other terrible experience coming home with Robin. I got on top of the hill, but now I had to face the icy blast more even than before. Somehow I reached the McCormack corner.

Now the wind was more on my back, and the snow not quite so deep, but I began to feel extremely tired. Dimly I began wondering if I could make it the rest of the way. Then it came to me that if I gave up, I surely would go to sleep and freeze to death, and my animals might starve to death. So I made a renewed effort. Again, that great instinct of direction guided me on. I thought back to the time of that other trip home. Then, I knew if I reached home there would be a light in the cabin, a warm room, a good hot supper, and my two children waiting for me.

Tonight, if I reached home, there would be an empty, ice cold, dark cabin waiting for me. I reached the foot of the little hill below my home. I fell in the deep snow. My legs were numb and at first I feared that I could not get up again. I forced myself up, half walking, half crawling; I reached the long driveway. If only I could hold out a few more rods. I had to waller through the deep snow to the back of the cabin as the front doors were closed inside. I could not even see the cabin till I was within a few feet of it. I had the door of the woodshed bolted outside. My hands were so cold and numb it took me some time to push the bolt back. Oh, joy, I was in the woodshed. I felt my way to the kitchen door, got in, shaking from head to foot. Somehow I found the matches, tried to light my lamp. One by one they went out.

Sophie Kussmaul

My fingers were so stiff and my hand shaking. At last the lamp was lit. I began to take off my wet frozen clothes. Luckily, I had a nice lot of kindling and dry wood in the kitchen. I started a fire, then took off the rest of my frozen clothes, and put on dry ones.

The clock was still running. It was just ten o'clock. The water pail was frozen, the windows a thick, white mass of ice. I soon had a good hot fire going. Made a hot drink and I had had a big pork roast the day before, so I cut a few thick slices of that cold roast, put it in the frying pan and heated it up. I was half starved, as I had not taken time to eat in Rome. I ate the rich, hot meat with bread, and drank a lot of hot Postum. My feet and legs and hands were aching terribly from the frost. I unpacked my heavy bag. My fruit was not frozen, as there were a lot of papers around them, and the constant motion of the moving bag kept them from freezing. At last, after filling up my stove with wood and feeding my cats and guinnea pigs, which were in the house, I went to bed near the stove and slept till daylight.

I woke up rested, but a little lame. There was still a good bed of red coals in the stove and it was not long before I had a good hot fire going. Ate my breakfast and got ready to do my chores. The ice and frost on the windows was so thick I could not look out. Luckily, I had my shovel in the woodshed. When I opened the woodshed door, I certainly was surprised. It must have snowed and drifted for hours after I got home. Now the wind had stopped blowing and also it had stopped snowing. I glanced at the thermometer. It was twenty-five below zero. The snow lay mountain high, not a sign of life anywhere. I worked myself to the little stable. I had to first shovel off part of the hard packed snow from the haystack, then dig out some hay for the cow and heifer. I had gotten my two hogs butchered a few days before. I fed my hens and ducks. Then shoveled a path to the pump; that was frozen. I had to melt some snow to get hot water to thaw it out. At last I got it thawed out, had to carry water to the cattle. They had none the day before. Ice would form over each pail full before I got it to their stable. When they had enough, I carried a few pails to the house.

I looked about me. Snow cold, a dark sky, a great aching loneliness stole over me. This was the day before Christmas; tonight would be Christmas Eve. The first Christmas in my life that I would be alone. I knew that as the road was impassable, the mail man could not get through, but a faint hope sprang up in my heart that perhaps a letter from my child had come for me the day before, as I had left home before the mailman had come. I was tired out from shoveling and wallering through the deep snow with heavy pails of water and other things and still lame from my exposure and overexertion from the day before, but I wallered through the deep, cold snow to the mail box. No letter. My heart was very sad. I got back to the cabin. I knew the next day, Christmas, was Saturday and the day after Sunday, so I could not get a letter from her till Monday.

I was so sure if she could not come to me for Christmas, she would write me a long, loving letter. My two cats looked at me, came to me, purred and rubbed their heads against me, tried to comfort me. Yes, they knew I was sad and my heart filled with grief. I took the toys and book I had gotten for my dear ones and put them in the bedroom so I would not see them before me. Darkness set in early. It was not quite so cold, just a little below zero. That night, as I lay in my lonely bed, darkness all about me, utterly cut off from all communication, all at once a great feeling of peace came over me. I felt the holiness of Christmas about me.

When morning came, the sun was shining. Christmas morning. I did my chores, gave my cattle some oats, and my poultry a pan of meat scraps I had saved up. Their Christmas treats. My cats and guinea pigs also got some extra tidbits. A peaceful silence hung in the air. All at once I heard some stamping in the woodshed. I quickly opened the kitchen door. There covered with snow, all out of breath, was John Covell. He brought in a big bag full of my groceries. He was so completely tired out that for a few minutes he could not speak. Then he told me he had worried himself half sick about me, thinking perhaps I had perished on my way home that awful night. He had started this morning with some of my groceries. There were at least fifty pounds in that bag. The Flanagan road was now open, but he had to waller every step of the way from the McCormack corner to my place. When he saw smoke from the cabin, he knew I must have gotten home. I made him some hot coffee; he would not stay for dinner.

Well, his kind interest in me cheered me up greatly. That was a very long and lonely Christmas week. On the twenty-ninth was Joe's birthday. He was now two years old. On the sixth of January, my little daughter was twenty-one. In a way it seemed only a little while ago since I, too, had been twenty-one. Yes, in spite of the hard and rocky road over which I had traveled through the years since then, here and there had been a few bright spots along the trail.

Chapter 35

The rest of that winter was not too bad. Mr. Covell went back to Camden and his job soon after New Year's. But he sent one of his boys up to my place twice a week to see if I needed anything. So the winter passed by. I had not heard a thing about my inheritance since November. Then on the fifth day of April, I got a letter from the Oneida Savings Bank telling me they had received two thousand and three hundred dollars for me, which was at their bank at interest. Well of course I was glad, but I lacked the joy I would have had had my children been with me.

I sent word to Mr. and Mrs. Miner telling them about my getting some of my money and asking them to take me to Oneida. I was to receive the balance later, but I never did. Now I am not at all superstitious, but if I were, I would surely say there had been a curse on that money.

All my life I had been very saving. I often have heard people say that I could make one dollar go as far as other people could two. But whatever I undertook with this money, things went wrong. Later, gossips said I gave my money to John Covell, but that was ridiculous. There was no truth in this story whatsoever.

On the eighth day of April, Mr. and Mrs. Miner took me to the Oneida bank. I drew one hundred and twenty-five dollars and paid Mr. Miner in the bank for the work he had done building the cabin and furnishing some of the materials to build. I drew seventy-five more dollars and went to the post office and sent that amount to George Dana at Camden. I drew some more to pay up a few other debts, such as a grocery bill that I owed since the house had burned to Homer Page at Jewell.

Sophie Kussmaul

Now I planned to build a good barn, with a basement first of all, then a good house over the old cellar. Mr. Miner was to do all the carpenter work. Mr. Covell to build the basement. Both Mr. Miner and Mr. Covell thought five hundred dollars would build a good barn, buy all the material and pay for the labor. They both agreed that one thousand dollars would build a house as I had planned. I thought that would leave me a few hundred in the bank. As the fences were all down, I bought a lot of wire, hired Dick Kenney, George Smith's son-in-law, to rebuild them, bought a few tons of lime, hired Mr. Miner to plow over half my cleared land, made some other improvements on the farm so as to be able to make a living from it later on. I took Mr. Miner, or rather had him take me, to Camden to Stereling's Sales Stable to buy a good horse. I thought he would be an expert in picking one out.

Well, there was a beautiful dark bay, weighing about twelve hundred pounds. He was fat, sleek, shiny. His head held up high, a deep chest, perfect legs. He seemed full of life, yet had a gentle look. Mr. Miner whispered to me, "That horse is worth two hundred dollars." We were so completely taken up with him that neither one of us looked in his mouth. Stereling said I could have him for one hundred and fifty dollars. Miner kept nodding at me. I bought him, thinking he would last me many years.

The next day, Stereling delivered him to me. He fairly danced on the way to the stable. I filled up his manger with good hay. Two hours later, I saw he had not touched it. I drove him to North Bay and back. He was a good roader. I thought perhaps there was something wrong with the hay. I cleaned out the manger, put in some from the other side of the hay stack. He looked at it, then at me, and whinnied. I brought him some feed. I had bought a hundred pounds of ground oats and corn. He ate it greedily, but in the morning I saw the hay had not been touched. Then I examined his mouth. He had no grinders at all. I fed him the ground feed and drove to Miners, had Mr. Miner look his mouth over. I had been right. The horse was very old and full of arsenic. I wrote to Stereling about it. He brought me out a black mare, Molly. He said she could eat hay. She did. She weighed about ten hundred.

Well, she walked just a tiny bit funny. Not really lame, but as if there was something wrong in her hind quarters. I drew manure, stones, some wood with her. She was very gentle and willing to pull a heavy load, but each day I noticed she walked a little stiffer. Came a day about two weeks later when she could hardly walk. I discovered she had a large hard lump inside one of her hind legs. I sent for Dr. Boshart. He said it was an absess, and when it was ripe, he would lance it. He looked at her mouth and said she was not over ten years old. A week later he came and lanced it and assured me she would be all right. Of course each time he came, it cost me five dollars. Now I know Boshart is a good veterinarian, but for once he was wrong. Molly died a few days after.

John Covell and Elmer were working on the basement, bringing their dinner. Howard Covell and his wife Viola came to live with me. They boarded themselves and quarreled all the time. Then something happened that I never mentioned, something I never liked to talk about, or even think about. It was when I went to Oneida with both Mr. Miner and John Covell to the Ruby Lumber Company. We had talked over the amount of the materials we would need for the barn. Mr. Miner, as the main carpenter, and John Covell as helper, picked out the stuff. Boards two by fours, four by sixes, planks, rafters, joists, beams, roofing boards, tracks for the rolling barn doors, fourteen rolls of heavy roofing paper, and eight sets of glass windows. There also were a lot of other things to be used in the building of the barn.

We were there some hours. To my horror, the whole amount delivered at my place came to five hundred and fifty dollars. Well, I thought I would have a beautiful barn and would build a much cheaper house. I do not remember just how many truck loads there were. They neatly piled each kind of lumber up by itself, but touching each other. I also remember buying a lot of paint, as I intended to get the barn painted as soon as it was built.

Howard and Viola went to Syracuse for a couple of days to visit her mother. Mr. Covell and I went to Rome to buy a car. I wanted a car I could drive myself. I had intended to get a cheap one, but I really fell in love with a Chevrolet coupe. It looked like new, ran very smoothly, and if I could pay cash, I could have it for two hundred dollars. I bought it. I also bought a few hundred pounds of nails in nail kegs for my barn. The dealer I bought the Chevrolet from took me around by Oneida so I could draw the money to pay him for the car, another man following in a car to take the dealer back to Rome. Now even before John Covell and I had left home, a heavy thunderstorm was raging in the south west. As we were on our way to Rome, the thunder and lightning west of us was terrific. But when we came back at last, we had been gone a good many hours and the sun was shining brightly. But to this day, what I saw on reaching home makes me fairly sick. My entire pile of new lumber gone. Just a mass of smoking embers left. I know it was caused by lightning. John Covell hinted strongly that Mr. Miner had set it afire, as he had wanted to build the basement. This was a hard, bitter blow. Now I only had a little over seven hundred dollars and nothing done except my basement stone work.

As I said, there seemed to be a curse on that money. It so happened that the very next day, Fred Bigley and his family came out from Oneida. They said they had intended to go to Niagara Falls, but their car was on the bum and so they would have to give it up. Like a flash, a thought entered my mind. I proposed to them that they drive my car out and I go along. I wanted to get away from my troubles. So the three of us went. Their children, grown, stayed in Oneida. We certainly had a wonderful trip out. I began to feel reckless. Everything had gone to the Devil.

I began to drink a little. The weather was hot the latter part of June, and we would often stop and drink beer and a little wine. We spent a happy day at the Falls. I had been there before. I wanted to forget my troubles. That night we all got drunk. About eight next morning we started for Lewiston. I also had been there before. We took the Gorge route near the river. We felt a little dull, stopped at a place, and drank and drank. Good wine, better whisky, smooth brandy. We got back into my car. Mrs. Bigley went to sleep. Fred Bigley drove zig-zag. I laughed myself sick. We got back to Niagara City. I wanted dinner.

Just how this horrible thing happened, I really do not know. All at once there was an awful smashing, crashing, screaming, yelling, swerving. I was thrown on the hard pavement. I was so stunned that everything seemed like a dream to me. I dimly saw a giant five ton truck, loaded high with something, looming up skyward before me. Heard the ear piercing shrieks of pain, loud voices, crowds all around me. I felt no pain, just stunned. But there was one thing I made out through all the confusion. My lovely shiny Chevrolet was only a mass of debris.

It was proved by everyone that the large trailer truck had had the right of way and Bigley was entirely to blame. The outcome of the whole thing was that Bigley had a broken leg, three or four smashed ribs, and a lot of cuts and bruises. Mrs. Bigly had internal injuries and outside cuts and bruises. My car smashed completely. I escaped all injuries except the shock. I think, though I never knew exactly, that the door next to where I sat was not securely closed and when that tremendous impact with the heavy truck came, it probably flew open and I half fell, was half thrown, out.

Everything was a muddle. All bystanders, including a traffic cop and the truck driver, agreed the driver of my car ran into the truck. An ambulance came and loaded up Mr. and Mrs. Bigly. I did not want to go, but they insisted I must be examined for internal injuries. I went to the thing that had been my car. I was looking for my purse. The day we left home, I stopped at the bank and drew one hundred and twenty-five dollars, fully intending not to break into the one hundred, just carry it as a precaution and return it to the bank on my way home. Well my purse was gone. Also the wallet Bigley had in his pocket.

At the hospital they declared I was all right. I sent a telegram to the Oneida Bank for seventy-five dollars. That left me just five hundred at the bank. They kept me at the hospital till the next day. In the first place, so I could pay for my examination. Bigleys, too, had to send home for funds, but they had to stay at the hospital for weeks.

As I said, there was a curse on that money. I have not the least idea what became of the wreck of my car. I had a wild idea that everything was going to the devil. I would go home by airship. In those days, very few people went that way. I could only go as far as Syracuse, then take a train to Oneida and another one from there to North Bay. When I got to Oneida, I spent another fifty dollars for the only thing I still have--a good set of upper teeth.

When I got home at last, Howard and Viola told me the first thing that John Covell had a sort of shock. It came on him all at once. A short time after that, the Covell family moved away from North Bay, and after that I only saw John a few times. I bought the large old barn from Leroy Page at Jewell, got a couple of men to take it down and truck it over to my place. Now I forgot to mention that my allowance had stopped a short time before I got my inheritance. Also, I want to say that when I got notice of my money being sent to me, it was understood that that was only a small part of it, that later on I would get the rest. That was partly the reason I spent it more freely.

Sophie Kussmaul

By the time I had the old barn moved, bought another horse, a farm wagon, and a Ford car, living expenses, and lending Howard and Viola fifty dollars, which I never got back, I had less than two hundred in the bank. Mr. Miner brought me my winter wood, for which he charged me an enormous price. Then he did something else, which I am sure his wife never knew. I had him put up a sort of roof over my haystack, out of the old boards from the barn I had bought. He charged me twenty-five dollars for putting it up, and also handed in a bill for each time he had brought me a bag of feed. Of course, I paid for the feed. I paid him up and told him never to come to my place again unless his wife wanted him to bring her to me. I still loved her and knew very well he never told her how he had overcharged me.

Now here was September. I had seventy-five dollars in the bank and no building done. Lost my allowance from New York City. My children gone. Howard and Viola moved to Syracuse. Mr. Covell a cripple and also moved. I missed him very much. He had some Indian blood in him and that probably accounted for our mutual liking.

Now out of all that money, I had bought no clothes at all for myself. I drove my old Ford a few times to Camden, leaving it to McLaughlin's. I had no driver's license. I began to reason things out. No allowance, all that to me big money gone, car smashed, horse died, winter coming. I must keep on living. At least I had my winter wood. I had paid very dearly for it. I would have my potatoes, beans, milk, butter, eggs, and two hogs to butcher. Of course there would be school taxes, land taxes, some groceries, always some other little expenses, but I would get through the winter all right. I must have cash to buy pigs in spring, feed, get plowing done.

Now the latter part of October, a new thing came into my life. It was a new romance. But here I must go back to another thing. When Mr. Miner built my cabin, I thought, of course, it would only be temporary. I would soon have the money to build a good house. So I had no chimney built, just the stove pipe sticking through the side of the building. A number of times the winter before, I had had an awful fright thinking the cabin might catch fire. One of the first things I bought in spring was a brand new oil stove and oven. So of course I had no fire in my big cook stove all summer and early fall. But with the first hot fire in late October, the old trouble started all over again. So for safety sake, I had an outside chimney built. That, together with

361

the fall school taxes, feed to fatten my hogs, my groceries, a collar for Dan my horse, reduced my bank money to fifty dollars. I knew in January my land taxes would come to about ten dollars, and to live as cheap as I could, it would cost me at least five dollars a month.

Now according to this, I would be entirely on my own by spring and there was all that big pile of lumber to build my barn with. Well, I went to picking Princess Pine to sell. After I had about one hundred pounds picked, I sent a post card to Cleveland to McCluskey, the man to whom I had sold it last fall. The answer came back that he was not buying any this year. I wrote to Gewenis, to whom I had sold three years before. He, too, had quit the business. Two or three others were the same way. I asked West, our mailman, if he knew of any buyer. He thought a few moments, then said, "There is a young fellow back of Williamstown who is buying up all he can get, and when he has gotten a ton of it collected, he ships it to New York City where it is made up into Christmas wreaths." He told me the man's name was Donald McDougle, a farmer's son, and that the address was Williamstown, R.F.D. No. 2. So I sent him a post card telling him to go to North Bay. From there, anyone could direct him to my place.

A few days later he came. Drove a coupe Oldsmobile. I was not in the least interested in the man, but from some inborn sense studied his face, his every feature, so that in no matter how many years went by, I would still know him. He was of medium height, rather strongly built, a plain but honest face, gray eyes, and rather light brown hair. He bought my pine and said he would buy all I could pick till the twelfth of December. So he agreed to come out twice a week after it, unless the snow should come so I could not pick any.

Each time he came, he would stay a little longer, tell me about his family and himself. He was an only child, his grandparents on both sides had come from Scotland. He lived with his parents on a small farm. The weather stayed quite pleasant. A few times it snowed but it never stayed on the ground long. Came the twenty-seventh of November, Wednesday, the day before Thanksgiving. Donald came to buy my pine. Asked me if I was invited out for next day's dinner. I said no. He said he had told his mother so much about me, and said she had sent me an invitation for Thanksgiving dinner. I asked him how many would be there. He told me no one besides his father, mother, and himself. He came after me the next day about ten o'clock.

Sophie Kussmaul

The day was cold, but clear. I was wondering if todays dinner would be like the last Thanksgiving dinner I had at Covell's. The McDougle's were farmers through and through. Poor, hard working people, but seemed well fed. We certainly had a real Thanksgiving dinner, turkey and all. I ate as I had not eaten in a long time. The old people were not old at all, still in their middle forties. I was nearly fifty-five, but they kept telling me what a wonderful good boy Donald was.

He brought me home, and as it was dark, helped me to do my chores. On the sixth of December, winter set in. That ended my picking princess pine, but it did not end Donald's visits. As long as the roads were passable, he came every Sunday afternoon. But at that time the back country roads were not kept open the way they are now, that is, not good enough for automobiles to travel. Mr. West got through most of the time with his horse and cutter.

Chapter 36

Came the twenty-first of December and my fifty-fifth birthday. Not even the mailman got through that day, and I was very, very lonely. That night I dreamed of my little Sophie. I was happy in my dream, but in my heart felt more lonely than ever when I woke up.

My Missing Daughter

Only in dreams I see her
As in the olden days
Her big eyes full of wonder
A smile upon her face

Only in dreams I hear her
Voice so soft and sweet
Only in dreams I hear
The patter of her feet

And now in dreams I
As we wandered hand in hand
From the golden land of childhood
To the one of grownup land.

Christmas, too, was lonely, filled with bittersweet memories of other days, days that would never return. Donald came once during the Christmas week, got stuck on our road, had to get Reamore to pull him out. I saw no one. Mrs. Covell wrote to me saying John was getting much better, but as he would not be able to drive a car for a long time to come, they would not license their car. Dear, good Mrs. Miner wrote to me very often, but

John made all kinds of excuses not to bring her. I heard from the Millers. They had moved to Rochester.

It was the fifteenth of January, a cold, clear day. No autos had gone by for a couple of weeks, but the road was open for sleighs. I was just coming from the little stable towards the cabin when I saw a man turn into my driveway. We both got to the cabin about the same time. I saw the man was Will Norman. I knew him slightly. I had known his wife a little better. She was part Indian and about sixty-five years old. He was about fifty and had been born and raised in Kentucky. I was a little surprised to see him, but we talked about the weather, the bad roads; I inquired about his wife. He acted a little uneasy. Absentminded, he would look at me as if he wanted to say something then lapse into silence.

At last I said to him, "Have you something on your mind?" He looked at me quick and said, "Yes." Then he told me his troubles. They had been living in one of Westcott's tenant houses. Westcott owned the Stone barn. He had had no work since September and had not paid a cent of rent for four months. Westcott had been very patient, but now he had a family that bought the house and wanted to move in at once. He had given the Normans a weeks notice, and tomorrow was their last day. He said he had walked to Cleveland, Camden, North Bay, all over, but could not find a house, or even a room, as he could not pay a cent down and knew of no job. Then he hesitated and asked me if I would let them move in with me. I said yes. He was really pleased. Said he would get Brockway to move them out in the forenoon. This was about ten o'clock in the forenoon now. I got him something to eat and he left for home.

I had plenty of potatoes, pork, beans, and cabbages. Some groceries, but I wondered how we would manage, three of us to eat instead of one. I cleaned out the bedroom. To my great surprise, at four o'clock that afternoon Brockway brought them to me, his sleigh piled up high. Both Mr. and Mrs. Norman walked, also Brockway. I had another surprise. Just a few hours before, Will had told me they had not a thing to speak of left to eat in the house, and here they were unloading two large boxes of good groceries. They told me afterwards that when Will got back from my place that morning, Mrs. Norman had received a letter from her daughter, who was an actress in New York City, with ten dollars. Right after she told him the good news, Brockway stopped at their house on his way to Cleveland. So

365

Mr. Norman went to Cleveland with him and invested the ten dollars in groceries.

Brockway told him that if he, Norman, wanted to get moved, to pack at once, as he had another job for the next day. So by four o'clock they were at my place. We got along lovely. After only two days, Will got a job cutting wood for Collins at North Bay. Then there was not a day that he did not bring home something extra for our supper. The only thing I did not like was that they brought their dog along. He was very well behaved, but he and my three cats did not like one another. But I really felt sorry when they left. They stayed with me until the twentieth of March then moved to Verona Beach, where Mr. Norman had a job.

All this was before our road was rebuilt, and so when the snow went away, each spring for weeks the mud and the frost in the ground thawing out made it entirely impossible for automobiles. Yes, even a horse or team could only get through with a light rig, so I had seen Donald only once since New Years.

Well I cannot say that I really missed him. Still, in my great loneliness, it was very pleasant for me to have him come, and I knew he had done his best to be agreeable. Now, I thought he probably would not come again until fall, when it was time to buy princess pine. Came the twenty-sixth of March, a warm, sunshiny day, much more like the latter part of April than March. Not a sign of the deep winter snow left, robins singing.

A man came to my cabin. I remembered to have met him before. He was an adopted son of Jake Miller's father. This man had no Indian blood in him. He told me a story. He had not been working all winter, had no home, could not get a job. This was the beginning of the Great Depression. He claimed to be a good carpenter, heard how I had so much old lumber on hand to build a barn. I told him I could not hire him, as I had no money to pay him with. He said if I let him stay, gave him his meals and a bed to sleep in, he would wait for his pay if it took years before I had the money to pay him. Again he said he had no place to lay his head.

Now to tell the truth, I did not like the man. What I ought to have done was to have drawn up a paper to that effect, gotten Mr. and Mrs. Miner as witnesses, and made this Roland Miller sign it. But I was green. Now I know much better. Well, I let him stay. He would work a few hours every day, each night sit down and write and figure in a little notebook. He claimed he needed a man to help him, which seemed reasonable as no one man could lift and handle those heavy timbers. I got Jake Meinhart to help him and so about six weeks went by. The work went very slowly, and though I am no carpenter, I knew things were not done right.

One night after supper (it was the twelfth of May) he studied his little notebook for hours, acted very strange. Next morning at breakfast, he could not look me in the face. Then he said he was going to Rome. Said he might not be back that night. Well, he left without looking at me. At night he did not return, nor the day after. The following day in the afternoon, a new shiny automobile drove into my yard. A man with a badge on his coat came to the door, asked me my name, and then handed me a large sealed envelope. Then before I had time to open it, or ask any questions, he had again gotten into the car and his driver started out of my yard.

To make a long story short, it was a summons to appear at the Rome Court House the day after and settle up with this Roland Miller, who had a bill against me for ninety-five dollars for work he had done on my barn. This was a blow. I had drawn out my last cent in the bank to buy roofing paper for the barn and not a cent coming in. I had thought as long as I had eggs, milk, butter, raised my own potatoes and other vegetables, I could manage. My huckleberry money would buy the feed to fatten my two hogs and a few groceries. My princess pine money would pay the taxes and buy more groceries.

Here I was all alone, no money, and supposed to be in Rome the next morning at ten o'clock. I had a slow old horse that had no shoes on his feet. Now I did not want to run to Miners. A thought flashed through my mind. I would walk out to Vienna and see Elmer Routh. He always had acted friendly. So I got my chores done a little earlier and walked to Vienna. Luckily I found Elmer at home, and told him my troubles, and asked him to take me to Rome in the morning. He promised to get me there in time. Next morning I was up early and ready to go. I waited and waited. It was fifteen minutes after nine o'clock when Elmer came.

He laughed when I told him we would be too late, said he could easily drive out there in half an hour. He did drive fast, but just this side of Herder's Bridge we had a flat tire. As he only had one good leg, it took a long time to change tires. At last we got started again and drove fast, but we did not get to the court house in time. They told me Miller had been there, the case had been called, and as I had not appeared, would be adjourned. A few days later, to my horror, a lawyer and a sheriff came to me. The lawyer was not quite so bad, but that sheriff had a heart of stone. He served me a notice, and as I had neglected to come to Rome at the date stated, my bill, now with the added costs, would be one hundred and twenty-five dollars. I was given three days to raise it in.

May nineteenth, at not one minute after twelve o'clock noon. If I did not have the money there by that time, the following would happen. They would advertise my stock and farm for sale by one o'clock. Then the sheriff walked around, wrote on a paper one cow, one heifer, one horse, fifteen hens, two pigs, some hay. Cattle at that time were the lowest in years. He said the cow, heifer, and horse at a sacrifice sale would not bring over fifty dollars. The hens, pigs, and what little hay there was, old hay left over from last year, would not bring over twenty dollars. My wagon would not bring over twenty dollars. So they would also have to sell the place. He added, and I suppose he thought he was being generous, "Whatever is over from the sale of the place will be yours." This was bad. Of course I did not cry. The lawyer was kind. He came to me, said he was very sorry, said I should surely be able to raise the money from some of my friends.

Well, I again went to Elmer Routh, had him take me to a dozen different ones, amongst them Monroe Bushnell and Edith Ennis. The next day he took me to George Skinner, the lawyer at Camden. This was my last day. Mr. Skinner told me if I only had come to him at once, I could have sued Miller for charging a high price and doing such poor work. But said now it was too late. The only thing left for me to do was to raise the money before tomorrow at eleven o'clock, as it would take an hour to get there. This was a little after three o'clock. He told me that the Camden bank was now closed, but to come to him in the morning and bring the deed of my place and he would go to the bank with me and see to it that the bank would loan me the money on a mortgage. I had slept hardly any for the last two nights. Before I went to bed this last night, I opened my New Testament at random.

This is what I read: *Ask and ye shall receive, and whatsoever ye shall ask in my name, that will I do, so that the Father may be glorified.* I ran down to my mother's grave and prayed, really prayed.

Said to Jesus, as if he were near me, "I do ask this in your name. Please help me." I felt better, went to my cabin and slept till morning. Ate my breakfast, did my chores, got ready to go to Camden. Elmer got me to Skinner's office by nine o'clock.

Mr. Skinner and I went directly over to the bank. A girl clerk asked what she could do for us. Mr. Skinner told her that I wanted to get some money and give a mortgage. She informed us that she had nothing to do with that kind of business and we would have to wait for Mr. Dorrance. She said he would be in by ten o'clock. We went back to Skinner's office. It seemed hours of waiting for me. We went back at ten, waited fifteen minutes after ten, Dorrance came. Mr. Skinner did his best to talk him into giving me the money and taking a mortgage, but Dorrance absolutely refused to do that. Skinner and I walked back to his office. I said, "This is the end. I will lose my home." Skinner said, "You will not lose your home. I will give you the money and take a mortgage." I felt very, very thankful, but looking at the clock, it was not twenty minutes to eleven. I said, "But isn't it too late?" Mr. Skinner said no. He started to dictate a letter to his stenographer and at the same time unlocked his safe, took out one hundred and twenty-five dollars, put it in the letter, and rushed to the Post Office.

My heart was beating wildly. The clock said five minutes to eleven when Skinner rushed off. Would he, could he, make it? Well after a while he came back, said he got it off in time. Then he made out the mortgage, putting in a clause that if I could pay it within a year, there would be no interest. I was happy. Instead of being sold out at once, I had a whole year before me. I did manage to pay back twenty-five dollars that fall. I took part of my berry money and sold one of my two hogs.

Now I will have to go back in my story again, to the latter part of March. As I said before, spring had come much earlier than usual. Even before the Normans had left me, Donald had started coming again. The first few times he left his car up at the Loomis Corner. That was a few years before our road was rebuilt. So regular each Sunday afternoon, he would appear. On Easter Sunday, the sixteenth of April, he came after me, took me to his parents' house. They were rather uneducated people, but by no means dumb. Poor, but not desperately so.

Through Sophie's Eyes

Well I admit I felt myself very superior to them, but still liked them. It certainly pleased me the way they acted. The father told me that he was going to give his son a jersey cow and a horse when he got married. Then he added, "And if the woman had a horse, too, there would be a team." Poor Donald, his face was as red as a beet, and he looked shyly at me. His mother smiled at me and said she would give him a dozen Plymouth Rock hens and a setting of turkey eggs. Then the father said, "He is our only child and after we pass on, he will have all we got." They made things so plain I could not help knowing what they meant. After this, Donald came twice a week, Sunday afternoons and Wednesday evenings.

He kept hinting, awkwardly making love, but as yet had not said anything directly. The weather continued lovely and as Roland Miller either went to North Bay each night after supper or directly into his room, he never interfered with our visits. We generally sat out under the little apple tree before my cabin.

Came the eighth of May, a lovely Sunday. About four in the afternoon, Donald drove in. I saw something in his face that told me at a glance that today he meant to come to a point. Now I had thought things over very carefully for some time past. I had made up my mind that even if I did not love him, I would marry him just as soon as he asked me to. I knew he was a good, decent young man, healthy and strong, a good worker, a born farmer. I fully realized that I could not do all my farm work alone, and also knew I could not afford to hire it done. In this way, we could make a living on the little farm. Then, too, it would be pleasanter for me than to live all my life alone.

Donald owned a little coupe car and that would give us many a little ride. Yes, I certainly would accept him. But naturally I pretended that I did not know or suspect that was why he was calling. So on this lovely May afternoon, we first sat under the little apple tree, neither one of us talking much. About six o'clock, I put supper on the table. Ever since Donald had started eating Sunday night supper with me, he always brought something from home along. A nice, large, freshly baked cake or pie or perhaps a dozen or so of good cookies or fried cakes, always saying his mother sent them to me. Of course, Roland Miller ate with us. But as always, took himself off right after. Donald helped me with the chores, then we went back under the apple tree. The sun was still shining. Now I very seldom had any callers, but we had not been seated for more than five minutes when Mrs. Blanche Mathews and her daughter Lena Howe came.

Any other time, I would have been glad to see them, but not tonight. Well, they stayed and stayed, long after the sun went down and the moon came up. At long last they left, and now I knew Donald would speak. Well, he did. Just as I had expected, he proposed we should get married at once, get married at the home of his parents, then go somewhere in his little car for a few days trip, and come back to my place so he could start at once to plow and put in a lot of crops. He said that man Miller could look after my few chores, I had no baby chickens yet, for the few days we would be away. All this sounded just right to me, just as I wanted it. But to my own surprise, I told him I wanted two days to think it over. I said, "Come again Tuesday evening, and I will then give you my answer. It will probably be yes, still I want those two days to think it over." I saw he was a little disappointed and he urged me to give him my answer that night, but I was firm. Just before he left, he kissed me, the first and only kiss he ever gave me.

I went to bed and thought how foolish I had been not to get things settled at once for surely I would say yes to him Tuesday night. All day Monday I worked very hard, had a good night's rest, and worked the next forenoon fixing the fence around my little pasture. After dinner, I sat down with a big Ward Montgomery catalog and picked out a cheap, light blue crepe dress to get married in. I must be saving. Luckily, I had a pair of white silk stockings and a pair of white, low, kid shoes Mrs. Fairchild had sent me over a year ago that I had never put on. Yes, tonight I would tell Donald yes.

About seven o'clock that night, one of the worst thunderstorms came and raged for hours. Wind, pouring rain, thunder and lightning. I knew it was impossible for Donald to come, especially as the worst of that terrible storm seemed to hover north of us. Roland Miller acted frightened half to death. About midnight it stopped. Roland went to his room, and I lay down on my sofa bed in the kitchen. This little bed stood near the front door. My head was near the door, so I was facing north. The terrible wind storm had ceased. The rain also had stopped, and in a few minutes I was asleep. Suddenly I woke up. The room was dark and perfectly still. I lay there wide awake, and dark though it was, I could make out the shape of the stove, the table, and the chairs. As I said, I was facing north, straight towards my north

371

window. Of course that, outlined against the sky, was much lighter than the room.

As I lay quietly there facing this window, I saw slowly the form of a tall man developing first very, very dimly, then clearer and clearer. Head, shoulders, body, and though the window was closed, he seemed to be floating through it. Then this shadowy being was in my kitchen room, coming silently towards me. Now instead of being frightened, a great sense of happiness came over me. Nearer and nearer he came to me, then bent over me, softly, tenderly put his arms about me, then just touched my cheek with his lips in a sweet kiss and whispered, "Sophie, I love you." Then as silently as he had come, he again floated to the north window, through it, and vanished. But he left such a great wave of happiness with me that I cannot put it into words. I made up my mind then and there that if such a man existed, I could never, never marry Donald.

Now as I have said before, this is my true story of my life, and this vision also is absolutely true. I was not dreaming; I was wide awake. I lay down again, but did not go to sleep for hours. At dawn, I dropped off to sleep. When I awoke, I felt happy and light hearted. I said to myself that if such a man as I had visioned in the night really existed, I would never be happy with Donald.

So I firmly decided not to accept him. It just seemed that that severe thunderstorm had come to keep him from coming the night before. Also, now I felt that it was providence that made me tell him to come back for his answer in two days. Yes, that must have been the reason, as I had really asked him to. I was happy that day, and when Donald came that night I met him with a smiling face. He came after supper, asked me to take a ride with him. We went to Cleveland and when we were almost there, he asked me if I had decided. I said, "Yes, I have, and although I do like you very much, I cannot marry you."

Naturally he asked me if there was someone else. He wanted to know why. I said there was someone else. He wanted to know who. I told him I did not know. He stared at me. But that was the truth. This was the eleventh of May. After that, as I have already put into this book, the trouble with Miller started. I was so worked up over that business, as I related, that I came, you really could say, within a few minutes of losing my place, so I hardly had time to even think about my affair with Donald, and hardly ever again gave a thought to the beautiful happy vision I had had of the man floating to me.

As I have said, the day Mr. Skinner gave me the money to pay off that terrible debt, I was very happy. Elmer Routh got me home a little past noon, and right here I want to say that he never charged me one cent for the many little trips on which he had taken me. Well, home, my home, seemed very good to me. The dark shadow of despair had lifted. I did not feel like rushing into hard work that afternoon, so I built a cute little chicken coop, then puttered about my flower garden, had an early supper, did up my chores, and was just about to go in front of my cabin to sit under the little apple tree when I saw a very tall, thin man coming into my driveway. He really looked more like an overgrown boy than a man. He walked straight up to me, looked at me, and said, "You do not remember me?" I gave him that long, searching look I was so in the habit of giving, then said, "Yes, I do. You are Leo Chesbro."

When he had been between fourteen and fifteen, he had worked for me a few days. So I asked him to sit down. The sun was still high up. We sat there till it got dusky, then went into the house. He had given me a long history from the time he was fourteen up to now. He had just turned twenty-two a month ago. He said he went to live with his mother in Oneida for a while; then they went to Utica. Later on, he went as a helper to a carpenter at Lake Saranac. After that, for the last two years, he had been staying at David Oughterson's, a farmer near Oneida whose family I had known for some years.

His mother had been keeping house for Charles Dixon for about six years. Now, he said, he had rented Matt Dixon's house for a couple of weeks for a little rest and vacation, then would go back to Oughterson's. Matt Dixon's empty house was known as the Mogsley house, and before I go any farther in this story I want to say that although Leo's mother was not well liked, his father and all his father's people were highly respectable people. Also, all the people on his mother's side. My father and mother had known and loved his grandparents. I remembered how fond he had been of music as a boy, so I brought him my accordion, which we had saved from the fire, and I also played many of my records on my phonograph. So the evening passed swiftly by and before we realized it, it was midnight. I asked him to call again before he went back to Oughterson's.

But I really was so full of my own plans, immensely relieved about my trouble with Miller, but still, of course a little worried just how to pay off that mortgage now that I had no longer my New York City allowance and had lost all my other money. So in a way, I did not give another thought to Leo Chesbro. Really, I was a little surprised when two days later, at nightfall, he again came calling.

Somehow, I told him more about my troubles than I had ever told Donald McDougle. Now I mentioned the fact that I had bought the roofing paper for my barn with my very last money and had no way to get it put on. I really did not think for one moment that he, Leo, might do this job. In the first place, as he had told me, he was out here for a two week's rest, and now about ten days of those two weeks were over. In the second place, I had told him in what a bad shape I was in, no money left or any more coming in. So to my great surprise, he offered to put it on for me. I again told him I had no way to pay him. Still, he said he had nothing to do and was getting tired of loafing around. I knew he would not play the same trick on me as Miller had, so I let him go ahead. Up to now, he had always come after supper, but of course while putting on the roof, he ate dinner and supper with me, and always spent a long evening with me.

One night I said to him, "Leo, I thought you only had two weeks out here. It is nearly three now." He looked at me and said, "I am not going back. I spoke to Clayton Montross and hired out to him until the first of October as an automobile mechanic." I said nothing, but thought perhaps he and Mr. Oughterson had a falling out. But the following Sunday afternoon, while Leo was at my house, Mr. Oughterson drove in and asked why Leo had not come back. But all Leo told him was that he had hired out to Clayton until the first of October. I must say here that Clayton never had much work after the summer people left their cottages.

The roof got done at last and Leo started to work for Clayton Montross. About three times a week he came to spend the evening with me, always coming late as he first went to the Mogsley house, about two miles from North Bay, got washed up, changed his clothes, got his supper, and then hurried to me. It was generally nine o'clock, sometimes later, when he came. He also came every Sunday afternoon and stayed for supper, but each time he would bring something along to eat, such as a pound of coffee, a pound of pork chops, a can of fish, some sliced ham, and so on.

Sophie Kussmaul

It was very pleasant, and so the summer went by. I really began to dread the first of October to come, as I took it for granted that then Leo would go back to Oughterson's. On the twenty-eighth of September, it was Sunday, Mr. and Mrs. Oughterson came out. Of course, Leo was at my house. They wanted him to go back with them to stay. To my joy, Leo told them he had made up his mind to stay around here, said Matt Dixon and some others wanted him to cut wood for them.

About the middle of November, he brought a bag of good groceries and said he thought it would be pleasanter for us both to eat supper together each night. He said, "You have to cook your supper, then eat alone. I come back after working in the woods, cook, and eat alone, and then come to you to spend the evening." So we had our supper together and spent each evening together until twelve or one o'clock.

On Thanksgiving Day, he got his mother to invite me to Charles Dixon's house. We had an enormous dinner. They made me stay, and after a late supper, Leo walked home with me. December brought bad weather, so about ten o'clock each forenoon, Leo would come. He always did bring something in the food line. He stayed for dinner and supper and about midnight went back to the Mogsley house.

Chapter 37

Came the twenty-first of December and my fifty-sixth birthday. Christmas I spent with Leo at his mother's place. New Year's Day we ate and stayed at my home. When the weather was halfway fair, Leo would cut wood for someone, but always came to me for supper and our long evening together. The fore part of January was not bad winter weather, little snow on the ground and not very cold. Leo, who never had been very strong, coughed more or less, but kept on cutting wood for a few hours each day.

Then came the sixteenth of January, a pouring rain. It rained all day and still rained at midnight when Leo went home. On the seventeenth, it still rained a little and when Leo came, about noon, he coughed terrible, said he had got soaking wet the night before on his way to the Mogsley house, a little over a mile from my home, and got chilled, as the house was damp and cold. As I said, it still rained a little and Leo as always stayed with me till midnight. He came back to me about ten o'clock the next morning.

This was the eighteenth of January. It had stopped raining, but I really think there was the heaviest fog I had ever seen. I had to keep my little kerosene lamp lit the same as at night. Leo shivered, sat close to my fire, and coughed worse than ever. So the day passed. Late that afternoon, the weather suddenly got much colder. The fog did not really disappear, but seemed to turn into a frozen snowstorm. By five o'clock, I finished my barn chores and could hardly battle my way to the cabin. It was snowing, blowing, and freezingly cold, and already quite dark.

Leo had carried in the wood from the woodshed. I was lucky enough to have a good supply on hand. I got our supper. Soon after, my lamp went out, so we sat together in the dark. Each hour the storm got worse. The very cabin shook with the icy blasts. Leo thought there might be a lull in the storm by midnight, but instead it was even worse. The night, pitch dark. I could not have put a dog out that night. We had been sitting close together on my sofa bed for hours. About one o'clock Leo got up and went into the woodshed, north of the kitchen. I was very tired and flopped back where I had been sitting. But I was wide awake. As I said, the night was very dark. Still, with what little light came from the north window and the faint glow of firelight which seeped through the cracks in the stove, I could make out the outlines of the furniture, table, stove, chairs. Leo came back from the woodshed. I could dimly see his tall figure coming towards me. Then for the first time I vividly recalled that beautiful vision I had about eight months before of that tall man floating towards me through the north window. Everything really was exactly the same.

I lay in the same position as then, facing the north window, the north door close to the window. Now, as in my vision, this thin, tall, shadowy man came slowly, silently towards me. He bent over me, tenderly put his arms about me, then gave me a light kiss again exactly as in that vision. "Sophie, I love you," in the same soft whisper as at that other time, and the very same words. I put my arms about his neck. We hung together a moment. Now for the evil minded, we spent the rest of that night in adultery. But for the pure in heart, it was spent in love, the good and great human love of one man for one woman. These were the words whispered into my ears. "There shall never be anyone but you, and wherever I go, you will go with me." As this is the true story of my life, I know that he meant those words, and for nearly the next eleven years, those words were kept.

In the morning we both felt very happy. I made the coffee and fried the meat. Leo baked the pancakes. We pulled the little table close to the stove and happily ate our breakfast. Leo proposed that we get married at once, said, "Mother will be delighted. We can get married there." I said to Leo, "Leo, I have no money left at all." He looked at me very tenderly and said, "I have none either, but I will get a job and be able to take care of us both." I know he meant it.

Well, it was still bitter cold, but the snow had stopped falling and the wind did not blow so bad. After a while, Leo went to the Mogsley house and came back loaded. He was completely tired out and coughed terribly. He brought a suitcase full of his clothes, a bran bag full of edibles, and a bottle of kerosene for our lamp. He said he intended also to go and tell the good news to his mother, but the condition the roads were in, and being half sick, he felt he could not do that today.

The day went by like a dream of happiness. The next day he joyously said he would go to his mother, tell her about us, and of course she would be glad and would want us to get married at her place. He said he had no good clothes, but as long as it was to be such a quiet family affair, his best suit, badly worn, would do. A few hours later, Leo came back, a sad faced Leo. He said he started to tell his mother about us, but she was not well and did not seem to understand. A few days later, he tried again. Said she was very bitterly opposed to it. But he told me he had a plan. Just as soon as Clayton Montross started to hire him, about the first of April, he would save his first pay and buy a car, and we would go to Halstead, Pennsylvania, and get married there. There were some of his one time high school friends there, and then we would comeback and tell his mother all about it, and then she, of course, would forgive him.

So the winter passed. My fifth honeymoon. Now I will say something that may shock my readers, but as every word I wrote is the truth, this is the truth too. Now strange as this may seem to most people, the five gloriously happy weeks I had spent with Earnest Galway at dear old Frisco and the first few months I spent with Leo seemed much, much more like a honeymoon to me than the three other times I was legally married. The little affair I had had with Fisher was just a little passing incident in my life.

To go back to my story. I kept writing to Mrs. Fairchild and after nearly two years, she again sent me a very small monthly allowance. Leo got a days work here and there, and so we got through the winter. Of course Leo's mother knew that he was living at my place, but did not know that he was living with me.

Came the sixteenth of March, Leo came home saying his mother was sick. Next day she was much worse. They sent for the North Bay doctor, Dr. Chattle. By the nineteenth, they had a doctor from Camden, Dr. Allison. He gave little hope, so they sent a telegram to Battle Creek, Michigan, to Leo's brother and his wife, one to Detroit, Michigan, to his sister Viola and her family, and one to Morrisville, New York State, to his other sister Vera and her family. Leo was there much of the time in daytime, but came home to me at night. They all left as the doctors thought there was a little improvement.

On the night of the twentieth to the twenty-first, they all had left and Leo stayed with her that night. That was the first night I again was alone. I went to bed early and had a good refreshing sleep. A little after one o'clock, I looked at the clock afterwards, I woke up suddenly. What awakened me was the voice of my little daughter Sophie calling my name. Although now nearly three years had passed by since I had last seen her, or heard her sweet voice, it came to my ears so clearly, so very distinctly, that I raised up from my sofa bed with a start into a sitting position. Now before I go any farther, I want to describe the night. There was no moonlight, but a clear, starry sky, no wind and not intensely cold, just a frosty late March night. So my kitchen room was not too dark and besides, as I had a low fire in the cook stove, that too gave out a faint glow. When I raised myself up into a sitting position, there not over four or five feet from me and about the same distance from the front door, sitting in a rocking chair, facing me, I plainly saw my little daughter. I spoke to her, asked her why she had come. Somehow it did not seem strange to me that she was there. Neither did I wonder that she had come into my cabin with the door bolted on the inside. Or though it was winter that she was sitting there just in her dress, no wraps at all.

She answered me in her sweet clear voice, just said, "I wanted to see you." I was eagerly looking at her. Even in the dim light, I could see her every feature. She looked the same as when we two were all in all to each other. Then, even while I was gazing at her, the vision faded, got dimmer and dimmer, and then was no more. I got up, looked at the clock. It was half past one o'clock. At that time I did not even know where my daughter was. Not until some years later did I find out that on that very night a girl, Jinni, was born.

Leo came home and told me his mother was getting better, wanted me to go and see her. I went that very day. She slowly got better. I often went there. She told me how unhappy she was at Charles Dixon's. Two more happy months went by. Leo had started to work for Clayton Montross the beginning of April, but his mother kept at him for extras, so our marriage was again put off. Leo brought home good food, but never made enough to buy himself any clothes.

About the twentieth of May, I went to visit his mother. She was crying, said she had had another bitter row with Charles Dixon. That night at supper I told Leo about it. Leo looked at me very tenderly, then said, "Honey, if you were willing, there is nothing I would like better than to have my mother come and live with us." For me this was an entirely new idea.

Well, my mother had been so kind, so loving, a truly wonderful mother. Albert's mother was a true mother to me and I had loved her the same as if she were my own, and although I knew she was opposed to Leo's marrying me, she really had used me very well the many times I had been there the last six or seven months. So I thought, if she was living with us, saw how much her son loved me, she would not object to our marriage. Leo seemed to have the same idea, for he said, "If mother is here, she cannot help loving you, if only for my sake." I thought what a beautiful thing it would be again to have a mother.

I had my chores all done before supper, so I said to Leo, "Let us go to your mother at once and tell her our plan." So on this lovely May evening, we walked hand in hand to Charles Dixon's house. The sun was still shining, the birds sweetly singing, and everywhere the sweet fresh odor of spring time. I think it would have been hard to find two happier people than Leo and myself.

When we got to Charles Dixon's house, we found Dr. Chattle there. Leo's mother had had a heart attack. But later on I was to learn that each time something went wrong, she would fly into a screaming rage, then exhausted call it a heart attack.

The doctor said she must keep in bed for a few days absolute rest, and after that, for a few more days, keep as quiet as possible. After the doctor left, we told her our plan. Charles Dixon was not in the house. She was delighted. She pulled me down with an awfully strong powerful arm, not like a sick person, kissed me, started crying for joy. She said that would be like heaven. But she did not want Charles Dixon to know she was leaving, said she wanted to move out some day when he was not at home.

That little trip home that night is one of my sweetest memories. The air was filled with the May perfume. In the low places the frogs were happily singing. From here and there floated the haunting song of the whip-poor-will. Above us shone a million stars. Leo had one arm about me and so, slowly, we went back to our little home, sweet home.

Life was sweet and beautiful in those days. After breakfast, Leo would go to his work at Clayton Montross's garage. I would hurry around and do my chores, work for a couple of hours in the garden, and then briskly walk to Charles Dixon's house, get something to eat for Leo's mother and do a dozen little things for her. But to my surprise, I saw that Charles Dixon went about the rest of the housework with an ease as if he was accustomed to it, and when I remarked about this to Leo's mother, she very reluctantly admitted that he helped her a little about the daily housework.

So after she was up again, and Charles not about his home, she had me unpack and repack her trunks, one very large one, the other one of medium size. On the thirtieth of May, Decoration Day, Leo, who worked that day--a holiday was always the busiest at the garage--came home much excited. He said he overheard Charles Dixon, who was at the garage, tell a neighbor that he was going on an all day spree with Albert Cole the next day to Utica.

So the coast would be clear for his mother to move out. That same night he walked over to Robert Holmes, engaged him to come and meet him at Charles Dixon's at ten o'clock with his truck. Then he went to Kate Kinney and asked her for the coupe to bring his mother home to us. We talked about her coming half the night and as glad as we were about it, there arose one little difficulty. Leo and I had been sleeping together in my kitchen, on a narrow sofa, for over four months now. With his mother occupying the bedroom, she would of course discover us together. But we had a plan. We would put up a cot bed in the basement of the barn. That basement was spotlessly clean. I still kept the cattle in the little stable. I kept my milk, butter, and eggs in a cupboard down there. So the next morning, the thirty-first of May, Leo did not go to work for Montross.

After breakfast Leo helped me to put up a cot bed in the northeast corner of the basement. I put a large soft rug in front of the bed, got a little stand with a nice cloth on it, and a chair, and put up a line to hang up some of our clothes. Our idea was this. At night, I would unroll my bedding on the sofa as if ready to use. Then after Leo's mother was in bed, run out to our basement. I always was up first, would run in the house, roll up by bedroll, and start breakfast. Leo would come in and just before I put breakfast on the table, Leo's mother would come in from her bedroom.

381

We did this until the sixteenth of December when the first bitter cold wave and a heavy snowstorm drove us out and into the cabin. We had had near zero weather before and also some snow, but after the sixteenth the weather got so rough and cold we had to move in, and I had to keep a fire going all night. I put up another cot for Leo in his mother's bedroom and put a curtain between, making two little rooms. I really think she never suspected my going out to Leo at night.

Each night, just before she went to her bed, she would close the door between her room and the kitchen with an awful bang. But I left most of the bedding on the cot bed in the basement and very, very often during the winter we would visit down there.

I am getting way, way ahead of my story. So on the morning of the thirty-first of May, Leo went to Kinney's, borrowed her little coupe car, and to my joy came back to my cabin with it. He said I should just jump into it and we would get his mother together. I was very happy. I said to Leo, "This is our first ride together." He gave me a look filled with so much tender love it went straight to my heart and said, "Yes, but it will not be the last ride we will have together." Oh, how true that proved to be. For later on we traveled many, many thousands of miles together, and always we two close together on the front seat. But, oh merciful God in Heaven, if only I could forget the last ride we had together.

Naturally we found his mother much excited. I helped her pick up a few little things, such as a lamp or two, some dishes and a few other things, that might get broken on the truck. Leo got her suitcase, a couple of old satchels, and some bundles of her clothing. Then we both helped her into the little car and hurried off. It was already nine o'clock, so after we got home, Leo quickly unloaded and took the car back to Kinney's. Then ran to Charles Dixon's house, where Robert Holmes already was with his truck. I was surprised at the amount of things on that truck. There was her large iron bedstead, springs, mattress, feather bed and a lot of bedding. A small bureau, her large rocking chair. The enormous trunk and the smaller one. An old fashioned washing machine. Washtubs, large stone jars, a box of kettles, frying pans, all sorts of pots and pans. Another box of dishes, glassware, her big cabinet phonograph, Leo's radio, and a lot of other things.

Sophie Kussmaul

I thought we never could put the half of them into my cabin. Yes, there also was a chunk stove and an oil cook stove. After the load was unloaded before my cabin and Robert Holmes had left, I put a lunch on the table. It was a little after one o'clock. I had heard so much about how sick this woman was that I could scarcely conceal my amazement at the amount of food she consumed. She ate more than twice as much as Leo and I together. The thing I could not understand was, she did not seem to either chew or swallow her food. There was a rapid throwing of it into her big mouth. Of course I had eaten at her house. I mean at Dixon's house a few times during the last half year or so. I had noticed that she kept filling and refilling her plate, but I always was so busy with my own food and visiting with Leo, yes and generally Charles Dixon, too, would be there at mealtimes, that I had never noticed the magic of her just throwing her food into her mouth as fast as she could get it from plate to mouth.

Now being a sick person, she laid down on my kitchen sofa and Leo and I started to find places for the small mountain of her things. After we had her bedroom furnished, we carried the rest into the basement. At four o'clock she asked me for something to eat, as she had had no dinner, only lunch. In spite of a number of very disagreeable things that developed during the next few days, the three of us really had a very happy week together. Leo and I had our breakfast alone together each morning. After he went to work, she would get up and I cooked her morning meal. She generally went back to her room and lay down again. I never worked harder than that summer.

I had the biggest garden I ever had. Made butter, raised chickens, a heifer calf, and two pigs. Picked and sold over sixty-five dollars worth of huckleberries. Worked in the hayfield and canned berries. I worked at canning fruits and vegetables, besides doing my housework. My meals always were on time. For the next five years that Leo's mother was with us, she never did five minutes work to help me. She has now been resting in her grave for nine years, so I will not say too much about her, but here is a sample of her utter laziness.

She had been sitting in the kitchen while I was out milking. A porcelain kettle with string beans was on the stove cooking. I smelled them burning out at the barn, quite a distance from my cabin. I rushed in. The black smoke was pouring from the kettle. She was complacently rocking back and forth in her chair. Not only were the beans completely spoiled, but that good kettle, too, was ruined. I asked her if she had not smelled it burning and she said, "Yes, I did, but I did not come here to do the work."

Another time, I had the supper table all set, all but the hot stuff, which was on the stove, but there was bread, butter, cheese, three sauce dishes with pudding, and a pitcher of milk on the table. I left her, as usual, rocking away in her chair. I saw I would have a few minutes of time left before Leo came to supper, so I went to feed the pigs. When I got back, there were four hens on the supper table. There was a large hole in the screen door. They had knocked over the milk pitcher, eaten, and made a general mess of the entire table. I asked her why she had not shooed them out. She insolently told me she was not going to do any work here.

Well, as I said, the first week went by very happily and each night Leo would tell me how wonderful I was, that his mother seemed to like me better than she ever had anyone else. I think at first she did. Just one week after she came, the three of us were happily eating our supper together. I had taken great pains with it, and amongst other things, I made a nice, light Johnny cake. Leo always had been fond of it. All at once, Leo turned to his mother, a tender smile on his face, and said, "Mother, don't you think my honey girl makes delicious Johnny cake?" In one moment, there came such a look of hate into the old lady's face as I had not imagined could come into a human face. She struck her enormous fist with full force on the table and yelled out, "Leo, I never want to hear you call Sophie that again." Leo turned very pale, but said firmly, "I love Sophie and intend to marry her."

There is only one phrase that I can use to express just what followed this. Hell broke loose. She stamped on the floor, pounded on the table until part of the dishes fell down, screamed, swore, yelled. When she had exhausted herself, she went into her room, slammed the door, and threw herself on the bed. That was one of her heart attacks.

That night while I was clasped in Leo's arms, I said what a terrible thing that had been. Leo said, "Mother is sick. She will get over it and then I will try and reason with her." Well, he did try. One evening after supper I was washing the dishes and Leo went, put his arm around his mother and said, "Mother, if you love me, love the girl I want to marry. I want Sophie more than I shall ever want any one."

Well the same thing happened again. She had another heart attack. Only this time, she screamed and yelled for hours. Did not speak to either one of us for about a week or more.

So the summer went by. I toiled from early in the morning till late at night, tried very hard to please and win the old lady's love, and during the hours when Leo was away, put up with thousands of little meannesses from her. When Leo was present, she just was coldly indifferent to me.

But I was repaid for all this when at night Leo held me close to him, and I went to sleep in his arms. But I must now go back to one little incident that happened in June, to be exact on the nineteenth of June. This has nothing to do with either Leo or his mother, and I felt they would not understand the thing I saw. In order to give a complete picture of this, I must carefully describe my surroundings.

My cabin stood quite a ways back from the road. As I have said, I was not using the basement as a stable, but a little north east of this big barn was the small stable which I have already mentioned in this book quite a few times. It might have been about one hundred and fifty feet from the cabin. In summer I had always milked out of doors, but this black cow I had did not stand still. She never kicked, but kept stepping. So each morning and night, I put some good grass in her manger and led her into the stable. While she was eating, I milked her. The manger was at the east end of the little stable, so of course the cow was facing east and the open door through which she had come in was at the west end of the stable. I, sitting there to milk, was naturally a little closer to the open door than the cow's head was. Besides, the way I sat at the cow, I was facing north.

To complete the picture, I will say that the sun was still nearly an hour high in the blue, cloudless June sky. The cow was greedily eating her grass, and I had begun milking, perhaps for two or three minutes, when suddenly the cow gave a little start, abruptly stopped eating, and turned her head quickly toward me, not at me, but looking out through the wide open door, with bulging eyes. Of course I looked too, to see what caused her to stop eating, and as it were to look behind her. I certainly got an eyeful. There coming from the direction of the cabin, slowly, very slowly, came my father and mother walking towards me hand in hand. They would walk a few steps, then stand still and gaze about, then come a little nearer, then again stop and look around.

They were dressed exactly as they used to be. I clearly saw their every feature.

Their faces were very sad looking. I sat there motionless. On they came till they were within a few feet of my open door. The cow, with a big mouthful of grass in her mouth, stood rigid, never moved a muscle, did not eat the grass in her mouth, just stared at what we both saw plainly. I wanted to speak, but like the cow, stared motionless. I was not in the least frightened. No, I rather felt a glad sensation of peace and security steal over me. This seeing my dear parents lasted perhaps a full minute, maybe longer; then slowly they seemed to dissolve. The cow started chewing her grass, gave one more quick, searching look about, and again turned her head to the manger and went at her supper with a zest. I finished milking her.

So the summer passed by. Came the sixth of October, a cloudy, dark day, but still the weather was warm. I saw at a glance when Leo came in that something troubled him. I said nothing to him about it, and he ate in silence. Then after supper he told us his troubles. It was really only what we had been expecting. Still, it came as a shock. Each spring, Clayton Montross hired a helper for the first few weeks. The farmers brought in their farm machinery to be repaired for spring and summer work. Then followed the brisk and busy season, the dozens and dozens of cottagers with their cars. But by the middle or latter part of September, they returned to their cities. Of course there was some work going on at the garage the year around, but not more than what Clayton could do himself. Today Clayton had told him he would not need him again until spring. We had lived well during the spring and summer of course. Leo had a few dollars left, but this was during the Depression and jobs were very hard to obtain.

I had been hoping and striving that now, with my little allowance from New York City and my berry money, I could pay off my mortgage by fall, but I began to see that no matter how good we lived, Leo's mother was not satisfied. In the first place, she consumed more food in one meal than Leo and I together in two meals. Also, she wanted and demanded good, rich food. Little by little, laying a little aside, I thought I could at least make a small payment. I had bought and paid for the pigs, paid for all their feed during the spring and summer, and would still have to buy feed for the next two months, pay the school and State taxes.

Sophie Kussmaul

I tried to cheer my poor Leo up, telling him what a lot of vegetables we had, that Queen Victoria was going to come in and then we would have two cows; that I had a lot of young roosters to kill, and so on. But the old lady stamped her foot and yelled out, "I got to have clothes, vegetables. To heck with that stuff." I knew Leo tried his best to get another job, but jobs at that time were hard to procure. So he got Luckcherham to come and cut wood on shares in my woods. At least we could get our winters wood cut without buying it.

I had one of my pigs killed the last of October. That would save me buying so much pig feed, and as I thought, keep us in meat until Christmas. But that meat just vanished. The pig dressed one hundred and twenty pounds, but the old lady insisted on having meat three times a day. Sometimes I made a large roast for dinner, thinking there would be enough for supper and also for the next few days for breakfast. But during the afternoon, she would find it, and eat up every bit of it.

On the twentieth of November, there was not a bit of the meat left. I had the other pig killed before Thanksgiving. That dressed one hundred and seventy five pounds. I kept telling her that after that it was gone, that Leo and I could not buy any more meat. To lengthen this out, I had my roosters killed. But in spite of all I could do, there was no meat left for Christmas.

Chapter 38

Came the twenty-first of December, and my fifty-seventh birthday. About this time both Leo and I came down with the flu. I do not mean just a hard cold, but the real flu. From then until April, I think looking back over all the winters of my life, these three months were in every respect the hardest I ever lived through. Leo, who never had been strong and rugged, now wasted away to a mere skeleton. In March he weighed only one hundred and fifteen pounds. A man who was six foot three inches tall in his stocking feet. He and I both coughed day and night. Neither one of us could eat. If we managed to swallow a mouthful or two, we were taken with such coughing spasms that we would throw up what little food we got down.

My black cow was dry and Queen Victoria would not freshen until spring. I was longing for a little milk. The few dollars Leo and I had saved up were all spent by the middle of January. We bought coffee, the one thing we could keep down, and the thick, sweet condensed milk. Leo and I would each drink a cup of coffee with a spoonful of the milk. Leo's mother would eat the rest of the entire can at one meal. Luckily the winter was not too severe. Our wood was drawed up in pole length. Each forenoon and each afternoon, Leo and I would stagger out. He would saw and split a few armfuls of the wood, then stagger in with it, shake, tremble, and almost cough himself to death. I would do the most necessary chores and somehow crawl back to the cabin.

We took turns in getting our water. Many, many times I fell down in the snow on my way back from the barn to the cabin, from utter weakness. Once Leo fainted at the sawbuck and fell over. I rubbed snow on his face, then staggered in the house, got a few drops of ammonia, forced it between his cold lips and into his nostrils, and got him back into the cabin.

Now all this would have been easy to bear, but here was the hard and bitter part. Leo's mother never helped. I was so weak I actually had to steady myself going from the stove to the table. She wanted things to eat. We had nothing to speak of left. She would go each day and open and eat one to two cans of the things I had canned for all of us. Kept saying I was just lazy, there was nothing the matter with me.

One day she read an advertisement in the Rome Sentinel. They wanted men at the brass and copper mill. She said, "Leo, I want you to go and get to work there." Leo said nothing. I said Leo would not last a day there. "He might as well die there than here. I got to have money." Those were her very words. At night I would dimly wonder if through my coughing spasms I would be alive in the morning.

In the morning Leo and I together would bake a huge pile of pancakes. Neither one of us could eat even one of them. She would come into the kitchen furious saying we both kept her awake with our everlasting coughing. I was beyond arguing. Leo would say, "We surely do not cough on purpose." She yelled at him and said, "If you tried, you could control yourselves." She said Leo and I did not eat just to be stubborn. I got so terribly weak I really did not care anymore about her everlasting taunting. Poor Leo would say, "Mother don't you see how sick Sophie is?" She would give a snort and say, "There is nothing the matter with her."

At last I wrote to Mrs. Fairchild, asked her for some good food. She sent box after box, but Leo and I got very, very little of it all. Leo would unpack a box, hand me some extra choice thing, say, "Here, honey, maybe you could eat this." Then she would snatch it out of my very hand and say, "I need that." Well, I could fill an entire book about this winter of horror, but will say no more about it.

At last spring came and we both slowly got better. Leo went back to work for Clayton Montross. Charles Dixon would come. She would tell him what a terrible winter she had, that I did not want to do any work. That Leo lay around all winter and she needed money, needed food. He would bring her candy, bananas, cookies, lots of other good things. She ate them greedily, never offered either Leo or I even a taste of her good things.

Through Sophie's Eyes

As I have said, Leo had some wood cut on shares, in pole length, and our half had been drawed up in a big pile near the woodshed door. Slowly, day by day during this horrible winter, Leo had cut some of it up. Most of that pile had consisted of medium sized poles. But there happened to be one log, Leo told me, that he could not cut up with the bucksaw, would have to use a crosscut saw on it. So that one log was left. It really was in the way, and now that the snow was all gone, and I felt better, I tried to roll it off a little way, but there was a slight rise in the ground, so I gave it up. One day I was picking up a pan of chips when the old lady came out. She stumbled over the log, swore, bent down, and to my utter amazement, picked it up, carried it a few feet, and tossed it on the ground. That was the woman who was so sick she could not sweep a room, wash a dish, or set a table.

The spring and summer and early autumn went by like the year before. Leo worked for Clayton Montross every day, Sundays and all. I did the housework, chores, had a big garden, picked berries to sell and can, and worked in the hayfield. During the day what little time I spent in the house, the old lady always found a way to taunt and torment me. But after Leo got home, she generally was very quiet. But our nights together in our love nest were very beautiful.

We would talk and visit and after a while go to sleep, clasped in each others arms. There was one little difference this year. We had Jeanie Walters with us, Leo's sister's little girl. I had an enormous amount of huckleberries this summer and hired a lot of pickers. I told Jeanie I would pay her the same price as the other pickers, but all the berries she picked were out of my baskets and into her mouth.

Well I stopped that. I told her she could eat all the berries she wanted but would have to pick them herself. She sulked and went without her berries rather than pick them. Came the twelfth of August, the day passed by like all the rest of those happy, busy summer days. The night was warm and still, no wind and noiselessly quiet. Like all other nights, I had fallen asleep in Leo's arms. Then suddenly I woke up. Leo's arm still clasped about me, his warm body close to mine, he was softly breathing in his sleep. I was wide awake. There was such a wonderful light all about me, not the horrible red glare of fire, not the dim gray of early dawn, nor yet the brightness of sunshine. Neither could I make out from whence it came. Had I not the assurance of Leo's presence, I would have felt sure that I was far, far away from home in some enchanted land.

Sophie Kussmaul

I gently put Leo's arm from me, slowly raised myself to a sitting position, and gazed at the marvelous beauty all about me. It seemed as if the lighted country stretched for miles and miles into the distance. The light kept shifting, from blue to silver, then to gold, green, rose. Stretching far away to a distant mountain range. There were no dwellings, but here and there clumps of trees. Not a sound. I wanted to wake Leo up, then hesitated, thinking perhaps this was only meant for me. I sat there gazing, perhaps five minutes, maybe longer. Then slowly the light grew dimmer. Then it faded quite away. I struck a match. The clock said two o'clock. Yes, I was still in the basement with my sleeping Leo. I snuggled down and thought to myself, that is, or will be, my heaven.

So another summer faded into eternity. A busy, happy summer in spite of all the countless little aggravations from Leo's mother. This year, Leo's work lasted all through October. I, too, was earning a few dollars picking and selling princess pine. The weather remained fine until the first of November. Here I want to relate one little incident, more to show the old lady's disposition than what the thing itself had amounted to.

Up to now the weather, though of course not warm like summer, had really been quite agreeable. Each morning when I went out to do my barn chores, and later in the day to pick pine, I just slipped on a very thin little sweater. But this morning the ground was frozen, a bitter cold, strong northwest wind was blowing, and a fine shower of frozen snow was in the air. The three of us had breakfast together. Leo had finished his work at Clayton's the night before, but had a few hours of picking up around the shop left and also to draw his last pay from Clayton, so he did not take his lunch, as he was expected home by one o'clock.

Well, as I had no sandwiches to make, I was going directly out to do my barn chores. I grabbed my thin little sweater and was just about to put it on when Leo looked at me and said to wait a moment. He ran into the bedroom. We still slept outside, but most of his clothes were in a little closet. He came back with a beautiful little sweater I had often seen, slipped it over me, looked happily smiling at his mother and said, "Mother, it just fits Sophie." I glanced at her. There was such a look of hate on her face that Leo, who saw it too, said, "You know I have not been able to get into it since I was seventeen and why should I keep it year after year." Well, she said

391

no more. I went out and did my morning chores. Leo went to North Bay. I came in and hung the sweater on a nail back of the stove with my other things. Then I washed up the dishes and did a few things, the old lady, as always, rocking in her chair. Then I went into the woodshed with the big iron kettle, in which I boil the hogs' potatoes. It took me a few minutes to sort them over and again to cover them up. When I came back into the kitchen, there was such a look of diabolic joy on her face as I had never before seen on a human face. I lifted the kettle on the stove, raised the lid, and there amidst the heavy cloud of smoke, I saw what was left of the beautiful, warm sweater.

So the time rolled on. Leo got Orville Holmes to cut wood on halves this fall. Orville took the good wood, we got the poor wood. But this time, it was buzzed up in the woods. Came the twenty-first of December and my fifty-eighth birthday. How swiftly the years were speeding past.

This winter I kept well. Leo got a few days work cutting wood. Made very little, but with what I got from New York City, and our own potatoes, and other things, we got through the winter. I milked two cows now, and so we had plenty of milk and butter. Leo had belonged to the North Bay firemen. In fact, a few years before he had organized them. They were going to put on a play to raise money to build a firehouse. So all through the month of March and nearly up to the middle of April, Leo and about a dozen or more of the younger women and men met two nights a week at the Central Hotel hall to practice the play. This did not interfere with any ones work, as they always met at night. The time for the play to be given was the fifteenth of April. Of course we often spoke of the play, Leo telling us about the different people in it. I knew them all.

Leo himself had rather an unimportant act in the play. Naturally I had intended to attend it. Leo said they had not really decided just where to give it, but said he felt sure it would be given in the North Bay Central Hotel hall, as all the actors, excepting himself, lived in North Bay. Besides, George Johnson, the son of the owner of the hotel, and his wife were in the play. So I would just have to walk to North Bay the night of the play, and on my way home, Leo would be with me.

Now neither Leo nor I had made a secret of my going to that play, but as it turned out, it seemed that Leo's mother did not know about my going. So a few days before the last rehearsal, Leo came home from work and said they had decided to have the play at McConnelsville, in the Community Hall. The posters were already printed ready to stick up, so they got someone to mark out Central Hotel at North Bay and type in the correction. I really forget their reasons for changing their plans, but think it was because their stage setting would have taken up at least half the floor space in the rather small North Bay hall.

We were at supper when Leo told us about the change. I looked up at him and said, "How will I get there? It is a good five miles, ten to come and go." Leo, eating away happily, looked at me and smilingly said, "I thought of that right away and tomorrow I will go and see Wallace Moore, hire him to come and get you and bring you back." The old lady started pounding the table, stamping her feet, and then yelled out, "Sophie is not going. I will not have it." Neither one of us answered her. She gave yell after yell, so loud that if anyone had passed by, even in a noisy car, they would have heard her, though my cabin was quite a long distance from the road. She went through the same old performance. Yelling, screaming until exhausted and then slamming her bedroom door, threw herself on her bed. A heart attack., Poor Leo. He left the table and went out. About an hour later I went to the basement. Leo had gone to bed.

The next morning she did not come in to breakfast. That is, she marched in her face quite distorted with rage, grabbed the dish filled with pancakes in one hand and the platter of fried eggs in the other. Took them into her room, came back, snatched the coffee pot, milk pitcher, and sugar bowl, went to her room and again slammed the door so the whole cabin shook. I hurried up and baked a few more pancakes, fried us some eggs. She had taken the last of the bacon. I made us some coffee in an open kettle. After Leo went for work, I went to her room to get the dishes. They were all empty, though I had filled them for breakfast for the three of us.

At lunch she did the same thing, but at supper time she came to the table sullen silent. The play was not mentioned again before her, but at night when we were alone, Leo told me he had hired Wallace Moore to come after me the next night at seven thirty. The play was to start at eight o'clock. The next day I was to have supper ready for Leo at half past five instead of our usual seven o'clock supper. So at five o'clock Leo came home, bathed, changed his clothes, shaved, and was all ready by half past five for supper. You see, he was to help

Russell Phelps to collect the furniture for the stage setting and help to arrange some of it on the stage at the hall. Russell was the only one of the actors who had a truck, so all the men in the play were to ride out with the truck. Later on George Johnson would bring out all the women actors in his automobile.

It seems the old lady had not heard that the play was not to start before eight o'clock. So when Leo left a little before six and she saw I had in no way started to get ready, she must have thought she had won out. Ever since the night she had heard Leo tell me about his hiring Mr. Moore, she had not spoken a word to either one of us. So tonight, she began to thaw out. She did not speak to me yet, but after Leo left and she saw me going about my dish washing in a leisurely way, instead of going into her room and slamming the door, she got one of my books. It was the *Shepherd of the Hills* by Harold Bell Wright. She sat in her big rocking chair reading, a look of great satisfaction and triumph on her large, coarse face. After I had the dishes done, I went out to do my chores.

I had always done them before supper, but as we had had our supper one and a half hours earlier, I did them afterwards. It was just seven o'clock when I came back into the cabin. The old lady was rocking away singing to herself, holding the book on her lap. Now she felt sure that she had won out. I washed my face, powdered it, and combed and brushed my hair. She kept watching me, but as I had done exactly the same thing every evening before Leo came home, she never dreamt that I still thought of going. It was now fifteen minutes after seven. I got my best dress and started putting it on. Then in one moment, her face turned red, then purple. She screamed at me, "You cannot go. I forbid it." I looked at her calmly and said, "I am going." I just got my best stockings on when I saw Mr. Moore drive into my long driveway. But where she sat, she could not see him coming. She was yelling, gave loud, horrible half choked screams of rage, was stamping her feet and pounding the table with her enormous fists. I ran to the door. Wallace had driven right up to the doorstep. Poor old Mr. Moore. All his life he had been a quite, peace loving little man. He sat there pale and frightened. Now that Leo's mother saw there was someone at the door, she had stopped her yelling. I said, "Hello, Uncle Wallie. Come in. I will be ready in a few minutes." He looked at me and said, "What happened?" I smiled and said, "Nothing at all." He stepped shyly into the kitchen. The old lady was rocking back and forth, her face purple with rage. Wallace, gentle Wallace, spoke to her, said, "Good evening." For an answer, she replied, "Shoot." Then with great force, she threw the book across the room. It landed in the water pail. I pulled it out, shook it, and put it on the stove shelf, put my hat and coat on, and said, "I'm ready now for a good time." For a few minutes we both rode on in silence; then Wallace said, "That woman is dangerous."

Well, we got to our destination in plenty of time. Leo had given both Wallace and myself a ticket. When the play was over, Leo came to us and said that he wanted to ride home with us, if he went back on Russell's truck, he would have to walk up from North Bay. So we waited until the stage settings were all dismantled and loaded on the truck. It was a little past midnight when we arrived home.

The night was a trifle chilly and as we had had such an early supper, we prepared for a midnight snack. Leo started a fire and made the coffee. I had baked some nice, fresh bread, and churned out a few pounds of good butter, and as a special treat, had made a large three layer cake. Maple sugar filling and a chocolate frosting on top. I had taken great pains with that cake, in a way as reward for Leo's hiring Wallace to take me to the play and as a finishing to our lovely evening. The cake was so large that I had figured that even if I cut three huge hunks out of it, a good half of that cake would be left for tomorrow so I could put one piece in Leo's lunch pail, one each for Leo's mother's and my lunch, and still have one apiece for the next night's supper.

I went into the woodshed where I kept a big tin box with a tight cover in which I always kept such things as cake or cookies. Leo opened the bedroom door, called to his mother to come out and eat a lunch with us. She yelled at him to get out and used some cuss words at him. Well, I found out why for once she did not want any lunch with us. She had eaten the entire cake. For over two weeks, she never spoke to us.

So another spring faded into summer. In spite of the old lady's constant nagging, fault finding, and trouble making, in spite of my endless work, I was happy. The long nights spent together in love with my Leo fully repaid me for all the happenings of the day.

Now I will go back to two things. First I want to say that it might seem strange that I wrote so much about the West, of my intense longing for it, and now for so many years never have mentioned it again. But really my thoughts still were with it much of the time. Towards night, when the sun was sinking westward, that old, old longing to follow its trail came sweeping over me, perhaps not quite as strong as in my childhood and girlhood, but still stronger than I could ever put into words. But I knew all we could do now was to keep us alive. In summer we lived well, and both Leo and I got a little money ahead, but when late fall and the long winter came, it was soon spent. I got some help from New York City, Leo got a few days work here and there, but that was during the Great Depression. Really, the old lady ate much, much more than Leo and I together, so I knew it was out of the question to make plans to go west.

Still, I always felt that some time I should make another trip to my beloved West. There was one thing I discovered to my dismay, and that was that Leo did not care to travel, could not understand why anyone should want to see the mountains, the desert, the ocean. So I seldom spoke to him about how I felt about the West, thinking there might in the years yet to come be a change.

Early one evening in January, there came a knock at the door. A man entered. He introduced himself as Arthur Kum. He was a near neighbor of ours. They were very poor people and the Welfare was paying their rent in the same place I used to own. He had a wife and two small children. This man was quite different from any I had ever met. He was thirty-eight years old, of medium height, rather of stocky build, brown hair with just a touch of gray at the temples, and brown eyes. A very intelligent looking man.

Though he was clad poorly and on relief, I could not but help notice his perfect English, no grammatical mistakes. He said he had been told that we had a lot of reading matter on hand, and as he had at present nothing to do, would appreciate a loan of some of it to while away the time. I think I have already mentioned the fact that Leo spent all his idle time tinkering about radios. That night he had a dismantled radio on a little stand. Mr. Kum kept looking towards it, then went over and deftly assembled the parts. "It seems you understand radios, Mr. Kum." He answered, "I ought to. I worked for ten years in a radio broadcasting station in Philadelphia."

Naturally Leo became interested and Leo always a great talker, told him about the different things that he did not understand about radio. Before Kum realized it, it was near midnight. So he promised to come over the next day and not only assemble the radio Leo had taken apart, but assemble and overhaul the one we were using. Leo was delighted. From then on, this man practically lived with us. He taught Leo a thousand things about radios. Told him that in a few more months he could get him a position on one of our big ocean liners at a hundred dollars a month, with board and state rooms for himself and me.

In the spring, in the middle of March, we moved into our basement. Leo would hold me close and say in that way we could save most of the money and in a few years time have enough put by so we could come home and really start living. Leo had intended to get his mother boarded somewhere.

Came April and Leo went back to work for Clayton Montross. But for some time now Mr. Kum had no longer shown any interest in Leo's radio work. Still he was at our house most of the time, though Leo was away all day. So one day I asked him why he had stopped helping Leo. He looked at me, hesitated then said, "Because I cannot get him any further. I never was so disappointed in anyone in my life before. I thought to myself, here is a man who will go far. At first he was so receptive. I explained a thing to him once and he understood readily. Very bright. But after I got him into a few more little difficult matters, he could not grasp them. I spent the better part of two weeks trying to teach him." Here he mentioned something about amplifiers. "But at the end of two weeks steady explaining, he had not yet in the least the faintest meaning of what I had tried to teach him." Then he went on to tell me about a dozen other little things that Leo just could not master. He said again, "He got as far with radio as he ever will." Yes, the later years proved that he was right. People would bring their radios to be fixed. If there was not much the matter with them, Leo would fix them, but if there was something the least complicated about them, he would either take them to Camden to Heine or to Phelps. These two men also tried to help Leo, but he could not follow them.

Now I want to say something about Mr. Kum. I was not in love with him. My whole heart belonged to Leo. Neither was he in love with me, but there was a very strong attraction on both sides, for each other. This man was, with the exception of my own child, the only person who had ever understood me. This may seem strange. My father and mother loved me with all their hearts, better than most parents love their children, but neither one of them in the least understood me. No, in a way, we were strangers. . My Aunt Sophie meant well by me, but the life she planned for me would have been horrible. None of my husbands in any way understood me. My one good and true mother-in-law, whom I so dearly loved and whom I think loved me the same as if I had been her own daughter, did not know me more than if I had been a stranger. Good Mrs. Fairchild from New York City, who had done so very much for me and been so kind, to her, too, I was a stranger. The only one so far who had understood me had been my child.

She could understand that I could be bad as the world might call it and still be good as God might see me. Yes, she could see how I might reason out a hard problem of life and at the same time go and enjoy catching a bright colored butterfly or go wading knee deep in the mud for pollywogs. Now this man, too, completely understood me. It was only the second day when he came to us that he frankly told us the reason he had called the night before.

He had come into this town a stranger, inquired for the Welfare officer, who lived at Fish Creek, and he told him, "Yes, there is an empty house I can rent for you. Sophie used to own it." From then on, it was, wherever he went, "So you live near Sophie, or have you seen Sophie yet?" He went to Camden and in one of the stores they asked him where he lived. He said near North Bay. Then they said, "Then you must know Sophie." So that was the reason he had taken the excuse the night before to come to our house. I asked him what he had heard about me, if it was good or bad. He just laughed and said both. So as time went on, we became very good friends.

When April came and Leo was away all day, I found out that there was one more thing we had in common. It was plants. He brought down two large books, plant books, giving both the Latin and English names of all our common weeds. Also, for what they were good, in a medical way. We spent many happy hours together strolling through the fields and pastures, picking flowers here, pulling up weeds there, and then comparing them with those in the books, and seeing for what they were good as medicine.

Of all the many little trips we made together in search of, for us, new plants, there was one trip I shall never forget. It will always stand out in my memory as a bright, happy moment of a rather drab life. We had seen some pictures of plants that only grew near shaded woodland streams, and which were supposed to be a wonderful cure for certain liver troubles. I, who had always had such a keen desire to know all the wild plants, told Kum I felt sure that that very plant grew near our brook in the woods.

So one perfect afternoon in May--it was the twenty-first of May-- we, with the big plant book, strolled out into the woods. I had traveled that lonely, tree overhung woodland road for many years, yes, made that same little trip on many a beautiful May day before, but never had it seemed so much like a picture out of a fairytale book. Yes, it seemed like an enchanted woodland trail leading us into a better land. Neither one of us spoke. I sensed that my companion, too, felt that magic spell. The sun was shining warm and bright from a blue and cloudless sky. The trees along both sides of the roadway, with their branches of young new leaves entwined above our heads, formed a bowered archway through which the golden sunbeams flickered sunlight and shadows on our path. The air was filled with the sweet odors of the spring woods. Song birds were singing above and around, butterflies flitting from flower to flower. So we reached the brook.

Silently, I gathered the plants of which I had spoken to Arthur Kum. We sat down on the very edge of the little brook. Arthur found the page and description of the plants in his plant book and read me their Latin and English names, also for what they could be used as medicine. Then he closed the book and in silence we sat there gazing into the clear, swiftly running waters of the brook.

I can, in memory, still see the scene before us. At our backs, the tall dark hemlocks of the Hackabaum, on either side masses of dense trees, both great and small, and at our very feet, the rippling brook, the water clear and shallow. Through this sun-flecked water, we could see the sandy bottom, the many, moss grown stones and pebbles, with here and there a water plant growing and swaying in the waters of the brook. Just across the brook, the mighty trees of the dear, thickly grown forest again shut us in. Beautiful beyond description. I cannot say just how long we sat there in utter silence. Then, not looking at me but still gazing into the depths of the little brook, Arthur said these words. "No, I know this cannot last. You will have to go back to your toil, to the fault finding, the daily aggravations. This is only a glimpse of the life you would love to lead, free and wild like the child of nature you are." I looked at him. He returned the glance. I said, "How did you know?" He only said, "Because I know you."

Through Sophie's Eyes

Yes, he certainly knew me well. To prove this, I must relate another incident which had happened some weeks before, in fact on the second day of April, the very day on which Leo started work again for Montross. But to give a perfect picture of this, I must go way back in my story. When I was between eighteen and nineteen, I wrote a poem about the West. I named the poem "My Beautiful West." I was very proud of it and thought it was the best I had ever written. I shyly handed it to my mother. She read it out loud in her light sing-song way, laid it down, and smilingly said to me, "Very pretty." I could see she had forgotten all about it the moment she laid it down. Now I knew my father loved poetry and understood a good one when he read one. But as he and I never had been friendly, I could not bring myself to take and hand it to him. So I left it on the table, where I knew he would find it as soon as he entered the room. I busied myself about the room, as I knew he would come in now any moment. He came in, saw the paper on the table, picked it up, read it, tossed it down again, and said, "Not bad for a child, but she lacks my talent, will never amount to anything." Oh, how that hurt. I, a child? I was nearer nineteen than eighteen. So he thought his poems were better. My mother never answered. I knew just what she was thinking. It was, what difference will it make if I could write good poetry or not. But I was very deeply hurt. Well, it could not have been too bad. In later years, I sent it to *The Utica Daily Press* and they published it. So I knew it was not bad.

Now to go on with my story. After I was married to Charles Estey, that was before the Utica paper printed it, I read the poem to him. I read it slowly, impressively, with all the feeling in my voice. When I got done, he said, "What made you write such foolishness?" I choked down my tears and left the room. Now although I had never yet told this Mr. Kum the intense longing I had always felt for the West, even before I really knew what the West was, I gave him this poem to read. He read it over, very slowly, then once again, handed it to me and said, "You are a great poet." What a thrill passed through me. I felt happy. I told him that *The Utica Press* had printed it. He said such poems should bring a good price. He picked it up again, slowly reread it, then looked me squarely in the face and said, "There is longing and heartbreak in every line. There was sorrow and tribulation in your heart when you wrote this, and maybe almost subconsciously your mind traveled westward. It must have been that for a long, long time you had been dreaming of that West, and then when the burden you were under became too great to bear, you wrote that poem."

It was a day in late October, the first cold, windy, rainy day of that month. I well remembered the day I had written that poem. My father had started in with his first so called arithmetic lesson that forenoon. I mean the first lesson of that fall. He stated I must learn, I must study; he would make me. To finish off, he turned to my mother and said, "If she does not master arithmetic, she will just be like these ignorant girls, marry a laborer, and she might better be dead than just the wife of a laborer."

He went out to do some chores. The rain had stopped. So I smuggled some paper and pencil and rushed off to my woodland retreat. I was angry, bitter. Why should I put up with another five or six months of that intolerable thing called arithmetic lessons. Yes, why should I. Then the great love I had for Joe again swept over me. What heavenly bliss it would be to have a tiny home with him, my laborer. Again I fell into a dream of longing for the West.

Oh, how strong that pull at my heartstrings grew for the West. All the pent up emotions within me found release in that poem. Now when I had hastily snatched up that scrap of paper, I did not have the slightest idea that that day I would write this poem, but always after such an outburst at home, when I got by myself, I wrote some poetry. Well, dinner was eaten in grim silence. Then, because the sun had come out, my father went to work on the farm. Late that afternoon, I showed the poem to my beloved mother. I have already told the rest. Yes, Mr. Kum understood me fully and truly.

Here is one more little incident. This was in April. I had just told him that some of the neighbors did not like me. He said, "That is because they do not know you." I looked at him and replied, "I grew up with all of them, lived a lifetime amongst them, and you only know me more for a few months." His reply was, "Still I know you better than they do." He was right about that.

In June I had a great surprise. I received a letter from my daughter. It would be impossible for me to describe the feeling that surged through my heart at the mere sight of her handwriting. Each word seemed like a message from beyond the grave, from another world. Both gladness and sadness seemed to overwhelm me. The long years of separation seemed suddenly to have shortened. Yes, she was still my child, my little Sophie. The rest of the day went like a dream.

The dear, busy, happy summer faded into autumn. In September, the Kum family moved away. I missed him, his understanding, helpful ways. Here I want to say that Leo, who had always been so fond of music and had never owned an instrument of his own, had for over a year practiced with the Holmes boys, he, Leo, playing on a borrowed violin, Harold Holmes on a guitar, and Elmer Holmes on a banjo. After a while they got Clyde Matthews to join them. Clyde's favorite instrument was the piano, but he also could play on any other instrument. So when they practiced all together, Clyde would play the bull fiddle.

During the long fall and winter evenings, they would take turns in meeting once a week. Two weeks at the Holmes' place, as there were two boys there, one week at Clyde's house, and one week at mine. I enjoyed these evenings very much. I went with Leo to Clyde's house once, but there was such a bitter row afterwards, I did not go again. Slowly they formed an orchestra, intending some time to play for money. During the busy summer months, their practicing stopped, or nearly, but once in a great while they came together. By this fall they took it up more seriously again, determined to make some money out of it. I think Clyde boosted them on.

Chapter 39

I was happy. I had Leo, got a letter once in a while from my daughter, and still had some help from New York City. Came the twenty-first of December and my fifty-ninth birthday. But really I felt young. Yes, I felt younger than in my dreary girlhood days. Around Christmas time, the old lady kept complaining that she did not feel well. For some time, I paid little attention to that as I had noticed during the years she was with me that if the slightest thing was the matter with her, such as if she burned her mouth on hot coffee or tea, she would make a fuss about it the rest of the day, and for days after bring it up how she had suffered.

Now her appetite was surely not impaired. I will just give one little item concerning that. In spring, I had made quite a large amount of maple syrup, but I had found out I had to hide the bulk of it as she would drink it. So I concealed a few gallons in the basement and each morning filled a pint pitcher for use on our pancakes. Leo and I would put a little of this on the pancakes on our plates. She always finished the pint. One morning instead of taking the little pitcher down to the basement to fill, I brought up a quart can to the kitchen. She generally did not come in to breakfast till it was all ready to eat, but for once she came in, spied the can of syrup, opened it, and drank the whole quart without even taking it from her mouth long enough to breath. A few minutes later she sat down to breakfast, and like every other morning, made an enormous meal.

A short time after New Year's, she had a sore on her back. Daily I washed it, put on healing salve, but just the same it grew worse from day to day, thick yellow matter running out of it. I knew it was not cancer, but I also knew that it was something that I did not

403

understand, so on the twenty-second of January, I told Leo he must get a doctor to come at once. It was a cold, blustery morning and Leo walked to Sylvan Beach to get the town doctor. About half past ten, he and Dr. Hall arrived. The doctor, after a careful examination, said the old lady had sugar diabetes, caused by too much sweet, grease, and starch, and she would have to be taken at once to the Rome Hospital. Leo went to Rome with his mother. When he came home that night and we two were alone again, it seemed so much like our first winter together. This was the twenty-second of January and then followed a very, very happy winter for me. We both kept well and lived in peace and love together. Clayton Montross sent for Leo once in a while for a day's help in the garage. I still got some help from New York City, and as the old lady had eaten much more than the two of us, we had plenty to eat this winter. Leo got Matthews to take us to Rome every two weeks so we could go to the hospital. I, too, went with Leo to hear the boys practice.

This winter was not as severe as generally. We often walked together to visit the Holmes, and other places, to spend the evening. Before we really realized it, spring had again come. Every few weeks I exchanged letters with my far away little daughter. In May, Leo's mother was so much improved I knew she would soon be with us again. I will say after my happy winter, I had fully made up my mind that I would do my utmost to live in peace with Leo's mother. I thought if I tried real hard, we could not help but to live in peace together.

On the second of June, a lovely Sunday afternoon, Orville Holmes, whom Leo had again hired as Clyde's old Ford was once more out of commission, took us to Rome to bring Leo's mother home. She was delighted to come back and really was quite well again. She claimed they half starved her to death, but her back was entirely healed up, and she admitted that she felt fine. So for a little while things ran quite smoothly, like the way they did the time she first came to live with us.

Now once more I will have to go back in my story. As I have already said, Leo and the boys had long been practicing together and at last thought they were now good enough to make their first public appearance. Naturally they were all very much excited about their adventure. Their little band now consisted of six members. Lewis Holmes, a young man from Camden whose name I have forgotten as he only belonged a short time, Elmer and Harold Holmes, Clyde

Matthews, and Leo. They had decided to call themselves the Hill Billy Boys. As to their uniforms, they thought it would be the most appropriate to get new blue overalls, new blue work-shirts, and a new red bandana handkerchief to wear around their necks. Also they all, with the exception of Lewis Holmes, were one might say penniless, and those garments would be the cheapest and later on could be used for work clothes.

Everything now seemed to be settled excepting the place where to give their first dance. They had so taken it for granted that George Johnson would only be too glad to let them use his hall, free of charge, as naturally that would bring a big crowd to his bar that they had not spoken to him till they were ready to have their posters printed. To their amazement, he refused. Yes, even when they offered to pay cash in advance for that one night. For some reason that they never found out, all the other small towns did the same thing. In Camden, they could have hired one for ten dollars. So Elmer and Harold Holmes asked their father's permission to use the large loft in his new barn. They had their posters printed and distributed. Had it advertised in the *Rome Sentinel*.

Of course all these things cost money, but they were so confident of their success, thinking the more they advertised it, the more people would come. The price of the tickets was a dollar a couple. The date was to be the sixteenth of June. The last rehearsal was at our house, the night before their first performance. They really played very well and to my surprise, Leo's mother enjoyed it. Leo, who was working at Montross, said he would be home shortly after two in the afternoon for a late dinner, as he and Clyde Matthews would have to wire the barn for lights.

Now I must relate a very strange thing. Since that winter, when I had been so terribly sick, I really had not had a sick day. On the day before the performance, I was as well as ever. But in the morning of the sixteenth, when I woke up, I was so deathly sick I could hardly get their breakfast. Of course I did not eat a mouthful. I had no pains, just a dizzy weakness. As I said, I did not have to put up Leo's dinner, as he was to come home to eat at half past two. Leo had spoken to Ira Howe to drive around this way as Clyde would be busy at the barn with Leo till almost the last minute. Both Leo and Clyde took their uniforms along. I thought now that she and I were on such good terms again, she would not make a fuss about my going.

Through Sophie's Eyes

Somehow I got dinner. Luckily I had cooked and baked a lot of things the day before or I never could have gotten that meal. I was so intensely weak it was almost impossible for me to move. Of course I had given up going out that night, but sick as I was, I could not but help to see the joy in the old lady's eyes and face. About four in the afternoon, Clyde came after Leo. They also had to build some benches and a ticket booth. Lewis Holmes's wife was to sell the tickets. It was just five o'clock, and a sleepiness came over me. Strange, I never slept any in the daytime. I said to Leo's mother, "I am sleepy. Will go and get a nap." Even in my misery, I saw her delight. She rubbed her fat hands together, said, "Yes, yes, go and sleep." I staggered down to the basement. It was a hot day, but oh how cool and pleasant that basement looked. Spotlessly clean and a snow white soft bed.

I just remember half falling down on that bed, then I was sound asleep. All at once I woke up, but Leo was not with me. I had always gotten up first. Then I saw I was dressed and on top of the bed, and then the whole thing came back to me. I saw the sun shining through the cracks. We were having our longest days. I felt quite well, was hungry. Jumped up and almost ran up to the cabin. The old lady was rocking away and reading. She looked up surprised to see me. It was just seven o'clock. I hustled around and got supper on the table. We ate in silence; then I went out and did my chores. When I was all done, it was just twenty minutes after eight.

The dance was to start at nine, but I knew it would not take me long to get ready, and in Howe's car, we could make it in five minutes. Everything was exactly the way it had been a little more than a year before when I got ready to go to that play. While I washed myself and combed my hair, and changed my clothes, she yelled, screamed, stamped her feet, pounded her fists on the table. At last, exhausted, she was gasping for breath. I turned to her and in a quiet voice said, "If you feel like that about my going, I will go out a lot oftener." When a fiendish look of triumph crossed her fat face, I knew she thought she had scared me out. The only way I can describe what happened was to say hell broke loose. Before, her screaming and yelling was that of a very willful child. Now her screams and yells of rage were those of a maniac. I went about just as if I did not even know she was in the room. I left. It was now dusky, a few minutes to nine. Walked to the road and sat down under the big maple trees. A few minutes later, the Howe family picked me up. I am sorry to say that the dance was a flop, a complete failure. After ten o'clock a few car loads of people came, looked in, did not buy any tickets, and drove off.

The old lady stayed angry for weeks to come. So another summer and autumn went by. My little girl wrote, saying they might come out in spring. How good that seemed. Came the twenty-first of December and my sixtieth birthday. Fast as the years had been coming, still this seemed different. I had, in a way, gotten used to the fifties, but now I had left them behind, too, and forever. At times, for a few fleeting moments, a feeling of the loss of all the years behind me, years that would not, could not, be lived again. But though these thoughts tugged at my heart, with a little sting of regret, I was swept on. These were happy, busy years. All the nagging and fault finding of Leo's mother was easy to bear as long as I had Leo's love. At night when clasped in his arms, the troubles of the day vanished like mist before sunshine.

Came the fifteenth of February, a dark, dreary day. But really for mid-winter not bad. There was hardly any wind and only about ten degrees below freezing. Right after breakfast, Leo left for Gene Holmes's. They were to buzz wood there that day, and I knew he would not be back until after they had supper there. All the forenoon, the old lady was on the warpath, acting meaner than usual. I tried not to pay any attention to her continuous nagging and fault finding.

As to the weather, we had a blizzard in the later part of February; each day the drifts grew deeper and deeper. The intense cold packed the snow so hard that even the large snow plow could no longer move it. For nearly a month Mr. West, our mailman, had not been able to get through. Every two or three days, a man on snowshoes with the mail bag over his shoulders would come by with the mail. I had not heard from my little girl in many weeks and was anxiously waiting for a letter again from her. On the fifteenth of March, the weather again took a sudden turn. A warm rain set in and the snow started melting. No mailman on the sixteenth.

Came the seventeenth of March, Saint Patrick's Day, a warm, bright, sunny day, but the roads were just a mass of water and mud and soft snow. Oh, joy, about two o'clock in the afternoon Mr. West came with a horse and sleigh. He had a whole bundle of mail for us and to my delight a letter from my little daughter from Glendale, California, a suburb of Los Angeles.

They had lived there for some time past. This letter contained three pieces of interesting news. The first was that my little Sophie had given birth on February 23, and they had named him Eugene Philip. The next news was that Ray's mother had died and the last, as a post-script, was that they intended coming east and make me a visit. How happy I was. She told me they were all living in a large house car that Ray had built himself, and as they were coming in that, they would not make me any trouble.

I began to figure out about when they would come. I thought they might be able to start on their long journey about two months after the baby had been born and, as it would take them about three weeks to make the long trip, by easy stages, I thought it would probably be somewhere around the middle of May. The snow kept melting fast, warm rains at night and sunny days. So by beginning of April, there was not much snow left, but instead of warmer weather with the coming of April, the weather became cold and rough. At night a few inches of snow would fall, the next day melt, and so on, making a continuous wet soggy ground or mud.

Something had gone wrong between Leo and Clayton Montross. Leo had started to work for him as usual, on the second day of April, but after only a few days, he quit, or as the saying goes, was fired. Although he tried his best, he could not obtain another job. This was during the midst of the Depression, so we, like millions of other people, were on relief. Of course when I had received my daughter's letter, I wrote to her at once. I asked her when they intended to come. But to my disappointment, I received no reply. I began to think they had given up coming out.

Came the sixteenth of April, a bright, sunshiny day. But there was a cold, cutting, northwest wind that might almost have been called a gale. The ground was soaking wet and cold, and as yet, not a green thing anywhere. There now were patches of dirty snow. The time of day was about four o'clock in the afternoon. Leo's mother, as usual, was in her bedroom laying on her bed. Leo sat near the stove reading. I was binding a book. We had received a year's free subscription from Father Coughlin to his very interesting newspaper, and I was trying to make a book out of it. Strange, with all our after fires and losses, I still got that huge volume.

As I said, the cold wind was roaring outside. But in spite of that and that my cabin stood so far from the road, I heard what sounded like a heavy truck go by. About fifteen minutes later, I heard a queer little noise at the front door. It did not sound like a person knocking, and besides, as it was a glass door, I would have seen the man or woman who had knocked even from my low rocking chair where I was sitting. A few moments later, I again heard that odd sound. I became a little curious, as I knew it was not made by my hens. So I got up, walked across the kitchen, and to my amazement saw a little boy of six or seven years, bareheaded, bare armed, bare legged, and dressed in thin summer clothes, going from my cabin to the road, but not along the driveway, but around back of the tall cranberry bushes. For a moment I was stunned. A strange child, little more than a baby, in thin summer clothes, out in this icy cold wind and, above all else, whose child, and where did he come from?

I knew none of our neighbors had a child like that. All of these thoughts rushed through my mind in a second. I called to Leo, who sat quite near the door, to look. He jumped up, looked. I asked him if he thought it might be a child from North Bay. By this time, the child was out of sight, the high cranberry bushes and other trees and shrubs hiding most of the road. We stood at the glass door waiting to get another glimpse of him. We knew that on reaching the road, if he went either up or down he would again come into sight. But he did not appear again. I said to Leo, "There must be an older boy or girl in the road waiting for him. A child as young as that would not be so far from home alone. I'll put on my rubbers and coat and go see where he went to." Leo spoke up and said, "I'll go."

I went back to my book binding. After a few minutes, Leo came back, smiling and a little excited. He said to me, "Who do you think is out there?" Of course I said, "How should I know?" Leo said, "It is Ray Wilson and the whole family on a large house car and trailer."

This news came entirely unexpected for I had felt so sure that they had not yet left California. It still shot through me like electricity. I jumped up, forgetting to put on my rubbers or a coat, and rushed out. Yes, there close by the road stood the largest house car I had ever seen. It was not what we generally see, a house car trailer. This thing was built on the chassis of a heavy truck. What in lumber wagons is called "the reach" was much lengthened out.

Through Sophie's Eyes

Standing close by the huge car was a little four year old girl, rather short but built stocky, with the reddest cheeks I have ever seen in a child. She had very long flaxen hair that hung down, uncombed. Her eyes had a haunted sadness, but were very blue. So this must be Jinni. I stepped into the car. The door was open. There I saw the little boy I had glimpsed before. This must be Rocky. And then another little thin, pale faced boy. Oh, that must be Joe. Joe, the tiny babe I had so loved and tenderly tended for seventeen happy months, and for whom I had suffered such heart breaking anguish when he had been taken away. Another swift glance and, oh, God, I saw my child again.

The last time I had seen her, now only a few weeks of being seven years, she had stood on the cabin doorstep bidding me hasten to go to Rome. Then she was round and plump, rosy cheeked, with the face of a child. Now there she stood, painfully thin and white and oh, so little and frail. Only her big gray eyes were still the same. I cannot find the right words to describe the feelings of sorrow, and sad surprise that flooded my heart at the sight of my child.

Then I spied hanging a basket, a cradle. I looked into it and there lay a beautiful round, fat baby boy. He had a few brown hairs and lovely shaped head and face. I could write a whole chapter about this happy reunion, but will not say more about it here.

Now, as to the weather, it remained cold and windy. Each day we had more or less rain and hardly any sunshine, but on the fifth of May another sudden change came, almost over night. It became unseasonably hot. Then up to May twenty-fourth the grass got green and growing fast. There were millions of wild strawberries. Every huckleberry bush, from the tiniest low bushes to the medium and high bushes, were a complete mass of white flowers. Every apple and pear tree was laden with bloom. What a promise for an abundance of berries, apples, and pears, though we did not have a drop of rain since May fourth. The ground had been so soaked that though rather dry now, nothing had suffered for moisture. I was so glad since for many years my little Sophie and I had really lived amongst the huckleberry bushes for ten weeks each summer.

At daybreak, before the sun was up, we would wander up the dear old lane, sometimes start picking on ours, the wild land, sometimes on LeGrand Cleveland's or Jim Dixon's. Oh, the glory of seeing the first golden rays of the rising sun, how it turned the lowland mists into shimmering gold. How sweet the odors arising from nature's

410

wilderness were, dew laden fragrance. How joyous were the songs of the woodland birds in the early mornings. We would hurry, fill our pails, pick at the same bushes, and visit happily together. Talking of the future, our plans were always linked together with a golden chain. Then our pails well filled, we would hurry home, hungry, and eat breakfast, do our chores, and hurry back to spend most of the day in the wild, free wilderness of the berry patches, which to us were all free hunting grounds.

We knew every bush and knoll, every tree and rock, for we lived amongst them. Each one of us averaged a crate a day, thirty-two quarts, sixty-four quarts for the two of us, and often, very often, we each had eight or ten quarts more than our crates. Oh, those were happy golden days. I had so missed my child's companionship in the years when she no longer was with me in berry time. But I had to keep on picking for the sake of the money the berries brought me. I could no longer go out in the early dawning after Leo came, as I had to cook breakfast and get him off to work. But many a time, when I was out there alone in the silence of the great solitude about me, it seemed as if I saw my child near me, as if I could sense her presence. Her spirit seemed near me, though I knew she was thousands of miles away from me.

Even on the first day of her return, she spoke about the huckleberries, how she had missed them, in the midst of all the abundance of semi-tropic fruits. How often she had told her children how good they were, and on the way out here, how they would enjoy them this coming summer. On the twenty-fourth of May, the weather suddenly turned colder. That night we had a light frost, just enough to kill the wild strawberry blossoms on low land. But to everyone's dismay, the next day, the twenty-fifth, we had a much harder frost. That night it froze thin ice, and all next day the thermometer never got much above thirty-three or thirty-four. That night it froze thick ice. The thermometer stood at twenty-four degrees in the morning of the twenty-sixth of May.

We all knew that would end the strawberries, huckleberries, cherries, apples, plums, and pears. Now it is a well known fact that after three frosts, there is rain. But not this year. It again come off hot and dry. Now I had always had a good garden, and had intended to have a larger and better garden this summer than usual. Ray and little Sophie, too, were going to put in a garden, as they intended to stay with us until the latter part of September. We had tried and tried to get someone to plow for us in the beginning of May, but could not get a team to do the work until the eighth of June. Besides our gardens, we got a piece of ground plowed for potatoes and beans and sweet corn.

Well, we got our things in the dry, dusty ground at last. No rain and each day the weather grew hotter and hotter. In the beginning of June, the blackberry bushes blossomed. But after the berries were set, this summer there was no rain, so of course they all dried up. Often it looked like rain, but after a few minutes of a light sprinkle, the sky would again clear off, and the blazing red sun came out again.

Now I will have to go back again a little way in this story. First of all, I want to say that in the beginning of May, for the first time in my memory they were really working on our road. About once a year a few stones were picked up, or a few loads of gravel dumped into some mud-hole, or a few bushes cut down. Each spring the road was for a time impassable. Now this spring they started to rebuild it. First they scraped and scraped the sides, then formed ditches on either side so the water could run off. Then started what they called paving. They drawed hundreds of truck loads of medium sized stone on the road to an average depth of six to eight inches deep, and on top of these stones, a layer of fine gravel, another eight to ten inches deep, and the last act was the big steam roller that went back and forth over the gravel about a dozen times. Although there were many men and trucks working, they only got from the McCormack corner to the old Brown place, now known as the Charles Clark farm.

This work was started the first week in May, and on account of bad weather, stopped the fifth of November. Both Leo and Ray tried to get on this job, but for some reason could not.

Another thing I want to mention here was that all at once the little help I still had been getting from New York City had stopped. I wrote to Mrs. Fairchild a number of times, but did not receive any answer. Here, too, I must say that Ray was a great worker and had always been able to obtain a job where others had failed. So this spring he was not in the least dismayed not to get on this road work. He just said he would find something else to do.

He made countless efforts to obtain work, but without success. So when their little horde of money they had brought with them was exhausted, they, too, had to go on relief. Came the first of June, as every day, the weather was hot and dry. I was at the pump after a pail of water. Ray also had come to the pump at the same time for water. He said to me, "This is very unhandy for you to carry the water so far. What made you build your cabin so far back?" I explained to him that when I had the cabin built, I had expected to get that money from Europe soon after, then build a good house over the cellar of where my former big house had been. Told him how that money had vanished. Then added that Leo and I had often spoken of getting the cabin moved back on over the cellar, but had to give it up. Ray asked me why we had to give it up. I explained to him that Orville Holmes had offered to move it for seventy-five dollars with his father's oxen, we to pay Gene Holmes for the use of the oxen. We, also, to hire a truck and go to Oneida and rent some rollers, which of course would have to be returned. So we had figured out that the moving would cost us a hundred dollars or more.

Ray listened; then said, "If you want it moved, I'll move it for you and it will not cost you a cent." I just stared at him; then said, "But you have neither oxen, horses, or a tractor." Ray said, "I would not need any. I have a chain fall." I knew that Ray knew perfectly well that neither Leo nor I had even a dollar. Once more I said, "But we have to obtain rollers and that would cost a lot." Ray said, "All I would need would be two heavy timbers and a long, strong rope." We walked to the old cellar, which was only about eight or ten feet from where we had been standing at the well. Ray said the top of the wall was crumbling and needed to be re-laid. I asked timidly how much the lime would cost to make the mortar. Again Ray said he could lay up a dry wall, just the stones.

I really was quite excited about the prospect of getting the cabin moved. We quickly walked over to my cabin and told Leo all the plans. Leo had been tinkering with a radio, but put that away quickly, and he and Ray began to discuss the subject. Ray went to his house car and fetched a measuring tape, measured the length and width of the cabin, and then the length and width of the cellar. The measurements showed that, with a few alterations of the wall, the cabin could be placed on the old foundation.

Then came the question about the heavy timbers and long, strong rope. I remembered the old Meinhart barn that had fallen to pieces a few years before, and that we might borrow some of those timbers. Leo was sure that Clyde Matthews would lend him his hay rope. But how to draw the stones for the cellar wall and bring home the long, heavy timbers. But Ray easily overcame that little difficulty too. He said he thought he could borrow Gene Holmes's truck. So it seemed that all difficulties were overcome, everything settled. The three of us walked back to the cabin.

Ray crawled under the cabin. It was not built close to the ground, but at each corner, and also between each corner, rested on some heavy stones. When Ray had crawled out again, he looked very sober and thoughtful. Then he remarked, "This cabin had never been intended to be moved." Then he explained to us in a few words the way it was put together and that it might collapse in moving. This indeed was a blow. I thought a few moments, then said, "Are you sure it would collapse?" Ray replied, "Why, no, it might hang together and it might not." I thought for another moment then asked, "How many chances do you think there would be in getting it moved without it falling to pieces?"

Ray whistled, said, "The chances would be about equal." I spoke up, "This is my cabin and I will take the chances." By now it was about eleven o'clock. We had just started eating when we saw Ray walking down the road very fast, in a short time coming back with Holmes's little truck.

Ray and Leo drawed a few loads of flat stones, and stones with a face, for the wall, then went to the Meinhart place and fetched some heavy timbers, and Leo stopped to Matthews and borrowed their hay rope, which I am sorry to say was never returned to them. That same evening, after supper, Ray and Leo started to clean out the old cellar, as in the ten years since the fire, there was a lot of rubbish in it.

Leo and I, as always, slept in the basement. Early next morning we were awakened by the sound of stones being handled. We both jumped up. Yes, there was Ray, working on the wall. Both Ray and Leo worked that day till nightfall, but they also had to rebuild the hatchway. Next morning the real moving of the cabin started. Leo's mother had slowly, very slowly but steadily, been failing. She still could hear as well as ever and knew nothing about our moving, but she did not seem in the least interested in anything going on about her. Instead of using her knife, fork, or spoon at the table, she just picked up her food from her plate with her fingers.

It took two days to move the cabin, as after each move the length of the rollers, the chain falls, as well as the rollers, had to be re-adjusted. As the ground was too rough to go cross lots, the cabin had to be moved along the long driveway nearly to the road, and then turned half way around and moved eastward to the cellar. But after a while it was accomplished. It seemed wonderfully good to be again near the road, near the mail box, and above all, near the pump. Now in this hot weather, almost under the very large, shady maple trees. Also, I again had a cellar, which I had missed very much.

I measured the distance from where the cabin had stood to the basement of the barn, and from the basement to where the cabin now stood, and to my surprise it was exactly the same. Yes, everything was much better, handier, excepting one thing. We had to leave the woodshed behind, as that could not be moved. Ray tore it down and brought the pile of old boards and rafters near the back of the cabin.

Now I will run ahead a little in my story and then come back here where I have left off. In October, long after my daughter and her family had left, Leo Kinney gave us four large French windows, the kind that can be opened and closed like a door. He also gave us a large two sash window and a heavy wood door, also quite a few clapboards as good as new, and enough light planks to lay a good floor in the woodshed.

I was delighted. Leo and I built the frame work for the new woodshed out of the old stuff from the old one. There were the rafters and roof boards, and we built the west and north side out of them, cutting and fitting a place on the west side for the two sash windows, and a place on the north side for the door. Then we took the four large French windows and they nearly made the east side, just lacking about four feet. Then laid the plank floor and made a hatchway door. Then took the good clapboards and covered over the west and north sides. We had to buy a few new rolls of roofing paper. This was our only expense. I collected a lot of pasteboard boxes and lined the inside all over with them, excepting of course, where all the windows were. I called this my sun parlor. I put a table at the west window where I did most of my work. It was warm enough in here so I could do all my washing all winter. This woodshed never saw a stick of wood. I loved this little room.

Now I must go back to where I left off. June continued hot and dry. I carried water for my garden and Ray and little Sophie carried water for their garden. We did our best, put up a fight against the dry weather. Came the twentieth of June, the day had been hot as usual, and now the red sun had gone down in a cloudless sky. The time was about half an hour after sundown. But at this time of the year, the longest days, it was still as light out of doors as before sunset. Inside the cabin, there was just a little dimness creeping in. Now after the great heat of the day, the evening brought a little welcome relief. A great silence, broken a little by the hum of summer's insects, drifted on the air.

Ray and Leo were sitting together on the doorstep in quiet conversation. Joe, Rocky, and Jinni were happily playing together in the yard. Leo's mother, as always, was lying on her bed in her room. Little Sophie and I were visiting together in the kitchen. I was sitting quite near the open door where the men sat on the steps. About eight or ten feet away from me, towards the middle of the cabin, stood the basket cradle in which little Philip slept. This basket was very light and fastened on two standards, so little Sophie sometimes brought him down cradle and all, as it was easier for her than to hold him. She herself sat on the other side of the cradle, but not in line with it.

We two visited together for a little while and naturally I kept looking towards her, when all at once I seemed to see a faint light just a few inches above the baby's little head. I kept looking. Yes, there it was, a little more plainly now. The light was a circle just about eight inches above the sleeping baby's head. A halo. A feeling as of being in the presence of something holy came over me. I could not speak for a little while. Then after it had vanished, I told my little Sophie about it.

Now again I will have to run way ahead of my story. Seven years later, I was with them for a little while and to my surprise, Philip was very religious. Quite different from the rest. In his sweet, childish way, he would talk about the Angels, about his conception of Heaven, very beautiful thoughts. Although he lived in an atmosphere far, far from being religious, he himself lived in a little sphere of his own.

Chapter 40

Now I will return to that unforgettable summer. July came in with increasing heat and dryness. Once I went back into my wild huckleberry lot, from there all over Dixon's, then Congden's, in hopes I might find at least a few huckleberries, but all in vain. This was, indeed, a great disappointment. Of course I had fully realized that my little Sophie and I could not now spend all our days together in the dear wilderness searching and picking huckleberries. She had a baby, besides her other children and housework. I had Leo's mother to look after, for by now she needed constant watching. Once she started down the road thinking she was headed for the toilet. Often, very often, she would fall down while walking a few steps.

Still, I had hoped we could go back together once in a while just for the sake of the dear old times. How good it would seem to revisit the same bushes that we had picked together so many times. So many years, too, I had pictured in my mind what joy I would derive from seeing the children sitting under my big shady trees, each with a half filled pail of huckleberries and eating their fill. For to me it always had seemed that the next best thing to eating berries from the bushes was to sit on the ground under some shady tree and have a well filled pail near you, and dive into that with your hands. Then eat and eat till you cannot hold any more. This sitting at a table eating berries out of a dish with a spoon is too artificial.

Well, July faded into August. Another hot, dry month. Both Leo and Ray had a days work now and then, but we all were still on relief. I knew Ray had intended to stay with us until the latter part of September or the first of October, but as he could not obtain a steady job, he was now planning to leave much sooner. Still, as there had not been any time set, I did not worry much about their going. It was still something a long ways off. My little daughter and I spent most of the daytime hours together. Of course we never could again relive those golden bygone days, but in a measure we again grew close to one another.

Came the twenty-fifth of August. I had made some succotash a few days before and my little Sophie tasted it and found it good. She had never made any. I started to tell her how I made it and then said, "The best way for you to learn how to make it will be for you to watch me from start to finish." So on this day, the twenty-fifth of August, I said, "Tomorrow forenoon I will have to do a washing. I always go to the basement right after dinner and lie down from twenty minutes to half an hour. Right after my rest, we will go together and pick the beans and sweet corn, then sit under my trees and shell the beans together, husk, silk, and cut off the corn from the cobs together, then you can watch me put them all together. And after seasoning these things, I will put them on to slowly simmer, and when supper time comes, put in the milk and butter, then divide the mess and you can take half of it home and we will eat the other half."

That evening after supper, as usual Ray and little Sophie, Leo and I sat in the comparative cool dimming light of a hot August day. We were out in the front yard of my cabin. The children were playing nearby. The baby was asleep and Leo's mother in her room. The conversation went on as usual. About nine o'clock they were getting ready to go back to their house car. Suddenly Ray spoke up and said, "Tomorrow is my day to go to Fisher Creek and get my grocery order. I will go in the morning, come back by noon with the groceries, tinker around the house car in the afternoon, and next morning on the twenty-seventh bright and early, we will pull out."

It just seemed as if an icy hand had clutched my heart. Yes, I had known they were going, maybe soon, but still this came as a shock. Then they left for the night, and Leo and I went to our basement bedroom. I lay awake a long time. Yes, I was planning how we could spend the last day together. We would both do our washing side by side, as I knew she would want to wash up every garment before leaving on their long, long trip. Ray had built a stove outside of stones, with a heavy tin cover on which we heated our washing water and boiled some of the white clothes. Yes, we would be together all the forenoon at our washings.

Sophie Kussmaul

Next morning, right after breakfast, Leo left to go and work that day at Orville Holmes, not to be back till supper time. Ray also left to make his last trip after groceries. I shall never forget that forenoon. We washed side by side and talked, telling one another little things that we wanted the other to know before the parting, perhaps forever. At eleven o'clock we both had finished our washings. Ray came home loaded down with groceries. My little Sophie went to cook their dinner. I went and prepared a lunch for the old lady and myself. After lunch I went to the basement for my half hour rest then we would be spending a long afternoon and evening together.

But I had hardly been laying down perhaps about five minutes when I heard a light step and my little daughter's clear, sweet voice saying, "I know you do not like to be disturbed during your noon rest, but Ray is going to leave here in fifteen minutes, and I thought in that case you would rather miss your rest than to find us gone." I jumped up, though a rather numb feeling came over me. I said these words: "And so cometh death."

I followed her around as in a dream. We took her clothes off the line, carried them to her house car, and picked up the rest from the ground where they lay on the grass to bleach. I saw her dinner dishes were still on the table, unwashed. Like a drowning man grasping for a straw, I asked her, "Will you not wash up your dishes before you go?" thinking that would let them stay a few minutes longer. But Ray spoke up quickly and said, "She can wash them after the car starts." Ray gave the boys a quick order to pick up all their playthings. It all seemed like a bad dream to me, that I would soon wake up and find her still with me. Then Ray said he had to do something about the motor that would take about ten minutes. My little daughter picked up the baby and came into my cabin. She nursed him and was rocking him to sleep, rocking him once more in the chair in which I had often rocked her, one we had saved from the burning house. I know we both felt depressed. We tried to tell one another that this parting was not forever and that we would meet again.

But in those few minutes, besides my great sorrow of parting with my beloved little daughter, there were two things that impressed themselves into my mind. Little things, perhaps in their own way, but to me things that burned themselves into my heart forever. The two little boys were joyously running about collecting their treasures. They were full of the great adventure before them and did not seem to regret leaving. I suppose that is the youthful way, always looking ahead. Then all at once they ran down to the spring. They realized there could not be over three or four minutes left, but they wanted once more to see if the lizards at the bottom of the spring were still there, wanted to see if the tiny bridge they had built over the mud was all right. To me, pictures of bygone days came flashing into my mind. First, when I was a little girl and had spent so much time down there by that spring, and later that happy summer with my Indian friends, and after how my own child and I had played there together. Then the long years when I seldom went there. This summer when my grandchildren had spent so many happy days there. The other thing that also will forever stay in my mind was just back of the cabin, where later on we built that glorified woodshed, was a small amount of sand. Jinni had been playing there most of the forenoon. Now the back door of the cabin stood wide open, and I sat near the open door. Remember, the last minutes were fast ebbing away. But Jinni was rapidly finishing what she had been doing in the forenoon. I saw her, as in a dream. She was building some tiny inch high houses out of chips. She had made roads to them. Then the last call came. Ray tooted the automobile horn. Jinni got up, looked longingly at her play work, and said to me, "Grandma, will you finish my last house for me after I am gone?" I knew she hated to leave this undone. Of course I promised and did finish it, though I knew the first rain would wash it all out. Even so, we worry about our unfinished tasks when we are departing for the next world.

My child got up with her sleeping baby in her arms. I followed her to the house car. So did Jinni. The boys came running up too. Ray had already turned the car around and headed it up the road; the motor was running. Ray sat at the wheel. I went in and once more clasped my child into my arms. How thin she was. I stepped out again, the car slowly started, my child stood at the back door and waved to me. It seemed as if my heart would break, must break. If I live to be a hundred years old, this picture, this scene, will never fade from my mind. There she stood, thin, pale, and oh, so little. She was waving a tiny little white hand, her face looked thin and old and white. The car, though moving very slowly as yet, was taking her farther from me each moment, going westward.

I stood there, half numbed, waving back to her. I climbed on a stump. The car was now going past the Cleveland house. I could still see her. Now past Nash's, and gone out of sight. I sank to the ground trembling. Then other pictures rose to my mind. In memory, I again saw before me as clearly as if it were today, my little Sophie going up this road with her little lunch pail to school. I would stand on the same spot where I now was and wave to her. She, a little short, plump, rosy cheeked child, would turn around every few steps, look back, and wave a small, fat little hand. When she got past the Cleveland place where I could no longer see her, I would run back into my house, hurry up with my work, and plan a good supper for her, as she would be running in happy and hungry late in the afternoon.

Well, I got up and walked unsteadily towards my cabin. I knew there would not be a happy returning from my child tonight. How empty the cabin seemed. How lonely the rocking chair looked. I went out again up where the house car had stood. There were so many little reminders everywhere I looked--an old shoe of Joe's, a ragged sweater of Rocky's, a broken doll of Jinni's; other things: a homemade bow, a broken arrow. I wandered down to the spring. There in the mud were their footprints, bare footed tiny footprints. I slowly walked home and finished the last tiny chip house. The afternoon seemed so long. I did not make any succotash. I could not bring myself to do that.

I cooked supper about seven o'clock. Leo came home. He looked surprised and said, "Where is the house car? Where is Ray?" I said they left. Leo said, "Why, they were not going till tomorrow morning." I said, "I know." Well, I never knew for sure if the old lady realized that they had gone or not. So time went on. That very night after they had left, we had our first real rain since the beginning of May. The great drought was broken. Of course we had a light rain once in a while during that time, but this was the first soaking rain, and how quickly things started to grow. From then on for weeks, we had lovely, hot summer weather, bright sunny days, and light warm showers at night. If only we could have had a little more rain while they were here, they could have had some garden vegetables to pay them for their many hours of toil.

The other change that started that very night was that as helpless as Leo's mother had been for so long, she still had managed to walk from her bedroom to the table and back three times a day. She also could use the pail in her room. But from this night on, she could not walk anymore, neither could she feed herself. We had to put the food into her mouth. She also lost complete control of her bowels and kidneys, doing everything in her bed. I had to change her sheets and blankets three and four times a day, twice during the night. That kept me at the washtub.

Luckily the weather in daytime was always sunny, so the things dried quickly. Leo and I had to move in from the basement, as I could not lift her alone. We got Dr. Hall again. He assured us that she suffered no pain whatsoever, just got into a sort of coma. On the sixth of September, I sent for Vera, her daughter, who lived in Morrisville. I thought perhaps that would arouse her a little, but when she came and bent over mother and said, "Mother, I am Vera, your child. Do you not know me?" she just stared at her without the least recognition in her gaze. So the days went by. On the seventeenth of September, Leo got Dr. Hall in the morning. He looked at her and declared that she must be taken at once to the hospital at Rome. Said I could not keep this up. In the hospital there would be three shifts of nurses, and even they would not have to do that laundry work.

This was about nine o'clock. Dr. Hall said he would stop at North Bay and telephone to the Rome Hospital to send out an ambulance at once. He also would get in an order to have her cared for at the County's expense. By eleven o'clock the ambulance arrived, but as only the driver had come, there was this problem. The old lady was very heavy, weighed over three hundred pounds, and Leo was not strong.

Neither was the driver. But for once we were fortunate. As I have mentioned, they had been rebuilding our road, and the road men were now just up to the Cleveland place. Leo walked up briskly and came back with Clyde Mathews, Grover Brockway, and Walter House. The driver fetched in a long narrow cot bed. We put this side of the bed and they gently lifted her from her bed onto the cot bed. Then the driver touched a spring on each side of the cot and a fence, or railing, sprang up so the patient could not roll off. The three men carried her to the ambulance. Leo and the driver helped a little to lift her in. Leo went to Rome with his mother.

When he came home, I asked him if he thought she realized about going. He said no. Right after they left, I took three of her bed quilts, which she had pieced and quilted herself, and carried them out and burned them up. They had been so saturated with filth and were so large and heavy I never could have washed them. I cleaned and scrubbed her room and although the doors and windows had been open all summer, there still was a bad smell in the room, a body odor. I burned up a lot more things. A good rug I had given her to step on near her bed, all the clothes she had lately worn, and when Leo came back, he helped me to carry out her big mattress, which we also burned.

Of course after a few days this horrible odor died down. The next morning at seven o'clock, Leo and I were through eating breakfast but still sitting at the table when a car drove into the yard. The man's name was Rice, a farmer who had bought the farm near Vienna known as the Rowell farm. He said his son, who had been driving one of the gravel trucks for our roadwork, had been taken sick in the night and could not take the truck out for a few days, and would Leo take his place. Well, we both were delighted.

This was fortunate for us. Leo could stop in for dinner, as they were still working close by. He went back with Rice and in short time returned with his first load. The gravel came out of Gene Holmes's gravel bed. Leo did not have to load up, as there were men at the bed to load the trucks as they came in. So the days passed by. It seemed as if I had nothing to do now. I got busy and made three or four kinds of pickles and we bought a bushel of pears from a peddler. The weather was beautiful.

Came the twenty-fourth of September, Thursday, and just a week to a day when Leo's mother was taken to the hospital. Leo was still driving the gravel truck. He stopped to tell me he would be in to dinner at half past eleven instead of twelve o'clock, as there would not be time to go after another load. This was ten minutes after eleven. I was busy at the cook stove. Fifteen minutes after eleven, five minutes after Leo had stopped, a car drove in. It was Clayton Montross. He told me he had just received a telephone message from the Rome Hospital that Leo's mother had just died. She had died just one week to an hour after leaving our home. Clayton asked me where Leo was. I told him up the road. I saw him drive up that way.

Now it would be impossible for me to describe the feelings that surged through me when I heard of the death of the old lady. I was not good enough to feel sad, sorrowful. Neither was I bad enough to feel glad. I think the only words that will describe my feelings will be to say that I was immensely relieved. She had lived with me for five years, with the exception of those four months that she had spent in the hospital a few years previous. She and I had always been together, as I had scarcely ever gone out. Five years. Five years is a short space of time when we are looking back to them. But, oh, how long they can be if lived in strife, part time hunger, and love. After all, she had been Leo's mother.

I got my dinner ready to put on the table when Leo came. I saw at a glance that Clayton had told him. He looked deathly pale. I was standing near the stove and said to him, "Did Clayton tell you?" He nodded his head, and then did a strange thing, but I suppose that was human nature, the urge for sympathy. He came to me, put his arms around me, and kissed me. I put the dinner on the table, but Leo said he could not eat. Neither could I. I just was not hungry. Now I know that if Leo had eaten, I could have also eaten, but sitting there and looking at his grief stricken face took my appetite away. So we both just swallowed some coffee.

After the time was set for the funeral, Leo telephoned to his sister at Morrisville and asked her to send a message to his sister, Leitha, at Utica. And telegraph a message to Battle Creek, Michigan, to his brother Guy, and another telegram to his sister Viva, who lived in Detroit, Michigan The agreement was that all of them should meet at our place and from there go all together to Lock's Funeral Parlor, from which place the funeral services were to be held. Lock wanted some of the old lady's clothes to lay her out in. I knew she only had had cheap house dresses, called wrappers, and they were badly worn. So what to do? After Mrs. Fairchild died, some of her folks had sent me three large boxes of her everyday dresses. Still, they all had been far, far better than my best had been. Mrs. Fairchild had been a very large woman. I had tried to cut down some of those dresses. But there had been one exquisitely beautiful dress, heavy black satin, trimmed with yards and yards of black silk ribbons, and made up beautifully. I had showed it to Mrs. Gleason, a dressmaker, and she declared it must have cost at least one hundred and twenty-five dollars. Now I knew I would never be able to wear this dress. In the first place, it had been made for a woman who weighed over three hundred pounds. If I had it made over to fit me, it probably would have cost more than to buy a more suitable best dress. So I went and gave it to Lock.

Sophie Kussmaul

The old lady was being buried by the town in a cheap casket in a dress of a near millionaire's wife. Mr. Wheeler, our road commissioner who lived on the farm next to Rice, towed the gravel truck home and explained to Rice why Leo had to quit. We were sitting in our little cabin kitchen, dimly lit by a kerosene lamp about two hours later, when another car drove into our yard. It was Mr. Rice. I shall never forget how kindly he looked at us, how tactfully he said that he had heard about our affliction and thought perhaps we could use what money Leo had coming. He insisted on paying him for this whole day, although Leo told him that he had not worked in the afternoon. That was the first and only time that I had ever seen him, but I heard afterwards that he and all his family were exceptionally good people.

Leo walked to the Mulholand place to see Leo Kinney. He was very nice and said of course he would act as bearer, and as we had no transportation to get down ourselves, he would come after us in his coupe car. Florence Mulholand, too, was very nice. She offered to go down and sing. She had been a famous singer for years in New York City. Leo hurried down to Lock's to see if everything was being done all right. He told Lock that so far he had only two bearers. Lock just said not to worry, as he would just pick out two more men from the assembled crowd at the funeral.

I had a very busy day. I scrubbed and cleaned the cabin, baked nice fresh bread, baked a large layer cake and an apple pie, churned out some cream into good butter. We had taken it for granted that Leo's brother, Guy, and his wife, Leo's sister, Viva, and her husband and two children would surely come in the forenoon and be with us for dinner. Perhaps his sister from Morrisville and her whole family and the one from Utica might come in time for dinner or come back after the funeral.

Early Saturday morning I had Leo kill four young roosters, which I dressed and half cooked so when they would be all here, I could finish cooking them while the potatoes and other vegetables were cooking, which I had all cleaned and washed. Eleven o'clock came. No one here yet. Twelve o'clock, I got us a quick lunch, waiting for the crowd. One o'clock, no one here. We thought they were delayed, would all be here for supper. Half past one and Vera, her husband, their oldest daughter, and the sister from Utica drove in. We waited and a few minutes later, Leo Kinney came. We waited till ten minutes to two, and then the two cars, the Walters family with Leitha, and Leo Kinney, drove down to Locks.

To our surprise, there was no one there. Florence Mulholand had walked down and the minister was waiting. No one else. At the last moment, Orville came. The minister waited till ten minutes after two then he made a sign to Florence. She sang a hymn, sang it beautiful. At the end of the services, Lock handed Leo and Arnold a pair of black gloves and said, "You two will have to be bearers." Also, of course, Orville and Leo Kinney. At the cemetery, we all had to walk as the only cars were Leo Kinney's and Arnold's, and the hearse. At the cemetery, while Florence sang one more hymn, we were joined by May Woodard, with her bread basket on her arm. Orville brought us home, Leo Kinney took Florence home, the Walters went back to Morrisville, and everything was over with.

Well, the weather continued beautiful all the rest of September and October, to the sixth of November. The first week in October, we built that glorified woodshed together which I mentioned before. Then Orville came again and cut wood on halves. I must mention that after Leo had those few days of road work, we could not get back on relief. Fells claimed that as long as we no longer had the old lady to support, we must get along the best we could.

Leo tried and tried to obtain a job, but this was still during the big Depression. Once in a while he got a days work here and there amongst the farmers, but though we had to go without most of the groceries we did not really go hungry. In the first place, the two of us did not eat as much as the old lady had consumed, and we now had our potatoes, cabbages, turnips, and carrots. As soon as the weather got cold in November, we had our pig killed. We also had a little milk and a few eggs. The two of us were happy together, as both of us together ate less than the old lady had eaten, we got along quite well.

Beautiful weather continued to the sixth of November, Election Day. This day was unbearably hot. I made as little fire as possible to cook our dinner. We had the door and windows wide open. After dinner, I worked in the front yard. At two o'clock, someone came after us to go and vote. When we got home, the west was black and it began thundering. In a short time one of the worst thunderstorms I ever saw broke. The lightning flashed and the thunder rolled and crashed. The rain fairly poured down.

Sophie Kussmaul

At five o'clock it was pitch dark, and I opened the front door. A cold wind blew in and the rain had turned into snow. In fact, there already was about an inch of snow on the doorstep. At nine o'clock, there was a strong wind, no longer from the southwest, but coming now directly from the northwest. There was a blinding snowstorm. In the morning, we were snowed in. Still the snow kept coming faster and faster. By noon, the thermometer had dropped to zero. By night, ten below, and the wind kept on roaring. More snow was falling and the drifts were getting higher and higher. Of course no mailman that day or the next.

The large snowplows were going day and night. Three shifts of men. As soon as the roads were passable, we had our pig killed. But this kind of weather continued for many weeks. At Thanksgiving, we had an extra cold spell, with a blizzard following. We both were thankful for our woodpile so near the house, as it now would be impossible to work in the woods, much less possible to get a team there even if the wood there was ready to be drawed out. We had plenty to eat though often were without bread as there was no money to buy flour. Sugar, coffee, and some other things we just had to go without. The cow dried up and my few hens stopped laying as soon as the snow came.

Chapter 41

Came the twenty-first of December and my sixty-second birthday. Then on the twenty-fourth of December, the day before Christmas, another big change came in the weather. A warm south wind began blowing with mild showers of rain, and by New Year's Eve there was no snow left, just bare, muddy ground.

Just a few days after New Years, I began to feel poorly. I knew I was again coming down with the flu, the same thing I had just six winters before. Each day I felt a little worse. But I kept up, and did what little housework there was to do. The weather continued mild and beautiful.

On the fifth of January, Robert Holmes stopped and told Leo that he had bought a wood lot on the Hall place, about a mile and a half beyond the Miner farm. He wanted to hire Leo to cut wood. He was to stop for him mornings about eight o'clock and bring him home at five. The pay was to be twenty cents an hour. These days that would be ridiculous and even then it was far below average wages, but as things were, Leo accepted the offer. We did not have a cent in the house, were getting low on food, and there was no prospect of any other job.

So for weeks I would stagger up in the morning after having coughed most of the night and get Leo's breakfast and put up his dinner pail. If I tried to eat a few bites, I had such a coughing spasm that I would almost strangle to death. Somehow I got to the barn. I only had one cow and a few hens to care for. In the afternoon I often sat for one or two hours on the doorstep in the warm sunshine. I would sit there sunning myself and watching the hens. They were happily walking about on the bare, muddy ground.

428

Sophie Kussmaul

After the sun got low in the west, or it got a little cloudy and I became chilly, I would go in and slowly, very slowly, start to prepare supper. As long as I sat perfectly still, I would cough the least. But if I started moving about, or talked or ate or drank, and especially if I tried to lie down, I would almost strangle. But I was happy, very, very happy. I think, looking back over the many, many winters of my life that, strange as this may seem, this winter will always stand out as one of the happiest I ever had. We were desperately poor, I was sick and weak unto death, and had to do my housework somehow. Still, I was far, far happier than in those winters of my girlhood days when I seemed to have everything.

So the weeks passed by. Came the eleventh of February; the day started like all the others had. I was getting better. Still extremely weak and coughing, but still I was steadily gaining in strength. As usual I had sat on the sunny doorstep, and though the sun was still bright and clear, a chill seemed to be creeping into the air. So at three o'clock I went back into the cabin. In the morning I had boiled a small kettle full of little potatoes in their jackets. Now I took them and started peeling them and cutting them up to fry for supper. I sat on a kitchen chair near the cook stove facing the west window. The glass door was on my left side, but of course by turning my head the least little bit, I could see out that way too. I was about ten feet from this door. Next to me, just a little bit nearer the door, stood a small rocking chair, the same one in which my little daughter had rocked her baby to sleep just before leaving. I was busy peeling my potatoes when suddenly I saw a shadow falling across the floor, coming from the glass door. There stood my little Sophie.

Now I do not remember if she opened the door or just came through, but although I had received a letter from her only a day or so before, I was not in the least surprised now to see her here with me in my cabin. Neither did it seem strange that she would be walking in from a distance of nearly four thousand miles without a coat or hat or rubbers or even her little handbag. She was bareheaded and just had her everyday work dress on. Of course a great wave of joy came over me at sight of her, but I felt no surprise. She said to me in her beautiful clear, sweet voice, "I see I got here in time." I nodded my head. I knew she had meant that she had gotten here while I was still alive. Then she sat down in the little rocking chair, close to me, and we looked at each other. Oh, how good it was to see her dear face again and her little hands. I can recall that neither one of us spoke again, but it did not seem necessary. We were reading one another's hearts. I cannot say how long we sat there, gazing at each other, and then slowly she vanished again. The sun was still brightly shining and as we mortals measure time, it was now only four o'clock. Well I never told Leo about this. Somehow I felt he would not understand. So the days and weeks went on. I got well again and the weather continued very mild. We had a rainy day once in a while, but no snow. Saturday nights, Leo would take a feed bag, walk to North Bay, and bring it back full of our week's groceries.

Came the eighth day of March, a dark, unpleasant morning. Robert called for Leo as usual. Soon after they left, a blinding snowstorm set in from the northeast. Before ten o'clock they came back. From then on, winter set in again. I did not get my maple trees tapped till the last day of March. Still I had a good run of sap and made gallons of delicious syrup and some sugar. The snow and cold weather stayed till late, about the middle of April. But when it began to warm up, for once it did not change back again to cold weather. We got Mr. Teal, Mrs. Storm's husband, to plow the garden on the twenty-eighth of April, and I had him make it a little larger. He also plowed a little over two acres for us in the lot, plowed, dragged, and marked it. Leo helped him back to pay for the team work. I got my garden all planted and the things up weeks before we generally got it even plowed.

I helped to plant the things in the lot too: field corn, sweet corn, pop corn, and potatoes and beans. Everything got into the ground early, as we had no frosts. Things grew as I never had seen them grow before. Everything else, too, seemed to make up for last summer's unfortunate weather conditions. It seemed as if every wild strawberry plant was blooming. The huckleberry bushes were so laden with their blossoms they looked as if covered with snow. Later on, the blackberry bushes were the same way. Every one of our apple trees was a mass of pink and white. Gloriously beautiful to see, and what a promise for a good harvest. The butternuts and grape vines, too, bloomed as never before. I think this was the first spring I could remember when we had no frost or even a cool spell to set back the growing plants. I worked very hard, but as I now had regained perfect health and was happy, and everything looked so good, I did not mind the work. The cow had a blue and white heifer calf, which of course we kept, and we bought a little red heifer calf from Teal.

Sophie Kussmaul

Leo helped Nick Dixon a few days on the farm and brought home two tiny little red pigs. I got a setting of duck eggs and had four litters of baby chickens. Everything went on lovely excepting one thing. Leo was very unhappy, completely discouraged. He took very little interest in all these things for which I was so thankful. He got a day's work at Matt Dixon's, a day now and then to Mrs. Gleason's, and at Teals, but he hated, hated farm work, and to tell the truth, this kind of work was very hard for him as he was not strong enough to do such work. He looked for a job everywhere. At Rome, Oneida, Sherril, and Camden.

Came the eleventh of June, a lovely day, rather hot. Leo left after breakfast to work for Mrs. Gleason. I put in almost the entire day in my garden. At five o'clock there was not a weed left. Everything looked beautiful. I was warm, sweaty, and very dirty, so I took a cool sponge bath, combed my hair, put on a clean, cheap dress and clean slippers. I wanted to look good for Leo's return.

I just started supper when a nice, shiny coupe car drove into the yard. A man about fifty years old, with a rather red face and dressed in a spotless clean business suit, got out of the car. I stepped to the open door and said, "I do not want to buy anything." The man smiled and said, "I am not selling anything." Still, I thought if he is not peddling, he must be some agent. Again I said, "We do not want a thing. We have no money." I thought that would send him away. Well he only smiled again and said, "Does Mr. Chesbro live here?" I said, "Yes, but he is not at home now." The man told me that his name was Teelan, that he owned and operated a repair automobile shop in Camden, also a garage, and said Leo had been there a number of times looking for a job. I had heard Leo tell me about this, but at those times he did not need any more help. But now he needed a man at once. If Mr. Chesbro could leave his other work, he would like to have him start work next morning at eight o'clock. He added, "I can only pay him $18 a week to start on, and if he makes good, I will raise his pay." My heart began to pound furiously.

During the busiest part of the summer, Leo had never gotten over $10 a week from Montross, and most of the time he worked there not over $8 a week. On the farms, $1.25 a day. Why this would be riches. Then Teelan said, "I suppose he has a car?" I said no, and Mr. Teelan whistled, and I thought everything was all over. Then he said, "I guess I can fix him up with an old car to drive back and forth till he can buy

431

one." Again he asked me, "I suppose he has his own tools to work with?" I told him that Leo had none. Another long whistle, then he said, "I think we got all the necessary tools at the shop. Tell him to be there tomorrow morning ready to start work at eight o'clock."

I said, "How can he get there? He would have to walk and it is eight miles." Mr. Teelan said he would send his nephew after him in his coupe car. He would be at our place the next morning at half past seven. Then he left.

I was terribly excited at the good news. I hurried around to prepare our supper and kept looking down the road to see if Leo was coming. Supper was ready and Leo came in. I might say, dragged himself in. He was dirty, tired, deathly pale, and lifeless. He dropped down in the big rocking chair and sat there with his eyes half closed. I went to him, sat down on the arm of his chair, and said, "Leo, what do you intend to do tomorrow?" He answered, in a tired, lifeless voice, "Oh, I will go back to Mrs. Gleason's and help George draw manure. All I will ever be fit for will be to shovel manure for the neighbors." I said to him, "I think you will go to Camden tomorrow." Leo answered in that same tired tone, "What should I go to Camden for?" I said to start working for Mr. Teelan. Leo grunted, saying, "He doesn't want me. I was there two or three times looking for a job, and he told me he could not use me." Then I said, "But now he does want you. He wants you to start working tomorrow morning at eight o'clock at $18 a week." Leo just stared at me then said, "You are just kidding me." Then I told him how Teelan had come, what he had said, and how he was going to send a car after him the next morning. Leo jumped up, walked briskly about the room, washed himself, combed his hair, and looked young and rested.

After supper, I went out to do my chores and for the first and only time, Leo followed me around, step by step, talking and asking me over and over again to tell him just what Mr. Teelan had said.

I always had had a lot of trouble to get him up in the morning, but the next morning he jumped out of bed the moment I got up. He kept saying, "Maybe he won't send for me." Well after breakfast I got his lunch ready to take, then at exactly half past seven the shiny little coupe car drove in, a young man driving. Leo was gone.

I did my chores then hoed potatoes. At fifteen minutes to six, Leo drove up in an old Oldsmobile coupe car. He was covered with grease and oil, but looked happy. He called to me, "Jump in and we will go to North Bay and get something for supper." I said I had supper all ready and he laughed and said, "We got to have something extra tonight." I hopped in, and although the little old car looked dilapidated, creaked and groaned and sputtered, and was smelly, I do not think I ever enjoyed a ride so much in my life before. I had ridden with Leo before, twice, in Kate Kinney's trim little Ford coupe. A few times in Orville's Chevrolet car. Once Leo had borrowed Clyde Mathew's Ford sedan and we had gone to Morrisville, and a few times Leo and I went to Oneida in Clayton Montross's Hudson. But this was different.

After supper, I hurried through my chores and then we went to Mrs. Gleason's to tell her why Leo had not come that day and would not be able to come and work for her any more. Mrs. Gleason, the good woman she always was, seemed glad for our good fortune. She said they would manage somehow to get their work done. But not so George Ellis. Oh, no. he thought Leo was making a great mistake. He said he could have given Leo quite a few days work during the summer. Then, too, he highly disapproved of the little car. He thought a horse would have been so much better.

The next night was Saturday night and we went to Oneida. First we bought a lot of good groceries, and then Leo took me to the theatre. This was the first time we had ever gone to a show together, though we had, by now, lived between seven and eight years together. The show happened to be an extra good one too. The picture was *The Life of Robert Burns*. Naturally the scenes were all laid in Old Scotland. The coloring was exquisite. After the show we went to Mike Pansica's place and had a real spaghetti supper and a lot of beer. It was after one o'clock when we got home.

The next day, Sunday, we went to Morrisville to Vera's, Leo's sister. So the golden summer went by, far the happiest I had ever had. Each Saturday night we went to Oneida, got a week's supply of groceries, and then had either a fish supper with beer or a spaghetti supper with beer. About every two Saturday nights, we went to the Theatre. Every Sunday, either to Morrisville or Fulton, and a few times to Oswego. I should say here that Leo only drove the little old smelly Oldsmobile car a few days, then bought a blue sedan Essex from Teelan, with which we had a queer experience. We had it less than a month when one Saturday night, coming home from Oneida at about one o'clock, we had almost reached the South Bay corner when the car gave a few jumps and then seemed to shiver and made for the ditch. Leo turned off the motor, and there we were. He examined the car and said the steering gear had gone to heck.

We had about eight dollars worth of groceries in the car and were wondering just what to do, when to our great surprise and joy a car came along and stopped, and it happened to be Mr. Teelan. He told us that he hardly ever went to Oneida and had not been there at night for over ten years. Well, he towed us home, and Monday morning sent a tow car for Leo, took this Essex back, and Leo traded it in for the dearest little black Essex coupe. Of all the cars we had later on, I always liked this one the best. But in late November, when the weather got cold, it just would not start. Leo then got a convertible coupe, a sturdy Studebaker. I never liked this car so much but it seemed to stand anything.

I must go back to where I left off. That Sunday we did not go out of course. I had known Mr. and Mrs. Drake and Mr. Wallace Moore for about twenty-five years. We never had been intimate friends, but just acquaintances. To my great surprise when my dear sweet mother died, Mrs. Drake, who had hardly known her, made and sent us a beautiful cross made out of daisies. From the time my mother had died, they came up once in a while. Mr. Moore, who lived with them, had an old car, and so the three of them came up once in a while. This Mr. Moore was the man that Leo had hired to take me to that play in McConnelsville. Long years before that, when I actually had to go somewhere, he always took me and would never take any pay.

He bought cider apples, old scraps of iron, cabbages, squash, and a lot of other things from me, and poor as he was, he always paid me a little more than the things were worth. After Leo's mother died, they came up often to spend the evening. If they happened to have something good to eat, they would always bring it in to share it with us. Twice Mr. Moore came after us and took Leo and me to Oneida. This was after Leo's mother had died. He would not take a cent pay for gas and oil. Both times, took us to Drakes on our way back, where those dear people had dinner ready for us. We knew, although they never guessed it, that it was all the food they had in their house.

Mr. Moore drove and owned a car ever since he was twelve years old. Cars of all kinds. Drove hundreds of thousands of miles and never had an accident. But it so happened that the very day Leo got his first car, or rather the use of one, Mr. Moore came through Sylvan

Sophie Kussmaul

Beach with Mr. and Mrs. Drake. A dog ran across the road in front of him. The owners of the dog were rich people from Utica, Mr. Moore and the Drakes extremely poor. The long and short of the story was that the Utica people had Mr. Moore arrested for reckless driving and also claimed that he had deliberately run into their dog. The two Drakes and Wallace Moore swore that the dog got across the road without being even touched by the car. But Moore's drivers license was taken away from him. He was told that he could easily get it back by taking a new test, but he would have to have a better car to take that test. Up to the time he died, he never gave up the hope that someday he would again have a car of his own.

Now it might seem that this had nothing to do with the story of my life, but it certainly made a vast difference to me. Now that there was no longer a car at Drakes and we had one, on our countless Saturday night trips to Oneida we would stop for them. When we had the coupe car, Bert Drake and Wallace Moore would ride in the rumble seat, Maud Drake with us. Somehow during the week, poor old Wallace would scratch enough money together to buy the gas. Yes, and always a few gallons over. Then he would buy part of the beer, Bert Drake the other part.

When we had a regular supper with the beer, they would insist on paying most of it. They all had grown up near Fulton and Oswego, so once in a while on Sunday we would all go to one of these places. Wallace always bought the gas and oil and filled up the tank when we got back to North Bay. Of course we always found a good diner at those places. We also went to Baldinsville to see Mrs. Drake's old father. As if this was not enough, poor old Wallace would come up and work for us all day besides and under no condition accept a penny. I truly think that this was without any exception the happiest summer I ever had. I was in perfect health and did more than twice as much work that summer as ever before. Everything at home turned out wonderful. The calves and pigs were rapidly growing. My pullets started laying in October, the few little ducks, too, grew up fast. We had plenty of milk and cream, and I kept making good fresh butter every few days.

My garden and field crops were marvelous. I canned a dozen cans of peas, a dozen cans of string beans, fifty cans of tomatoes. We had all the fresh vegetables we could eat. I made a lot of sauerkraut. Pickles of all kinds. I put dozens of heads of cabbage in the cellar,

435

bushels of turnips and carrots. I dried a lot of sweet corn. We had over two bushels of hard popcorn. I had dozens of large Hubbard winter squash. There were onions, beets, and cauliflower. A bushel of dry, white beans and fifty bushels of potatoes. On one of our Fulton trips, we bought a bushel crate of large red cherries and strawberries, and in the fall a bushel of pears, two bushels of peaches, and a peck of plums. I canned them all up. Also made a lot of applesauce and jellies of all kinds.

Everything was very early, so I found a few nice large strawberries near by on the fourteenth of June. I remembered that there used to be some in the old Yager lot back of our woods. So I went there, and at first I thought I must be dreaming. The ground was red with them. I had a ten quart pail, of course thinking I might get a couple of quarts. But in a short time I had it heaped high with the wonderful berries. I picked them in the cluster so when I got home, under my shady trees, they were easy to hull, not sticky or messy. After that for just two weeks, excepting Sundays, I went out there every day and brought home my ten quart pail heaped up. In the cluster they laid lightly, and each night there was a delicious wild strawberry shortcake for supper. We would eat half of it for supper, then just before going to bed another chunk, and what was left, I would have for my lunch the next day. I also had enough berries left each day to make a pint can of strawberry jam.

We never had had many wild red raspberries around here, but I had discovered a lot of bushes near and around the old Yager house and where the barn used to be. By making numerous trips out there, and as no one else picked there, I got enough to make ten quart cans of delicious red raspberry preserves. The huckleberries, every single bush, both low and high, were loaded down. I sold over two hundred quarts. Canned up twenty-five quart cans. Of course we had plenty of huckleberry pies too. Blackberries always had been very scarce around here. I knew where there were a. few on Jim Dixon's and on the old Kit Dixon place, but this year I found a small patch of them just at the head of my lane, over on Congden's. I do not think Charles Congdon ever knew about them. They were away from his huckleberries and must have covered less than an eighth of an acre of ground.

But there they hung in dense masses. The big, long, thimble berries, sweet and luscious. I picked enough to fill twenty-five quart cans. We had a blackberry pie every night for two weeks and I made five gallons of blackberry wine, the first I had ever made. We had more grapes than we ever had before, and every apple tree was so loaded down with apples that I had to prop up the limbs so they would not break. I picked eighteen bushels of choice winter apples. Leo kept bringing home barrels and boxes from Camden. I put a table in the cellar and put up some shelves and filled them with my canned goods, from maple syrup to the fall canned fruit. There were so many barrels and boxes full of potatoes, apples, and all kinds of winter vegetables there was scarcely room to move about.

Mr. Moore gave us a fifty gallon barrel and a ten gallon keg. I picked up and bagged enough apples to fill those barrels with cider. I would get about fifteen bushels ready in daytime, and at night we would take them down to Drakes, where Wallace had his cider mill. Of course Wallace took no pay for making the cider. Still there were so many apples that each day I picked up a few pails of the sweet ones for the pigs to eat. When we had the first real frost in October, I took a bag and large pail and went to the old Yager place, back of our woods, to where their buildings used to be and gathered and carried home between six and seven bushels of butternuts. I had to make six trips that day, each trip home with a little over a bushel of butternuts. It was a clear, cool day and I felt that if I did not bring them all home that day, maybe someone else might find them.

I do admit that I was good and tired when I had carried home my last load of nuts, but it was a happy tired. I spread them all out in the sunshine to dry, turning them all over a few times each day, and when they were thoroughly dry I put them into boxes in my little woodshed. There was just one thing that took some of the joy out of all my marvelously abundant harvest, and that was that the last summer had been an entire failure. We had nothing and this summer there would have been everything for the children. That hurt me a little.

This wonderful summer and early fall faded .away. November brought colder weather and occasional snow. This year Leo could not spend time to cut wood, so he put a coal crate into our large cook stove and bought a small secondhand heating coal stove, which we set up in our bedroom. He bought the coal in one hundred pound bags in Camden and so it cost us nothing to have the coal delivered. Oh what comfort it was to get up in the morning and dress in a warm bedroom, put on warm clothes, then step into a warm kitchen, just shake down the old coals, open up the drafts, and in a few minutes have a hot fire. Some different from getting up in a cold room, putting on cold clothes, going into a cold kitchen, and starting a slow wood fire. It took about an hour each morning to warm up the kitchen.

So time went happily by. I got Leo off each morning in time to get to work at eight or just a little before eight o'clock. About the middle of November, on a cold, frosty day, Bert Drake and Wallace Moore came up and butchered one of our pigs.

Now on the twentieth of November, I will leave this story for a while and go back to relate a few things I did not mention before. In winter, a family by the name of Tifft moved into the old Wilson place. We got acquainted with them through Mrs. Gleason and Mr. and Mrs. Teal, with whom at that time we were quite intimate. This family consisted of Mr. and Mrs. Tifft and two little daughters aged eight and ten years. Two of the best behaved children I ever saw. But there was one more being kept there. They had taken him out of the County House to give him a home. He was very tall and would have had broad shoulders if he had had any flesh on his bones. As it was, there was just a frame on which some old ragged clothes hung. He had a large, bald head, hollow eyes, hollow cheeks, no teeth, and his lower jaw seemed very loose. His skin was quite yellow and he walked with a slinking limp.

I eyed him carefully, fearing he would collapse and fall to pieces. As there were only two bedrooms, one for Mr. and Mrs. Tifft and the other one for the girls, the phantom, as I called him, was allowed to lay down on the floor near the big chunk stove with the three cats. Well, that saved him the time to dress and undress. So in the morning all the master of the place had to do was to stick his head out of the bedroom and give orders. The bony creature would arise, build the kitchen fire, and go and feed the horses. Mrs. Tifft got breakfast and Mr. Tifft helped to dress his children.

The phantom was ordered to saw and split wood. After the Tifft family and their three cats were through with their breakfasts, the phantom was called in to eat. Then Mr. Tifft took him out into the woods to cut wood. After they had felled a good sized tree, together, Mr. Tifft would sit down and start whittling little wooden dolls and the tall lanky one would saw off block after block of wood. So the winter passed by. When spring came, Mr. Tifft took his car and went to North Bay, engaging himself to plow people's gardens. So he would send down the phantom to plow them, and he would drive down in the car and see to it that the work was done right. Was on hand to receive the pay. Everything went on beautiful till one morning they found that the "ungrateful one" had left and returned to the poor house. But as neighbors, the Tiffts were number one. Friendly, accommodating, agreeable people.

Now I want to tell of one little incident that I experienced that summer. It was in the forepart of July, and for once I do not remember the exact days. After our supper, Rose McCormack and her sister Gertrude Corcoran called to tell us that one of their relatives whom Leo and I both had known, but who had not been any particular friend of ours, had died and was going to be buried the next day, and they thought they would let us know as perhaps we might, want to attend the funeral. Leo told them that he could not very well leave off work, but I said that I would come.

The next day after I had my chores all done, I got ready and started over to the little church cross lots. It was a good many years since I had walked across this wild, quiet stretch of field and pasture land. In years gone by, I had sometimes, in spring and summer, walked with my dear mother over these lonely stretches to attend Sunday morning Mass at the little church. Yes, that must be about fifty years ago. Why, I thought, it only seemed such a short time ago.   When I was seated in the church, I missed the old people of those days. There used to be so many snowy haired, bowed old heads on bent shoulders and with wrinkled faces sitting on the pews with their hardened, folded hands. But those pews were not empty. Other aged people occupied them now. Why, yes, these old people were the youngsters of that other time. Still, though all this deeply impressed me, I did not quite sense the advantage of time until I was standing near the open grave. While the Priest was saying the last prayer, and the casket was slowly being lowered, I glanced about me, and there, all around me, I saw young familiar faces. At first glance I thought I was looking again into the youthful faces of the boys and girls of my own young days, but at the second glance, I saw my error. These were the grandsons and granddaughters of my friends of fifty odd years gone by.

As the crowd about me jostled me, and someone's shoulder would brush against mine, for a fleeting second I thought my father or mother were near me, for the three of us had all stood together on that very spot of ground many a time when one of the older members of

439

the Corcoran family were being laid to rest. I glanced above at the deep, clear blue sky. The golden sunshine warming the earth. My glance wandered southward. Yes, there far below in the distance lay the Oneida Lake. The sky above and the lake below had not changed. Neither had the pine grove on Scullian's pasture, nor the light green of the lowlands on the other side, nor yet the Madison hills beyond. Only the people.

Well, it was all over and folks were scattering, going home. I felt as if I was in a dream. I left the cemetery and was just going across the road to return home the way I had come when Mrs. Gleason called to me. She and George Ellis brought me home in their old buggy.

When I reached home, the spell was broken. My cat met me with a purring caress, the pigs were squealing lustily, demanding their dinner, the cow was softly mooing a welcome, the calves wanted a drink, and the chickens and ducklings clustered around me. Yes, this was real, the other only an act out of time.

Now there is another thing I must not forget to mention, as it proved to be of great importance to us later on. From the very first, when Leo started his work at Camden, he kept telling me how good Mr. Teelan was, how on different occasions when Leo had finished a repair on a car in the forenoon and there had been nothing else brought in the rest of the day, Mr. Teelan would just smile and say, "Take it easy." Tomorrow morning another car will be brought in. While all through the years Leo had worked for Clayton Montross and been idle for one hour, Clayton would deduct that out of his pay.

Every once in a while Leo would bring back his lunch, saying that Uncle Henry took him to the restaurant and treated him to a full dinner. Each Saturday night he told Leo to fill up his gas tank free of charge. During the week, he gave Leo two gallons of gas a day to drive back and forth with. Of course it did not take that much. I could mention a dozen other little things, too, such as telling Leo to take and bring home all the kindling wood he wanted. But there was one thing there that Leo did not like. It was Mr. Teelan's nephew. Also from the very first, Leo kept telling me that the young upstart tried to boss him. This nephew was a great favorite of Teelan's. Teelan's only sister had begged her brother, on her dying bed, to raise and educate her baby. The boy was less than a year old. Mr. and Mrs. Teelan brought him up as if he was their own, and after a college education Mr. Teelan took him into partnership. This was about a year before he hired Leo. Teelan himself was away a good share of the time and this nephew stayed at the office and salesroom. These were upstairs, the repair shop downstairs in a large basement. So sometimes when Leo was working on a Ford, this young man would come down and tell Leo to stop working on the Ford and get a Chevrolet fixed, or perhaps the other way around.

Leo greatly resented these orders and would tell me that he always did just the opposite from what this nephew told him to do. Yes, he went much further. He would, in dozens of little ways, aggravate and even insult him. I tried to reason with Leo, told him over and over again to control himself, to remember that after all, this nephew was much nearer to Mr. Teelan than, he, Leo, was. Also, as he was Mr. Teelan's partner, he would naturally in his uncle's absence have the right to give orders. I kept telling Leo how hard he had tried to obtain a job, and if he lost this one, we would again be where we were before he went to Teelan's. I reminded him that never before in his life had he made so much money, how he, himself, kept telling me how kind Mr. Teelan always was, the best boss he ever had. But what I said made no difference. Leo would just say he was not going to take any orders from that young snot. So I said no more, but each month Leo carried his insults a little further. On the first of September, he got a two dollar a week raise. He now got twenty dollars a week.

On the twenty-fourth of September, just a year to the day our old lady had died, she appeared to me. Yes, not only once but continuously all that day. In the entire year, I had never seen her, and neither did I ever again in all these years since. The weather, too, was exactly like that of the year before. When I was outdoors and came back towards the cabin, I could plainly see her sitting in her large rocking chair, under the shade tree, where she used to sit so often in summer.

Yes, even when I got close up to where I saw her, the vision remained. This was daytime, in the bright sunshine. While I was busy in the kitchen of my cabin, at least a dozen times that day I saw her coming from her bedroom with that heavy, lumbering gait of hers, remain with me a few moments, and then walk back to her room. I even could hear her when she threw herself heavily on her bed. Now all this did not in the least frighten me, neither did I feel surprised. It all just seemed to me as if a live person was there to spend a few hours with me.

Chapter 42

So the golden days of autumn went by, and now I will resume the story where I left off on the twentieth of November. It was a clear, cold day, about a foot of snow on the ground. The sun was shining brightly, but it threw out little heat. It was Sunday and we were eating our twelve o'clock dinner. We were not going on a long trip today, but had intended to go to back of Taberg, to a Mr. Phelps, after a radio in the afternoon. A car drove into the yard and Roland O'Dell came into the house.

Now I must give a very brief description of him and his mother. His mother's name was Mrs. Bertram, as she remarried after Roland's father died. They came from Virginia about two years before. Stayed in Cleveland for some time. Then Mrs. Bertram hired out as a housekeeper for Florence Mulholand, the singer. Her son Roland worked in Sherril, in the silver department, and boarded at Florence Mulholand's. As Leo and I called at Mulholand's, we were introduced to them. Roland had a guitar and really played well. He also had a good voice, and I loved to hear him play and sing. He came over to our place twice, and Leo and he played together. Then a short time before Leo went to work in Camden, they bought the George White farm, just beyond the old Shwartz place.

Now Mrs. Bertram had never been to our place and as we had not seen either one of them for over half a year, and really never had been friends, we were somewhat astonished when after a few moments young Roland said that his mother had sent him down to invite us for Thanksgiving dinner. He must have seen that we both were surprised, so he hastily added that she would have come herself to invite us, but had a headache and so sent him as she feared, if she waited with her invitation, we might accept someone else's invitation and that would be a terrible disappointment to her. At the door, he turned around once more and asked us to be sure to come. I asked him if there were a lot of people invited besides us. He assured me there was no one else invited besides us, except George White, the former owner of the place.

After he went, Leo and I thought it was very strange that of all the people we knew, this woman who was really a stranger to us should send such an urgent invitation to what had always been, to my way of thinking, more of a family dinner. We had never even called on her, and she had never been to our house either. What made it seem all the stranger was the fact that with the one exception, the time Leo's mother had invited me for Thanksgiving dinner eight years before, I had never received a Thanksgiving dinner invitation. I knew that for at least the last nine years, neither had Leo. Of course during the five years we had the old lady with us, it would not have been possible to leave her alone

Well, next day, Monday, in the forenoon, George Ellis drove into the yard with Mrs. Gleason's old horse and said Mrs. Gleason had sent him to invite us for Thanksgiving dinner. Of course I told him why we could not accept. That same afternoon, Mr. and Mrs. Teal drove in with their old rattling Ford. They, too, brought us a Thanksgiving dinner invitation.

That night at supper while I was telling Leo about Mrs. Gleason's and Mr. and Mrs. Teal's invitations, another car drove in, Mr. and Mrs. Tifft and their two little girls. They, too, invited us for Thanksgiving dinner. Tuesday morning a letter came from Morrisville. Leo's sister invited us out there for Thursday dinner. In the afternoon, Wallace Moore walked up, said that Mr. and Mrs. Drake wanted us to be sure and come down there for dinner. Next day, the day before Thanksgiving, Patsy Loftus drove in with his shiny coupe car and very formally invited Leo and me for next day's dinner. How strange. Seven invitations this year and I might say, never any before.

Now I had felt from the very first that Mrs. Bertram must have some reason for inviting us. Well, the next day was lovely for the time of year. The weather had warmed up the last few days. The ground was nearly bare again and the sun was shining warm and bright. We got to Mrs. Bertram's house a little before twelve o'clock.

Sophie Kussmaul

The dinner was to be served at one. Well there was no one else there excepting Mr. White. I really must mention the things we had to eat. Just to say we had a grand dinner would not half convey the meaning of that feast. Still it would be impossible to put into words how delicious every single thing had been cooked and served. We well knew that these people were poor. All their earnings had gone to make a first payment on their farm. Then after moving on it, Mrs. Bertram's earnings had stopped. Most of Roland's pay each month went to make regular payments on their farm.

So to my amazement, this is what we had for dinner. First a small dish of raw oysters, with lemon juice on them, and crackers. Then there was a perfectly roasted turkey with stuffing, slices of cold roast ham, and a large spare rib with thick, well done meat on it, and dressing, mashed white potatoes, baked sweet potatoes, mashed turnips, tender baked cauliflower with hot butter sauce on it, mixed pickles, sweet green tomatoes, pickled, tiny green spiced cucumber pickles, gravy, cranberry jelly, currant jelly, celery, olives, and grated horseradish, tiny, hot, light white biscuits with good fresh butter, hot Boston brown bread with honey, apple pie, pumpkin pie, custard pie, two kinds of cheese, a rich fruit cake, tea, coffee, and lemonade. The dinner lasted an hour. The rest of the people jabbered, but I ate in silence. When I saw how the big table was loaded and a small serving table also, I went about the business of eating with a system. I ate slowly, but steadily, all through that happy hour. I could hardly move when at last I left the table. I sank down into a cushioned chair and stayed there for hours.

At five o'clock, Leo said it was time for us to go home. Mrs. Bertram jumped up and said to wait a few minutes. She went into the kitchen and brought an enormous white layer cake, with whipped cream filling and frosting, and a large dish of delicious homemade ice cream. Oh, it was good. That night we ate no supper at home.

So the next few weeks went by, Leo never late to get to Camden. For two or three times a week, we would run down to Drakes for a little visit after supper. Then came the twenty-first of December and my sixty-third birthday. I really felt much younger, and far, far happier than I did on my twenty-third birthday. Life was a beautiful thing, and I in my happiness was enjoying it to the fullest extent.

Now I want to speak about Christmas Day. This was a day I shall never forget, one of those rare days that will linger in my memory forever. Ever since the days had grown short, I had been getting up by lamplight about six o'clock so as to be able to cook a good breakfast and give us time to eat it together leisurely and still enable Leo to start at half past seven, and when the roads were not so good, a little earlier. But this morning, Christmas morning, I was wide awake at five o'clock. Our rooms were warm and cozy, but the windows were covered with thick ice and white frost. I stirred up the fires and went outdoors. The air was clear and cold. The sky a dark blue, with a million stars shining and twinkling above. In the east was the largest of all the stars, the Bethlehem Star. A feeling of holiness, of utter peace seemed in the air. I walked down to the graves and sent up a little prayer. It seemed almost as if my father and mother were with me, and also my child though I knew she was nearly four thousand miles away.

I felt happy, yet a sharp pain pierced my heart at the thought of those other Christmas mornings when she, my child, and I were all the world to one another, and now a continent divided us. I went to the barn and felt my way in, as I never carried a lantern into it for fear of fire. The cow mooed a low, soft welcome, and I gave her an extra big feeding of hay, first because it was Christmas, secondly because I knew I would be away all day. I did not milk her now. I only milked once a day, at night. I went back into the cabin and mixed up a big pail of warm pig feed and took that out to the one remaining pig in the pen. He got up grunting and started eating in the dark. I carried a large pan of corn out to the little hen house. They were all snug on the roost, but I knew that as soon as daylight came, they, too, would find a bountiful meal.

Then I started our breakfast, changing into my best clothes at the same time. I got Leo up and we ate and right after, left for Morrisville. The darkness of night was now melting into the light of day. It was dawning. All the stars had vanished, all but the faint light of the Bethlehem Star. That was still visible. As we drove through North Bay most of the houses were still in utter darkness, but a few were lit up. As we reached the top of the little hill of the Y, a rosy streak shone in the eastern sky. Soon the golden sun would be shining on the ice covered, the snow covered country.

Well, I will not stop to describe our day at Morrisville. It was a happy day. At night, I again did my chores by the light of the stars. So Christmas was over with again.

Sophie Kussmaul

We ate New Year's Day dinner at Drakes. I roasted the meat, made a pumpkin pie the day before, which we took down. I also took some milk and butter and pickles along. So those busy happy days went by too swiftly. Came the tenth of January, a clear, rather frosty morning. As every day, Leo had gone to work. I had just finished my morning outdoor chores and got back in the cabin when Mr. Moore came. We always called him Uncle Wally. He seemed to like to be our uncle. He told me that the people in the Campbell house, for once I forgot their names, wanted to buy a bushel of carrots and if possible wanted them at once. They had no car, but I told Wallace we would bring them down that night.

I took him into the cellar and we picked out a bushel basket of the nicest ones, which he carried upstairs for me. While we were in the cellar, I showed him all my canned things. There were over two hundred cans of it, my barrels and barrels of lovely apples, and all my other winter vegetables. Wallace looked at all this and said, "Sophie, you would have plenty for a family of six people."

That night at supper, Clyde Mathews walked in to invite Leo and I to come down and play cards. We said we would, but would first have to deliver the carrots. We were just putting on our coats when we had another caller. It was Bob Dunham, Roscoe Armstrong's grandson, who lived with his grandfather. He came in out of breath and very much excited. Said his old car got into a ditch, and he had worked two hours to get it out, but could not budge it. The car was stuck right near his grandfather's place, over two miles from our place. Leo asked him why he did not get Roland O'Dell to pull him out, but he said Roland O'Dell was now working on the nightshift in Sherril and he, Bob, was to be in Rome tomorrow. He was to be there at eight o'clock at the Brass and Copper Mill. So Clyde, Bob, and Leo and I first went up to the Armstrong place and pulled out Bob's car. Came back to our place, put on some more coal on both fires, and as we three left, I glanced at the clock. It was exactly fifteen minutes after nine o'clock. Our big gray and white cat was, as usual curled up in a large cushioned rocking chair in front of the cook stove. We took the carrots down to the Campbell's house. Then, instead of coming home, we drove to Clyde's house. We had scarcely got our coats off when Blanche Mathews came in from the other part of the house and said these very words: "I hate to frighten you people, but there is a big fire over your way. I jumped up like lightning and rushed to the window, and oh, horrors! The big red flames were shooting skyward, and I was sure they came from either my cabin or barn. All this took only a few seconds before I, Leo, and Clyde, with our coats half on, were rushing out and into our Studebaker.

I had glanced at the clock in rushing out. It was just twenty minutes to ten. Why that meant that it was five minutes less than half an hour since we left home. At that time, everything seemed so safe, both coal stoves shut up tight. Well, I do not think we were over a minute going home. The car just seemed to fly along. When we got as far as Reamore's, we all thought it must be our barn, but a few moments later, when we got to the Cleveland place, we knew it was the cabin. Although it was still less than half an hour since we had left, there was now nothing left of our little home. Just the outside walls were standing, and they were just falling in, as we got there. There were about twenty people there and six or eight automobiles parked at the roadside. Yes, even the little fire engine from North Bay was there, but that, too, had arrived too late.

Soon most of the people left. They had a house, a home, to go to. A few of them remained a little longer and said they were sorry for us. Wanted to know how it happened, asked carefully if we were insured. But after a little while, Leo, Clyde, and I were alone. We waited there, in the cutting cold northwest wind, to make sure that no flying sparks would be carried to the barn. There really was but little danger, as now the whole burning mass was in the cellar, and only an occasional cinder or spark came flying up. Besides, where the wind now was, the sparks would be carried in the opposite direction of the barn. Still, the wind might shift and blow harder in that way, fan the burning embers into more activity. There was no danger of the fire running on the ground as there was between one and two feet of snow everywhere.

Well, I stood there, gazing at what just a short time before had been my happy home, and a multitude of thoughts surged through my mind. I thought of the well stocked up cellar, my whole spring, summer, and autumn toil and pride now all destroyed. Of the beautiful parlor glass, those hard earned butternuts and a few hundred pounds of pig and chicken feed. Of all the good groceries that we had been getting ahead and stored in large boxes in the bedroom. I thought of our good bedding, soft feather beds, downy pillows. Of our clothes, dishes, silverware, and furniture. Musical instruments. Yes, and a lot of other things. But what hurt the most was to think that the oil paintings and other framed family portraits that my child had rescued out of our burning home, that they, with our photograph albums and a few other family heirlooms, were gone, too. They never could be replaced. Then there was that terrible fear in my heart about our cat. Did he, could he, have gotten out of that inferno.

That other time, when the barn burned with all our dear animals, next day, towards night, Twilight came to us, though he had never been to our new home. So I thought maybe this cat, too, got out somehow, would stay hid now, but in the morning would be at the barn. Still, I knew there was only one chance of that in a hundred. So tearless, but with a heart filled with sorrow, I stood there. Leo and Clyde were talking. When there was absolutely no more flying sparks or embers, Clyde told us to come home with them. It was after eleven o'clock now. Of course there were no cards played. At two o'clock they prepared a supper. I forgot what it was, only there was very little food, and that was badly cooked.

They told us they did not have an extra bed, but gave us a blanket and the use of their big couch in the living room. There was a big chunk stove there and at least we were in a warm room. Of course neither Leo nor I closed our eyes. Now the Mathews family always had been, and still were, late in the morning, but it so happened that both Clyde and Pearl were to appear the next morning in Utica at Court at nine o'clock and as they, at that time, only had a broken down old Ford car, they had to leave home about seven o'clock. So a little after five, the household was up and stirring about. We had been up all night. After a poor and very scant breakfast, we left for home. The sun was not up. Now in the hours of the night, Leo and I had talked things over. There was no house in the neighborhood that we could rent. Leo said the only thing to do was to sell the cow and hens and rent a few rooms in Camden, where his work was, until spring. Then buy another cow, a few hens, and build a small house or cabin.

I did not like this idea at all. I knew that if we sold the cow and hens now, in a hurry, we would get next to nothing for them, while when spring came we would have to pay twice as much for a cow than she would be worth. Besides, I felt that if we once left my little farm, Leo would never want to come back to it. Still, as things were, I saw no other way out. It was in the heart of winter, and we had to have shelter. Leo would have to keep on with Teelan's job. When we got home, I fed the cow. The hens and pig were demanding their breakfast, too, but as their feed had been in the woodshed, that, too, was destroyed. I had always made a practice of taking my handbag with me wherever I went, but last night for once I forgot to take it. So what little money I had in it, together with my reading glasses and a few other trinkets, was also gone. But I had the dollar I took in last night for the carrots. So I told Leo I would buy a dollars worth of corn for the hens and pig till we could sell them.

We went to Camden and Leo told Mr. Teelan why he could not work for him that day. Then we started out to hunt a place to stay. We inquired everywhere, in stores, at the feed mill, in offices. Leo asked a dozen men whom he slightly knew of a place where we could stay a few months. At last we found a place on Second Street. Three rooms upstairs at twelve dollars a week, and they were unfurnished. We got back into our car. I told Leo my plan. It was to try and fix up the little cow stable back of my barn. We still had an old cook stove out under the trees, on which I used to cook when the weather was real hot. I said that even if it would cost a few dollars, it would come to less than one week's rent. As we had plenty of hay, we could then keep the cow and calf. I told him that if we could fix it up warm enough for him to sleep there, he would be at Camden in a warm shop all day. I would much rather be cold all day, and be home, than be even in a warm, comfortable place in the village. Besides, if we took that place on Second Street, we would have to buy some furniture at once.

For once Leo agreed with me. Then, being twelve o'clock, he proposed going into a restaurant. Again I made another suggestion. I said, "Let us buy a little meat, a loaf of bread, a few cookies, and go to Drakes and eat there. They will in some way help us." Well, we did so. When we got to Drakes, I laid the things on the table and said to Maude, "Here is some meat. Will you cook it for us, as we have no way to cook it?" She stared at me, then said, "What is the matter with your stove?" Then we told them what had happened the night before. Then all three, Mr. Bert Drake, Maude Drake, and Wallace, all of them, in the same breath, said, "You must stay right here with us. This is your home." We told them that would not do as we had the cow and hens at home and intended to fix up that little shack.

Maude spoke up quickly. "All right, both of these men will go right up with you and help, and tonight you come right home and stay here." I asked her for a pail, a clean cloth to strain the milk, and a couple of quart cans to put it in. The men got shovels and an axe. All our things like that had been in the woodshed. By the time we got home, it was two o'clock and fifteen below zero. We found the shack in much worse condition than we had expected it to be. The door, a rough stable door, was partly open, froze in. A few boards on the sides and a roof board was torn off, so first the rain had poured in and frozen, then the snow. It took the men some time to chop the ice and frozen snow at the door so it could be opened. Inside, we found mounds of old cow manure saturated with rain and now a frozen mass like a rock. All this, viewed in a cold north wind with the thermometer at fifteen below zero.

While Bert was trying to clear out one corner of the shack, I mean chop out some of the ice and frozen snow, I showed Leo and Wallace where the old cook stove was. It had been entirely covered with the frozen snow as, where it stood, the snow had drifted. But I saw a little of the stovepipe sticking out. Leo and Wallace dug it out, and then Bert, Wallace, and Leo carried it into the shack, stopping often, as the inside of the stove was completely filled with hard, frozen snow, and it was a long ways to the shack. Then Leo took the car and went to North Bay to get some stovepipes. The men cut a hole for the pipe and lined it with tin. I did my chores.

By the time the pipe was fitted, it was getting dark and we went back to Drakes. I could see that Maude had done her very best to prepare a good supper for us. I also could see that they had very little in the house to eat, but oh, how glad they all were to share what they had with us. There were boiled potatoes with water gravy, baker's bread without butter, tea without sugar, some canned blackberries and cucumber pickles. They gave us a little bedroom above the kitchen with the stovepipe going through. Later on, I discovered that they had taken quilts and blankets from their own beds to put on ours. They piled coats and strips of clean carpets on their own. Now these people in winter had not gotten up in the mornings until eight o'clock or after. But as Leo told them, in order to be at Camden at eight and first drive around by our home so he could bring me and the two men up to work on the shack, and the back roads being now none too good, he ought to leave there by seven.

Next morning, I heard Bert stirring about in the kitchen at five o'clock. He told us afterwards he wanted to warm up our little room so we could dress more comfortable. He called us at six. Breakfast

451

was on the table, consisting of oatmeal, baker's bread without butter, and the coffee we had taken there the day before. Also the milk I had taken down. Bert said what meat and cookies were left from what we had brought I should put into Leo's dinner pail. Of course Leo's dinner pail and thermos bottle had been destroyed. But Wallace gave Leo his, saying he would probably never use it again. Maude made us, Wallace, Bert, and myself, a few thin sandwiches out of baker's bread and jelly. She put a drawing of tea in a tea pot, so I could just pour boiling water on it.

Bert put an armful of kindling wood in the car, a bottle of kerosene to start the fires, and a wash boiler to heat water to scald the pig. Also his butchering tools. Wallace got his blowtorch, hammer and nails, saw, and axe. We left Drakes' at seven o'clock. The sun was not up yet. In fact, it looked as if it would stay hidden that day. The thermometer had dropped to twenty below zero. Of course it was impossible to start a fire in the stove as it was full of frozen snow and ice. So Wallace took his blowtorch and thawed, or rather cut, the frozen snow out of the fire pot of the stove. Bert cut down a small maple tree for firewood in the stove. Also to use for an outside fire to heat the scalding water. No one could realize the intense cold. There was no way to warm our freezing faces, hands, or feet. At last the fire slowly burned, or I should say smoldered. There seemed to come no heat from that little weak blaze in the still ice covered fire pot of the stove.

The men started a fire outside. That, too, kept going out, but at last it got going. They had to carry the water from the spring as our pump was all froze up. If the ground had been bare, they could have found old boards, sticks, something to burn. As it was, everything was now covered over with frozen snow. I helped all I could. Carried the wood as the men cut it, did the barn chores, and tried to keep the fire alive in the stove. While Wallace was waiting for the water to heat outside, he took the blowtorch and cut through the frozen manure inside the shack.

Well after a while the outside fire burned good and the water got hot. The pig was killed and scalded, but the cold was so intense the water froze on the pig, so there was a poor job done in scraping it. I had found an old tin dish in the barn and heated the water for the tea. After the pig was all dressed, about one o'clock, we had our dinner. I found three old tin cans into which we poured the tea. Then each one of us had one thin, frozen sandwich. Of course we just stood on the snow, ice covered floor around the fire. We laid our solidly frozen sandwiches on the stove, but the inside of them stayed frozen. I got Bert to cut a few pounds of the tenderloin to take to Drakes for our breakfast and to make sandwiches for us all the next day.

Leo brought sugar and butter and some other things, pancake flour, so I thought tomorrow we would have a grand breakfast. I had had about half enough to eat this morning and stayed in the horrible cold all day. The stove, as yet, threw out but little heat. We only had green wood to burn, the shack was still filled with ice and snow, and each icy blast from the north would bring in another gust of fine snow. Bert carried hay from the barn to stuff into the places where the boards were entirely gone. As I said, our dinner had consisted of one thin frozen sandwich and a little tea.

When we got to Drakes, Maude had supper ready, and I went upstairs soon after. In the morning, Bert called us at six o'clock. I must here say that Bert always cooked the breakfast. I smelled the meat cooking, a good smell. But when I got downstairs, I saw a large dish of good light pancakes and hard, scorched meat. He had fried it to a crisp, the good, juicy tenderloin. Of course I said nothing, but made up my mind that that would not happen again. So after breakfast, I asked Maude for a roaster, pepper, salt, and a big sharp knife. This morning it was thirty below zero. Maude wanted me to stay with her, said the men should go up alone. But I said the captain stays with the ship.

Now I must mention something to make the story clearer. Our cabin burned down Monday night. The next day, in the afternoon, we just got the stove set up. Wednesday we had the pig killed and West, the mailman, came to the shack. He was horrified. Thursday, while the men were starting the fire, I cut and sawed off a chunk of frozen meat. Had to use the axe as the knife could not cut it. I left the broadside on the ribs. The meat and fat were about three inches thick. Rubbed salt and pepper on it and put the frozen mass into the icy oven by eight o'clock. I knew it would take hours to thaw out before it would start to cook. The men cut down another small maple tree. I have said that our winter beans had burned up. Yes, but I had a bushel basket of beans in their pods left in the basement. I got them and while leaning over the stove, started to shell them with half frozen fingers. Every little while the men came in. Wallace would use the blowtorch to cut through the icy masses. Bert would use the pick axe and shovel. The fire burned better today, and close up to the stove, there was a little warmth.

About ten o'clock I heard the sound of sleigh runners on the frozen snow, the stamping of horse feet, and the creaking of harnesses. Voices. I opened the stable door and there was Teal's team at our very shack door. In marched Mr. and Mrs. Teal, said West had told them about our misfortune. They fetched in half a bushel of potatoes, which I laid on the back of the stove. If I had laid them near the stove, on the ice, they would have frozen solid. It was thirty below zero outside and in the open. Ice filled the shack. It probably was fifteen to twenty below zero just a few feet from the stove. Mrs. Teal, the former Mrs. Storm, also gave us a pail and some clean rags to use as towels, but oh joy, they brought us a whole cord of seasoned hardwood. They could not stay as their horses were out in the terrible cold, but they said Mr. and Mrs. Tifft and Annie Gleason were going to bring some things too.

Well, I put some of the potatoes in the oven. Now what I am going to say may not sound like an appetizing meal, but I cannot recall a dinner that ever tasted better to me. We had no plates, knives or forks or spoons. I went into the basement, found a pasteboard box, and tore off enough to make three plates. They were just ragged, uneven pieces of rough pasteboard. I cut huge chunks of the now well done roast, put one chunk on each piece of pasteboard. Put three or four baked potatoes on with the meat. Laid the bread on the back part of the stove, poured the coffee into the same tin cans we had yesterday, and so we stood there and feasted. Yes, it was good. Our hands were unwashed, but we ate with them just the same. Right after dinner, Mr. and Mrs. Tifft drove up in their car. They, too, brought potatoes, a few onions, sauerkraut, and cabbages. Later in the day, George Ellis came with Mrs. Gleason's horse and cutter. The poor old man was so nearly frozen to death he could at first not speak. I made him a little coffee. Mrs. Gleason sent us two feather pillows and a warm bed quilt. We had to put them into the basement as there was not even a box in the icy shack. Of course that night we took the roast to Drakes for our supper and breakfast and Leo's sandwiches. Also the potatoes and other vegetables or they would have frozen like rocks.

Next day was Friday, about twenty below zero. I, after getting another frozen chunk of meat in the oven, again was busy shelling beans with my numbed fingers. The men were trying to stuff up the biggest holes and banking the shack with snow. The wind was still in the north. All at once I heard a car at the door. I opened the door and in came Patzy Loftus. He was dressed like a millionaire and over his beautiful suit wore an expensive fur coat. He stepped into the little, bare, icy shack, gave one quick look around, then came to me, took me into his arms, and kissed me. Then I shed my first tears. Patzy's salute was not that of a fresh kind. It was just a brotherly way of showing his sympathy. Then he said he had brought me a few things. He went out and fetched a wooden box in, put it on the still ice covered floor, as there was neither a chair or table in the little shack. In this box were lovely dainty dishes, gold and flower trimmed plates, saucers, and cups. Vegetable dishes, milk pitchers, sauce dishes, and also some glassware. Half a dozen silver knives, forks, and spoons. When I remarked about his not giving me such expensive tableware, he said that those things were all spare articles not belonging to his sets. Then he ran out again and brought in another wooden box. This one contained six quart cans of peaches, six quart cans of pears, six quart cans of cherries, and six quart cans of strawberries. He proudly told me that he had canned them all himself. Then he made another trip to the car and carried in a huge pasteboard carton. In it were two brand new bed quilts, two downy pillows with lace edged pillow slips. Of course all this, excepting the canned things, had to be taken into the basement. Then he told me that in about half an hour a truckload of furniture and other things would be coming up, as the boys had been collecting things for us.

Just before leaving, he put a five dollar bill in my hand, saying, "Maybe you can use this." Really a short time after, a large truck drove in loaded with a good bedstead, springs, mattress, more quilts, a lovely feather bed, a small table, a small bureau, a big Morris chair, two little kitchen chairs, and a rocking chair. Three boxes of clothing, some for me, some for Leo. Yards and yards of carpeting, both old and new. A large box of dishes of all kinds. Kettles, frying pans, pans, pancake griddle, pails, dippers, and also china dishes. A lamp, broom, mop, a large box of tinned goods, meat, fish, soups, vegetables of all kinds, a sack of flour, some sugar, tea, coffee, and a lot of other things.

The driver of the truck was George Deo, but the spokesman was Will Brown. I certainly was surprised, as George Deo was practically a stranger to us, and although I had always known Will Brown, had never considered him as a friend. Then Will Brown said to me, "The boys also made up a little collection for you." He handed me twenty-six dollars and a half, which each person's name who gave. He, Will Brown, headed the list with five dollars. The rest of the men gave either one dollar or a half dollar. Then, carpenter that he was, he glanced about, saying, "You will need new floorboards. These seem eaten away. Some boards on the sides to cover up those huge cracks where the hay is, and a few more roof boards, and about three rolls of roofing paper. I will bring them right up." Then he measured the floor space and they left. Yes, about an hour later they were back, had the boards, roofing paper, hammers and nails, and two extra men.

Luckily, by now the stove had gotten all the ice thawed out and we kept it going red hot. There was a little warmth in the shack, but the ice and snow on the floor that had not all been scraped up did not melt, no, not even under the stove. Two of the men would go out and work on the roof and sides a few minutes, then come in with half frozen fingers and lean over the hot stove while the two others went out. While these four men worked in relays outside, Bert and Wallace laid the nice, clean, dry boards on the old icy ones.

The men also brought a window, for which they cut a hole on the south side, near the stove, and under which I was going to put my little table. There was one window in the shack high up. It was getting dark when they got done and left. As usual, when Leo came, around six o'clock, we all went back to Drakes for supper and to spend the night there. Saturday morning was not quite so cold, only around zero. Wallace put two large rolls of some kind of paper into the car to line our walls and ceiling with. I had never, before or after, seen paper like this. It was white, almost glistening white, and thinner than pasteboard. Wallace told us he had obtained it in a paper mill where he had once worked. It was made to make up into paper drinking cups.

Well he and Bert got busy and they lined the sides and ceiling with this lovely paper. Now the bare, rough, almost black board walls and ceiling were pure white. Then Bert built a sort of primitive cupboard while Wallace built a bench for the water pail and wash dish. I laid the warmest of the carpeting in the part where our bedroom was to be. Then on a wire hung some of the carpeting to curtain this part off from the kitchen. The men then carried in from the basement the bedstead, springs, and mattress, and also the large feather bed, and put these up. There was enough room to put the small bureau and a little rocking chair in this room. I put a nice white scarf I found amongst the clothes on the bureau and put the clock Mr. West had brought on it together with one of the lamps. It all looked lovely.

While the men were out cutting wood, it was getting dark now, I made paste and papered the cupboard with clean newspaper. I put the beautiful dishes, glass, and silver on the shelves. Put the oilcloth table cover on the new little table near the stove and under the window. Set the table for two, as Leo wanted to start staying here beginning the next day, Sunday. I forgot to mention that in the forenoon Chester Yager brought us a half a cord of hardwood and Arthur Nash brought a brand new quilt his wife had made. The mailman fetched in two huge bundles. One from the Dennis family which contained mostly clothing. The other one from Libby Shwartz, which bundle was a twenty yard brand new carpet. Just to say I was astonished would hardly describe my feelings. This woman had never been in our house, we had never called on her. In fact, we had never been introduced to one another. Besides, she was a very poor woman.

In the afternoon, Florence Mulholand drove in. She brought a lot of canned fruit and jams and jellies. Now I must say this. Leo never realized the hardships Bert, Wallace, and I went through in those last five days. In the morning he would just stop long enough so we could unload the things we brought from the Drakes. Then he rode in his heated car to Camden. In the basement where he worked, there was a giant furnace in which the fire never went out at night. On his way home to pick us up, he would either not get out of the car at all, or just step in a moment to see how much headway we had made during the day. But tonight I wanted him to see the almost magic transformation. I lit both lamps, the one in the tiny bedroom, the other one on the dainty, set, tiny table.

The weather, too, had warmed up. It was now ten above zero. Having closed up all the great holes, covered them with boards and paper, both outside and inside, the little building was fairly warm now. How surprised he would be. How glad how happy.

For over seven months now, in fact from the time Leo had started to work for Mr. Teelan, each Saturday I made out a full list of the groceries we would need through the coming week. Each time I would hand Leo the list with this remark, "Did I put down too much?" His answer was always the same, "No, you did not put down enough." So when he came home this night, he glanced about the neat, clean, lovely little home in complete silence, showing no joy or admiration whatsoever. His face was deathly pale. I said to him, "Are you sick?" He just shook his head. I handed him my grocery list. He slowly read it; then I said as always, "Did I put down too much?" He answered in a low tone, "Yes, we can only get the most necessary things. I got fired today."

This indeed was a hard blow. The men had not heard this, as they were busy putting their tools and things in the car as now they were all done here. We got into the car and on the way Bert and Wallace tried to talk to Leo. He either did not answer them at all or only in a short way. Supper was ready for us as usual. Maude, too, tried to be pleasant to Leo. We ate in silence. After supper, Leo told them that Teelan had fired him. Oh, how much those dear good poor people took it to heart.

Since the weather had gotten cold, they no longer went with us to Oneida. But we both knew the real reason. They had no money, either for food for themselves or to buy our gas, or treat us to beer or suppers. So they just said they could not stand to go out in the cold. So after Leo and I got into the car, he told me how things were. He said Teelan had not been there in the forenoon and that young nephew had come down and given him orders about the work. I told him to get the heck out of my shop and stay out, or I will kick you out. Leo said he never answered him, but went upstairs where, Leo said, he belonged. In the afternoon, Uncle Henry came back. He came to Leo's place where he worked and calmly told him that he no longer needed him. He, Leo, should hunt up another job. We did not go to the show or to our beer place, just to Drakes. Then that night sitting in their poor shabby kitchen, I saw one of the most beautiful sights I have ever seen, something I will not ever forget.

I must first of all give a brief description of the surroundings. The floor was bare, but the old, well worn boards had been scrubbed clean. The walls and ceiling were much in need of new wallpaper. In one corner of this little kitchen was the table with its clean, but shabby, oilcloth. The table on which we had eaten so many, many meals, but had been so welcome, not only to share their humble food, but always given the best and the most of it. There were three old kitchen chairs standing in a sort of semi-circle. On one of them sat Maude, next to her, Bert, and next to him, Wallace. Leo and I each sat in an old rocking chair facing those three. We were perhaps eight or ten feet from the trio.

Both men were dressed in much worn, much patched old working clothes. Maude, immaculately clean, also had on an old, faded, much mended dress. On a little shelf just above the table stood a small kerosene lamp turned rather low to consume less oil. There was silence. Leo, I knew, was in deep thought of how and where to obtain another job, a way to make a living. This was plainly written on his face. I glanced at the three people facing me. There they sat with their heads partly bowed, their thin, work hardened hands folded in the laps. Their pale, wrinkled faces showing the effect of long, semi-starvation, undernourishment.

But I also saw, in each of their faces, that hard up as they were themselves, they were now deep in thought and plans to help us. Then glancing up, I saw plainly a light, a circle of light, just above each one of their heads. A thrill passed through me. I felt as if I was in the presence of something holy, for that light was a perfect halo. Yes, it remained there over their heads. I glanced around at Leo. He did not have it, or see it. His glance was not directed towards them. After a while it vanished, and each one of the three spoke. Each one of them proposed a way to help us.

This was our last night at the Drakes. Next day, Sunday, we stayed at home. Monday morning we went to Rome. Leo again went from place to place trying to get a job, but it was the old story. I insisted on taking $17 from the money the men had collected for us to buy new license plates for the car, for I knew if we did not get them now, the money would go anyway. Leo tried Sherril, Oneida, Utica, but could not obtain any work. He tried to hire out at Lyle Richie. Richie told him that now during the winter months he could not use him, but by the middle of April he might want him.

For a few weeks, we had plenty to eat. There were the things that had been brought in, and Leo still had some money left that he had earned at Teelan's. But by the middle of March, we were all out of food again. Leo cut wood on shares for Mrs. Gleason, bringing our share home each night. Sometimes Mrs. Gleason would hire him for a few hours. That bought a little food for us.

Through Sophie's Eyes

One day while Leo was at Gleason's, Howard DeForest drove in the yard. He had been Teelan's salesman for years. He brought a sweater that Leo had left in the workshop and did not want to go back for it again. He told me how sorry he was about our fire and about Leo's losing his job. He said Uncle Henry was sorry, too. Said he never had a better mechanic. Also that Leo had been strictly honest but that it was impossible to keep him any longer as he had ordered his nephew out of the shop a number of times, had swore at him, and had continuously insulted him. Mr. DeForest told me he had repeatedly warned Leo, but it had done no good.

We had given up our pleasant Saturday night trips to Oneida, but Leo had heard that they wanted help in the casket factory at Oneida. This was about two weeks after we had been living in the little shack. Both Leo and I had gotten a terrible cold. We both coughed so hard we almost strangled to death. The day we went to Oneida was a bitter cold, raw day, a strong northeast wind blowing. Of course Leo did not get a job in the casket works, but on the way back we stopped at Oughterson's. Coming into their house out of the bitter cold into the warm heated rooms, we both started to cough. It seemed impossible to stop. We were fairly fighting, gasping for breath. Mrs. Oughterson said to me, "Where did you catch such an awful cold?" As soon as I could control myself, I gasped out, "I suppose [cough] we caught it [cough] because we [cough] moved into [cough] the pigpen." For a moment there was silence. Mr. and Mrs. Oughterson stared at me, at Leo, looked at themselves. Then Dave Oughterson spoke to me. "What did you mean, about moving into the pigpen?" I looked him straight into the face and without smiling, soberly answered, "Just what I said." Another pause, then Mrs. Oughterson said to me, "But why did you do that?" Again I kept my face sober and said, "Because we had no other place to move into."

By now Leo got over his coughing spell and told them about our fire. Then Dave yelled out, "Arthur, go down cellar and bring up a bushel of potatoes." Arthur fetched them up. Then he said, "Go into the smokehouse and get a ham." He carried in a lovely smoked ham that weighed twenty-eight pounds. Then he said to his wife, "Julia, what are you going to give them?" She went downstairs and brought up some canned peaches and a five pound jar of butter. We stayed for dinner and then came home. This was the first week in February.

460

Chapter 43

Spring came at last. Wallace Moore had been coming up to us every few days refusing to eat with us, always saying he was not hungry.But from the first of April, he came to stay with us altogether.
He got on relief, meaning he got a $4 grocery order each week. He brought the food up and cut wood, fixed fences, did a dozen jobs for us. He brought his bed roll and slept on the haymow. The fifteenth of April, Leo started to work for Lyle Richie. But from the first, things went wrong there. Lyle would deduct every half and even quarter hour Leo was not working.

Our Studebaker car had, for some time, been making queer noises and was getting harder and harder to start. Just one week after Leo had started to work for Richie; the car would not start at all. Uncle Wallace and Leo both worked at Jewell. They came after the Studebaker with the crane. Richie got Leo to trade in the Studebaker for a Peerless, with Leo to pay Richie $60 to boot. As Leo had no money, Richie agreed to take it out of Leo's wages, and so Leo never got over $6 to $7 a week, and would have to let Richie take half of it; we fared rather slim.

Mr. Teal plowed and dragged a few acres of ground for us. Wallace and I planted it to corn, potatoes, and beans, Wallace doing most of the work. He also helped me a lot in the garden, but things did not flourish the way they had the last year. The first of May, the weather became hot. I put the cow out to pasture every night, as well as days. I got Wallace to help me clean out the basement. We scrubbed and mopped it out. The next day when the floor was dry, we moved our big bed into the basement. I laid a strip of carpet in

461

front of the bed, stood a small stand at the head with a nice cloth on it, and put a couple of chairs and the big round table in the center of the basement. That table had been too big to put into the shack. We put a cot bed in the shack where our bed had been and Wallace put his bedding on that. Wallace and I moved the cook stove from the shack under the young maple trees just below the barn.

Now we had a cool place to sleep and keep our food in. Wallace could have the shack all to himself. Wallace gave me a three burner oil cook stove, which we put in the shack so when it rained, I used the oil stove, and other times the outdoor wood cook stove. Now this was all very nice, very pleasant, but it meant endless trips for me. Some of our dishes were in the basement, but most of them still in the cupboard in the shack. We also had most of our clothes in the shack and the little bureau was also full of things we daily needed. So each meal I cooked, I had to keep running all over.

The well, too, was quite a little distance from where we now lived. Uncle Wally, when he was not working in the field, always helped. We went out Saturday nights, but we could not spend so much money this summer and did not get out very often on Sundays as we had the last summer. Mr. Teal mowed for us. I raked the hay, and Teal, Wallace, and I drawed it in. Wallace worked for Teal to pay him back for what he did here. I sold some huckleberries, but they were not as plentiful as the year before, and there were no blackberries. We got along fairly well.

Uncle Wallace, besides all the work he did for us, got little jobs around North Bay, and that always meant some extra food for us and beer on Saturday nights. Came the twenty-third of August, an unusually hot day. All through the afternoon, black thunder clouds appeared in the southwest then would vanish and some more would form. Once in a while there was distant thunder. Leo came home from Richie's at the usual time. The heat was still almost unbearable. The air seemed so hot and by now the thunder was much worse, and the lightning flashes came from all over the southwest, west, and northwest, but as yet no rain had fallen.

It was just half past seven when the three of us got into the car to go to North Bay after a few groceries. We only were in the store for a few minutes, then started back home. Leo said he wanted to see Orville Holmes about something. Orville was now married and living in one part of Ira Howe's house. So we drove around that way.

As I knew Leo would not stay there long, I stayed in the car, which was parked in the front yard. I was sitting in the front seat and Wallace was in the back seat. By now the entire sky, excepting the direct east, seemed filled with electricity. Crash after crash of thunder came nearer all the time. The lightning was now continuous. Wallace and I were watching what really was a grand display of nature. I had never in the least been afraid of lightning. We might have been thus sitting there for ten minutes when glancing northward, we saw a blue ball of fire drop out of the sky and the very next moment a flame of fire shot up. I, who know all the directions so well, gave a quick start, saying as I jumped out of the car, "That is our barn." I flew to the open door, yelled, "Leo, for God's sake, come home. The barn is on fire!"

Leo got into the car, drove at record speed. We got home and the barn was all right, but the shack back of it was half gone. Attached to this was the little hen house. Most of the hens were flying out, a few of them burned up. It had not rained for a long time and the grass was all brown and dry, but almost miraculously just then the rain started pouring down in torrents. If that had not come just then, nothing could have saved the barn, and the fire would also have spread, perhaps for miles. Now I must relate two little incidences connected with that fire.

That very night, Leo had brought home five gallons of kerosene to use in the oil cook stove, and left it just outside the door of the shack. We hardly reached home when the flames found the can. There was one mighty bang and then a great shower of flaming sparks, some of which flew thirty feet in the air. The other thing that impressed itself upon my mind was that after poor Wallace once got in his head that it was the barn, that idea stayed with him. I had put the calf in the upper part of the barn before we left, as I thought we would have a heavy rain. Now, as we drove into the driveway, we saw the barn was not burning, that it was the building back of it. We, Leo and I, stood there a few moments. There was nothing we could do. I saw Wallace staggering to the barn. I followed him in. He was trying to untie the calf's rope. His hands shook and trembled so badly he made little headway. I said to him, "The barn is not burning. It's the shack," and he had plainly seen himself that it was the shack, but he kept on working. I repeated it a number of times, but he did not seem to hear me. At last he got the rope untied and led the calf out. Next day, he declared that he had neither seen nor heard me, only thinking to save the calf out of the burning barn.

Poor Wallace. All his earthly belongings went up in that fire. His treasured tools, some of which he had since his boyhood. All his clothes, his bedding, and a lot of little things he had brought to us, such as his razor, mirror, a few silver teaspoons, together with our things we had left in the shack. But he never even once complained about his loss. No, he only felt sorry for us. We, at least, still had our bed, and as luck would have it, our best clothes. Of course, most of our dishes, and they had been so nice, were gone. Also the yards and yards of good new carpeting, the radio and clock, and a lot of other things.

Next day, Leo went to work as usual at Richie's. He told him what had happened to us the night before. Richie laughed, said, "Well you are sort of getting used to it." No one said or sent anything this time. In fact, we were told that that lightning story was too thin. A few nights later we were down at Drakes. They, of course, believed about the building being struck. Wallace had seen it himself, and though they were poorer than all the rest, Maude gave us the things we needed the most. I noticed she gave us their wash basin. They used an old one which had been so often soldered it got old and bent and still leaked. She gave me their only towels. They used rags to wipe their faces and hands on. I could mention a dozen other things which they really needed themselves that they gave us. They had an almost new broom, and an old worn out one. They gave us the good one.

Well, we were discussing just what to do in winter. We well knew that it would be impossible to live in the basement in winter. Surely we could have slept there, even with the cow there, but if we had put a stove in there and heated up the stable, the smell of the cow manure would have been unsanitary. We had thought of fixing up the upper part of the barn to live in, but as we could only use a stove pipe, that would have been too dangerous near the hay. Both Bert and Maude said we should bring the hay and cow and hens down to them and stay with them till spring.

This was in the last week of August. We were again seated in the little old kitchen, and while they were talking, I was thinking of their great kindness, their wonderful unselfishness, of all the many things they had done for us. Now, when no one else gave us a thing, they gave us things that they really needed themselves. Then for the first time it came to me that in winter, when we had so many, many things given to us, that with the exception of the food and money, all the other things were such as the people no longer needed themselves. Now I do not for a moment mean to belittle or criticize them, far from it. Still, compared to Drakes, there was a vast difference. They gave out of their plenty, Drakes gave us the things we needed the most, regardless of themselves. While I was thinking about these things and remembering the holy light that had hovered over their heads, all at once I distinctly heard a voice. It said, "I was hungry and ye fed me. I was thirsty and ye gave me drink. I was naked and ye clothed me. I was homeless and ye took me in." Yes, they had done all this, and a great deal more.

We considered their kind offer, but did not accept it. At least we wanted to wait and see just how we would come out. It would be no little matter to move the hay, cow, hens, and move back again in spring. I would much rather be at home, only there was no place to live in winter, and no money to build. Mr. and Mrs. Teal made us the offer to bring the cow, hay, and hens to them for the winter and Leo to pay them $10 a week for our board, when Leo averaged a lot less than $5 a week. Mrs. Gleason, too, said we should bring the cow, hay, and hens to her place, sleep in one of her upstairs rooms, and have the big, black kitchen to cook, eat, and live in. Said Leo could have all the wood we needed for the cutting. But as their road was so often impassable in winter, Leo could not have gotten to Jewell each morning.

So the time went on and we still did not know where or how we would get through the winter. Came the third of October, a nice warm day. Leo as always was at Richie's, Uncle Wallace was digging the last of our potatoes. I had been washing and brought the clothes to the pump to rinse them out. While I was there, Mr. Tifft, who was mowing the roadside with his team, stopped for a drink of water. He asked me if we had now made up our minds where to spend the winter.

I told him we were still undecided. Then to my intense surprise, he said, "If I were in your place, I would put a roof on the cellar and live there this winter." I stared at him, thinking he meant it for a joke, but I saw he was in earnest about it. We walked the few steps from the pump to the cellar. He said it could easily and cheaply be done. Yes, it did sound reasonable. I told Wallace about it. He, too, approved of it. Of course now it was always dark when Leo came home, but we told him what Tifft had said. Leo thought that would be a good plan.

Right after supper, we went to Drakes. Of course, they were glad that we had found a way to stay on the place. Bert Drake said he would be up early in the morning to help Wallace clean out the cellar. So, the next morning, long before Leo started for Jewell, Bert and Wallace began to clean out the debris from the fire. Both stoves, iron bedsteads, tin cans, hundreds of broken glass cans, dishes, and so on had to be taken out. A lot of dirt, stones, chunks of blackened beams, and all sorts of other things lay in the cellar. Now this was very hard work for two feeble old men because all of that stuff had to be lifted up. I sent a post card to Oneida, to a junk man. He came out the next day. The men wheeled away seventy-five wheelbarrows of dirt, stones, broken dishes, glass and tin.

Bert came up again the next day, as the weather now being lovely, might not last long, now being the fifth of October. That day, they finished that much of the job. Before Leo left in the morning he measured the width of the cellar for rafters. On the third day, the sixth of October, I took Bert and Wallace back into my woods, near the creek, and showed them where to cut the hemlocks for the rafters. That night we went to Mr. Tifft to hire him to bring his team the next day and draw out the rafters. He would not take a cent pay. Of course Bert and Wallace had both worked for no pay also.

Now another question arose. Where would we get roof boards and side wall boards for three sides and some sills and plates? Leo barely made enough to keep us in food. Now that the Peerless was at least paid for, Lyle Richie cut down on Leo's wages, but Leo well knew, and so did Richie that Leo could not get another job, so it was stay with him or starve. I had an inspiration. I knew that down at the corner, what had been left of the old McCormack house had been torn down and piled up. Sarah Dixon owned the place. I would go to her and being old friends, get enough of what we needed for a low sum of money.

Next morning I walked over to see her. She told me I could have all the boards we would need for nothing. So that night after supper, we again went to Tifft's to get him to fetch up the things. Next morning Sarah and I met at the corner and waited there for Mr. Tifft. Now so far it had not cost us a penny. But now we needed roofing paper and nails. So we cut down on our groceries and went to Utica after the paper. We had wonderful luck as to the weather. For two whole weeks it had not rained. Leo did not go to Richie's for a few days and did the first work on the building himself. He and Wallace put on the roof. But we needed a floor and stairs and window sills. Leo got the lumber from Richie, for which he charged an enormous price, also automobile door glasses for windows.

Of course that kept Leo in debt again to Richie's, so he got two dollars a week cash until those things were at last paid for. Wallace and Bert laid the floor, built the stairs, built another so called cupboard, a wash bench, and made two partitions at each end, one to be our bedroom, the other Wallace's. Of course, we still slept and ate in the barn. I cooked under the trees. It had gotten much colder, often rained lately. Wallace had put a sort of roof over my outdoor stove, but that only kept off the worst of the rain. On the twenty first of October, it started snowing. Wallace moved his bed; Bert had given him another cot bed into his little bedroom in the cellar. I moved the cow and yearling into the upper part of the barn.

We could not very well move into our new quarters until we had a chimney, and Leo could not build one till it stopped raining and snowing. So I continued to cook out of doors, running back and forth from the stove to the basement in the rain. I was wet, yes, drenched, half the time. At last, on the first of November, we had a clear, bright, sun-shining day. Leo stayed home and he and Wallace laid the chimney. Now last winter when we had so much given to us, there was amongst other things a beautiful blue and white cook stove, which had only been used a few months. Mr. and Mrs. DeForrest had given us that stove. All this time it had been stored in the barn. It was large and heavy and now arose the question to get it from the barn and down the stairs and set it up.

That night we went to Drakes and got Bert to come up in the morning and help with the stove. It was a clear, but cold morning. Bert, Wallace, and Leo got it to the house, as we now called our new habitation, in comparative ease. But as the stove was heavy and not one of the three men strong, there arose the question of how to get it downstairs without anyone getting hurt or letting the stove drop and break. While they were discussing ways and means to get it downstairs, a car drove into the yard. Mr. and Mrs. Evans and Billy from Waterville. Billy was strong, and with his help the stove was gotten downstairs and set up in a short time. I cooked dinner outdoors once more, but we ate in the basement as all the dishes and foodstuffs were there.

After dinner, Leo hurried off to Richie's. It was steadily getting colder, the ground beginning to freeze. Wallace built a fire in the blue and white stove. I carried dishes, kettles, and food into our new living quarters. Wallace and I took our big bed apart, carried it in and set it up. Together we brought down the table, chairs, and so on. It was now getting quite dark, the ground frozen hard, and a cold wind blowing. Wallace had kept the fire going and carried in a big pile of wood. I lit the little kerosene lamp. That was before we had electric lights. Really, things, though crude, looked homey.

I started cooking supper on the beautiful stove. Though this cellar has now been transformed, glorified, the blue stove is still the same, and this very minute, while I am writing this, I am sitting close to it.

So when Leo came home that night, we ate our first meal and spent our first night in the new home. Thanksgiving, we again went to Drakes. I took a large pork roast and a pumpkin pie down. A few days later, the Peerless gave out. Leo traded it in with Richie for a Willis, this time a good car, but of course Leo had to pay quite a big sum. So with his low pay during the winter, that again would leave us very little for food.

Uncle Wallace started to cut wood in the woods for us. Teal drawed it home in pole length, Wallace sawed it up by hand, and Wallace and I helped Teal to buzz wood at his place to pay for the team work. Teal handled the engine, Wallace fed the saw, and I threw the wood away from the saw. Mrs. Teal was afraid of the saw.

So time went on. Came the twenty-first of December and my sixty-fourth birthday. Really the last happy birthday I have had. There had been some snow, but most of it had melted. But now the air was clear and cold. After breakfast we started for Waterville, to the Evans. It was a lovely ride. Bright, clear sunshine, good roads. We had a bountiful twelve o'clock dinner. I should have mentioned that my birthday had come on a Sunday.

About two o'clock in the afternoon, we left and went over the hills to Earlville and from there to Morrisville. Had a good supper, left there about ten o'clock for Oneida, had some beer and wine, and got home at one o'clock. A lovely full moon was shining. The air was icy cold, but in our heated car it was warm and snug. Wallace had done the chores and kept the fire going so we found a warm, comfortable house.

Sophie Kussmaul

Came Christmas and I got up a good dinner, and we went down after Bert and Maude Drake. New Year's Day, we stayed at home. There had been a frozen rain all night, was still raining and freezing, and the roads were impassable. About the middle of January, I received a letter from my little daughter Sophie. She told me that on the eleventh, she had another baby born, a little girl named Noreen. So the winter went on. Sometimes we just went to Camden on Saturday nights for our week's groceries, sometimes to Oneida and had some beer. In February, Wallace got sick. He started with a head cold, but that was not all. He got the diarrhea and a touch of pneumonia. We took him back to Drake's. There he got good care, a warm room, and Maude made him stay in bed. Bert did not allow him to go out to the toilet, but waited on him. They got a doctor for him and he forbade Wallace to do any work; that was after he was up again, for at least six weeks. I think he came near dying.

In April my little daughter wrote to me that they were intending to come out again this spring. Of course I was more than happy to think I should see her again, and the new little grandchild too. They were now living in Glendale, California.

Came the nineteenth of May. On that day the Wilson family arrived from California. Philip, who had been the babe in arms when they left here, was now a sturdy, chunky little fellow of four years, almost as broad as high, very short for his age but well and rosy cheeked. Today I got my first glimpse of Noreen. She was now five months old. Tiny and very dainty looking, more like a doll. Of course I was the most pleased to see my beloved child again. All these years I had carried the picture in my mind and heart of the last time I had seen her going up the road in their house car and waving a thin, tiny white hand arm. Today she was still thin, but had a better color. Yes, she looked healthier. Oh, how I had wanted to see her again. Since she had written to me about their coming out, I had thought of countless little things I wanted to tell her, little happenings from our neighborhood, her childhood and girlhood home. Little news items such as concerning her one time school mates, give her a full account of our two fires, and so on.

Of course I had kept writing to her, but letters alone were not giving all the little intimate happenings of our daily life. I had pictured to myself the happy summer we would be spending together, a renewal of our old time life, our old time intimacy as it were, for I was sure they would stay with us until the fall, probably until the beginning of October. Those were happy dreams of anticipation, but they never came true. There had been a change, a subtle change. For one thing, my child no longer felt as she and I were the closest beings on earth. She was all mother, entirely wrapped up in her family, her life amongst so many new surroundings. To my great sorrow, I felt that I no longer was to her what I once had been. Also, she took little interest in all the many changes of her one time friends and acquaintances. But the hardest, saddest part of it all was that it was practically impossible for me to visit with her even for five minutes.

I do think that if she had realized my bitter disappointment, she might have arranged it that we, for the sake of the olden, golden times, might have spent a few hours together, alone. For how could we know that but that this summer might be the last one on earth that we could see one another? They had not come out this time in a house car. Ray put up a tent, in which they lived while he built a log cabin. This log cabin was just a little way below our dwelling, and only about twenty feet north of our graves. Now the children played out of doors all day long. But when I ran down to visit a few minutes with my little daughter, they would rush in and demand her attention, talk, and I am sorry to say my child seemed to have ears only for them. They never came to visit me, but the very moment their mother came up, they would follow her in and make a lot of noise so we could not talk together.

When they had been here four years ago, they all tried to please me, followed me around, and wanted me to play with them. But this time, from the very first, they all tried to tantalize me, aggravate and torment me. So I really saw very little of my child. There were quite a lot of huckleberries. The Wilsons and I picked to eat, can, and sell them. But during the entire huckleberry season, my little Sophie and I only picked together once, for about two hours. How good it seemed roaming around once more over the old wilderness together where in the bygone years we had practically lived, had spent most of our summers. We joyfully recalled things that day, like this: oh here is the bush where we used to hide our pails. Oh, this is the bush with those sweet large black ones, the ones I always liked the best. Here is the little tree where I used to tie my pony. So those two happy fleeting hours went by. I thought we could often pick together again. But this, too, was impossible. She would pick with Ray or some of her children.

We divided up the garden space. They had half and I had half. The garden things turned out fairly well, but not as well as that one wonderful summer. No, this was not a happy summer for me. There were other things, too, other disappointments. Now for nine years, Leo and I had been very happy together. In all those years, we had never quarreled once, had always been loving together. But for some reason, ever since the Wilsons had come out, things seemed different. I certainly do not mean to imply that their coming had made any difference. We still loved each other, made up after our quarrels, went out together but I was not quite so happy after each quarrel.

Then there was one other thing that saddened my life, something for which no one was to blame. For years, Maude Drake had not been really well, but she was not the kind of person ever to complain. Always cheerful, happy acting. She would worry about Bert and Wallace, yes, and if I had a cold, she would feel bad for me. But I had noticed, ever since early spring, that once in a while, even while she was trying to entertain us, a great spasm of pain would show in her face. She would clench her hands and controlling her features, go on talking. I had also noticed that her skin was getting a little yellow. Then in August, one night when we were there, she said she had the doctor come up, and he said she must go to the Rome Hospital and have an examination there, and an x-ray. My heart almost stood still. Would my worst fears be realized? Why should this good woman have to suffer?

A few days later, she went to Rome. Bert came and paid Leo to take him and Wallace to Rome. We went, and how glad Maude was to see us. She told us that the x-ray had proved that she had cancer and in an advanced stage. The doctor in Rome said there was just one chance in ten to save her by going to Buffalo to that great Cancer Institute. But as she had been run down so much, been undernourished, she would have to stay in the Rome hospital for a week or ten days to get built and fed up enough to stand the trip. Maude did not complain. A week after, we again went there and she begged the nurses and doctor to let her come home with us. She came home. The Rome doctor made arrangements with the Buffalo hospital, and on the twenty-first of September, she was taken to Buffalo in an ambulance. Poor Maude, poor Bert, poor Wallace. I hope I shall never again see so much grief. Yet the worst was still to come.

Maude wrote to me often, cheerful letters, little anecdotes of the nurses. Asked me how my flowers were, my cat, little messages to give to Bert and Wallace. But never a word about herself. Wallace came up often. Both he and Bert got letters from Maude every few days. Bert wrote to her every day. So time went on. Came the twentieth of October, a hot day, much more like a day in midsummer than a fall day. All day long the air seemed oppressive, as if a heavy thunderstorm was brewing. Both Leo and I were half sick. I did not want Leo to go to work that morning. Neither one of us could eat any breakfast, just a cup of coffee. We both had fever and coughed continuously. Leo went and laid down, then said, "I ought to go to bed, but Lyle's got to get the Hartman car done, so I suppose I have to go." I felt miserable too.

Though I could not do any more than my chores, something seemed to urge me on, seemed almost to compel me to bake bread and two pumpkin pies. Both the bread and the pies turned out good. In the afternoon, I took some cream out under the shade trees and turned it into butter. Leo came home, ate a few bites. I, too, could eat scarcely anything. It had been thundering for the last few hours, but as yet had not started to rain. Being late in October, the night, especially being so cloudy, set in early and by eight o'clock it was, as the saying goes, pitch dark.

We, both feeling so sick and miserable, went to bed soon after eight o'clock. The rain started, first lightly; then amidst the rolling, crashing thunder and the sharp lightning, the rain was pouring down. We lay there listening to it when all at once we heard voices and pounding on the door. Leo jumped up saying who in the heck can be out there on such a night. He did not stop even to pull on his pants, but rushed upstairs to let in whoever was out of doors. That was before we had electric lights. Of all people, in came Bert and Wallace, each carrying a flashlight. Both men were soaking wet. They told us at once what had brought them up. Bert had just received a telegram from Buffalo that if he wanted to see his wife, to come out at once.

As they knew of no one else that would take them, they asked if Leo could go in the morning. There was a pause; then Leo said he could not go. I was up and dressed by this time. I said, "Leo, we have to go." Leo explained that in order to make such a long trip, we would have to spend five or six hours working on the Willis. I knew that was so, as for the last week or ten days, each day Leo had spoken about a certain thing that was wrong with the car, saying I must get it fixed, or it might give out before I get to Jewell.

I asked him if he could not borrow a car from Lyle Richie. He said Lyle had refused to lend him one for us to go to Oneida. Yes, I knew that was so. Leo said, "Besides, I would not undertake such a long trip without at least fifteen dollars between us. Right now, I have less than a dollar in my pocket." Then he turned to the men and said, "Boys, how much have you got?" Bert said, "I only have fifty cents, but I know I can borrow five dollars from Charlie French." Wallace spoke up, "I have a little over a dollar, but I am sure I can get three or four dollars from Jim Hollenbeck."

While we were talking, the rain was still pouring down, and the thunder rolling. I made a cup of coffee for the men. I said, "I am sure I can borrow a few dollars from my daughter in the morning." Then Leo said, "I ought to be in bed and stay there tonight and all day tomorrow." I knew he was really sick, but I also saw the despair on the faces of Bert and Wallace. I said, "Leo, I know you are sick, but do you remember how these two men, when the weather was between twenty and thirty five below zero, worked out of doors for us for nothing to rebuild our shack? Do you remember how they and Maude took us in, made their home our home, when no one else asked us in? Now this is literally a matter of life and death. Try to get them to Buffalo."

There was a long silence. My heart was in my mouth. It was not ten o'clock and still raining, but not so hard any more. At last Leo got up and said, "Boys, I will take you home and then go to the shop and see what I can do about the car. It will probably take me most all night." I was unspeakable thankful, but at the same time very sorry for Leo. I went back to bed, but could not get to sleep. I, too, was sick, a high fever, a racking cough. My great sorrow about Maude. In my heart I knew that she was the best woman friend I now had left on earth, and she was now, even now, on the borderland of the great beyond.

At twelve o'clock the rain had stopped. I had a few catnaps; then at half past three, I heard the car drive into the yard. I jumped up. Leo came downstairs covered with dirt, oil, and grease. I got the wash basin ready for him. He said he did not want to wash or eat, just get a little sleep. Told me to be sure and wake him up at half past five, as he wanted to run up to Matt Kirk's and see if he could borrow ten dollars. I asked him if he had not asked Richie, as he owed him a weeks pay. Leo said he had asked him, but could not get a cent. He actually dropped asleep as he was lying down. I did not go to sleep any more, but stayed in bed till a little after four o'clock.

By lamplight I got a large clean pasteboard box, lined it with clean paper, cut one of my nice, fresh loaves of bread into slices, spread them thick with the new butter I had made. Wrapped these up and put them into the box. Cut both pumpkin pies into four pies and packed them in their tins. I boiled a dozen eggs hard and made some coffee to fill the thermos bottle. Also put in a can of my young cucumber pickles. By this time it started to get daylight. I milked the cow and filled a quart can with the new milk to take along. I saw a light in the cabin and knew my child was up. She always was the first one up. So I went and told her what had happened and asked her to lend me a few dollars. She let me have three dollars which she had saved up for Christmas. I told her I would use it only in extreme need. I told her that we could not get back home until the next night, this was Friday morning, and asked her to do my chores for me for the time we were away.

Then I woke up poor Leo. I had a hard time to get him up. He seemed drunk with sleep. He started for Matt Kirk's, dirt and all. I started to cook breakfast, changing my clothes at the same time. Leo came back in a few minutes with ten dollars. He washed and shaved and changed his clothes. We ate, but I left my dirty dishes. It was just seven o'clock. When we got to Drakes, both men were ready. They, too, had packed a little box. Canned beans, a can of salmon, a dozen cookies, and a few apples. Bert had borrowed five dollars from Charles French and Wallace got four from Jim Hollenbeck. I do not think either Bert or Wallace had slept any during the night. Both Leo and I coughed most of the time.

The weather had changed wonderfully. The air was clear, not a cloud in the sky, no wind, and a warm, not hot sun shining. A perfect day. This was the first long ride I had ever taken with Leo, and under other circumstances I would have enjoyed myself to the utmost. But the knowledge that Maude was dying, yes, might even be dead now, took all the joy out of me. I knew I was losing a good and true friend, that no other woman would ever take her place in my heart. In the back seat were two silent, grief stricken, old men, their anguish written in their faces. Beside me sat Leo, sick, tired, and afraid that he could not hold out, as he called it, to drive till night. At twelve o'clock noon, we reached Seneca Lake and ate our dinner on the very brink of it. A little after three we reached Buffalo, but it was four before we had located the hospital. It was a huge building, built out of dark stones. Five stories high. Even Aburn Prison to my way of thinking did not look so cold and formidable. There was something sinister about it that I cannot describe.

At the office, we found out that Mrs. Drake was on the third floor. We went up in the elevator, then along a long passageway, meeting nurses wheeling patients from the operating room. We came to Maude's room. She was propped up in bed, half sitting. She gave a glad little cry, reached out her arms, and said, "Oh, Bert, you did come." Bert seemed to make a spring, put his arms around Maude, and they clung together a few moments. Then he said, in a trembling voice, "Did not papa's baby know that papa would come to his baby girl." Then she greeted the rest of us. She never spoke of herself., but wanted to know if they, Bert and Wallace, were having enough to eat, how the house plants were, the cat. If Wallace was making cider. Told them both to be sure and put on their heavier underclothes as soon as it got colder. Asked me how my daughter and her family were, said Noreen was such a dear baby. Asked me about my plants, my cat. Wanted Leo to go and see a doctor before we left for home, but not one word about herself.

Bert went to see the head nurse of that floor and asked permission to stay with his wife that night. To my surprise, she readily granted the permission. We, Wallace, Leo, and I, left her about half past five, telling her we would be back in the morning. We drove outside the city, out of the business part of it, to a quiet street, and found what we had been looking for. Rooms to let. Leo engaged two really nice rooms, one for Wallace and one for us. We left the car there and hunted up a restaurant. Yes, we could eat again. Walked back to our rooms. I noticed a lovely bathroom and though I was ready to drop with fatigue, took a hot bath. Oh, that felt good. Leo was fast asleep when I got to bed. It was not ten o'clock.

Next morning we both felt better. Went out to get our breakfast, and then started back to the hospital. We got there by nine o'clock. Bert had not slept. Most of the many night hours he had sat by

Maude's bed, holding her hand. When Maude was awake they would talk to one another. Well I could see that change in her face, that change that never changes back. After she had greeted us, she motioned to Wallace to come close. She took one of Bert's hands, one of Wallace's, and said, "I want you two boys to stick together, be good to one another." Then she motioned to Leo and me to come up to her, took one of Leo's hands and one of mine, looked at both of us, thanked us for coming, then said, "We had many happy times together." Then releasing us, she waved her hand over us all and said, "I want you four to stick together. Be good to one another. Have good times together." Then giving a tremulous sound, she added, "There used to be five of us." We stayed a few minutes more; then Leo said it was getting late, and we had a long ways to travel. One more good-bye and the four of us left.

We walked together down the long hall and Leo, Wallace, and I got into the elevator. Bert had one foot in it, too; then all at once he turned around and ran back to Maude's room. Of course we all thought he had forgotten something, so we three got out, too, and waited in the hall for him to come back. While we stood there waiting, we saw the nurse who had been taking care of Maude. I asked her just where Maude's cancer was. She told me it was one of the worst cases they had ever had. Her entire liver and stomach were eaten away and part of her intestines, yet she never complained.

Well, Bert did not come back. After about fifteen minutes waiting, Leo sent Wallace back after him. Well, he got him, but Wallace told me afterwards when he got back in the room, he found Bert with his arms around Maude. We got started at last. When we reached Batavia, Wallace bought four quart bottles of beer. When we got outside of town, we parked the car at the roadside and ate the food we still had in the car, washing it down with the beer. This was about one o'clock. We got home just before dark, and I was glad to be able to give back the money I had borrowed from my child the morning before. This was Saturday night.

Late Sunday afternoon we drove down to Drake's. Bert said he had gone to North Bay to ask the minister, Reverend Baker, to take up a collection for him to go back to Buffalo and stay with Maude. It seemed poor Bert still thought she would get well again. He could take care of her himself. Of course, Monday Leo went to work as usual. Wallace came up, said Bert felt so sure if he only had Maude home, she would get well. Again Tuesday morning Wallace came up, said the minister had brought Bert fifteen and a half dollars he had collected for him. As a train was to leave Oneida for Buffalo a little before seven in the morning, Bert had started from home on his wheel in the pitch darkness for Oneida at four in the morning.

Chapter 44

Then came Thursday, the twenty sixth of October, a day I shall never forget. Soon after Leo had left for work, Wallace had come up. He was all broke up. Bert got to Buffalo at one o'clock Tuesday, took a taxi cab to the hospital, telling the driver to drive fast. When he reached the hospital, he went directly to Maude's room. It was empty. He called a nurse, asking her where they had put Maude. She told him that she had died Monday night. They sent him a telegram early that morning. Bert could not believe it, demanding to see Maude. Well, the nurse took him to the cooler. There he saw Maude, packed in ice. Wallace told me that they had sent Kenneth Locke after Maude's body, he was the North Bay undertaker, and that the funeral would be on Saturday afternoon at two o'clock.

Now I will have to go back a little in my story. Ray had intended to leave here the latter part of September, or not later than the first of October. But his old car was in bad shape. He kept saying it would never make that long trip. He had gone to Syracuse a few times trying to trade it in for something better, but as he had little money to give to boot, he could not find a suitable car to make that long trip. So for a long time he had kept tinkering with his old car. This day, the twenty-sixth of October, he had kept working most of the forenoon at his car, swearing and cursing it. Soon after Wallace had left, he came to my place saying he could not start out with that heap of junk. I said, "Then you made up your mind to stay here this winter?" He looked at me, gave a quick laugh, and said, "No, I will pull out of here yet before this month is over with." I did not know what he meant.

About half past five, it was getting dark. I had one lamp lit and was cooking Leo's supper when Ray came in again. He said the best

478

way would be to talk Leo into going to California, too. His car, the Willis, could make it all right. All that was wrong with the Willis was two poor tires, and the only good thing about his car was that it had three good tires and the same size of tires fit both cars, so if he put his tires on our car, we would be all set to go. I told Ray that I would be delighted to go for the winter, but that Leo would not go. Ray went back to the cabin, and I almost forget what he had proposed as, of course, I had not the least idea that Leo would even listen to him.

In the ten years that we had been together, I had often mentioned to him about my longing for the West, telling him about the warm, pleasant climate of southern California, how cheap and abundant fruits and vegetables were out there, and so on. He either did not answer me at all, or merely said, "I do not ever want to see that country. New York State is good enough for me." So after a while I said no more about it. Tonight I was all unstrung about Maude, and my heart was aching for Bert and Wallace, for I knew that few people loved one another the way these people had. So when Leo came home, I started right in to tell him what Wallace had told me. We were eating supper when Ray came in again. He told Leo about his plan and talked so persuasively. He knew Leo hated the cold winters here, so he pictured the warm climate, no expense for either coal or wood, no drifted, blocked roads to travel to Jewell, easy, well paying jobs near by wherever we would stay, meat prices down to one half that they were here. So on and on.

To my utter amazement, Leo said, "I got the Willis all paid up and Lyle will give me enough work so I can get all the groceries we will need. We have two good sized hogs almost ready to kill. They will keep us in meat all winter, and even next summer. There are vegetables and Sophie canned up a lot of things. There is the cow and young heifer, hens, ducks. Why fool all that away to go on a wild goose chase?" Well down in my heart I knew he was right, but the old call of the West was strong in me. I was grasping for a straw, as it were. I said lightly, "We can sell the cow and hens and board the heifer out somewhere." I helped Ray to talk Leo into going, but still did not think he would.

After Ray went home, and we were in bed, Leo had partly agreed to go. Next morning while we were at breakfast, Ray again came in, urging and hastening Leo to accept the new proposals. Leo said he would have to go to Richie's for the forenoon, but would be back for dinner, then we would start out to sell the cattle and hogs. That afternoon, Friday, the twenty-seventh, the weather had turned much colder. A cold rain accompanied by a northwest wind was blowing.

We went to see Beach Eckel. He said cattle were way down in price and so were hogs. He did not want to buy them. On the way home, we stopped at Gene Holmes'. He said he would buy the hogs. Next forenoon, Leo went once more to work for Lyle and settle up. After dinner, Ray, my daughter, and their baby, Leo, and I went to Maude Drakes funeral. The weather had turned even colder, there was snow in the air, and the ground was freezing. A sad funeral.

When we got home, I watered my cow and heifer in a snowstorm. My heart was aching. I loved them so, and now in a day or so I would have to see them go into unknown hands. Little Sophie's kids were delighted they were out, scraping up the snow and making snowballs. Next day, Sunday, the twenty-ninth, the weather was a little milder. Leo and I went to Morrisville to bid Vera good-by and also to see if Harry Brown, a cattle buyer near Peterboro, would buy our cattle. He said he had more on hand now than he knew what to do with. That night the Tifft family came to spend the evening with us. They were greatly surprised to hear about our going away so suddenly. They now lived in North Bay in that old house next to the James Louden place, almost opposite Fullers grocery store. I told Mrs. Tifft if they could come tomorrow forenoon, I would give the girls my rabbits and her all my houseplants, and asked her to help me dig my gladiolas and dahlia roots and store them for me in her cellar.

That night after we got to bed, Leo carried on so terrible. He said we were throwing everything away, would no longer have a home, moaned and acted as if he was losing his mind. I said to him, "If you feel that bad about going, let us give it up. We still got the animals. We can yet back out." But he said, "No, now we will go." Next morning, Leo went to see about selling the cattle. The Tiffts came up. I gave them my plants and rabbits. She helped me with my bulbs. Jim Hallenbeck came and bought my ducks. Leo came back and said the Worthmans would buy the hens that night.

This was Monday, the thirtieth, and Ray said we must leave next day. Ray and Leo spent a few hours taking off the old tires from the Willis and putting on Ray's better ones. I got dinner. After dinner, Leo and I went to see Justin Skinner, now living beyond Camden. He agreed to buy the cattle. Would come out next morning. That night

Sophie Kussmaul

Gene Holmes got the hogs and the Worthmans the hens. Leo was heartbroken, kept saying it was the last night we have a home. Well, next morning I got us a good solid breakfast, as I knew we could only have a hasty cold lunch. I finished our packing, also putting our coffee pot and frying pan into the box with the things that we were going to take.

A strange thing happened during our breakfast. I felt as if it was an omen. Ever since the Teals had given us their cat, he would sit near us at breakfast, and I would hand him a bite of this or that. Then afterwards I would go out to milk, and he would follow me out, sit near me till I got all done and wait for his dish of warm milk. But this morning he wanted to go out just when we were sitting down to eat. I watched him. He went as far as the road, turned, looked back, and then went across the road. Of course I expected him to come right back when I went to milk, but he did not come. I filled his dish with the warm milk and called and called him, but he did not come back. We had spoken to Bert and Wallace. We were to bring him down just before we left, together with a few things we did not want to leave at the house and could not take with us. Both men loved cats, and we knew they would be good to ours, and our cat liked them. Well, I never saw that cat again.

About ten o'clock, Skinner and another man came with a cattle truck. This was very hard for me. Soon after, I said good-by to Mr. West. Then about eleven, Leo, Ray, and I got into the Willis. First we went up and I paid my school taxes. From there we went to say good-by to Mrs. Gleason. Of course she had not yet heard of our going. She was not only surprised, but very much opposed to it. She kept telling us over and over again that no good would come from it; that we were making a big mistake; that we all would be glad to get back, and so on. That it was wrong to sell the poor cattle not knowing what would become of them. Now all this did not help to make our outlook more cheerful.

From there we went to Drakes. We did not go in. Ray kept hurrying us. I told them about the cat and they both promised to come up and call it, take it home. We left our silverware, my new rubber boots, Leo's tools, and a few other things there. Then came the parting. Bert started trembling. His jaw and lips moved, he clutched our hands, turned his head and looked away. Poor, dear old Uncle Wally. He broke down entirely. He tried to control himself, but started sobbing. We tore ourselves away from them. When we got into the road, I looked back once more. There at the back door they stood, two old, bent, lonely old men, seeing us go. Words cannot describe the sadness in their thin old faces. A feeling of guilt came over me. It was just ten days before that we four had stood by the bedside of Maude, and her last wish, her dying request, had been that we four stick together. Now just three days after her funeral, two of us were going many thousands of miles away.

It was twelve o'clock. Leo and I hurriedly ate a cold sandwich, which I had prepared after breakfast, and a glass of milk. We filled the trunk of the car with canned things. As we could not take it all with us, we had told Bert and Wallace to take what was left and left the keys with them. We had two big suitcases and a little one. We fastened the two large ones on the outside of the car. The Wilsons had three big suitcases. They, too, were fastened on the outside. The Wilsons spread their bedroll on the back seat to sit on. We spread ours on the front seat. Then there was a good sized pasteboard box into which we packed eight tin plates, eight tin cups, spoons, and knives. No forks. There were nine of us, but Noreen did not yet use these things. Also a coffee pot, frying pan, salt, pepper, sugar, and as we stopped here and there, bread, cookies, and other things. Potatoes, meat, and so on. We also carried an axe, hammer, butcher knife, and automobile tools along. Then at the last minute I ran down to the graves once more and said good-bye.

Into the back seat went my daughter, her baby, Joe, and Jinni. They rode there all the time. In the front seat, Leo and I rode all the way. In the forenoon from breakfast till our noon meal, we had Rocky with us, Ray being in the back seat, and from noon till we stopped to camp for the night, Ray was with us on the front seat and Rocky on the back seat. The reason for this was he was quiet, did not talk much, and sat without moving around. But the first afternoon we pulled out at one clock. Leo drove till night, and we had Rocky with us. As we pulled out of our driveway, a fine cold rain started to fall. When we reached Central Square, it turned into snow and kept on snowing till we stopped for the night at Batavia, where we took cabins. I kept thinking all the time about the poor cat. He probably came home, hungry and cold, the house closed up, waiting for us to return for his warm milk. It spoiled my peace of mind.

Sophie Kussmaul

As I have said before, I will not describe my travels, so all I will say is that we, after leaving Ohio, went by the southwestern route, over some of the roads I had traveled before with Albert, but most of the way was new to me. In spite of the fact about feeling guilty concerning the cat, the cattle, leaving my home, my sorrow about Maude, hating to have left Bert and Wallace, but in spite of it all, after I was out a day or so, the old call of the road was growing ever stronger.

The sight of western cattle, the vast ranches, the almost endless spaces, the distant mountains, the desert, everything seemed to beckon me on, to sooth my spirit. Still there were a number of things that made this trip not so pleasant. Ray was forever hurrying us, driving us on. Both Leo and I would have loved to sleep a little later in the morning, say till seven. But each morning even before daylight, five or half past five, Ray would pound on our door; we always had two cabins close together, saying it was getting late, we should hurry.

I would be half dead for the want of sleep, would stagger about getting breakfast. While we were eating, he would come and say they were all ready to go, grab our bedding, rush back asking if we were going to eat all day. I knew he was bitter against packing dirty dishes, so I would start to wash up our dirty dishes so as to finish my breakfast at the same time. We would tumble into the car, generally just before sunrise, and each morning he would say, "Late again. Half the day is gone."

At noon we would stop a short time. Ray would build a small, quick fire. Even in the great desert he would find a little dead sagebrush, use a little gas on it, and in a few moments there was a hot blaze. We would heat a little water, which we carried with us, and make some coffee. Sometimes heat up some soup or anything that did not take long. Then hastily swallow our food and rush on again. About five o'clock, I became desperately hungry and would say to Ray, who was now driving, "There are some good cabins." Ray would say, "We do not want to stop in the middle of the afternoon." So six, seven would come and go by. We were still racing onward. At last we would stop; I had been hungry so long by now I felt weak, half sick then had to start to cook our first real meal of the day. I generally boiled potatoes, cooked some kind of meat and another vegetable. We had some of our sweet canned fruit from home and of course bread, butter, and coffee. Sometimes we had beer with this meal.

After supper, no matter how weary I was, I had to wash up the dishes and prepare for a quick breakfast as much as I could at night. So it generally was ten or after before I got to bed. Now I said then and I still say that there was no use in this awful rushing. What difference would it have made if we had been on the road a few more days? How much easier it would have been. At last we entered Yuma and had our things inspected. An easy matter. Soon after we glimpsed the Salton Sea, a relic from pre-historic times, and a strange feeling came over me at the sight of that body of gleaming water laying there in the hot desert sun. Yes, the same as it had millions of years before.

Well I must not dwell on our trip. It was the eleventh of November, Armistice Day, when we reached Glendale. The Wilsons had camped there before, so before we hunted up a place to stay, they took us to a very large market known as Rogers Market. In that part of the country, any stores that carried food, be it groceries, meat, vegetables, fruit, or baked goods, are called markets. The word store is only used for clothing, shoes, or hardware, also drug stores. Well this market contained very many kinds of meat, fish, vegetables, fruits, groceries, baked goods, candies, nuts, ice cream, and both soft and hard drinks. We bought a modest supply of necessary food for a few days supply.

Ray took us near to where they had camped. We went into a large automobile camp. This camp was right on the edge of the San Fernando Road, a four lane road that runs about six hundred miles and I think is the most traveled highway in the United States. Running alongside of this highway are the double tracks of the Southern Pacific Railroad, and just a few feet from that, also going in the same direction, is the old road, the San Fernando Road. So, no matter at what time, day or night, there was an endless stream of travel going both ways. For miles there ran a sidewalk on either side of the main road. Only a little ways from here, across this mesh of roads, is Griffith Park, where a lot of motion pictures are taken. Our automobile camp was on the other side of those roads. There were twenty cabins and about a dozen stationary house cars. Also people who had come in their own housecar trailers. In the center of this extensive camp was a building containing a free laundry for the use of any of the people living in the camp. There were eight stationary washtubs, with hot and cold water. A few electric washing machines, but to use those, a person had to pay. Also the use of electric flat irons. Connected with this building on one side were toilets for men, also shower baths. On the other side, toilets for ladies and also free shower baths. At the lower end of this camp was another free building, a regular bath house, both tubs and showers.

We took cabin number eight; the Wilsons took cabin number nine. But between these two cabins were two stationary housecar trailers, each with a small yard. Of course we parked the Willis at our cabin. Leo carried in our things. Ray and the boys took their things to their cabin. Then while I got settled, Ray took Leo out to find a job. I started to cook our supper on the gas stove that was part of the cabin's furnishing and before I had it done, Leo came back, and for the first time since before we left home, looked happy. He told me he and Ray both had obtained a job in a wrecking yard within five minutes walk from our cabin, their work to begin next morning at eight o'clock.

I was so glad. Now instead of going five miles night and morning through blizzards and deep snow, and eating cold lunches, Leo would be in this lovely warm climate, five minutes from our camp, and be home for a good hot dinner at noon. This was Friday night. Next morning Leo left cheerfully for his work. I took a nice long walk, came back at twelve and had dinner on the table. But to my surprise and disappointment, Leo came in and looked dejected, saying the work was much harder here than at Richie's. He feared he could not stand that kind of work. He went back after dinner, but by night was utterly tired out. Ray did not seem to mind the work at all.

The next day being Sunday, Ray took us on a sightseeing trip, of course using our car. We drove around for hours, all over Hollywood and Beverly Hills, Ray pointing out where some of the most important actors and actresses lived. Some lovely bungalows clinging to the very edge of mountains, overhanging high precipices. We went to Venice, Santa Monica, and some interesting places along the beach. I had been to these beach places twice before.

So the weeks went by, Leo working at the wrecking yard part of each day, Ray putting in full time. Right here I must say that Ray not only divided up their pay each Saturday night, but gave Leo the biggest part of their earnings. Still, Leo could not stand the work. He was so lame at times I had to take off his shoes. The worst of it all was he hated the place. Every minute he was home, he would say how he regretted coming out here, how he disliked the heat here, although at home, he always had dreaded the winter. He even threatened to commit suicide.

When I reminded him of the cheap fruits and so on, he would only say, "We always got along without them all right." Added to this, I began to feel sick. I do not just know what it was. I would cough day and night, lost my appetite, got weaker day by day. I would sit for hours in the hot sun, take walks, sometimes alone, sometimes with Leo, sometimes with my daughter. If Leo could possibly spare the money, we would attend a movie. It was only about half a mile to the business part of Glendale. There was a long street, perhaps a mile or more, running one way back to the Mother City of Los Angeles and the other end into the great Mojave Desert. Now when I said a mile or so, that was where about a dozen theatres were; at the end, running towards the desert, the street was lined by endless stores and shops. The street on both sides had been planted with palm trees. A strange combination, a city street shaded by desert palm trees.

About the first of December Leo gave out. He could no longer even work at the wrecking yard for a few hours. His back, hips, and neck were in such a condition he could hardly get about. All the time, he was saying that he knew we would now starve to death. I got more and more miserable each day. Once in a while he got a radio to repair, meaning a few things to eat, although I could eat next to nothing. I swallowed my pride and went three times a week to the Salvation Army for bread and whatever else I could obtain there.

Came the twenty-first of December and my sixty-fifth birthday. Sick as I was, we went that night to the theatre in the car. I never could have walked there and back that night. Although I went at least to a dozen movies while in Glendale, the picture I saw that night is the only one I can now remember. It was *The Life of Stephen Foster*, in color. A very beautiful picture. Two days later, it was the twenty-third of December and Leo and I went up to this street again. It was afternoon, a warm bright day. The golden sun was shining from a deep blue cloudless sky. Every store, every shop, was in full Christmas array. Every window in its green and red trimmings, its countless toys, tiny Christmas trees in their trimmings. Presents for old and young. Little and big Santa Clauses, piles of green fir Christmas trees at the street corners. Overhead, endless ropes of red and green, which even in daytime were beautiful to behold. Crowds of happy faced Christmas shoppers, laughing little children.

Sophie Kussmaul

I felt a little better today, but still so weak I fairly trembled with the exertion of walking. By my side was Leo, limping along. He was lame, sick, and entirely discouraged. So we slowly walked along. I felt the glory of the Christmas Spirit all about us. I said to Leo, "How beautiful everything looks." He gave a little sniff and said, "Things look all right, but to me it does not look like Christmas at all. Christmas to my way of thinking is connected with cold weather, snow, bare trees, winter in general." Then at that very moment, an inspiration was born within me. I looked up at Leo and said, "Leo, this is like the first Christmas, a clear, blue sky above, palm trees, and there is the desert like the one over which the wise men came on camels, and here, too, in the early morning we can see the Bethlehem star shining in the east." There was silence. I never knew if this sank into Leo's heart or brain or not.

The next day I felt worse again. At night, Christmas Eve, the camp was blazing with colored lights and almost every cabin had a tree. The Wilsons had one for their kids, and although it was only about one minutes walk to their cabin, I did not feel like going to see it. While I lay propped up in my bed, I could not lie down as my cough was strangling, from everywhere floated the Christmas music. Very beautiful indeed, and though so far from home, yes, and further from my childhood and though sick unto death, poor and destitute, and witnessing Leo's growing misery and discontent, still I felt the glory, the divineness, of Christmas about me.

In the morning, the Wilson children rushed happily in, showing me their presents. I had staggered up and got Leo's breakfast, but I could not eat a thing. About ten, my little daughter came running in and said to me to hurry up and get ready, we were all going to the Mason's to spend the day. This family lived near Roscoe about fifteen miles from Glendale, but still belonging to Los Angeles. The Wilsons had known them for some time and we had been with them once to make a short call. I told my child I was not able to go, but she insisted, said as they were such plain people I need not change my clothes. So we went with them.

Now I think the real reason for their wanting us to go was they had no car, and so I think it was a polite way to get our car to take them there. When we arrived there were three or four men there besides Mr. and Mrs. Mason. There was just one long room. I spied three things when I entered. First, a lovely, brownly roasted turkey. It smelled good, and at the far end of that room three kegs of beer, near them a huge old easy chair. I started for that chair as I knew I could not sit on one of their crude wooden benches or hard chairs. I was so weak I staggered about clutching at chair backs to keep from falling. A kindly man gently took my arm and guided me to the big chair. I knew he meant well, but the thing he said to me made me furious. He said, "It is hard to be old. I always feel sorry for old people." I turned to him and said, "I am not as old as you are, but I happen to be sick." Well I got settled in the big chair, coughing. I sat there viewing the people, the turkey, and the beer kegs. If I had been well, how I would have gone in heavy at the meat and beer.

Soon after we got there, they started to pass the beer around. Instead of joyously drinking it down in long healthy draughts, and happily knowing that there would be more and more to follow, I slowly sipped mine between spasms of hard, choking coughing. About three o'clock they had dinner on the long table. They wanted me to come and sit down with them. I absolutely refused, thinking I could not eat a bite. This same oldish man went and filled a large dinner plate with all kinds of food and brought it to me, also another glass of beer. I looked at the food. The meat looked good. I tasted it. Yes, I could eat that. I ate all the meat and drank the beer. The old man came back, fairly hovered over me, urged me to eat. I shook my head and said, "More meat." He was delighted, got another hunk of turkey, more beer. Again I said, "More meat," and for the third time he brought me meat and beer. This was the first real meal I had eaten in weeks. So Christmas Day came to an end.

For some time Leo and I had tried to get on relief. We had to go to different places, sign papers, have an investigation. A man called at our cabin a few times, but after a while we got in. I forget the exact amount, but it was enough to keep us in the most necessary food. We got our first check on the second of January. Of course our rent had to be paid out of this money. I do remember this, the rent for the cabin was five dollars a week. But that included our lights and gas for cooking and heating. There was a lovely little gas range in the kitchen, and we also had a little gas heater, which we only used on cool mornings.

We, like all the rest in that auto camp, had the free use of the laundry, bathrooms, and toilets. But save as we might, we plainly saw that we could not get any money ahead towards coming home. Leo got a few hours work once in a while; I collected fruits and vegetables from the big markets three times a week. They gave me vegetables that were slightly wilted and fruits that had a few spots and weren't saleable. I spent as much time as I possibly could sitting in the warm golden sunshine. I did manage to get our simple meals and walk about. But I slowly, steadily kept getting weaker, more sick, all the time. I often wondered how I kept going. I ate next to nothing, and if I did manage to swallow a little food, I had to vomit it up. There was that terrific cough. Instead of pleasant surroundings, Leo would forever declare that we would never see home again and lament about our coming out. I knew he, too, was sick in body as well as mind. So time went on. Came the fifteenth of January. That day I felt too weak to take even a short walk. Somehow I got a little food ready for Leo. I did not even try to eat anything. Leo washed up the dishes. I went to bed about six o'clock. That is, propped up in bed, I lay there listening to Leo tell me how sick he was. Yes, I knew he was in a bad shape, so lame he could hardly move about. Then, between coughing, I got a little sleep, Leo lying beside me. I woke up and saw the lights were on. Leo was in the kitchen heating up some of his rubbing liniment. I felt queer. I just cannot say how I felt. For once I was not coughing, but I just seemed to have no body. I lay, or rather half sat, there. I could think clearly, but I did not even seem aware of my arms or legs or hands. I surely thought my end had come. I thought I wanted to see my little daughter once more. I asked Leo what time it was. He said it was half past two. I hesitated. Should I send for her? I knew she worked every moment and needed her night's sleep. I knew Ray had a job, had to leave before seven. She had to get up about half past five. Perhaps I would still be alive then. So I did not send for her. I did not tell Leo how I felt. In fact, I felt more as if I was in a sort of dream.

Then the next thing I knew I woke up. It was daylight. Leo was sleeping by my side. I felt better. Slowly I could move my legs and arms, and I was not coughing. After a while, Leo woke up. I told him he would have to cook his own breakfast. After he was up, I tried to dress. I put on one stocking, had to rest, as that slight effort made me dizzy. Then the other stocking, another rest, a shoe, the weakness overpowering me. At last I was dressed, staggered into the kitchen and sipped a half cup of hot coffee, got back to my bed shaking, trembling, dizzy. But still I felt better. At that time I did not know it, but this was the turning point of my sickness. The crisis. About nine o'clock, my little daughter came in. She told me how cute Noreen had been, what Philip had said, what they had for their breakfast, what she was going to cook for their supper, and so on and on. After about half an hour, she got up, went as far as the door, turned around and said to me, "Well, how are you this morning?" I said, "At half past two this morning, I thought I was going to die. I was going to send for you but did not want to disturb your sleep." All she said was, "Oh, I guess you will be all right now." She left me. After that, I really started to get better again. I coughed some yet, for a long time, but I could eat and resume my walks besides doing my little household chores.

So we got into February. It was the tenth day of February and for some reason I cannot now recall, it was necessary for Leo to go to the Court House. Now I have said so often that I would not describe my travels. But although I had daily seen the beauties, the flowers, trees, shrubs of all kinds, been in the golden life giving sunshine, yet what I saw this morning was so absolutely ahead of anything else, I felt fairly overpowered with it all.

I had given no thought as to that Court House. If I had, I would just have made a mental picture of some large, square, cold looking building. But when we stopped near a small fairy like park, I saw an enormous white, glistening building that probably was constructed of imitation marble that looked like the real thing, I just stared at it. Exquisitely carved cornices, balconies, large, odd shaped windows with frescoed window ledges, graceful porches, little delicately chiseled side entrances. To me it looked like a castle out of a fairytale story. Breathtakingly beautiful. I heard later on that that building cost three-and-a-half million dollars. I strolled into the little park like yard. Though I had been wandering all about Glendale for weeks enjoying the lovely flowers and shrubs, the sight that met my gaze fairly took my breath away. I will try and describe that yard, though I know that no mere words could portray the glory that was spread before me.

Above, there was a deep blue, cloudless sky, and the warm golden sunshine seemed to purify and glorify everything. Never have I seen greener, softer grass. There were three fountains playing, splashing their silver spray back into their crystal pools. In the larger one of these pools, were a pair of snow white swans. At the edges of the other two were pond lilies and water hyacinths. In the middle of this lawn was a very large rose arbor, inside of which were a few rustic seats. This arbor was completely covered with climbing roses of different shades of color. Here and there were large rose bushes, or I should say rose trees, literally covered with blooming roses. There were shiny white paths winding about all over this lawn. They were flanked by dozens of camilla bushes, all laden with their rich burdens of blooms. Here and there were flower beds scattered about, and they contained what I had always classed as hothouse flowers. Some of them were planted to cyclamen, some to primrose, others to great double fuchsias. Besides, there were many, many more. Scattered about were orange trees with both golden fruit and fragrant, waxy flowers. A little in the background on two sides were tall, dark palm trees. On the third side in the background stood that magnificent crystal white castle the Court House. Now added to all this splendor was the music of many singing birds, birds that were unknown to me. The very air was sweet with the many perfumes of the flowers. I walked about almost as if in a dream.

After a while Leo came out, and we went back to our cabin. Now the question was still before us of how to get home. I knew that many families got sent home. I mean the State paid their fare back. Leo and I talked this over with Ray. He told us what authorities to see about it. We were sent from place to place. An investigator called at our cabin a number of times. After some time, we were told they would send us home by train. They would bring some men, appraise our few belongings, sell them, and together with what they brought, add enough money to buy our tickets home. We were allowed to keep two suitcases. Now we well knew that our car, though still in good condition, would not bring over five dollars at such a sale. Our dishes, bedding, radio, Leo's violin, all together perhaps another five dollars. Then when we finally landed at Oneida, the nearest place they would send us, we would be stranded. No more car, bedding, dishes, and even most of our clothes would have to be left behind. That was not all. For months I had collected and carefully rooted plants to bring home, plants I could not get at home. I also had collected stones and small rocks and picked up sea shells from the Pacific Ocean beach, and should I have to leave all those things behind.

Leo had tried to sell his violin and box of tools. He was offered a ridiculous small sum, not the twentieth part of what they were worth. Things indeed looked black to both of us. But somehow I still felt there might be a way out of our troubles. Leo had given up, said there was no further use to try to get sent home with our car, as they had told us we were going by train. I remembered that the Wilson family had been sent across by auto, taking all their possessions along, so why could not we be sent that way too.

Leo and I again made the rounds of all the different offices connected with the business of transportation of transients like us. But to no avail. They all agreed that the rule, or custom, was if they sent one or two people across the country, it was much cheaper for the State to send them by train. If a whole family was to be sent home, they would let them keep their car and give them gas and let them have oil tickets and enough cash to buy food for a certain amount of days in which to cross the country.

Then just why this idea came into my head, I never knew, but all at once I felt I must go and see the headman, or manager, of the Young Men's Christian Association. A men's society of all places. Yes, I knew it sounded crazy, but still I felt I must try. Next morning I started out. I told Leo I was going for a walk, which of course was the truth. I knew if I told Leo where I was going, he would stop me, as he did not believe in anything religious. Well I admit it took some courage on my part to take that step.

I entered the enormous hall and felt that it was strictly a man's place. At the furthest end was a desk, at which a man sat writing. I went up to him and asked to see the head man of the association. He really did not seem surprised and told me to which door to go. I know my legs trembled, and I felt so entirely out of place, but I went to the slightly opened door and walked in. A tall, broad shouldered man of about fifty sat at a desk looking over some papers. He glanced up at me and said the usual thing. "Is there something I can do for you?" At one glance I saw that he really was a good kindly man. Just how I told him, I do not know, but I told him how much we wanted to get home. I explained to him that if they sent us by train, we would be completely stripped, and that my husband would need the car to get to work with after we got home.

The man listened carefully and then said, "I have nothing to do about such cases. That's completely out of my line." I looked at him pitifully. After a few moments, he said, "Sit down. I will see what I can do." Then he started telephoning to all the places where we had already been told that they could not let us keep the car and our few possessions, also to a number of other places. After a while he said,

"Those fellows seem rather stubborn. I will go downtown this afternoon and see some of them in person." Then he said I should come back next morning at ten o'clock.

So promptly at ten I was back. The man was all smiles and the moment I glanced at him, I knew he had good news. He told me that he had quite a time with the transportation people, and that I should bring in my husband at four that afternoon. I went home feeling more lighthearted than I had for weeks past. Then I told Leo where I had been the last two days. That afternoon we both went to see this man once more. Again he started telephoning and putting down addresses and handing them to us. One was to the Chamber of Commerce. We were to stop in there and hand them the card he gave us. Another one was to an address way down in the heart of the City, to a place to have our car inspected.

When we got home and told Ray about our good luck and showed him the address where we were to have the car inspected, he gave a loud snort and said, "That ends it." Then he told us that at least a dozen persons had been to that place and not one of them ever had any success in getting their cars to pass inspection. He said, "In the first place they never allow a car to pass over a year old, and your car is nine years old. Then, too, it has to have four new tires and a new spare. Even then you are not sure if they will let it pass. One of the men will drive it around the block and if he can hear the least little flaw in the motor, he will not let it pass." Well Ray said it was only a waste of time and gas to take our ten year old Willis down there. "Why," he said, "they would not even leave their office to look at it. One glance through their windows and they would say, "Get that old wreck out of our yard before it falls to pieces."

I looked at Leo. He said nothing, but I could see he was ready to give up. I, too, felt discouraged, but I turned to Ray and said, "We have been trying everything now for about a month. Let us try one more thing." Ray said, "Well maybe you will know more about it after they get through with you."

Leo asked Ray to drive us down to that place the next morning. It was a good ten miles through the city and we both knew that Ray was better acquainted with Los Angeles than we were. We were supposed to be at the inspection place at ten o'clock the next morning. For once next morning, instead of California golden sunshine there was a heavy fog and a fine misty rain. Really I never saw our poor old Willis look so drab and cheap, really shabby.

Well Ray drove us down there. There was quite a pretentious gas station and some rather stylish looking offices connected with the gas station. On one of these office windows was printed, in large gold letters, Car Inspection Office. Ray and I stayed in the car and Leo went into the office. Ray turned to me and said, "I bet they will not even step out of their darned office." Well a few moments later, Leo came out again, accompanied by a very sour faced man. I must say my heart seemed to stop beating when I looked at that surly faced man.

I forgot to mention that I had prayed and prayed a dozen times during the past night, imploring God to let the car pass so we could bring it and our things home, but when I saw that man's face, I had little hope left. He walked around the car just once, did not even seem to look at it, and strode back into the office. Leo followed him. Ray turned to me again and said, "Just as I thought. He would not even look at it much less start up the motor." By this time the man came back with a little slip of paper in his hand. He stuck it on the windshield. It said this car had been duly inspected and passed inspection.

I sent up a silent prayer of thankfulness and Ray said, "Well I will be darned." Now of course, I never knew just what that kind man at the Y.M.C. had done or said, but he certainly must have been the cause of our getting that inspection slip. My heart was overflowing with happiness. From there we went to another address which the man at the Y.M.C. had given us. There they consulted road maps in search of the best route to send us home. They figured out how many miles it would be to Oneida. Of course North Bay was not on those maps. Then they figured out how many gallons of gas and oil it would take to make the trip. But they did not give us the money to buy the gas and oil. They gave us a gas and oil coupon book to cover the first thousand miles to a place in New Mexico called Tucumcari. There they told us we were to go to the police headquarters, and they would give us another coupon book for the next thousand miles, which place was Joplin, Missouri, and the city where we were to stop next was Indianapolis, Indiana.

They gave us the cash to buy food. I do not remember how much, but they figured we would eat our three meals in restaurants and allowed that it would take fifteen or sixteen days to make the trip home. But Leo had bought a cute little gasoline stove that folded up like a suitcase. Of course we still had our dishes we had been using in our camp. So we left the heart of Los Angeles and on the way back we stopped at Rogers Market, where we had been getting our food supplies since we came to Glendale.

I cannot remember all we bought, of course, but I do remember we got a side of bacon, sugar, coffee, pancake flour, a box of vegetables, and a box of fruits, canned milk, and a few baked things, thinking this would take us through the desert. Now for some reason Ray urged us to move to Rosco. Rosco was about twenty miles from Glendale, the last suburb of Los Angeles. Really more of an outpost than a settlement. A few scattered huts, a tiny general store with a post office, and on three sides the great, vast, open desert, and about one hundred miles eastward the blue outline of the distant Rockies.

Ray had gotten himself a job near there and was going to move his family out there that day to live in a tent. So we collected all our belongings out of our little cabin in Glendale, which had been our home for about four months, and piled them in and over the car and on both running boards, and followed Ray's huge car and belongings east of Rosco. I was quite well again now and before me lay the glistening, sun drenched, silent desert.

Chapter 45

All the worry, anxiety, uncertainty about how, if ever, we would reach home, now settled beyond our fondest hopes, and before me lay the long, long trail to be journeyed alone with my beloved Leo. Still there would be the parting with my child, perhaps forever. Also, leaving behind the ever summer land of Southern California.

Ray had a job on a dam a few miles away. We unloaded our things in the sand, cooked our meals on an open campfire, and Leo took out the two seats of the Willis and in some way I forget now, hinged them so that at night we could turn them into a bed in a few minutes and get them into the smallest possible space. I still marvel at the amount of things we managed to get into that car. Besides, we had six good sized suitcases fastened on the fenders and a ten gallon can on one side and a ten gallon can of water on the other side, on the running boards.

Now I want to speak of something, something that really has nothing to do with this Western trip, but something I have observed all my life. It is not the big things in life that always leave the deepest impressions in our mind. Often, very often it is the little things, things apparently of no consequence. I will allude to one here. Those three days spent near Rosco, on the very edge of the desert, were naturally filled with things of great importance. The wonder of how we would be able to make that nearly four thousand mile trip with an old car, the problem of what to do in case it broke down and left us stranded. The wonder of just how we would find things after getting home. The twinge of heartache of leaving my beloved foster home, Southern California. Also my beloved little Sophie and her family.

496

Sophie Kussmaul

Although I had crossed the desert a number of times, yes, lived in it for weeks, I shall always recall those three days spent on the very edge of it. Two things will ever stand out more clearly than the rest. One of them was my daughter's children had taken two little bantams from home, a little red hen and rooster. I had seen them all summer at home, every day on our long trip to California, many times a day each day in Glendale, but now to see them on the sand, amongst the sage brush, sent such a queer sensation over me that I cannot describe. As long as I may live, in my mind I shall always see those two tiny little busy fowls going hunting, scratching amongst the desert herbage.

The other thing was that Leo and I slept in the car at night. There was a full moon over the ever cloudless desert sky and through the night hours, far out in the desert, I could hear the mournful, wailing, howl of the coyotes. Shortly before daybreak they became silent, and then the little red bantam rooster started crowing lustily and cheerfully.

Well on the fourteenth of March, we cooked our last breakfast there on the campfire and said our last farewells and started for San Fernando. All day we traveled through grapefruit, orange, and lemon groves, all watered by irrigation ditches. In the afternoon, we passed through Altadena and Pasadena, and then through less and less cultivated country. By nightfall we had covered over two hundred miles and camped in the vast open desert. Now although I would enjoy to give a full account of that trip, I will only mention a few things.

I want to say that from the very hour we two started on that long trail, till we finally landed at home, I truly can say those few weeks were about the happiest of my life. They compensated me for much of the sorrow through which I had passed in former years. I will not undertake to describe this trip across this continent, but there are a few little things I feel I must mention. Here is one of them.

During about ten months of the year, the great desert is one almost endless stretch of white, glistening sand, laying there under burning heat of the sun. Here and there are various species of cactus, and no other vegetation, not even one spear of grass. There are spaces of perhaps fifty or a hundred acres where there is not even a cactus plant growing. But through the month of February, there are quick drenching showers. Not like our eastern rains, lasting for hours, but suddenly a black cloud, then minutes later, the hot sunshine out of the blue cloudless sky. The result of this is that tens of millions of desert flowers spring up and into bloom in a surprisingly short time. Mile after mile, as far as the eye can reach, the sand floor has changed to a dense carpet of red, pink, and white flowers, perhaps three or four inches high. They are at their best only a few weeks, then the intense heat scorches and burns them up, and a very short time after that, there is not a vestige of them left, not even the tiniest stalks. But they have fulfilled their mission. They dropped countless of millions of their seeds into the dry sand, where they will remain dormant for another ten months. Then the rains will awaken them into life and so on and on through the centuries as we mortals count time. The rains also kissed the cactus plants into bloom. Through this wonderland the two of us journeyed, during the daytime under the deep blue sky, with the life giving sunshine warm and golden about us, during the silent nights, sleeping in one another's arms.

Out in the desert, the stars look much larger and brighter, seem nearer to the earth, than in the eastern states. The reason for this is because the air in the desert is much clearer. Oh, how good our bacon and eggs and coffee tasted, with plenty of fresh fruit in those early desert mornings. Yes, I repeat, though Leo and I had been married over eight years, this was our first real honeymoon.

We traveled over many miles of desolation called desert. Entering New Mexico, the country changed a little. Still desert, all unsuitable land, but more uneven rocky hills and patches of pinion trees. These trees are a sort of cousin to our cedar trees, but they bear an abundance of delicious, soft shelled nuts. Also here and there were small adobe huts inhabited by Indians. The country was becoming higher and higher, more and more rugged. Ever before and beyond us a dim mass, which at first we thought were low lying clouds. But as the miles brought us nearer, we saw it was a vast mountain. At the foot of it, or rather on the beginning of the steeper ascent, was the small town of Preston, a mining town.

We followed a narrow, winding road up and up, ever higher, steeper, as the air grew thinner and rarer. The radiator on the car started to boil. We could only proceed a few rods and then wait for it to cool off a little. The scenery was sublimely grand, simple beyond description by mere words. In places, we traveled on narrow winding shelves over a mile and a half high. The slightest accident would have hurled us to eternity. But oh, the pureness of the air. Still we were climbing. After we reached the summit and began our downward way, once in a while we saw a tiny hut clinging to the very edge of the cliffs, a mountaineer's dwelling. As long as I may live, that picture will always stay fresh in my mind. The thrill of danger, but also the greater thrill of the Glory of God, who made this wonderland. Later on, I heard these particular mountains are called The Superior Mountains.

Then much later on, on this trip, there was one more thing, again of no apparent issue, yet to me it came like a divine promise. The night before Easter Sunday, we camped on a lonely, brush grown back road not very far from the State highway. Somewhere in Illinois. I awoke from a long, sound sleep, the golden sun shining into our car windows. But what really did awaken me was lovely Easter music. At first I was a little bewildered, there on that lonely spot. But after we had breakfast and started out again, I found that just a few rods away from where we had camped, around a bend on the State road, and hidden by a thick clump of trees, stood a small Catholic church. Thus came the glorious music.

After a few more days, we reached Buffalo in a raging snowstorm. The weather had turned bitter cold, and we had to take a room there for the night. Next morning we started, but oh what drifting snow. Cold, dry snow. More snow coming down. Every few miles we met a snow plow. At times we were tempted to stop at the first little town we came to. Then again, we thought every mile would bring us near to home. At Syracuse, we were told that the road to Central Square had not yet been plowed. The roads toward Canastota and Oneida were passable. At last, at dusk we reached Oneida. There we were told that the road to Durhamville was not yet opened. Somehow we got to Aughterson's, cold, wet, tired, and hungry.

We were received warmly, as if we had been one of the family. We stayed there five days. Then got as far as Drake's. Bert and Wallace told us that the Flanegan road was not yet opened. We stayed there two days. Yes, the Flanegan road was still unplowed. We went to the next crossroad. It was open. When we got to our road, to our joy we saw a big snowplow going down our way. We followed down to our yard. The snow was drifting high. We left the car on the road, walked to our home over the mountain of snow. Across the road, Arthur Nash's fence posts just showed over the endless snow.

Through Sophie's Eyes

We opened the door. The place was almost dark. The snow outside had covered the windows. Still, we could see how the snow had drifted through the windows. Little snow drifts were on the floor, patches of ice, where some time the snow had melted on the roof, drifted down the leaks in the roof. That was home. Cold, dark, dismal. Well, we went back to the Drakes for the night. Next morning the sun was shining. We came back and Uncle Wallace came back with us. We built a fire in the blue stove and Wallace shoveled out the driveway, also shoveled the snow off the roof and windows. I cleaned and cleaned. We had the lights put back. It was home. Soon the snow outside got less, the sun shone brighter.

On the fifth of April, I started tapping maple trees. I still had to wade through the deep snow from tree to tree. After a month, May, the snow was gone. I got two hens, a cat, the early, muddy ground smelled good, a bit of grass was coming up, the robins came back to their olden trees and sang cheerfully. Everything was calling for new life, new hope. Daffodils bloomed, then new lilacs. I was home.

So life went on and on. Another summer, another winter. Many more years came swiftly, and I stopped to write this book for a while, a few years. After, I just drifted on. Therefore my story skipped a few years, a span of time as man measures time.

Well, I think it is about twelve years since I wrote my last chapter concerning my life story. How swiftly those years went by. Just when I got comfortably settled into my seventies, I found myself in the eighties. Sometime there will be an end even to this. As a child I lived a sort of Eden. No care, no worry, no responsibility. All I knew was love, kindness, protection. Slowly came the awakening, slowly I entered the threshold of life. Fairies seemed less real, while other things seemed more real.

When I came back home from the West fifteen years ago, I thought that great longing, that great call for the West, was not as strong within me as it had been in my younger days. I still felt it. I felt it in the mornings at sunrise; I felt it at noontime, but most of all when the sun was low in the west. But now there was another lure for me, calling, calling me westward. It was the call of my children. So I made that long western trip there and back again twice since I thought I had said good-bye to the distant land of my dreams. People ask me, "Will you go west again?" I answer them that I cannot tell. Time and circumstances will decide that. I live in the same place where I was born, yet looking back at all the people I knew when I was a child there are now only two of my neighbors left. Sometimes when I am lying in my swing under the heavy branches of my giant trees, I am half lulled to sleep, just drowsiness by the hum of bees or other insects. I gaze at the road, the little winding hillside, and there I see the vast procession going past in silence, the people of other years, men, women, and children. They all seem so real, yet only phantoms.

So many people have asked me if I had my life to live over again would I make any changes. The answer is yes and no. Under the same circumstances, the same surroundings, I would live the same life again, maybe make worse mistakes. But I would not submit to fourteen winters of arithmetic again, come what may.

I love this country. I love the rugged mountains, the lakes and rivers, the wilderness of the western plains, the vastness and, strange to say, the desert. There is a strange attraction about it, a lure, a thing left over from yesteryear. It is like an unsolved mystery. These thoughts come to me each time I cross it.

> Voice of the voiceless desert
> Calling unto me
> Out of bygone ages
> Unto eternity
>
> A million years of sunlight
> Have shone on this desert land
> A million years of moonlight
> Made this enchanted land
>
> Why is the desert calling
> Forever unto me
> With a tone so full of meaning
> And a voice so sweet and low
>
> I think I know the answer
> For it's written on my heart

Epilogue

Life, oh, how beautiful life really is if we could only understand the great loveliness of nature, see the glory of God's world.

Here is one more thing I want to talk about. It is about my lovely visions. I do not mean my dreams, although I have been blessed with heavenly dreams. More so, I think, than most of us have. But all my visions have come to me in daytime. I have had twelve of them, but all of them have appeared right here on my dear old home. Nowhere else have I had even one of them. I love my humble home so much that even after I have given up my bodily life, I feel as if my spirit will never leave this place.

Now I will close my last chapter with this one remark. I can truthfully say I love all my grandchildren, including my grandchildren by marriage. They are all my beloved children. This story of my life is a true picture of my ancestors' lives as well as my own. Farewell, my dear ones.